G20 GOVERNANCE FOR A GLOBALIZED WORLD

Global Finance Series

Edited by
John Kirton, University of Toronto, Canada,
Michele Fratianni, Indiana University, USA, and
Paolo Savona, University of Rome Guglielmo Marconi, Italy

The intensifying globalization of the twenty-first century has brought a myriad of new managerial and political challenges for governing international finance. The return of synchronous global slowdown, mounting developed country debt, and new economy volatility have overturned established economic certainties. Proliferating financial crises, transnational terrorism, currency consolidation, and increasing demands that international finance should better serve public goods such as social and environmental security, have all arisen to compound the problem.

The new public and private international institutions that are emerging to govern global finance have only just begun to comprehend and respond to this new world. Embracing international financial flows and foreign direct investment, in both the private and public sector dimensions, this series focuses on the challenges and opportunities faced by firms, national governments, and international institutions, and their roles in creating a new system of global finance.

Also in the series

European Union Economic Diplomacy
The Role of the EU in External Economic Relations
Stephen Woolcock
ISBN: 978-0-7546-7930-1

The New Economic Diplomacy
Decision-Making and Negotiation in International Economic Relations
Edited by Nicholas Bayne and Stephen Woolcock
ISBN: 978-1-4094-2541-0

Financial Crisis Management and the Pursuit of Power
American Pre-eminence and the Credit Crunch
Mine Aysen Doyran
ISBN: 978-1-4094-0095-0

Full series listing at the back of the book

G20 Governance for a Globalized World

JOHN J. KIRTON
University of Toronto, Canada

ASHGATE

Published by
Ashgate Publishing Limited
Wey Court East
Union Road
Farnham
Surrey, GU9 7PT
England

Ashgate Publishing Company
110 Cherry Street
Suite 3-1
Burlington, VT 05401-3818
USA

www.ashgate.com

British Library Cataloguing in Publication Data
Kirton, John J.
G20 governance for a globalized world. – (Global finance series)
1. Group of Twenty. 2. International organization – Case studies. 3. International economic integration – Case studies. 4. Economic history –21st century.
I. Title II. Series
337.1-dc23

Library of Congress Cataloging-in-Publication Data
Kirton, John J.
G20 governance for a globalized world / by John Kirton.
p. cm. – (Global finance)
Includes bibliographical references and index.
ISBN 978-1-4094-2829-9 (hardback) – ISBN 978-1-4094-2830-5 (ebook) 1. Group of Twenty. 2. International economic relations. 3. International economic integration—Case studies. 4. International organizations—Case studies. 5. Economic history—21st century. I. Title.
HF1359.K574 2011
337.1–dc23

2011048773

ISBN: 978-1-4094-2829-9 (hbk)
ISBN: 978-1-4094-2830-5 (ebk – PDF)
ISBN: 978-1-4724-0450-3 (ebk – ePUB)

MIX
Paper from responsible sources
FSC® C018575
FSC www.fsc.org

Printed and bound in Great Britain by the MPG Books Group, UK.

Contents

List of Tables

Preface

The research for this book began more than a decade ago, as part of my ongoing work on Group of Eight (G8) governance. When the Asian-turned-global financial crisis struck in 1997–99, the finance ministers of the Group of Seven (G7) and the G8 leaders endorsed a new body—the G20 finance ministers' and central bank governors' forum in 1999—in what appeared to be the latest of many extensions of the G8's global governance reach. The new G20 remained a subject of particular interest amidst rising concern about governing globalization at the start of the twenty-first century and then combating terrorism after al Qaeda attacked the United States from Afghanistan on September 11, 2001. Enriched by concerns about legitimacy and effectiveness in global governance, my research on the G20 continued until 2005, when I systematically assessed G20 governance over its first five years. That assessment and its broader concern with legitimacy and effectiveness in global governance, well used by scholars, students, and other stakeholders to this day, suggested that the G20 was not only here to stay but also worth a closer look.

However, my attention turned to the G8's efforts during that decade to include emerging powers and international organizations in its annual summit and governance system beneath. This process took a great leap forward when the Group of Five (G5) of Brazil, China, India, Mexico, and South Africa joined the G8 leaders as participants in the latter's Gleneagles gathering in 2005. There followed the Heiligendamm Dialogue Process at the official level in 2007, the meeting of the Major Economies Forum (MEF) as part of the G8 summit in 2008, and efforts at more inclusive, more variable participation culminating in 2009.

Even before the American-turned-global financial crisis erupted in full force in the autumn of 2008, my attention had turned back to the G20, first in the form of a separate G20 Research Group, which I created, and then with a book, co-edited with Madeline Koch, to commemorate the first decade of G20 governance on the occasion of its annual autumn ministerial meeting in São Paulo, Brazil. By the time that book arrived, so had G20 summitry, with the first encounter in Washington DC on November 14–15, 2008. That started an intense sequence that continued with its fourth summit in Toronto on June 26–27, 2010, which is where I have chosen to end this book. By the end of the Toronto Summit, I had written 50 articles, chapters, and edited volumes on the G20 in its various parts. Yet, in doing so I was frustrated by the fact that within the great global outpouring of commentary on the G20, there was no single work that reliably—comprehensively, continuously, and in detail—told the story of the G20—a group whose leaders had, at their Pittsburgh Summit in September 2009, proclaimed it to be theirs and thus the world's permanent, premier forum for international economic cooperation. This book has been written as a result.

Approach and Methods

This book seeks to be the first full, comprehensive, independent, authoritative, analytical account of the G20 from its birth at the level of finance ministers and central bank governors in 1999 through to its fourth summit in Toronto in 2010. It avoids the popular, proliferating program of advising G20 governors what they should do or criticizing them for not using it differently. Nor is it a sanitized account as seen from the inside, as is the G20's own valuable history, published in 2008 before the G20 became a summit club. Instead, it draws on the best concepts and theories of international relations and global governance to offer an account of G20 governance and the G20 itself.

This purpose imposes demands of evidence far greater than those adopted by the many who engage in the abundant advisory, advocacy, or assessment tasks. Such evidence comes from the usual sources: scholarly works on the G20, accounts of think tank analysts, publications by practitioners, biographies of G20 participants, policy commentaries, and, importantly, newspaper and other media accounts. In addition, this book has benefited from more than 100 private interviews and participation in policy dialogues with key G20 governors, several of whom have reviewed drafts, taking place from 1999 to 2011 and embracing those from almost all the member countries and multilateral organizations of the G20, from the level of leaders on down. I remain the proverbial pygmy standing gratefully on the shoulders of those giants who have offered inevitably instant or early analyses so I could begin the task of explaining and understanding the G20 and its work. I thus begin each empirical chapter with a summary of their arguments to show the reader where my analysis fits and to allow others to decide for themselves who offers the more convincing account. To be sure, at this early stage before the archives are open and before practitioners are willing to tell all in publishable form, much of relevance is no doubt missing. But the evidence assembled for this work is sufficient to achieve its purpose of providing the first and most comprehensive, reliable, detailed, independent, and scholarly account of G20 governance for the moment, and as the foundation for others that will follow and build better accounts of G20 governance in the years ahead. This is not a work that will last for all time—only until a better one comes along.

Acknowledgements

In producing this book I have acquired an enormous debt to many individuals in many ways. My first debt is to those G20 leaders, finance ministers, central bank governors, their officials, and their colleagues in leading intergovernmental organizations who agreed to be interviewed by me, to review my draft chapters, or to write for my publications, often several times. I am also grateful to Newsdesk Media, which allowed me to include contributions by G20 practitioners from the present and past in the books that I co-edited and that they have published for each G20 summit that has taken place. Kirstin Howgate, Margaret Younger, and their colleagues at Ashgate were a joy to work with, as they always are. I appreciate the willingness of Ashgate Publishing to allow me to draw on portions of my previously published work. I also thank the important assistance of the Canadian embassies, academic relations programs, and scholarly partners in several capitals and countries, including Belgium, Turkey, Korea, and Indonesia, for hosting my G20-related visits there and putting me in touch with G20 governors who helped broaden and balance my understanding of what went on within the G20. David Shorr and his colleagues at the Stanley Foundation in the United States were exceptionally helpful in assembling and inviting me to several workshops where key practitioners and observers freely exchanged information and views about the G20.

I owe much to the exceptional support of many colleagues at the University of Toronto, the home hub of the global network of scholars, students, and professionals that make up the G20 Research Group. Professor Peter Hajnal, Dr. Ella Kokotsis, the Honourable Michael Wilson, Ivan Savic, Kathryn Kotris, Lida Preyma, and Sandra Larmour served in important ways. Carol Moore, head librarian of the University of Toronto Libraries, hosted the G20 Information Centre website. Linda Corman, head librarian of the John W. Graham Library of Trinity College, oversees the G8 and now G20 archives, reading room, library collection, and artefacts. Professor Louis Pauly, first as director of the Centre for International Studies and subsequently as deputy director of research of the Munk School of Global Affairs, always offered wise counsel, assistance, and reminders of the high standards that we scholars are obliged to meet. My many other scholarly colleagues at the Munk School, starting with Joe Wong and Jeff Kopstein, were always ready to help. At Trinity College in the University of Toronto, provost Andy Orchard, dean Derek Allen, and bursar Geoffrey Seaborn, and Bob Bothwell and then Mairi McDonald, directors of the International Relations Program, have been essential pillars of strength and support. In my home Department of Political Science, chair David Cameron was too. At Simcoe Hall, President David Naylor and his team provided the strategic global vision and leadership essential to our work. And outside the

University of Toronto, the help of my good friends Andrew F. Cooper and John English were vital in intellectual and material ways. So were my key international partners in the G20 Research Group's global network, above all Paolo Savona in Rome, Michele Fratianni in Bloomington, Domenico Lombardi in Washington DC, Marina Larionova in Moscow, Dries Lesage in Ghent, Lee Dong-hwi in Seoul, Zhu Jeijin in Shanghai, and Xu Ting in Beijing.

I am most grateful to Heather Keachie, who served as the lead researcher for this book during the crucial summer of 2010, and to Irena Erema, who did so during the summer of 2011. Marissa Semkiew, Sophie Langlois, and Aleksandra Susak were a constant source of inspiration as we shared ideas in a summer reading course on G20 governance. Zaria Shaw, Robin Lennox, Caroline Bracht, Maria Marchyshyn, Ryan Hilmoniuk, and Julia Kulik were tireless in generating the data for the appendices and assisting with other tasks. And Jenilee Guebert, Director of Research, and Madeline Koch, Managing Director of the G20 Research Group, were there, as always, to help when the hard work needed to be done.

This book could not have been written had the G20 itself not been conceived, created, and continued in ways that led it to become a summit-level success. While many made their contribution, this ultimately happened because two men were smart enough to have the vision and wise enough to work together to bring it to life. It is for that reason that this book is dedicated to the Right Honourable Paul Martin of Canada and Lawrence Summers of the United States.

John Kirton
Mile Island, Morrison Lake
August 2012

Abbreviations and Acronyms

3G	Global Governance Group
AFL-CIO	American Federation of Labor and Congress of Industrial Organizations
APEC	Asia-Pacific Economic Cooperation
ASEAN	Association of Southeast Asian Nations
ASEM	Asia–European Union Meeting
AU	African Union
BCBS	Basel Committee on Banking Supervision
BIS	Bank for International Settlements
BJP	Bharatiya Janata Party (India)
BRIC	Brazil, Russia, India, and China
BRICS	Brazil, Russia, India, China, and South Africa
BSE	bovine spongiform encephalopathy (mad cow disease)
CAC	collective action clause
CCL	contingent credit line
ECB	European Central Bank
EITI	Extractive Industries Transparency Initiative
FATF	Financial Action Task Force against Money Laundering
FSAP	Financial Sector Assessment Program (of the International Monetary Fund)
FSB	Financial Stability Board
FSF	Financial Stability Fund
G5	Group of Five (Brazil, China, India, Mexico, and South Africa)
G7	Group of Seven (Canada, France, Germany, Italy, Japan, the United Kingdom, the United States, and the European Union)
G8	Group of Eight (G7 plus Russia)
G10	Group of Ten central bank governors (Belgium, Canada, France, Germany, Italy, Japan, the Netherlands, Sweden, Switzerland, the United Kingdom, and the United States)
G20	Group of 20 (Argentina, Australia, Brazil, Canada, China, France, Germany, India, Indonesia, Italy, Japan, Korea, Mexico, Russia, Saudi Arabia, Turkey, the United Kingdom, the United States, and the European Union)
G22	Group of 22 (Argentina, Australia, Brazil, Canada, China, France, Germany, Hong Kong, India, Indonesia, Italy, Japan, Korea, Malaysia, Mexico, Poland, Russia, Singapore, South Africa, Thailand, the United Kingdom, and the United States)

G33	Group of 33 (Argentina, Australia, Belgium, Brazil, Canada, Chile, China, Côte d'Ivoire, Egypt, France, Germany, Hong Kong, India, Indonesia, Italy, Japan, Korea, Malaysia, Mexico, Morocco, the Netherlands, Poland, Russia, Saudi Arabia, Singapore, South Africa, Spain, Sweden, Switzerland, Thailand, Turkey, the United Kingdom, and the United States)
G77	Group of 77 (now 131 developing-country members of the United Nations)
GAB	General Arrangements to Borrow
GDP	gross domestic product
GNP	gross national product
HAP	Heiligendamm L'Aquila Process
HIPC	heavily indebted poor country
IASB	International Accounting Standards Board
IBSA	India, Brazil, and South Africa
IEA	International Energy Agency
IFI	international financial institution
ILO	International Labour Organization
IMF	International Monetary Fund
IMFC	International Monetary and Financial Committee (of the International Monetary Fund)
IOSCO	International Organization of Securities Commissions
JODI	Joint Oil Data Initiative
L20	Leaders' Twenty
LIBOR	London inter-bank offered rate
LTCM	Long-Term Capital Management
MAP	Mutual Assessment Process
MDB	multilateral development bank
MDG	Millennium Development Goal
MEF	Major Economies Forum on Energy and Climate
MEM	Major Economies Meeting on Energy Security and Climate Change
NAB	New Arrangements to Borrow
NAFTA	North American Free Trade Agreement
NATO	North Atlantic Treaty Organization
NEPAD	New Partnership for Africa's Development
NIE	newly industrializing country
NGO	nongovernmental organization
O5	Outreach Five (see Group of Five)
ODA	official development assistance
OECD	Organisation for Economic Co-operation and Development
OIS	overnight indexed swap
OPEC	Organization of the Petroleum Exporting Countries
R2P	responsibility to protect
SARS	severe acute respiratory syndrome

SCO	Shanghai Cooperation Organisation
SME	small and medium-sized enterprise
SOA	Summit of the Americas
SDR	special drawing right
SDRM	sovereign debt restructuring mechanism
SPP	Security and Prosperity Partnership
TARP	Troubled Assets Relief Program (in the United States)
UN	United Nations
UNCTAD	United Nations Conference on Trade and Development
UNDP	United Nations Development Programme
UNGA	United Nations General Assembly
UNSC	United Nations Security Council
WTO	World Trade Organization

PART I
Analysing G20 Governance

Chapter 1
Introduction

The Significance of G20 Governance

On December 15–16, 1999, the finance ministers and central bank governors of the world's 19 most systemically significant countries and the European Union gathered in Berlin for the first meeting of the Group of 20 (G20) (Kirton 2001a, 2001b). They gathered in response to the decisions made earlier that year, endorsed by the Group of Seven (G7) finance ministers and Group of Eight (G8) leaders, to create such a group. These decisions flowed from the initiative of two individuals: the finance minister of the G7's smallest power, Paul Martin (2008) of Canada, and the treasury secretary of the G7's largest power, Lawrence Summers (2008) of the United States. Martin, Summers, and their colleagues were reacting to the Asian-turned-global financial crisis that had erupted in Thailand in July 1997, engulfed Indonesia and Korea by the end of 1997, and spread to Russia in August, then the United States, with the collapse of hedge fund Long-Term Capital Management (LTCM) in September and finally to Brazil by the autumn of 1998. These cascading crises demonstrated the inability of the G7/8 and the International Monetary Fund (IMF) acting alone to provide financial stability for a world of increasingly globalized finance. In the view of Martin and Summers, the world needed a new, broader, permanent group of established and emerging countries to serve as a global financial and economic steering committee. They thought that each member of this group would operate as equals in the collective provision of essential global public goods. All the countries they chose as members agreed to join this new group. The G20 was thus established at the level of finance ministers and central bank governors just as the twenty-first century was about to dawn.

Almost a decade later, on November 14–15, 2008, the leaders of the same systemically significant countries and the European Union gathered in Washington DC for the first G20 summit. Similar to the birth of the G7 summit among six leaders in 1975, this first meeting featured France as the initiator and the United States as the decider. The immediate call for the G20 summit had come from French president Nicolas Sarkozy, whose predecessor Valéry Giscard d'Estaing had requested and hosted the first G7 summit in November 1975. Support for such a G20 summit soon came from the United States, led by President George W. Bush. As in 1975, the United States insisted that a broader group of countries be brought to the table, from beyond the established, exclusive Eurocentric and Atlantic club, in order to mobilize new, rising global powers whose contributions were now needed to confront the compounding crises adequately in the world. Bush decided in October 2008 that the new summit must be composed not only of

G8 members and a few other countries, but also of all members of the established G20 finance ministers' and central bank governors' forum, and that it be hosted and chaired by the United States. Just as the finance ministers and bank governors had done a decade earlier, all G20 leaders agreed to attend. They believed that a global response was needed to the destructive American-turned-global financial crisis that had erupted in the US mortgage markets of "main street" and then Wall Street, and that had reached across the Atlantic to engulf Europe too. These shocks showed the need for a new, summit-level centre of global governance to foster financial stability, economic growth, trade liberalization, and development for the poor. These issues already constituted key components of the core G7/8 summit agenda, but they now needed a broader G20 to address them effectively. Managing crises that affected the global system required greater participation and equality than the G7/8 allowed. Together, the G20 members contained 65 percent of the population, 80 percent of the trade, and 85 percent of the gross national product (GNP) of the world.

The first G20 summit in Washington set key directions to mitigate the financial and economic crisis, initiated a process to apply them, and took concrete decisions to put them into effect. It agreed on a follow-up summit to be held in just over four months' time. This second G20 summit, hosted by UK prime minister Gordon Brown in London on April 1–2, 2009, led many to conclude that the new leader-level G20 should and would become a permanent institution to reinforce, rival, or even replace the G7/8 as the centre of global economic governance in the twenty-first century. The third G20 summit, hosted and chaired by new US president Barack Obama in Pittsburgh on September 24–25, 2009, took the next step along this path by proclaiming that the G20 henceforth would be the permanent premier forum for its members' international economic cooperation. The fourth G20 summit, chaired by Canadian prime minister Stephen Harper in Toronto on June 26–27, 2010, underscored the continuing need for such intense G20 summitry, for it confronted and contained the newly erupting European-turning-global financial crisis sparked by the spiralling sovereign debt of Greece. This Eurocrisis had quickly expanded beyond the control of the powerful regional EU to become the third global financial and ensuing economic crisis in just over ten years.

Competing Assessments of G20 Governance

The leaders of the world's key governments quickly decided that among all the international institutions available or imaginable, the G20 was the most appropriate to lead the global response to the 2007–10 financial crisis. This suggests that they judged the earlier G20 finance ministers' and central bank governors' forum to have been successful during its first decade, and saw the G20 being so yet again at a higher level. The G20 seems, in retrospect, to have been the obvious international institution to mobilize a new configuration of collectively predominant economic powers to meet the needs of a rapidly globalizing, more equally vulnerable world. At the same time, the much greater speed, scope, scale, simultaneity, and societal impact of the 2007–10 crisis, relative to the 1997–99 one, as well as the former's outbreak after only a decade of G20 efforts to produce financial stability at the level of ministers and bank governors, suggest that there were serious shortcomings in the G20's earlier performance. Such shortcomings could be sufficiently large that a simple rise of the same club to the leaders' level might be insufficient to overcome them.

Which of these two possibilities proved most accurate is a matter of critical significance for the many whose financial security, economic prospects, and daily lives have been devastated by the events of 2007–10 and their aftermath. It is equally important for scholars and practitioners of international politics and global governance seeking, respectively, to understand and to shape the G20 and other informal plurilateral summit institutions by specifying the workings of an effective, legitimate, and enduring global governance architecture for a now tightly wired world where major power shifts and changes in the connectivity of countries are underway.

To date, judgements about the course, causes, and consequences of G20 governance at the level of finance ministers and bank governors and now leaders have offered few convincing conclusions that command consensus by the standards used by scholars and others. In their place has come a wide-ranging, often poorly disciplined, prescriptively and normatively oriented debate among several schools of thought (see Appendix A). This debate often focuses in the first instance on the general question of the relationship between the new G20 and the old G7/8 (Hermawan et al. 2011).

Redundant

The first general school in this debate sees the G20 as redundant in the long term, because it is too large and diverse in its membership and too informal in its institutionalization, or because it has inspired the G7/8, other informal plurilateral bodies, or the Bretton Woods/United Nations organizations to revive and reform to meet the new global governance needs. Assuming a zero-sum global governance competition, this school first finds support in the G20's birth alongside the British-guided, legally entrenched International Monetary and Financial Committee (IMFC) and the German-designed Financial Stability Forum (FSF). It adds that the minister- and governor-level G20 failed to predict or prevent the 2007–09 US-centred crisis that challenged its core mission of providing global financial stability and making globalization work for all. Even at the leaders' level, the G20 did not prevent the onset of the 2010 European crisis from arising in Greece. Indeed, it was the G7 finance ministers who first responded to the erupting crisis in May 2010, leaving the G20 ones to follow a day later in less detail. After the fifth G20 summit in Seoul, Korea, on November 11–12, 2010, the G20 faded from being a twice-a-year gathering to only an annual encounter. This left the G7/8 and others to govern the ever more challenging global economy for the following year until G20 leaders were to assemble again in Cannes, France, on November 3–4, 2011, and in Los Cabos, Mexico, on June 18–19, 2012.

In this view, the G20 stands as an inherent rival of a G7/8 that has rapidly adapted to the competition from the G20 by expanding its own membership and participation through to 2009. At its finance ministers' and central bank governors' meetings and its summits in 2009, the G7/8 returned to dealing seriously with the financial and economic issues that its summits had largely abandoned during the decade before. The G8 summit routinely and expansively includes other countries and international organizations. With G20 leaders having done no better than their G8 counterparts to get the overdue Doha Development Agenda of trade liberalization done, with finance and economics a core part of the 2009 and 2010 G8 summits, with the new Financial Stability Board (FSB), old Basel Committee on Banking Supervision (BCBS), and the IMF doing the detailed reform work, and with the leaders of Brazil and Australia choosing not to come to the fourth G20 summit in Toronto, the G20 summit could become redundant and fade away as the self-proclaimed premier or even consequential global economic governance forum. At best, the existing finance G20 could be left to do its lower-level work alongside such other G7/8-catalysed finance-oriented bodies as the 1989 Financial Action Task Force against Money Laundering (FATF) and the 1999 FSF (Bayne 2003).

A particularly strong, prescriptively oriented strain of the "redundant" school sees the G20 as a great danger to the kind of global economic governance the world needs. A leading G20 abolitionist, Anders Åslund (2009) argued after the 2009 Pittsburgh Summit that the G20 was a threat to the international architecture and must be "stopped." He questioned the legitimacy of an institution that arrogantly named itself the premier economic forum, without clear criteria for membership, agreed rules of governance, or authorization from excluded powers. In Åslund's view, the G20 breached the principle of national sovereignty by usurping power for global finance governance while expecting the remaining 173 countries excluded from the G20 to follow its rules. Åslund's alternative is the IMF, since it has the needed universality, hard legal status, and staff. He would make the G20 an informal "consultative forum" at best. Many traditional, hard law multilateralists associated with or sympathetic to the IMF or United Nations shared this view. Indeed, the IMF itself had long followed this approach, seeking to destroy the G20 since its 1999 start until its elevation to a leader-level club in 2008. Even after the 2010 Seoul Summit, IMF managing director Dominique Strauss-Kahn warned of the continuing risk that the G20 could become a largely irrelevant institution (Talley 2010).

Rejection

The second general school rejects the pre-eminence but accepts the continuation and contribution of the G20 (Beeson and Bell 2009). Such rejectionists, conceding the possibility of positive sum coexistence and cooperation among international institutions, conclude that although the G20 will endure, it has failed to perform as the primary centre of global economic governance, in part because it contains many of the flaws that have afflicted the G8. Such claims about poor G20 performance arose soon after its start and came especially from those who shared a hard law, legalization approach (Abbott et al. 2000). They predicted that another informal ministerial meeting was destined to fail due to the superior power or performance of the existing or reformed hard law multilateral bodies (Culpeper 2000; Foster 2003; Scholte 2003; Bryant 2003). They highlighted the formidable institutional defects of the G20, while conceding its competence on immediate narrow tasks. They insisted that the G20 was incapable of dealing with the much different global economic architecture the world needed. Leonardo Martinez-Diaz (2007) saw imbalances in G20 outcomes arising due to G7 dominance, arguing that the finance G20 did not work equally well for its emerging economy members due to a reliance on consensus rather than majority voting and to the G7's dominance in capability, coherence, and continuity as an established concert within the new G20.

Rejectionists also emerged in response to the first G20 summit in Washington. They insisted that the leaders fell well short of their objectives due to a misdiagnosis of the financial crisis, denial of their own culpability for it, and failure to deliver what they had promised at prior ministerials (Duncan 2008; Lander 2008; *Economist* 2008c, 2008d, 2008a, 2008b). After Pittsburgh, rejectionists still doubted the group's performance (Giles 2009; Donovan 2009; Winning and Parkinson 2009). Some pointed to differing dominant domestic ideas and interests across key members as causes of the summit's failure to agree on key issues (Schirm 2012). In the lead-up to Toronto, Kenneth Rogoff (2010) presciently asked the self-proclaimed international financial regulators of the world to explain their failure to control the sovereign debt crisis spreading through Europe and beyond. He insisted that the global challenges modern society faced, from regulating complex technologies to managing ever increasing financial risks, as well as crises such as the 2010 BP oil leak in the Gulf of Mexico, necessitated a much more concerted and inclusive organizational response.

More analytically, Paul Masson and John Pattison (2010) found that international financial cooperation after a common shock might suffer because of a free-rider problem. They wrote that "regulation is an international public good that is under-provided, since some of the benefits and costs spill over to other countries." While the G20 as a whole might work better than the G8, it is less beneficial for G8 countries to be involved in the larger group. Some additional members may not add much value to financial regulation, and their involvement in the group dramatically increases cooperation costs. Thus, the size of the G20 "has lowered the chances of agreement on major reforms." Furthermore, it is difficult for the informal G20 to transform international consensus into domestic law, which renders the group toothless.

Anthony Payne (2010) also wonders how the G20 can work well with a "marginalized" majority left out. Thomas Wright accepts the G20's "transformation in the architecture" of global governance, but similarly questions the legitimacy of a group with an "arbitrary" membership (Shorr and Wright 2010). With 173 countries left out, accusations of "global economic apartheid" could arise. Agreement is difficult to reach in a group of so many equal members who confront complex issues and do not share the same values. Wright's solution is stronger US leadership in developing deeper relationships with countries that share its interests.

Other critics also reject the G20 due to an absent Africa and the missing poor of the world (Payne 2010). After the 2009 Pittsburgh Summit, Senegalese finance minister Abdoulaye Diop remarked that the leaders could not "continue to ignore hundreds of millions of Africans" (Agence France Presse 2009a). The ministers of the heavily indebted poor countries (HIPCs) called for the G20 to remedy the fact that no genuinely poor country was represented in the group.

Some rejectionists are ultimately reformers. Those in this reform sub-school reject the G20 in its current form and conduct, but would see it as effective, legitimate, and adequate if several changes were made. Sylvia Ostry (2010) claims that the G20 as an informal steering committee has suffered from the lack of trust that inspired the G7, having no criteria for membership and an American desire to reduce its membership. It needs "significant changes in structure and process in handling the ongoing global economic challenges." A host of analysts, largely in the rejectionist school, have offered a multiplicity of suggestions for such institutional improvement (Bradford and Lim 2010). But they often disagree on the desirable reforms, offer an internally inconsistent array of proposals, and fail to show, analytically and empirically, how their preferred proposals would produce the particular governance results they want.

Reinforcement

The third general school sees G20 governance as a valuable reinforcement of what the G8 and other similar bodies do (Kirton 2005a, 2005b, 2010b; Alexandroff and Kirton 2010; Griesgraber 2009; Kharas and Lombardi 2012). It argues that the G20 works well in its own distinct domain of serving as a permanent, primary centre of international economic cooperation among its members, especially with the established G7/8 members, the IMF, the World Bank, and other hard law multilateral organizations operating as committed components of the new G20. It does not see, expect, or hope that the G20 will or could serve as the only centre of effective and legitimate global governance, even for its own members, let alone the global "G193" as a whole.

This school begins with the "distinctive mission" sub-school. It argues that the provision of financial stability, sustained growth, and globalization that benefits all is the G20's core mission and the proper standard by which its performance should be judged.

A second, "expanded representation" sub-school argues that the addition of the G20 to a continuing G7/8 brought the important emerging country buy-in that the older body lacked.

A third "conditional potential" sub-school judged the ministerial G20 during its first few years to be a promising institution with a potentially valuable contribution to make if several substantial challenges were met (Porter 2000; Johnson 2000, 2001; Helleiner 2001; Kirton 2001a). Pierre Marc Johnson (2001) saw a "promising organisation that could play a significant role in global governance." Its promise rested on its combination of several assets: the 19 member countries plus the EU, the European Central Bank (ECB), the IMF, and the World Bank; its representation of more than 85 percent of the world's gross domestic product (GDP) and 65 percent of its population; its expert economists and finance ministers; its comprehensive and flexible agenda; and its first chair's focus on an expansive agenda that included poverty reduction and other measures to ensure that the benefits of globalization were widely shared. The G20 could thus foster a revised north-south bargain to start a new round of multilateral trade liberalization, to embrace and integrate trade, environment, development, and social issues, and to design and foster a comprehensive and coherent new system of global governance.

A fourth "proven performer" sub-school saw the G20 as "an effective and legitimate institution that had delivered significant achievements" during its first several years of work (Kirton 2002; Martin 2004; Crockett 2004; Meyer et al. 2004; Knight et al. 2004).

A fifth "summit governance for globalization" sub-school advocated at an early stage the addition of a top-level Leaders' 20, or L20, perhaps as one of many enhancements to respond to a process of globalization that was gathering force (Le Boucher 2003). Their proposed summit could be an ad hoc meeting to address a particular pressing global issue (Martin 2004). Alternatively, it could be a permanent body with a more comprehensive agenda (Johnson 2001; Schwab 2003; O'Neill and Hormats 2004; Kirton 2001a). Anne-Marie Slaughter (2005), who saw the finance G20 forum as "a network specifically created to help prevent future crises," proposed that it be institutionally extended in several ways.

When the G20 did leap to the leaders' level in 2008, the reinforcers arose in full force (Kirton 2008, 2009; Cooper 2010a, 2010b). In a sixth "here to stay due to the G7" sub-school, Risto Penttilä (2009) concluded that G20 summitry was too big and diverse to be efficient, with the synergistic co-dependent result that "the G7 will become an executive committee while the G20 will assume the role of an assembly."

A seventh "G20-G8 cooperative co-dependence" sub-school emphasized the important cooperative interaction between the G20 and G8, with the G8 being able to offer valuable advice on critical issues and the G20 catalytic innovation (Postel-Vinay 2011). Andrew F. Cooper (2010a) insisted that the G8 could "act as a model and catalyst for setting out innovative paths for the G20 in its long moment of transition from a crisis committee to a new more comprehensive steering committee." Nicholas Bayne (2010, 228–89) concluded that "the early summits have been productive beyond expectations and established positive interaction between the G20, the IMF and the reformed Financial Stability Board."

But he cautioned that their subsequent program of macroeconomic coordination went beyond anything tried in the previous three decades and that the G7 members must learn to share power with the other G20 ones.

In an eighth "contingent G20 primacy" sub-school, Cooper and Paola Subacchi argued that the G20 summit was an innovative, indispensible, flexible network as a "systemic risk manager, and a bulwark against restrictive forms of unilateralism," but required improvements in legitimacy and efficiency to work well (Cooper and Subacchi 2010; Cooper 2010b). Wongi Choe (2010) argued more ambitiously and forcefully that the financial crisis of 2007–09 signified a shift in the balance of power and the established economic neoliberal policy paradigm, and thus the emergence of the G20 as "the only game in town." Yet it would still face significant challenges in the near future, including how to maintain its momentum as the economic crisis receded, and how to govern without formal institutionalization and accountability mechanisms of its own.

Replacement

The fourth general school sees replacement, as the G20, engaged in a zero-sum global governance competition, substitutes for a G7/8 that had, would or should soon fade away as an effective central forum (Ernst Weltke, quoted in Porter 2000; Beauchesne 1999; Bradford and Linn 2004; Jim Peterson, quoted in Dean 2004; Paul Heinbecker, quoted in McCarthy 2004; Carin and Mehlenbacher 2010; Heine 2010).

The early replacers formed a first sub-school focused on the failure of the G7/8 as the primary cause of why the new G20 would replace the former G8. They argued that the G20 was "useful," "important," "inclusive," "experienced," "successful," and "effective," whereas the G8 had become an "inadequate," "obsolete," "exclusionary," "antiquated," "anachronistic," "stale," "ineffective" forum for the "mere exchanges of views and pleasantries" (Bradford and Linn 2004). G20 performance had been sufficiently robust that it was starting to replace the G8, institutionally and operationally, at both the ministerial and leaders' levels for global governance.

These early replacers, composed largely of retired practitioners, often advanced their claims on the basis of internally contradictory, selectively supported, or unproven assertions about current and future transformations in the international system. They spoke of the failure of the G8 and UN in response to crisis, and assumed the advantages of a more representative L20. Almost never did their call for a G20 replacement come from a close analysis of what the existing G20 finance ministers' and central bank governors' forum had actually done, why it had done it, and what leaders alone could add, or from a similarly disciplined and detailed analysis of the G7/8 since 1997.

Once G20 summitry started, replacers' claims grew. A second sub-school emerged, as causal emphasis shifted to changing relative capability among countries and the value of "inclusiveness" itself (Celso Amorim, quoted in Agence

France Presse 2009b; Choi 2009; Baker 2010; Shanghai Institutes of International Studies Working Group 2009; Hermawan et al. 2011; Persaud 2010; Wang 2009). Paul Kelly (2009) argued that the shift to the G20 was only a matter of time because the rise of the G20 as the premier economic governance forum was an overdue recognition of the relative shifts in the global power balance. Others highlighted the tremendous benefits that countries such as Australia accrued from a "seat at the top table." Although the group was large and divided, and it was a challenge to reach consensus, the G20 was necessarily inclusive and might be too symbolically important to fail in its mandate.

A third sub-school stressed the leaders' innovation as the dominant causal force. In the immediate lead-up to the Toronto Summit, Paul Martin asserted that the G20 summit had "done very, very well" by having leaders sit down together in person to develop the kinds of innovative responses required for new financial challenges (Grant 2010). He foresaw a future in which G20 summitry would replace the G8 one.

In a fourth "institutionalized informality" sub-school, David Shorr emphasized that the G20, based on countries' political and economic significance, was not an arbitrary creation, and that the lack of a solid institutional structure kept "the focus on the discussions of the deciders" (Shorr and Wright 2010; Wang 2009). Indeed, the G20's informality was crucial for encouraging both domestic and international compliance. The shared expectations and interests that face-to-face meetings can build generated positive pressure and momentum for the leaders to return home with. Bruce Jones, Carlos Pascual, and Stephen Stedman (2009) agreed, seeing the "G" processes as "a mode of institutionalized dialogue that can improve policy ... to find a path toward consensus."

Even more expansively, in a fifth "proven primacy" sub-school, Jennifer Hillman (2010) argued that the G20 had "defied its doubters in reaching consensus on specific approaches to a number of critical and controversial issues." She proposed it should be used by the United States and Europe to create a "council of governors" for global economic institutions as a whole. Russian scholar and G8 sous-sherpa Vadim Lukov (2010a, 2010b) similarly emphasized the G20 summit's success in stopping the 2007–09 financial crisis by mobilizing historic fiscal and other stimulus, in reforming the international financial institutions (IFIs), and, above all, in starting an unprecedented dialogue on different philosophies of government and economic management across many highly diverse divides. Jing Wang and Matthew Goodman (2012) added financial regulation as a G20 summit "unsung success."

A sixth highly optimistic "UN revitalization" sub-school suggested that a G20 summit could not only replace the G7/8 but also revitalize an otherwise immobilized UN, or even replace in practice its ineffective central command institutions such as the Permanent Five members of the UN Security Council (UNSC) (Janice Stein, quoted in McCarthy 2004). When, in August 2010, French president Nicolas Sarkozy first announced his plans for the sixth G20 summit, which he would host in November 2011, he suggested more modestly that it would be used to reform the UNSC.

Puzzles

From this rich debate alone, it is difficult to determine which schools' and sub-schools' claims are more analytically persuasive and empirically correct. Each of the four general schools presents serious puzzles for scholars and analysts of G20 governance in the past, at present, and for the years to come. Moreover, none of the schools is based on a close, detailed, systematic examination of actual G20 behaviour. Few are informed by concepts or theories of international relations that examine how and why international institutions should and do behave. Few assess G20 governance across a full array of international institutional performance dimensions, such as domestic political management, deliberation, direction setting, decision making, the delivery of these decisions, and the development of global governance as a whole. Few offer a clear, well-specified, systematically tested explanation for the emergence, evolution, and performance of the G20—one that could serve as a foundation for predicting or prescribing how it would and should operate in the years ahead. In particular, while many claim that the rise of emerging powers makes the G20 necessary and inevitable, few have offered arguments from the overall structure, issue structure, power cycle, or other systemic theories to show that this claim is logically convincing. Few have carefully considered the realists' supply of changing relative capability together with the vulnerability bred by the emerging intensely interconnected global system and the converging, compounding demands thus placed on all international institutions claiming to meet the need. Above all, while some have noted the causal relevance or even centrality of crisis in generating G20 governance, none has explained why the G20 continued and in some ways strengthened during the financial crisis-free years from 2002 to 2007. And even in the crisis-scarred years from 1997 to 2001 and from 2008 to 2010, none has explained why the unique G20 prevailed over all other present and possible international institutional alternatives. Without a detailed look at the particular causal configurations and pathways, it is too soon to predict if continuing, compounding crises will reinforce or reduce the rising power and influence of the G20's emerging powers, or do so in a way that creates greater commonality and consensus among all its members. It remains to be seen how selectively globalized yet acutely vulnerable countries such as China and Saudi Arabia will fit into this new global governance architecture and how well countries that are not members of the G8, the Organisation for Economic Co-operation and Development (OECD), or the BRICS grouping of Brazil, Russia, India, China, and South Africa perform as G20 summit hosts.

Despite the rich debate on G20 governance, no one has yet analysed, alone or in a comparative context, the full performance of the G20 finance ministers' and central bank governors' forum over more than a decade, or the performance of the new G20 summit at its first four meetings that arose from this continuing core to govern as an integrated whole. Nor has anyone credibly connected the G20's alleged advantages in weight, inclusiveness, representativeness, and legitimacy and its apparent disadvantages in diversity to its particular patterns of performance. Several puzzles arise as a result. Why did the G20 prevail over the new IMFC and FSF created alongside it in 1999, especially when the initial crisis that catalysed all three faded away? Why did the new Bush administration in 2001 bond with the Clinton-created G20? Why did the G20 summit take so long to emerge, despite the clear logic and energetic entrepreneurship of Paul Martin as Canadian prime minister in 2004–05? And why did George Bush, the great resister, become the founding father of the G20 summit in 2008, after he had vetoed its creation in the autumn of 2005? A close, systematic examination of the design, evolution, operation, and impact of the finance G20 meetings and summits can offer a cogent account of how the G20 has grown and governed, what it has accomplished, and the causes of its particular evolutionary path and performance thus far.

The Aim and Approach

To provide such an account, this book systematically assesses the G20's emergence, evolution, and performance in response to growing systemic demands for global governance across a wide, interconnected policy agenda. This book draws on classic and contemporary international relations themes and concepts to explain the causes of observed G20 governance, and on this basis offers some concluding predictions about its future path. In particular, the book offers an account of G20 governance, grounded in the competitive, co-dependent, and cooperative dynamics among international institutions in a crowded world, rather than a conception based only on the older models of "forum shopping" among states and the "nesting" of their international institutions in an anarchic system (Kirton 2005b).

This book offers the first full, independent, authoritative scholarly account of the G20 from its birth at the finance ministers' and central bank governors' level in 1999 through to its fourth summit in Toronto in 2010 (see Appendix B). It does not take up the popular enterprise of advising G20 governors what they should do with their forum or criticizing them for not using it to quickly solve the many problems present in the world. Nor is it a carefully vetted account from the inside, as is the G20's useful history of its work at the ministers' and central bank governors' level, published in 2008. This book focuses instead on systematically describing what the G20 did and explaining why it did it, using the best theories and concepts that scholars of international relations and global governance have in their analytic repertoire. Here it seeks not to test competing international relations theories with evidence from G20 governance, but to use the key concepts from these theories to help provide a more disciplined and insightful account of the G20 as an institution from those that currently exist.

This purpose imposes demands of evidence far greater than those accepted by many who engage in an advisory, advocacy, or assessment way in the growing G20 governance debate. Such evidence comes from scholarly works on the G20, publications by and biographies of G20 participants, policy commentaries, and, importantly, newspaper and other media accounts. In addition, this book has benefited from extensive private interviews, conversations, participation in policy dialogues, and discussions of drafts with key G20 participants, taking place from 1997 to 2012 and embracing those from almost all country members of the G20. At this early stage, before all the archives are open and before most practitioners are willing to tell all, much of relevance remains missing and some evidence comes with less strong, authoritative confirmation than scholars would prefer. But the evidence assembled in the book is sufficient to support its purpose of being the first comprehensive, reliable, detailed, independent, scholarly account of G20 governance to date, and the foundation for others to build on in the years ahead.

The Argument of Systemic Hub Governance

This book argues that the G20 has emerged as a systemic hub with a performance at the ministerial and now leader level that has generally grown to a high level across a widening policy agenda and array of global governance dimensions. The G20's expanding, effective, legitimate global governance is due in the first instance to proliferating shocks that have exposed new, non-state, equalizing vulnerabilities afflicting all systemically significant member countries. The shift to the new G20 centre of global governance also flows from the inability of older multilateral organizations and newer plurilateral institutions to cope with such shocks on their own, from the rising relative capabilities of non-G7 countries, from their increasing democratic character, from G20 representatives' domestic political control, capital, continuity, competence, and commitment, and from the G20's growth toward being a club that its members personally care about, at the hub of a growing global governance network for the world.

This is not the first work to suggest that the G20 is a flexible network for global economic governance and one catalysed by the outbreak of unprecedented global financial crises (Slaughter 1997; Alexandroff and Kirton 2010; Kirton 2010a; Cooper and Subacchi 2010; Heine 2010). It is the first work to specify what the concept of a network means in its full application to the G20, whether, how, and how much the G20 is the hub of a global network, and how it has grown to achieve that status and centrality now. It is not the first to suggest that crises of various sorts are essential catalysts for creating institutionalized global governance (Ikenberry 2001; Gamble 2009). However, it is one of the few to take seriously the view that crisis, relative capability, and democratic commonality alone are not enough to shape specific global governance creations and outcomes in the institutional and ideational sphere. The agency, visions, calculations, and choices of individual leaders, alone and together, are required as well. This work thus systematically identifies, arranges, and traces the six key causes that, in an interactive combination, produced the particular path and pattern of G20 performance over its first 11 years. Here, as led by the analytics and evidence, it highlights the importance of agency, the role of the individual, and the prescient vision of global governance that the G20's creators and continuing custodians have had.

The Course of G8 Governance

This book argues that since 1999 the G20 has grown quickly and flexibly to govern much of the broad economically related agenda long addressed by the G7/8, including a few core political-security issues such as terrorist finance, money laundering, transnational crime and corruption, and good governance. By 2001 and especially with the advent of G20 summitry in 2008, the G20 has moved from its initial achievements in domestic political management, deliberation, and direction setting into robust decision making, delivery, and the development of global governance. The G20 has also since the start quietly supported and succeeded in protecting and promoting economic and political openness and thus democracy around the world, by encouraging learning, socialization, and economic, regulatory, and political reform among once closed member states. Yet it still has not met the challenge of democratizing its own governance appropriately to broadly include civil society or develop adequate accountability mechanisms, in order to reinforce its democratization from the top, or to meet the demands for greater legitimacy from all around.

The Causes of G20 Governance

The particular course of G20 governance has been driven in the first instance by shocks, initially from finance from 1997 to 2001 and again from 2007 to 2010, from terrorism since 2001, and, finally, from energy and the environment since 2007. These shocks grew in their speed of eruption and contagious spread, their geographic and policy scope, and their scale of impact within sovereign states, up to those at the very top of the relative capability scale. The sources and targets of such increasingly non-state initiated shocks changed, from an emerging Asia in 1997, to a once hegemonic but now highly vulnerable America and Europe by 2007–10. The sequence and shift showed that globalization had transformed the world, socially as well as materially, into a complex, adaptive system characterized by compounding interconnectedness, complexity, and uncertainty.

Such shocks exposed and equalized the vulnerability of the major powers to such a degree that the formal multilateral organizations America and its Atlantic allies had constructed for the still Westphalian world in the 1940s and their subsequent informal plurilateral international institutional enhancements could no longer protect them to the necessary degree now. Unlike its many international institutional alternatives, the G20 alone comprised as full, equal members the countries that increasingly contained the collectively predominant and internally equal capabilities required to respond effectively to the growing shocks and vulnerabilities of a globalized world. These systemically significant members, including both the leading producers and consumers of systemic security, increasingly became more politically open polities, driven by economic growth, globalization, G8 guidance, and G20 socialization. The G20 further benefited from the sustained domestic political control, capital, continuity, competence, and commitment of its finance ministers, central bank governors, and leaders. These began with its founding visionary, Paul Martin, who steered it from 1997 to 2001 and encouraged its summit-level version from 2004 to 2005, and his colleague Larry Summers, who contributed critically to the finance G20 forum at its start and to G20 summitry in its formative years from 2009 to 2010.

The G20 slowly moved toward becoming a club whose unchanging membership and limited participation reduced transaction costs and engendered trust. It fostered learning and socialization among established and emerging countries and conferred the status, identity, and new conceptions of systemic interests, such as "enlightened sovereignty," on members of a prestigious top-tier group from which many benefits flowed. Group identity, attachment, and socialization were fuelled by the increasing intensity of interaction among members. In particular, the 2008 American-initiated crisis brought the group together at the leaders' level twice a year for two years. The G20 also became a hub for a growing global governance network. Many of its members also met at summits and ministerials of globally relevant plurilateral institutions, where they had a further chance to speak, share views, come to consensus, and collectively decide. There was ongoing participation on many levels by member governments in processes that culminated in leaders' summits. As a result, the G20 gained centrality, effectiveness, and legitimacy as the hub of a global network and as a valued group moving to become an internally cherished club.

The Phases of G20 Governance

More specifically, G20 governance evolved through three distinct phases, each with a particular pattern of performance and configuration of salient causes behind.

Phase 1: The Crisis-Catalysed Canadian-American Co-creation, 1997–2001

The first phase was the crisis-catalysed Canadian-American co-creation of the "finance G20" from 1997 to 2001. During that time the world was struck by three unprecedented sequences of shocks: the Asian-turned-global financial crisis, the 9/11 terrorist attacks and their aftermath, and the financial shocks in Turkey and Argentina. The G20 was formed to cope with these financial shocks and rapidly expanded into a group with an economic, social, and security agenda too. However, these crisis catalysts were transformed into the specific G20 governance result, among the many international institutional alternatives available, largely due to two G7 finance ministers, Paul Martin and Lawrence Summers. They foresaw and rationally calculated the changing relative capability that would come from rising powers and the growing vulnerability for all and crafted a new group of systemically significant equals in response. It was a group initially generated and guided by G7 members when the G7/8 was at its victorious post-Cold War peak and had just decided to admit a now democratically devoted Russia to the G8 in 1997–98.

Phase 2: The Emerging Countries' Club, 2002–2007 The second phase of G20 governance saw the G20 genuinely become an emerging countries' group from 2002 to 2007. Hosting and chairing responsibilities and rights moved to non-G7 members, which became more attached and influential as a consequence and cause. The agenda shifted to these countries' priorities of development and IFI reform. Germany and China became G20 enthusiasts and leaders. The group produced its initial architectural achievement by giving rising powers a larger institutionalized place through an agreement on the first stage of IMF voice and vote reform—an achievement that had eluded other forums. This outcome was driven less by new shocks, such as the terrorist attacks in Britain on July 7, 2005, than by the slow response and shortcomings of the G7/8 and other international institutions in accepting as equals the rapidly rising emerging countries. It was also driven by deepening democracy among G20 countries, by Martin's campaign for the G20 to rise to the summit level, and by the growing global institutional network around the G20 hub, such as the Major Economies Meeting on Energy Security and Climate Change (MEM). Once the crisis necessary for the G20's creation had subsided, the initial design continued internally to produce some of the important results intended by the founders and have the group gather strength as a systemic hub of global relevance and reach.

Phase 3: The Core Crisis-Catalysed Central Summit Club The third phase of G20 governance saw the G20 rise to the leaders' level to become, in self-proclamation and in practice, the premier forum for its members and thus the world's economic governance as a whole. The G20 summit stopped the American-turned-global financial and economic crisis of 2007–09 and the European-going-global aftershock that erupted in the spring of 2010. The Eurocrisis advanced to new levels the difficult processes of securing fiscal stimulus and sustainability, balancing global growth through mutual assessment and adjustment, opening trade despite global economic contraction, strengthening common domestic financial regulation and supervision, financing development, and advancing the second stage of IFI voice and vote reform.

The years from 2007 to 2010 brought an almost perfect storm of non-state shocks, in global finance and economics, in terrorism in Moscow, Mumbai, and elsewhere, and in energy and the environment with the historic oil price spike in 2008 and America's Macondo oil leak in the Gulf of Mexico in April 2010. But once again, shocks alone were not enough to drive and determine the G20's response, if only because, as in 1997–99, there were many unilateral, bilateral, regional, or other international institutional alternatives present and proposed. Moreover, the September 2009 decision to make the new G20 summit "permanent" and "premier" as its members' preferred forum came after the initial crisis had been contained, before the Eurocrisis erupted, and while most of the other half-century old architectural issues were still waiting to be addressed. Once again, American leadership and domestic politics do not directly drive the result. As in the 1997–2001 formation, the 2008–10 elevation to the leaders' level was a bipartisan effort with a lame duck US president of one party and his fresh successor from another contributing in quick succession to the G20's rapid creation and growth. In both cases, an American was the key "decider," but the initiative came from elsewhere in the G7. Moreover, the decision was taken within a field of possibilities that was importantly and increasingly constrained by actors and forces beyond.

The G20 summit was chosen as the solution to the crisis in 2008 in part because it had been designed so well at the ministers' and central bank governors' level in 1999 and had worked well since. All G20 members save a hesitant President Bush had agreed it should be elevated to the leaders' level even before the 2008 shock struck. Proclaiming it permanent and premier at Pittsburgh was a step further along a path-dependent process started in 1997–99 when the G20's founders chose the right route to cut through the twenty-first century forest of interconnectedness, complexity, and uncertainty and chose the right companions to blaze what became the superhighway for the first responders and subsequent reconstructors to arrive on time when the 2008 shocks struck. In a tightly wired world where the less powerful could quickly take down the strongest, the right global governance response required equality among all the systemically significant countries, whether new or old, and increasing openness among and within each, to foster the fast flexibility and learning needed to cope with the complex, uncertain, connectivity, and challenges of the new age. This time the great global power transition was also different than in the Westphalian past because now almost all the rapidly rising powers were democracies, thanks in large part to the G8 and then the G20's work. Even China was slowly moving toward the greater economic, social, and political openness needed to thrive in a networked world. It was thus doing its part to make the G20 a genuine global governance hub that was becoming an interpersonal as well as an institutional club.

The Future of G20 Governance

During its first 11 years from 1999 to 2010, the G20 focused on key financial, economic, trade, and development issues that increasingly demanded global governance. It quickly reached out flexibly to address other issues, notably terrorism in 2001 and climate change in 2006. An important feature of the G20 has been the growing consensus on common economic, political, and social principles within the group, which has created a commitment to greater political openness at the core.

This may result in the long term in reciprocity, replication, and an ultimate fusion between the G20 and a G8 devoted to open democracy and social advance at its existential core. Because democracy breeds economic growth and vice versa, the resulting virtuous cycle should make the democratizing G20 a more effective economic, social, and political global governance club (Friedman 2006). Because open democracy has dominant global appeal as the form of "right rule" for the future, the G20 will become an increasingly legitimate club. In the number and composition of its members and participants, the G20 has led the G8, while in the policy agenda, range of governance functions and core mission of democratization, the G8 has assisted the G20 to slowly become more like an interpersonally cherished club. In the long term, an institutionally dominant G20 and an ideationally dominant G8 may well merge into one, especially if the G20 can reach down to involve civil society more inclusively and improve its accountability along the lines that the G8 has.

The Approach

To arrive at this conclusion, the analysis in this book unfolds as follows. Chapter 2, "The Systemic Hub Model of G20 Governance," outlines the specific conceptual contributions taken from a wide range of international relations theory to guide this analysis of G20 governance. These theories and concepts have been combined to create a model of "systemic hub governance" that systematically describes and explains how and why the G20 has evolved and performed in the particular way it has.

Part II, "Generating the Group, 1999–2001," outlines the original crisis-catalysed conception and operation of the G20 during its formative first three years. Chapter 3, entitled "Creating the Group, Berlin 1999," examines how and why the G20 emerged from the 1997–99 Asian-turned-global financial crisis, against several alternatives and alongside the IMFC and FSF, through the leadership of Canada's Paul Martin and America's Larry Summers, to take life at its first ministerial meeting in Berlin. Chapter 4, "Governing Globalization, Montreal 2000," charts how the G20 quickly broadened its ambitions, agenda, and achievements once Martin served as host as well as chair. Chapter 5, "Combating Terrorism, Ottawa 2001," shows how the G20 flexibly and effectively became a global security governor, taking terrorist finance as its focus, and briefly bonding as an interpersonal club when the new Bush administration was assaulted by the unprecedented al Qaeda attacks on America in the autumn of 2001.

Part III, "Equalizing the Influence, 2002–2007," charts the mid-course correction and evolution that made the G20 an emerging countries' group during its second phase of work. Then the G20 became in operation, as well as in conception and institutional architecture, a more genuine group of equals, while the 2004–05 campaign to elevate it to the leaders' level almost met with success. Chapter 6, "Driving Development, New Delhi 2002 and Morelia 2003," shows the G20 turning to development when its non-G7 members first took the chair. Chapter 7, "Bonding Berlin, Berlin 2004," shows how a once reluctant Germany became an effective G20 leader, paving the way for the G20's contribution to reforming the IFIs to give emerging country members a greater place. Chapter 8, "Capturing China, Xianghe 2005," charts the path as the largest non-G8 member of the G20 assumed the chair and leadership of the group. Chapter 9, "Strengthening Sustainability, Melbourne 2006 and Kleinmond 2007," accounts for the move to include sustainable development on the G20 agenda, as energy and climate change arose as critical issues in the world.

Part IV, "Creating the Summit Club, 2008–2010," examines how and why the G20 was chosen to leap to the leaders' level, become institutionalized, and performed effectively as the permanent, premier centre of its members' international economic cooperation during its first two years. Chapter 10, "Soaring to the Summit, Washington 2008," traces how and why this G20 leaders' governance started amidst the unprecedented US financial crisis erupting in the autumn of 2008. Chapter 11, "Containing Contraction, London 2009," charts the G20 summit's continuation as the "Great Recession" assumed full force in the established, emerging, and developing countries alike. Chapter 12, "Institutionalizing Summitry, Pittsburgh 2009," addresses the G20's evolution into the self-proclaimed permanent, premier centre of its members' international economic cooperation. Chapter 13, "Controlling the Eurocrisis, Toronto 2010," shows how it fulfilled this larger ambition as a new sovereign debt crisis erupted in Europe from Greece in the spring of 2010.

The book concludes in Part V with Chapter 14, "The Future of G20 Governance." It summarizes the book's central arguments about the course and causes of G20 governance and the contribution to international relations theory that this analysis makes. On this basis it briefly considers the future of the G20 at its subsequent and forthcoming summits and its impact on global governance as a whole.

References

Abbott, Kenneth W., Keohane, Robert, Moravcsik, Andrew, Slaughter, Anne-Marie, and Snidal, Duncan. 2000. "The Concept of Legalization." *International Organization* 54(3): 401–20.

Agence France Presse. 2009a. "African Ministers Demand G20 Seat." October 4. Available at: www.pambazuka.org/aumonitor/comments/2564. Accessed: July 2012.

Agence France Presse. 2009b. "Brazil Sees Chance to Alter World Decisions at BRIC Summit." June 14.

Alexandroff, Alan S. and Kirton, John J. 2010. "The 'Great Recession' and the Emergence of the G20 Leaders' Summit." In *Rising States, Rising Institutions: Challenges for Global Governance*, eds Alexandroff, Alan S., and Cooper, Andrew F. Washington DC: Brookings Institution Press, 178–95.

Åslund, Anders. 2009. "The Group of 20 Must Be Stopped." *Financial Times*, November 26. Available at: www.iie.com/publications/opeds/oped.cfm?ResearchID=1549. Accessed: July 2012.

Baker, Andrew. 2010. "Restraining Regulatory Capture? Anglo-America, Crisis Politics, and Trajectories of Change in Global Financial Crisis." *International Affairs* 83(3): 647–63.

Bayne, Nicholas. 2003. "Impressions of the Evian Summit, 1–3 June 2003." June 3. Available at: www.g8.utoronto.ca/evaluations/2003evian/assess_bayne030603.html. Accessed: July 2012.

Bayne, Nicholas. 2010. *Economic Diplomat*. Durham UK: Memoir Club.

Beauchesne, Eric. 1999. "Martin Warns against Complacency." *Montreal Gazette*, September 26, p. A9.

Beeson, Mark and Bell, Stephen. 2009. "The G20 and International Economic Governance: Hegemony, Collectivism, or Both?" *Global Governance* 15(1): 67–86.

Bradford, Colin I. and Lim, Wonhyuk, eds. 2010. *Toward the Consolidation of the G20: From Crisis Committee to Global Steering Committee*. Seoul and Washington DC: Korea Development Institute and Brookings Institution.

Bradford, Colin I. and Linn, Johannes F. 2004. "Global Economic Governance at a Crossroads: Replacing the G7 with the G20." Brookings Institution Policy Brief 131. Available at: www.brookings.edu/papers/2004/04globaleconomics_bradford.aspx. Accessed: July 2012.

Bryant, Ralph C. 2003. *Turbulent Waters: Cross-Border Finance and International Governance*. Washington DC: Brookings Institution Press.

Carin, Barry and Mehlenbacher, Alan. 2010. "Constituting Global Leadership: Which Countries Need to Be Around the Summit Table for Climate Change and Energy Security?" *Global Governance* 16(1): 21–38.

Choe, Wongi. 2010. "The Role of Korea in G20 Process and the Seoul Summit." Paper prepared for an international conference on "G20 Seoul Summit: From Crisis to Cooperation," Korean Association of Negotiation Studies, May 20, Seoul. Available at: www.g20.utoronto.ca/biblio/choe-kans.pdf. Accessed: July 2012.

Choi, Hee-nam. 2009. "Enhancing Korea's Standing through the G20." *Korea Herald*, June 9.

Cooper, Andrew F. 2010a. "The G8-G20 Partnership." In *G8 & G20: The 2010 Canadian Summits*, eds Kirton, John J., and Koch, Madeline. London: Newsdesk, 306–07. Available at: www.g8.utoronto.ca/newsdesk/g8g20. Accessed: July 2012.

Cooper, Andrew F. 2010b. "The G20 as an Improvised Crisis Committee and/or a Contested 'Steering Committee' for the World." *International Affairs* 86(3): 741–57.

Cooper, Andrew F. and Subacchi, Paola. 2010. "Overview." *International Affairs* 86(3): 607–17.

Crockett, Andrew. 2004. "Progress towards Greater International Financial Stability." In *The IMF and Its Critics: Reform of Global Financial Architecture*, eds Vines, David, and Gilbert, Christopher L. Cambridge: Cambridge University Press, 36–58.

Culpeper, Roy. 2000. "Systemic Reform at a Standstill: A Flock of 'Gs' in Search of Global Financial Stability." Paper presented at Critical Issues in Financial Reform: Latin-American/Caribbean and Canadian Perspectives, Munk Centre for International Studies, University of Toronto, June 1–2, Toronto. Available at: www.g8.utoronto.ca/scholar/culpeper2000. Accessed: July 2012.

Dean, January. 2004. "Trade Minister Says PM's Right on Expanding G7." *Mississauga News*, April 21.

Donovan, Paul. 2009. "What Is the G20 Really Fighting For?" *Jakarta Post*, October 19.

Duncan, Richard. 2008. "Bring Back the Link between Gold and the Dollar." *Financial Times*, November 23. Available at: www.ft.com/intl/cms/s/0/ba673d22-b977-11dd-99dc-0000779fd18c.html#axzz215UCNXWY. Accessed: July 2012.

Economist. 2008a. "The Coddle and Protect Policy." November 20. Available at: www.economist.com/node/12636308. Accessed: July 2012.

Economist. 2008b. "Miss World Goes Missing." November 20. Available at: www.economist.com/node/12641700. Accessed: July 2012.

Economist. 2008c. "No Time to Waste." November 20. Available at: www.economist.com/node/12637027. Accessed: July 2012.

Economist. 2008d. "Where's Angela?," November 20. Available at: www.economist.com/node/12637035. Accessed: July 2012.

Foster, Peter. 2003. "Far More New Faces than New Ideas." *National Post*, December 13.

Friedman, Benjamin. 2006. "The Moral Consequences of Economic Growth." *Society* 43(2): 15–22.

Gamble, Andrew. 2009. *The Spectre at the Feast: Capitalist Crisis and the Politics of Recession*. Basingstoke: Palgrave Macmillan.

Giles, Chris. 2009. "G20 Yet to Deliver on Early Promise." *Financial Times*, November 8. Available at: www.ft.com/cms/s/0/8e834f02-cc63-11de-8e30-00144feabdc0.html#axzz1B4rYIUhT. Accessed: July 2012.

Grant, Kelly. 2010. "Paul Martin." *Globe and Mail*, May 31.

Griesgraber, Jo Marie. 2009. "Reforms for Major New Roles of the International Monetary Fund? The IMF Post-G20 Summit." *Global Governance* 15: 179–86.

Heine, Jorge. 2010. "Will They Have Table Manners? The G20, Emerging Powers, and Global Responsibility." *South African Journal of International Affairs* 17(1): 1–11.

Helleiner, Gerald. 2001. "Developing Countries, Global Financial Architecture, and the Group of Twenty: A Note." Prepared for the Governance Working Group of the Global Financial Governance Initiative. Available at: www.

globaleconomicgovernance.org/wp-content/uploads/Helleiner%20on%20G20.PDF. Accessed: July 2012.

Hermawan, Yulius P., Sriyuliani, Wulani, Hardjowijono, Getruida H., and Tanaga, Sylvie. 2011. *The Role of Indonesia in the G20: Background, Role, and Objectives of Indonesia's Membership*. Jakarta: Friedrich-Ebert-Stiftung Indonesia Office. Available at: library.fes.de/pdf-files/bueros/indonesien/08365.pdf. Accessed: July 2012.

Hillman, Jennifer. 2010. "Saving Multilateralism: Renovating the House of Global Economic Governance for the 21st Century." Brussels Forum Paper Series, March. German Marshall Fund of the United States. Available at: www.gmfus.org/wp-content/files_mf//galleries/ct_publication_attachments/EconJenniferHillmanBFPaperSavingMultilateralism.pdf. Accessed: July 2012.

Ikenberry, G. John. 2001. *After Victory: Institutions, Strategic Restraint, and the Rebuilding of Order after Major Wars*. Princeton: Princeton University Press.

Johnson, Pierre Marc. 2000. "Beyond Trade: The Case for a Broadened International Governance Agenda." *Policy Matters* 1(3): 4–36.

Johnson, Pierre Marc. 2001. "Creating Sustainable Global Governance." In *Guiding Global Order: G8 Governance in the Twenty-First Century*, eds Kirton, John J., Daniels, Joseph P., and Freytag, Andreas. Aldershot: Ashgate, 245–82.

Jones, Bruce, Pascual, Carlos, and Stedman, Stephen John. 2009. *Power and Responsibility: Building International Order in an Era of Transnational Threats*. Washington DC: Brookings Institution.

Kelly, Paul. 2009. "Shift to G20 Was Matter of Time." *Australian*, September 27.

Kharas, Homi and Lombardi, Domenico. 2012. "The Group of Twenty: Origins, Prospects, and Challenges for Global Governance." Brookings Institution, Washington DC. Available at: www.brookings.edu/research/papers/2012/08/g20-global-governance-kharas-lombardi. Accessed: July 2012.

Kirton, John J. 2001a. "The G20: Representativeness, Effectiveness, and Leadership in Global Governance." In *Guiding Global Order: G8 Governance in the Twenty-First Century*, eds Kirton, John J., Daniels, Joseph P., and Freytag, Andreas. Aldershot: Ashgate, 143–72.

Kirton, John J. 2001b. "Guiding Global Economic Governance: The G20, the G7, and the International Monetary Fund at Century's Dawn." In *New Directions in Global Economic Governance: Managing Globalisation in the Twenty-First Century*, eds Kirton, John J., and von Furstenberg, George M. Aldershot: Ashgate, 143–67.

Kirton, John J. 2002. "Global Community Outreach: The G20 and Africa." G8 Online, Lecture No. 9. Available at: www.g8.utoronto.ca/g8online/2002/english/2002/09.html. Accessed: July 2012.

Kirton, John J. 2005a. "The Future of the G8." In *G8 Summit 2005: Mapping the Challenges*, ed Fraser, Maurice. London: Newsdesk Publications. Available at: www.g8.utoronto.ca/newsdesk/G8-2005.pdf. Accessed: July 2012.

Kirton, John J. 2005b. "Toward Multilateral Reform: The G20's Contribution." In *Reforming from the Top: A Leaders' 20 Summit*, eds English, John, Thakur, Ramesh, and Cooper, Andrew F. Tokyo: United Nations University Press, 141–68.

Kirton, John J. 2008. "The G8's Democratic Governance." ["In Portuguese."] *Cadernos Adenauer* 9: 39–60.

Kirton, John J. 2009. "London Summit: Acting for Change." In *The G20 London Summit: Growth, Stability, Jobs*, eds Kirton, John J., and Koch, Madeline. London: Newsdesk Publications, 26–27. Available at: www.g20.utoronto.ca/newsdesk/london. Accessed: July 2012.

Kirton, John J. 2010a. "The G20 Finance Ministers: Network Governance." In *Rising States, Rising Institutions: Can the World Be Governed?*, eds Alexandroff, Alan S., and Cooper, Andrew F. Washington DC: Brookings Institution Press, 196–217.

Kirton, John J. 2010b. "The G20 Summit as an International Negotiation Process: Shaping the Systemic Summit Club for Toronto and Seoul." Paper prepared for a conference on on "G20 Seoul Summit: From Crisis to Co-operation" hosted by the Korean Association of Negotiation Studies and sponsored by the Institute of Foreign Affairs and National Security, May 19, Seoul. Available at: www.g20.utoronto.ca/biblio/kirton-kans.pdf. Accessed: July 2012.

Knight, Malcolm, Schembri, Lawrence, and Powell, James. 2004. "Reforming the Global Financial Architecture: Just Tinkering Around the Edges?" In *The IMF and Its Critics: Reform of Global Financial Architecture*, eds Vines, David, and Gilbert, Christopher L. Cambridge: Cambridge University Press, 124–56.

Lander, Mark. 2008. "World Leaders Vow Joint Push to Aid Economy: Big Decisions Delayed." *New York Times*, November 16, p. 1. Available at: www.nytimes.com/2008/11/16/business/worldbusiness/16summit.html. Accessed: July 2012.

Le Boucher, Eric. 2003. "Pourquoi les antimondialistes gagnent du terrain." *Le Monde*, November 9.

Lukov, Vadim. 2010a. "G20 and G8 in Search of Solutions: Global Problems of Economy and Society." *International Affairs* 56(5): 58–76.

Lukov, Vadim. 2010b. "Parnership for Progress: From the 2010 Muskoka-Toronto Summits to the Seoul Summit." Conference on "Partnership for Progress: From the 2010 Muskoka-Toronto Summits to Seoul Summit" at the State University Higher School of Economics, October 27, Moscow.

Martin, Paul. 2004. "Speech by the Prime Minister." Address at a luncheon hosted by CORIM, CERIUM, Institut d'études internationales de Montréal at UQAM and the Montreal International Organization, Montreal, May 10. Available at: epe.lac-bac.gc.ca/100/205/301/prime_minister-ef/paul_martin/05-10-06/www.pm.gc.ca/eng/news.asp@id=201. Accessed: July 2012.

Martin, Paul. 2008. "Time for the G20 to Take the Mantle from the G8." In *Growth, Innovation, Inclusion: The G20 at Ten*, eds Kirton, John J., and Koch,

Madeline. London: Newsdesk, 22–27. Available at: www.g8.utoronto.ca/newsdesk/G20at10.pdf. Accessed: July 2011.

Martinez-Diaz, Leonardo. 2007. "The G20 after Eight Years: How Effective a Vehicle for Developing-Country Influence?" Global Economy and Development Working Paper No. 12, Brookings Institution, Washington DC. Available at: www.brookings.edu/papers/2007/1017development.aspx. Accessed: July 2012.

Masson, Paul R. and Pattison, John C. 2010. "Financial Regulatory Reform: Using Models of Cooperation to Evaluate Current Prospects for International Agreement." Rotman School of Management, University of Toronto, Toronto. Available at: www.g20.utoronto.ca/biblio/G20reforms.pdf. Accessed: July 2012.

McCarthy, Shawn. 2004. "Ottawa Still Supports UN, Graham Says." *Globe and Mail*, May 1.

Meyer, Laurence, Doyle, Brian, Gagnon, Joseph, and Henderson, Dale. 2004. "International Coordination of Macroeconomic Policies: Still Alive in the New Millennium?" In *The IMF and Its Critics: Reform of Global Financial Architecture*, eds Vines, David, and Gilbert, Christopher L. Cambridge: Cambridge University Press, 59–105.

O'Neill, Jim and Hormats, Robert. 2004. "The G8: Time for a Change." Global Economics Paper No. 112, Goldman Sachs, New York.

Ostry, Sylvia. 2010. "Pessimism of the Intellect, Optimism of the Will." August 7, Available at: www.g20.utoronto.ca/biblio/ostry-cipa.html. Accessed: July 2012.

Payne, Anthony. 2010. "How Many Gs Are There in 'Global Governance' after the Crisis? The Perspectives of the 'Marginal Majority' of the World's States." *International Affairs* 86(3): 729–40. doi: 10.1111/j.1468-2346.2010.00908.x.

Penttilä, Risto E.J. 2009. "Multilateralism Light: The Rise of Informal International Governance." Centre for European Reform, London. Available at: www.cer.org.uk/pdf/penttila_essay_july09.pdf. Accessed: July 2011.

Persaud, Avinash. 2010. "The Locus of Financial Regulation: Home versus Host." *International Affairs* 86: 637–46).

Porter, Tony. 2000. "The G7, the Financial Stability Forum, the G20, and the Politics of International Financial Regulation." Paper presented at the annual convention of the International Studies Association, March 15, Los Angeles. Available at: www.g8.utoronto.ca/g20/biblio/porter-isa-2000.pdf. Accessed: July 2012.

Postel-Vinay, Karoline. 2011. *Le G20, laboratoire d'un monde émergent*. Paris: Les Presses de Sciences Po.

Rogoff, Kenneth. 2010. "Technology, Complexity, Economy, Catastrophe." *Globe and Mail*, June 2. Available at: www.theglobeandmail.com/news/opinions/technology-complexity-economy-catastrophe/article1588565. Accessed: July 2012.

Schirm, Stefan A. 2012 (July). "Global Politics Are Domestic Politics: A Societal Approach to Divergence in the G20." *Review of International Studies*: 1–22. doi: dx.doi.org/10.1017/S0260210512000216.

Scholte, Jan Aart. 2003. "Governing Global Finance." In *Governing Globalization: Power, Authority and Global Governance*, eds Held, David, and McGrew, Anthony. Cambridge: Polity Press, 189–208.

Schwab, Klaus. 2003. "Address to the Plenary Session of the World Economic Forum: Africa Economic Summit 2003." June 12, Durban.

Shanghai Institutes of International Studies Working Group. 2009. "The Reform of International Financial System and China's Policy Options." *Global Review* (3): 40–54.

Shorr, David and Wright, Thomas. 2010. "The G20 and Global Governance: An Exchange." *Survival: Global Politics and Strategy* 52(2): 171–98.

Slaughter, Anne-Marie. 1997. "The Real New World Order." *Foreign Affairs* 76(5): 183–97.

Slaughter, Anne-Marie. 2005. "Government Networks, World Order, and the L20." In *Reforming from the Top: A Leaders' 20 Summit*, eds English, John, Thakur, Ramesh, and Cooper, Andrew F. Tokyo: United Nations University Press, 281–95.

Summers, Lawrence. 2008. "The Birth of the G20." In *Growth, Innovation, Inclusion: The G20 at Ten*, eds Kirton, John J., and Koch, Madeline. London: Newsdesk, 29–31. Available at: www.g8.utoronto.ca/newsdesk/G20at10.pdf. Accessed: July 2012.

Talley, Ian. 2010. "IMF Chief: Global Financial Crisis Has Washed Away Old Economic Order." Dow Jones, December 8.

Wang, Guoxing. 2009. "Financial Crisis: Its Impacts on International Economic System and Geopolitics." *Global Review* 3: 24–38.

Wang, Jing and Goodman, Matthew P. 2012. "Prudence and the G20." *Global Economics Update* 1(6): 1–2. Available at: csis.org/files/publication/120802_Simonchair_newsletter_August2012.pdf. Accessed: August 2012.

Winning, Nicholas and Parkinson, Joe. 2009. "G20 Fin Mins Come Up Short on Climate Change." Dow Jones, November 7.

Chapter 2
The Systemic Hub Model of G20 Governance

The Approach to Analysis

Explaining the particular path of Group of 20 (G20) governance requires a compact, multicausal model that coherently combines key causes and clearly connects them to the particular outcomes that took place and, where possible, to those that did not. To construct such a model this chapter draws on concepts from classic and contemporary theories of international relations. It also mobilizes the established models of Group of Eight (G8) governance, with appropriate adjustments for the distinctive characteristics of the G20 and the specific tasks G20 governors have been called upon to perform in the changed systematic context they have faced. The result is a model of systemic hub governance that adapts and extends the proven concert equality model of G8 governance by selectively drawing on concepts from international relations theories of realism, liberal institutionalism, Gramscian political economy, constructivism, complex adaptive systems, clubs, and networks.

International Relations Theory

Applications to the G20

The work of mobilizing international relations theory to explain G20 governance began with Tony Porter's (2000) analysis of the origins, early operation, and future prospects of the finance G20 (see also Schirm 2012). He argued that the concept of legitimacy, as opposed to standard realist, liberal-institutionalist, and Gramscian explanations, was critical in accounting for the creation of both the G20 and the Financial Stability Forum (FSF). Realist theories could account for American leadership in creating the earlier Group of 22 (G22), which consisted of Group of Seven (G7) members, Australia, and 14 emerging countries selected unilaterally by the United States. But the subsequent G20 could not be seen as a direct benefit to the United States alone or to its G7 colleagues, especially in relation to the non-G7 powers that had their relative power enhanced by membership and that apparently made no bargaining concessions to secure admission to the new group. Similarly, liberal-institutionalist approaches could account for the G20's role in reducing transaction costs, creating economies of scale in learning, reducing uncertainty, and enhancing monitoring in the wake of the 1997–99 financial crisis. They could also account for the use of the G7 as an international institutional regime "nest." However, the absence of rational bargaining among G7 or other G20 members, the absence of concessions from non-G7 members to secure membership, and the momentary crisis-induced weakness of developing country members at the time of their admission constituted important departures from the core theoretical claims of the liberal-institutionalist as well of the realist repertoire.

Gramscian approaches failed as well. Despite the G20's capitalist-friendly appearance, it increased the autonomy of member states relative to markets and the business community, saw business groups play no consequential role in the group's formation or operation, and emphasized two key ideas—private-sector burden sharing and slow capital account liberalization with selective capital controls—that were antithetical to the interests of the wealthy classes. The G20's efforts to minimize the frequency and severity of financial crisis and instability were indeed in the interests of wealthy investors and the broad mass of newer ones. But these interests were shared by the crisis-affected countries and classes and by the broader international community as well. A superior explanation flowed from the dynamics of legitimacy—the way the G20 and FSF provided technical and political legitimacy on economic, professional, and democratic grounds.

Porter's (2000) account properly points to the crucial role of crisis, in particular the successive shocks of the 1997–99 global financial crisis that delegitimized the prevailing institutions (the International Monetary Fund [IMF], the Group of Ten (G10), the Basel Committee on Banking Supervision [BCBS], and even the G7 on its own) and prompted a call for a new, more broadly representative forum that shifted the prevailing pre-crisis neoliberal doctrine to a more socially sensitive approach to globalization (Kirton 1999, 2000). Yet a detailed examination of the evolution and early operation of the G20 suggests a somewhat more robust, if still incomplete, role for realist, liberal-institutionalist and Gramscian political economy contributions than Porter allowed.

Realism

Standard accounts of the G20 begin implicitly or explicitly with the core realist assumption about the primacy of relative capabilities among the territorially exclusive Westphalian sovereigns that count in shaping outcomes in the international system, global governance, and world order (Morgenthau 1948). Drawing implicitly on power cycle theory in its various forms, such accounts highlight the rapid rise of emerging powers and conclude that they need their proper place in the central global governance forum if world stability and order are to be maintained and reformed and, by extension, if many of the world's problems are to be solved in an effective and legitimate way (Organski and Kugler 1980; Doran 1971; Cooper 2010). Realism in the form of hegemonic stability and leadership theory points to the essential role of the predominant power, most recently post-World War Two America, in creating international institutions and still leading them in its "after hegemony" moment with a little help from its ranking allies, as the American-plus-one leadership model of G8 governance affirms (Keohane 1984; Putnam and Bayne 1987; Hajnal 2007).

To be sure, such accommodating American leadership did arise in 1997. The initiative to create the ad hoc G22 was a personal initiative of a few American officials rather than a US state interest overall (Krasner 1978). The experience with the G22 gave the US government, along with its fellow members of the G7 concert, a shared interest in creating a regularized, institutionalized forum with a permanent, fixed membership and proper reporting relationship to the G7 and the other established international institutions in which it was nested. Even with the apparent decade-long "Goldilocks" economy and the 1997–99 crisis-driven resurgence in relative US power against G7 countries other than Britain and Canada, the resulting G20—as with the G7 itself in 1975—mobilized systemically predominant capabilities to combat a now much more global threat and one that a post-hegemonic United States could no longer combat alone, as revealed by the crisis catalysed by the collapse of Long-Term Capital Management (LTCM) in September 1998 in America (Kirton 2000).

Realism remains more broadly relevant in explaining G20 governance. The countries included in the G20, with few exceptions, were the most relatively capable ones in the world at the time, while less capable candidates such as Thailand and Chile were not admitted. Each member, regardless of its G7 or Group of 77 (G77) status, soon combined with many others in flexible balancing coalitions that cut across old divides to get the outcomes it thought were best and were needed to make the G20 work as a club of equals. As number one, America helped lead the creation of the G20 both in 1999 and 2008. It did so with the support of a strong second—Canada in 1999 and France and Britain in 2008. America may have caused the 2008 crisis but it could be argued that it had the most specialized capabilities required to comprehend and cure it, residing in its sophisticated financial centre of New York. And both declining relative powers with their defensive positionalist desires and rising ones revising the foreign policy conceptions of their rights and responsibilities had a common interest in creating an expanded group to protect their top-tier position, rather than becoming revolutionaries to overthrow an order that had allowed them each to rise at different times.

Yet the causal links connecting relative capabilities to international institutional creation, operation, outcomes, and impact are seldom straightforward. Moreover, realist theory has been much better at theorizing the world order effects of unipolarity, bipolarity, and multipolarity in the form of a pentarchy (and the respective "powerness" that lies behind) than it has been in addressing how a world of 20 leading powers can create a continuing international institution that has autonomous effects, beyond allowing the "balancing" behaviour of each of the 20 to proceed in more efficient ways. Realism requires Westphalian states equipped only with relative capability and rationality as its theoretical building blocks. It cannot cope well with their vulnerabilities as well as capabilities, with the interconnections among them, with the importance of horizontality as well as verticality in the international state system, with the equal importance of those formerly relegated to the realm of middle powers, and with the reduced relevance of territoriality in a fast-moving globalized age. Relative capability, changes in relative capability, and a concern with defensive positional stability in the face of systemic shocks remain relevant in accounting for G20 governance. But the realist repertoire provides only a few essential components, rather than a complete toolkit for constructing a comprehensive model of how and why the G20 works. The fast-moving twenty-first century world is very different than the slow-moving one of Westphalia in 1648. In this new world, relative connectivity counts alongside the relative capability that once did all alone.

Liberal Institutionalism

Liberal institutionalism also offers conceptual contributions. Its initial emphasis on reducing transaction costs by providing a focal point, lengthening the shadow of the future, creating transparency and trust, and catching cheating are important in showing why the G20 prevailed over the initial and subsequent ad hoc assemblies created or proposed by a leading power or multilateral organization (Krasner 1978; Keohane 1984; Cooper 2010). These features help explain why the institutionalized G20 won out over the IMF's ad hoc 25-member New Arrangements to Borrow (NAB-25), the G22, and the Group of 33 (G33) in 1999, why the G20 continued with unchanged membership after the creational crisis had passed, and why it was chosen as the group to leap to the leaders' level when a mega-crisis came in the autumn of 2008. Moreover, the G7/8 provided an important international institutional nest to incubate and nurture the new G20—by approving its creation in 1999, providing internal guidance and leadership throughout, offering lessons about why a leader-level G20 was useful, and having its experienced members host and chair the G20 at both the ministerial and leaders' levels during its formative years.

But liberal institutionalism, especially in its legalization extension, cannot account well for why the G20 won out over and came to guide and govern the highly legalized IMF and its International Monetary and Financial Committee (IMFC) (Abbott et al. 2000). Nor can it explain why the informal, lightly legalized G20 often performed well for over a decade without its own secretariat or legal charter to provide the theoretically desired precision, obligation, and delegation or the legitimacy that the United Nations and the IMF claimed to have as a result. Such fixed attributes may be far less important in a densely interdependent world where fast, flexible, innovative, interconnected responses are at a premium in determining which global governance centres will work and win. In the end, the informal G20 reformed the formal IMF in its key "voice and vote" feature, rather than the other way around.

Gramscian Political Economy

Political economy concepts, especially from the Gramscian and historical materialist tradition, also add a little but leave out a lot (Wallerstein 1979). As with the more elite G7/8, the G20 was a case of group hegemony—governance of and by the top 20 for the lesser 173 Westphalian sovereigns that were left out (Bailin 2005; Soederberg 2002; Best 2003). Moreover, most G20 members in 1999 were rich or rising enough to have a vested interest in the status quo, and thus the group goals of financial stability, counterterrorism, and the creation and continuation of a top-tier governance group where their equal position was secure. All had come to accept the basic premises of globalization, market capitalism, and the real rather than caricatured Washington Consensus, and, above all, the importance of open trade and investment for export-led growth (Williamson 1997). Countries that did not accept those premises, such as Mahathir's Malaysia, did not get in. The unity created by the primacy of this economic and ideational consensus did not extend to classic security issues, a policy domain that the G20 did not take up at the start (Arrighi and Silver 1999).

However, some of the G20's leading members, starting with China and India, saw themselves as representing the still dispossessed developing countries and did so with demonstrable reformist, if not revolutionary, effect, especially on issues such as climate change. More broadly, while the G20 recognized the logic that the single-world capitalist system now needed global capitalist governance from a single political centre, China and Saudi Arabia were hardly the "captured" capitalist countries that historical materialists had in mind. Moreover, the important architectural debates within the G20, including those over zero-sum voice and vote at the international financial institutions (IFIs) and which variety of market-state capitalism was now appropriate, were the essence of G20 politics. The G20's great failure to predict or prevent the 2007–09 crisis erupting in America and the leading Atlantic powers, without exposing the contradictions that created a new ideational order, also challenges key historical materialist claims.

Constructivism

Constructivism in its many varieties has concepts to contribute but remains an incomplete account. It adds the important social dimension, allowing conscious, committed, goal-directed actors that interact intensely with one another in response to new problems to construct new consensual knowledge, interests, identities, and even international institutions that become what might be called "stability communities" or financial, economic, and social security communities in a changing world (Adler 2002, 1997; Adler and Barnett 1998; Baker 2006, 2010).

Constructivism first invites scholars to transcend the crumbling pillars of Westphalianism and to highlight the epistemic dimension and autonomous power of ideas, from embedded liberalism to democracy, human rights, and the rule of law. Indeed, John Ruggie's (1983) initial insight that shared social purpose as distinct from material power can maintain and change international regimes highlights how the evolving ideational consensus of the G7/8 and then the G20 helped create and continue the G20, especially during the crisis-free years of rapid change in relative capability. Here the consensus of "embedded ecologism" played a role (Polanyi 1944; Kirton 2002). Redistributional principles were relevant too (Kirton 2005). Constructivism focuses ideationally on direction setting as a component and on common principles and practices as a cause of what international institutions such as the G20 do.

Second, the G20's agenda dealt with highly technical, specialized issues of domestic financial regulation and supervision, international finance, and the work of the IFIs. Here new consensual knowledge in response to new problems was at a premium (Adler and Haas 1992). This helped the G7, which initially had an advantage in new knowledge construction but not a sufficient share, to lead and need the G20, rather than to invoke old, fixed interests to dictate its course.

Third, in the great crisis that created the G20 in 1999 and elevated it in 2008, member countries increasingly confronted a world and agenda of interconnectedness, complexity, and uncertainty that they struggled to comprehend. They had few well-known fixed interests of any specificity to defend in G20 debates about non-bank asset-backed commercial paper, credit default swaps, and various instruments invented for the mortgage market in the United States. Crisis easily killed inherited positions. New ones had to be intellectually and politically invented domestically, and internationally, beyond a due regard for what the ever-changing international traffic would bear to avoid loss through regulatory arbitrage. Positions thus had to be socially constructed in an intense process of international interaction to define a new regime and within it domestic preferences beyond loss aversion, at a time when crisis meant that the status quo was no longer an option.

Yet constructivism leaves much out. The socially constructed new economic order created by the G20 was more like the status quo than the far-reaching alternatives that French president Nicolas Sarkozy and British prime minister Gordon Brown had heralded as the "new Bretton Woods" when the 2008 crisis struck. The trust and sociability within the old G7 remained much greater than in the new G20, especially where China, Saudi Arabia, and Argentina were concerned. And while some lesser powers such as Canada and Korea found it easy to adopt a new identity of a "G20 member," it was harder for the most powerful United States. And the leaders of longstanding "middle powers" Australia and Brazil did not even show up for the summit in June 2010. By then no G20 community or club had emerged in an interpersonal sense.

Key Concepts

To account for such shortcomings and for the demand for and supply of a new form of global governance for the twenty-first century world, the insights of three additional theories need to be added to the analytical repertoire.

Complex Adaptive Systems

The first addition, accounting for the demand for a new form of global governance, is complex adaptive systems (Holling 1973; Homer-Dixon 2001; Dewitt and Kirton 1983; Ostrom 2009). This concept highlights a world with no stable equilibrium, few constant, proportional, linear causal relationships, path-dependent processes, multiple feedback loops, sudden and step-level jumps to new states, and a changing structure as a result.

In such a system, actors face an environment of interconnectedness, complexity, and uncertainty, over which they have, and know they have, very incomplete comprehension and control. Their task is less to operate within a fixed, simple, well-understood system to preserve or promote their own well-known established interests and identities, as either possession or milieu goals (Wolfers 1962). Rather, it is to come together to comprehend how the new system works, and how much and how it can be controlled, before it takes all of them down in a short time. This is especially true if the recurrent crises come not from a known, nasty, offensive country or even from Westphalian states that can often calculate the cumulative effect of their interactions (if not the outbreak of accidental wars), but rather from many non-state actors, including all living things and physical processes beyond. Such a system regularly generates shocks that make all aware of their shared vulnerabilities and triggers a common and collective loss-aversion instinct. It is thus the changing complexity, not the constant anarchy of the system, from which the demand for new global governance flows.

Clubs

The second addition is the concept of clubs. In its rationalist, incentive-oriented, institutional expression, this concept helps explain why the G20 was not a concert, such as the G8 with merely more powers added, but a different kind of group that had arisen to govern a changed world. The G8 is a concert—a very particular kind of club. The G20, with its many non-major power members, including a few non-democratic ones, is not. But it is still compact, continuing, clear, and consciously constructed enough to constitute not merely a continuing coalition of convenience, but a club with known members with well-understood collective responsibilities and rights. Moreover, like a concert, it is a club that has not expelled or seen any of its members leave in its first 11 years.

The concept of a club was first developed by James Buchanan (1965) to account for cooperative membership and behaviour and do so by bridging the gap between purely private goods and public goods. Clubs are voluntary and exclusive, with non-members excluded from the benefits of membership. The benefits of belonging must outweigh the costs (Sandler and Tschirhart 1997). Michele Fratianni and John Pattison (2001) argue that the concept has significant explanatory power for international institutions. As the cost of hegemonic leadership for the United States has increased, “today’s incentive structure suggests collegial leadership, not hegemony." There are strong incentives to being included in and thus to maintaining and strengthening such a group, particularly for the relatively less powerful member countries that are less able to exert influence on the basis of relative capability alone.

This shift in incentive structure also helps explain the rise of the G20 (Hermawan et al. 2011). Larger and more powerful countries tend to have larger costs for—but also larger benefits from—group membership. As the benefits decline, so does the incentive for such a country to lead the group. That the G20 was conceived as a club of equals may in part be explained by the declining incentive of the United States to play the leading role in international cooperation. There are also significant benefits to being a member of such a club, starting with the prestige of being one of the systemically significant countries, the domestic political rewards that can accrue from attendance at its meetings, the confidence that encourages all to contribute, and, above all, the ability to shape the new global order in the way a member thinks best. Beyond the direct club benefits are those that flow from producing the broader global public goods that only the club can, and that its members need.

A second dimension of a club, the social-psychological aspect, is also important (Stephens 2010). The G8 is a club of a particular kind—a small elite group, often gathering in isolated or resort settings with time for spontaneous personal encounters where everyone at the working meals and sessions is seated around the table close enough to touch a colleague's shoulder, whisper to a neighbour, and engage in personal and informal collective conversation. With the G20, the room is substantially expanded, the members seated far apart from one another, the time for informal conversation much reduced, the meetings shorter, and the languages spoken by the leaders more diverse. However, the number of members still remains limited. The opportunity for personal interaction is sufficient for the emergence of a valued, shared collective identity as a member of a cherished club. At a minimum, G20 meetings, especially through their increased frequency since 2008, can increasingly foster enough of a relationship among ministers and central bank governors so that a member can telephone others when a crisis looms, as in May 2010. Even the diverse collection of G20 leaders can forge such interpersonal bonds.

Shocks are an important galvanizing factor in increasing international cooperation within clubs, with the effect depending on the relative impact of the shock on different countries (Masson and Pattison 2010). Where the shocks are comparable, the result will be increased benefits from cooperation and coordination of policy. Yet if one country experiences a larger shock than another, it will benefit less from coordination unless contagion is an issue, as indicated by the differing responses of G20 members to a proposed bank levy in 2009–10. Severe, sequential shocks produce a particular incentive to reach out to one's familiar and ever more trusted colleagues, to share and reduce one's uncertainties and fears, and to work collectively to devise a common response.

In short, shocks activate the first, instrumental dimension of club behaviour as the members realize that if they do not all "hang together" they will each hang alone (Putnam and Bayne 1987). The second social-psychological dimension is triggered as the members come together to struggle to solve the problems the shock creates and the shared sense of elation and triumph when they succeed.

Networks

The third conceptual addition is that of networks (Zacher and Sutton 1996). The G20 is not just an institutional and emerging social-psychological club to cope with continuing, compounding, complex crises, but is a club that serves as the hub of a global network. In this network, the combined established and emerging powers are members of the G20 club at the hub of other global groups that radiate to bring insights and influence into and out of the hub. In this way, every member of the network is represented in G20 governance even if it is not a full member or ad hoc participant of the club at the hub. The G20 is thus the most well-connected club in the world. As the club at the hub of a network, the G20 can perform at least adequately in providing global governance even in the absence of new shocks.

Anne-Marie Slaughter (1997, 2004, 2005, 2009) asserts that the world is no longer composed of formal hierarchies, but of spider web-like networks that confer benefits on the basis of connectivity rather than inclusion. She argues that global governance will increasingly be the result of transnational intergovernmental interactions among executive branch members, regulators, and members of the judiciary and legislatures forming consensus beyond and below the traditional level of the executive branch. The old world as a system of hierarchically stacked "black box" states of different sizes subject to rules created by themselves with a little help from international institutions is giving way to a world of national government components—executive, judiciary, legislature—interacting with each other internationally, transnationally, and domestically.

G20 governance was a network at its inception when it was composed of finance ministers, central bankers, and their deputies and officials. It soon spawned numerous working groups and study seminars composed of experts consulted for their knowledge in a particular field. The equalization of knowledge through the simultaneous diffusion of information through the network, increasingly made possible by the internet, reinforced these network effects through the G20's preparatory and follow-up processes and among regulators at what became "its" Financial Stability Board (FSB).

On the demand side, globalization means that the world needs much more global regulation. But on the supply side, its Westphalian sovereigns do not want a classic centralized authority with decision-making power (Slaughter 2005). Robert Keohane (2002) saw that globalization, which creates a dense network in the nongovernmental world, "creates potential gains from cooperation" if institutions can be created to harness those gains, adding that institutions themselves can be "oppressive." Slaughter (2005) argued that a leader-level G20 could meet demands for accountability and transparency by demonstrating that a government network is more inclusive than the UN or the World Trade Organization (WTO) in terms of the balance in the locus of power and more transparent in its aims. A G20 summit "can be a catalyst for change and creating problem-solving … as well as being at the centre of its own network of networks" (Slaughter 2005). The advent of the G20 summit, its increasing inclusion of invited countries and international organizations, and the growing outreach of the host have increased these network characteristics and effects. Even leaders at the very top of their national hierarchies can successfully engage in network governance with their peers outside.

The Model of Systemic Hub Governance

Describing and explaining the G20's performance requires a causal model that compactly and coherently accounts for the G20's creation, evolution, and performance as the consequence, as well as the forces that combined to cause this particular pattern of behaviour. The concert equality model of G8 governance, first developed by John Kirton (1989, 1993, 2000, 2001), offers a suitable starting point. But adaptations and extensions are needed to capture the distinctive character of the G20 as a systemic club (Kirton 2010). The G20 is not just the G8 concert writ large, with the existential membership criteria of major-powerness and democratic polity relaxed. Rather, it is a different kind of club, defined by the systemic significance of its members in a world where the connectivity among as well as the relative capability across countries is a central feature of the system that matters much more than it did in the slow, separated world of Westphalia in 1648.

The Dimensions of G20 Governance

As with the concert equality model, the G20's international institutional performance can be charted along six dimensions (see Appendix C).

Domestic Political Management

The first dimension is domestic political management (see Appendix D). It occurs first through the prestige that comes when a country's participation or membership in the G20, or its chairing or hosting of the G20, is announced and happens, and as its priorities for its summit or ministerial participation become known, approved, and applauded at home. These components are joined at the summit or ministerial meeting by compliments for a country encoded in the collective communiqué and at its end by the editorial approval, immediate increase in domestic public opinion support, and ultimate electoral reward that a country or its representative receives. They extend to references to the meeting in national policy addresses and the national image conveyed in its branded accomplishments, such as the Montreal Consensus or the Seoul Development Consensus. In addition, hosting a summit or ministerial meeting can have, and be seen to have, economic and other benefits such as image enhancement, offset by its financial and other physical and political costs.

Deliberation

The second dimension is deliberation (see Appendix E). It occurs privately and internally through the face-to-face discussions and conversations the members have at and during the meeting, in the lead-up and follow-up to the meeting, in other venues, and even through plurilateral and bilateral conference calls and email exchanges. This private dimension is accompanied by the public and external dimension of the G20's deliberation, as encoded in the collective communiqués issued in the members' names.

Direction Setting

The third dimension is direction setting (see Appendix F). Central to this dimension is the G20's affirmation of shared principles and norms, with principles defined from classic regime theory as statements of fact, causation, and rectitude and norms defined as more specific statements of prescription ("thou shall"), prohibitions ("thou shall not"), or permission ("thou may") (Krasner 1983).

The initial acceptance or creation of facts shows G20 governors' ability to comprehend the operation of the complex adaptive system they are steering, and the basis of their ability to predict and prevent a crisis in advance.

Their mental causal model shows how well they map the system's ontological "reality" or at least match any prevailing consensus of outside "experts" in the field. They, along with other stakeholders, thus help determine the epistemic credibility of the G20. At this point, the internal consensus and coherence of their causal model as well as its fit with the prevailing one outside become important for external credibility.

Complete internal consensus can coexist with a complete absence of a match with any external one. Indeed, the G7-focused false new consensus model suggests that G20 members can be in complete agreement that they are now powerless to take any effective action aimed at governing globalized financial markets even if outside experts believe this is empirically incorrect (Bergsten and Henning 1996; Kirton 1999). On the other hand, creativity and innovation in G20 comprehension, well beyond outside consensus, can show G20 leadership at its best.

From facts and causation flows rectitude—a consensus on the right thing to do or have done. This is the core of legitimacy, which is defined simply as right rule. If the G20 is seen to be doing the right thing for everyone, it matters less who is at the table to do it on their behalf. If it is seen to be trying to do the right thing in the right way, it matters less if it is fully effective in getting it done. Who governs and who gets what is less important than the substance of what is being done. The "right to rule" derives from the superior concept of right rule (Buchanan and Keohane 2006).

Important also for the G20's inherent rectitude and thus legitimacy are its affirmations of democratic values. In the narrow sense, the principles of open democracy, individual liberty, and social advance flow from the G20's nurturing by G7/8, which has these values at its core. In the broader sense of political openness, democratic values such as transparency, accountability, and the rule of law are procedural principles on which most can agree and that ensure G20 governance is open to the broader community. Most broadly, there is an empirical case that these values are more acceptable to all countries and citizens in the world than the alternatives that have now been defeated in most consequential countries, or the ones that have arisen in their place. Since its start in 1975 the global democratic revolution has largely proceeded down a one-way street, with the small-scale reversals in Venezuela and Bolivia being but small speed bumps on the superhighway that global democratization has become.

Decision Making

The fourth dimension is decision making—the provision of credible, clear, collective commitments with sufficient precision, obligation, and delegation to serve as a reference point, a source of moral suasion, or a deterrent threat for outside actors who respond to G20 commitments in the intended way, even in the absence of further implementing action by G20 governments (Abbott et al. 2000; Kokotsis 1999) (see Appendix G). The soft law embodied in G20 statements offers a credible expression of determination and self-binding, while avoiding the generality, ambiguity, or obsolescence in the face of fast-moving circumstances that the principles, norms, and rules entrenched in formal charters of ratified intergovernmental treaties can suffer from (cf. Simmons 2000). Commitments may vary in their ambition, significance, and the number of members to which they explicitly apply. But by extending G20 governance into a global executive branch as a source of prescriptive authoritative action, they make the G20 more than a photo op for domestic political management, a global hot tub party for deliberation, or a preacher's pulpit from which to sermonize about good things.

Delivery

The fifth dimension is delivery, starting with the compliance with those decisional commitments and extending to their effective implementation by members and others to produce the intended results in the intended or other ways to effectively address the problem at hand (see Appendix H). Here G20 governments initially faithfully follow their collective consensus through "first order" implementing actions designed to fulfil their commitments (Kokotsis 1999). An extensive body of evidence points to widespread variation across time, members, and issue areas in the extent of member governments' efforts to comply with their G7/8 commitments (von Furstenberg and Daniels 1992; Kokotsis 1999). This evidence suggests that informal, soft law institutions like the G7/8 and G20 can be their own "judiciary," without a police force to back them, as a genuine group that binds members and whose commitments count. There is also emerging evidence that leaders can craft their commitments in ways that include catalysts to improve compliance. It remains to be determined which accountability mechanisms enhance compliance and how they work in this regard.

Development of Global Governance

The sixth dimension is the development of global governance—internally the creation, continuation, and evolution of the G20 as an international institution and externally of those to which it relates. It is in this category that the key components of the G20's institutional evolution, as distinct from its ongoing operations, are contained. Internally, the creation and use of summit, ministerial, official, and civil society components stand at the core. Included here is the incubation by the G7/8 and G20 of spin-off plurilateral summit institutions or those at other levels involving subsets of G20 members, notably the BRICS grouping of Brazil, Russia, India, China, and South Africa.

Externally, of particular importance is the G20's ability to maintain its identity and operate as a group within broader international institutions, such as the IMF, and other forums to which its members belong, in order to extend its intra-G20 consensus and collectively receive the inputs that these broader bodies send to the G20 as a global network hub. In this respect G20 members are not constrained by the particular regimes embedded in these other institutions, but use these institutions as delivery vehicles or legitimating mechanisms to forward the consensus within a broader group.

The Configuration of the Performance Dimensions

These six dimensions of G20 governance lie along a scale in two ways. The first is temporal, ranging from immediate to very long-term impacts. Domestic political management takes place immediately, starting long before a summit or ministerial meeting occurs, when it is learned that a country has been included or chosen to host. The development of global governance has the most long-range effects in changing the institutional and even constitutional architecture and structure of how the world is governed and thus how the world works, as with the G20's creation of voice and vote reform at the IMF.

The second dimension is a spatial one, ranging from the local site of the meeting or summit up to the international, supranational, and global levels. Domestic political management is, by definition, focused on governing within the domestic, geographically determined, and territorially restricted Westphalian state and society, starting with the meeting site, although it may extend to efforts at the influence of and within targeted states and societies beyond. Deliberation, direction setting, and decision making take place at the intergovernmental level among the members of the group, although these dimensions can extend to outsiders as participants or targets of influence. Delivery can be done by others beyond those who made the decision. The development of global governance embraces the planet as a whole (Putnam and Bayne 1987).

Overall, G20 governance can also be assessed by its comprehensiveness—the provision of effective performance and institutional capacity to address the full range of global challenges, either by reforming existing international institutions or by helping create new ones within and outside itself. Comprehensiveness can be assessed in several ways: spatially, according to the full set of global countries or geographic regions included and affected; functionally, according to the range of issue areas dealt with; temporally, according to the crisis response, repair, and prevention to post-crisis reform conducted; and vertically, according to the degree of domestic intrusiveness sought and obtained. Its full realization takes maximum advantage of the G20's unique character as a flexible forum with an expanding mandate and agenda, able to link issues in innovative ways, to create large package deals that enhance general welfare, and to set new directions for the global community as a whole.

The G20's collective performance can also be assessed according to its overall coherence. Coherence can be conceived of as the provision of an internally consistent, logically credible, complete, and effective system of global governance, in response to the demands of the global system at any time. G20 governance may work well in some components. But if it acts at cross purposes at the same time, it may not be internally consistent, efficient, or comprehensive enough to cope with the global challenges at hand.

The Causes of G20 Governance

The model of systemic hub governance explains G20 governance as the proximate result of a process of fluid coalition diplomacy that has four characteristics: any member will lead; any member will support or oppose; a full array of coalitions that cut across conventional criteria or existing blocs will flexibly arise according to the issue; and even the most powerful member will eventually adjust to and abide by the collective result. Such a process of fluid coalition diplomacy arises from six underlying causes: shock-activated, equalizing vulnerability; the failure of older international institutions acting alone to protect members' national interests and preferences and to provide global public goods; collectively predominant and internally equal capabilities; common core domestic characteristics; domestic political control, capital, continuity, competence, and commitment; and controlled club participation as a global network hub.

This model represents an adaptation and extension of the concert equality model constructed to explain G8 governance (Kirton 1989, 1993). Similar to the revised concert equality model, it starts with the claim that in an intensely globalized world, the equalization of inter-vulnerability, more than capability, requires the involvement in an expanded group of those countries that can contribute resources in the face of contagious threats affecting all or, as importantly, can infect all directly through vulnerabilities within their national systems (Keohane and Nye 1989). In 1999 the G20's outer, non-G7 ring of emerging or middle powers mattered in multidimensional terms, unlike those in the Organization of the Petroleum Exporting Countries (OPEC), the Group of 77, the Consumer-Producer dialogue from the 1970s, the Cancún "global negotiations" members of 1981, or the Group of 15 developing countries that began meeting in at the G7 Paris Summit in 1989. They mattered both for the destructive vulnerabilities and reinforcing capabilities they possessed in a tightly wired world. They mattered equally when they changed categories in the great reversal taking place within a decade's time, with the United States, the United Kingdom, and Germany moving from being providers of financial security in the 1997–99 crisis to being consumers of financial security in the 2008–10 one. Countries such as Indonesia, Korea, Russia, and Brazil moved the other way. The global geographic extent, speed of contagion, and domestic destructiveness of the new globalization dramatically displayed by the 1997–99 global financial crisis required the response and mobilization of a predominance of capabilities far greater than before, as well as many more states inside the core group, to lead in implementing the domestic measures to prevent such systemically and socially destructive crises from starting in the first place.

Furthermore, unlike the divided world of the Cold War era, the international community now included enough representative democratic polities, or enough moving toward more democratic degrees and forms of governance, to make possible a permanent institutionalized association for effective global governance based on shared domestic characteristics (Ikenberry 2001). It was from this democratic or proto-democratic stratum that the G20's outer members were almost entirely drawn and from which a common purpose was in part forged. Such growing political openness gave members accessibility, interaction, and opportunities for learning within the governments of all other members, thus deepening and reinforcing the cohesion of the group.

Empirically, since its start, the G20 was marked by significant bargaining over fundamental issues in its creation and early operation. The most profound issue was the overall architectural question of whether the G20 or the rival IMFC would emerge as the effective political centre of economic governance for the new era that had dawned in 1999. A second was the question of membership, with different G7 members having distinctive preferences, and two enjoying some success as they sought to secure their national preferences in the new institution and bring into being their preferred approach to world order. The third issue, as shown by the early debate over the new principles of private-sector participation and controlled capital account liberalization, was the way that the initial division between G7 and non-G7 members showed signs of yielding to a reciprocal flow of influence and to fluid coalitions of G20 members that crossed the divide from the G7 to the non-G7 members.

In short, in the post-Cold War, intensely globalized world of the twenty-first century, an adjusted and expanded form of the concert equality model that explains the emergence, operation, and effectiveness of the G7/8 accounts to a considerable degree for the creation, continuation, evolution, activity, and impact of the G20. In its initial years, the new G20 forum was defined by multifaceted inter-vulnerability rendered visible by six factors: a sequence of shocks; the failure of other international institutions in response; the predominance and equalization of members' capabilities; converging characteristics of political openness; the political control, capital, continuity, competence, and commitment of its agents; and its controlled club participation as a network hub without and equality within. This gave rise to a fluid pattern of forming internal coalitions, in which any member could combine with any other on the basis of enduring interests, distinctive national values, and changing preferences. As with the concert equality model, the embryonic reservoir of common purpose, the role of coalitional fluidity in bringing together the large collection of members beyond the confines of a K-group, and the G20's resistance to expansion showed that the cause of constricted participation remained relevant (Snidal 1985). Yet unique to the systemic hub model was the G20's status as a network hub, as a club of an institutional sort if not permanently of an interpersonal one.

Shock-Activated, Equalizing Vulnerability

In the model of systemic hub governance, the first cause of the G20's evolution and performance along all six governance dimensions is shock-activated, equalizing vulnerability (see Appendix I). Shocks, like acute international crises, come with a high level of surprise and constitute a high threat to national values but do not necessarily require a short time to respond. Moreover, shocks can come not only as a bolt-out-of-the-blue assault with no precedents or warning, but also as one instalment along a cumulative causal chain whose latest link is more or less dramatic and damaging than those before. Even 9/11, as America's twenty-first century Pearl Harbor moment, was the second occasion in less than a decade in which al Qaeda-affiliated terrorists had attacked the World Trade Center in New York City to kill innocent civilians there. It is because leaders of the most capable countries, relative to models of analytical rationality, are generally slow, selective, cybernetic learners, that second and subsequent shocks have escalating, at times non-linear, step-level effects (Steinbruner 2002; Welch 2005).

Such sequential shocks awaken leaders to their vulnerabilities—harm within the societies and states of their sovereign polities that cannot be contained by their own unilateral changes in national policy (Keohane and Nye 1977). Of particular salience are the shock-activated, equalizing vulnerabilities arising from non-state or even non-human sources, launched with no consciousness, intentionality, targeting, or control but able to intrude into even the most powerful polities anywhere at any time to quickly kill or hurt many humans and do much other damage there. The 9/11 terrorist attacks on America had a few attributes of this new vulnerability. "Swine" influenza and climate change have more. The financial market meltdowns of 1997–2001 and 2008–10 had the most, including the slow death of the newly deprived and dispossessed that they brought.

Such shock-activated, equalizing vulnerabilities can easily arise from and arrive in small poor states and communities, which often live in such a world of new vulnerability every day and lack the adaptive resilience required to respond (Dewitt and Kirton 1983). But they can also arise from within the small or large to make even the most capable countries as vulnerable as the small. The 1997–2001 crises largely showed the first dynamic, at least until the LTCM hedge fund in America collapsed. The 2008–10 financial crisis showed the second, as the most capable country, America, became almost as vulnerable as the much less capable, if not quite to the same degree as internationally bailed-out Iceland, Ireland, Greece, or Portugal.

In this world, countries count if they are either controllers or causes of the shocks and vulnerabilities that lie behind. They are systemically significant on either count. They are too interconnected to be left out of any effective response.

International Institutional Failure

The second cause of the G20's evolution and performance is the failure of other international institutions acting alone to respond adequately to such shock-activated, equalizing vulnerabilities (see Appendix J). These included both the old formal, hard law multilateral organizations from the 1940s and the newer, more informal, soft law plurilateral ones, including the G7/8 itself, and those with secretariats too (Wicks 2003). These institutions fail not only in their prescience, processes, and policies, but also in their inclusion, as equals in their governance centres of the countries with the capabilities needed to cope with the shocks and the vulnerabilities they expose in an intensely interconnected world. Multilateral organizations can work well for their founders long after hegemony has left, but eventually pathology and obsolescence will arise (Barnett and Finnemore 1999, 2004). The failure of the old multilateral organizations, as well as unilateral, regional, and other plurilateral alternatives, to protect members' interests and provide needed global public goods can catalyse G20 cohesion and action. The failure of other governance alternatives to act adequately is a strong impetus for the G20 to govern instead.

It is here that the great debate over the G20's "representativeness" can be addressed. As everyone reserves the right in public as well as private life to form groups to which not everyone belongs or attends, the pertinent criterion is relative representativeness rather than representativeness according to some arbitrary ideal. The appropriate question is thus: compared to other relevant international institutions does the G20 have a better number, balance, and diversity on various dimensions of the actors included in its governance core?

The G20 contains as members more than double the number of countries in the G8, and contains two more multilateral institutions. Non-G7 and non-G8 countries predominate numerically. There is a rough balance between developed and developing countries, and between members and non-members of the Organisation for Economic Co-operation and Development (OECD). G20 members come from all major geographic regions, with particularly robust representation from Asia and especially the Asia-Pacific, and from all of the world's major geopolitically grounded civilizations. Relative to the IMFC, the G20 can be criticized on geographic, linguistic, and relative capability grounds. Specifically, it under-represents Africa and the francophone world and small, poor states, and over-represents traditional western European middle powers, in part because of the still unoccupied, initially identified Nigerian seat. However, the ex officio membership of the IMF and the World Bank in the G20 gives the G20 a claim to at least a second-hand representation of the universal membership of the global community, over the broad and expanding array of finance, development, and many related international and domestic issues these Bretton Woods institutions now address. However, as with the G7 and G8, the unique presence among regional organizations of the European Union, while deepening the G20's democratic character, constitutes an imbalance that privileges developed and European countries rather than the broad array of emerging, smaller, developing, and less developed countries from most other regions of the world (Larionova 2012). More broadly, the G20 was not created with an architecture for broadly incorporating civil society representatives, nor has it yet devised such a process, even in the classic form that international institutions such as the OECD or the International Labour Organization have long had. The greatest lack of representativeness in the G20 is its overwhelming predominance of democratic politics, a characteristic that few have criticized. How and how much particular dimensions of the G20's changing representativeness matter is an issue best left for the evidence from 1997 to 2010 to decide. Comparative representativeness is but one component of international institutional failure. More important are prescience or anticipatory performance, the institutional capacity to address as well as comprehend the problem, and the speed of response when shock sequences arise.

The failure of other international institutions on these and other components means that many of the same countries that belong to many of these institutions look to the G20 to do the job. Over time the G20 thus comes to prevail over its older international institutional alternatives. Yet from the start the G20, ratified by the G7/8 with the IMF and World Bank as integral members, succeeds when these particular institutions cooperate in providing essential support to G20 governance, even as they fail when acting on their own.

Collective Predominance and Internal Equality in Capabilities

The third cause of the G20's evolution and performance is the collective predominance and internal equality in overall and specific relevant capabilities of the country members (see Appendix K). The collective predominance of the members provides the resources that assist compliance. The G20 leaves out no consequential countries that might have the incentive or ability to create a challenging counter-club. It induces outside actors to accept the G20's reference and deterrence points as those likely to prevail. It enables the G20 to assemble the most capacity to respond to the shock and challenge at hand.

Internal equality among members produces the sense of responsibility and resources that enhance performance because it is more likely that G20 members will exert dominant influence and assume formal management responsibilities within the broader multilateral organizations in keeping with G20 goals. Such resources and responsibility will also induce comprehensiveness, as this collective hegemon has the resources and incentive to pioneer governance arrangements in new fields.

Increasingly, equalizing capabilities make it likely that markets and outside actors will respond to collective G20 consensus, rather than that of the United States or the G7/8 alone. Moreover, such equality, by offering each member a credible threat of retaliation for any member's defection, increases the prospects of compliance in general and consistency in particular, and increases the collective provision of more comprehensive governance (Kirton 1993).

In the case of both predominance and equality, relative capability must be assessed according to not only the classic Westphalian calculus but also according to the equal importance of connectivity in a tightly wired world. The key questions are whether the G20's collective predominance in capabilities is adequate to govern the system and whether there is effective internal equality in capability and connectivity across and among the members of the group.

Converging Domestic Characteristics

The fourth cause of the G20's evolution and performance is the converging political characteristics of openness to which most or all members of the group are domestically attached (see Appendix L). Here political openness and ideally democracy take pride of place, for these characteristics allow open, accessible, multilateral, network governance among G20 governments and societies to occur. Such shared domestic attributes are both institutional and ideational. Institutionally, domestic democracy makes countries more pacific polities, more open economies, and more international cooperators, as many classic and contemporary democratic peace theorists have affirmed (Kant 1991; Oneal and Russett 1999; Ikenberry 2001). Ideationally those polities that have durably and deeply adopted and accepted democratic principles can be considered members of the democratic club. Yet even the oldest constitutionally committed democracies have had setbacks, and indeed have never lived up to their ideal, as the Watergate-scarred America of the early 1970s shows. In practice, democracy is always a work in progress (United Nations Development Programme 2010). In principle, it is not.

Political Control, Capital, Continuity, Competence, and Commitment

The fifth cause of the G20's evolution and performance is the members' domestic political control, capital, continuity, competence, and commitment (see Appendix M). Leaders or ministers in control of their executive, legislatures, central banks, and regulatory agencies and in possession of a sufficient popularity and electoral freedom at home have a margin of political control and capital that enables them to overcome dominant societal interests or ideas to address distant global problems, of a long-term, structural, or emerging nature and to adjust to others abroad to get a deal done (Baker 2010; cf. Schirm 2012). By extension, should such leaders have a similar popular appeal in countries beyond the G20, they will be looked to for leadership there. Their proposed solution will produce a responsiveness and legitimacy and thus have an impact among publics, even should other national governments and intervening international organizations prove resistant. Low political control and capital at home might make a G20 leader seek greater performance on the dimension of domestic political management, but will diminish collective performance on the other five dimensions of G20 governance.

Continuity gives agents greater experience and expertise, and casts a longer shadow of the future. It also produces the personal relationships and sense of responsibility that help make a group an interpersonal club. Competence acquired from education and previous professional experience in finance, economics, and business, which are the core issues dealt with by the G20, enhances the influence of those who have it within the group and of the group as a whole in the world outside (Porter 2003; Baker 2010). Commitment is a personal property of agents, referring to the importance they attach to particular issues and to G20 governance overall, their vision of how it should unfold, and their will and skill in bringing this vision to life.

Controlled Club Participation as a Network Hub

The sixth cause of the G20's evolution and performance is controlled club participation as a network hub (see Appendix N). Control of the size and quality of participants increases the attachment to the exclusive club and its prestige. Limiting the group's size allows for more deliberative conversation, direction-setting consensus, and decisional commitment and delivery through compliance. The intensity of interaction increases and mutually reinforces these characteristics and consequences of the group.

Together these dynamics mean that agents' conceptions of interest and identities are increasingly constructed collectively as a consequence of the intense, personal interaction among the same counterparts in the group. With high continuity and intensity, personal bonds arise. While personal dislikes can be fostered as well, the sense of attachment to the group and its fellow representatives as a whole can prevail. The institutional group thus becomes a personal club.

Such a club becomes the hub of a global network when combinations of its established G8 and emerging non-G8 members are key members of other plurilateral groups that count. This is not the imperial hub-and-spoke sociogram where a single country at the centre radiates influence and interaction along separated spokes to which it alone belongs and that it alone controls (Galtung 1964). Rather, overlapping combinations of those in the club at the hub are leading members of other institutions. They thus spread information, interaction, and influence around in more reciprocal and resilient ways. Given the summits or finance ministers' forums of the Commonwealth, la Francophonie, the Asia-Pacific Economic Cooperation (APEC) forum, and the Summit of the Americas, the G20 began life in 1999 on a firm foundation in this regard. With many more such bodies added afterward, by 2010 the G20 became more of a club at the hub.

Conclusion

The successive shocks activating the new vulnerabilities brought by globalization, erupting in the Asian-turned-global financial crisis of 1997–99, catalysed the creation in 1999 of a broader, more collectively capable, and intensely interconnected G20 to help the G7/8 and others provide global governance in finance and related fields. The G20's expanded number and range of systemically significant countries as members increased the capacity, representativeness, effectiveness, and legitimacy of this new centre of collective leadership. In 2008, the much greater American-turned-global financial crisis inspired the G20 to leap to the leaders' level, a move that brought new opportunities and levels of performance in these regards. Just how much, how, and why the G20 seized these opportunities from 1999 to 2010 constitute the core of the story that the following chapters tell.

References

Abbott, Kenneth W., Keohane, Robert, Moravcsik, Andrew, Slaughter, Anne-Marie, and Snidal, Duncan. 2000. "The Concept of Legalization." *International Organization* 54(3): 401–20.

Adler, Emanuel. 1997. "Seizing the Middle Ground: Constructivism in World Politics." *European Journal of International Relations* 3(3): 319–63.

Adler, Emanuel. 2002. "Constructivism and International Relations." In *Handbook of International Relations*, eds Carlsnaes, Walter, Risse, Thomas, and Simmons, Beth A. London: Sage Publications, 95–118.

Adler, Emanuel and Barnett, Michael, eds. 1998. *Security Communities*. Cambridge: Cambridge University Press.

Adler, Emanuel and Haas, Peter M. 1992. "Conclusion: Epistemic Communities, World Order, and the Creation of a Reflective Research Program." *International Organization* 46(1): 367–90.

Arrighi, Giovanni and Silver, Beverly. 1999. *Chaos and Governance in the Modern World System*. Minneapolis: University of Minnesota Press.

Bailin, Alison. 2005. *From Traditional to Group Hegemony: The G7, the Liberal Economic Order, and the Core-Periphery Gap*. Aldershot: Ashgate.

Baker, Andrew. 2006. *The Group of Seven: Finance Ministries, Central Banks, and Global Financial Governance*. London: Routledge.

Baker, Andrew. 2010. "Restraining Regulatory Capture? Anglo-America, Crisis Politics, and Trajectories of Change in Global Financial Crisis." *International Affairs* 83(3): 647–63.

Barnett, Michael and Finnemore, Martha. 1999. "The Politics, Power, and Pathologies of International Organizations." *International Organization* 53(4): 699–732.

Barnett, Michael and Finnemore, Martha. 2004. *Rules for the World: International Organizations in Global Politics*. Ithaca: Cornell University Press.

Bergsten, C. Fred and Henning, C. Randall. 1996. *Global Economic Leadership and the Group of Seven*. Washington DC: Institute for International Economics.

Best, Jacqueline. 2003. "From the Top-Down: The New Financial Architecture and the Re-embedding of Global Finance." *New Political Economy* 8(3): 383–84.

Buchanan, Allen and Keohane, Robert O. 2006. "The Legitimacy of Global Governance Institutions." *Ethics and International Affairs* 20(4): 405–37.

Buchanan, James M. 1965. "An Economic Theory of Clubs." *Economica* 32(125): 1–14.

Cooper, Andrew F. 2010. "The G20 as an Improvised Crisis Committee and/or a Contested 'Steering Committee' for the World." *International Affairs* 86(3): 741–57.

Dewitt, David and Kirton, John J. 1983. *Canada as a Principal Power: A Study in Foreign Policy and International Relations*. Toronto: John Wiley and Sons.

Doran, Charles. 1971. *The Politics of Assimilation: Hegemony and Its Aftermath*. Baltimore: Johns Hopkins University Press.

Fratianni, Michele and Pattison, John C. 2001. "International Organisations in a World of Regional Trade Agreements: Lessons from Club Theory." *World Economy* 24(3): 333–58.

Galtung, Johan. 1964. "Balance of Power and the Problem of Perception: A Logical Analysis." *Inquiry* 7(1–4): 277–94.

Hajnal, Peter I. 2007. "Summitry from G5 to L20: A Review of Reform Initiatives." CIGI Working Paper No. 20, March, Centre for International Governance Innovation, Waterloo ON. Available at: www.cigionline.org/publications/2007/3/summitry-g5-l20-review-reform-initiatives. Accessed: July 2012.

Hermawan, Yulius P., Sriyuliani, Wulani, Hardjowijono, Getruida H., and Tanaga, Sylvie. 2011. *The Role of Indonesia in the G20: Background,*

Role, and Objectives of Indonesia's Membership. Jakarta: Friedrich-Ebert-Stiftung Indonesia Office. Available at: library.fes.de/pdf-files/bueros/indonesien/08365.pdf. Accessed: July 2012.
Holling, Crawford. 1973. "Resilience and Stability of Ecological Systems." *Annual Review of Ecology and Systematics* 4: 1–23.
Homer-Dixon, Thomas. 2001. *The Ingenuity Gap: Can We Solve the Problems of the Future?* Toronto: Vintage.
Ikenberry, G. John. 2001. *After Victory: Institutions, Strategic Restraint, and the Rebuilding of Order after Major Wars*. Princeton: Princeton University Press.
Kant, Immanuel. 1991. "Perpetual Peace: A Philosophical Sketch." In *Kant: Political Writings*, ed Reiss, Hans Siegbert. Cambridge: Cambridge University Press, 93–130.
Keohane, Robert O. 1984. *After Hegemony: Cooperation and Discord in the World Political Economy*. Princeton: Princeton University Press.
Keohane, Robert O. 2002. *Power and Governance in a Partially Globalized World*. London: Routledge.
Keohane, Robert O. and Nye, Joseph S. 1977. *Power and Interdependence: World Politics in Transition*. Boston: Little, Brown.
Keohane, Robert O. and Nye, Joseph S. 1989. *Power and Interdependence*. 2nd ed. Glenview, IL: Scott, Foresman.
Kirton, John J. 1989. "Contemporary Concert Diplomacy: The Seven-Power Summit and the Management of International Order." Paper presented at the annual convention of the International Studies Association, 29 March–1 April, London. Available at: www.g8.utoronto.ca/scholar/kirton198901. Accessed: July 2012.
Kirton, John J. 1993. "The Seven Power Summits as a New Security Institution." In *Building a New Global Order: Emerging Trends in International Security*, eds Dewitt, David, Haglund, David, and Kirton, John J. Toronto: Oxford University Press, 335–57.
Kirton, John J. 1999. "Economic Cooperation: Summitry, Institutions, and Structural Change." In *Structural Change and Cooperation in the Global Economy*, eds Boyd, Gavin, and Dunning, John H. Cheltenham: Edward Elgar.
Kirton, John J. 2000. "The Dynamics of G7 Leadership in Crisis Response and System Reconstruction." In *Shaping a New International Financial System: Challenges of Governance in a Globalizing World*, eds Kaiser, Karl, Kirton, John J., and Daniels, Joseph P. Aldershot: Ashgate, 65–94.
Kirton, John J. 2001. "Guiding Global Economic Governance: The G20, the G7, and the International Monetary Fund at Century's Dawn." In *New Directions in Global Economic Governance: Managing Globalisation in the Twenty-First Century*, eds Kirton, John J., and von Furstenberg, George M. Aldershot: Ashgate, 143–67.
Kirton, John J. 2002. "Embedded Ecologism and Institutional Inequality: Linking Trade, Environment, and Social Cohesion in the G8." In *Linking Trade,*

Environment, and Social Cohesion: NAFTA Experiences, Global Challenges, eds Kirton, John J., and Maclaren, Virginia W. Aldershot: Ashgate, 45–72.

Kirton, John J. 2005. "Toward Multilateral Reform: The G20's Contribution." In *Reforming from the Top: A Leaders' 20 Summit*, eds English, John, Thakur, Ramesh, and Cooper, Andrew F. Tokyo: United Nations University Press, 141–68.

Kirton, John J. 2010. "The G20 Finance Ministers: Network Governance." In *Rising States, Rising Institutions: Can the World Be Governed?*, eds Alexandroff, Alan S., and Cooper, Andrew F. Washington DC: Brookings Institution Press, 196–217.

Kokotsis, Eleanore. 1999. *Keeping International Commitments: Compliance, Credibility, and the G7, 1988–1995*. New York: Garland.

Krasner, Stephen D. 1978. *Defending the National Interest: Raw Materials Investments and US Foreign Policy*. Princeton: Princeton University Press.

Krasner, Stephen D. 1983. *International Regimes*. Ithaca, NY: Cornell University Press.

Larionova, Marina, ed. 2012. *The European Union in the G8: Promoting Consensus and Concerted Actions for Global Public Goods*. Farnham: Ashgate.

Masson, Paul R. and Pattison, John C. 2010. "Financial Regulatory Reform: Using Models of Cooperation to Evaluate Current Prospects for International Agreement." Rotman School of Management, University of Toronto, Toronto. Available at: www.g20.utoronto.ca/biblio/G20reforms.pdf. Accessed: July 2012.

Morgenthau, Hans Joachim. 1948. *Politics among Nations: The Struggle for Power and Peace*. New York: Knopf.

Oneal, John R. and Russett, Bruce. 1999. "The Kantian Peace: The Pacific Benefits of Democracy, Interdependence, and International Organizations." *World Politics* 52(1): 1–37.

Organski, A.F.K. and Kugler, Jacek. 1980. *The War Ledger*. Chicago: University of Chicago Press.

Ostrom, Elinor. 2009. "Beyond Markets and States: Polycentric Governance of Complex Economic Systems." Nobel Prize lecture, December 8. Available at: www.nobelprize.org/nobel_prizes/economics/laureates/2009/ostrom_lecture.pdf. Accessed: July 2012.

Polanyi, Karl. 1944. *The Great Transformation: The Political and Economic Origins of Our Time*. New York: Farrar and Rinehart.

Porter, Tony. 2000. "The G7, the Financial Stability Forum, the G20, and the Politics of International Financial Regulation." Paper presented at the annual convention of the International Studies Association, March 15, Los Angeles. Available at: www.g8.utoronto.ca/g20/biblio/porter-isa-2000.pdf. Accessed: July 2012.

Porter, Tony. 2003. "Technical Collaboration and Political Conflict in the Emerging Regime for International Financial Regulation." *Review of International Political Economy* 10(3): 520–51.

Putnam, Robert and Bayne, Nicholas. 1987. *Hanging Together: Co-operation and Conflict in the Seven-Power Summit*. 2nd ed. London: Sage Publications.

Ruggie, John G. 1983. "International Regimes, Transactions, and Change: Embedded Liberalism in the Postwar Economic Order." In *International Regimes*, ed Krasner, Stephen D. Ithaca: Cornell University Press, 195–232.

Sandler, Todd and Tschirhart, John T. 1997. "Club Theory: Thirty Years Later." *Public Choice* 93(3): 335–55.

Schirm, Stefan A. 2012 (July). "Global Politics Are Domestic Politics: A Societal Approach to Divergence in the G20." *Review of International Studies*: 1–22. doi: dx.doi.org/10.1017/S0260210512000216.

Simmons, Beth. 2000. "The Legalization of International Monetary Affairs." *International Organization* 54(3): 573–602.

Slaughter, Anne-Marie. 1997. "The Real New World Order." *Foreign Affairs* 76(5): 183–97.

Slaughter, Anne-Marie. 2004. *A New World Order*. Princeton: Princeton University Press.

Slaughter, Anne-Marie. 2005. "Government Networks, World Order, and the L20." In *Reforming from the Top: A Leaders' 20 Summit*, eds English, John, Thakur, Ramesh, and Cooper, Andrew F. Tokyo: United Nations University Press, 281–95.

Slaughter, Anne-Marie. 2009. "America's Edge: Power in the Networked Century." *Foreign Affairs* 88(1): 94–113.

Snidal, Duncan. 1985. "The Limits of Hegemonic Stability Theory." *International Organisation* 39(4): 579–614.

Soederberg, Susanne. 2002. "On the Contradictions of the New International Financial Architecture: Another Procrustean Bed for Emerging Markets?" *Third World Quarterly* 23(4): 607–20.

Steinbruner, John D. 2002. *The Cybernetic Theory of Decision: New Dimensions of Political Analysis*. Princeton: Princeton University Press.

Stephens, Gina. 2010. "Information and Communication: G8 Institutionalization and Compliance in the DOT Force." In *Making Global Governance Effective: Hard and Soft Law Institutions in a Crowded World*, eds Kirton, John J., Larionova, Marina, and Savona, Paolo. Farnham: Ashgate, 201–15.

United Nations Development Programme. 2010. "The Real Wealth of Nations: Pathways to Human Development." Human Development Report 2010. Available at: hdr.undp.org/en/reports/global/hdr2010/chapters/. Accessed: July 2012.

von Furstenberg, George M. and Daniels, Joseph P. 1992. *Economic Summit Declarations, 1975–1989: Examining the Written Record of International Cooperation*. Princeton: Princeton University Press.

Wallerstein, Immanuel. 1979. *The Capitalist World-Economy*. Cambridge: Cambridge University Press.

Welch, David. 2005. *Painful Choices: A Theory of Foreign Policy Change*. Princeton: Princeton University Press.

Wicks, Nigel L. 2003. "Governments, the International Financial Institutions, and Cooperation." In *The New Economic Diplomacy: Decision-Making and*

Negotiation in International Economic Relations, eds Bayne, Nicholas, and Woolcock, Stephen. Aldershot: Ashgate, 261–74.

Williamson, John. 1997. "The Washington Consensus Revisited." In *Economic and Social Development into the XXI Century*, ed Emmerji, Louis. Washington DC: Inter-American Development Bank, 48–61.

Wolfers, Arnold. 1962. "National Security as an Ambiguous Symbol." In *Discord and Collaboration: Essays on International Politics*, ed Wolfers, Arnold. Baltimore: Johns Hopkins University Press, 147–65.

Zacher, Mark and Sutton, Brent. 1996. *Governing Global Networks: International Regimes for Transportation and Communication*. Cambridge: Cambridge University Press.

PART II
Generating the Group, 1999–2001

Chapter 3
Creating the Group, Berlin 1999

Introduction

The Challenge

The 1997–99 Asian-turned-global financial crisis catalysed several new American and Group of Seven (G7) member-centred international institutions at the ministerial and official levels in the field of finance. The process began at the meeting of Asia-Pacific Economic Cooperation (APEC) leaders in Vancouver, Canada, in November 1997. Here US president Bill Clinton announced the ad hoc, short-lived, officials' level Group of 22 (G22) to discuss the unfolding Asian financial crisis that had erupted in Thailand in July and consider ways to strengthen the international financial architecture in response. The process continued with the somewhat larger but equally ad hoc Group of 33 (G33), which included several smaller states. In 1999 at the International Monetary Fund (IMF), a new International Monetary and Financial Committee (IMFC) was formed with 24 members. In the autumn of 1998 and formally in the spring of 1999, the G7 created the Financial Stability Forum (FSF), first made up of the G7 countries but soon adding four smaller members.

By far the most ambitious attempt to create a new forum for global financial and economic governance came with the creation of the Group of 20 (G20). It was endorsed by G7 leaders at their Cologne Summit on June 18–20, 1999. The formal agenda of this new political-level forum centred publicly on financial matters, but embraced a wide range of economic issues along with their social and political implications. Its members collectively contained a predominant share of the world's economic capabilities at the time.

With the systemically significant emerging countries included as equals alongside the established G8 powers, the G20 offered great potential. But it was not at all clear how important this particular new group would be, or what place it would occupy in a world filled with long-established and more recently created international institutions to govern global finance. Would the G20 lead a major move into more inclusive global governance? Or was it just one more of the proliferating informal, consultative bodies struggling to find a significant role in a world where existing international institutions, while under a new assault, still held the predominant place?

Competing Assessments

Assessments of the new G20 varied considerably across several competing schools of thought. The first school, skeptics, saw American dominance. Its adherents pointed to the G20 as a promising but potentially transitory, US-initiated response to the 1997–99 financial crisis, as an effort to institutionalize American unilateralism in a way that reflected and reinforced G7 dominance, and to the restricted novelty of its agenda and actions during its first year (Helleiner 2001; Culpeper 2000).

A second school saw a soft law loser. Its adherents accepted the G20 as a genuine group of equals for crisis response. But they felt it was destined to fade in the face of competition from its formidable hard law competitor embedded in the oldest, heavily legalized, and most powerful part of the multilaterally organized order, the new IMFC at the IMF (Abbott et al. 2000; Brown 2010).

A third school saw a more permanent, potentially promising, broader club (Porter 2000; Germain 2001). Its authors agreed that because the G20 had a broader membership than the G7, it had a better chance to acquire the legitimacy needed to work as an informal global governance group.

A fourth school, of optimists, argued that the crisis-ridden world of the coming twenty-first century, much like that of the early 1970s, needed a new centre of global governance to combine the capabilities of a fresh set of leading countries to address new, global, systemic vulnerabilities (Kirton 2000). The G20 was that centre.

A fifth school, of visionaries, recalled that the G7 itself had been founded amid financial crises containing inherent linkages to a wide range of central economic, social, and, ultimately, political concerns. The G7 had also been created by forward-looking finance ministers inside and outside the United States, who wished to continue their informal meetings when they became leaders (Putnam and Bayne 1984, 1987; Baker 2006). The visionaries suggested that the G20 too might someday rise to the top. The G20 quickly generated claims that it would soon supersede the G7/8 as an effective centre of global governance (Beauchesne 1999). Indeed, an authoritative, well-positioned participant, Ernst Weltke, president of Germany's Bundesbank, declared at the time of the G20's first ministerial meeting in Berlin in December 1999 that this new institution could replace the G7, or at least take over its leading role.

The Argument

This chapter argues that the optimists proved to be correct. In its creation and first year of operations, the G20 got off to a sound start, in part because the visionary conceptions of its Canadian creator, Canadian finance minister Paul Martin, and his American colleague, treasury secretary Larry Summers, were central to its shape and work. During its first year, the G20's founding custodians consciously and successfully designed and steered the group in a direction that led to a solid success at its first meeting in Berlin and that would lead it to the breadth, novelty, and ambition appropriate for leaders themselves.

The G20's conception, creation, and early operation are well accounted for by the model of systemic hub governance. The G20's systemically significant countries responded to the sequential shocks of an interconnected, complex, uncertain, more equally vulnerable world where old, formal multilateral organizations and newer plurilateral institutions failed, and where competent and committed individuals constructed and led, amid considerable competition and collegiality, a new group of globally predominant, internally equal, domestically convergent countries that ultimately prevailed.

To be sure, the G20 was conceived and created in the view of some to help ensure that the G20's initiatives were understood, accepted, and implemented by a broader group of consequential countries. But the G20's creators sought at a minimum to ensure reciprocally that its G7 members had full sensitivity to the perspectives, positions, and domestic political priorities of a broader group of countries that counted in the post-Cold War globalizing world, where the G7 could no longer govern global finance alone. The G20, more than the IMFC, had the flexibility and the lateral and vertical linkages as a network hub to emerge as the leading centre of sensitization, legitimization, and timely, well-targeted action in an increasingly globalized, crisis-prone world. Moreover, Paul Martin, the G20's primary conceiver and custodian, constructed the G20 with the political authority and broad, innovative, ambitious agenda that made it effective as an inclusive leadership forum. The distinguishing feature of the G20 was its membership. No other institution brought together such diverse, systemically significant countries, in the persons of ministers and governors from capitals, for an informal dialogue among equals in a compact group. The G20 thus filled a great gap in the architecture of international financial governance (G20 2008).

The G20 was catalysed by a sustained sequence of financial shocks that first erupted in Asia but spread globally with unprecedented speed, scale, and scope. These shocks ultimately affected newly democratic Russia and, even briefly, the other classic superpower, the United States. Neither the multilateral IMF, the plurilateral G7/8, nor the United States acting alone had predicted, prevented, contained, or coped adequately with this full sequence of shocks. It became clear that the successful response required a new group of systemically significant countries with globally predominant capability and considerable internal equality. Its members would be brought together by their growing domestic preferences and practices of financial stability, economic growth, and economic and social stability, supported by growing political openness in virtually all. Behind these principles lay the will and skill of the two men who first conceived of it and brought it to life (Brown 2010). Lawrence Summers had led the US Treasury's international affairs work since 1993, became treasury secretary in 1999, and would stay in the job for another year. Paul Martin, a veteran finance minister since 1993, would chair the group for its first three years. The group of 20 members, while less constricted than the G8, was still sufficiently compact and globally connected as a network hub to start deliberating, setting new directions, and making decisions for an increasingly inter-vulnerable world.

The Process of Creation

The Initial Vision and Institutional Path

The vision of what was to become the G20 first arose in a politically consequential way at the 1988 G7 Toronto Summit. There leaders first identified in their communiqué a new process they called "globalization," which had intensifying global economic interdependence at its core (G7 1988). In response to economic globalization and the changing balance of power in the world, they called for a new forum for dialogue. In their highly prescient conception:

> Certain newly industrializing economies (NIEs) in the Asia-Pacific region have become increasingly important in world trade … With increased economic importance come greater international responsibilities and a strong mutual interest in improved constructive dialogue and cooperative efforts in the near term between the industrialized countries and the Asian NIEs, as well as the other outward-oriented countries in the region. The dialogue and cooperative efforts could center on such policy areas as macroeconomic, currency, structural and trade to achieve the international adjustment necessary for sustained, balanced growth of the world economy. We encourage the development of informal processes which would facilitate multilateral discussions of issues of mutual concern and foster the necessary cooperation (G7 1988).

The initial institutional realization of this vision, with Europe excluded, came a year later, with the creation of APEC among finance and foreign ministers in 1989. APEC was elevated to the leaders' level in 1993 at the initiative of the new administration of President Bill Clinton in the United States. It became a plurilateral summit institution with established and emerging countries in a network where the G20 would eventually become the hub. Four years later, the annual APEC leaders' meeting took place on the shores of the Pacific Ocean in Vancouver, where it was able to respond to the Asian financial crisis erupting in July 1997, and to serve as the initial nest for a new process of international institution creation, culminating in the G20.

The G20 also emerged from earlier efforts during the 1990s to broaden the traditional G7 and Group of Ten (G10) centres of international financial governance. This process of including countries with rapidly growing capability and systemic relevance was designed to help stem the deepening, broadening, and quickening shock-activated inter-vulnerability of a rapidly globalizing world. It began with the emergence of the IMF's New Agreements to Borrow (NAB), a body larger than the existing G10-dominated General Arrangements to Borrow

(GAB), in the aftermath of the 1994 Mexican peso crisis from the Americas (Kirton 1995; Summers 2008). It continued with the creation of the G22, its expansion into the G33, the IMFC, and the FSF in response to the Asian-turned-global financial crisis of 1997–98. It culminated with the creation of the G20. Throughout there were recurrent efforts to combat an intensifying succession of shock-activated, contagious vulnerabilities, and to institutionalize, constrain, and replace unilateral and discretionary US-centred leadership with a system-wide approach to global governance, tailored to the needs of a rapidly globalizing world. At the centre of this process was Martin, who had first conceived of such a group in the wake of the Mexican crisis and had settled on the number of 20 as its membership after the G22 had been formed.

The New Arrangements to Borrow, January 1997

The first step in broadening the G7 to include major emerging countries that were newly consequential for global finance came in the mid 1990s. The shock of the Mexican peso crisis in December 1994 catalysed the creation of the NAB. At their 1995 Halifax Summit, G7 leaders called for the G10 to double the money available to the IMF under the GAB (Bergsten and Henning 1996; Kirton 1995; Fréchette 1995). The IMF Executive Board finally approved the NAB on January 27, 1997. It entered into force on November 17, 1998, more than a year after the Asian crisis had started in Thailand in July 1997. The NAB, whose secretariat was housed at the IMF, was similar to the longstanding GAB, but included more funds and additional contributors such as Korea.

The NAB had 25 members, more than double the 11-member GAB. Those with the lowest NAB contribution of 340 million special drawing rights (SDRs) were Korea, the Hong Kong Monetary Authority, Malaysia, Singapore, Thailand, and Finland. Canada, the lowest ranked G7 member, had 1,396 SDRs, more than four times as much. The US, the top-ranked G7 member, had 6,712 SDRs, almost six times as much as Canada and 20 times as much as Korea and its colleagues on the lowest tier. Both the NAB and older GAB were used during the 1997 crisis. The fact that the NAB had more money and more flexibility than the GAB proved essential to the successful containment of the crisis. The 1994 peso shock from the Americas thus eventually produced a new effective club of 25 members, containing both established and emerging countries, if not in an equal way.

The G22, November 1997

The second step toward moving beyond the G7 and the even older G10 came with the formation of the temporary, official-level G22. The G22, also called the Willard Group after the Washington hotel where it first met, included finance and central bank representatives from the G7 members and 15 others: Argentina, Australia, Brazil, China, Hong Kong, India, Indonesia, Korea, Malaysia, Mexico, Poland, Russia, Singapore, South Africa, and Thailand (Hajnal 2007; G20 2008; Jokela

2011; Costello 2008). It was created as a personal initiative of the US president Bill Clinton and Singaporean prime minister Goh Chok Tong, who had met at the November 1997 APEC leaders' meeting in Vancouver.

The G22 was an idea hatched at the US Treasury. It grew out of the 1997 financial crisis, the IMF meeting in Hong Kong, and the rejection of the idea to establish an Asian monetary fund. Clinton had proposed the G22 immediately after the Asian financial crisis had engulfed Thailand and Indonesia (Kokotsis and Kirton 1997). There was general support among G7 countries for such American leadership. The subsequent Korean crisis culminating on December 24, 1997, appeared to justify the move (Kirton 2000). Martin had no role in picking the G22 members. But the US had a large role, as it convened the first meeting in April 1998.

The G22's activities over the subsequent year and its three meetings centred on producing reports on particular aspects of the international financial architecture. It produced some useful analytic studies. Here Canada's contribution to the group stood out. This contribution fuelled Martin's belief in the value of a G20 and Canada's reputation in taking the lead in bringing the G20 to life.

The G33, March 1999

The third step came in March 1999, when the G22 was expanded to become the G33. The G33 added 11 countries to the G22: Belgium, Chile, Côte d'Ivoire, Egypt, Morocco, the Netherlands, Saudi Arabia, Spain, Sweden, Switzerland, and Turkey. The expansion came importantly because the European G7 countries did not like leaving their European G10 colleagues out of the game, as the G22 had.

Such an expansion did not improve effectiveness. It did not satisfy Washington's growing frustration with the Europeans and the international institutions they dominated (Blustein 2001). Moreover, as predicted by liberal-institutionalist's legalization theory, there was widespread concern within the US Treasury and among other G7 members about whom the new ad hoc, informal G22 would report to, what its mandate and membership would be, and how its work would relate to those of other established international institutions (Abbott et al. 2000). Within Canada's Department of Finance the experience with the G22 and G33 highlighted the need for a "regular international consultative forum with a broader membership than the G7" and one integrated into the governance structures of the IMF and World Bank (Canada, Department of Finance 2000). These conclusions led to initiatives to create a more institutionalized and permanent body, initially known as G-x. It would have a defined role among established institutions and new forums, such as the IMFC. Thus the G33 quickly died.

This prospect probably inspired some in the US and elsewhere to draw up lists of who should be in a new group. France played an unusually limited role because the energetic Dominique Strauss-Kahn had left as finance minister. Australia was active in pushing for its inclusion in such a group, for while it was analytically good, it was not an obvious choice.

The Financial Stability Forum, February 1999

The fourth step was the creation of the FSF by the G7 finance ministers, first at their meeting on October 3, 1998, and then formally at their meeting in Bonn, Germany, on February 22, 1999 (Helleiner et al. 2010). The first G7 meeting had reached a decision in principle but could not agree on how to implement it. The second one did. The FSF's purpose was to "promote information exchange and co-ordination among the national authorities, international institutions and international regulatory or experts' groupings with responsibilities for questions of international financial stability" (FSF 1999).

The FSF had originally been proposed at the G7 finance meeting. Hans Tietmeyer, the highly respected German central bank governor at the meeting, rejected the proposal immediately, although US Federal Reserve governor Alan Greenspan asked him to study it and return with a more considered response. This Tietmeyer agreed to do and did, producing three months later a proposal to create the new forum. Its initial membership was based on a formula composed by Tietmeyer, with the key criterion being those polities that contained the world's major capital markets. The FSF consisted in the first instance of representatives from the finance ministries and central banks and leading supervisors of G7 countries, along with the chairs of the nongovernmental international regulatory organizations and representatives of international financial institutions (IFIs).

In keeping with the contents of Tietmeyer's report, the FSF's aim and approach was to maintain the free flow of capital, but now with adequate frameworks and regulations to ensure this capital was going to productive purposes and was properly monitored to this end.

The FSF first met at the IMF in Washington on April 14, 1999. At the Cologne Summit on June 18–20, 1999, G7 leaders agreed to expand the group to include "systemically important emerging economies," a sign that the concept of systemic significance was taking pride of place (G7 1999). The established and emerging global financial centres of the Netherlands, Australia, Hong Kong, and Singapore were thus added for the FSF's subsequent meeting in Paris on September 15, 1999, giving the FSF 11 members.

Martin had proposed that all members of the emerging G20 be included in the FSF (Ibbitson and Perkins 2010). But he was told informally that he was lucky to get his G20 and should not push his luck. His call for the FSF to be given much more authority, resources, and staff was similarly refused. European reluctance to expand and strengthen the FSF flowed in part from the fact that the Eurocentric G10 was now being pushed aside. The Germans and the French had been criticized and lobbied hard by their smaller European colleagues about their exclusion from the FSF. The admission of the European Union and its rotating presidency had been a response to these concerns. The Europeans were further worried about their influence being diluted in a broader, non-European group. The 11-member FSF was a particular humiliation for democratic Russia. It had just been admitted to the G8 but was still left out of the G7 finance forum and now also the FSF, while semi-sovereign Hong Kong and small Singapore made it in, due to the presence of their capital markets.

The International Monetary and Financial Committee, June 1999

The fifth step was the simultaneous creation of the IMFC, endorsed by the G7 leaders at their summit in Cologne in June 1999. In order to encourage strengthening and reform of the governance structures of the IFIs, the IMF's Interim Committee was superseded by the IMFC in September. The IMFC acquired many of the Interim Committee's previous responsibilities, such as advising the board of governors and managing the international monetary and financial system. It also obtained an expanded advisory role and had fiscal issues under its purview.

The IMFC was required to hold preparatory sessions before its spring and fall meetings, in addition to the twice-annual meetings that the Interim Committee had held. Its 24 members reflected the composition of the IMF executive board. Its value came in part from its representation of both developed and developing countries. Participants were finance ministers, central bank governors, or comparable figures. The IMFC's inaugural chair was Gordon Brown, Britain's chancellor of the exchequer, who continued in the role for several years.

The IMFC won out over two alternatives for strengthening the IMF. One was the creation of a ministerial council, as envisaged in the original Articles of Agreement that established the IMF. The other was the creation of a leaders' IMFC, an alternative energetically pursued by IMF managing director Michel Camdessus from 1996 to 1998.

The G20's Creation

The sixth and final step was the creation of the G20 itself. This forum of finance ministers and central bank governors was endorsed by G7 leaders, alongside the FSF and IMFC, at the 1999 Cologne Summit. In their June 18 communiqué, the leaders noted the need for new institutions and affirmed the central role of the IMF and the World Bank (G7 1999). They also welcomed the establishment of the FSF to enhance international cooperation and coordination in financial market supervision and regulation.

The G20 was thus born not as the one and only prized, G7-endorsed, international institutional response to the 1997–99 crisis, nor one that commanded the complete confidence of all its members. Rather, it came to life as one of three new bodies, as an infant that would have to find and follow its comparative advantage, and cooperate and compete with the German-designed FSF and the British-chaired IMFC within a French-led IMF, in an increasingly institutionally crowded world (Fratianni et al. 2005).

As outlined by Paul Martin, who chaired the G20 for its first few years, the G20's public, formal mandate was in the first instance a deliberate one—to "promote discussion, and [it] will study and review policy issues among industrialized countries and emerging markets with a view to promoting international financial stability" (Canada, Department of Finance 2000). The initial 19 country members included the G7 countries plus Argentina, Australia, Brazil, China, India, Indonesia, Korea, Mexico, Russia, Saudi Arabia, South Africa, and Turkey. Canada would chair the first meeting in Berlin in December 1999, a location chosen as part of the overall compromise, and chair and host the second meeting in Canada in 2000. The chair and host would then rotate annually among participants, given that the hosts and chairs for the first two years had come from the G7 countries.

Format

The G20 was not created as a pure US-led initiative, unfolding according to classic realist models of benign hegemony in international regime formation or the American leadership model of G7 governance (Keohane 1984; Putnam and Bayne 1987; Cohn 2000). In the creation of the earlier ad hoc G22 and G33, the US had indeed identified the demand for a new body, created the momentum, set the agenda, hosted the gatherings, and largely chosen the members. But with the G20, the inspiration and initiative came from Canadian finance minister Paul Martin (2008a, 2008b; see also Summers 2008; Sautter 2008; Amato 2008; Brown 2010). He approached Lawrence Summers, who readily agreed. They then met to design the club in Summers's office in Washington on April 27, 1999, just two weeks before Clinton would announce on May 12 that Summers would succeed Robert Rubin as treasury secretary of the United States (Ibbitson and Perkins 2010).

The American desire for a new process, or even institution, to cope with the new world exposed by the 1997–99 Asian-turned-global financial crisis was driven by several forces. Here Summers was the key individual defining and driving the American response to the crisis and the Treasury's entire international work (Rubin and Weisberg 2003). First as deputy treasury secretary and then as treasury secretary after his Senate confirmation on July 2, 1999, Summers sought—along with some Treasury officials—to create a compact group of systemically significant countries that would take the governance of the G7 and extend it in a broader group (Rubin and Weisberg 2003). They were reacting primarily to the financial crisis and the strong congressional, specialist, and public criticism that the IMF had received in response. This criticism included calls for the abolition of the IMF or a dramatic narrowing of its mandate. Such frustration had first arisen at the start of the Clinton administration's first term with the IMF's slow, inflexible, and legally constrained response to the December 1994 peso crisis in Mexico, a country that was the partner of the US and Canada in the new North American Free Trade Agreement (NAFTA).

In the wake of the Mexican peso crisis, the US Treasury came to view the IMF, with its large and powerful staff, as a technocratic body that resisted US proposals for rapid, badly needed response and reform. The Treasury tended to regard the

IMF's Interim Committee as a forum whose agenda was set by IMF staff, with all issues resolved by prior consultation among officials. The nominally responsible and often democratically accountable finance ministers merely flew in from their capitals for a brief meeting to deliver their statements, endorse a communiqué prepared by others, and then quickly leave. In the G20, the US Treasury sought to escape such legalized, organizational constraints, both to better secure American preferences and to cope more effectively with the new form of financial crisis for the broader public good.

Yet American frustration with the IMF's inadequacies during the Mexican crisis did not account alone for the creation of the G20, or predominantly determine the shape of the body that emerged. The G20 was the product of a consensus between Summers and Martin. Martin, having served as Canada's finance minister since 1993, had a well-developed vision of how best to reform the international financial system. Following the Mexican peso crisis, he had conceived of creating a group of finance ministers, including those from major Asian countries and a Muslim country, to respond to such crises in the future. But as a relatively new finance minister he made no progress in advancing his idea then. The G7 summit hosted by Canada at Halifax in 1995, which focused on IFI reform in response to the peso crisis as well as the collapse of Barings Bank earlier that spring, underscored the need for additional moves (Kirton 1995; Fréchette 1995). From an early stage Martin and his officials thus supported the American instinct to do things differently. They actively pushed forward the American thrust for a broader, more institutionalized, consultative group, and proposed Martin as its chair.

The British and the Japanese joined the Americans and Canadians as the most enthusiastic advocates within the G7 for the creation of a new group. Britain, however, was concerned that the G20 not diminish the prominence of the new IMFC, where Brown (2010), whose term as chancellor of the exchequer had begun in 1997, wished to be—and was—the first chair.

The Germans were reluctant about the creation of the G20. They felt that the technical, G7-controlled FSF held the key job. As chair of the G7 and G8 in 1999 and the dominant economic power in Europe, they did not see the need for another broader, informal, institutional global body in which their position might be diluted. Moreover, after a process that had complicated US–German relations in global financial governance, Horst Köhler—a German national—had just become the managing director of the IMF. The Germans acquiesced to the creation of the G20 as part of a compromise, which included allowing them to host the G20's first meeting, with Paul Martin in the chair.

As German finance minister Hans Eichel had become chair of the G7 finance forum on January 1, 1999, he and his officials had ample opportunity to make their views known to their American counterparts about the emerging G20. But no detailed, reliable evidence has been found to support the claim that they inspired the creation of the G20 or defined the shape it took (cf. Wade and Vestergaard 2010b, 2010a). With regard to the G20's members, it has been asserted that

> they were selected in 1999 by Timothy Geithner at the US Treasury in a transatlantic telephone call with his counterpart at the German Finance Ministry, Caio Koch-Weser. Geithner and Koch-Weser went down the list of countries saying, Canada in, Spain out, South Africa in, Nigeria and Egypt out, and so on; they sent their list to the other G7 finance ministries; and the invitations to the first meeting went out. (Wade 2009)

It is likely that this telephone call, on an unidentified date between the two senior-level subordinates, took place after the principals—Summers and Martin as ministers—had decided the membership at their face-to-face meeting in Washington on April 27 (see below). More broadly, the Asian crisis had led to much discussion among many about the need for a new financial architecture and what the optimal group at the centre might be.

The French were also reluctant about the creation of the G20, as they were pressured by the Dutch and Spaniards as fellow Europeans who were excluded from the new group (Brown 2010). The French were comfortable with the IMF, then headed by their compatriot Michel Camdessus, and the new IMFC. Throughout 1999, the French, along with Britain's Gordon Brown, sought to strengthen the IMF's Interim Committee. They wanted ministerial working groups of the IMFC to deal with specific issues such as transparency. Under this concept, five to six ministers would meet two to four times a year and report back to the full IMFC on options for decisions needed at the ministerial level. This could be done on the development and implementation of standards. As 1999 ended, the acceptance of these proposals remained possible, although they had not been officially endorsed. France also pushed to turn the IMF's Interim Committee into a new council of ministers at the heart of the IMF.

The IMF itself was opposed to the G20's creation, life, and work. This attitude is reflected in Brown's (2010, 79) assessment, a decade later, that "the truth is that, in its original conception, the G20 was an attempt to bypass the IMF, and at the same time to balance the group toward Asia, where the economic crisis was then raging." Indeed, for the G20's first decade as a finance forum, the IMF sought to destroy it as a serious competitor to its own core competence in governing global finance. Only in 2008, when the G20 leapt to the leaders' level, did the IMF, which had never met at that level, admit defeat. It switched to a strategy of controlling rather than destroying the G20. From the start, however, Camdessus was always very cooperative with Martin as the first chair of the G20.

The G20 was, in this limited sense, the result of a Franco-American accommodation, with the remaining G7 members lined up somewhat predictably on each side of the trans-Atlantic divide. These coalitions played into the selection of Martin as inaugural chair. Most G7 members saw that the new G20 body would look too much like a US creature if, as with the G22 and the G33, the US chaired it or if its first meeting was held in the United States. The US canvassed other G7 countries for candidates for a chair. Some suggested Brown, since the G7 ministers were not in competition with the IMFC and wished to maintain its legitimacy as a consultative, advisory, and potential decision-making committee of the IMF. But Martin emerged as the preferred American and British choice and an acceptable trans-Atlantic and trans-Pacific one. Both Martin and Brown thus became the chair of the body for which they had done the most work to create—and that each wanted to chair and that they had agreed they would.

In the end there was a converging view among G7 members on the need for a balanced and representative institution at the ministerial level that remained small enough to foster open dialogue on global economic and financial matters and thereby generate consensus on major issues. The work of the G22 and the two G33 officials' seminars, when juxtaposed against the cascading global financial crisis that was devastating emerging markets, suggested the need for a more potent, effective, higher-level forum. It further suggested that such a forum should focus on reducing vulnerability to crisis by creating appropriate exchange-rate arrangements, liability management, and international codes and standards. Many inside and outside the G7 felt that weaknesses in those areas had compounded the crisis at hand.

More broadly, there was a functional consensus on the potential value of having a third leg of the stool that constituted the new international financial architecture, with ministers after the Tietmeyer report having a comprehensive view of the comparative advantage of each of the new forums. The FSF would address banking, securities, insurance, and the financial sector. The IMFC would assert itself with the formal governing structure of the IMF, with ministers from capitals exerting much more direct control over the resident executive directors and the staff. The G20 would be a caucus for common vision and consensus building and thus effective decision making, to get acceptance for action by the bodies of jurisdiction—national governments at home, the IMFC and the Bank for International Settlements (BIS) at the international level, and the FSF in the domestic and private self-regulatory domains. This meant the G20 was designed to do deliberation through open conversation and direction setting through consensus building and buy-in, with its participants taking these results to the authoritative bodies abroad and at home for actual formal decision making as required, and delivery in the form of compliance and implementation there.

Membership

The G20 was designed to include the most economically capable, vulnerable, and connected countries in the world. The G7 communiqué specified that a G20 member must be a "systemically important country" or a "key emerging market" (G7 1999). Behind these simple phrases lay several criteria. The first was systemic significance in both a vulnerability and capability sense. Whereas FSF membership had been based on specialized capability—where the world's major capital markets were—the G20's membership flowed from both overall global capability and vulnerability. Vulnerability meant a consideration of which countries were so exposed by debt or other channels that their failure to follow the right advice and policies could have contagious consequences for the system as a whole, as Thailand, Indonesia, and Korea in turn had recently shown. Countries such as Argentina and Turkey should be there to help them from taking the global system down with them should they collapse. Vulnerability, capability, and connectivity were the combined criteria above all.

The members beyond the G7 countries were further expected to have a different viewpoint than that of the developed countries and to come from the various geographic regions of the world, even if a non-member country might have a larger economy on a single global scale. The right balance thus joined the biggest risks as the criterion of choice. A key criteria was buy-in—which countries needed to be at the table to join in the task of coming to consensus on the best ways to strengthen the financial regulations and system to prevent or otherwise protect against the global financial shocks that globalization now brought. Given the Asian crisis caused hostility to the IMF, which was seen to be preaching from above on issues from fiscal austerity to stronger standards and codes for finance, it was now felt that a sufficient range of the intended recipients of IMF advice needed to be at the table and feel that they were part of the process of advice making for all.

There were also geopolitical concerns. The regional weight of several countries was a significant factor. So was their political character. There was a clear desire on the US side to protect and promote political openness and democracy. For Canadians the focal point was financial stability, recognizing that domestic political openness could enhance the domestic financial stability of countries that were so connected to the system that their domestic failure could pose real risks to all.

The members of the new group were ultimately selected jointly by Martin and Summers, rather than by the United States alone (Ibbitson and Perkins 2010). Within the US government, Summers's Treasury officials consulted the State Department and very probably the White House on the membership, as there were political considerations. Martin did not consult with his prime minister on the choice.

On April 27, 1999, Martin and Summers, then Clinton's nominee for Treasury secretary, met in Washington to decide who would be in the new forum (Ibbitson and Perkins 2010). With economic crises multiplying over the past five years, Martin was convinced that major emerging countries needed a seat at the global governance table. He suggested that the G22 had been a great success and that they should elevate it to the level of finance ministers and central bank governors. The two men drew up a list of countries to be included in the incipient G20, beginning with a consideration of those already in the G22. The choice was then based not on a systematic statistical calculation, but on an intuitive sense of which countries were most systemically significant (Ibbitson and Perkins 2010). After Summers and Martin had decided which was admitted, the list was circulated to the selected members. Others offered their own lists and views. These had no important effect on the outcome.

Beyond the G8 members, the most obvious candidate for Summers, Martin, and others was China. India was also a clear choice. Brazil and Mexico were included from the outset. Then much discussion arose. Some lists excluded Australia, Korea, Turkey, and Saudi Arabia.

Although Saudi Arabia had not been a G22 member, it was an obvious choice for US Treasury officials, given its position as an associate member of the G10. Moreover, it provided abundant oil-backed funding, was critically located in the Middle East, and was a close ally of the United States, which had become vulnerable to the energy exports Saudi Arabia sent to the US, Japan, and the world. Both Summers and Martin largely agreed that every global region should be included, but Summers felt strongly that Saudi Arabia was the first clear choice from the Middle East.

Turkey, another country not in the G22, was easily agreed upon by both Summers and Martin. It was accepted due to its large role as a military ally of the US and of the North Atlantic Treaty Organization (NATO) and the overall strategy of linking it more firmly to the West (Kirton 2010b; Lesage 2010). The case for G20 membership as one important component of this strategy proved persuasive. The calculation was that such a move was needed, given the precarious probability of EU membership for Turkey. A G20 association would also help deepen Turkey's democratic tradition, begun in 1950. Turkey was thus admitted to the G20 in part to sustain its character as a stable, Muslim democratic polity in a Muslim non-democratically dominated Middle East. It may also have benefited from the non-admission of Poland (see below). The inclusion of Turkey helped pave the way for it to receive significant new IMF financial support when the country was struck by a financial crisis in 2001, as it would be politically impossible to let a G20 member fail.

Indonesia was the third state with a Muslim majority to be admitted. Even with a crisis-devastated economy that made its vulnerability and contagious systemic significance clear, Indonesia had acknowledged capability in the categories of gross domestic product (GDP) and population. It was also influential in Asia and the Association of Southeast Asian Nations (ASEAN). Relevant to American thinking was the country's position as the largest Muslim state that was moving toward democracy. Although Indonesia was admitted, it was subsequently afflicted by political instability, with the result that its invitation to the first G20 meeting was deferred until its governance problems were resolved (Martin 2010). However, they were resolved in time for Indonesia to participate at Berlin.

Argentina, which was already a G22 member, made it in. It was still unaffected by its financial crisis that came in 2001. The country had what was considered at that time in 1999 to be a good economic policy and performance.

Elsewhere in South America, Chile, which had declined to participate in the NAB, was not on the US list of G20 candidates. Martin admired Chile as by far the economically best-run country in Latin America. Its case also received sympathy from Canada as its new free trade partner. During the free trade negotiations, Chile had convinced Martin that selective capital controls had their place. In the most lengthy discussions about individual members, Summers agreed that Chile's economic credentials were very strong. But size counted, both in the weight and number of countries in the new group. Chile was left out.

South Africa's admission began with Martin's conviction that every region of the world must be included. Summers agreed that for that continent, South Africa was the obvious first choice. This was in part because of Trevor Manuel, its highly respected finance minister. The US considered South Africa, Nigeria, and Egypt. Egypt's fate was related to Turkey, which, for political reasons, got in.

Nigeria was chosen as the second significant state from Africa. On the US side, it appears to have arisen as a candidate of the State Department for political reasons. Treasury officials knew it was not a G22 member and thought its economic performance was too poor. Martin (2010) felt it should be selected, and it was. But then, like Indonesia, Nigeria encountered domestic political instability—which, unlike in Indonesia—was not resolved by the time of the Berlin meeting. Nigeria was thus not invited. Even when its domestic difficulties were resolved, it was not given its initially identified seat.

Japan sought very strongly to have robust Asian representation in the G20. Malaysia was not considered for several reasons: its imposition of capital controls, its broad attack on the IMF and globalization during the 1997–99 financial crisis, its attachment to what it heralded as "Asian" values, its support for a proposed regional Asian monetary fund, and its growing disregard for democratic values, human rights, and the rule of law (Katada 2001; Martin 2008a).

Thailand, although a G22 member, was also not admitted. As it had been with Chile, Canada was sympathetic. Canada had provided Thailand with exceptional financial support in the spring of 1998 when Indonesia, by then consumed by the crisis, was unable to fulfil its earlier regional pledge (Kirton 2000). Some G7 members subsequently felt that its inclusion was warranted by its size and by its rejection of currency controls during and after the crisis, and by the need for another Asian country, especially a member of ASEAN, to reduce the Euro-centricity of the prospective G20 and old centres such as the G10. In the end, however, small size mattered for Thailand, as it also did for Singapore and Hong Kong, which had been G22 members as well.

From Europe, Poland was eliminated at an early stage. When the US proposed it, the Europeans vetoed it due to their problem with Spain.

The admission of the EU and the European Central Bank (ECB), as the only regional organizations allowed in, represented a victory for the European members of the G7. Initially, Martin and Summers included no international organizations apart from the IMF and World Bank, which often attended G7 meetings. The Dutch and Spanish complained bitterly to the French about their exclusion. The French approached Martin with their plea. The Scandinavians argued for a rotating seat, given their high proportion of donated official development assistance (ODA) as a percentage of GDP. The EU's existing place in the G7 made it difficult to deny it. This was despite US impatience, evident here and in simultaneous discussions about the place of the EU and the ECB in the G7, and in the initial discussions at the IMF over reforming quota share arrangements, with the inherited and now excessive Eurocentricity of so many allegedly global economic governance groups. The Europeans had also wanted the EU's Council of Ministers to participate, as it did at the G7. The US refused, wanting no more Europeans, both for geographic balance and for restricting the seats at the table to those with political influence directly from national capitals.

With this success in the G20, the US then turned to the task of reducing the weight of the Europeans in the IMF and its executive board by reconfiguring the quotas to reflect the new weight of developing countries. This reconfiguration would come at the expense of relatively declining France, Britain, Italy, and the smaller European countries, in favour of rising Japan, Korea, China, and Germany. This proved to be more than a decade-long pursuit, as realism's defensive positionalism, prospect theory's loss aversion, and liberal institutionalism's legalization combined to beat the most powerful country's preference. The IMF was thus left to be governed for another decade largely as it had been since 1944, until the G20 at the summit level sprang to life.

When the April 27 Martin–Summers meeting ended, the G20's membership was set in stone. Some members still offered alternative lists of members, and several outsiders sought to get in, but the initial Martin-Summers list endured for several reasons. No one wanted to open a Pandora's box by raising the issue of membership after the meetings had begun. Another factor was the absence of agreement on who should be added and, given the logic of systemic vulnerability, the subsequent reluctance to eliminate any country, such as Argentina, no matter how poor its economic performance and policy became. As with a concert, membership was for all time. As with a club, membership had its privileges in this most meaningful way. The large numbers and multidimensional diversity of the starting roster, relative to the G7, produced a disinclination to add more members, while the dominant norm of equality reduced the incentive to invite others as partial participants. Above all, the founding 19 countries constituted a prescient choice of the systemically significant countries, as producers and consumers of systemic stability, for the next decade and beyond.

Martin and Summers decided to call the new club the "G20," despite it having only 19 country members, to reduce a barrage of claims for the still apparently empty 20th spot. The 20th chair was for the Bretton Woods bodies, to be shared by the IMF and the World Bank, which would always attend. Once Martin and Summers had determined the membership, Martin asked the prospective members' finance ministers whether they wanted to participate and encouraged them to agree. He spoke most with G7 ministers, arguing that their closed group was not going to work anymore in all global financial issues, and that emerging market economies, especially Asians angry at the IMF's handling of the 1997–99 crisis, would simply not listen to what the G7 alone agreed. He also spoke with potential G20-only members and ensured their support.

Institutional Design

The G20 was designed as a deliberative and direction-setting forum that would have, in practice, an increasing decision-making effect just as the G7 finance forum did. It was tailored to encourage the "formation of consensus on international issues" (Canada, Department of Finance 2000). Moreover, it had a policy focus, given its mandate to promote international financial stability. The G7-specified subject area for the G20 to address was finance. Yet Martin suggested from the start a far more comprehensive and ambitious mission and agenda for the new body. It was one with a substantive core that represented a major revision of the neoliberal orthodoxy with which other international financial institutions were so strongly associated in their critics' minds. Martin took a strong personal interest in designing and developing the new forum in accordance with his vision. He announced at the outset that the G20 would "focus on translating the benefits of globalization into higher incomes and better opportunities everywhere," including for working people around the world (Beattie 1999). The distributional and broad social ideals were clear, for the new forum would foster stable and sustainable global growth. Martin signalled from the start that the G20's core mission was both promoting financial stability and making globalization work for all.

Martin envisaged a flexible and comprehensive agenda. Skilfully employing the prerogatives of chair, he declared at the outset that there was "no major aspect of the global economy or international financial system that will be outside of the group's purview" (Canada, Department of Finance 1999). Eight months later, Martin elaborated: "The G20 has a mandate to explore virtually every area of international finance. This includes the devastating effects of financial crises, the growing gap between the rich and the poor, and a system of governance—and on this I would insist—that has not kept pace with the sweeping changes that are taking place in the global economy" (Canada, Standing Committee on Foreign Affairs and International Trade 2000). As the first G20 ministerial and bank governors meeting hosted in Canada approached in the autumn of 2000, Martin added that the time had come for the G20 to "tackle the broader problems associated with globalization."

Martin further saw the G20 concentrating on longer-term prevention as well as immediate crisis-response policy. The G20 was thus conceived of as more than a technically oriented, limited, issue-specific forum.

The G20's relationship with other international institutions also suggested its potentially robust, if organizationally constrained, role. It would operate within the framework of the Bretton Woods bodies, fully involve their representatives (including the chairs of the IMF's Interim Committee and Development Joint Committee) and the EU in its substantive discussions, in order to ensure that its work was "well integrated." It would "help co-ordinate the activities of other international groups and organizations, such as the Financial Stability Forum," "facilitate deliberations" in the IMFC, and potentially develop "common positions on complex issues … to expedite decision making in other fora" (Canada, Department of Finance 2000).

Designed to guide the work of other key institutions both new and old, it would act as a hub of a new global governance network for finance and economic affairs. However, in practice there was no initial link to the FSF.

The G20's potential importance was further suggested by other institutional features. These included the firm control of the chair by a G7 country at the start, a one-year rotational cycle for the chair after the first two years, the linking of its meetings to those of the G7 at the start of each year, deputies gatherings' to prepare for and support the ministerial meetings, the ability to call on the resources of the IMF, World Bank, and outside experts, and the power to form working groups to study and make recommendations related to its mandate.

Importantly the G20 included its members' central bank governors as equals alongside their finance ministers. This was a carryover from the central banks' strong role in the G22 and G33, the latter a result of the personal initiative of US Treasury official Edwin Truman. In the G20 the central bankers played a larger role than they did in the G7.

Martin sought to develop the new institution into a very influential forum. The Canadians initially considered holding the second ministerial meeting in Toronto in June 2000, a mere six months after the first one in Berlin. There were fears that this could detract from the lead-up to the G7 finance ministers meeting and G7/8 Okinawa Summit in Japan in July. But the Canadians hoped that the envisaged G20 timing and location would better enable the new group, whose conclusions could be recorded in a chair's statement, to influence the G7/8 meeting itself. In the end they chose to wait until after the G8 summit, thus establishing the G20 at the ministerial and governors' level as an annual, autumn event. But Martin's desire to have the G20 go first to guide the G7/8 was there from the very start. In his initial consultation with non-G7 members, about half raised this point. They were adamant that the G20 was not to be a body that ratified what the G7/8 had already decided to do on its own.

Canada also sought an inclusive, regionally balanced forum replete with differing perspectives, to avoid the body recreating and falling victim to traditional divisions, including those arising only on a geographically regional or older North-South divide. Canada preferred to keep the group focused on sharing experiences through open discussion, rather than members' stating hard, often inherited positions. Canada's instinct thus differed from the views of some, notably one newly included finance minister, who saw the G20 as an excellent opportunity for the South to press its issues against the North.

There was some skepticism about this potentially G7-dominated body. In Brazil, back in the mid-1990s amidst the mounting financial crises, Fernando Henrique Cardoso, president from 1995 to 2003, had called for global coordination to contain uncontrolled capital flows. But Brazil was a late convert to the G20 solution, seeing it as an initiative that might undermine traditional UN-based multilateralism.

Yet the non-G7 members took the group seriously and gave it a chance to succeed. They were led by the largest and potentially most problematic country,

China. Its open attitude and rising weight were important in ensuring that the G20 would become a forum for meaningful reciprocal influence across the G7–non-G7 divide. As an Asian power that had largely escaped the 1997–99 financial crisis, China would deal from a position of strength in the new forum.

There were, nonetheless, questions about whether this fledgling group could do much more than legitimize G7/8 positions. Some participants saw the G20 as part of the crisis-bred "G7-ization" of the world, with the G20 created to secure a broader consensus for G7/8-generated ideas and thus make them more palatable to the wider world. In this view, the G20's 11, heavily crisis-affected, non-G7/8 members were destined to be informed of G7/8 initiatives, to be given some semblance of participation, and to affect outcomes merely at the margin. The G20's creation further showed that the G7/8 did not want to leave the reform of the international financial system to the IMF or the World Bank, where poorer developing countries had a longstanding, institutionalized role and could call upon the capacity of a large and well-equipped international staff. But China proved reluctant to become a member of a fixed developing country coalition. This helped prevent the G20 from becoming a new North-South dialogue, or a collection of small, dependent, neoliberal, committed or confirmed countries echoing the views of a US-led, unified G7/8.

Mission and Agenda

The mission and agenda of the G20 immediately grew well beyond its initial formal focus on financial stability. The 1999 German-hosted G8 summit, under the impact of successive financial shocks, had just pioneered a new "Cologne consensus" on socially sustainable globalization. It was distinctly different from the "Ronald Thatcherism" or commonly understood Washington Consensus that had dominated the earlier G7 as well as the current IMF (Kirton 2000). Promoting global growth appealed to many, inside and outside the G7, who had not yet shared the locomotive-led benefits that had been so impressively produced by the American "Goldilocks" economy—which was not so cold that it caused a recession, and not so hot that it caused inflation. Moreover, within the finance core, an analysis of the recent crises showed many that exchange rates, liability management, and international codes and standards were the key issues for the G20 to address.

Plans and Preparations

Vancouver, November 1999

The G20's work began with the first preparatory meeting of its deputies in Vancouver in November 1999. The meeting, chaired by Caio Koch-Weser, the secretary of state at Germany's Ministry of Finance, was designed to determine the rules of the game, for adjustment and approval by the finance ministers and bank governors the following month in Berlin. It sought to have the new body sustain, rationalize, legitimate, and globalize things that were neglected in the G7.

At their first session, the deputies reached general agreement on several basic points. The G20 should focus on an efficient exchange of ideas on the key issues of finance, build consensus on these ideas, and demonstrate leadership by example. The group would deal with selected economic issues that the G7 did not. There would be one meeting of ministers and bank governors and two of deputies each year. The World Bank and the IMF would provide input for the G20's work and assist in its implementation. The G20 was not a formal decision-making forum. It would work on a confidential basis, without a secretariat or working groups.

Beyond these basics, a difference of opinion arose over what the agenda, and by implication the ambition, of the G20 should be. The IMF led one position, arguing that in order to add value to a system already replete with institutions, the G20 should focus on difficult issues where the IMF's own executive board had not been able to agree. This agenda included capital account liberalization, private sector participation in sovereign debt rescheduling, and contingent credit lines (CCL). Such an agenda would ensure that the G20 was useful and would take hard decisions.

The alternative position, led by Canada, was to start gently, by focusing on issues where there was already a substantial measure of existing, emerging, or prospective consensus from all within the group. This agenda included some important issues, such as appropriate exchange rate regimes and private sector involvement in rescheduling. The Canadians were particularly firm on their preferred approach, arguing it was needed to build momentum for, comfort with, and confidence in the new body. This approach prevailed.

The second deputies' session dealt with exchange rates, capital account, and financial sector debt management. It did little beyond what the G7, the IMF Executive Board, and the Organisation for Economic Co-operation and Development (OECD) had already done.

Session three dealt with the role of the international community. The IMF argued that the issue of CCLs should be examined by the G20, with a view to securing a G7-G20 agreement on its reform. Similar processes were recommended for debt standstill, for collective action clauses for modifying bonds (where a joint public–private sector working group was suggested), and for debt standstill. These ideas were not adopted.

Although nothing controversial or radical emerged from the meeting, several important procedural decisions did. The discussions would serve as the agenda for the ministers and bank governors in Berlin. At that meeting, there was to be no communiqué and therefore no drafting session, just a relatively informal concluding chair's statement. As the Canadian chair wanted, the G20 ministers and bank governors would start with the issues on which there was some reasonable prospect of securing consensus. Deliberation and direction setting, not hard decision making, would be the G20's initial thrust.

At the Meeting

Berlin, December 1999

The first meeting of the G20 came physically from a compromise. It was held in Berlin to placate the reluctant Germans. It was chaired by Canadian Paul Martin, in part to forestall any argument that it was too American led.

The topics, issues, and background documentation for Berlin came almost entirely from other international institutions. In Berlin, the IMF-led coalition once again asked the G20 to deal with issues where there was no consensus in the IMF Executive Board, the IMFC, or the international community at large. The Canadians again countered that the G20 should start with the issues on which there was minimum agreement in order to build momentum. The Canadians, with the support of host Germany and the US, drove the discussion in favour of this latter approach. It was antithetical to any earlier hope that the G20 would be a forum for the rapid legitimization of US-bred ideas for IMF and international financial system reform. In keeping with Canadian desires, the G20's agenda focused on exchange rate arrangements, financial sector regulation, and supervision and prudential liability management. These were, in Martin's judgement, "all areas of architectural reform in which national governments working collectively have become increasingly prepared to take the steps required to reduce vulnerabilities to crises" (Martin 2000). Shock-bred vulnerability reduction thus took pride of place.

The direct documentation for the Berlin meeting was prepared by the Canadians and Germans and, to a lesser extent, the United States. The meeting, which was designed to be informal and issue only a one-page chair's statement, was to serve as a round table to "get to know you," set the rules of the game, and identify the purpose of the group.

The meeting started in the evening and proceeded for the following full day. It dealt with standard broad topics and featured an open floor. Martin encouraged ministers to speak up, ask questions, and share their point of view. In its discussions of macroeconomic trends and prospects, the discussions tended to be thematic, focusing on areas where the global economy as a whole was vulnerable, rather than on the situation in, or performance of, individual countries. Systemic vulnerabilities, not country-specific problems and responsibilities, were the focus here.

Some representatives from emerging countries read prepared statements. But most participants were pleased with the informality of the discussion, although it repeated the dialogue from other forums. The meeting featured free-flowing discussion, as Martin had hoped, even if the conclusions were familiar. This underscored the importance of putting diplomacy and discussion above hard decision making at the start. The fact that the meeting was held in Europe made it more difficult for the European members to speak with anything other than a single voice. This reinforced the reluctance of some non-European members to add more European claimants to the group.

The first G20 meeting did not create any working groups, although some would later emerge. Nor did it request extensive work from other international institutions. More contentious issues, such as those raised on the eve of the meeting in a public call by Summers for reform of the IMF, were discussed only a little as part of the dialogue on "vulnerabilities" in the international system. Most discussion of Summers's proposal took place in the corridors. Summers's call was an effort at domestic political management, in the form of a US attempt to show Congress that the administration was addressing concerns about the IMF and the work of the International Financial Institution Advisory Commission, chaired by Allan Meltzer and established by Congress to recommend US policy toward multilateral institutions. But it helped put the architectural issue of IFI reform on the G20's informal agenda at the very start.

The meeting showed some signs of the challenges, but registered some success, in bridging the potential established-versus-emerging country divide. On issues such as codes—an "Anglo-Saxon"/German project—Canada and the US felt Turkey and others agreed with their approach. Others seemed to agree, in contrast to the hesitancy that they had shown at the IMFC and IMF Executive Board.

The developing countries, however, saw the dynamics somewhat differently. They viewed the meeting as a way to learn and exchange views rather than as a negotiation out of which decisions would come. They continued to insist that on major issues more work needed to be done. They set clear limits to any co-optation and buy-in for any G7-led program.

The G20 meeting did not immediately change any minds of resistant emerging country representatives about transparency, codes, and governance. The US, UK, and Canada regarded these as the core foundations of the new international financial architecture. Following the meeting, China and Brazil continued to express deep concerns about IMF programs and, along with Mexico and Argentina, about the strong conditions imposed from this external source. Arrayed against them still stood the three "Anglo" countries (Canada, US, and the UK), Germany, and, to a lesser extent, Japan, which wanted clear codes adopted by all. More broadly there were also divisions within the G7, where Martin was pushing strongly to have the G20 instruct the FSF to take a tough line on banking regulation. Other G7 members then deregulating their banks stood opposed.

Yet there were concrete signs of consensus. All G20 countries agreed to ask the IMF and the World Bank to examine how their respective national financial rules measured up to international standards and how those rules might be strengthened. International surveillance of domestic financial regulation would begin. With appropriate follow-up, this could indeed represent "an important breakthrough in the establishment of generally accepted principles of global governance" (Canada, Standing Committee on Foreign Affairs and International Trade 2000). On issues such as standards and codes, direction-setting consensus thus flowed into decisional commitment, as there was a clear discussion and conscious choice to implement the consensus domestically, and thus lead by example, rather than preach. Participants were aware that because of their weight in the world and their central positions in the IFIs, their governance through consensus and leadership by example in delivery would probably constitute a de facto decision for all.

Dimensions of Performance

At Berlin, the G20 got off to a solid start, especially with a strong performance as intended in the deliberative and direction-setting domains (see Appendix C-1).

Domestic Political Management

There was little effort to use the first G20 meeting, beyond Larry Summers's speech to manage its members' domestic politics. There were no compliments offered to any member in the communiqué (see Appendix D).

In fact, the first G20 meeting may have harmed some members back home. *The Globe and Mail* (1999), Canada's elite daily newspaper, criticized finance minister Martin for heading off to Berlin when there were problems to deal with at home. Its editorial concluded that "Martin is off to Berlin this week, where he will chair the first meeting of the G20, which focuses on international financial systems and flows, but he has a great deal of repair work to do at home." Other assessments were less negative, but remained skeptical that the G20 would be able to accomplish anything worthwhile (Cook 1999).

Deliberation

In its deliberation, Berlin was a solid success. Publicly, on paper it produced a very short chair's statement of 472 words in six paragraphs, substantially shorter than any of the statements produced at the scheduled meetings over the next decade (see Appendix E). The Berlin statement was heavily rooted in macroeconomics and trade. It was the shortest document ever produced at a scheduled meeting. When the ministers met the following year, the length increased more than four times. However, within the meeting room itself, Berlin's discussion led to a somewhat open exchange, as the chair had sought.

Direction Setting

In its direction setting, Berlin was a strong success. With Canada at the helm, democratic principles in their most general form were endorsed. The G20 made three references to three such principles: transparency, the mobilization of ideas, and the importance of access to ideas in all countries (see Appendix F-1). Berlin thus laid the core normative foundation for the group. The importance of distributional outcomes and the social protections of embedded liberalism were affirmed as well.

Decision Making

On the dimension of decision making, Berlin was a solid start. It made four concrete commitments (see Appendix G). Two related to macroeconomics and two related to international financial institutions. This was the second lowest number and the lowest spread of commitments made by the ministers' and governors' group over the next decade.

Delivery

In the delivery of the Berlin decisions, there was an emphasis on embedding accountability mechanisms. Commitments were crafted with concrete intrinsic guidelines contained within. Three of the commitments were placed under the responsibility of the G20 finance deputies. The fourth emphasized the importance of clear and transparent data reporting in the IMF and the World Bank.

Development of Global Governance

In its development of global governance, Berlin took some solid steps (see Appendix C-1). Internally, members institutionalized the group in four references and by publicly committing to meet again in Canada in 2000. In two of these references Berlin mandated the deputies to work on several issues that would be reported back to the ministers at the next meeting.

Externally, the ministers agreed to continue to work with and through existing international forums, notably the FSF, the IMF, and the World Bank to tackle the financial crisis. The IMF and the World Bank had pride of place but the World Trade Organization received one of the six such references too. With four references to its own institution and six to those outside, the Berlin G20 focused on both developing its own institution and on complimenting, supplementing, supporting, furthering, and enhancing the work that had been done and could be done in other forums.

Causes of Performance

The causes of the creation and initial performance of the G20 are captured well by the model of systemic hub governance. The model's systematic synthesis in its first three causes is consistent with the even more compact trilogy of causes highlighted by Gordon Brown's (2010) assessment a decade later: the Asian economic crisis then raging, the G20 as an attempt to bypass the IMF, and an effort to balance the group toward an Asia where many countries were clearly vulnerable but some rising countries—led by China and India—were not. Yet beyond shock-activated, equalizing vulnerability, international institutional failure, and equalizing relative capability lie the model's important three additional components of domestic democratic convergence, political capital, control, continuity, competence, and commitment, and the G20's position as the hub of a growing global network.

Shock-Activated, Equalizing Vulnerability

The first cause of the G20's creation and its solid success at Berlin was the sequence of shocks that showed the emerging, equalizing vulnerability of many members to new non-state threats. After the earlier small shocks of the 1994 Mexican peso crisis and the 1995 Barings Bank failure and then a two-year interval of stability, the Asian-turned-global financial crisis from 1997 to 1999, which had started in the property markets in Thailand, was the catalyst for creating the G20. The geographic and functional scope of the crisis spread throughout and beyond Asia, assaulting Thailand in July 1997, Indonesia that autumn, Korea in December, Russia in August 1998, the United States with the collapse of the hedge fund Long-Term Capital Management (LTCM) in September 1998, and Brazil two months later. Moreover, its speed intensified. The first phase, in distant Asia, had been a slow burn, taking half a year to bring down three small, if increasingly large, countries. But after a seven-month springtime sabbatical that bred complacency, the second global phase struck rapidly, hitting two "superpowers" and Brazil, in Europe and the Americas, within three months.

It became increasingly clear that the emerging international system was much more interconnected, making countries more vulnerable to swiftly spreading external shocks than it had been in 1944, 1975, or even at the time of the precursor shocks of Mexico in 1994 and the collapse of Barings Bank in the spring of 1995. The new shocks first arose from non-state financial firms within sovereign polities and only subsequently from the sovereigns themselves. They spread across sectors and regions over two years to affect the United States itself. Both consumers and producers of financial security were now systemically significant, and both were deliberately included in the G20. The 1994 Mexican peso crisis alone had not brought Paul Martin's concept of a group of systemically significant finance ministers to life. Only the second sequence of shocks from the Asian-turned-global financial crisis of 1997–99 did.

International Institutional Failure

The second cause of the G20's creation and initial solid performance was international institutional failure elsewhere. In the face of the cadence of contagious Asian-catalysed shocks from the increasingly integrated and complex international financial system, each usually greater in scale than its predecessor, the formal multilateral organizations from the 1940s, all headquartered in the US or Europe, and the newer informal plurilateral institutions from the 1960s onward failed to respond adequately on their own, both in the actual damage that came from the crisis and in the view of many countries that the crisis consumed (see Appendix I). The compounding complexity and uncertainty caused by the contagion led first to two years of experimentation with the single-purpose NAB, the ad hoc G22, and the G33 and finally to the three new bodies created in 1999.

The IMF was the first to fail along the full spectrum of performance, starting with prediction and prevention, through containment, to conducting reforms that would prevent another crisis arising again. The IMF's inadequacies started with the 1994 Mexican peso crisis that it failed to predict and prevent. The IMF did predict the Thai crisis in September 1996 and the managing director sought unsuccessfully to induce Thailand to take preventive action. However, the IMF was unable to convince the G7 to provide the resources required to cope with the Thai crisis. The IMF then required and secured new resources from the G7's second line of defence to respond to Korea on December 24, 1997. It imposed conditions that most Asians believed worsened the impact of the crisis.

With the creation of the G20, the IMF sought to improve its performance. As the chair of the IMFC Gordon Brown (2010, 80) "sought to get the balance right between the G20 and the IMF: the G20 would take a strategic role and look at long-term issues, and the IMF would deal with the more immediate problems that required decisions to be made … However, an initiative by the IMF to deal with global imbalances fell by the wayside."

The G7 was the second established international institution to fail when acting alone. At the Denver Summit and the finance ministers' lead-up meeting in the first half of 1997, it too failed to predict or prevent the coming crisis (Kirton 2010a). The G7 offered an inadequate response at its autumn ministerial in Hong Kong on September 20, after Thailand had gone down but before Indonesia and Korea did. And it similarly failed at the Birmingham Summit in 1998 and in its G7 finance ministers' lead-up meeting to predict or prevent the second stage of the crisis, with Russia defaulting in August, American financial markets seizing up in response to LTCM's collapse in September, and Brazil requiring a rescue later that autumn. Where G7/8 governance did perform with great success during the crisis, in accordance with its core mission, was in defining a response that protected and promoted democracy—in Indonesia, Korea, Russia, and Brazil. But in the "lower" politics of promoting financial stability alone, it failed. During the crisis, the G7 finance ministers had tried but failed to convince the emerging countries to adopt the G7 rules and frameworks on financial regulation. Emerging countries ignored the G7 suggestions primarily because they had not been a part of their formulation (Martin 2008a). After two years the G7 rationally recognized the need for a broader body and responded with the FSF and by endorsing the IMFC and the G20 as well.

Clearly, there was a new institutional need but no confidence that a single institution would be effective alone. The result was a search for international institutional comparative advantage, collegiality, competition, and insurance by creating new bodies, rather than forum shopping among established ones. The

G7/8 itself did not add any newly systemically significant countries. The FSF reluctantly added to its G7 members only a few small countries—Australia, the Netherlands, Singapore, and Hong Kong. The IMF was more universal and legalized, and gave Brazil, Mexico, and Argentina seats on its executive board. However, it was hampered by obsolescent Eurocentric over-representation in its inner councils, and too self-contained to be a forum for open, informal discussion. It was confined by its 1944 charter, its national composition of IMF senior staff, and its organizational expertise and culture to respond to the new demands. Moreover, none of these bodies gave central bank governors from all members the equal role alongside their finance ministers that the G20 did, and allowed the bank governors to speak for their country on matters within their domain. At the IMFC the governors usually sat behind their finance minister, rather than at his or her side. Thus the G20 was also needed and ultimately prevailed.

Predominant, Equalizing Capabilities

The third cause of the G20's creation and solid performance at Berlin was the collectively predominant and internally equalizing capabilities of the countries and the EU in the new group. The failure of the old multilateral and newer plurilateral institutions in the face of sequential, severe shocks revealed that emerging countries were increasingly becoming a necessary part of international financial governance just as they were also the causes of a global crisis whose cure lay at its source in reforming the financial regulations, supervision, and "crony" capitalism within their sovereign states. They were emerging not only as consumers of financial security but also as producers of it, as well as of global trade and growth, with the rise of China and India. Yet despite their rising relevance, in both categories, they were absent from the G7/8 in 1997–99, virtually absent from the FSF, and underrepresented at the IMFC and IMF's Executive Board. The G20, with all those emerging countries in from the start as equal members, recognized that considerable changes had occurred in the structure of international economic capabilities over the past decades (G20 2008). Compared to its 1999 colleagues, it had the advantage in globally predominant and internally equalized capability combined (see Appendix K). The G20's advantage was greater still if the population of its member countries was added, as a component of the population-resources-technology factors of production or capability triad, and as a post-Westphalian key component of international legitimacy (as distinct from power) (Dewitt and Kirton 1983).

In 1999, the G8 alone represented 67 percent of the world's GDP, but only 14 percent of the world's population. Its largest economy, the United States, was vastly larger than its least powerful one, Russia. Moreover, while the G8 had predominant, equalizing capability, it suffered on connectivity. The crisis caused Russia to default in August 1998 and drove the currency of its next weakest member, Canada, to a historic low of just over 62 cents to the US dollar at the time.

The FSF included the G7, excluded Russia, but included four small rich polities that added little to the G7's predominant, equalizing capability. The US was vastly larger than the smallest member. The IMFC's 24 members included the G7 along with Belgium, Denmark, the Netherlands, Switzerland, Algeria, the United Arab Emirates, Gabon, Thailand, and others. It represented almost the same percentage of the global economy as the G20. Yet its largest member was vastly more powerful than its smallest.

The third candidate from the class of 1999 was the G20. Its 19 country members represented 81 percent of global GDP and two thirds of the world's population. It included several large rising powers unscathed by the crisis, notably China and India (Kirton 2000). Given current and projected growth rates, such as Korea's 9 percent growth in 1999, it was clear then that the G20 would be an even weightier institution soon. Its largest member, the US, was 70 times larger than its smallest one, South Africa. The G20's Gini coefficient, as a measure of equality among its members, was 0.54. The G20 thus had the clear advantage in the combination of globally predominant, equalizing capability outside and international equality inside. This helped it work as a club of equals whose conversations, consensus, and commitments were produced, accepted, and owned by all its members, without the direct use of threats, sanctions, inducements, or other incentives that were relied upon in intergovernmental bargaining forums.

Democratic Convergence

The fourth cause of the G20's creation and initial solid success, especially in direction setting, was the domestic democratic convergence of its members. The G20 was a very heterogeneous group in its members' geographical regions, levels of development, languages, religions, cultures, and legal and political systems. However, both the established and emerging country members had an interest in national and hence global financial stability, sustained growth, and social stability through making globalization work for all. Some, led by a China with vivid memories of the shock of the Tiananmen Square uprising and massacre in 1989, needed such financial stability and strong, stable, sustained growth to combat the domestic social instability that could threaten their closed political regimes.

Beyond domestic commitment to social stability lay an increasing convergence on political openness and democracy in the commitment and character of their domestic systems. The G7 had acted to defend somewhat democratic Mexico in 1994 and Korea in 1997, and Russia and Brazil in 1998 (see Appendix L). The US in particular sought to strengthen this success by including them in the G20. It used G20 membership to entrench democracy in Turkey and secure it in Indonesia and Nigeria through inclusion. With only Saudi Arabia and China left as devoted non-democracies by the time of the first G20 ministerial, the G20 was born as an overwhelmingly democratic group. Its members were systematically significant not only for financial stability as a start but for protecting and promoting the global democratic revolution in the end.

The G20 had the advantage of political openness among the new bodies born in 1999. The G20's 19 country members included non-democratic China and Saudi Arabia (see Appendix L-2). This produced a democratic ratio of 89 percent, which was even higher if the EU and all its member countries were included, as all were on the G20's democratic side. The FSF had nine democratic members and two doubtfully democratic ones (Singapore and Hong Kong) for an assured democratic ratio of 82 percent. The IMF's 24 members contained several non-democratic polities.

Domestic Political Control, Capital, Continuity, Competence, and Commitment

The fifth cause of the G20's creation and solid performance at Berlin was the breadth and depth of its representatives' domestic political control, capital, continuity, competence, and commitment, beyond the relative capabilities of their countries as a whole (see Appendix M). Within Canada co-founder Paul Martin's Liberal Party enjoyed a secure parliamentary majority dating back to 1993, a divided opposition, and strong popular approval ratings. Martin himself was expected to assume the position of prime minister when Jean Chrétien, the long-serving incumbent, left. Martin had been finance minister since December 1993 and the chief executive officer of a multinational corporation, Canada Steamship Lines, with operations in major emerging countries before. By 1999, his fellow finance ministers were ready to hear and accept his call to create a new group.

Within the US, Lawrence Summers served what some saw as a lame-duck administration under Bill Clinton that did not control Congress and whose standing with the public had been bruised by the Monica Lewinsky affair and the resulting impeachment proceedings against the president. Yet Summers was a highly acclaimed professional economist with extensive Treasury experience prior to his recent appointment as secretary. He was regarded as the second most powerful person in the Clinton administration with immediate access to and influence in the White House. Despite low political control, capital, and prospective continuity, Summers offered high continuity from the past and very high competence in the present.

In the UK, the new Labour government, elected in 1997 under Tony Blair (2010), had a majority in parliament and strong popular approval. Gordon Brown was a finance minister with a deep commitment to poverty reduction and education. In Germany, Gerhard Schroeder's Social Democratic Party had swept to power, with its Green Party coalition partners, in 1998. In France, the experienced government of Jacques Chirac, elected in 1995, was firmly in command. In these consequential countries there was a left liberal majority, with only Chirac's France standing outside.

Controlled Club Participation as a Network Hub

The sixth cause of the G20's creation and solid performance at Berlin was its controlled club participation as a network hub. As the discussions about the membership of the new G20 revealed, the status and selection of the countries that counted were by no means self-evident. The first criterion, quite explicit, was systemic significance, recognizing that the new world of contagious interconnectedness had replaced the self-contained billiard ball-like sovereigns containing only relative capability based on their territory from the Westphalian world of old. A second, less explicit criterion was democratic commitment. The criteria that had dominated the 1940s architecture—relative capability, wartime victory, and land-based geographic representativeness—remained relevant, but less so than in the past.

The G20's first and fundamental advantage, as an institutional club, was the full equality among its members from the very start. They were each fully equal in an institutional and operational sense, even if behaviourally some were more important than others in practice before, during, and after the Berlin meeting took place. Even here, however, there was an operational and epistemic equality among the ministers, governors, and deputies, reinforced by the extensive experience the individual participants, such as Brazil's Pedro Malan, had acquired as their country's executive directors at the IMF.

This was reinforced by the G20's second advantage, its geographically mobile hosting and thus venue each year, rather than a largely fixed chair and place. This helped ensure that all G20 members were and thus felt equal, for each could assume the rights, responsibilities, and prestige of chair and host at some time. In contrast, the IMFC was continuously chaired for its first several years by Gordon Brown and met in Washington except when the annual meeting was held elsewhere once every three years. The FSF tended to meet in Basel, Switzerland. Even the G7 finance ministers tended to meet once or twice a year in Washington DC in the United States at the semi-annual meetings of the IMF and no longer met at their leaders' rotating annual summit after 1997. And with German Horst Köhler as head of the IMF, an American—James Wolfensohn—as head of the World Bank, and the Germans having designed the FSF, these bodies looked like the exclusive Euro-American world of the 20th century, rather than the Asian and emerging country world of the twenty-first century.

The G20's third advantage, as a controlled club, was the continuity of its membership. In sharp contrast to the ever expanding G7 from its start as the G4 in July 1973, the G8 from its start in 1975, the G22 that became a G33, and the FSF in its move from seven to eleven, the G20 kept the same members since its start. This was a deliberate decision in the design, reflected in the choice of the number 20 for the name of a club with only 19 country members (Ibbitson and Perkins 2010). This antipathy toward expansion is why a subsequently democratic Nigeria was not given a seat. This continuity helps create an exclusive, compact, high-status club, valued by those within.

The G20's fourth advantage, again as a controlled club, was the tightly constricted membership and participation in the compact club. With its 19 country members, the EU, IMF, and World Bank, and with each country sending a finance minister and central bank governor to the annual meetings, the G20 had more participants than the G7/8 and FSF. But the G20 was still smaller than the 24-member IMFC and IMF Executive Board and the 25-member (and later larger) NAB, and both the G22 and the G33. Moreover, the number of representatives at G20 meetings made it about as large as those of the FSF, given the many officials each member sent to the FSF. The G20 reinforced this advantage by starting with open discussion and moving on to more consensus and commitment in later years.

The G20's fifth advantage, as a compact club, was its informal, soft law character, directly delivered from capitals by ministers and bank governors who thus felt they owned it, rather than being a body run by international civil servants bound by an international bureaucratic culture and international law. The G20 thus avoided the problem of bureaucratic capture, the inflexibility of a legal mandate and large organization, and the pathologies that flowed from these (Barnett and Finnemore 1999, 2004). One reason the G20 was created was that influential figures in national capitals did not like those at the IMF telling them what to do.

Furthermore, unlike in the IMFC's constituency model, the G20's major emerging country representatives had the freedom to act, along with the G5 members, as individuals, rather than as agents of a fixed consensus of their constituency where they would have to repeat the established lowest common denominator line. At the IMFC, Turkey was included in a constituency represented by a continental European middle power. Brazil, Argentina, and Mexico represented several other Latin American countries. The G20 was able to separate these countries from such constraints. Together with its more constricted participation, this made the G20 a forum for more open, flexible deliberation and consensus formation.

At the same time, the presence of the IMF and World Bank, as continuing participants representing the institution if not necessarily its executive board, endowed the G20 with a built-in link to these Bretton Woods bodies. The G20 thus inherited some of the IMFC's legal legitimacy, global accountability, and extensive organizational resources, even if these were limited back in Washington by the G7's dominant weight in the Executive Board and the European-American character of the executive heads. Yet the IMF and World Bank were no more important than South Africa, Indonesia, Korea, or any other country member. This was different from what happened at meetings of the World Bank and IMF in Washington. The G20 also mobilized the formidable national resources of its chair for the effective preparation and implementation of its consensus.

The sixth G20 advantage was the intensity of interaction within the institutional club. As its annual meeting inspired deputies' meetings and workshops, the increasing intensity of interaction could incubate the group dynamics and identity, through social-psychological constructivist dynamics, that could also make the group an interpersonal club. Its ministers and governors also met face to face with their colleagues in various outer nodes of the network many times a year. But at the start, the intensity of interaction at the hub was modest, as were the Berlin results.

However, there was a respectful collegiality among Paul Martin, Gordon Brown, and Hans Eichel and no sense that they were competing as individuals or as guardians of the respective forums they most preferred, respectively the G20, the IMFC, and the FSF. All three led successful economies that served as examples for the world. Indeed, as the G20 and IMFC were being formed there was some consideration of Brown being made chair of the G20 and Martin of the IMFC, even though it was clear to both that it was the other body that each preferred to lead. In a conversation between the two, each made it evident that he did not want to chair the body that the other wished to chair.

The G20's seventh advantage was its location, externally, at the hub of a global network of other plurilateral groups. These groups were often led by combinations of established and emerging countries from within the G20. Thus Britain, Canada, Australia, India, and South Africa connected the G20 to the Commonwealth, the world's oldest global plurilateral summit institution, started almost a century earlier. France and Canada did so with La Francophonie, which had started its biennial summits in 1985. Many G7 countries along with Turkey connected the G20 to NATO, whose summits intensified in the 1990s. Many also linked it to APEC, whose leaders' meeting began in 1993, to the Summit of the Americas (SOA) that started in 1994, and to the Asia–European Union Meeting (ASEM) that started in 1996, as the Europeans responded to the Pacific powers that had created the APEC leaders' meeting in 1993.

At the finance ministers' level, the creation of the ongoing NAB with Korea, the ongoing FSF with Australia, and the ongoing IMFC strengthened the position of the G20 as the global network hub. Beyond lay the OECD, now with Mexico and Korea as members, the APEC finance ministers' forum, the western hemisphere finance ministers' forum, and the older BIS, its Basel Committee on Banking Supervision (BCBS), the G10, and the Commonwealth finance ministers forum. The BIS had successfully moved beyond its former G10 dominance before the G20 arrived. The BCBS met at the BIS but was no longer controlled by the G10 governors. Each G20 member was thus too interconnected with key groups and constituencies to be left out, through its key position in the overlapping membership of international institutions that radiated influence in, out, and around to form a global financial governance network as a whole.

This distinct character of the G20 as a systemic club that served as the hub of a global governance network explains why some popular criteria from past concepts are less relevant in explaining its success. In an age of fast-flowing globalization, fixed geographic regionalism mattered far less that it did when the Treaties of Westphalia were signed in the middle of continental Europe in 1648 (Ruggie 1993). To the extent that it did, the IMFC's membership was heavily weighted toward Europe, the Middle East, and Africa, as befitting the IMF's origins in 1944 and its adjustment in the wake of the 1973 oil shocks. The G20, in contrast, contained

Korea and Turkey, increasing representativeness along several dimensions such as religion and language beyond geographic location alone.

The G20's status as the club at the hub of a global governance network fostered cooperation more than competition. Securing acceptance for the new codes and practices of transparency and surveillance did show the G7's leadership, with the G20 and IMFC serving as legitimating bodies, as the G22 had been before. Yet, as more difficult issues emerged, the flexibility, smaller size, and individual country freedom of the G20 suggested that this body could provide a more timely and balanced result.

Conclusion

The future of the fledgling G20 depended on the ability of its early custodians to realize the ambitious goals they had set. They also depended on the G20's chair finding the appropriate answers to several challenges.

One challenge was the G20's ability to supersede older and recently created consultative groups, while resisting any temptation to add any of its Eurocentric members to a globally balanced G20 that already contained the four European G7 members and the EU. Here the pro forma nature of the G10 meeting in Washington in April 2000 soon suggested that the G10 could easily be terminated, its agenda folded into that of the G20, and its European members such as Switzerland left outside or represented through innovative arrangements with the EU.

The second challenge was to keep the constricted participation, functional fit, and high status of the G20 as a systemically significant top-tier group, by resisting entreaties to expand the global reach, geographic balance, and weight of the G20 by adding new members or participants.

The third challenge was to increase downward representation and democratic legitimacy, by demonstrating benefits to and involving civil society. This was a call that would predictably come once the clear and present danger of the crisis had passed (Canada, Standing Committee on Foreign Affairs and International Trade 2000). The need was seen at the IMF meeting in Washington in April 1999, where civil society representatives had been left to protest on the outside. It would soon be addressed by the G8, which started to seriously engage in civil society dialogue at the Okinawa Summit in 2000.

References

Abbott, Kenneth W., Keohane, Robert, Moravcsik, Andrew, Slaughter, Anne-Marie, and Snidal, Duncan. 2000. "The Concept of Legalization." *International Organization* 54(3): 401–20.

Amato, Giuliano. 2008. "From Bretton Woods to the G20." In *Growth, Innovation, Inclusion: The G20 at Ten*, eds Kirton, John J., and Koch, Madeline. London:

Newsdesk, 29–31. Available at: www.g8.utoronto.ca/newsdesk/G20at10.pdf. Accessed: July 2011.

Baker, Andrew. 2006. *The Group of Seven: Finance Ministries, Central Banks, and Global Financial Governance*. London: Routledge.

Barnett, Michael and Finnemore, Martha. 1999. "The Politics, Power, and Pathologies of International Organizations." *International Organization* 53(4): 699–732.

Barnett, Michael and Finnemore, Martha. 2004. *Rules for the World: International Organizations in Global Politics*. Ithaca: Cornell University Press.

Beattie, Alan. 1999. "New Forum to Supplement G7 Work." *Financial Times*, September 27.

Beauchesne, Eric. 1999. "Martin Warns against Complacency." *Montreal Gazette*, September 26, p. A9.

Bergsten, C. Fred and Henning, C. Randall. 1996. *Global Economic Leadership and the Group of Seven*. Washington DC: Institute for International Economics.

Blair, Tony. 2010. *A Journey*. London: Random House.

Blustein, Paul. 2001. *The Chastening: Inside the Crisis That Rocked the Global Financial System and Humbled the IMF*. New York: PublicAffairs.

Brown, Gordon. 2010. *Beyond the Crash: Overcoming the First Crisis of Globalization*. New York: Free Press.

Canada. Department of Finance. 1999. "Finance Minister Paul Martin Chosen as Inaugural Chairperson of New Group of Twenty." Press Release 99–080, Washington DC, September 25. Available at: www.g8.utoronto.ca/finance/fm992509.htm. Accessed: July 2012.

Canada. Department of Finance. 2000. "New G20 Forum: Backgrounder." Available at: www.g20.utoronto.ca/g20backgrounder.htm. Accessed: July 2012.

Canada. Standing Committee on Foreign Affairs and International Trade. 2000. "Evidence." Ottawa, May 18. Available at: www.parl.gc.ca/HousePublications/Publication.aspx?DocId=1040280&Language=E&Mode=1&Parl=36&Ses=2. Accessed: July 2012.

Cohn, Theodore. 2000. *Global Political Economy: Theory and Practice*. New York: Longman.

Cook, Peter. 1999. "Time Will Tell Whether There's a Need for a G20, Peter Cook Says." *Globe and Mail*, December 15.

Costello, Peter. 2008. *The Costello Memoirs: The Age of Prosperity*. Melbourne: Melbourne University Press.

Culpeper, Roy. 2000. "Systemic Reform at a Standstill: A Flock of 'Gs' in Search of Global Financial Stability." Paper presented at Critical Issues in Financial Reform: Latin-American/Caribbean and Canadian Perspectives, Munk Centre for International Studies, University of Toronto, June 1–2, Toronto. Available at: www.g8.utoronto.ca/scholar/culpeper2000. Accessed: July 2012.

Dewitt, David and Kirton, John J. 1983. *Canada as a Principal Power: A Study in Foreign Policy and International Relations*. Toronto: John Wiley and Sons.

Financial Stability Forum. 1999. "Announcement of the First Meeting of the FSF, Washington." April 6. Available at: www.financialstabilityboard.org/press/t_990414.htm. Accessed: July 2012.

Fratianni, Michele, Savona, Paolo, and Kirton, John J., eds. 2005. *New Perspectives on Global Governance: Why America Needs the G8*. Aldershot: Ashgate.

Fréchette, Louise. 1995. "The Halifax Summit: A Canadian Perspective." *North American Outlook* 5(3): 7–13.

G7. 1988. "Toronto Economic Summit Economic Declaration." Toronto, June 21. Available at: www.g8.utoronto.ca/summit/1988toronto. Accessed: July 2012.

G7. 1999. "G7 Statement." Cologne, June 18. Available at: www.g8.utoronto.ca/summit/1999koln/g7statement_june18.htm. Accessed: July 2012.

G20. 2008. "The Group of Twenty: A History." Available at: www.g20.utoronto.ca/docs/g20history.pdf. Accessed: July 2012.

Germain, Randall D. 2001. "Global Financial Governance and the Problem of Inclusion." *Global Governance* 7(4): 411–26.

Globe and Mail. 1999. "The Surprising Legacy of the Minister of Finance Paul Martin's Triumph on the Deficit is Shadowed by Wrong-headed Policies Elsewhere." December 19.

Hajnal, Peter I. 2007. *The G8 System and the G20: Evolution, Role, and Documentation*. Aldershot: Ashgate.

Helleiner, Eric, Woods, Ngaire, and Griffith-Jones, Stephany. 2010. "The Financial Stability Board: An Effective Fourth Pillar of Global Economic Governance?," Centre for International Governance Innovation, Waterloo ON. Available at: www.cigionline.org/sites/default/files/FSB%20special%20report_2.pdf. Accessed: July 2012.

Helleiner, Gerald. 2001. "Markets, Politics, and Globalization: Can the Global Economy Be Civilized?" *Global Governance* 7(3): 243–63.

Ibbitson, John and Perkins, Tara. 2010. "How Canada Made the G20." *Globe and Mail*, June 18. Available at: www.theglobeandmail.com/news/world/g8-g20/news/how-canada-made-the-g20-happen/article1609690. Accessed: July 2012.

Jokela, Juha. 2011. "The G20: A Pathway to Effective Multilateralism?" Chaillot Paper No. 125, April 21, European Union Institute for Security Studies. Available at: www.iss.europa.eu/publications/detail/article/the-g-20-a-pathway-to-effective-multilateralism. Accessed: July 2012.

Katada, Saori N. 2001. *Banking on Stability: Japan and the Cross-Pacific Dynamics of International Financial Crisis Management*. Ann Arbor: University of Michigan Press.

Keohane, Robert O. 1984. *After Hegemony: Cooperation and Discord in the World Political Economy*. Princeton: Princeton University Press.

Kirton, John J. 1995. "The G7, the Halifax Summit, and International Financial System Reform." *North American Outlook* 5 (June): 43–66.

Kirton, John J. 2000. "The Dynamics of G7 Leadership in Crisis Response and System Reconstruction." In *Shaping a New International Financial System:*

Challenges of Governance in a Globalizing World, eds Kaiser, Karl, Kirton, John J., and Daniels, Joseph P. Aldershot: Ashgate, 65–94.

Kirton, John J. 2010a. "The Group of Eight's Legacy, Limitations, and Lessons." In *The New Dynamics of Summitry: Innovations for G20 Summits*, eds Bradford, Colin I., and Lim, Wonhyuk. Washington DC and Seoul: Brookings Institution Press and Korea Development Institute, 17–60.

Kirton, John J. 2010b. "Potential Partnership in Global Economic Governance: Canada's G20 Summit from Toronto to Turkey." Paper prepared for a presentation at TEPAV, Ankara, and DEIK, Istanbul, Turkey, June 7–8, Available at: www.g20.utoronto.ca/biblio/kirton-turkey-2010.pdf. Accessed: July 2012.

Kokotsis, Eleanore and Kirton, John J. 1997. "National Compliance with Environmental Regimes: The Case of the G7, 1988–1995." Paper prepared for the annual convention of the International Studies Association, March 18–22, Toronto.

Lesage, Dries ed. 2010. "The Future of the G8 and G20" [Special issue]. *Studia Diplomatica* 63(2).

Martin, Paul. 2000. "Statement by the Honourable Paul Martin, Minister of Finance for Canada, to the Institute for International Economics." Washington DC, April 14. Available at: www.collectionscanada.gc.ca/webarchives/20071122055106/www.fin.gc.ca/news00/00-031e.html. Accessed: July 2012.

Martin, Paul. 2008a. "Speaking Notes for the Right Honourable Paul Martin." Canada 2020 and Financial Times: View from the Top, Toronto, September 29. Available at: canada2020.ca/files/Canada_2020_Martin_Speech_FINAL.pdf. Accessed: July 2012.

Martin, Paul. 2008b. "Time for the G20 to Take the Mantle from the G8." In *Growth, Innovation, Inclusion: The G20 at Ten*, eds Kirton, John J., and Koch, Madeline. London: Newsdesk, 22–27. Available at: www.g8.utoronto.ca/newsdesk/G20at10.pdf. Accessed: July 2011.

Martin, Paul. 2010. "Address to the 2010 Couchiching Conference on 'Watershed Moment or Wasted Opportunity'." August 6, Geneva Park, Canada.

Porter, Tony. 2000. "The G7, the Financial Stability Forum, the G20, and the Politics of International Financial Regulation." Paper presented at the annual convention of the International Studies Association, March 15, Los Angeles. Available at: www.g8.utoronto.ca/g20/biblio/porter-isa-2000.pdf. Accessed: July 2012.

Putnam, Robert and Bayne, Nicholas. 1984. *Hanging Together: Co-operation and Conflict in the Seven-Power Summit*. 1st ed. Cambridge MA: Harvard University Press.

Putnam, Robert and Bayne, Nicholas. 1987. *Hanging Together: Co-operation and Conflict in the Seven-Power Summit*. 2nd ed. London: Sage Publications.

Rubin, Robert E. and Weisberg, Jacob. 2003. *In an Uncertain World: Tough Choices from Wall Street to Washington*. New York: Random House.

Ruggie, John G. 1993. "Territoriality and Beyond: Problematizing Modernity in International Relations." *International Organization* 47(1): 139–74.
Sautter, Christian. 2008. "Fundamental Principles for Global Financial Governance." In *Growth, Innovation, Inclusion: The G20 at Ten*, eds Kirton, John J., and Koch, Madeline. London: Newsdesk, 32–34. Available at: www.g8.utoronto.ca/newsdesk/G20at10.pdf. Accessed: July 2012.
Summers, Lawrence. 2008. "The Birth of the G20." In *Growth, Innovation, Inclusion: The G20 at Ten*, eds Kirton, John J., and Koch, Madeline. London: Newsdesk, 29–31. Available at: www.g8.utoronto.ca/newsdesk/G20at10.pdf. Accessed: July 2012.
Wade, Robert. 2009. "From Global Imbalances to Global Reorganisations." *Cambridge Journal of Economics* 33(4): 539–62. doi: 10.1093/cje/bep032.
Wade, Robert and Vestergaard, Jakob. 2010a. "Judging G20 by Output Ignores Input Problems." *Financial Times*, October 22. Available at: www.ft.com/intl/cms/s/0/2581209c-5f0b-11e0-a2d7-00144feab49a.html#axzz1mClv38ck. Accessed: July 2012.
Wade, Robert and Vestergaard, Jakob. 2010b. "Overhaul the G20 for the Sake of the G172." *Financial Times*, October 22. Available at: www.ft.com/intl/cms/s/0/a2ab4716-dd45-11df-9236-00144feabdc0.html#axzz1mClv38ck. Accessed: July 2012.

Chapter 4
Governing Globalization, Montreal 2000

Introduction

The Challenge

The Group of 20 (G20) held its second meeting in Montreal, Canada, on October 24–25, 2000. Paul Martin was again chair and now host for the first time. At Montreal the fledgling G20 confronted the challenge of carving out a specific role that would generate effective and legitimate governance in a mutually reinforcing way, now that the Asian crisis that had catalysed its creation had passed and no new shock to galvanize action had yet come. In the absence of an acute crisis the G20 had to define its distinctive role and prove its worth amidst the well-established informal plurilateral institutions with their distinct, if overlapping, membership, led by the Group of Seven (G7) and the Group of Eight (G8), and the formal, broadly multilateral organizations led by the International Monetary Fund (IMF) and its new International Monetary and Financial Committee (IMFC).

Unlike the IMFC, embedded within the long-established, powerful IMF, and the technically oriented Financial Stability Forum (FSF) closely related to the Bank for International Settlements (BIS), the G20 lacked an international organizational "nest" beyond the powerful national bureaucracies of most of its members. It floated alone as a forum for finance ministers, bank governors, and deputies in a world densely populated with powerful bodies of all kinds. These included informal plurilateral bodies, leading national governments, multinational corporations, private authorities, and fast-moving markets themselves (Cutler et al. 1999).

Beyond mere survival, through holding a second meeting, the future influence and ultimate importance of the G20 depended on which of three possible paths the fledgling institution would take in forging a relationship with the old and new institutions at the centre of global financial and economic governance.

First, the G20 could become a body trying to legitimize a G7/8-bred consensus among a broader influential group of emerging countries. It would do so by inducing them to support G7/8 positions, thus allowing the G7/8 to dominate the new order, through either the appearance or the reality of broader legitimacy and buy-in.

Second, the G20 could evolve into a secondary body, destined to fade away as an effective centre once the crisis that had catalysed its creation had passed. With its busy member ministers and bank governors meeting so often elsewhere and thus losing interest, it could yield to a new IMFC mobilizing the formidable resources of formal organization possessed by the IMF. These would be backed by the heavy influence of major European powers through the governance regime and rules for voting rights established long ago, by Britain's chair of the IMFC, by the support of continental France for this IMF-embedded body, and by the unique veto held by the United States at the IMF.

Third, the G20 could become an autonomous effective and legitimate centre for defining and delivering new directions, decisions, and institutions in global economic governance in a post-Cold War, shock-scarred era of intensified globalization. It could do so by bringing together as equals G7 members and other key developed and emerging countries, empowering the latter's distinctive voices and dealing in a more integrative, forward-looking, effective, and legitimate way with the central challenges of globalization. Taking up these larger tasks would be essential to the G20's influence and impact, with the fading importance of its initial focus on the 1997–99 crisis response and the consequent construction of a reformed international financial architecture. The remaining challenge was the much broader one of governing globalization to ensure that it would benefit all, or at least recognizably offset the distributional inequalities that a market logic left to itself would likely bring.

Competing Assessments

Among scholars there has arisen a debate between two main schools of thought about which of these paths would and did prevail, about the fledgling G20's performance in its second year, and about the causes of the pathway pursued and the performance achieved.

The first school, composed of skeptics, saw little in the second meeting's centrepiece achievement of a new "Montreal consensus" on socially sustainable globalization. To Andrew Baker (2006) this was "little more than a loose recognition that tackling poverty and deprivation in the developing world is a priority," with the result that "the way forward remains uncertain and doubts remain as to whether this meagre but important recognition represents another false dawn."

A second school saw G20 success in setting directions to guide globalization, due to the G20's soft law character and the will and skill of Paul Martin as chair (Kirton 2001b). It claimed Montreal made the new G20 a more effective and legitimate institution that delivered significant achievements, primarily the Montreal Consensus on socially sustainable globalization, to replace the old, now widely contested, commonly understood Washington consensus. The Montreal meeting tackled the difficult question of globalization, and openly recognized that globalization could give rise to economic difficulties and social dislocations. Martin stated that this meeting was the first time that an institution of importance had discussed the pros and cons of globalization (Paul Martin, quoted in Scoffield 2000). These discussions and directions were backed by some specific decisions and new institutional processes. These considerable achievements compared favourably with those of its old and new international institutional competitors and colleagues that year.

The Argument

This chapter argues that the G20 in 2000 proved its worth, producing a Montreal meeting of significant success. It successfully put at the forefront of its work the broad, integrative agenda of globalization that preoccupied citizens of the global community as the twenty-first century dawned. It set new principled directions and gave the G20 a new core mission of governing globalization. More specifically, Montreal was a significant success in three ways: its agenda broadened substantially to cover the wide array of issues raised by globalization; it moved from deliberation to direction setting, creating the innovative Montreal Consensus to reflect the concerns of its emerging country members; and it moved more into decision making, too.

This performance flowed less from the immediate impact of recent or new shocks than from the comparative advantages of the group, including its particularly powerful and representative membership, flexible mandate and procedure, and highly competent, committed chair. The G20 thus passed its first critical post-crisis test. Its advances at Montreal were driven by the failure of the IMF to respond well to the challenges and concerns of globalization, the failure of the G8 to expand its participation at the 2000 Okinawa Summit, the robust revival of emerging country capabilities, and, above all, the high continuity, competence, and commitment of Paul Martin as its host and chair.

The International Institutional Competitors and Colleagues

The challenges of shaping a new international financial order in the wake of the 1997–99 global financial shocks and calming the broader anxieties about globalization bred by those shocks were central to the agenda of the G7, the IMF, and its new IMFC, as well as the G20 as the twenty-first century began (Kaiser et al. 2000; Kirton et al. 2001b). The G7 took up the challenge, starting with its finance ministers' meetings in January and April 2000, continuing with its preparations for the G8 summit in July in Okinawa, and culminating in its post-summit meeting in Prague in September 2000. At Prague the IMFC also weighed in, in an important way.

The G7

In the months leading up to the Okinawa Summit, finance deputies and their officials worked with increasing intensity to develop agreements that their ministers and leaders would adjust and approve. The G7 finance ministers met in post-crisis Asia, in Fukuoka, Japan, on July 8–9, to decide on narrow finance issues themselves and send to their leaders reports on the international financial architecture, debt relief for the poorest, and other items needing the attention of heads.

At Fukuoka the ministers reviewed the world economy and Russia. On the world economy and its management, there was little disagreement. The Japanese economy, along with much of Asia's, had resumed its growth. The world economy was moving toward sustained growth. While poor consumer confidence in Japan was noted, no minister wished to emphasize such risks. The macroeconomic downturn from the crisis had clearly passed.

On the international financial architecture, the ministers did not go into detail or offer new initiatives. They discussed reform of IMF facilities, following the compromise proposals presented by US treasury secretary Lawrence Summers in response to the report of the International Financial Institutions Advisory Commission chaired by Allan Meltzer (2000). They also discussed reform of the multilateral development banks (MDBs), notably the respective roles of the World Bank and the regional banks. An earlier US proposal that the IMF should offer short-term finance and the World Bank long-term development funding had led to a compromise. After this few difficult issues remained.

In Okinawa a few weeks later, the G7 leaders met first. They gathered on the afternoon of July 21 before the opening of the G8 summit itself. Their agenda, broader than that of their finance ministers, focused on financial architecture, heavily indebted poor countries (HIPCs), financial crime, and nuclear safety (Bayne 2001). They did not attempt to guide globalization as a whole.

When the G7 finance ministers later assembled in Prague in September for their first post-summit meeting, oil prices took centre stage. The G7 wanted to develop language they could take into the subsequent IMFC meeting for broader endorsement. The US in particular sought and largely secured an agreement welcoming recent supply increases from Saudi Arabia, as a responsible ally. There was general agreement, too, on the reform of the international financial architecture. The G7, in accordance with the generally understood Washington Consensus, recommended that developing countries rely on private capital markets rather than public sources for their financing needs.

Another important issue was the HIPCs. Here progress had stalled. This was a frustration for Canada, which sought to go faster than its partners. Without consulting its G7 colleagues, Canada unilaterally declared a moratorium on interest payments—the only G7 country to do so. It adopted a technique previously employed only by the Americans and British, who would regularly go public with actions beyond the consensus arrived at by the G7 finance ministers as a group. Summers and British chancellor of the exchequer Gordon Brown strongly criticized Martin for doing so, objecting to the unilateralism rather than the substance of what the Canadian finance minister had done. Martin was not deterred. His actions also caught the attention of "celebrity diplomat" Bono. They met for the first time, at Bono's request, with the singer publicly praising Martin and his move.

Overall, however, during this last year of the Clinton administration, America adjusted well to its G7 colleagues. The G7 was driven by British and Canadian leadership, a new Japanese assertiveness, and a forceful and often successful

European resistance to major changes (Kirton 2000). But the G7 took few major steps to build a new international financial architecture, or to move forward the HIPC initiative to the target set at its 1999 summit in Cologne. Japan now demanded a louder voice for outsiders, particularly Asians, in the governance of the IMF and global finance. In addressing this demand, and in dealing with other issues such as money laundering, the G7 again served as the effective centre of leadership for the formally multilateral IMF. But it also gave way to the G20, as the central forum for meeting the demands for broader participation in global financial governance and for addressing the central challenge of governing globalization in more stable, shared, and just ways.

The International Monetary and Financial Committee

Canadian ambitions for its G20 Montreal meeting were fuelled by the experience of the IMFC at the latter's inaugural meeting in Washington in April 2000. Here there were several signs that the IMFC would become an effective forum. Under the decisive leadership and chairing of Gordon Brown, the IMFC moved through an ambitious agenda, including controversial items such as HIPC debt relief. Uganda, with its recent purchase of a prime ministerial jet, stood as the test case. The ministers' discussion was sufficiently spontaneous to produce several meaningful changes in the draft communiqué that had been prepared by the finance deputies and IMF officials. Perhaps the most consequential was the placement of a strong statement on the continuing, central role of the IMF at the beginning of the communiqué. This was in direct response to the thousands of protestors who had assembled on the streets of Washington in an effort to draw attention to the IMF's alleged defects and, for some, to prevent the IMFC from meeting at all. In a foretaste of the G20's London Summit in April 2009, the changes in the communiqué were supervised by Brown himself. He allowed his fellow ministers, but none of the regular officials, into the drafting room.

At the same time, there were few signs that the IMFC would surpass the G20 as the central forum for broader concerns. The IMFC agenda was largely confined to traditional finance subjects. It failed to solve the impasse over the HIPCs created by the Ugandan plane purchase. The meeting was fairly stilted, with many members making prepared remarks. In the view of some, Brown tended to be very directional and to end discussion prematurely. As a result of the street demonstrations, a few consequential figures failed to make it into the meeting at all. They included France's new finance minister Laurent Fabius, so that France was represented by its more experienced central bank governor Jean-Claude Trichet. In all, the IMFC ended up defending the IMF, leaving others to defend globalization and to make the IMF and globalization work for all.

The IMFC's next ministerial meeting took place in Prague on September 19–28 during the semi-annual gathering of the IMF and the World Bank. Despite initial hopes that the IMFC would empower members' ministers rather than the IMF's own staff, almost all the work for the meeting was prepared beforehand, most of it was done at the IMFC deputies' meeting in London, where the G7 deputies had also met.

There were more protestors at Prague than at Washington, with numbers rivalling those that had disrupted the ministerial meeting of the World Trade Organization (WTO) in Seattle in December 1999. They ultimately surrounded the buildings where the meetings were being held, refusing to let anyone inside leave. The new IMF managing director, German G7 veteran Horst Köhler, had initially welcomed the demonstrators, as a way of heightening awareness of the issues the IMF addressed. But he was upset by the level of violence he witnessed. He declared that the G7 countries must start to visibly defend the IMF's work.

At Prague the IMFC featured a new interactive format. The meeting opened with a presentation by the IMF on its *World Economic Outlook* and a discussion of the risks and vulnerabilities to the global economy. As chair, Brown kept the discussion moving. It was fluid, with almost no set statements read. But with 24 ministers in the room, representing very different points of view—approved in many cases by the constituencies that lay behind—it was a somewhat stilted dialogue.

The Americans and Germans advanced their preferred vision of a reformed IMF. In it they would still dominate in quota share and occupancy of the managing director's position. The IMFC, along with the IMF Executive Board, proved to be an effective instrument of American leadership on issues, notably the contingent credit line (CCL) where the personal reputation of US president Bill Clinton and the interests of US financial institutions were at stake.

However, Brown, who cared deeply about poverty, backed by a broad coalition of civil society organizations, supported by all G7 members save Germany and Japan, included poverty reduction in the new IMFC mandate. The IMFC thus secured what the Japanese-chaired G7 had failed to achieve that year—a firm commitment, subsequently fulfilled in a frenzy of action at the IMF, to get 20 countries into the HIPC process by year's end. Yet the IMFC proved generally to be a forum for reinforcing an American, and with it a British and European, vision of a new international financial order, rather than one in which a broader array of actors and values had a full place.

The G10

The G10 also held a very brief meeting at Prague. It focused on banking regulation and financial sector supervision. The discussion was very technical. The G10 served de facto as the ministerial meeting of the Basel Committee on Banking Supervision (BCBS) of the BIS and the General Arrangements to Borrow (GAB).

Plans and Preparations

The culmination of this effort to reshape global economic governance in 2000 came at the G20 ministers' and bank governors' meeting in Montreal, held on October 24–25. Its central tasks were to conclude the discussions that had been initiated in Berlin and to achieve consensus on the role of the G20 and the international community in guiding globalization. This task expanded Berlin's focus on financial crisis response. At Montreal the G20 moved, with greater success than the G7 or the IMFC, beyond the narrow, often technical issues of finance to confront the broad problem of an increasingly interconnected global economy and society. It also assured those outside the G7, many of those within, and those in global civil society that their concerns were being heard, understood, and addressed. Montreal took a crucial step in assuring the G20's continuing relevance, effectiveness, and legitimacy by setting new directions in global economic, social, and even ecological governance (Kirton 2001b).

During the G20's first year, the non-G7 members had asked how the new forum would work for them, while some G7 countries wondered if they would lose control in it. The G20 in response, guided by its Canadian chair, had focused on getting members to know one another and work together similar to the G7 members. The chair's key goal was to make the non-G7 members feel comfortable in the new group. The G20 had generated a growing consensus about the problems of globalization and an agreement to cooperate on standards and codes, if not regulations, on international and domestic banking and private sector involvement in financial bailouts.

More significantly, the G20 had generated a growing consensus that the group was needed, that there were serious social costs to globalization that must be addressed through new initiatives, and that limits on market-driven globalization must be set. A more precise consensus had emerged that the private sector must to some degree accept risk and be involved in the solution of crises, that codes and standards were needed, and that they could be shaped by developed and developing countries working together. There was a further consensus on exchange rates, with all agreeing that different approaches and mechanisms were required in different circumstances. Yet this emerging G20 consensus had not yet changed what member representatives argued at the IMF Executive Board or the World Bank, especially in countries where finance members were not in charge of their countries' position in the World Bank.

Paul Martin, along with emerging country members, felt that there was a shared interest in reducing the social costs of globalization, and in involving civil society in the task. That Montreal meeting thus focused on "governing globalization" and culminated in the Montreal Consensus. It broadened the G20's agenda and mission from a narrow emphasis on financial stability. Martin had never thought that the G20 at the finance ministers' level was limited to financial matters. He always believed that the underlying principle was that the world had changed and that it was only a matter of time before China and India would be major players. The sooner they got to the table, the better. Moreover, finance ministers in every government were the most powerful ministers because they held the purse strings. Finance ministers were thus involved in everything their government did. For example, they discussed trade issues regardless of what their trade minister colleagues thought.

The prevailing Washington Consensus, in the traditional IMF way, initially imposed by the prevailing US perspective, was interpreted as a very tight, conservative approach to what countries should do. In reality it was more liberal than the perception of it (Williamson 1997). It had more understanding and a greater degree of social concern than the very right-wing interpretation and the symbolism it had acquired by 1999. There was a feeling that a herd approach was being taken by supporters of market-based philosophies, such as the Chicago school of economists and the IMF. They recommended that a developing country in trouble would have to raise taxes and cut spending. However, Martin, as the finance minister of a developed country, felt he had the right to overrule his officials if he was told to take such a hard line. The developing countries, in contrast, had far less of an ability to override IMF economists and all the other G7 countries, especially where their ministers and bank governors had gone to the same schools as the staff of the IMF and had served with them.

An important related issue was the liberalization of capital markets. The IMF eagerly sought capital market liberalization. When "hot money" fled a country, the IMF prescribed austerity as the appropriate response. To say that capital should not be able to flow unimpeded was to challenge the dominant financial thinking at the time. Martin stated that the G20 should not stand for such a consensus. The non-G7 members of the G20 did not agree with it. G20 ministers were more than orthodox economists. Martin wanted a consensus that expressed their views, not the generally assumed, IMF-advocated Washington Consensus, although he expected to have a difficult time getting his alternative through. But he did not.

Among the developed G20 members, the Commonwealth anglophone countries of Britain and Australia were closest to Canada. France remained suspicious of any institution that might detract from the IMF. Summers also did not want to undermine the US veto at the IMF and World Bank, in favour of a forum where the US was just one of 20 equal members. But the US was comforted by the fact that a trusted, fellow North American chaired the G20, and was persuaded by analytic arguments in favour of the Canadian approach. Among the G20 countries that were not members of the Organisation for Economic Co-operation and Development (OECD), China was a very strong supporter, having recently decided to join the WTO. Martin and his allies succeeded in having the broad topic of globalization form the centrepiece of the G20 agenda at Montreal.

The Hong Kong Deputies' Meeting, March 2000

G20 deputies first met in Hong Kong in March 2000 to review the results of the Berlin meeting and begin preparations for Montreal. They met just prior to the

IMFC deputies' meeting to prepare for the first IMFC meeting in mid April 2000. The G20 deputies were pleased with the results of Berlin. This led the Canadian chair to adopt a more ambitious approach for Montreal.

The Toronto Deputies' Meeting, August 2000

At the subsequent round table of G20 deputies in Toronto in August, there were strong signs that the G20 had secured real buy-in from major emerging country members. Russia was more energized. South Africa was very active. Indonesia was variable and Saudi Arabia was a good team player. China remained a strong supporter of both the G20 forum and the preferred Canadian approach.

The participants agreed that the private sector accepted their inevitable role in the resolution of financial crises. Many members were, however, concerned with a lack of transparency and what seemed like a resort to unilateral actions by some.

At the Ministerial Meeting

As host, Canada wanted highly interactive sessions for the Montreal meeting, with no time for social activity, caucus groups, G7 meetings on the side, or scheduled bilaterals. It also sought to secure the future of the forum by identifying its meeting schedule and chair for the following year. In terms of substance, it sought a recognition that globalization had two sides—the finance and economic side and the social side, including health, education, welfare, and employment.

Martin felt very strongly that civil society organizations were raising real issues. He felt their views were very important, especially when they differed from those of his ministry. He agreed to meet with the nongovernmental organizations (NGOs) before the G20 meeting, to listen to and learn from them, and, where he agreed, bring their views forward within the G20 meeting. He would have liked more ministers to have met individually with their own civil society members in preparation for the Montreal ministerial. However, there was no consensus among G20 members to have representatives of civil society organizations broadly involved in any way.

The meeting dealt with four items: responses to the challenges of globalization, the state of the world economy, action on financial stability, and follow-up on reducing vulnerability to crises. Following the intense protests at the Seattle WTO ministerial meeting and the Washington and Prague IMF meetings, concerns about globalization were very much at the fore. The meeting itself was notable for its spontaneity and substantive discussions. Martin considered it one of the better and more open discussions of this sort.

Globalization

Going into Montreal the progress started at Berlin on standards and codes was modest, as there was little respect for what the IMF was telling the emerging countries to do. At the meeting, the latter's representatives and others asked how they could be expected to proceed when their citizens viewed such things as oppressive and socially counterproductive, and indeed would invite more anti-globalization protests. Martin and Australia's Peter Costello said that many had lived through similar struggles from closed to open economies and from structural adjustment. Alan Greenspan, chair of the US Federal Reserve, spoke about the value of creative destruction.

Montreal thus launched a process of reflecting on globalization. Each country was invited to reflect on its own experience with globalization. The exercise was intended to reassure all that each G20 country had lived through similar experiences. Over the next two years, 16 of the 20 members would produce reports on what had gone right and what had gone wrong with their country's experience.

Montreal featured an open, soul-searching discussion about the reasons for the recent violent reactions to globalization, and what the G20 could do to better engage the critics. A consensus emerged that the benefits of globalization outweighed the costs. Yet several speakers pointed to the marginalization of many countries and their citizens in the globalization process, the insecurity that it bred, and the invisibility of its benefits for many. Some argued that technological progress and other forms of globalization were increasing the distance between winners and losers across the digital divide, creating an increased demand for redistribution and insurance. Globalization simultaneously made it more difficult for governments to tax both their citizens and their corporations, which could and would leave in response. If they did, governments would have even less money to meet these demands.

Speakers also pointed to a loss of control, the feeling that individuals and institutions beyond borders and outside the electoral process were making decisions that affected them, and the lack of direct accountability of national governments to the citizens of their sovereign state. Globalization was thus infringing on sovereignty. In the view of one participant, it was leading to the victory of the Anglo-Saxon model of economic and social organization.

All agreed that globalization was increasing, would continue to do so, and would require collective action in response. While there was no simple solution, current developments had to be put into perspective to show the gains. More energetic efforts were required to reduce the imbalances caused by globalization. The G20 must deal aggressively with trade, including the impediments to market access in advanced countries. It must ensure that the rules kept pace with global integration and dealt with poverty, including through increases in official development assistance (ODA). G20 members had to speak forcefully on these issues. The G20 asked its deputy ministers to prepare reports for the next ministerial meeting on the costs and benefits of globalization, using country case studies to illustrate the key points.

World Economy, Exchange Rates, Imbalances, and Energy

The discussion on the world economy began with a presentation of the IMF's *World Economic Outlook*. There was some divergence among participants about the importance and implications of the US current account deficit. The most contentious issue was exchange rates. One G7 bank governor asked how much of a problem was posed by the deficit when, under floating exchange rates, incoming private investment rather than government deficits was causing the imbalance. Two European G7 bank governors countered that the combined European and US deficits and the exchange rates represented undesirable imbalances in the world economy and posed significant risk. They argued that the flow of world savings was moving from developing countries, where they were needed, to the United States, where they were not. The developing countries generally backed the Europeans, arguing that turbulence in G7 exchange markets was a particular problem for their own economic growth, and needed to be limited in some way. The Americans countered that given the inability of G20 ministers to understand why markets were pricing assets as they were, one could not conclude that there would be an abrupt correction. It would thus be far-fetched to consider action aimed at stabilizing exchange rates.

Developments in oil markets were also discussed. Both oil exporters and importers were concerned about the level and volume of prices. They agreed these were driven by political rather than economic factors. The oil exporters argued that producers were pumping at near capacity, that there was now an expectation of a modest surplus, and that prices should fall once short-term, politically driven developments had passed.

Financial Stability

Andrew Crockett of the FSF led the discussion on its financial stability. He pointed to its three new interests: market liquidity and volatility; e-finance, which would be examined by working groups; and the wind-up of complex instruments such as hedge funds, drawing on the work by the G10 deputies on consolidating the financial sector. Some argued that the FSF should expand its membership. If it failed to do so, it should at least be required to report to the G20.

Crisis Vulnerability

The last session dealt with reducing vulnerability to crises. It covered standards and codes, external liabilities, exchange rate regulation, and private sector involvement. On standards and codes there was some concern about setting a process that was too rigid. Developing countries argued that there should be more than one model. One innovative suggestion was that there be standards for delivering ODA. There were polar extremes on exchange rates, with more support for floating exchange rates as the only viable long-range option. Some exchange rate intervention was consistent with this approach. On HIPCs, the US gave a very positive assessment of the prospects for its legislation finally being passed by Congress, which it subsequently was. Here the G20 was primarily receiving an update from a key member on an initiative that had originated several years before, and was primarily the product of the other forums, above all the G7/8.

Achievements

The Montreal meeting was a significant success. It was important more for the new principles and directions it established than for the specific decisions it reached or the institutional processes it put in place. It offered what host Paul Martin called the Montreal Consensus on globalization, with shared benefits and social protections for all. While the name never caught on, its ideas importantly did.

In its broadest terms, this new consensus said that economic growth was not enough. It affirmed that economic growth was important, even necessary—but, without development in health care and education, not sufficient. In that way, it went a step beyond the conventionally understood Washington Consensus and built on the G7's "Cologne Consensus" from 1999. The Montreal Consensus consisted of a connected and balanced affirmation of three central points: that globalization was good for everyone; that its benefits had to be more broadly shared; and that the poor had to be protected from its costs. None of these individual elements was entirely new (Kirton et al. 2001a). But the Montreal Consensus marked an agreement among a representative group of systemically significant developed and developing countries to move from a single focus on stabilizing the global financial system and economy to sharing its potential benefits and safeguarding the world's poor. The 1940s compromise of embedded liberalism had returned and been extended to embrace modern social protections and the very poor (Ruggie 1983). The G20 thus added to promoting financial stability its second core mission of making globalization work for all and put the latter mission in the primary place.

Dimensions of Performance

A systematic review of the six dimensions of G20 governance confirms Montreal's significant, strong success.

Domestic Political Management

In domestic political management, the Montreal meeting was highly successful. It issued ten communiqué compliments to its individual members, the highest in G20 history through to the summer of 2010 (see Appendix D). Four went to G8 members and six to non-G8 ones, reflecting Martin's desire to make the latter feel at home in the new group.

The meeting worked directly for its host and chair in domestic politics. It took place on October 24–25, just two days after the prime minister and leader of Paul Martin's Liberal Party had called an early election for November 27. The decision on the timing and location of the G20 meeting had flowed from the normal cadence of autumn G20 ministerials and the fact that Martin's parliamentary constituency was in Montreal. While the popular Liberal Party did not need much help in Montreal or Quebec from a successful G20 meeting, in the general election a month later, the Liberals increased their majority in the House of Commons from 155 to 172 seats.

Deliberation

In the deliberative domain, Montreal's communiqué and its annex of 2,504 words were six times longer than Berlin's had been (see Appendix E). Montreal's agenda was also much broader, going well beyond crisis response and architecture construction aimed at financial stability. Montreal also addressed debt, development assistance, trade liberalization, health, agriculture, the environment, and social policy. It fulfilled Martin's earlier promise that there was no area of economically related policy outside of the G20's potential purview. As he noted, it would also make its conclusions the subject of discussion among many other ministers in national governments. It was an agenda whose wide, multisector breadth and high general ambition would be appropriate for the G20 leaders themselves to address.

Direction Setting

In the direction-setting domain, Montreal's performance was strongest and most important. It was the first time that the very diverse and influential countries assembled in the G20 all affirmed that globalization was the right direction for them and for the global community as a whole. They all agreed that "economic integration that is at the heart of globalization can continue to be an enormously powerful force contributing to improving the lives of hundreds of millions of people in industrial, transition[al], and developing countries alike" (G20 Finance 2000). Coming in the immediate wake of the 1997–99 global financial crisis and affirmed by China and Saudi Arabia, this was a remarkable consensus. Moreover, the voice of emerging countries and the importance of the distributional dimension of globalization were reflected in the call for "improved access for developing countries' exports to advanced economies' markets" and the affirmation that "governments have an important role to play." The consensus of embedded liberalism had returned to triumph over the "Ronald Thatcherism" that had displaced it during the two decades before (Ruggie 1983).

The specific concept of globalization endorsed by the G20 ministers and bank governors was also significant. They defined globalization in broad terms as "the increasing integration of national economies resulting from the greater international mobility of goods, services, capital, people, and ideas" (G20 Finance 2000). Globalization was more than the economic liberalization that lay at the heart of the neoliberal consensus. The G20's understanding of globalization did involve technology, the acceptance of market-based economic systems, and trade and capital liberalization. However, it was also infused with political content, in its celebration of globalization's generation of greater access to ideas. Here it built on the G8's Okinawa Summit communiqué, which specifically acknowledged the positive role that information technology, including across the digital divide, could have in sharing cultural content and ideas (Kirton et al. 2001a). The idea of increased mobility of people and even integration between economies also had political implications. The G20's normative contribution to globalizing the G8's core value of "open democracy" was thus advanced. Two affirmations of the principle of transparency were made (see Appendix F).

An equal and integral place was given to the distributional dimension. There was little new or specific content in the general promise to improve the effectiveness, transparency, and cooperative spirit of international institutions, although the pledge might have been of some small solace to those protesting on the streets. The G20 affirmed that liberalization provided the means to "attack income inequalities and reduce poverty," noted that it could create "economic difficulties and social dislocations," and championed a "globalization process that works for all of its participants" (G20 Finance 2000). In doing so it underscored the social dimension and the human face of globalization. Signs that the voices of the emerging countries were heard came in the passages calling for improved market access for developing countries. Thus the G20 echoed the G8's insistence that they must "maximise the benefits of globalisation for all" (G8 2000).

The Montreal Consensus built on and expanded the Cologne Consensus for socially sensitive and safeguarded globalization (Kirton 2000). The G20 took the idea beyond a closed group of developed countries to embrace emerging ones. It hastened the global normative shift from a singular focus on stabilizing the global economy to the need to share its benefits and safeguard the poor.

Decision Making

In the decisional domain, the Montreal meeting made seven commitments, almost double the number in Berlin the year before (see Appendix G). The issue area of macroeconomic policy led with three, followed by development with two and reform of the international financial institutions and social policy with one each.

The specific commitment on international financial architecture, also detailed in an annex, represented a small step forward at best.

Of greater importance, coming from finance ministers with considerable influence on national budget expenditures, was the recognition that "emerging market economies should be supported with technical assistance" and the pledge to "contribute to international efforts to increase the provision of other global public goods" regarding infectious disease, agricultural research, and the environment (G20 Finance 2000). The passage on HIPCs reaffirmed the need for a sharp focus on poverty reduction and economic reforms. It added a veiled reference for the US to contribute its share. Weak commitments but far-reaching social objectives characterized the call for trade liberalization to benefit the lowest income economies, to "promote domestic policies that help spread the benefits of integration to all members of society," and to design and implement social safety nets to protect the most vulnerable during liberalization. In the purely political realm, an important connection was made between financial abuse and "market integrity," on the one hand, and financial stability, on the other.

Delivery

In the delivery domain, Montreal's performance proved to be modest. None of the eight commitments included a catalyst that counted in improving compliance in the work of the closely related G8 summit. Delivery was not a major concern as this was only the G20's second ministerial meeting. Instead, participants focused on finishing the discussions they had started in Berlin on crisis management as well as on globalization in the wake of the recent protests. But Martin argued that the G20 was not only a discussion forum, but also "a forum which encourages the implementation of concrete policy measures" (G20 2008). The G20 communiqué's emphasis on implementation was a useful reminder of the work that remained to be done, especially in regard to international financial architecture. The concern with delivery had begun, if in a modest way.

Development of Global Governance

In the domain of institutionally developing the G20's global governance, Montreal also made its mark. Its communiqué made seven references to its own institution and 18 to institutions outside (see Appendix C-1). Internally, participants agreed to hold two deputies' meetings and one ministerial meeting in the following year. This helped ensure that the G20 became a permanent body, with a specific agenda of guiding globalization. It gave the G20 a mandate well beyond the initial one of crisis response and architectural reform. Moreover, with India slated to host the subsequent 2001 ministerial meeting, with the important prerogative of the host to set the agenda, the essential move from established to emerging countries' institutional leadership began.

At the official level, the Montreal meeting mandated three follow-up processes. The first was a series of case studies of countries' experiences in being affected by and responding to globalization. They were aimed at providing a common diagnosis and balanced evaluation to advance the debate and identify key factors. The second process was a study of international institutions, conducted by G20 deputies, to look at the gaps, overlaps, and functional responsibilities for global governance. The third process was a G20 seminar on exchange rate regimes aimed at providing concrete advice to guide policy decisions. Private sector representatives would be involved in these activities, as they had been when G20 deputies had met in Toronto in August. The emphasis thus shifted from Berlin's direction to other international institutions to Montreal's development of the G20 as an institution in its own right, including civil society participation of an expert sort.

Externally, Montreal's 18 references to other international institutions was three times as many as in Berlin. Montreal referred 10 times to the IMF, including three references to the IMFC, reinforcing an already established strong relationship between the G20 and the IMF. The G20 referred four times to the World Bank. It referred twice to the FSF, the first time the G20 had referred to this body, in which the G20's emerging countries were not members. Despite their absence, they could thus still guide its work from the G20 forum.

The Causes of G20 Performance

The causes of Montreal's significant performance are well captured by the model of systemic hub governance, with the relative salience of the component causes now shifting from shock-activated, equalizing vulnerability at the start of the list to the causes lower down.

Shock-Activated, Equalizing Vulnerabilities

The first cause of Montreal's significant success was the shock-activated, equalizing vulnerabilities, still coming from finance but also from energy and social cohesion now (see Appendix I). At Montreal, memories of the recent Asian financial crisis and the vulnerability it created remained strong, even if they were starting to recede. At the same time, concerns were mounting about a new crisis coming from Argentina. Argentina had entered a three-year recession in 1999, secured an adjustment program of $40 billion (including $14 billion from the IMF) in March 2000, and entered a political crisis when its vice president resigned in October 2000 (de Larosière 2005). It finally defaulted on a record $132 billion in sovereign debt in December 2001.

Crisis response was one of the two key themes for Montreal. To this end, preparations included identifying best practices in exchange rate arrangements, liability management, private sector involvement, and the implementation of international standards and codes. The final communiqué included an annex entitled "Reducing Vulnerability to Financial Crises," which addressed those issues directly.

Additionally, a new kind of crisis loomed beyond finance narrowly defined, in the form of the energy shocks that had long spurred the G8 into action. In the lead-up to Montreal, rising oil prices increased the vulnerability of the established members led by the US, Japan, and Germany. But increases in Saudi Arabian supplies showed that Saudi Arabia was a required and responsible member of the G20 and an ally of the United States.

Finally, a potential crisis of social cohesion came from the eruption of violent protests within the G7 countries, with the protests in Seattle, Washington, and Prague. The protests that had erupted in Asia during the crisis had now spread to America itself. Montreal thus addressed globalization and remained free of violent protests. The G20 thus shifted its attention to deal with broader, if less acute shocks, including those in the social and political realm.

International Institutional Failure

The second cause of Montreal's significant success was the failure of the old multilateral organizations to respond to the recent shocks, and the failure of the G7/8 to embrace the rising and badly affected emerging countries in the aftermath. The IMF failed to predict the strong global growth that appeared in 2000 (see Appendix J-1). In the view of many, including in time the organization itself, the IMF had performed poorly during the Asian financial crisis. Its reputation had not recovered by 2000. Some saw the crisis caused not by severely overvalued exchange rates or too much sovereign debt in emerging countries but by the "intrinsic instability in international lending" (Sachs 1998). The impressive growth of the Asian countries in past decades had been accompanied at international urging by some financial reforms that had left their financial institutions more exposed to international instabilities. In general, growth had not been matched by prudent regulation. The IMF's insistence on privatization and liberalization meant that some emerging countries were ill equipped to deal with an abrupt halt and reversal of capital inflows. Jeffrey Sachs (1998) argued that the countries attacked by markets were illiquid but not insolvent, and that the problem was that they were unable to borrow enough to cover their debt when foreign financing decreased. Additionally, when the flow of resources dwindled, the national governments and the IMF both made mistakes that deepened the crisis.

The WTO, born as a major multilateral organization in 1995, had still failed to launch a new round of negotiations for multilateral trade liberalization five years after the previous one had ended. Its ministerial meeting in Seattle saw violent street protests similar to those of the IMF–World Bank ministerial meetings that year, as citizens demanded that trade work for social and ecological concerns. While such protests may have driven some G20 discussions at Montreal, they did not loom large in the mind of Martin as host.

The Montreal Consensus was in part a response to the failure of the old, commonly understood Washington Consensus that dominated the thinking of the IMF, the World Bank, and WTO. The G20, as a still new group of finance ministers and central bank governors, without a secretariat or bureaucracy to entrench and enforce such a consensus, could oppose previous policies of strict free market economies and deregulation. At Montreal, the G20 thus expanded its agenda to tackle the broader question of globalization and its impacts, and affirmed the need for wider protection.

Early in the Asian financial crisis it had become clear that the G7/8 was not sufficiently flexible and sensitive to put in place the new international consensus on stronger regulation necessary to avert or contain a similar crisis in the future. Even with its new Cologne Consensus, at Okinawa it did not bring in others to broaden the conversation and buy-in. The Japanese host, with support from Germany's Gerhard Schroeder, had tried, but others in the G8 and the prospective invitees did not agree (Kirton 2001a).

Predominant, Equalizing Capabilities

The third cause of Montreal's significant success was the predominant, equalizing capabilities of the countries in the group (see Appendix K). In 2000, the G20 represented 82 percent of the world's total gross domestic product (GDP), the same as the year before. But the contributions of G8 country members had dropped from 67 percent to 66 percent, while those of the emerging countries had risen from 14 percent to 15 percent.

India, China, and Brazil, among others, were still considered developing countries. Yet their share in the world economy was steadily increasing, making the G20's internal equality slowly rise. In 2000, the emerging country members of the G20 were well on the road to post-crisis recovery. Rising oil prices boosted Russia's GDP and removed the chance that it would seek debt relief from the Paris Club. Having been a consumer of financial security in August 1998, Russia was turning into a potential provider of financial security, but was still frozen out of the continuing G7 finance club that had emerged in 1986 when Canada and Italy had been added to the old G5. A serious, balanced, and sensitive discussion about the benefits and drawbacks of globalization had to include those countries experiencing both sides of the economic integration coin.

Democratic Convergence

The fourth cause of Montreal's significant success was the substantial democratic convergence of member countries in their domestic principles and practices. Developing common ideas of the meaning of globalization and how it should be governed formed the first step in creating a more broadly shared vision for international regulation. This consensus was driven in particular by the deepening commitment to political openness among the G20 members at the domestic level.

One promising advance came in post-crisis Russia, with the peaceful arrival of a new, later duly elected, president in Vladimir Putin. Indonesia had held its first free elections in 1999 in more than 40 years (see Appendix L-1). It was now implementing democratic reforms, including presidential term and mandate limits. China's decision to join the WTO suggested it was much more willing to spread the rule of law at home. Korea and Argentina also showed a democratic advance. Brazil and Mexico did too (see Appendix L-2).

Political Control, Capital, Continuity, and Competence

The fifth and most salient cause of Montreal's significant success came from the strong political control, capital, continuity, competence, and commitment of the G20 finance ministers and central bank governors (see Appendix M). Here the enhanced continuity and competence and the continuing high commitment of the host, chair, and co-creator Paul Martin, stood out.

The Montreal meeting was attended by essentially the same individuals who had been at Berlin. But they now brought an additional year of experience. To be sure, public opinion polls on the US presidential election coming one month later suggested that G20 co-founder Larry Summers could soon leave after Montreal. But his Canadian counterpart seemed likely to remain for several more years as part of a renewed majority government, given the poll results when the Canadian general election was called on October 22. And a highly personally committed and motivated Martin, now with seven years of experience as a finance minister, as well as having been a private sector CEO, was now the G20 host as well as chair for the second time.

Controlled Club Participation as a Network Hub

The sixth cause of Montreal's significant success was its increasing controlled club participation as a network hub.

Internally, the group maintained its identical, compact membership for its second year. Martin and Summers returned for a second year and ten of their colleagues remained in their jobs. Maintaining consistent membership from year to year had a cumulative effect, as the participants began to build a personal relationship with each other.

Externally, members included the European Union, the World Bank, and the IMF to connect the group to the wider world. As the Washington and Prague gatherings showed, the Bretton Woods bodies served semi-annually as the nest for a dense set of plurilateral, established–emerging group meetings, where G20 members dominated the members and participants lists.

In addition, the global network with the G20 at the hub had recently been enlarged by a new set of trans-regional or global finance ministers' forums (see appendices N-3 and N-4). The Commonwealth, with five G20 members, met in Malta on September 19–20, 2000. La Francophonie's ministers for economy and finance, with two members from the G20, had held their inaugural meeting the previous year, in April 1999, to discuss trade and investment. The Asia-Pacific Economic Co-operation forum held its seventh annual meeting of finance ministers, with ten from the G20, in Brunei Darussalam on September 9–10, 2000. The western hemisphere finance ministers followed their second meeting in Chile in November 1997 with their third meeting in Cancún, Mexico on February 3, 2000, bringing five G20 ministers together again. OECD finance ministers, with ten G20 members including Mexico and Korea, also held their stand and annual general council meeting in late spring.

Conclusion

As 2000 came to a close, the 1997–99 global financial crisis, while rapidly receding as the dominant force, still had an enduring legacy, now in inspiring new directions in G20 governance. Among the emerging country members of the G20, the searing memory of the crisis and its consequences remained very much alive. Each of the old institutions at the centre of the established order and the newer institutions created in the immediate wake of the crisis in 1999 shaped that legacy in different ways.

The G7, having generated a new consensus on the need for socially sensitive and sustainable globalization at its 1999 Cologne Summit, moved at Okinawa in 2000 to address the information technology revolution at the heart of the current phase of globalization. It focused on how its benefits could be magnified and its digital divide diminished by new approaches to governance that involved civil society actors, and countries and institutions outside the G7 circle, even as it affirmed the role of the public sector in addressing distributional concerns.

The IMFC at Prague concentrated on affirming the American position on the very old issue of oil price increases, and on securing an endorsement for the new "lean and mean" IMF and the American-inspired CCL. It proved unable to engage successfully with civil society and address its concerns. But it did deliver the HIPC commitment that was most consistent with the British-inspired "poverty exception" the G7/8 had created. This constituted the latest instalment of the Toronto terms for debt relief for the poorest initiated at the G7's Toronto Summit in 1988.

In contrast, the G20 at Montreal focused on the broad question of globalization, reached out more effectively to embrace the concerns of developing countries and civil society, and forged a consensus distinct from the divisive fixed positions that the same countries still advanced within the IMF. The G20 affirmed among its broader constituency the Montreal Consensus that built on that of the G7 at Cologne, to give the social, ecological, human, and distributional side of globalization equal weight to the economic fundamentals to which the IMF remained largely confined. Only in the G20 was the full economic–social balance equalized and inclusively agreed. The impact of this direction-setting shift was seen in the fact that after

Montreal, the Washington Consensus was no longer an American government position, even if it continued to be an IMF one. In the longer term, the IMF itself shifted 180 degrees on the liberalization of capital markets. A decade later the proposal had died for good, never to be revived in its 1990s version at the IMF.

The primary cause of this distinct G20 path lay not in the mere fact of a recent common global shock, if only because that slow-moving shock sequence affected each of the G7 and major developing country members in different ways. These shocks brought about by a globalized financial system had created the conditions and catalysts for far-reaching transformation in the global governance response. But the degree and direction that change took demonstrated that autonomous international institutions and their custodians mattered in consequential ways. This was especially so in a rapidly changing world where globalization, with its corresponding interconnectivity, complexities, and uncertainties, led countries and international institutions to start reconstructing their interests and identities in intense interaction with one another.

As a new international institution, the G20 demonstrated its particular commitment to a broad, egalitarian, and distributive conception of globalization. It defined its mandate as guiding globalization for the benefit of all. In this way it established itself as a distinctive and thus influential, permanent, legitimate fixture of global governance. In so doing, it showed the importance of individual agency within international institutions. Even as one G20 co-founder, Lawrence Summers, was due to depart soon, a few weeks after the Montreal ministerial Paul Martin and his Liberal Party won a substantial majority government that allowed Martin to remain, at least for another crucial year.

References

Baker, Andrew. 2006. *The Group of Seven: Finance Ministries, Central Banks, and Global Financial Governance*. London: Routledge.

Bayne, Nicholas. 2001. "Managing Globalisation and the New Economy: The Contribution of the G8 Summit." In *New Directions in Global Economic Governance: Managing Globalisation in the Twenty-First Century*, eds Kirton, John J., and von Furstenberg, George M. Aldershot: Ashgate, 171–88.

Cutler, A. Claire, Haufler, Virginia, and Porter, Tony, eds. 1999. *Private Authority and International Affairs*. Albany: State University of New York Press.

de Larosière, Jacques. 2005. "From Mexico to Argentina: What Have We Learned from Two Decades of Debt Crises?" Monograph Series, Number 3, Princeton Institute for International and Regional Studies. Available at: www.asmp.fr/fiches_academiciens/textacad/larosiere/mexico_argentina.pdf. Accessed: July 2012.

G8. 2000. "G8 Communiqué Okinawa 2000." Okinawa, July 23. Available at: www.g8.utoronto.ca/summit/2000okinawa/finalcom.htm. Accessed: July 2012.

G20. 2008. "The Group of Twenty: A History." Available at: www.g20.utoronto.ca/docs/g20history.pdf. Accessed: July 2012.

G20 Finance Ministers and Central Bank Governors. 2000. "Communiqué." Montreal, October 25. Available at: www.g20.utoronto.ca/2000/2000 communique.html. Accessed: July 2012.

Kaiser, Karl, Kirton, John J., and Daniels, Joseph P., eds. 2000. *Shaping a New International Financial System: Challenges of Governance in a Globalizing World*. Aldershot: Ashgate.

Kirton, John J. 2000. "The Dynamics of G7 Leadership in Crisis Response and System Reconstruction." In *Shaping a New International Financial System: Challenges of Governance in a Globalizing World*, eds Kaiser, Karl, Kirton, John J., and Daniels, Joseph P. Aldershot: Ashgate, 65–94.

Kirton, John J. 2001a. "The G7/8 and China: Toward a Closer Association." In *Guiding Global Order: G8 Governance in the Twenty-First Century*, eds Kirton, John J., Daniels, Joseph P., and Freytag, Andreas. Aldershot: Ashgate, 189–222.

Kirton, John J. 2001b. "The G20: Representativeness, Effectiveness, and Leadership in Global Governance." In *Guiding Global Order: G8 Governance in the Twenty-First Century*, eds Kirton, John J., Daniels, Joseph P., and Freytag, Andreas. Aldershot: Ashgate, 143–72.

Kirton, John J., Daniels, Joseph P., and Freytag, Andreas. 2001a. "The G8's Contributions to Twenty-First Century Governance." In *Guiding Global Order: G8 Governance in the Twenty-First Century*, eds Kirton, John J., Daniels, Joseph P., and Freytag, Andreas. Aldershot: Ashgate, 283–304.

Kirton, John J., Daniels, Joseph P., and Freytag, Andreas, eds. 2001b. *Guiding Global Order: G8 Governance in the Twenty-First Century*. Aldershot: Ashgate.

Meltzer, Allan H. 2000. "Report of the International Financial Institutions Advisory Commission." United States Congress, Washington DC.

Ruggie, John G. 1983. "International Regimes, Transactions, and Change: Embedded Liberalism in the Postwar Economic Order." In *International Regimes*, ed Krasner, Stephen D. Ithaca: Cornell University Press, 195–232.

Sachs, Jeffrey. 1998. "Global Capitalism: Making It Work." *Economist*, September 12, pp. 23–25.

Scoffield, Heather. 2000. "Globalization Must Deal with Poverty: Martin." *Globe and Mail*, October 25.

Williamson, John. 1997. "The Washington Consensus Revisited." In *Economic and Social Development into the XXI Century*, ed Emmerji, Louis. Washington DC: Inter-American Development Bank, 48–61.

Chapter 5
Combating Terrorism, Ottawa 2001

Introduction

The Challenge

The third meeting of the finance ministers and central bank governors of the Group of 20 (G20) took place, unexpectedly, in Ottawa, Canada, on November 16–17, 2001. Paul Martin, also unexpectedly, served as chair. The meeting had been scheduled to be held in India, following Martin's suggestion that the G20 hold its meeting in an emerging country in its third year. However, after the terrorist attacks from the air on the United States on September 11, 2001, and the ensuing anthrax attacks on America on the ground starting September 18, all major international meetings were cancelled. G20 ministers were not allowed by their security offices to travel to India. Martin eventually offered to host the meeting of the G20 in Ottawa, and thus the semi-annual meetings of the World Bank, International Monetary Fund (IMF), and Group of Seven (G7) gathering, so that a preoccupied US treasury secretary and other colleagues could attend.

Martin as a finance minister emphasized that it was the World Trade Center in America's financial centre that had been the terrorists' target (Martin 2001). Stopping al Qaeda terrorism, in part by suffocating terrorist finance, thus immediately became the overwhelming finance and economic issue of the time. Even though no one wanted to travel to any major international meetings, Martin insisted on holding a G20 meeting: "I kept saying, 'You are letting these people paralyze us. This is exactly what they want'" (Martin 2008). He presented various options, including a meeting in Washington DC. The security forces of the US and other members adamantly rejected all of them. Paul O'Neill, the US treasury secretary, had been in Tokyo on September 11 and the administration did not want him outside America should al Qaeda strike again (Suskind 2004). Martin finally offered Ottawa as a host city, hoping that travelling to Canada would be acceptable for the United States and his other G20 colleagues.

No other country had offered to hold the meeting, although Britain's Gordon Brown seemed prepared to do so. But Ottawa was the only location all would accept. The fact that Canada came forward to host again showed Martin's asserted and accepted leadership within the group. It also showed the resilience of this group, in contrast to other international institutions, in the face of this unprecedented shock to the United States, to those many countries whose citizens had died in the twin towers, and to the whole world. Martin believed that it was fundamentally important to show that global institutions were responsive and capable of dealing with even the most severe shocks.

In having the meeting focus on terrorist finance and mobilizing the full G20—emerging and Islamic states included—to support an America under attack, the G20 bonded the new administration of Republican president George W. Bush to the still fledgling group. The Bush administration had just eliminated several other informal plurilateral institutions created by the just-defeated Clinton Democrats, such as the G8's Renewable Energy Task Force and the Digital Opportunity Task Force (DOT Force). Yet the new administration was very grateful that the G20, by holding its and the other meetings in Ottawa, set things in motion to get the world back to business. The Americans' response was "Thank God Canada took up the bit." Thus, on Bush's watch, the G20 survived. It was available for dealing with the new terrorist shock to America, and used to address both it and the next instalment of finance shocks elsewhere, when Turkey's and Argentina's financial crises peaked later in 2001.

Competing Assessments

Among scholars there is a debate about the content, causes, and consequences of what the G20 did in 2001. One school sees it acting too little and too late to prevent or contain al Qaeda's global terrorist threats, which soon arose again, notably to attack Britain in 2005. A second school concludes that the G20 acted effectively, because it was an informal institution that could swiftly turn to contain the global crisis at hand, using its competence in finance that had long been part of the security calculus whenever economic sanctions, war financing, or support for allies were involved (Kirton 2011; Freytag et al. 2011).

Yet such accounts, which recognize that a severely shocked and newly vulnerable United States now needed international support, do not fully explain why the United States accepted such help, if somewhat reluctantly, in the particular form of the G20. Nor do they explain why all G20 members gave it so fast, so freely, and so fully to the G20 rather than the more established international finance institutions, in a common cause for the group and the globe.

The Argument

This chapter argues that the G20 in 2001 was a very strong success. It swiftly refocused and vastly expanded its agenda to focus on the security subjects of terrorist finance and Afghanistan. In doing so, it moved swiftly from its dominant direction setting at Montreal to ambitious, intensive decision making and faithful delivery beyond. It thus bonded the new administration in the US to a body recently created by the Democrats that Bush had just defeated at the polls. Moreover, the Ottawa meeting showed that the G20 had superseded the International Monetary and Financial Committee (IMFC) and the G7 too, as it was only because of the G20 meeting that the latter bodies were able to assemble and operate at all. The September 11 shocks made the G20 the necessary hub of a network, including its old and new competitors and now colleagues, in a physical, indeed existential, way. It also turned the new group, however temporarily, into a genuine interpersonal club.

More specifically, the causes of Ottawa's very strong success lie first in the twin shocks of 2001—the second, unpredictably severe al Qaeda terrorist attack on the United States at its World Trade Center and now also at the Pentagon—and the emerging signs of new finance shocks that might come from the Islamic Middle East in Turkey and from the Americas in the new democracy of Argentina. The second cause came from the failure of all international institutions, especially those headquartered in terrorist-struck New York City and Washington DC, to function in that shell-shocked autumn and the absence of any component of the United Nations galaxy focusing effectively on terrorism, terrorist finance, and "skyjacking," including its International Civil Aviation Organization headquartered in Montreal. While the relevant financial capabilities later required to support Turkey and Argentina lay with the G7, those needed to cut the flow of finance to al Qaeda lay also within the Islamic and other countries uniquely a part of the broader G20. Especially with so many of their own citizens killed in the World Trade Center, most G20 members understood the terrorist threat to the rule of law and most to democracy in their own countries very well. While the Bush administration was new, Paul Martin and many of his fellow G20 finance ministers were not. After two meetings, the G20 was now a group with a chair whom all members trusted enough to attend and use to get the terrorist finance job done.

The causes of this great leap upward into the security sphere through terrorist finance, forward into intense decision making and delivery, and inward into much stronger internationally coordinated domestic financial regulation were thus the shock-activated, equalizing vulnerabilities of the September 11 terrorist attacks on America; the failure of the old multilateral and new plurilateral bodies on their own even to meet without the G20; the issue-specific, systemically significant capabilities of American allies, including Islamic Saudi Arabia, Indonesia, and Turkey; the G20 members' common abhorrence of the terrorist threat to the rule of law and to economic, social, and political openness; and the continuity, competence, and commitment of Paul Martin as chair of this group that suddenly became the world's essential global governance hub and a valued interpersonal club.

Plans and Preparations

The Ottawa gathering showed how high-level meetings, despite months of careful and conscientious preparation, can be hijacked by events just prior to the event. In this case, the September 11 terrorist attacks significantly shaped the location, agenda, and achievements of the G20 meeting. In the preparatory meetings leading up to Montreal, several issues had been scheduled to be addressed. But at Montreal, terrorist finance suddenly took centre stage.

The Choice of India

The 2001 G20 ministerial had been scheduled to take place in New Delhi, India. From the G20's start Martin had sought to chair the first two meetings to get the new body underway. Chairing and hosting should then move to a non-G7 member, to alternate between the two groups.

For many members, the obvious candidate to serve as the first non-G7 host and chair was South Africa. This was by virtue of the towering reputation of its finance minister, Trevor Manuel, who outshone the rest of his G20 colleagues. Although apparently willing at first, Manuel declined, on the grounds that South Africa lacked the bureaucratic capacity to serve. India subsequently offered, in part because its nationalist Bharatiya Janata Party (BJP), elected in 1998 to replace Nehru's internationally familiar and respected Congress Party and in power since Indian independence, wished to reinforce its prestige and credentials abroad and at home. This was especially the case following the international disfavour brought by India's nuclear explosion at the time of the G8's Birmingham Summit in 1998. No one else offered to host. India was thus a choice that Canada as chair and the other members made easily. But when September 11 came, India was judged to be too far away from America or anywhere else in the G20 and too close to al Qaeda's Afghanistan home.

The Change to Ottawa

After September 11, security officials in all G20 members vetoed any international gathering that might be an al Qaeda target. Jonathan Fried, Canada's finance deputy, communicated Martin's feelings that it nonetheless remained important for the G20 to meet. The Canadian view was that the terrorists would win if the IMF, World Bank, G7, and G20 meetings did not take place, to show that the international system was robust and whole. Even with only six weeks to prepare, Canada thought it could and should get this critical job done. Martin suggested a meeting in Canada under heightened security, and pushed for this at both the G7 level and, more strongly, at the G20 level, as he was still the chair. But both he and Fried were refused by their colleagues, whose security services felt that security trumped all. When the issue of terrorist finance arose, Martin concluded that it was an issue better suited to the G20 than the G7. Many agreed that the G20 had to deal with the issue. Resistance to holding a meeting began to thaw. Martin's suggestion of meeting in Washington was rejected by the Americans. British finance minister Gordon Brown seemed agreeable to a London location, but security officials vetoed the idea. Martin then offered Ottawa.

All the G20 countries agreed to come to Ottawa, but many had one condition: they did not want to meet if a G7 finance ministers' meeting were held immediately before. They did not want to be in a position where the G7 caucused first and the G20 subsequently simply ratified the G7's decisions. Martin insisted the sequence be for the G20 to meet first, after which the G7 and IMFC would adopt robust action against terrorist financing. The Canadians explicitly said no other groups could meet with the G20 during its breaks, nor could there be any meetings on the margins of the IMF gathering. When the Ottawa G20 meeting was announced, the G7 finance ministers decided to meet as well, and did so following the G20 meeting.

Deputies' Meeting

At the deputies' meeting held in October 2001 to prepare for the ministers' and governors' gathering, officials focused on three key areas: the vulnerabilities of the global economy, terrorism, and globalization. Argentina's financial crisis was addressed on the sidelines. The worry was that Argentina would restructure its sovereign debt in a way that amounted to a default, causing another blow to the international economy, already shaky after the September 11 attacks. The two shocks, one new and one old, interacted in a potentially menacing way.

The G20 members had discussed exchange rate regimes in Montreal in 2000. There had been a general demand for Canada to host an exchange rate seminar, which it did at the Ottawa deputies' meeting. There was no consensus on an optimal regime. There was, however, agreement that strong domestic policies were important, and that a managed floating regime was not appropriate for all emerging countries. Brazil in particular did not want a floating exchange rate regime. Canadian officials helped convince Brazil to go to a staggered devaluation instead.

The G20 deputies also held a round table with the private sector to discuss how to improve the efficiency and stability of international capital markets. The private sector representatives highlighted the importance of developing domestic capital markets, issuing debt in the local currency, and building strong financial institutions.

At the Meeting

Three issues dominated the finance ministers' and bank governors' meeting, which took place at Ottawa's Conference Centre: the post-September 11 slowdown of the economy, terrorist finance, and, very much at Martin's insistence, development.

Economic Growth

The first issue was economic growth. The continuing global slowdown remained a particular concern. The IMF had just released its predictions for the coming year, forecasting a meagre 2.4 percent growth in world output for 2002 and 2003 (IMF 2001). This slowdown was different than earlier ones, in that it was synchronous across all geographic regions and sectors, a sure sign that economic globalization had taken hold. Even before September 11, businesses and consumers were losing confidence and interest rates were falling. Emerging markets had also been affected and were having trouble raising liquidity, as contagion carried the initial shock from terrorism to finance and from America to non-G7 countries around the world.

On the issue of sovereign debt, Martin had been arguing for some time for an international regime to deal in an orderly way with debt refinancing. Although opposition remained, the attitude of his colleagues was starting to shift. Discussions did not focus specifically on Argentina or Turkey, but rather on how to deal systematically with the kinds of crises they might be moving toward. Instead of coping with crises as they came up, as the IMF tended to do, the Bank of Canada and the Bank of England—among others—pushed to develop a framework for prevention, including ways to involve the private sector earlier to reduce the need for a big IMF bailout after the fact.

Discussions on the flagging global economy and crisis resolution could not avoid the specific cases of greater concern. The G20 representatives sympathized with their colleagues affected by their looming crises. They recognized that the international community had a vested interest in well-functioning capital markets everywhere. But they did not offer any increased support to Argentina, beyond what the IMF and Spain had provided earlier in the year. G20 ministers also did not promise Turkey any new funds.

Terrorist Finance

The second issue was terrorist finance. Participants knew that they were one part of a larger response to the September 11 terrorist attacks and that the one thing they could do was cut off the terrorists' finance. At the meeting, the ministers and governors learned, many for the first time, about the facts and details of sharia finance and the informal money transfer systems used in the Islamic world. The month before, G7 finance ministers had agreed that they would ratify the UN resolutions on terrorist finance. Their G20 colleagues now did so too. They developed the detailed "G20 Action Plan on Terrorist Financing." Although most of the work had been done prior to the meeting by Canadian officials consulting with colleagues from all the members, the ministers and governors were left with some details to decide. Their action plan was a significant achievement, both in its own right and for the consensus that it represented.

The action plan was largely a Canadian initiative, due in part to the structure of the G20. With no secretariat, the host country was responsible for assembling the agenda, with input from all members. Canadian finance officials worked with those from the other countries to produce about 90 percent of the plan. The remaining 10 percent was done by the ministers and governors at the meeting.

This involved a trade-off. For some of the smaller countries, terrorist finance was not a priority. They were more concerned with health care or education. Moreover, taking the necessary steps to combat terrorist finance was often not possible without substantial reforms to their banking systems. This would require assistance from the richer countries.

The G20 reached an informal consensus: the emerging countries would agree on the action plan if the developed ones promised assistance in promoting the prime concerns of the emerging countries. Through such cross-issue bargaining, functionally driven bundling, and September 11–induced psycho-sociological bonding, the emerging country members' influence and the equality within the G20 increased.

Deliberations turned into decisions within the G20 and beyond. After reaching consensus on the action plan, the G20 sent it to the IMFC meeting, which took place subsequently in the same building. The next day, the IMFC adopted the "G20 Action Plan on Terrorist Financing" almost word for word. This was a significant step forward for the G20 as an informal group that had initially been brought together primarily for deliberative purposes. It also showed how the G20 could lead other, more formal, institutionalized, legalized bodies within the global governance galaxy.

Development

The third issue was development. All again agreed that globalization could be a positive force. It needed to be a public-private partnership. Recipient countries told donor countries that increased aid effectiveness and resources were necessary for development.

Afghanistan

The G20 finance ministers and bank governors discussed Afghanistan, which the US-led coalition had invaded at the beginning of October. They examined a possible reconstruction plan for the country. They concluded that it was too early to arrive at a total of the required sum. Martin presciently declared that the costs of reconstruction would be enormous.

The ministers discussed the possibility of meeting the following week to discuss reconstruction. A senior officials meeting, co-hosted by the United States and Japan, was indeed held in Washington on November 20, 2001—the first conference on rebuilding Afghanistan. Leaders from a dozen countries and international organizations attended. With its new actions on freezing terrorist finance and reconstructing Afghanistan, the G20 had become a global security governor in a direct and dual way.

Achievements

The key achievement of the Ottawa meeting was the "G20 Action Plan on Terrorist Financing." Annexed to the communiqué, it was almost as long as the main document itself. The action plan was immediately endorsed by the IMFC. In it the G20 countries committed themselves to implement the UN Security Council (UNSC) resolutions on terrorism and terrorism financing, and to ratify the UN's International Convention on the Suppression of the Financing of Terrorism and Convention Against Transnational Organized Crime. They also called for other countries and international organizations to implement the action plan. As chair, Paul Martin judged that the action plan demonstrated the flexibility of the G20 "to address urgent issues outside of the established work program" (G20 2008). The ministers promised to review their progress at the next meeting, showing their concern with delivery and with making terrorist finance an ongoing part of their agenda.

Getting agreement on terrorist finance was a significant achievement. Despite the international impact of the September 11 terrorist attacks on the World Trade Center and the Pentagon, many G20 countries were geographically and politically located far from the United States. In a sharp reversal of the balance of vulnerability in 1997–99, they were less directly affected by the attacks than America, although many had had some of their citizens killed there. Argentina had other pressing concerns. Not all member countries were able to afford anti-terrorism measures, particularly those needed to meet the anti-money laundering goals.

Political divergences also played a role. Saudi Arabia, the only G20 country from the Middle East, had not been cooperative outside of the G20. It continued to deny that 17 of the alleged hijackers in the attack were Saudi. Martin, however, wanted consensus on this issue and to make it the centrepiece of the Ottawa meeting. He was successful in getting all 20 members to sign onto the ambitious action plan, and do so in more than an acquiescent way. There was genuine buy-in, including from Saudi Arabia and Indonesia, to the directions and decisions.

The Ottawa meeting featured both innovation and iteration. The G20 showed it could respond to the new crisis while delivering its core, built-in agenda, as it continued its work on managing international finance and economics. The ministers and governors stressed that the terrorist attacks would not undermine their economic prospects, noting that they had already taken action to maintain liquidity and to stabilize the markets. The mounting economic crises in emerging markets were thus not hijacked by the security shocks of September 11.

The ministers asked their deputies to build on the private sector discussions and to report at the next meeting on how to improve the way financial crises were addressed. Led by Canada and the United Kingdom, the G20 moved toward a framework for crisis prevention. Canadian central bank governor David Dodge saw much progress on this issue. The meeting was not about how to solve the Argentine financial crisis: the ministers listened to the central bankers of both Argentina and Brazil since they were living through the implications of the crisis. Both made important contributions.

On the issue of globalization, the G20 continued to move forward. By the Ottawa meeting, most participating countries had completed their case study reports. The Canadian G20 secretariat had prepared a report based on those findings. The document found that globalization had contributed to increasing global prosperity and that successful experiences required strong and sound domestic policies to secure progress. But given the preoccupations flowing from September 11, serious discussion of these reports was deferred until the following year.

On globalization, the result was a positive but nuanced stance. The G20 accepted that globalization had a beneficial impact and had "led to demonstrable improvements in living standards for the vast majority of our citizens" (G20 Finance 2001a). Nonetheless, globalization also brought risks and challenges that required international cooperation to overcome. One major benefit of globalization within developed countries came from decreasing the trade barriers between them. For countries that were not members of the Organisation for Economic Co-operation and Development, those benefits were just beginning, as trade barriers between developed and developing countries came down. The G20 ministers recognized the need to work with international financial institutions and the World Trade Organization (WTO) to ensure that the poorest countries benefited from increased economic integration. But there were risks involved. As economic integration increased, so did vulnerability.

Dimensions of Performance

The Ottawa meeting was a very strong success on virtually all dimensions of G20 governance.

Domestic Political Management

In its domestic political management, Ottawa's performance was strong. On paper, the meeting issued no communiqué compliments to any of the G20 members (see Appendix D). However, in practice it enabled Martin to show Canada's terrified citizens, and those in the US next door and beyond, that the G20 countries were acting decisively on America's behalf to stop further strikes.

In holding the meeting in Ottawa, Martin was willing to run domestic political risks. One risk was a terrorist attack on Ottawa itself. Another was violence, like the protests that had afflicted the G8 Genoa Summit a few months before. Martin monitored his officials' discussions with the Ottawa police to reduce the risks of both.

Deliberation

In its deliberation, Ottawa was a very strong success. With a total of 1,646 words, it was the first time the meeting produced a second separate document, unlike the annex appended to Montreal's communiqué (see Appendix E). This was the "G20 Action Plan on Terrorist Financing" (G20 Finance 2001b). The shift to deal with terrorist financing, which had not been explored before, took more than half of the G20's overall communiqué. This surge in attention to terrorism at the 2001 meeting was not surprising, given the recent September 11 attacks.

In practice, at the same time, Afghanistan and development also came onto the agenda in an important way. Ample attention continued to be paid to macroeconomic policy and trade. However, attention to most of the issues discussed at the previous two meetings, such as domestic financial regulation, declined.

Direction Setting

Ottawa's performance in direction setting was very strong. The September 11 terrorist attacks, still fresh in everyone's minds, caused a surge in the G20's affirmation of old and new shared values (see Appendix F). Ottawa endorsed four democratic principles on four occasions, the highest number to date. It again affirmed transparency. It also noted for the first time the importance of good governance, accountable international institutions, and information and knowledge exchange (G20 Finance 2001a).

At Montreal the G20's affirmation of distributional principles was even stronger once again. Stronger still was its endorsement of the protections of embedded liberalism, whose frequency and spread rose to a new high.

Decision Making

In its collective decision making Ottawa's performance was very strong. It surged to make 24 commitments (see Appendix G). This was three times as many as in Montreal the year before and six times as many as at the inaugural meeting in Berlin. Thus September 11 and Ottawa moved the G20 from a deliberative and direction setting to a strong decisional forum.

Of these 24 commitments, 20 came on terrorism, two on macroeconomic policy, one on international financial institutions and one on trade. Martin thus achieved his goal of creating an ambitious new mechanism for tracking and freezing terrorist finance. He called this "an important counter-strike," and something that the G7 could never have achieved (Martin 2008). The consensus required some compromise among what different countries considered their top priorities. In the end, however, all 20 members agreed on a substantive action plan that could not have secured that level of support had it been designed by the more exclusive G7.

Delivery

In its delivery of its 24 decisions, Ottawa's performance was also very strong. The meeting led directly to the successful tracking of terrorist finance. It issued several remit mandates and follow-up meetings, showing that compliance was clearly on the members' minds. Concern with delivery was seen in its promise to review progress on its terrorist finance action plan at its next meeting, as well as to receive a report from the deputies on managing financial crises. However, those commitments contained only three catalysts that counted in the context of a G8 summit to spur members' compliance over the following year.

Development of Global Governance

In developing global governance, Ottawa's performance was very strong in several ways. Internally, the G20 flexibly adjusted its timing, location, and agenda to meet when other bodies could not. It did so not only to address the crisis at hand but also to address and broaden its built-in agenda. It involved the private sector in its preparations. And it spawned an officials' meeting in Washington the week after the meeting to implement its decisions in regard to rebuilding Afghanistan. Ottawa's communiqué made six references to institutionalizing the G20 (see Appendix C-1).

Externally, Ottawa's "G20 Action Plan on Terrorist Financing" was adopted by the IMFC the next day. The G20 communiqué made a new high of 31 references to outside institutions, compared to only six references to itself as an institution. The Financial Action Task Force (FATF), mentioned for the first time, took first place with eight references. Most notably, the G20 made several references to political-security institutions, including two to the UNSC. The UN had six references overall. At a lower level, the IMF had four references and the Financial Stability Forum (FSF) was now equal with the World Bank, with three references each. The reciprocal flow of inter-institutional influence was clear from the fact that the G20 supported the UN, while leading the IMF and G7 in the counterterrorism campaign.

Causes of Performance

Once again the systemic hub model accounts well for the surge to very strong, much more comprehensive performance along the particular path that the G20 took in 2001.

Shock-Activated, Equalizing Vulnerabilities

The first, critical cause was the shock-activated, equalizing vulnerability, first from the terrorist attacks on America itself and second from looming financial crises in Argentina and Turkey beyond. The terrorist attacks of September 11, 2001, were, in their surprise, scale, scope, and societal impact, an unprecedented shock on America, its allies, and the international system as a whole. Following al Qaeda's deadly attack on the World Trade Center in 1993, it had returned with a second shock, consisting of two much more deadly attacks on the same target and two others against Washington in a single day. These attacks sent a message to North America that it was no longer invulnerable to the rest of the world in its physical, national, and financial security, with the New York Stock Exchange and much economic activity in the US shut down for several days. The attacks compounded the cyclical and synchronized economic slowdown that was affecting the global economy. They were followed one week later by the outbreak of deadly anthrax attacks from an unknown source across the eastern US.

The second shock sequence arose from an emerging sovereign debt crisis in Argentina. It eventually brought the largest sovereign default in world history in December. Turkey also experienced financial difficulties. The combined effects spread to other regions and countries, raising the prospect of rampant and devastating global contagion once again. Reinforced by a sharp downturn in the internet-based "new economy," by rising oil prices and by increasing inflation, the United States, soon followed by Japan and Europe, entered a period of significantly slower growth. This, too, threatened a serious global slowdown that made it more difficult to respond to the autumn security shocks.

The terrorist shock and its tight link to an American and global economic downturn and to the looming financial crises in Argentina and Turkey explain well the G20's high performance on its new subjects of terrorist finance and Afghanistan and its advances on its built-in agenda of financial crisis response and macroeconomic management. But more than shocks alone are needed to account for why a G20 meeting was held, in Canada, and one that Bush's America and all other members agreed to come to and cooperate within.

International Institutional Failure

The second cause of Ottawa's very strong success is the failure of the other international institutions acting on their own to respond adequately to these shocks. The new security shocks made clear the inability of the other international institutions to act appropriately in advance to anticipate and prevent the assaults, or afterward to act on their own in response (Kirton 1993). After September 11, the UN did not hold its regular September meeting to open the General Assembly. The IMF and the World Bank were unable to meet in Washington and had to piggyback on the G20 meeting in Ottawa. The IMF's very optimistic prediction of global growth was inaccurate, failing to anticipate the shocks of the fall and setbacks later in the year (see Appendix J-1). Only the North Atlantic Treaty Organization (NATO) sprang into action immediately after the September 11 attacks with an effective response on the military front.

In Italy, the G8 had identified a potential terrorist attack on the Genoa Summit in July 2001 and successfully staved it off. But it did little to preview or prevent the attacks on America a few months later. Nor did protest-ridden Genoa's historic involvement of countries and international organizations outside the G8 help it focus on the terrorist threat or the financial ones emerging in Argentina and Turkey. The G8 had invited to Genoa only a few African countries, and none of those systemically significant countries for terrorism and finance elsewhere in the world.

On September 25, the G7 finance ministers had held a conference call to discuss the ramifications of the terrorist attacks on their countries. They spoke of their "common cause in strengthening the international fight against the financing of terrorism" and made plans to integrate their actions. They discussed scheduling a meeting early in October to pursue the "global campaign" against terrorist finance (G7 2001). But they could only do so on the margins of the G20 meeting in Ottawa, after the G20 meeting itself had been held (G20 Finance 2001b).

More broadly, the international financial system itself seemed to need a new generation of reforms. These were needed not only to mobilize more money for crisis response and to strengthen private sector responsibility, but also to sharpen the IMF's focus, reinvent it as a crisis prevention institution, improve its relationship with a reformed array of multilateral development banks (MDBs), and address such new globalization issues as the impact of derivatives and the process of dollarization (Fratianni et al. 1999; Salvatore 2000; Hale 2001; von Furstenberg 2001b, 2001a). But few reforms were forthcoming on time.

Together these failures evoked the spectre of a return to an alleged tendency, identified in the mid 1990s, for the G7/8 leaders to retreat to impotent inactivity in the face of globalized markets that they felt they could no longer control (Bergsten and Henning 1996). They even suggested to some that the world's major governments in the G7 had in fact been rendered relatively powerless by a world of rampant globalization and by the prevailing neoliberal Washington Consensus and "constitutional" confines it brought, and that recent efforts to counter with a socially sensitive approach to global governance were for naught (Gill 1993; Cerny 1995; Birdsall and de la Torre 2001; Kirton 2001). They raised the question of whether national governments, even acting together through the old IMF or newer G7/8, and recent offshoots such as the IMFC and the FSF, could offer a coherent governance response to the pressure of the market in an intensely globalizing age. Now these built-in challenges of globalization were threatened by the prospect of a security blackout, as all advanced countries turned to face the new security threat. In so doing they all largely failed.

The G20, however, despite being a new, finance-focused body and thus one more easily sidelined in the face of such shocks, was the only one to respond quickly and decisively, not only to terrorist finance but also to the other acute and chronic challenges on the security, finance, globalization, and development fronts.

Predominant, Equalizing Capability

A third cause of Ottawa's strong comprehensive success was the increasing external predominance and internal equality of G20 country members' relative capability (see Appendix K). The group continued to contain 82 percent of global gross domestic product (GDP), the level it had reached the year before. Its internal equality, as measured by the Gini coefficient, increased for the first time, to 0.55 from 0.54 in the previous two years, as the non-G8 members share of global GDP remained at 15 percent. However, the ratio of its highest to lowest members increased to 86.76 from 74.84 the year before, as falling oil prices lowered the GDP of Saudi Arabia at the bottom relative to the US at the top.

Beyond its overall capabilities, the G20 alone contained the countries with the issue-specific capabilities that counted to cope with the shocks at hand. The leading G7 countries controlled the world's formal financial centres and payment systems. However, Saudi Arabia, Indonesia, and Turkey were important in the informal ones also needed to control terrorist finance. Many G20 members quickly learned that they could not control terrorist finance without dealing with sharia finance and thus the countries where it flourished. And the G20, not the G7, contained as full members Turkey and Argentina, where the new financial crises were coming from.

Democratic Convergence

A fourth cause of Ottawa's strong comprehensive success was the democratizing convergence of G20 members in their political systems at home. In 2001, Russia and Mexico made a major advance in their democratization (see Appendix L). Korea, Indonesia, and Argentina continued the advances they had made before. India had taken a further step, as the Congress Party, its post-independence governing party, had been replaced at the polls by an opposition party for the first time. In addition, the shock of September 11 reminded all of their common, existential commitment to preserve their monopoly of legitimate force and the rule of law in the face of terrorist attacks, and their financial stability now under such severe attack.

Political Control, Capital, Continuity, Competence, and Commitment

The fifth cause of Ottawa's strong, comprehensive success was the continuing political control, capital, continuity, competence, and commitment where it counted among the G20 members. Considerable change brought greater political control and capital and a sharp rightward shift in several consequential countries. The shift began in the United States with the election of George W. Bush. His new treasury secretary, Paul O'Neill, had begun his tenure wondering about the value of the G7 finance ministers forum, G7 governments' provision of national "second lines of defence" to combat foreign financial crises, much of what the IMF and the MDBs had recently done (including support for a democratizing Russia), and the G7's success in fighting money laundering through the FATF. In Japan the spring brought a new prime minister, Junichiro Koizumi, to power. His bold promise to end an era of massive fiscal deficits and financial relief for ailing banks and to undertake genuine structural reform appeared to repudiate the patronage-reinforced deficit-spending Keynesian orthodoxy that had long prevailed. In Italy, the election of the government of Silvio Berlusconi in May 2001, following the early 2000 election of Vladimir Putin in Russia, seemed to confirm the rightward shift.

Among the non-G7/8 countries, in Mexico, at the end of 2000, Vicente Fox of the centre-right National Action Party replaced Ernesto Zedillo, ending the long rule of the centre-left Institutional Revolutionary Party. Elsewhere Australia was still led by John Howard and his centre-right coalition and Brazil by Fernando

Henrique Cardoso. India was led by Atal Bihari Vajpayee, leader of the BJP, a social and economic conservative party.

On the other hand, the re-election of the centrist majority government of Tony Blair's Labour Party in Britain in June 2001, following that of Jean Chrétien's Liberals in Canada the previous year, promised a politically secure and popular loyal opposition lodged in two of the G7/8's smaller countries. Germany's "Red-Green" coalition and France's leadership would remain in office for at least another year.

In South Africa, Thabo Mbeki had recently assumed leadership of the presidency, backed by the social democratic African National Congress and keeping Trevor Manuel as finance minister. In Turkey, Ahmet Necdet Sezer assumed the presidency in May 2000. Sezer's name had been put forward after no candidate could be agreed on in parliament. Despite no official political party affiliation, Sezer was known for his secular and liberal views, at odds with the official conservative opposition party. In Argentina, Fernando de la Rúa from the Radical Civic Union party assumed the presidency in December 1999 after the re-election attempt of Carlos Menem, who had led the country from 1989 to 1999, was deemed unconstitutional.

The overall change increased political control and capital. The resulting shift to the right made it easier for the G20 to focus for the first time on terrorist finance and related Afghanistan security. However, there was sufficiently strong centre-left continuity in consequential countries for globalization and development to be added to and integrated with the advances made.

Above all, the founding finance minister pillars of Canada's Martin, Britain's Brown, and South Africa's Manuel remained a long commitment. Martin, chairing his third G20 meeting, formed a September 11–driven bond with America's O'Neill. As O'Neill had wide responsibilities for border security, he and Martin, from neighbouring Canada, spoke intensively about border issues. They developed a friendship as a result.

Controlled Club Participation as a Network Hub

The sixth cause of Ottawa's strong, comprehensive success was the G20's increasing controlled club participation as a network hub. Internally, the shocks of September 11 bonded G20 ministers, governors, and officials together as a club in a common cause. They became closer colleagues to counter a common, compelling counterterrorist threat, even if there were differences on the appropriate priority for this issue and the particular instruments to be used. In the face of a new emerging financial crisis, when they met they offered economically struggling Argentina and Turkey not lectures but sympathy, if not actual financial assistance.

The sudden new sense of clubness was enhanced by Canada's logistical choices. In keeping with its G7/8 tradition, and making a virtue of necessity, Canada told each country that given the short time, hotel space, and security, each delegation could have only five members, rather than the normal 25. The much smaller size also made it easier for those who were there to bond.

Another sign that the G20 became an interpersonal club in Ottawa was the fact that so many who were invited made an exceptional effort to attend, and did. Everyone who needed to be present was there, as was nearly every member of the IMFC—despite the difficulties created by September 11 and the fact that some had to travel through New York or Toronto.

In the airport lounges en route, in the meetings corridors, and over meals, bonding occurred spontaneously. All felt this was a defining moment, a test of one's credentials—"us" against "them," and "you were either with us or against us." Even the Saudis, who were very nervous, wanted to prove that they were full members of the team. There was no dissent.

All were adamant that they would not let the terrorists win. The Canadians were equally adamant that this was not just about having a meeting in Ottawa but also about showing the world the determination to stick together to defeat a common threat. It was a test of the G20 and the international community. Everyone must come together to show clearly that they and their values would win.

At Ottawa participants felt this was the place to be, with the people who would make a positive difference. There was an intense sense of a common cause. It was a seminal moment when the G20 left behind its old identity to take up a moral imperative as a polity and group of people united against the devastation they had just seen. They believed deeply in the values that set them apart—democracy, transparency, and openness. Most G20 members, aside from Saudi Arabia, considered this the moment to define themselves as an open society willing to take on its foes, and do so with and for political openness, too. Many felt it was an extraordinary human experience, with ministers and governors reaching out to make a human connection, unlike at any G20 meeting before or since.

Externally, this Ottawa meeting served as the essential hub for the IMFC and G7 meetings to take place in the same spot immediately afterward, thus deepening the global network that had the G20 as its now necessary core. The G20 thereby became the priority, permanent forum for its members' cooperation on terrorist finance. The G20 became the only part of the broader, global network that worked on its own financial governance in the wake of the September 11 attacks. The western hemisphere finance ministers had met on March 29–30 and the finance ministers of the Asia-Pacific Economic Cooperation (APEC) forum, had met in Suzhou, China, on September 8–9, immediately before the terrorists hit. However, the autumn meeting of Commonwealth finance ministers, scheduled for after September 11, was postponed five times and then cancelled outright.

Conclusion

The G20's Ottawa meeting was a strong, comprehensive success in several ways. Meeting soon after September 11 to address terrorist finance sent a message that the G20 was a significant actor in responding to global shocks, in particular to a direct shock on America itself. The G20 was now a critical actor to counter security shocks, beyond the strictly financial and economic ones that had catalysed the group's creation in 1999.

Ottawa helped the new Bush administration, suspicious of international institutions created by the defeated Clinton administration, to bond with the group. The G20 secured greater buy-in from emerging country members, both by broadening the agenda to deal with their development priorities and by assisting them in combating terrorist finance at home. The quick, decisive, detailed, and rapidly delivered "G20 Action Plan on Terrorist Financing," immediately adopted by the IMFC, represented a shift in the G20 from a consultative, caucus body to an effective decision-making one with a clear and concrete agenda, with the political will and capital to get things done, and with the ability to extend its influence by directing broader bodies such as the IMFC. Holding the meeting at the same time as the IMF and the World Bank gatherings and immediately before the G7 meeting showed the indispensability of the G20 and lent it legitimacy, solidifying its position as the essential hub of the top-tier global financial governance groups.

Even before such a singular success, some had felt that the G20 should make the leap to the leaders' level. Paul Martin had thought that it should from the very start. Former Brazilian president Cardoso had argued this case publicly as well. While the idea was not widely embraced at the time, the group was moving in that direction. The G20 legitimately and effectively linked terrorism and finance as well as terrorism and development in Afghanistan. Such issues and linkages were appropriate for leaders as well as finance ministers to address and make.

Similarly the IMF's managing director, Michel Camdessus, had suggested to the IMF Executive Board that the IMFC should meet at the leaders' level. He had done so when the Interim Committee had discussed turning itself into a stronger IMFC. No one took up his idea. G7 countries were opposed and developing countries did not see it as realistic.

Yet before a major move could be mounted to make the G20 a leader-level forum, the G20 at the finance-minister level had to pass several tests. The first was to govern effectively the absence of new acute global finance and terrorist crises in the following years. The second was to do so after the shift of the chair and the host from a committed Paul Martin and the experienced G7 members to the non-G7 ones. And the third was to do so with the unexpected departure of Martin, its founding visionary and only chair for its first three years.

References

Bergsten, C. Fred and Henning, C. Randall. 1996. *Global Economic Leadership and the Group of Seven*. Washington DC: Institute for International Economics.

Birdsall, Nancy and de la Torre, Augusta. 2001. "Washington Contentious." *Politica Internazionale* 29 (January-April): 97–104.

Cerny, Philip G. 1995. "Globalization and the Changing Logic of Collective Action." *International Organisation* 49(4): 595–625.

Fratianni, Michele, Salvatore, Dominick, and Savona, Paolo, eds. 1999. *Ideas for the Future of the International Monetary System*. Boston: Kluwer Academic Publishers.

Freytag, Andreas, Kirton, John J., Sally, Razeen, and Savona, Paolo, eds. 2011. *Securing the Global Economy: G8 Global Governance for a Post-Crisis World*. Farnham: Ashgate.

G7. 2001. "G7 Statement." Genoa, July 20. Available at: www.g8.utoronto.ca/g7/summit/2001genoa/g7statement.html. Accessed: July 2011.

G20. 2008. "The Group of Twenty: A History." Available at: www.g20.utoronto.ca/docs/g20history.pdf. Accessed: July 2012.

G20 Finance Ministers and Central Bank Governors. 2001a. "Communiqué." Ottawa, November 17. Available at: www.g20.utoronto.ca/2001/2001communique.html. Accessed: July 2012.

G20 Finance Ministers and Central Bank Governors. 2001b. "G20 Action Plan on Terrorist Financing." Ottawa, November 17. Available at: www.g20.utoronto.ca/2001/2001communique.html#action. Accessed: July 2012.

Gill, Stephen, ed. 1993. *Gramsci, Historical Materialism, and International Relations*. Cambridge: Cambridge University Press.

Hale, David. 2001. "Have Hedge Funds Become an Agent of Monetary Policy?," Zurich Financial Services, 13 June.

International Monetary Fund. 2001. "World Economic Outlook: The Global Economy After September 11." December, Washington DC. Available at: www.imf.org/external/pubs/ft/weo/2001/03. Accessed: July 2012.

Kirton, John J. 1993. "The Seven Power Summits as a New Security Institution." In *Building a New Global Order: Emerging Trends in International Security*, eds Dewitt, David, Haglund, David, and Kirton, John J. Toronto: Oxford University Press, 335–57.

Kirton, John J. 2001. "Guiding Global Economic Governance: The G20, the G7, and the International Monetary Fund at Century's Dawn." In *New Directions in Global Economic Governance: Managing Globalisation in the Twenty-First Century*, eds Kirton, John J., and von Furstenberg, George M. Aldershot: Ashgate, 143–67.

Kirton, John J. 2011. "G8 Sanctioning Success." In *Securing the Global Economy: G8 Global Governance for a Post-Crisis World*, eds Freytag, Andreas, Kirton, John J., Sally, Razeen, and Savona, Paolo. Farnham: Ashgate, 157–80.

Martin, Paul. 2001. "Globalization, Terrorism, and the World Economy." Speech delivered at a luncheon organized by the Reinventing Bretton Woods Committee and The Conference Board of Canada, Ottawa, November 16. Available at: www.collectionscanada.gc.ca/webarchives/20071122093833/http://www.fin.gc.ca/news01/01-105e.html. Accessed: July 2012.

Martin, Paul. 2008. *Hell or High Water: My Life In and Out of Politics*. Toronto: McClelland and Stewart.

Salvatore, Dominick. 2000. "The Present International Monetary System: Problems, Complications, and Reforms." *Open Economies Review* 11(1): 133–48.

Suskind, Ron. 2004. *The Price of Loyalty: George W. Bush, the White House, and the Education of Paul O'Neill*. New York: Simon and Schuster.

von Furstenberg, George M. 2001a. "Assembling a New Financial Architecture: The G7's 2001 Role and Response." Paper presented at the conference on Assembling a New International Financial Architecture: The Deeper Challenges, LUISS University, July 17, Rome.

von Furstenberg, George M. 2001b. "US Dollarization: A Second-Best Form of Regional Currency Consolidation." In *Guiding Global Order: G8 Governance in the Twenty-First Century*, eds Kirton, John J., Daniels, Joseph P., and Freytag, Andreas. Aldershot: Ashgate, 45–54.

PART III
Equalizing the Influence, 2002–2007

Chapter 6
Driving Development, New Delhi 2002 and Morelia 2003

Introduction

Following its first three meetings led by Canada, the chairing and hosting of the Group of 20 (G20) passed to emerging country members. The fourth G20 ministerial was held on November 22–23, 2002, in New Delhi, India, where it had been planned to take place the previous year before it was relocated to Ottawa after the terrorist attacks of September 11, 2001.

A year after the New Delhi meeting, the G20 held its fifth meeting in Morelia, Mexico, on October 26–27, 2003. Morelia was a reflective gathering, where the finance ministers and central bank governors looked back at what they had accomplished and considered the future direction of the group. The agenda at Mexico included all the issue areas that the G20 had been addressing in previous years. It also added two new ones: preventing abuses in the financial system and future strategic priorities for the G20.

The shift to emerging country hosts and chairs marked more than a geographic change from the Atlantic to the Asian and Latin American regions. With it came a new focus on the substantive priorities and concerns of the emerging country members, with development in first place. To be sure, the G20 had previously addressed development, particularly at Montreal when the group had discussed the challenges of globalization for developing countries. However, in 2002 and 2003, the G20 took a closer look at the mechanisms of development itself.

The G20 was not the only international forum to address development priorities in those years. In March 2002, the United Nations held the International Conference on Financing for Development in Monterrey, Mexico. Here 50 heads of state and 200 finance ministers developed and adopted the Monterrey Consensus, which the G20 also took up. It embraced six areas of development financing, including international trade, increasing technical assistance for development, and broader issues such as monetary systems.

The Group of Seven (G7) and Group of Eight (G8) also took up development as a major theme in 2002. The G8 summit, hosted by Canada in Kananaskis that summer, took African development as its priority theme. It responded affirmatively to the New Partnership for Africa's Development (NEPAD) by establishing the G8 Africa Action Plan. The G8 also built on its previous summit's initiative for inclusiveness, by inviting the leaders of the four major African democracies and the UN secretary general to attend the summit as equals for the session on the final day.

The G8's now iterated and embryonically institutionalized outreach marked the start of a new, summit-level source of international institutional competition for the G20. The G8 during the first decade of the twenty-first century took up development as a key concern, and invited an increasing array of developing and emerging countries to its summits and to its ministerial and official forums in more institutionalized and equal ways. This process expanded from the African four of 2002 through to the Heiligendamm Dialogue Process of an equal dialogue among G8 and Group of Five (G5) members of Brazil, China, India, Mexico, and South Africa starting in 2007 (Kirton 2010a). In light of this new G8-plus competitor, the G20 ultimately prevailed, above all when it too leapt to the leaders' level to start its own summitry in 2008.

While the 2007–08 global financial crisis was the proximate cause of that great leap upward, the underlying conditions came from the advances the G20 had made at the level of finance ministers and central bank governors during its second phase from 2002 to 2007. During this time, the G20 more genuinely became a group of and for its emerging members, in its institutional leadership, agenda, policy initiatives, and outcomes. It also proved it could work where the International Monetary Fund (IMF) and G7/8 had long tried and failed, especially on reforming the IMF to reflect the rising power and demand of the emerging countries.

Starting in 2002 with India—a charter member of the Commonwealth since 1947—the G20 began to prove its value as a group of systemically significant equals, with emerging members now in the lead. It continued in 2003 with Mexico, next door to the United States, and a partner with both the US and Canada in the North American Free Trade Agreement (NAFTA)—and a member of the Organisation for Economic Co-operation and Development (OECD). In 2004, the G20 would bond at Berlin, as this initial opponent of the G20 in 1999 became an enthusiastic convert to the group. In 2005, the G20 would diplomatically capture China, as the host that initiated the G20's ultimate great success of the first stage of voice and vote reform at the IMF to give rising powers a large place. The G20's institutionalization as a group of equals, with hosting generally rotating among emerging and established countries, would intensify at Australia in 2006 and South Africa in 2007. The troika system for guidance from past, present, and future hosts took hold, to reinforce this equality between established and emerging states.

All this was done with no great new global financial, economic, or terrorist shocks to galvanize action. To be sure, social unrest and terrorism, as well as ecological and commodity shocks, continued to remind all of their growing vulnerability in an increasingly globalized world and to support the solid performance achieved during these years. However, the key causes of this more equal, effective performance during the G20's second phase were the willingness of emerging member democracies to assume the leadership in 2002, 2003, 2005, and 2007, with longstanding democratic, diverse members of the Commonwealth playing a leading role as chair of the G20 for six of its first nine years, including the first four. Also important was new leadership, notably in China and in Canada, where, after an absence in 2002 and 2003, Paul Martin returned as prime minister to campaign for a leaders-level G20 in 2004 and 2005. Above all, the G20 continued as a compact, closed group of equals. In sharp contrast, the G8 added only participants, not new equal members from the ranks of rising states (Kirton 2010b, 2010a, 2010c). In the end, representativeness did not matter much for group effectiveness. Equality did.

The G20's Advance in 2002–2003

The 2002 and 2003 meetings were a solid success, if a somewhat smaller success than those in the G20's first three years before. This was caused in large part because the meetings were hosted and chaired by emerging countries as equal members. This important step helped to solidify and legitimize the group's role for all members and the broader international community as seen in its growing, flexible agenda. The G20 was able to shift from crisis response to address broader global challenges beyond terrorist financing, particularly those priorities of emerging countries inside and outside of the narrow financial and economic realms. A second cause was the failure of other international institutions to embrace as equals the world's rising, systemically significant powers, to deal successfully with these issues and concerns. The G20 had already stepped in with such inclusive equality for consequential countries where others did or could not.

New Delhi 2002

The Challenge

Originally, the third G20 meeting was to have been chaired by and held in India. After the terrorist attacks on America on September 11, 2001, however, the meeting was moved to Canada (see Chapter 5). In February 2002, the members thus decided that the fourth meeting should be hosted and chaired by India. It took place in New Delhi on November 22–23, 2002.

Hosted by Indian finance minister Jaswant Singh, the New Delhi meeting was to address poverty alleviation, the global economy, and terrorist finance. Terrorist finance was a particular concern to both India, which suffered from continual terrorist attacks, and the United States, where the memories of September 11 were still very fresh (Ben-Ishai et al. 2002).

New Delhi was the first time that the G20 was chaired and hosted by an emerging country. It focused on four themes: crisis prevention and resolution, globalization, terrorist financing, and development. By this meeting, the members had started to discuss how the group could move beyond crisis response to address broader topics. The troika of past, present, and future hosts was established, an institutional innovation particularly important for the incoming emerging country hosts.

Reforming the Indian economy was also an important topic at the meeting. Britain pledged to support India's privatization plans. Meanwhile, US treasury secretary Paul O'Neill tried to reassure the G20 that the American economy was looking up and reported that George W. Bush planned to push Congress to pass reforms on job creation and economic stimulus (Ben-Ishai et al. 2002).

Competing Assessments

The New Delhi meeting inspired a debate about its performance among competing schools of thought. The first school argued that it was a success. Poverty in the G20 had declined substantially and inequality among the members was lessening. G20 members were successfully learning lessons from one another. The group was proving its value (Salai-i-Martin and Mohapatra 2003; Mukherji 2002).

A second school argued that the G20 failed to come to a consensus on the debt defaults of emerging economies. It also failed to make any significant progress on terrorist financing in 2002. This was because advanced and emerging countries were divided on issues (Luce 2002; Gupta and Friel 2002).

A third school argued that the G20 succeeded more strongly in coming to a consensus on broader themes. It also did well in making general commitments. Yet it failed to agree on specific, detailed measures (Mahapatra 2002).

The Argument

The 2002 meeting was successful in its structure, its agenda, and its achievements, as the first meeting hosted and chaired by an emerging country. The unique governing troika was established in the lead-up to the meeting. It was the first meeting where the G20 focused fully on development. It also institutionalized the G20's attention to and achievements on terrorist finance, proving this systemic issue was a priority for leading established country members such as the United States as well as leading emerging ones such as India.

Plans and Preparations

Preparations for the 2002 meeting in New Delhi had begun in the lead-up to the 2001 meeting. Given that the first two G20 meetings were chaired and hosted by advanced countries, Paul Martin and some members thought that it was time to meet in an emerging country. Martin had made it clear to his officials that in a spirit of buy-in, chairing responsibilities should rotate between emerging and developed countries. The deputies thus engaged in extensive negotiations to map out the rotation for the following 15 years. They assessed such factors as G7 and non-G7 status, geographic region, and timing of elections. A rotation was ultimately agreed, with the Indians chairing first. To assist India, which felt it might have difficulty chairing, Canada promised its support and pledged to bring to the table the host of the post-India meeting to allow it to start preparing in advance. Thus was created the first troika of present, past, and future chairs. This institutional innovation was adopted by the Asia-Pacific Economic Cooperation (APEC) forum in later years.

Yet, after September 11, the Canadian chair offered and members accepted to move the location to Canada. Thus, in February 2002, the chair officially transferred to India. As promised, the Canadians worked closely with the Indians to ensure a smooth transition and help develop the agenda. India relied heavily on Canada for much of the preparatory work. In a further expression of Commonwealth and G20 collegiality, the Reserve Bank of Australia and the Australian Treasury hosted a workshop on globalization, living standards, and inequality in Sydney on May 27–28, 2002 (Gruen et al. 2002).

At the Deputies' Meeting To prepare directly for India's 2002 G20 ministerial, India's secretary of economic affairs C.M. Vasudev hosted a G20 deputies' meeting in New Delhi on July 16–17, 2002. Four themes were on the agenda: globalization, crisis prevention and resolution, development and aid, and terrorist finance. Deputies also discussed the world economy, sovereign debt restructuring, domestic policy requirements for regeneration of capital flows, and standards and codes for the financial sector and corporate governance (G20 Finance 2003a).

The deputies established the G20 troika of Canada, India, and Mexico. This system to ensure continuity was particularly important for India, as the first emerging country to host a G20. It obviated the need for a permanent secretariat (G20 2008).

Thus, by the fourth meeting, the G20's perennial themes were firmly entrenched. But now development and aid had been added as a priority theme. Deputies prepared their notes on crisis prevention to give to the ministers for their own meeting.

At the Meeting

At New Delhi participants addressed a reasonably clear set of issues where views differed. They methodically went through the progress being made on standards and codes and on terrorist finance, and on the reports on globalization. The subtext of the latter was to provide the political basis for the other work to be done.

The 2002 communiqué offered an integrated vision. The ministers mainstreamed development, rather than separating the themes of globalization, trade, and development. After reviewing the results of their workshop on "Globalisation, Living Standards, and Inequality: Recent Progress and Continuing Challenges" in Sydney and the commissioned case studies on the topic, the ministers and bank governors concluded that the benefits of globalization could be maximized with both appropriate domestic policies and a healthy international system. Domestically this meant strengthening institutions, encouraging savings and investment, transparency and the rule of law, and investing in infrastructure and human capacity. Each subtheme was addressed in one paragraph under a consolidated heading. As with the "G8 Africa Action Plan," good governance had pride of place.

Members noted that reducing trade barriers would help spread the potential benefits of globalization. They did not, however, commit to reducing those barriers. That would come later, when the G20 had developed enough political cohesion to make those kinds of domestically difficult commitments.

On development, G20 representatives recognized the importance of the Millennium Development Goals (MDGs), which had been announced in 2000 by the United Nations, and reaffirmed their support for NEPAD. They noted that development assistance could play a "valuable catalytic role, including the provision of global public goods" (G20 Finance 2002). They welcomed the increases in official development assistance (ODA) by some countries as well as the Heavily Indebted Poor Country (HIPC) Initiative. They did not commit to increase ODA or reduce debt.

In the areas of financial stability, crisis prevention, and terrorist finance, the 2002 communiqué recognized and applauded existing action. It made few new commitments.

Globalization for Development from Good Governance The presentation of highlights from the Australian workshop on globalization prompted a rich discussion. The workshop had been based on the case studies on the impacts of globalization done by Australia, Canada, China, France, Germany, Korea, Mexico, Russia, South Africa, the United States, and the United Kingdom. These case studies, commissioned at Montreal for delivery a year later, had been delayed due to the preoccupation at Ottawa with terrorist finance. It was decided that they would be published so that the public and think tanks as well as governments could see the results. The G20 asked the World Bank to oversee their publication.

Having established in Montreal in 2000 that globalization had both positive and negative effects, and having globalization as well as development and aid as major themes in 2002, the G20 ministers concluded in New Delhi that "special attention needed to be paid by the international community to the condition of the world's poor" (G20 2008). They did not, however, minimize the role that recipient countries would play. Good governance, including high-quality institutions and appropriate domestic policies, was also deemed necessary for globalization to work.

Picking up on the Montreal Consensus, the ministers recommitted to achieving the MDGs. They recognized that for aid to be effective, it needed to result in a real transfer of resources to developing countries. They also agreed that capacity building in recipient countries should include institutional frameworks, appropriate government policies, and community participation.

Crisis Prevention In 2001, the G20 deputy ministers had been tasked to report on crisis prevention. They concluded that countries' increasing interconnectedness exposed them more to external shocks and made them susceptible to poor domestic policies in other countries. Accountable and effective international financial institutions (IFIs) and a system of international monitoring were judged essential to a healthy international financial system. The G20 ministers and governors took note of their deputies' recommendations.

Due to increasing economic integration among countries and shared vulnerability, domestic policies were coming more and more under the purview of international institutions such as the G20. The ministers and governors implicitly recognized this shift in the concept and manifestation of sovereignty by affirming the need for sound national financial systems, alongside strengthened international architecture, to maintain a healthy global economy and reduce the risk and damage of financial crises. They also called for a more orderly process of crisis management, allowing for swifter and more coordinated international action. They specifically endorsed collective action clauses (CACs), a sovereign debt restructuring mechanism (SDRM), and a code of good practice.

Combating Terrorist Financing In 2001, the G20 ministers and bank governors had committed to freeze terrorist assets, implement international standards, and exchange information and provide technical assistance. They had also promised to review the progress made on these commitments in 2002. Taking up this remit mandate at New Delhi, they concluded that countries had indeed moved toward implementing relevant UN resolutions and enacting domestic legislation that criminalized terrorist financing. The discussions focused on the need to strengthen the formal channels for transferring money in order to reduce the use of informal ones. They also discussed developing monitoring systems and warning signals.

Achievements

The 2002 meeting was, in some respects, less successful than the first three meetings. While it broadened the discussions to focus on development and made institutional advances, with no crisis imminent the G20 took less immediate action.

The New Delhi ministerial meeting expanded the G20's attention and agenda in important ways. The G20 had featured a core agenda of three subjects discussed at every meeting—global economic growth and conditions, trade liberalization, and international codes and standards. Apart from crisis-ridden 2001, two other subjects—financial system vulnerability and crisis response and prevention (the initial focus for the forum)—were always on the built-in agenda. The great leap forward in 2000 added two items that became yearly agenda items: poverty reduction and ODA. In 2001, the G20 added terrorist finance as a continuing issue. In 2002, the international agenda brought the MDGs and NEPAD to the G20 table. It also moved beyond financial stability and crisis response to the more macroeconomic concerns of sustainable and balanced global economic growth.

In addition, the G20 troika system was officially formed to ensure that the experience of past chairs would be passed to successors (G20 2008).

Dimensions of Performance

This modest success is seen in New Delhi's particular performance on all six dimensions of G20 governance.

Domestic Political Management In domestic political management, the G20 issued one communiqué compliment, to incoming host Mexico (see Appendix D-1). This was a small step up from the year before, when no compliments had been offered. Hosting the G20 also improved the prestige of the Indian government, as India had never before hosted such an elite economic event.

However, fewer ministers travelled to New Delhi than had to G20 meetings in the previous three years. The reduced attendance was due not to a lack of confidence in the G20 or dismissal of its relevance but a straightforward issue of logistics—distance and travel time. The IMF and World Bank meetings had been held at Ottawa at the same time as the G20 meeting the year before, whereas New Delhi was a standalone G20 event.

Deliberation New Delhi's deliberative performance was the second lowest in G20 history for the annual ministerials (see Appendix E). The ministers and bank governors issued a meagre 989 words in 10 paragraphs in their communiqué, below the previous levels in 2000 and 2001. New Delhi produced no annexes.

This initial indication of declining performance, however, is strongly qualified by the particular issues on the agenda, and the iteration and innovation this agenda contained. At first glance, the individual issues showed a slow start as in 1999, with only five issues on the agenda, a great leap forward in 2000 with 19, and then a fall-off in crisis-ridden 2001 to 13. In 2002 there was a return to a high-level, broad agenda with 19 issues. In restoring the Montreal-like breadth of the G20 agenda, New Delhi was a deliberate success.

Direction Setting New Delhi's direction-setting performance saw strong advances. In particular, on democratic principles and norms, the number and spread of affirmations rose to five (see Appendix F-1). New Delhi reinforced democracy as a G20 value, by making it a priority when the group was hosted by a poor emerging country, not just when it was chaired by a rich G7 one.

Over its first four years, the G20 had come closer to the G8's core normative commitment, through significant G20 extensions toward a new consensus on embedded liberalism under globalization in the economic and social domains, and on open democracy, if not individual liberty, in the political sphere.

Since its start the G20 had constantly affirmed that its ultimate core values or targets were those of stability, growth, and equity. The 1999 communiqué had noted that the G20 sought "to achieve stable and sustainable world economic growth that benefits all." Ottawa 2001 extended this to "growth, equity, and well-being for all our peoples." New Delhi in 2002 reaffirmed in more detail the importance of "a more stable, prosperous, and equitable global economy."

The first notable normative development came in regard to open democracy. The G20 started in 1999 on the fragile foundation of transparency alone. In 2000 it quickly added international mobility and citizens' access to ideas from all countries of the world. Since 2001, good governance had formed a new core. Long democratic India's meeting in 2002 added, for the first time, worldwide surveillance, the rule of law, and support for NEPAD.

Even more important was the way the G20 progressively linked these principles in an ever tighter causal model. New Delhi put the rule of law in first place as foundational. It proclaimed that "strong institutions, a climate that fosters savings and investment, transparency, and the rule of law, coupled with increased investments in infrastructure and human capital in developing countries are *essential* ingredients for promoting growth and reducing poverty" [emphasis added].

In this G20 consensus, democracy in the form of good governance and the rule of law had thus become necessary to produce the ultimate goals of growth, equity, social well-being, and poverty reduction. Democracy for development came first. The G20 had also become indispensible in forging the links among liberalized trade, aid and finance for development, and democratic good governance.

The second normative evolution came in regard to distribution or equity. The 1990s sparse distributional principle of "growth that benefits all" expanded in 2000 to focus on income inequality, poverty reduction, and benefits to the poorest countries, the most vulnerable groups of society, and all members as individuals. Ottawa in 2001 brought minor extensions. New Delhi in 2002 added, more specifically, the MDGs. The strong, sustained commitment to delivering benefits to the poorest, most vulnerable, and all members of global society was reinforced.

The third normative development came in regard to embedded liberalism under conditions of globalization (Ruggie 1983). This centred on changes in major values related to international opening/closure and domestic opening/closure and adaptation/strengthening, and the balance among them. International openness had been a constant value. The G20 had approved "well-sequenced" and then "appropriately" sequenced capital account opening in 2002. It added the domestic interventionist principle of "no safe haven" for terrorists from 2001 onward. This normative attachment to expansive forms of international openness was tempered from the start by an emphasis on domestic protections by national governments. The domestic emphasis shifted to sound policies that accorded with international best practices, sound structural policies, and efficient and solid markets. Yet these domestically adaptive neoliberal additions were balanced by an equally strong extension into strong institutions, sound social policies, investments in infrastructure and human capital, and appropriate management of the process of reform. The overall emphasis had shifted from the question of how much and what can and should a national government protect domestically to what a national government should build domestically. However, the embryonic addition of environmental values in 1999 and 2000 ended, stopping the G20 from evolving into the consensus on embedded ecologism that had become a hallmark of the G8

(Kirton 2002). The G20 had become a development club, but not an ecologically sustainable development one.

Decision Making New Delhi put in a poor performance in the decisional realm (see Appendix G). Since the start, the annual G20 meeting had generated a steadily rising stream of collective commitments. However, in 2002 it dipped to only two—the lowest ever. One commitment was on development and the other on terrorism. The G20 had reverted to being a deliberative and direction-setting forum.

Delivery In delivery, the G20 moved to strengthen its performance, if in a tentative way. With only two commitments at New Delhi, there was little to deliver, even with the use of remit mandates or, unknown to G20 governors, the compliance catalysts that counted in the G8.

Development of Global Governance In the development of global governance, the New Delhi G20 did much better. Internally, over its first four years, the G20 did much to develop as a thicker, still flexible, innovative institution of 20 equal members. It had met the liberal-institutionalist standard of providing a predictable transaction point, with a lengthening shadow of the future, from which efficient interaction, transparency, and trust could come. The G20 had evolved into an institution that met at the ministerial level once a year, in the autumn, for a two-day event that began with an opening dinner and continued for the full next day. It had largely avoided the distractions of social events or of subgroups caucusing on a G8, emerging country, or other basis. At New Delhi, hosting by an emerging member and the troika's leadership were added.

Externally, the New Delhi G20 gave less attention to other international institutions than its two predecessors had (see Appendix C-1). But its six references exceeded the two it made to itself. Those outward references added NEPAD for the first time and focused on institutions and instruments in the development domain, reinforcing a consistency across the six performance dimensions.

Causes of Performance

The systemic club model accounts adequately for the G20's performance in 2002. The absence of major new shocks that equalize vulnerability accounts for the drop to smaller, only solid success. The causes of international institutional failure, equalizing capabilities, and democratic convergence played the most salient part in producing the meaningful, if modest, performance observed.

Shock-Activated, Equalizing Vulnerability The G20 had its first genuinely shock-free year in 2002. The 2001 financial crises in Argentina and Turkey were contained, as least as systemic concerns that afflicted the most powerful countries in the group. Although the finance ministers and bank governors acknowledged terrorist shocks in Indonesia and Russia, there were no major terrorist shocks similar to the year before as the numbers of and fatalities from terrorist attacks declined (see Appendix I). Ecological disasters, such as the oil spill from the tanker *Prestige* that affected the shores of Portugal, Spain, and France, seemed like minor concerns after the great drama of the G20's first three years. The absence of serious shocks was consistent with the low decisional performance of New Delhi.

International Institutional Failure A second cause of the G20 diminished performance was the success of its rivals in producing results, if not the reforms that responded to global demands in ways that reflected the views of the emerging democratic countries. New Delhi's lower overall performance was consistent with the IMF's accuracy in predicting global economic growth, which was high for the first time since the G20's start (see Appendix J-1). However, as its failure to produce the SDRM showed, the IMF remained an unreformed G7-controlled club. Systemically significant states such as Argentina and Korea still saw it as a source of insensitive conditionality rather than effective support when crisis struck. The Financial Stability Forum (FSF), another G7-controlled club, had no money to help with crisis response and no real interest in development or other emerging country concerns.

A reforming G7/8, now reaching out to include developing African countries as participants, did offer some competition and catalysis. The G7/8's successful prompting of democracy supported the G20's direction-setting success here. However, with regard to the need for greater inclusion, the G7/8 learned late and little from the G20 in return. At the finance ministers' level, in 1988 the G7 had begun to invite the executive heads of the multilateral World Bank and the World Trade Organization (WTO) to participate in its meetings, but did nothing after that. Not until October 2004 did the G7 invite China to participate. It added India, Brazil, and South Africa only in 2005. At the leaders' level, the G8 in 2001 had started inviting international organizations (as in 1996) and countries, concentrating on Africa. But this ad hoc experimental thrust toward inclusiveness was at the discretion of the G7 and the G8, and continued to deny emerging powers an assured and equal place. Most notably, neither the International Monetary and Financial Committee (IMFC), the FSF, the G7, nor the G8 was ever chaired by an emerging country. The G20's New Delhi ministerial in 2002 was the first time for such leadership.

Predominant, Equalizing Capability The third cause of the G20's smaller but still solid performance at Delhi was the marginally decreasing external predominance and internal equality of the members' relative capability (see Appendix K). The group's external predominance declined slightly to 81 percent of the global total, from 82 percent the two years before. Its internal equality also decreased as the Gini coefficient rose to 0.56 from 0.55 the year before and the ratio between the highest and lowest member rose to 103.59 from 86.76 the previous year.

Democratic Convergence A fourth cause of Delhi's performance, especially in direction setting, was its domestic democratic convergence, led by the fact that the meeting was hosted by the most durable democracy among the G20's emerging country ranks. In 2002, democracy in G20 polities was becoming more established, by remaining at the same level in all established and emerging members (see Appendix L). The major change was having democratic India as host. Had relative capability alone been determinative, China should have been the G20's first emerging country chair and host. Because India was allowed and accepted, it was much easier for the G20 to develop as an institution in its early years on a firm, expansive foundation of democratic norms.

Political Control, Capital, Continuity, Competence, and Commitment The fifth cause, explaining the low performance in decision making and the development of global governance externally, was a lessening of the political control, capital, continuity, competence, and commitment among G20 members. The New Delhi meeting was the first ministerial that took place without its founder, Paul Martin, who had left the Canadian cabinet in June. He was replaced by John Manley as finance minister. From Britain, Gordon Brown, although still chancellor, chose not to come, sending a junior minister, Ed Balls. France, China, Korea, and Turkey sent brand-new ministers as well (see Appendix M). John Snow represented the United States for a second time, as did Masajuro Shiokawa for Japan. The only founding fathers present were Germany's Hans Eichel, Australia's Peter Costello, South Africa's Trevor Manuel, Brazil's Pedro Malan, and Saudi Arabia's Ibrahim Al-Assaf.

The highly competent economist Manmohan Singh was in the chair. Yet as this was his first time as a G20 host, chair, and participant, it is not surprising that New Delhi's performance resembled Berlin's in 1999. Singh was very smart and thoughtful. Given the traditions he had grown up with, he was a soft spoken, quiet consensus builder. At the meeting itself, many of the ministers and governors read statements prepared by their deputies. But in the corridors Singh effectively broke the logjams that had developed.

Controlled Club Participation as a Network Hub The sixth cause of New Delhi's modest overall performance was the slowly growing character of the G20 as a controlled club at the hub of a global network. For a fourth year, no outside countries were invited. However, no new spokes were added to the network to give the G20 a performance boost.

Internally, at New Delhi the G20 became a finance ministers' group of an emerging systemic community kind. Critics and even proponents of the G20 had questioned how such a diverse group of countries with different political structures and beliefs were able to discuss and agree on international issues. Part of the response of those involved in the meetings was that the G20 remained focused on technical aspects of the financial sector. The emerging countries' finance ministers and central bankers were knowledgeable and sophisticated individuals, even if the financial systems in the countries they represented varied in sophistication. There was a similar view and expertise across all the countries. David Dodge (2001), the governor of the Bank of Canada who had attended the G20 meetings in 2001 and 2002, reported that the ministers and central bankers, starting at the meetings in 2001, talked to each other as equals, and had a lot in common: "it's not as difficult as one might think because a lot of our backgrounds are similar and certainly we understand the issues in a similar way." The G20 was never supposed to be a forum where developing countries could learn from developed ones. This was a meeting of equals, with highly skilled individuals coming together to solve global economic problems that required an unprecedented degree of international cooperation and coordination. In 2002, with Singh in the chair, the epistemic community character of the group was advanced.

Externally, the global finance and economic network connected by the G20 at the hub resumed its routine functioning, following the suspension due to the September 11 terrorist attacks the year before.

Morelia 2003

The Challenge

The following year, in 2003, for the second year in a row, the G20 finance meeting was hosted by a democratic emerging member. Under Mexico's leadership at Morelia, two main themes were addressed—global economic recovery and sustainable economic growth—with the finance ministers and central bank governors seeking to address the imbalances among developed countries and between the developed and less developed ones. They continued to discuss issues that had been prominent when India was chair: crisis prevention and resolution, globalization, combating terrorist financing, and financing for development. Preventing the abuse of the financial system and promoting transparency and information exchange were added to the agenda. Members also reflected further on future priorities (G20 2008).

The American-led invasion in Iraq in the spring of 2003 created challenges for the group. Mexico and Germany questioned whether the world had become too dependent on the US economy. The US current account deficit and public deficit were raised as problems. Federal Reserve chair Alan Greenspan admitted that the US economy had experienced a setback due to recent conflicts such as the war in Iraq. John Snow, the US treasury secretary, pushed for initiatives to counteract terrorism and encouraged members to donate to Iraqi reconstruction. Snow placed the onus for economic growth on Europe and Asia. He discussed these issues in private bilateral meetings with officials from Russia, China, Argentina, Germany, Mexico, Turkey, South Africa, and France (Watson 2003). However, most members did not share the cause that drove this American military-inspired leadership.

Competing Assessments Morelia's performance was the subject of competing assessments among three major schools of thought. One school argued that the G20 failed because it was diverted from its intended discussions. Its proponents did not consider the G20 meeting an appropriate time or place to discuss issues such as Iraqi debt (ITAR-TASS 2003).

A second school argued that it was successful in getting the global economic recovery underway (Perez 2003).

A third school of thought argued that the Mexico meeting proved the G20 was an effective consensus-building forum, with a good mix of political and technical expertise (G20 2008).

The Argument This section argues that Mexico's G20 meeting was another small, solid success. It was most successful in its internal development of global governance by advancing the structural and institutional components of the G20. It did less well in dealing with the policy substance of the issues it addressed. The finance ministers and bank governors were able to move beyond crisis response and adopt commitments on issues such as corruption. However, they were preoccupied by different, distracting shocks that had hit their countries in the year since the New Delhi meeting. In addition, the recent, divisive, American-led invasion into Iraq stifled discussions and constrained decision making.

Plans and Preparations

The first plans for the Mexican meeting were announced days after the conclusion of the Indian one. The Mexican treasury department suggested that the working agenda include the topics of globalization and crisis prevention and resolution, with a particular focus on sovereign debt. It also proposed that tax havens be discussed (*El Economista* 2002).

To prepare for the annual gathering, several preparatory meetings, conferences, and workshops were held. The G20 deputies met for the first time in Cancún on March 3–4, 2003. Six themes were selected for the ministerial agenda: crisis prevention and resolution, prevention of abuse of the international financial system, promotion of transparency and information exchange, globalization and the role of institution building in the financial sector, financing for development, and the fight against terrorist financing. Several days later, on March 9, a conference was held in Paris to discuss proposals for improving the "international debt workout mechanism" (G20 Finance 2003c). On May 26, the G20 held a seminar on sovereign debt restructuring in Mexico City (G20 Finance 2003c).

The G20 deputies met for a second time in London on September 24–25. This time only four themes were selected for discussion: financing for development and combating terrorist financing from the earlier meeting, plus debt restructuring as well as globalization and economic growth (G20 Finance 2003c). For the first time, the G20 launched discussions on the importance of building financial institutions that would foster economic development and growth. These discussions would be taken up again in 2004 at a meeting in Ottawa, co-hosted by Germany and Canada (G20 Finance 2004).

For the October 26–27 ministerial meeting in Morelia, Mexico prepared discussion papers on crisis prevention and resolution, prevention of abuse of the international financial system, the promotion of transparency and information exchange, globalization and economic growth, and the role of institution building in the financial sector. The UK contributed to the paper on financing for development and the US helped prepare background material for the paper on combating terrorist financing (G20 Finance 2003c).

At the Meeting

The main issues at Morelia were crisis prevention and resolution, prevention of abuse of the international financial system, the promotion of transparency and information exchange, globalization and economic growth, and globalization and the role of institution building in the financial sector. Five less important issues were also on the agenda: the deputies had prepared a report on combating terrorist financing in addition to the one on financing for development; the Bank of Mexico made a presentation on the 16 case studies—from all members but Argentina, Indonesia, Saudi Arabia, and the European Union—on the effects of globalization; the future and effectiveness of the G20 was discussed; and participants formally decided on which country would chair the next year (G20 Finance 2003b).

In their 2003 communiqué, the G20 finance ministers and bank governors highlighted the importance of balanced growth. As at the APEC ministerial meeting on October 17–18 just a few days earlier in Bangkok, Thailand, the G20 focused on reviving trade talks again, after disappointing discussions at the fifth WTO ministerial conference in Cancún on September 10–14. They also reaffirmed their mandate on crisis prevention and resolution and reviewed progress on terrorist financing and money laundering, as they had promised to do in 2002. They reaffirmed their commitment to tackling global poverty and to implementing the MDGs and Monterrey development commitments. For the first time, the G20 announced who would host the next two summits—Germany in 2004 and China in 2005—reinforcing the developing tradition of rotating from an advanced country to an emerging one.

Certain participants also came with issues of their own. John Snow, having flown directly from an Iraq donors' conference in Madrid, Spain, pushed the G20 to help clear Iraq's debt. Not all, such as Russia's finance minister Alexei Kudrin, were enthusiastic about this proposal. Iraq was not mentioned in the final communiqué. Snow also encouraged China to adopt a more flexible currency system and asked the European and Asian countries to strengthen their economic growth, so that the United States would not have to be the sole engine of growth. Argentinean finance minister Roberto Lavagna met with representatives from the G7 on the sidelines to discuss the financial difficulties facing Argentina. German finance minister Hans Eichel—who would chair the G20 the following year—

pushed for a voluntary code of conduct for crisis prevention to be established by the end of the year (Authers 2003).

Achievements

The achievements at Morelia were limited. The main advance was achieving a consensus on resolving financial crises. The "key breakthrough" was the deputies' announcement of collective action clauses in an international bond at their meeting in March (G20 2008). CACs provide a framework for restructuring debt if a debtor cannot honour the loan commitments.

Dimensions of Performance

The limited achievements at Morelia were reflected in the G20's six specific dimensions of performance.

Domestic Political Management In its domestic political management, Morelia performance was limited. The G20 issued two communiqué compliments, the second highest number in the G20's first five years (see Appendix D-1). One went to Mexico for its "excellent leadership." The other went to Germany for offering to host the 2004 meeting. There was little evidence, however, that Mexico had effectively used its position as chair to advance its political agenda on the domestic front.

Deliberation In the deliberative domain, performance was limited as well. Morelia offered only a nine-paragraph communiqué, with no annexes. At 1,185 words, it was the third lowest to date, although higher than the previous year (see Appendix E). The focus was on macroeconomics, followed by trade and financial regulation. Earlier issues were dropped. The G20 thus continued to be a flexible forum, with a sound balance of iteration and innovation, in response to changing global demands.

Direction Setting Direction setting saw a retreat. The Morelia meeting made only three references to democratic principles: one to good governance and two to information and knowledge exchange (see Appendix F-1). The communiqué declared that "the G20 is uniquely placed to deepen the linkages between aid, good governance, financing and trade." The number and spread of affirmations of distributional and embedded liberal principles also declined.

Decision Making In the decisional realm, with six commitments the G20 bounced back from the low of the previous year (see Appendix G). Morelia's six commitments came in the areas of macroeconomics and corruption, with two apiece, and trade and terrorism. The finance ministers and bank governors made their first commitment on corruption, an issue particularly important to the Mexican host.

Delivery While there were not many decisions, delivery on those commitments was nonetheless strong. Most G20 members whose implementation was measured complied with their 2003 commitments to a high degree, with an average score of +0.42 (71 percent), on a scale from +1.00 to –1.00 (see Appendix H-1). The G20 meeting thus equalled the G8 summits in compliance at the same time. Indeed, the five measured non-G8 members of the G20 complied with the commitments made at the G8's 2003 Evian Summit to the same high degree (see Appendix H-2). These G20 members appeared ready for regular participation or even full membership in the G8 club. Compliance was strongest on financial abuse, terrorism, and trade. G8 members did better than non-G8 members in complying with their Morelia commitments, but not by much and not in each individual case. The G20 was becoming a group of equals in this critical respect.

Development of Global Governance In the development of global governance, the Morelia G20 moved ahead modestly. Internally, the G20's self-institutionalization advanced, when the participants declared what country would chair the meeting not only in 2004 (Germany), but also in 2005 (China). The rotation between established and emerging country members thus became the norm.

Externally, at Morelia the G20 doubled the number of references to other international institutions, producing twice as many as the year before (see Appendix C-1). These 14 references dwarfed the four to the G20 itself. The IMF, with five, regained its historic lead.

Causes of Performance

The systemic club model of G20 governance again accounts adequately for the performance of the G20 in 2003.

Shock-Activated, Equalizing Vulnerability The most salient shock was a deliberate, old-style, conscious state-driven one as the US-led coalition invaded Iraq in March 2003. This fuelled an inequality in the vulnerability among G20 members, few of which invaded Iraq alongside the United States. The price of oil rose to a new high of $37.96 per barrel, the highest since the G20 was created in 1999—although the peak came just before the invasion and its effects had worn off by the time the G20 met in the fall (see Appendix I). The number of terrorist attacks remained low.

Heat waves in Europe and India caused challenges in 2003. More than 40,000 Europeans and more than 1,200 Indians died as a result. Severe acute respiratory syndrome (SARS) was also a major concern. By the end of the year, more than 8,000 cases and 774 deaths had been reported (World Health Organization 2004). However, these shocks, which showed members' new vulnerability, were too new for the G20 to take up and forge a link from finance and economics on the one hand to health and the environment on the other, and the reverse.

International Institutional Failure There was less international institutional failure in 2003 than in previous years. The UN refused to approve the US-led invasion of Iraq. The IMF predicted global economic growth with high accuracy (see Appendix J-1).

Above all, the G8, expanding again to include more Europeans in its summit, finally reached out to invite emerging countries from the G20 as well. Among the many non-G8 members that France invited to its Evian Summit were China, India, Brazil, Mexico, and Saudi Arabia. But some still considered this to be second-class participation, on a one-time basis, at the discretion of the G8 host. Moreover, at the finance ministers' level, the G7 still froze everyone else completely out of its club (see Appendix J-3).

Predominant, Equalizing Capabilities There were marginal declines in the G20's global predominance and internal equality (as measured by the Gini coefficient) in gross domestic product (see Appendix K). The gap between its most powerful and weakest members plunged back to the 2001 level. Elsewhere, the G8's summit outreach was a rational response to changing relative capability in the world.

Common Principles of Democracy The G20's convergence to democratic principles remained constant in the 2003 meeting. There were no significant shifts in promoting democratic principles or practices at home (see Appendix L). All members remained relatively free, with the exceptions of China and Saudi Arabia, which remained undemocratic; and Russia, Indonesia, and Turkey, which continued to straddle the line between free and non-democratic. Cumulatively, another year of widely shared democracy among the members slowly strengthened the common principles of the club.

Political Control, Capital, Continuity, and Competence Political continuity at the Morelia meeting was low. Brand-new finance ministers came from the Brazil, China, Japan, Korea, and the US (see Appendix M-2). Attending for only the second time were those from Argentina, Canada, France, India, and Turkey. The inexperience showed in the case of the US, whose new treasury secretary, John Snow, forcefully sought to use the meeting to advance America's Iraq agenda shared by few others, to little effect.

Controlled Club Participation as a Network Hub Internally, at Morelia, the G20 continued for a fifth year to function as a compact group with the same countries as members since its start. But cohesion was disturbed by the approach of the new American treasury secretary.

Externally, the network around the G20 expanded. The Morelia ministerial saw an outburst of bilateral activity, especially on the part of the Americans. This negatively affected the tenor and impact of the meeting, but enhanced its status as a network node. More importantly, in 2003 G20 members headed all the major international financial institutions apart from the Basel Committee on Banking

Supervision (BCBS), which had moved from the US to Spain (see Appendix J-2). In August 2003 a group of developing countries, also referred to as the G20, came together on the issue of trade and met for the first time following the WTO ministerial meeting in Cancún in September.[1] The APEC summit and finance ministers' meeting was held in Bangkok just before the G20's Morelia meeting.

Conclusion

Even as the G20 expanded its hosting and agenda, it stayed close to the core principles it had adopted from its parent G7/8—open democracy, individual liberty, and social advance. It did so even after the shocks activating its members' equalizing vulnerability diminished and normalcy returned. After its first five years, the G20 thus had established itself as an institution with the capacity to address some of the more difficult systemic financial issues. Beyond strict financial regulation, the G20 had begun to extend its influence in the realms of globalization, terrorism, and development.

The achievements of its first three years largely endured, even as hosting passed from G7 countries to democratic emerging country members. In New Delhi in 2002, the strong emphasis on both development and democracy indicated that the G20's most democratic and second most powerful emerging country member had bought into the still fledgling group, where it would prove influential. In Morelia in 2003, Mexico's G20 meeting confirmed the trend. The stage was thus set for another strong advance when the G20 returned the next year to where it had started, Berlin.

References

Authers, John. 2003. "G20 Meeting Upbeat over Outlook for World Economy." *Financial Times*, October 28.

Ben-Ishai, Elizabeth, Aburto, Daniella, Fiorello, Carrie, Harrison, Judah, and Dolkar, Karma. 2002. "G20 in New Delhi: Fight Trade Barriers and Money Laundering." *G8 Bulletin*, November 18–24. Available at: www.g8.utoronto.ca/g8bulletin/vol6/issue12.htm. Accessed: July 2012.

Dodge, David. 2001. "Interview with Candida Tamar Paltiel." November 18. Available at: www.g8.utoronto.ca/oralhistory. Accessed: July 2012.

El Economista. 2002. "Mexico to Preside over G20 During 2003." November 25.

1 The G20 developing countries consists of 23 members: Argentina, Bolivia, Brazil, Chile, China, Cuba, Ecuador, Egypt, Guatemala, India, Indonesia, Mexico, Nigeria, Pakistan, Paraguay, Peru, the Philippines, South Africa, Tanzania, Thailand, Uruguay, Venezuela, and Zimbabwe.

G20. 2008. "The Group of Twenty: A History." Available at: www.g20.utoronto.ca/docs/g20history.pdf. Accessed: July 2012.
G20 Finance Ministers and Central Bank Governors. 2002. "Delhi Communiqué." Delhi, November 23. Available at: www.g20.utoronto.ca/2002/2002communique.html. Accessed: July 2012.
G20 Finance Ministers and Central Bank Governors. 2003a. "Economic Reform in this Era of Globalization: 16 Country Cases." Available at: www.g20.utoronto.ca/docs/economicreform.pdf. Accessed: July 2012.
G20 Finance Ministers and Central Bank Governors. 2003b. "G20 Communiqué." Morelia, Mexico, October 27. Available at: www.g20.utoronto.ca/2003/2003communique.html. Accessed: July 2012.
G20 Finance Ministers and Central Bank Governors. 2003c. "Mexico 2003: G20 Work Program." Available at: www.g20.utoronto.ca/2003/2003program.pdf. Accessed: July 2012.
G20 Finance Ministers and Central Bank Governors. 2004. "G20 Workshop on Developing Strong Domestic Financial Markets." April 26–27. Available at: www.g20.utoronto.ca/docs/financialmarketsworkshop.pdf. Accessed: July 2012.
Gruen, David, O'Brien, Terry, and Lawson, Jeremy, eds. 2002. *Globalisation, Living Standards, and Inequality: Recent Progress and Continuing Challenges*. Sydney, Australia: Reserve Bank of Australia. Available at: www.g20.utoronto.ca/biblio/rba-at-2002.pdf. Accessed: July 2012.
Gupta, Surojit and Friel, Terry. 2002. "G20 Nations Unsure How to Cut Money for Terrorism." Reuters, November 24.
ITAR-TASS. 2003. "It Is Premature to Discuss Donations to Iraq—Kudrin." October 27.
Kirton, John J. 2002. "Global Community Outreach: The G20 and Africa." G8 Online, Lecture No. 9. Available at: www.g8.utoronto.ca/g8online/2002/english/2002/09.html. Accessed: July 2012.
Kirton, John J. 2010a. "The G20 Finance Ministers: Network Governance." In *Rising States, Rising Institutions: Can the World Be Governed?*, eds Alexandroff, Alan S., and Cooper, Andrew F. Washington DC: Brookings Institution Press, 196–217.
Kirton, John J. 2010b. "The G20, the G8, the G5, and the Role of Ascending Powers." Paper prepared for a presentation at a seminar on "Ascending Powers and the International System," December 14, Mexico City. Available at: www.g20.utoronto.ca/biblio/kirton-g20-g8-g5.pdf. Accessed: July 2012.
Kirton, John J. 2010c. "The Group of Eight's Legacy, Limitations, and Lessons." In *The New Dynamics of Summitry: Innovations for G20 Summits*, eds Bradford, Colin I., and Lim, Wonhyuk. Washington DC and Seoul: Brookings Institution Press and Korea Development Institute, 17–60.
Luce, Edward. 2002. "G20 Countries Disagree on Debt Defaults." *Financial Times*, November 25.

Mahapatra, Rajesh. 2002. "G20 Ministers Agree on Early Removal of Trade Barriers and Phasing Out Subsidies." Associated Press, November 23.

Mukherji, Biman. 2002. "Worldwide Trade to Benefit from G20 Pledge." Agence France Presse, November 24.

Perez, Santiago. 2003. "G20 Summit Ends, Sees Global Economic Recovery Underway." Dow Jones, October 27.

Ruggie, John G. 1983. "International Regimes, Transactions, and Change: Embedded Liberalism in the Postwar Economic Order." In *International Regimes*, ed Krasner, Stephen D. Ithaca: Cornell University Press, 195–232.

Salai-i-Martin, Xavier and Mohapatra, Sanket. 2003. "Poverty, Inequality, and the Distribution of Income in the Group of 20." *Economic Roundup* Autumn. Available at: archive.treasury.gov.au/documents/580/HTML/docshell.asp?URL=Poverty_Inequality.asp. Accessed: July 2012.

Watson, Sheri. 2003. "G20 Bulletin." October 28. Available at: www.g8.utoronto.ca/g20bulletin/g20v2n1.htm. Accessed: July 2012.

World Health Organization. 2004. "Summary of Probable SARS Cases with Onset of Illness from 1 November 2002 to 31 July 2003." Geneva. Available at: www.who.int/csr/sars/country/table2004_04_21/en. Accessed: July 2012.

Chapter 7
Bonding Berlin, Berlin 2004

Introduction

The Challenge

As the Group of 20 (G20) finance ministers and central bank governors met for the sixth time, in Berlin on November 20–21, 2004, two paths lay ahead. The first took the G20 back to its core concern with financial stability, which had been the focus the first time an initially reluctant Germany had hosted in 1999. The second path, building on all that the G20 had done since, led down a wider road to become a greater centre of global governance, to make globalization work for all, and to promote development through more economic, social, and political openness in a globalized world.

The G20 had evolved over its first five years from a forum focused on finance and economics to one widening its agenda, setting new normative directions, and taking and delivering collective decisions. It was also developing global governance by thickening its own institutional structure and working in conscious cooperation as well as implicit competition with other multilateral organizations and plurilateral institutions. The G20 increasingly had an autonomous, direct impact by bridging differences between and within its developed and emerging members and in hastening agreement on important issues in outside forums.

The success of the G20 was based in part on working with the similarly constructed, much more experienced, and much more cohesive Group of Seven (G7) in support of the largely shared principles of transparency, openness, democracy, and social advance. A steady succession of shocks to these values had had a significant impact in deepening the G20 as an autonomous, well-guided institution, where increasingly emerging countries could lead, most members could exercise influence, and all could start to accept a growing array of democratic norms.

As 2004 began, the impact of the 1997–2002 economic shocks and the 2001 terrorist ones receded further, particularly as strong global economic growth returned. The International Monetary Fund ([IMF] 2004) reported that the world economy was picking up after the lows of 2003. Indeed, it forecast the best back-to-back years for growth in more than a decade, based on good fundamentals in Asia, including Indonesia, Korea, Malaysia, Singapore, and Thailand. There was also growth in some larger Latin American countries, particularly Argentina and Brazil. The G7 finance ministers and the leaders of the Group of Eight (G8), when the latter met at Sea Island in the United States in the summer of 2004, made much of this upward economic turn. For the G20, however, a further move away from severe financial and economic shocks meant a reconsideration of its core mission. Since members had come together to deal with the Asian-turned-global financial crisis of 1997–99, and stayed together to address the new challenges brought about by the 2001 terrorist attacks on America, a stable, secure global financial and economic system posed a potentially existential threat. Could the G20, created and continued as a crisis response group, survive sustained, strong, secure, global economic growth?

It could, and did, in part because such growth brought new challenges. The rising price of oil in particular was a considerable concern. The IMF had highlighted the resulting risks of an economic downturn. The warning was echoed by the G20 in its 2004 communiqué, as ministers noted that the risks had "increased due to oil price volatility, persisting external imbalances and geo-political concerns" (G20 Finance 2004a). The reference to geopolitical concerns suggested that the G20 was again broadening its agenda, and losing its reticence about embracing global security on a broader scale, doing so the year after an American-led coalition—without Germany, Japan, France, Canada, and almost all non-G8 members of the G20—had invaded Iraq.

Moreover, the global balance of economic power was shifting. Europe was still not growing strongly. Its structural problems of an older economy and population without an intense drive to innovate and expand contrasted sharply with a vibrant America and China, India, and the rest of the emerging world. Emerging markets in developing countries were increasingly where the economic action was. Russia was steadily growing due to strong oil prices. For 2005, the IMF ominously predicted a temporary slowdown in the world economy, but with still solid growth, in Asia above all.

This vibrant emerging country growth, the new challenges it brought and the G20's broadening agenda created the conditions for a move to the leaders' level, to become a summit-level group. The election of Paul Martin as Canada's prime minister provided the individual needed to start such a serious thrust.

Competing Assessments

As the Berlin meeting approached and in its aftermath, assessments of the G20 began to converge on several main views, inspiring a debate among four competing schools of thought.

The first school saw the G20 as a failure in addressing the critical issue of exchange rates, as it was difficult to achieve much consensus or action not already accomplished elsewhere, due to the lack of American interest. This school of thought felt foreign exchange rates were the most important issue, but that the G20 would issue only general statements because US interest in the issue was not as strong as Europe's (Thomas 2004a). The exchange rate question, which loomed large before the meeting but was not officially on the agenda, led some to conclude that the G20 was not effective on significant, pressing concerns (Brown

2004). The yuan had depreciated along with the dollar, making Chinese exports even more competitive elsewhere. Economist Huang Yiping did not expect that foreign exchange would be a priority of Chinese policy makers (Brown 2004). Just before the Berlin meeting, US treasury secretary John Snow said that the G20 was not the appropriate forum for discussing exchange rates (Reuters 2004). After the meeting, the G20 was criticized for its inability to calm worried markets, as it showed no interest in intervening in the foreign exchange market.

A second school felt that the Berlin G20 was a specialized success, performing well within its relatively constricted core field of financial regulation. Caio Koch-Weser, a secretary of state at the German finance ministry, downplayed the issue of exchange rate volatility, noting there was a need "to be realistic about what could be discussed in so large a gathering" (Agence France Presse 2004c).

A third school, led by Paul Martin, thought that the G20 was sufficiently successful that it should be a comprehensive, leaders-level governance centre for the future. Australia's treasurer Peter Costello supported transforming the G20 into a leaders-level meeting, noting that "it is very hard to discuss economic co-ordination without having China at the table" (Uren 2004). Gordon Smith (2004), a former Canadian deputy minister of foreign affairs, supported Martin's initiative, seeing a G20 summit as a means of better managing "our increasingly global interdependence." Similarly, Lawrence Summers, former US treasury secretary, said that the G7 was no longer the forum to discuss issues of truly global importance; instead, the G20 was the more appropriate body (*Business Times Singapore* 2004). World Bank president James Wolfensohn also called for a more important role for the G20, but without entirely sidelining the G8: "there is a need for an additional instrument, a need to have a G20 with China, India, South Africa and representatives from Islamic countries" (Agence France Presse 2004h).

A fourth school claimed even more expansively that the G20 would and should soon replace the G8. Colin Bradford and Johannes Linn (2004) argued that beyond population and economic weight, globalization had changed the way countries interacted with each other economically and that the integration of financial markets meant that a new kind of international governance was required. Governance could no longer be compartmentalized into different issue areas because policy domains increasingly overlapped. Only the G20 was sufficiently representative and had a broad enough mandate to deal with this new governance challenge. "At the highest political level, there was no other representative forum mandated to address these inter-sectoral and inter-institutional issues, which are part of the G-20's founding principles" (Bradford and Linn 2004, 4). In order to respond to the imbalances in the global governance structures, they advocated elevating the G20 to the leaders' level. Paul Heinbecker, Canada's former ambassador to the United Nations, also saw the G20 replacing the G8, but not competing with or challenging the UN: "the G20 could go a long way to get consensus among a diverse group of countries, but the UN will remain the international body with the most legitimacy by virtue of its broad membership" (McCarthy 2004).

The Argument

This chapter argues that the G20's 2004 Berlin meeting met most expectations for growing G20 governance, but not the leap to the leaders' level itself. It proved to be a strong success. It made major advances in agenda setting and policy adjustment on macroeconomic policy coordination, including exchange rates, debt restructuring, and reform of international financial institutions (IFIs). It set new highs in deliberation and democratic direction setting, and performed strongly on decision making and the development of global governance.

This strong performance was not primarily driven by new shocks, especially ones with sufficient strength to catalyse a G20 summit. It was driven more by the failure of the Bretton Woods bodies, and even the G7/8 to move on issues important to emerging countries, notably debt restructuring and IFI reform. Simultaneously, the American-hosted G8 Sea Island Summit demoted the systemically significant countries from their initial inclusion the year before in France. The rising relative capability of the G20's emerging members made their influence increasingly felt. The largely continuing democratic character of G20 members meant cumulating cohesion for the group. Founding veterans Hans Eichel as chair, Britain's Gordon Brown, South Africa's Trevor Manuel, Australia's Peter Costello, and Saudi Arabia's Ibrahim Al-Assaf—key figures from both the advanced and emerging economies in equal measure—guided the group toward consensus and collective success. Founding visionary Paul Martin, now Canada's prime minister, led a campaign to make the G20 a leaders-level group known as the Leaders 20 (L20). With such continuity, and especially with the conversion of a once skeptical Eichel into a G20 enthusiast, the G20 moved further toward becoming a non-crisis-created club in a social-psychological sense as well as in a rational instrumental sense.

Martin's Initiative for an L20

Paul Martin had long felt that the world needed a G20 summit. As finance minister, he had never discussed the idea directly with Prime Minister Jean Chrétien, because there was little support for the notion there. Chrétien and Canada's Department of Foreign Affairs and International Trade had doubts about the G20, based on the apparent dilution of Canada's influence relative to the G7/8 in a wider group. But Martin felt that the G20 must meet at the highest level, on the grounds that it made sense to include China, India, Brazil, and South Africa at the leaders' table, given the issues that had to be discussed.

When Martin became prime minister, he immediately put in place a process designed to bring a G20 summit to life. At a dinner in Ottawa on the night before he formally became prime minister, he raised the idea with China's Wen Jiabao (Martin 2010). He received strong support. The initial reservations among G8 members were eroding and the enthusiasm of the G20's non-G8 members was strong. But when Martin mentioned the idea at his first meeting with George W. Bush, the US president would not address the issue. At the Sea Island Summit, hosted by Bush, Martin (2010) argued it made no sense not to have the leaders of such emerging powers as China, India, and Brazil meet with them. The idea was raised and acknowledged at the collective leaders' table, but again Bush would not engage. Indeed, Martin referred to the issue of a G20 summit every time he met Bush, to no effect. But elsewhere Martin's global tour to press the case had a reward. Russia's Vladimir Putin showed an interest. Japan's Junichiro Koizumi initially opposed the concept but subsequently shifted, saying he would come to one such summit and, if it worked, would come to more.

It thus seemed possible that a G20 summit would emerge as early as the following year. Martin pressed his idea in Paris, Moscow, and Washington. Italian foreign minister Franco Frattini, after speaking with his Canadian counterpart Pierre Pettigrew, said that he supported the Canadian initiative to hold a G20 summit (Agence France Presse 2004d). German finance minister Hans Eichel said that "the G20 has not yet totally exploited its potential … I think that we can theoretically expect to see, at some time or another in the future, a G20 with heads of state and government" (Agence France Presse 2004a). After the Berlin meeting, Japanese officials supported the idea of an expanded, more representative leaders' forum, although some suggested that the G20 was perhaps too large a group (Waki 2004).

Officials in Washington also spoke in even more reserved fashion of the growing importance of the G20. A few days before US treasury secretary John Snow left for the Berlin meeting, a treasury official said that "each (G20) meeting has more and more significance as a forum for discussion," adding that "it's a very good forum for discussing emerging market issues, the success of collective action clauses, further reforms in the IMF" (Agence France Presse 2004g).

Plans and Preparations

To prepare for the Berlin ministerial, two deputies' meetings and three workshops were held. The first workshop, held in Ottawa on April 26–27, was on developing strong domestic markets. The second, held in Paris on July 1–2, was on demography and growth. The third workshop, held in Beijing on September 22–23, was on regional economic integration in a global framework.

The potential of the G20 was reinforced by the G7 finance ministers and the G8. The G7 finance ministers' meeting in Dubai in September 2003 had been somewhat of a hand-off to the G20. At the G7 finance ministers' meeting in Boca Raton, Florida, in February 2004, Ralph Goodale, Martin's newly appointed finance minister, proposed moving from the more exclusive G7 to a G20 meeting. At the American-hosted G8 summit at Sea Island on June 8–10, the issue of expanding the membership of the G8, or moving over to a leaders' G20 was collectively raised.

In November, Eichel said that the unexpectedly high price of oil would be a significant item at Berlin. He was less specific about exchange rates, saying that the G7 finance ministers would discuss dollar-euro exchange rates if the euro continued its upward trend. However, before the Berlin meeting began, Eichel confirmed that exchange rates would not be on the G20's official agenda. The high euro and weak dollar, however, were nevertheless expected to be discussed.

A day before the meeting, US treasury secretary Snow emphasized that the G20 would not discuss foreign exchange rates. British chancellor of the exchequer Gordon Brown was also expected to steer G20 discussions away from exchange rates, instead pushing his own priority of the demographics of aging societies. Officially, the G20 meeting was to focus on promoting economic growth and increasing trade liberalization, taking into account Europe's slow economic recovery.

At the Meeting

In his opening address at Berlin, Eichel stated that the major goal of the G20 would be to combat threats to the international financial system, including terrorist finance, money laundering, and unjust tax systems.

Economic and Development Issues

The first issue for discussion was current economic and development concerns. The IMF had prepared a note on the subject. US Federal Reserve chair Alan Greenspan spoke first, giving a balanced and positive view of the US recovery. He noted, however, that this recovery was not reflected in significant increases in capital investment. There was a flattening of profit margins in the private sector, and the high productivity rates of the past would likely slow down. There was also a temporary increase in core inflation. While higher energy prices had not yet affected wages, Greenspan said he would be watching closely. He was optimistic about reducing the American deficit. He expected revenue to increase with growth, although there were still long-term problems in Asia. He issued a warning about the dollar, particularly with the balance of payments showing aggregate demand for dollar assets falling below American financing needs. Current account balances would have to adjust. He was relatively optimistic that this could happen without massive exchange rate adjustments, provided capital and labour flexibility continued.

After Greenspan, the only other reference to exchange rates was made by Jean-Claude Trichet, president of the European Central Bank (ECB). He said there was no clear signal that a rise in the value of the euro would hurt recovery in Europe—contrary to his earlier public statements. The discrepancy revealed how the G20 had become a forum where members could speak freely with one another, able to offer opinions without fear of public reaction. After the meeting, many of the participants commented on exchange rates. Most, including Japanese, Turkish, Italian, and Saudi representatives, argued that rapid change in either foreign exchange rates or oil prices would only further upset the unbalanced economy (Reuters 2004).

With respect to global balances, Trichet noted that developing countries were financing the industrial countries with their savings, while it should be the other way around. There was consensus among all but the United States that the American current account and budget deficits were a major cause of macroeconomic instability. Europe and Japan both had account surpluses, supporting the American deficit. While one US official denied that the United States had been "put on the hot seat" with respect to its fiscal deficit, Snow acknowledged his commitment to the principles of budget balancing and his responsibility to the other G20 member countries: "I wanted my colleagues ... to know of the earnestness and sincerity and depth of our commitment to dealing with the deficit ... I wanted them to understand that this administration is absolutely committed to fiscally responsible behavior" (Agence France Presse 2004f).

The Germans challenged the other Europeans to match American productivity levels, and called for more international labour flows to this end. Snow was encouraged by what he called the more sophisticated treatment of issues than he found in the media. World Bank president James Wolfensohn presented research showing that recent oil price rises had a $25 billion negative impact on low-income countries. P. Chidambaram, India's finance minister, was also very concerned about rising oil prices, which had peaked at $55 a barrel earlier in the year. Yet the G20 finance ministers and bank governors, consistent with the IMF *World Economic Outlook*, predicted slower but stable growth of around 4 percent.

Development was a significant concern. Brown was very worried about the lack of progress in achieving the Millennium Development Goals (MDGs). He drew attention to the forthcoming 2005 MDG Summit at the United Nations, where it would have to be acknowledged that many African countries were "a century away" from meeting the goals. He wanted to resolve debt relief issues and provide financing for development. He was vocal about developing countries, outlining plans for the G8 summit that Britain would host in 2005 at Gleneagles and its focus on the concerns of developing countries, particularly in Africa. Brown's concern demonstrated how the G20 had become a forum where developing country issues and distributional norms, including those of the poorest countries not at the table, could be advanced by their G8 and G20 allies despite more reluctant members, including the United States.

Financial System Abuse

The second issue was combating the abuse of the financial system, with a focus on tax evasion. There was broad support for the considerable work of the Organisation for Economic Co-operation and Development (OECD) in trying to mobilize more international cooperation. On money laundering, Mexican finance minister Francisco Gil Díaz suggested that outgoing transactions be routed through an international centre, such as the IMF or the Bank for International Settlements, that would serve as a clearing-house to scan for suspicious transactions and communicate with national authorities. Many participants welcomed China's imminent membership in the Financial Action Task Force (FATF) as another sign of China's growing integration into global policy-making bodies. It was a move that would make the G20 group more of a network hub.

Demographic Challenges

The third issue built on the workshop held in July on the emerging demographic challenges for both developed and developing countries. For developed countries such as Germany, the concern was aging-related budgetary pressures. In developing countries, the issue was a rise in the working-age population. Participants at Berlin referred to the workshop, pointing out the importance of retaining a stable financial system that controlled flows at different points of demographic transition. Their communiqué called for more intensive monitoring and for the IMF to produce an integrated analysis of long-term challenges and an analysis every four years for every country. The IMF had not expected this request.

Sustained Growth and the Reform Agenda

The fourth issue generated two of the additional documents issued at the meeting—on sustained growth and on implementing policies in this regard. While some wanted to call the reform agenda a "consensus," others argued successfully that a Washington "consensus" was not a good thing to replicate. The reform agenda consisted of a collection of unilateral policy statements by each of the members. The most notable feature was the absence of any reference to exchange rate flexibility in the lengthy section on China. The list was mostly a reiteration of previous policies and commitments, much like the G7/8 agenda its members had been following. But the exercise showed growth in the structure and cohesion of the G20 as a group. Members now recognized they had to assess their own reforms on the basis of what they had written down. Self-assessment in a collective context, as an initial step in accountability, had begun.

Financial Sector Strengthening

There was no discussion of "regional economic integration" in a global context. Institution building in the financial sector, however, generated a fair amount of dialogue. The relevant report of the deputy finance ministers was welcomed by their ministers, who agreed to keep the issue on the agenda. The Australians pointed to the need for countries to have deep markets in domestic currency debt. David Dodge, Canada's central bank governor, pushed hard for adherence to international standards and codes. He argued that standards must be made less voluntary and enforced in some countries, implying that it was the role of the international institutions to monitor and enforce them. On the question of insolvency rights, most participants welcomed the World Bank's work in developing a set of principles.

China called for assistance from the World Bank, the IMF, and the G20 to help it urgently upgrade its insolvency regime.

Capital Flows and Debt Restructuring

In the discussion on capital flows and debt restructuring, several representatives participated in a free-flowing, productive exchange. Argentina, in default of its international loans, did not even attend the Berlin meeting, as it did not want to be criticized by colleagues demanding their money back. More importantly, Argentina objected to the code of good conduct agreed to by the G20. The principles of the code, strongly supported by Brazil, were to strengthen transparency by the issuer, maintain close dialogue in good and bad times, conduct good-faith actions during restructuring, and treat all creditors fairly. Argentina had violated all of these principles. The French welcomed them, as the code was in part their initiative. Trichet had helped start the process in 2002, when he was the head of the Banque de France involved in preparing for G8 summits. The treatment of this issue showed that the G20 had become both a consensus forum that could shun, if not shame, its sinners, and a forum where the old North–South divide was dissolving fast.

These principles of good financial conduct were presented as a complement to the collective action clauses (CAC) to be included in bond contracts to guide restructuring in cases of sovereign debt difficulty. Some countries complained that the principles did not deal with the issue of standstills, when countries simply stopped paying. Others regretted the omission of bearing creditors' costs, meaning that if a country stopped payment, the government would have to pay the costs of the restructuring as well as credit rating and legal fees. This issue was one of the reasons Argentina did not attend. The idea of CACs had been put to the G7 as a mechanism for quick action if countries defaulted on their debts. But it had not proved popular there. Paul O'Neill, Snow's predecessor as US treasury secretary, had asked the IMF to examine the issue. The IMF claimed it did not have the authority or impartiality to do so. In contrast, the G20 made progress in the area, including through a voluntary approach to debt restructuring. The mandate to deal with this issue was directly passed from the G7 to the G20, in part because of the G20's mixed membership between debtor and creditor countries. The G20 thus succeeded on an issue where both the G7 and IMF had failed.

The announcement that the Paris Club would reduce Iraqi debt by 80 percent was made on the sidelines of the G20 meeting, although the G20 itself did not directly address it. The technical aspects of the debt deal had been discussed at the Paris Club meeting in Paris. It had been a compromise between Russia, France, and Germany, which had refused to go beyond a 50 percent reduction, and the United States and the United Kingdom, which had been pushing for a 95 percent reduction (Weiss 2005; Agence France Presse 2004e).

IFI Reform

The final issue was the strategic reform of the Bretton Woods institutions. Here the G20 made major agenda-setting advances. At the recent G8 summit, leaders had launched a review of the IMF. The Germans thought the G20 would be the appropriate forum to deal with IFI reform because the most important shareholders were there. America's Snow supported the idea and underlined the critical importance of having the G20 discuss the issue. All the participants welcomed the UK's assurance that the issue would be on the agenda of the Gleneagles Summit in 2005. China, as the incoming G20 chair and host, committed to keep IFI reform on the agenda. The aim was not to be critical but to keep the IFIs relevant in a changed world and to make sure they pursued their missions effectively. The shared agenda went well beyond that of the G7/8, which had wanted more efficiency, more scrutiny of budgets, only modest—if any—increases in budgets, and clear aims and rules for use of the financial resources of the World Bank and IMF.

IMF managing director Rodrigo de Rato made several significant interventions. The IMF was trying to analyse itself and take ownership of this issue so as not to have reforms dictated by the G7/8 or G20. Apart from institutional sovereignty, it wanted to ensure that all voices were heard and not just those of the subset of the membership that belonged to the G20. James Wolfensohn of the World Bank was a little defensive, but agreed that changes needed to be made.

The British were adamant that the IFIs should not review themselves. They wanted the G20 to ask very fundamental questions, examining the very mandate of the institutions and whether their structure remained relevant. Mervyn King, governor of the Bank of England, was upset that such a review had not been done 10 years earlier, on the occasion of the 50th anniversary of the founding of the Bretton Woods bodies. He did not want these issues ignored this time around.

The Canadians also insisted on a G20 review of the Bretton Woods institutions. David Dodge, making a link to the delicate exchange rate issue, said the problem for the IMF was managing the uneasy coexistence between traditional Bretton Woods' adjustment mechanisms and a floating exchange rate regime with a well-defined adjustment path.

Emerging market members, notably Turkey and Brazil, asked who would make the decisions if there were to be a fundamental review process. Brazil claimed that the G7/8 had impeded the creation of a proper crisis prevention facility at the IMF for emerging countries, because the countries that needed the IMF's help were those increasing their integration into the world economy. Brazilian finance minister Antonio Palocci wanted to include a precautionary arrangement at the IMF to prevent crises. He challenged the G7/8 to come up with a position next year.

The Asian countries also contributed to the debate, generally supporting the idea of G20-led reform. Korea and Japan ambitiously demanded a discussion of representation, pointing to the over-representation of European countries and the significant under-representation of emerging countries in the governing structures.

The Europeans were not receptive. However, China vowed to make this a priority when it hosted the G20 in 2005.

Plans for 2005

Toward the end of the meeting, the Chinese signalled their intentions and priorities for the next year. They would hold the annual G20 meeting outside Beijing on October 15–16, 2005, and two deputies' meetings, one on March 14–15 in Chongquing and the other on September 1–2 in Dalian. The theme would be strengthening global cooperation and balance in the world economy. They would focus on three key issues: first, a more appropriate flow of the factors of production; second, the continued development of the world economy, including IFI reform, mechanisms for trade and development, and the coordination of international economic institutions; and third, developing laws to govern a balanced world economy. The G20 also decided that Australia would host the ministerial two years hence, in 2006, confirming the two-year shadow of the future and institutionalizing the precise advanced–emerging member annual rotation for the first time.

Achievements

The Berlin G20 meeting achieved a great deal. In policy substance it made important advances in macroeconomic policy coordination and the first stage of IMF voice and vote reform. Institutionally, it confirmed its reach into the future and the rotation among advanced and emerging members as host and chair. And on the personal level, it saw the conversion of Hans Eichel, the skeptical host at the start in 1999, into an accomplished, committed enthusiast leading the G20 in its post-crisis phase.

Dimensions of Performance

A systematic review of the six dimensions of G20 performance confirms that the Berlin ministerial was a strong, comprehensive success.

Domestic Political Management

In the realm of domestic political management, some ministers, starting with Argentina's, did not attend. But five communiqué compliments were issued, the second highest to date (see Appendix D). Three went to G8 members and two to emerging ones.

For Australia, being chosen to host in 2006 was a major boost in prestige. Australian treasurer Peter Costello emphasized the importance of the G20, calling it the "key forum of international economic and financial policymakers" and playing up Australia's role as the host in setting the agenda for the meeting (*Daily Telegraph* 2004).

Canada's effort to elevate the G20 to the leaders' level had an impact on political management at home. In the speech from the throne Governor General Adrienne Clarkson, as advised by a deeply committed Prime Minister Paul Martin, declared that "the government will work to bring about a meeting of G20 leaders to address common and pressing concerns" (Canada, Governor General 2004). This national policy address presented Canada as an important international player to Canadian citizens.

Deliberation

In its deliberation, the Berlin meeting was, by a substantial margin, the most productive to date in its public written record (see Appendix E). It produced four documents and a total of 3,971 words.

The communiqué had 11 paragraphs, accompanied by three additional documents that contained an additional 29 paragraphs. All included, Berlin marked a new high of 40 paragraphs, slightly above the previous peak of 38 at Montreal. Macroeconomic policy as a subject had a strong lead.

In private, the dynamics of the discussion showed how far the G20 had come as an effective, deliberative forum. Berlin had eight major agenda items. A few were discussed in real detail and produced unexpected results.

At the meeting itself, discussions were frank and open. Although exchange rates were not officially part of the agenda, the ministers were able to broach the topic on the sidelines. Zhou Xiaochuan, governor of the People's Bank of China, indicated that China was "prepared to talk with other G20 countries about long-term economic policy, including its exchange rate" (Dow Jones Chinese Financial Wire 2004).

Direction Setting

In its direction setting, the Berlin meeting contributed very strongly to the diffusion of democratic principles and norms. Its six affirmations of democratic values were the highest of any annual G20 meeting thus far (see Appendix F-1). The core communiqué affirmed the democratic norms of transparency above all, as well as information and knowledge exchange, surveillance and monitoring, and accountability, while adding creditors' rights. The texts of the three accompanying documents affirmed a broad set of democratic norms. They gave equal prominence to the values of "sustained growth," "reform" of each member's economy, and "transparency and exchange of information." In the communiqué, principles of distribution and embedded liberalism were also affirmed, if with less frequency than all previous meetings since 1999.

Decision Making

In the decisional realm, Berlin's strong and rising performance stood out. There were 10 commitments made in the core communiqué, the second highest thus far (see Appendix G). This compared with an average of five a year in the main communiqué and 14 a year in the documentation overall. The G20 in 2004 thus matched the number of commitments produced by most G7 finance ministers' sessions from 1999 to 2004 (notably the average of 15 per meeting from April 20, 2002, to May 17, 2003). At Berlin, macroeconomic policy led the commitments.

Three key agreements came out of Berlin. The "G20 Accord for Sustained Growth" generated momentum for domestic economic reform within member countries (G20 Finance 2004b). The consensus for that reform was solidified by the endorsement of the agreement, which emphasized the G20 members' commitment to effective macroeconomic frameworks, competitive markets, and strong domestic institutions. In the "G20 Reform Agenda," members agreed to implement the ideas in the accord and translate them into concrete policy measures, and to review these measures regularly (G20 Finance 2004c). Finally, the "G20 Statement on Transparency and Exchange of Information for Tax Purposes" was a further expression of the G20's commitment to fighting terrorist finance (G20 Finance 2004d).

Delivery

In its delivery, Berlin also did well. There was a strong effort to ensure compliance with the commitments made. For the reform agenda, there were reviews and a recommitment to implement the policies outlined in the accord for sustained growth in the annual meetings in 2005 in China and in 2006 in Australia. Only after the G20 moved to the leaders' level was the accord replaced.

Development of Global Governance

The development of global governance was also strong at Berlin (see Appendix C-1). The G20 came of age institutionally. Internally, it institutionalized its two-year shadow of the future for chairing and hosting and the precise annual rotation between advanced and emerging members. It made eight references to its own institutional development, more than ever before.

Externally, the G20 made 21 references to outside institutions, the second highest number to date. These were led by the FATF with five and—in a great new surge—by the OECD with five as well.

Momentum had also started for a leap to the leaders' level. In April 2004, Martin had delivered a major foreign policy speech in Washington, arguing that the world needed a global leaders' forum like the G20 to solve the difficult problems it faced (Fagan 2004). Canadian officials described the White House as receptive to the idea. Although the Canadians sounded others out in the corridors at Berlin, the topic did not arise in the meeting itself. The Americans were reluctant to spend scarce political capital where they did not expect much return for their investment.

Causes of Performance

Once again the systemic hub model well accounts for Berlin's strong, comprehensive success. That performance came, for the first time in G20 history, not from big, sequential shocks from outside, but largely from forces and active agents inside the group.

Shock-Activated, Equalizing Vulnerabilities

The first cause, shock-activated, equalizing vulnerabilities, did not directly contribute much to Berlin's success. In 2004, such shocks were subdued (see Appendix I). The Asian-turned-global financial crisis and September 11 terrorist attacks were long past, even if their effects lingered. Many of the Asian countries that had been affected still mistrusted the IMF because of its poor handling of the financial crisis. They thus supported the push for its reform. China took up the issue for its meeting the following year.

A new shock emerged in energy. Just a few weeks before the Berlin meeting, oil prices had risen to a new high, having steadily come back after their post-September 11 slide. The rising oil prices were the result of political and ecological mini-shocks—strikes in Nigeria and Norway and hurricanes in the United States—along with more systemic mismatches between supply and demand.

Coupled with that stress, the dollar was weakening, especially against the euro. The week before the meeting, the euro reached a new high of 1.30 against the dollar, triggering concern from European countries. Europe criticized the US for its slow economic recovery.

In all, however, the increasing pressures on the international financial system and economy in 2004 did not constitute a shock sequence nearly as severe as in 1999 or as politically significant as September 11. Yet G20 members still considered the forum for addressing the global economy, including the sensitive and difficult topic of exchange rates.

International Institutional Failure

The second cause, international institutional failure, was a major driver of Berlin's strong success. The IMF had failed to predict the vibrant growth of 5.1 percent in the global economy in 2004 (see Appendix J-1). Despite some discussion that a bubble might be developing in financial matters, such concerns were readily dismissed. The inability of the Bretton Woods bodies or the G7/8 to reform the IFIs or the debt-restructuring regime led the G20 to take up these causes. Moreover, with the failure of the World Trade Organization (WTO) and the G8 to break the deadlock of the Doha round of trade negotiations, the G20 addressed the thorniest trade issues too. EU trade commissioner Pascal Lamy and WTO director general Supachai Panitchpakdi met not with the G8 leaders at Sea Island but with the G20 finance ministers to discuss how to advance the development-oriented trade talks (Bradford and Linn 2004). In development, despite the continued competence of the G7 and the Paris Club in addressing the Iraq debt program, the G20 was becoming increasingly important.

As part of the argument for a G20 leaders' level forum, Australian treasurer Peter Costello claimed that the G20 had been formed due to the IMF's failure to respond adequately to the Asian financial crisis, and that the IMF had continued to miss important warning signs in Asia and not focus enough attention on that region (Uren 2004). Canadian officials promoted the idea of an L20 in Washington on even broader grounds. Foreign minister Bill Graham described the UN system as a "very formalized, very bureaucratized institution that doesn't allow for informal discussion among leaders" (McCarthy 2004). His observations highlighted the importance of possibilities such as the G20, which was more representative than the G7/8 or the Security Council, and yet still much smaller than the General Assembly, allowing for more informal and spontaneous discussion.

The G7/8 system in 2004 also failed in key respects as a global financial and economic governor. To be sure, G7 finance ministers for the first time invited China to their meeting in October 2004. But no other systemically significant countries were invited, even in this second class way (see Appendix J-3). Bush as G8 host devoted his Sea Island Summit to the new Broader Middle East and North Africa Initiative, African development, and security, leaving little space for finance and economic concerns. Above all, he failed to invite Brazil, India, China, or Mexico, the year after they had attended the G8 for the first time. This demotion of the systemically significant countries in the G8 in 2004 was a powerful thrust for Paul Martin's L20 campaign (Kirton 2010).

Predominant, Equalizing Capabilities

The third cause, predominant, equalizing capabilities, was potent as well (see Appendix K). While the G20's collective predominance declined slightly, it was still a formidable 80 percent. Moreover, its internal equality grew in all respects but the Gini coefficient (Bradford and Linn 2004). Its G8 members' share of the global economy declined from 65 percent to 64 percent, while that of its non-G8 members grew by one percentage point to 17 percent. The ratio of gross domestic product between its most and least powerful members continued to decline from its Argentinean-induced peak of 2002.

Domestic Convergence

The fourth cause, domestic democratic convergence, contributed a little (see Appendix L-2). By 2004, the G20 contained 14 members classified by Freedom

House as fully free, two as partially free (Indonesia and Turkey), and three as not free (Russia, China, and Saudi Arabia). Thus over half the non-G8 members were deemed to be fully free. This collective accumulation of a democratic tradition was enhanced by the presence of Germany, now containing a more fully absorbed democratic Eastern Germany, in the G20's chair.

Domestic Political Control, Capital, Continuity, Competence and Commitment

The fifth cause of domestic political control, capital, continuity, competence, and commitment was important, above all in the case of the Berlin meeting's chair and host and Paul Martin's initiative beyond.

Hans Eichel was a G20 founder, now attending his sixth ministerial in a row, and the host of the first and now sixth meetings. He became only the second G20 finance minister, along with Paul Martin, to host the G20 for a second time. The G20 skeptic of 1999 had now become a committed leader of the group. He was supported by his fellow founding, continuously serving veterans—Britain's Gordon Brown, South Africa's Trevor Manuel, Australia's Peter Costello, and Saudi Arabia's Ibrahim Al-Assaf (see Appendix M-2). However, five finance ministers did not attend Berlin, including rookie finance minister Nicolas Sarkozy of France, Sadakazu Tanigaki of Japan, Alexei Kudrin of Russia, and Lee Hun-jai of Korea. Sarkozy was reportedly busy with his election campaign, and Kudrin was ill. The ministers from Japan and Korea were preoccupied with their domestic budgets. They sent representatives in their place.

Argentina's Roberto Lavagna did not attend. Argentina was in the middle of launching a $103 billion debt restructuring. He reportedly feared reproach from his G20 colleagues regarding Argentina's debt default. Officially, the Argentinian embassy in Germany cited a "scheduling problem" (Agence France Presse 2004b). Eichel noted that Argentinians' decision was unfortunate and regrettable because they were "backing themselves into a corner," but he would leave the door open for future talks (Thomas 2004b). Argentina also disagreed with the rules relevant for a significant part of the proposed agenda for the meeting. Argentina was the only G20 member that did not send a representative at all.

The actual attendance affected the outcomes on some issues. Oil prices were a significant item and the G20 brought together several key oil-producing countries, including global kingpin Saudi Arabia. But when the ailing Russian finance minister was unable to attend, the G20 was less able to develop a broad and coherent position on the future price of oil.

At the leaders' level, Paul Martin had long been personally and politically committed to the G20 and to raising it to the leaders' level. Now as prime minister he sought to build consensus for an L20 along with his other foreign policy priorities of UN reform, peace and security, the economy, human security, and promoting the principle of the responsibility to protect (R2P), which would be supported at the UN General Assembly in 2005.

Controlled Club Participation as a Network Hub

The sixth cause, controlled club participation as a network hub, was the most important cause of all. Internally, the presence of the five founders, especially with Eichel's conversion, began to make the G20 a club in the non-shocked social-psychological sense as well as a rational instrumental one. There was still more cohesion among the G7/8 members than any other coalition within the G20, but there was no other natural bloc. A counterbalance to the G7 was developing between China and Brazil. They were both large powers, despite being from different continents. Both were suspicious of the United States, and eager to improve relations with each other. Within Asia, the Chinese, Japanese, Koreans, and Indians were divided in many ways. New relationships across the non-G7 divide were forged within the group.

The G7 remained more important than the G20 in some ways. The G20, however, included both debtor and creditor members, making it a unique grouping within the international financial architecture. The G7/8 had cohesion, a long history, regular meetings, and the ability to make powerful decisions based on quick consensus. Increasingly, however, the G20 had important work to do and the capacity to get it done. It thus acquired the issue of IFI reform and agreed among all, save for absent Argentina, on codes of good conduct in debt restructuring.

Externally, the finance ministers' network around the G20 club strengthened as a hub. The finance ministers were invited with their leaders to a special Summit of the Americas in Monterrey, Mexico, on January 12–13, 2004, the first such summit since Quebec City in 2001. In the autumn finance ministers of the Asia-Pacific Economic Cooperation (APEC) forum met on September 2–3 in Chile, and the Commonwealth finance ministers met in St. Kitts and Neves on September 28–30.

Above all, with the defensive positionalist, loss-aversion blow suffered by the G20's non-G8 members due to George Bush's refusal to invite them to the G8 summit again, and the opportunity offered by Paul Martin's campaign for an L20 of equals, it was clear that the G20 and not a "G8 plus" offered the best chance of becoming a summit-level hub for global governance.

In addition, the so-called "Progressive Summit," begun by Tony Blair and Bill Clinton and supported by Jean Chrétien, brought Martin and several G20 and other leaders together in 2004 and 2005. Their discussions came to focus on R2P.

Conclusion

By 2004, the G20 had become established in the global governance architecture. It successfully showed that it could govern important financial issues and broader topics, including terrorism, financial crime, trade, development, and energy. It had carved a post-crisis path for itself beyond the 1997–99 Asian financial shocks. Both advanced and emerging economy members save for Argentina were now fully and equally engaged in the group. The G20 had started to work more closely and cooperatively with other institutions, including a G7/8 and IMF that still largely shut the emerging powers out.

The campaign for a leaders' level G20 had begun. Whether it should or could start and continue, what issues it would address, and whether it should include the same membership of the existing G20 were all uncertain. Discussions on these issues grew in 2005. The 2005 G20 meeting would be chaired by a rapidly rising China, which furthered the G20's potential accomplishments, particularly on the issue of IFI reform. At the same time, the G8 summit struck back, by inviting the leaders of not only China but also India, Brazil, Mexico, and South Africa to its Gleneagles Summit in 2005.

References

Agence France Presse. 2004a. "After Five Years, G20 Forum Still Teething." November 16.

Agence France Presse. 2004b. "Eichel Criticizes Argentina's Pullout from G20 Meeting." November 19.

Agence France Presse. 2004c. "Exchange Rate Developments Could Come Up at Central Bankers' Meeting." November 10.

Agence France Presse. 2004d. "Italy Supports Canadian Plans for a G20 Summit, Cooperation on Africa." October 15.

Agence France Presse. 2004e. "Russia Blocking Paris Club Debt Relief for Iraq." November 21.

Agence France Presse. 2004f. "Snow Pleased by G20 'Broad Endorsement' of Pro-growth Agenda." November 21.

Agence France Presse. 2004g. "US Sees Growing Importance of G20; Wants to Avoid Dollar Spat." November 16.

Agence France Presse. 2004h. "Wolfensohn Says Economic Powers Should Formalize G20 to Consult." September 24.

Bradford, Colin I. and Linn, Johannes F. 2004. "Global Economic Governance at a Crossroads: Replacing the G7 with the G20." Brookings Institution Policy Brief 131. Available at: www.brookings.edu/papers/2004/04globaleconomics_bradford.aspx. Accessed: July 2012.

Brown, Owen. 2004. "China Watch: Yuan Grumbles at G20, But No Moves Likely." Dow Jones International News. November 19.

Business Times Singapore. 2004. "US Dollar Danger Ahead." October 8.

Canada. Governor General. 2004. "Speech from the Throne to Open the First Session of the 38th Parliament of Canada." October 5. Available at: www.pco-bcp.gc.ca/index.asp?lang=eng&page=information&sub=publications&doc=aarchives/sft-ddt/2004_2-eng.htm. Accessed: July 2012.

Daily Telegraph. 2004. "G20 Host Adds to Status." November 22.

Dow Jones Chinese Financial Wire. 2004. "China Central Banker: Prepared to Talk on FX Rates at G20." November 19.

Fagan, Drew. 2004. "PM's Plan Pushes UN to Sidelines." *Globe and Mail*, April 30, p. A1.

G20 Finance Ministers and Central Bank Governors. 2004a. "Communiqué." Berlin, November 21. Available at: www.g20.utoronto.ca/2004/2004communique.html. Accessed: July 2012.

G20 Finance Ministers and Central Bank Governors. 2004b. "G20 Accord for Sustained Growth." Berlin, November 21. Available at: www.g20.utoronto.ca/2004/2004growth.html. Accessed: July 2012.

G20 Finance Ministers and Central Bank Governors. 2004c. "G20 Reform Agenda." Berlin, November 21. Available at: www.g20.utoronto.ca/2004/2004reform.html. Accessed: July 2012.

G20 Finance Ministers and Central Bank Governors. 2004d. "G20 Statement on Transparency and Exchange of Information for Tax Purposes." Berlin, November 21. Available at: www.g20.utoronto.ca/2004/2004transparency.html. Accessed: July 2012.

International Monetary Fund. 2004. "World Economic Outlook: Advancing Structural Reforms." April, Washington DC. Available at: www.imf.org/external/pubs/ft/weo/2004/01. Accessed: July 2012.

Kirton, John J. 2010. "The G20, the G8, the G5, and the Role of Ascending Powers." Paper prepared for a presentation at a seminar on "Ascending Powers and the International System," December 14, Mexico City. Available at: www.g20.utoronto.ca/biblio/kirton-g20-g8-g5.pdf. Accessed: July 2012.

Martin, Paul. 2010. "Address to the 2010 Couchiching Conference on 'Watershed Moment or Wasted Opportunity'." August 6, Geneva Park, Canada.

McCarthy, Shawn. 2004. "Ottawa Still Supports UN, Graham Says." *Globe and Mail*, May 1.

Reuters. 2004. "Highlights: G20 Delegates' Comments on FX." November 21.

Smith, Gordon. 2004. "An Idea Whose Time Has Come." *Globe and Mail*, October 22, p. A19.

Thomas, Andrea. 2004a. "Dollar Decline Bedevils G20 Officials, Little Relief Seen." *Globe and Mail*, November 18.

Thomas, Andrea. 2004b. "Germany's Eichel Sees G20 Progress on Debt Restructuring." *Globe and Mail*, November 20.

Uren, David. 2004. "Costello Backs Bid to Power Up G20." *Australian*, May 3.

Waki, Natsuko. 2004. "Japan Says G20 Too Large But Possible to Expand G7." Reuters, November 21.

Weiss, Martin A. 2005. "Iraq: Debt Relief." March 11, Federation of American Scientists, Washington DC. Available at: www.fas.org/sgp/crs/mideast/RS21765.pdf. Accessed: July 2012.

Chapter 8
Capturing China, Xianghe 2005

Introduction

The Challenge

In 2005 the world was plagued by several shocks, from tsunamis, hurricanes, soaring energy prices, avian influenza, and terrorist attacks. But it was also a year of stability and opportunity in the crisis-free fields of economics and finance. The emerging powers led by China leapt ahead in their relative capability. The Group of Eight (G8) responded to their rapid rise, as Britain's Tony Blair showcased their priority of development and invited China, India, Brazil, Mexico, and South Africa as the "outreach" Group of Five (G5) to participate in the G8 summit he hosted at Gleneagles in July. The Gleneagles Summit produced a standout performance in the development issues cherished by the emerging economies. It also created the new ongoing G5 to work with the G8 at the summit level and increasingly the ministerial level too. It further showed that with China, India, and others at the table, progress could be made on the challenges of climate change and energy, where the formal multilateral United Nations process had largely failed to advance.

In the face of these G8 moves, how would the Group of 20 (G20) respond, using its built-in advantage of having the emerging countries as equal members from the start in its finance ministers' and central bank governors' forum? The first strategic, summit-oriented response came at the initiative of Canada's Prime Minister Paul Martin, who continued to campaign for the G20 to be raised to the leaders' level, to form the Leaders 20 (L20). Martin culminated his campaign by informally discussing with China the possibility of co-chairing, with Canada, a G20 leaders' session at the United Nations General Assembly (UNGA) and the Millennium Review Summit in September 2005. He did so on the grounds that China was serving as chair of the G20 finance ministers' and bank governors' meeting that year, and that Chinese assent would make it more likely that all the other members would attend. China soon signalled its willingness to co-lead such a G20 summit.

In the end, United States president George Bush, whom Martin had informally sounded out at the leaders' meeting of Asia-Pacific Economic Cooperation (APEC), refused to attend even a very short G20 session, even one focused on the current crisis of pandemic disease. Thus no G20 leader-level encounter took place. Yet the comparison of Martin's 2004–05 campaign with his earlier initiative to launch the G20 at the ministerial level in 1997–99 was striking, for now he started not with the most powerful G8 member—democratic America—as his sole partner, but with the most powerful non-G8, non-democratic one—China. In both cases, China readily agreed to create the new group of equals. This time America was not the first co-leader but the last laggard. It delayed the G20's leap to the leaders' level for three years, until a financial shock erupted in a vulnerable America in the autumn of 2008 to change Bush's mind.

The second G20 response to the G8's Gleneagles challenge came at the finance ministers' and bank governors' level. The year 2005 marked a major advance in G20 governance, as the group succeeded in more fully capturing China politically as an interested and involved member, and one able and willing to lead. Thus on October 15–16 in Xianghe, Hebei, China, for the first time the annual G20 meeting was hosted by the group's most powerful emerging country and a non-democratic member. China took its hosting responsibilities seriously. It set out a broad, ambitious agenda. Chinese president Hu Jintao, who had arrived in office in 2003 gave the opening speech to the assembled ministers and governors. The Chinese ensured that the issues they highlighted, above all the commitment to reform the International Monetary Fund (IMF) by 2008, would continue when the G20 chair passed to Australia in 2006 and South Africa in 2007.

Competing Assessments

The performance of the first G20 meeting China hosted and China's role in the G20 inspired a debate among five major competing schools of thought.

The first school doubted China's abilities to chair a successful G20, due to China's stark differences from the other members of the group. While its hosting in 2005 was considered a sign of the larger global power shift that was taking place, there was considerable skepticism that China could meet the internal test and outside challenge of hosting a comprehensive and robust meeting (Holbrooke 2005).

The second school saw China's growing inclusion in the finance ministers' forum of the Group of Seven (G7) and by implication in the G20 one as a sign that it was a worthy as well as necessary associate in the economic sphere (Whyman 1995; Hodges 1999; Baum and Shevchenko 2001). To some, it was a legitimate member of the ministerial finance-focused Group of Seven (G7), if not the leaders' politically focused G8 club (Jayawardena 1989; Smyser 1993; ul Haq 1994; Commission on Global Governance 1995; Brzezinski 1996; Bergsten 1998; *Economist* 1998; Desai 2006).

The third school saw Xianghe as the start of a new era. The Chinese-chaired meeting highlighted important, indeed architectural issues that would remain on the G20 agenda in the years to come (de Brouwer and Yeaman 2007).

The fourth school argued that the 2005 G20 meeting was a partial success. On energy, the ministers and governors rose to the challenge and dealt effectively with rapidly rising oil prices. But the lack of consensus and discussion on China's currency was seen as a major shortcoming (Wheatley and Love 2005).

The fifth school argued that China was an internationally engaged, fully equal member and embryonic leader in the G20 and in the world. It was thus able to host and chair a successful ministerial and to join with Canada and eventually almost all other members to agree to create a leaders' level club (Martin 2005b; Kirton 2007, 2005a).

The Argument

This chapter argues that the 2005 G20 was a strong success, both at its annual meeting and in the almost successful Canadian-Chinese campaign to create a leaders-level club. At the annual G20 meeting, China satisfied emerging and advanced countries alike by highlighting issues that appealed to all. The meeting successfully started serious negotiations for IMF and World Bank reforms, which these institutions had been unable to do themselves. The G20 thus evolved from being a largely deliberative forum setting new normative directions and taking collective decisions on immediate, often crisis-bred issues to developing global governance by broadening its agenda, solidifying its structure, working collaboratively with and through the G7 and other multilateral organizations, and, above all, initiating the ultimately successful process to reform the 1944 Bretton Woods institutions. China not only became more engaged in the group as a result of its chairing and hosting responsibilities, but also showed it would lead and win. This success was most strikingly seen three years later when the Canadian-Chinese campaign to make the G20 a leaders-level club finally had the intended result.

These advances were caused by new shocks, even if the most prominent shared one of avian influenza ultimately failed to convince George Bush to bring a G20 summit to life in 2005. Another key cause of the G20's ministers' and bank governors' success was the failure of the old multilateral organizations, above all the IMF, to give the now rapidly emerging powers the voice and vote that their expanding capabilities warranted. Democratic convergence grew, as in Asia Indonesia took a substantial step toward democratization. Chinese finance minister Jin Renqing chaired, drawing on his experience from his two meetings before. Above all, the G20 was increasingly becoming the hub in the spreading network of global governance, at the level of finance ministers and other portfolio ministers. The membership of the Gleneagles Dialogue on climate change, clean energy, and sustainable development, launched at the G8 summit, largely overlapped the G20. Health ministers from all the G20 countries—with the exception of Saudi Arabia—with the addition of several others met for the first time to deal with the shock of avian influenza.

At the leaders' level, despite the 2005 arrival of the G8 Plus Five, the slow response of the G8 to include all the rapidly rising emerging powers and to include any as equals, as well as the intensification of the G20-centred global network, exerted a strong pull that almost created a G20 summit. Whereas the G8 at Gleneagles allowed only partial, discretionary, issue-specific participation for the G5 countries, including the four that were fellow democratic polities of G8 members, the G20 emerged as the preference of all but America, and was the ultimate international institutional winner in 2008. This was because the G20 alone contained as equals, and flexibly adjusted to, the rising, emerging, systemically significant powers in the world. Moreover, the addition in 2005 of new plurilateral summits, notably those led by the United States with Canada and Mexico in North America and by China in East Asia, strengthened the leaders' level network that had G20 countries at the hub. The rational response of raising the G20 itself to the leaders' level thus acquired a rationale as well as a consensus that was almost complete (Martin 2005b, 2005a; Canada 2005a, 2005b; Ibbitson 2005; Cooper 2007).

However, individual agency in the form of America's George Bush ultimately mattered in delaying the G20's rational response to shifting relative capability, cumulating systemic connectivity, and the resulting need for a new summit-level institution in the world. The G20 ministerial thus flourished only as a finance ministers' and governors' group at the hub of a global network, until a mega shock arrived in America three years later to change Bush's mind and bring Paul Martin's vision to life.

Canada's Campaign with China for an L20 in 2005

In January, as 2005 began, Chinese president Hu Jintao and Indian prime minister Manmohan Singh welcomed Canadian prime minister Paul Martin's proposal for a G20 leaders' meeting, perhaps because they had a particular interest in avian influenza (Canada 2005a, 2005b). Their bilateral meetings with Martin focused on terrorism, development, public health, and the environment (Martin 2005a; Canada 2005b). By February, Russia, France, Britain, Mexico, and Brazil backed the initiative for a G20 summit, too. Remaining reluctant were Germany, Japan, and the United States (Ibbitson 2005). After the US, Japan was the most reluctant. It warily watched its rapidly rising Chinese neighbour and cherished its established G8 club (Dobson 2004; Kirton 2007). However, in the end Japanese prime minister Junichiro Koizumi agreed to come to one G20 meeting and, if it worked, to come to more.

In 2005, along with hosting the meeting of G20 finance ministers and central bank governors, China became more involved in the G7 finance ministers' process (Kirton 2008; Desai 2006). It was invited for the second time to meet informally with the G7 finance ministers and central bank governors at their meeting in London on February 5. They exchanged views on fiscal and monetary policies in the G7, the Asian economy, and exchange rate flexibility (G7 Finance 2005b). China was invited again to an "outreach session" of the G7's September 23 finance meeting. This time Brazil, India, Russia, and South Africa were invited for the first time (G7 Finance 2005a). In December, at a special G7 finance meeting, China, Brazil, and India were invited again (Brown 2005).

China also started to participate regularly at G8 summits. The 2005 Gleneagles Summit was the second in which China participated, following its first in 2003 (Kirton and Panova 2007; Blair 2010). At Gleneagles China became entrenched in the process—with invitations subsequently arriving to participate in the following four G8 summits (Åslund 2006; Vickers 2006). China was a founding member of the new Gleneagles Dialogue on clean energy and climate change, which included Australia, Brazil, Canada, China, France, Germany, India, Indonesia, Italy, Iran, Japan, Mexico, Nigeria, Poland, Russia, South Africa, Spain, the United Kingdom, the United States, and the European Union. The dialogue's mandate extended until 2008.

The terrorist-shocked G8 Gleneagles Summit confirmed for Paul Martin (2010) the value that a G20 summit would have. He had made the point to his G8 colleagues that treating the G5 leaders as second-class, part-time participants would not build collegiality with them. Moreover, the G5 leaders were likely meeting on their own to prepare for participating in the G8 summit, so the G8—by including them—was effectively preventing the creation of a counter institution in the form of the G5.

At their lunch the leaders of the G8, the G5, and the World Trade Organization (WTO) discussed trade, including the Doha round of trade negotiations and its critical component of agriculture. Pascal Lamy, director general of the WTO, urged cooperation, thereby catalysing a debate between America's Bush and India's Singh, a debate that others joined. The leaders were so engaged that they ignored reminders of the other issues on the agenda still to be dealt with. Bush and Singh told each other that they learned things in that discussion that they had not known. But before such "spontaneous combustion" could lead all leaders to instruct their officials to get Doha done, the session came to its scheduled end. The G5 leaders were abruptly dismissed from the G8 summit.

Martin's desire for a G20 leaders' forum was thus reinforced by several broad calculations. One was the desire to prevent the emergence of a G5 summit that would serve as an alternative to, or antithesis of, the G8. A second was the rapidly rising power of the "BRICs," in the concept coined and calculations confirmed by Jim O'Neill of Goldman Sachs to refer to Brazil, Russia, India, and China. A third was a fear that a new G group would arrive out of the blue that Canada would not be part of. The solution was to lead in taking an institution that Canada was already a core part of—the G20—and upgrade it to the leaders' level to govern the new world that globalization had brought.

Following the Gleneagles Summit, Martin made the final push. The leading idea was to hold the first L20, co-chaired by Canada and China, as a dinner at the UN summit in New York in September, which most G20 leaders were already scheduled to attend. The calculation was that with the Chinese and so many other big players at the table, America's George Bush would feel he needed to come, despite his general dislike of so many summits and his belief that there was no need for a G20 one. The agenda would include issues such as the recent avian influenza pandemic, of particular concern to a China and a Canada shocked by severe acute respiratory syndrome (SARS) in 2003—but not by terrorism, a key concern of Bush's. The smaller members of the G20 were willing to come to the dinner, as were the Europeans overall. The Canadians were flexible about the timing and format. Yet, in the end, Bush, who never directly addressed the issue with Martin, did not agree. American officials suggested that Bush, having sat through several summits with large numbers, such as the Summit of the Americas (SOA) earlier in the year in Argentina, and UNGA, did want to change his schedule even for a few hours to attend another unproductive meeting where participants simply read prepared speeches to one another.

When this American resistance became apparent, the Canadians called off their initiative. Given the close US–Japanese relationship since 1945, the close personal relationship between Bush and Blair, and the central purpose of building global consensus at such a summit, there was no case for having it without Bush present. Moreover, all perspective attendees were busy at the UN summit, trying to advance the Millennium Development Goals (MDGs), reform the UN Security Council, improve peacekeeping and human rights, and endorse the revolutionary principle of an international responsibility to protect.

Martin, who had returned with a minority government in 2004, and was defeated in the general election of January 2006, could not hold the meeting he intended to, had he won again. Only three years later, in the midst of an unprecedented financial crisis that arose in America and erupted in New York City itself in September, did a now responsive George Bush bring the G20 summit to life at the White House in Washington DC in a meeting focused on financial reform, rather than the one at the UN in New York focused on UN reform.

Plans and Preparations

As the G20 chair, China set the theme of the 2005 meeting as "Global Cooperation: Promoting Balanced and Orderly World Economic Development." To prepare, China held two deputies' meetings, in March and September, and three workshops, all in non-G8 countries.

The first workshop was on "Innovative Financing Mechanisms for Development," held in Brazil on June 29–July 1. The second was on economic growth, held in South Africa on August 4–5. The third was on demographic challenges held in Australia on August 28–29. This last one followed the first workshop on this theme, which had been hosted by France in 2004. In France, participants had explored the impacts of demographic change on economic growth. The 2005 follow-on focused on the role of migration in dealing with aging populations.

There were several video conferences held among the members of the troika of Germany, China, and Australia to help determine the finance ministers' and bank governors' agenda. The subjects chosen were economic and development issues, reviewing the Bretton Woods institutions after 60 years, the MDGs, development assistance and innovative financing mechanisms, and the G20 Accord on Sustained Growth—one of the significant accomplishments of the 2004 Berlin meeting, which members had pledged to review in 2005.

High oil prices, which remained a concern, were included in the category of the economy. The review of international financial institutions (IFIs), which had also been initiated in Berlin, was of particular interest to the Chinese. They had committed themselves to address the issue as chair. The G20 also wanted to maintain continuity with its previous agenda, and so included migration and remittances in the context of changing demographics. On the G20 accord, the Chinese continued trying to translate promises into policy actions and included a separate session on sustained growth.

Development was a major emphasis. This was not surprising, as this topic was high on other summit agendas throughout the year. At the G8 Gleneagles Summit in July, it was a priority theme. The UN's 2005 World Summit High-Level Plenary Meeting on September 14–16 discussed the progress that had been made on the MDGs after their first five years.

Bilateral and multilateral meetings took place ahead of the G20's annual meeting. US treasury secretary John Snow met with Japanese finance minister Sadakazu Tanigaki to discuss oil prices, reform of the Bretton Woods institutions, and the effect of bovine spongiform encephalopathy (BSE, or mad cow disease) on US beef imports to Japan. European finance ministers met to discuss the possibility of increasing interest rates, oil prices, reform of the Bretton Woods institutions, and Basel II.

At the Meeting

President Hu Jintao opened the annual meeting with a speech on "Strengthening Global Cooperation to Promote Common Development," given on October 15 in Beijing (Costello 2008, 183). He suggested that there were four ways the G20 could strengthen international cooperation to promote balanced economic development. The first was by understanding and respecting the fact that different development models could work well in different countries. Second, the G20 should increase its dialogue on and coordination of macroeconomic policy. Third, all could benefit by further improving global economic and trading rules. Fourth, the G20 needed to assist accelerated growth in developing countries (Pan 2005).

The first day of discussions in Xianghe focused on three issues: prospects for the global economy, international development—particularly the MDGs—and IFI reform. Demographic changes and migration as well as innovative development were on the agenda for the second day. Other priority items included high oil prices, trade, and China's currency.

At the end of the meeting, the G20 released four documents. In addition to the communiqué, it issued statements on reform of the Bretton Woods institutions, global development, and the G20 reform agenda, which focused on country-specific initiatives. The communiqué itself covered global imbalances, oil prices, trade and completing the Doha Development Agenda, the reform of the Bretton Woods institutions, aging populations, tax evasion, and progress on collective action clauses. It discussed development and the MDGs and Monterrey commitments, and how development approaches fit within the G20 Accord for Sustained Growth (G20 Finance 2005a).

Achievements

IFI Reform

The G20's statement on reforming the Bretton Woods institutions highlighted the vital role that both the World Bank and IMF continued to play in economic and financial governance. These IFIs were presented as complementary to, not competing with, the G20. However, they were also portrayed as out of date and not reflecting how the world had evolved since their creation in 1944. The finance ministers and bank governors agreed that their quotas, representation, management, and operational structure all needed reform (G20 Finance 2005d).

Development

The G20's statement on global development focused on the MDGs. It emphasized that individual country strategies were appropriate. It welcomed donors' timetables to achieve the target of 0.7 percent of gross national product for official development assistance. It endorsed the G8's Gleneagles commitments on debt relief. It encouraged enhancing aid effectiveness and promoting trade for development (G20 Finance 2005c).

Domestic Economic Reform

On the G20's domestic economic reform agenda, the United States acknowledged that future tax, health, and pension policies could further improve economic growth. Canada committed to focus on jobs and maintain balanced budgets and sound monetary policy. Japan pledged to advance its postal services reform and fiscal sustainability. The European Union committed to reform labour markets, to consolidate public finances and pension systems, and to enhance innovation. Germany pledged to make its tax system more competitive and to reform its labour market, health, and pension policies. France committed to strengthen its labour market. Italy indicated it would simplify administration procedures, liberalize energy markets, and invest in research and development, science and technology, and innovative education. The United Kingdom promised to entrench stability, to strengthen science and innovation, and to improve public services. Russia pledged to improve its investments in human capital—particularly health and education—and to improve its investment climate.

Among the non-G8 members, Argentina committed to correcting imbalances. Brazil pledged to strengthen its macroeconomic framework. Mexico committed to reach equilibrium between public revenue and expenditure. Turkey pledged to reform its financial sector, social security, tax system, and investment climate. South Africa committed to increasing investments in infrastructure and human capital. Saudi Arabia pledged to diversify its economy, reduce its dependence on oil, and improve its investment climate. India committed to infrastructure and agricultural reform. Indonesia pledged to improve its public debt management and to reduce poverty. Korea promised it would strengthen social safety nets and expedite its economic recovery. Advanced economy Australia said it would focus on raising employment and productivity.

China was the only member not to make new pledges. It merely acknowledged a number of initiatives that had already been initiated and implemented (G20 Finance 2005b).

Exchange Rates

Representatives of G7 countries—led by the US—pushed China for a more flexible exchange rate. The Chinese refused. The ministers and governors were left to issue a general statement about their determination to "implement the necessary fiscal, monetary and exchange rate policies, and accelerate structural adjustments to resolve these imbalances and overcome these risks" (G20 Finance 2005a). Following the G20 gathering, China and the US held their 17th Sino-US Joint Economic Commission meeting, where they discussed the renminbi exchange rate and volatile oil prices again.

Trade

On trade, the G20 went beyond its traditional discussions of multilateral trade negotiations. It embraced South–South trade, trade and investment, and trade for development (see Appendix G). An independent analysis concluded that trade was an issue area where the G20, in balanced fashion as a forum of equals, sided with neither the previous positions of the G7 nor those of the G24 (Martinez-Diaz 2007, 11).

Dimensions of Performance

A systematic review of the six dimensions of G20 governance confirms Xianghe's strong performance.

Domestic Political Management

In domestic political management the 2005 ministerial did well. Many finance ministers felt it was in their domestic interest to attend. Coming from the G8 were finance ministers John Snow of the United States, Sadakazu Tanigaki of Japan, Thierry Breton of France, and Alexei Kudrin of Russia. (Germany's Hans Eichel remained in Berlin because of the deadlock in Germany's parliamentary elections, so Caio Koch-Weser attended instead. Koch-Weser, who had been deputy finance minister since 1999, had been involved in the G20 since its first meeting in Berlin.) The G5 finance ministers' attendees included Jin Renqing of China, P. Chidambaram of India, and Francisco Gil Díaz of Mexico. The other finance ministers included Peter Costello of Australia, Roberto Lavagna of Argentina, Ibrahim al-Assaf of Saudi Arabia, and Jusuf Anwar of Indonesia.

As chair of the meeting, China benefited domestically most of all. President Hu took advantage of the occasion, unusual for a G20 meeting, to give the opening speech. This Chinese initiative signalled that the G20's work was directly relevant to leaders themselves. Hu acknowledged the benefits and opportunities associated with globalization. But he also highlighted the importance of respecting state sovereignty and each country's right to choose its development path, a key domestic priority. Hu emphasized China's own reform successes.

There was only one country compliment in the communiqué (see Appendix D). It went to the host. The G20 not only thanked China for chairing the meeting, which was now a common practice, but also for its "excellent stewardship" over the year (G20 Finance 2005a).

Deliberation

In its deliberation, the 2005 meeting took a slight step back in its public performance from the new peak set at Berlin the year before. Xianghe produced four documents, the same as in 2004, but they included a total of only 3,462 words (see Appendix E). Xianghe produced a significant 35 paragraphs in its four documents. But again this was fewer than the 40 produced at Berlin and the 38 at Montreal.

The communiqué concentrated on macroeconomics. For the first time, the ministers and governors also held a substantial discussion about IFI reform. It was a strong second, leaping to a much higher share than ever before. Trade was also a significant theme, taking third place.

Discussions at the meeting were productive. With oil prices reaching $62.61 a barrel the day before the meeting opened, the G20 used the forum to try to calm the resulting concerns. While exchange rates were once again not officially on the agenda, the participants discussed them on the sidelines and in bilateral meetings before and after the meeting.

Direction Setting

In direction setting Xianghe continued to diffuse democratic principles and norms (see Appendix F). Its six democratic references tied it with Berlin for the highest number made at a meeting to date. Transparency, good governance, and information and knowledge exchange were the three democratic principles affirmed. Even with non-democratic China in the chair, the embedded democratic values of the G20 came through.

Decision Making

In decision making, Xianghe made eight collective commitments (see Appendix G). This was down from the 10 made in 2004 and the 24 made in 2001. Yet it was still the third highest to date. The promises came in the areas of trade with four and development and IFI reform with two each.

The most substantive commitment was on IMF reform. G20 members (2005d) committed specifically to "identify principles for quota reform which could be an important input into the IMF's Thirteenth General Review of Quotas, scheduled to be completed by January 2008" (G20 Finance 2005d).

Delivery

Xianghe did less well on delivery. The commitments made in China were generally weak. A large number were not due for completion for several years and evidence from G8 summits has shown that such multiyear targets and timetables tend not to catalyse compliance during the year after such commitments are made. The MDGs were still 10 years away from their target in 2015. IMF reform was still at least three years off. Instead, the intention was that Australia would take responsibility for revisiting the commitments as the chair in 2006.

Yet there were some sound reasons to believe that China as host would keep the commitments made at the meeting it chaired (Guebert 2008). With the 2003 G20 Morelia commitments, at +0.67 (83.5 percent) China had the highest compliance score of all of the non-G8 countries measured, coming in well above the non-G8 average of +0.36 (68 percent). China's score was also higher than the average of +0.51 (75.5 percent) for the four G8 countries assessed. Indeed, overall China stood second only to Russia, which had an average compliance score of +0.75 (87.5 percent). In 2003, the first year that China participated in a G8 summit, it again came out on top, with an impressive compliance score of +0.73 (86.5 percent). This was significantly higher than the non-G8 countries' average of +0.48 (74 percent) and also higher than the G8 average for that year of +0.51 (75.5 percent) (Kirton and Kokotsis 2004; Kokotsis 2005; G8 Research Group 2004).

However, a year after Xianghe, in 2006, where the G8 and G5's compliance with their climate change commitments were assessed, China had the lowest average compliance score of all the participating countries (G8 Research Group Oxford 2007). China was tied with India at –0.20 (40 percent) for last place. This was lower than the very poor G5 average of –0.04 (48 percent) and the G8 average (including the EU), which at +0.20 (60 percent) was still rather poor. China performed poorest on the commitment to "work with the private sector to accelerate utilization of innovative technologies that advance more efficient hydrocarbon production and reduce the environmental impact of its production and use" (G8 2006). Nonetheless, it still managed to perform above the rest of the G5 on the commitment to promote the "environmentally sound development and use of energy, and deployment and transfer of clean energy technologies which help to tackle climate change" (0.00 compared to –0.40, or 30 percent). Mexico performed the best (+0.20 or 60 percent) that year, while Brazil and South Africa tied for second (0.00 or 50 percent).

In 2007, on G8 and G5 commitments for climate change, investment, energy, and development, China performed much better, at an average +0.71 (85.5 percent), to take first place among the G5 (G8 Research Group LSE/Oxford 2007). This was much better than the G5 average of +0.40 (70 percent) and even than the G8-EU average of +0.48 (74 percent). China complied fully with all commitments measured, except for the two on energy efficiency.

Taken together, China, save for its low score in 2006 on climate change, had positive compliance each year. It consistently had top compliance scores since 2003 when it first was invited to participate in the G8. It consistently led its G5 counterparts, and even the G8 and other outreach participants, including the "developed" ones of Australia, Indonesia, and Korea. Given this record of Chinese compliance, the case for a G20 leap to the leaders' level on a wide range of subjects seemed clear.

Development of Global Governance

In the development of global governance, Xianghe did well. Internally, there were eight references to the G20 itself, as there had been the previous year (see Appendix C-1). It also confirmed the annual rotation between advanced and emerging members as host, with South Africa taking on hosting responsibilities in 2007 following Australia in 2006.

Externally, 2005 saw a strengthening of the relationship at the level of finance ministers and bank governors between the G7 and the G20, with a peak of 39 references to international institutions. Finance ministers from China, Brazil, India, and South Africa, as well as Russia, were invited to participate in G7 finance meetings that year (see Appendix J-3). The G5 leaders were invited to the G8 summit. A large number of non-G8 countries from the G20 were also included as full members in the Gleneagles Dialogue on climate change, clean energy, and sustainable development. The G7 recognized that global governance, particularly of finance and energy, required more than just the old exclusive G7 club, although the G7 did not go so far as to endorse the G20 as a whole.

Causes of Performance

Once again the systemic hub model accounts for Xianghe's strong performance, with shocks activating members' equal vulnerability returning to spur strong action.

Shock-Activated, Equalizing Vulnerabilities

The G20's strong performance in 2005 was driven in the first instance by new, non-state shocks that erupted to affect all members, above all the most powerful Asian ones, but America and Britain too (see Appendix I). They came in a comprehensive way outside the finance and economic field.

The year began with the devastating Indian Ocean tsunami of December 26, 2004, fresh in the minds of citizens around the world, above all in Asia itself. With more than 230,000 casualties, it was one of the most deadly natural disasters ever recorded. The tsunami had the biggest direct impact on Indonesia and India. But as one of the worst natural disasters to hit the planet, a global response was required. The G20 countries rallied to provide assistance, including humanitarian relief and financial support.

In August 2005 a second deadly natural disaster from the sea struck a powerful G20 country, with deadly and destructive force. This time the victim was the United States, when Hurricane Katrina took out New Orleans, in a way military planners had only imagined in their Cold War nuclear games. Hurricane Katrina struck America's Gulf Coast on August 29. Doing more than $200 billion in damage, with at least 1,833 deaths, it was the costliest natural disaster in the United States (Dolfman et al. 2007; Knabb et al. 2006). Katrina also exacerbated America's energy insecurity, and drove energy prices up. Oil prices climbed to new highs in 2005. The day before the G20 met in China, oil was at $62.61 a barrel, almost reaching its $69.91 high for the year. This was a major jump from the price of $46.30 a barrel before the previous G20 meeting in 2004.

A third, much smaller shock sequence came from avian influenza. It started in China, but became a contagious concern for many other G20 countries. The number of cases grew from four in 2003, and 46 in 2004 to a total of 98 in 2005 (World Health Organization 2012). By the end of 2005, 43 deaths had occurred, with the most in Indonesia and China. The number of cases of avian influenza continued to rise into 2005, in China, Asia, North America, and beyond. The ecological and health shocks arising in Asia provided new incentives and motivation to elevate the G20 to the leaders' level.

A fourth terrorist shock sequence also had an impact. The number of terrorist attacks increased nearly fourfold in 2005 (DeYoung 2006). In July, during the G8 summit, London fell prey to a major al Qaeda-modelled terrorist attack, in which 56 people including the bombers were killed and more than 700 injured (MI5 2006).

As Asia, America, and Europe all suffered from these serious shocks, coordinated, global responses through the G20 were appropriate. Xianghe responded by dealing directly with several of the issue areas in which these shocks had arisen. However, the one major shock to America, Hurricane Katrina, came only on August 28, just two weeks before the UN 2005 World Summit was to begin on September 14. But by then, Paul Martin's proposed G20 summit had chosen health as its focus rather than hurricanes or energy. There was thus no proximate, crisis-specific incentive for George Bush, preoccupied with the ecological attack on New Orleans and the terrorist attacks on America in 2001 and Britain in July 2005, to attend even a brief G20 summit in New York. And without his presence, the Canadians concluded there was no point in proceeding with such an event, to form an all-but-America group that left out the US.

International Institutional Failure

The second cause, international institutional failure, importantly drove Xianghe's strong success.

Multilateral Organizations Multilateral organizational failure was evident in the field of finance, which had been the G20's core competence from the start. The IMF's weaknesses were on open display in 2005 when the G20 took up the issue of IMF reform. With the IMF unable to deal with its own internal architectural defects, the G20 took on the task, which was becoming urgent as the relative capabilities of the rising powers grew. The 24 members that made up the International Monetary and Financial Committee (IMFC) in 2005 were less economically capable than the G20. This gave China and others an incentive to rely more on the G20 to lead in IFI reform.

The IMF poorly predicted the global economic outlook once again (see Appendix J-1). In the spring of 2004, it predicted that global gross domestic product would be 4.4 percent. In the fall, it adjusted its prediction to 4.3 percent. Growth in 2005 came in at a notably stronger 4.9 percent.

Another inadequacy, shared with all international financial institutions, as well as the G20, came in financial regulation. While a few individuals wondered if a bubble might be forming, the dominant response was that well-functioning, even more sophisticated financial markets were merely operating the way they should.

Beyond finance, other multilateral organizations had also failed. The World Health Organization, which had performed poorly in response to the SARS outbreak in 2003, was struggling now to cope with avian influenza (Cooper et al. 2007; Cooper and Kirton 2009). And the UN's process of conferences and meetings of the parties to the United Nations Framework Convention on Climate Change seemed to move too slowly to mobilize consequential countries for the climate change control cause, especially as its Montreal meeting in December approached.

The G7/8 The G7/8 proved more responsive to the shock-activated, systemic need to include the rapidly rising emerging powers in its governance core. But its response was still too little too late, especially where China was concerned. The G7/8's actual treatment of China from 1975 to 2000 had shown that it was increasingly embracing China (Kirton 1999, 2001a). There had been a change in the attitude toward the country between 1975 and 1999. Then China's responsible position in the 1997–99 financial crisis, its approach to international financial system reform in ways that coincided with the position of some G7 members on some core issues, its role in the G20, and the contribution of Hong Kong to the Group of 22 (G22) finance ministers and the Financial Stability Forum (FSF) warranted a move toward association with the G7/8 at the leaders' level. Thus, in 2000, the G8 invited China to a pre-summit dinner dialogue (Kirton 2001a). The Chinese did not accept. It was not until 2003, once President Hu Jintao had arrived in office, that China would participate in its first G8 summit, along with many other emerging and developing states. After the absence of an invitation in 2004, China returned as part of the G5 in 2005, 2006, 2007, 2008, and 2009 (Åslund 2006; Vickers 2006).

The G8 Plus Five By 2005, it was increasingly evident that the G7 and G8 needed emerging economies at the table, particularly for discussions on finance, energy, and climate change. Specialized capability was shifting. The idea of elevating the G20 to the leaders' level gained much support (Ibbitson 2005; Martin 2005a; Canada 2005a, 2005b). Yet it was not the only proposed solution, as the G8 Plus Five formula also came to life.

Tony Blair's decision to invite China, India, Brazil, Mexico, and South Africa, in what became the G5 to portions of the 2005 G8 Gleneagles Summit set a precedent. In 2006, the novice Russian hosts were convinced to follow the formula. The Germans continued in 2007, adding also an official-level, issue-specific Heiligendamm Dialogue Process that affirmed the equality among all 13 members at a third tier. The Japanese in 2008 and Italians in 2009 both followed their predecessors. The perceived success of the "Gleneagles G8 Plus Five" when it first arose in July 2005 diminished the attractiveness of a G20 summit, even as the subject-specific focus of the former increasingly left issues arising from the new global financial system off the agenda.

Despite all this G8 outreach, however, never were the rising powers, whose relevance was increasingly recognized, allowed to participate as full equals in all discussions at the G8 summits. Even on July 7, 2005, when the invited leaders of China, India, Brazil, Mexico, and South Africa stood shoulder to shoulder with Tony Blair and his G8 colleagues to condemn the terrorist attacks on London that very day, such an impressive display of "G13" solidarity on the central security issue did not inspire the G8 to upgrade the status of the G5 members in the still G8-only club. Democratic India, which some thought deserved a place by 2005, was left out (Kirton 2005b; Thakur 2007).

The Finance Plurilaterals At the ministerial level, China alone stood out. It had begun participating in G7 finance ministers' meetings even when its G5 partners were not there. In December 2005, it did so when Mexico and South Africa were missing. In June 2006 Brazil did not attend, although G20 members Korea and Australia did. For those times when China was absent, no countries other than the G8 members came.

In the field of finance, the G20 remained the only institution that gave emerging economies an opportunity to lead. All other major financial forums, notably led by the G7, the G8, the IMF, the IMFC, the Bank for International Settlements, the Basel Committee on Banking Supervision, the Organisation for Economic Co-operation and Development, the Group of 10, and the FSF, failed to embrace all the critically important emerging economies. Moreover, they continued to be led or dominated by advanced, mostly G8 countries.

The G20 thus began winning out over other bodies with fewer, greater, and different numbers, at the level of leaders, ministers, and officials and across a wide range of policy domains (Bradford and Linn 2004; Cooper et al. 2006; Cooper and English 2005; Fues 2007; Gurría 2005; Kirton 2001b, 2004a, 2004b, 2005a, 2010; Lesage 2007; Martin 2005b; Wilson and Purushothaman 2003).

Predominant, Equalizing Capabilities The third cause, predominant, equalizing capabilities, also helps a little to explain the G20's strong performance in 2005. To be sure, its globally predominant, equalizing capability slipped marginally to 79 percent and its internal equality rose, as measured by the Gini coefficient (see Appendix K). However, the relative capability ratio between its strongest and weakest members dropped, creating increased equality within the group.

Democratic Convergence The fourth cause, domestic, democratic convergence, increased in 2005. That year Indonesia improved its political rights and civil liberties to become a fully free democracy (see Appendix L). Now, 15 of the 19 countries in the G20 were considered fully free democracies. Russia, China, and Saudi Arabia were still not free. Turkey was still considered only partially free. Indonesia's advance in 2005 showed that Asian democracy was on the rise. This advance was consistent with Xianghe's strong affirmation of democratic principles even though non-democratic China chaired the group.

Domestic Political Control, Capital, Continuity, Competence, and Commitment

The fifth cause of domestic political control, capital, continuity, competence, and commitment was also a strong spur of G20 representativeness.

A highly committed Paul Martin now had his own mandate as prime minister, if a minority one. He accelerated his campaign for a G20 summit, although it lasted only until his electoral defeat in January 2006. Britain's Tony Blair and his reappointed chancellor of the exchequer Gordon Brown won a third majority mandate in the spring of 2005.

Continuity was substantial. Finance ministers from Australia, Germany, Saudi Arabia, South Africa, and the UK had all been in power since the first G20 meeting in 1999 (see Appendix M-2). The finance ministers from China and the US—the most capable of the non-G8 and G8 countries—both came to the Xianghe meeting, each for the third time. They were joined by their colleagues from Mexico, India, Russia, France, and tsunami-hit Indonesia.

While not all finance ministers attended the Xianghe meeting, it assembled the most experienced ministers of all the G20's annual fall meetings from 1999 through to 2009. In total, the finance ministers in China in 2005 had 56 years of G20 experience. Of this, 35 years came from non-G8 members and 21 from G8 ones. The balance of experience and continuity had shifted to the emerging country members of the group, even as the equality in core continuity fostered the movement from a group toward a club.

Controlled Club Participation as a Network Hub

The status of the G20 as the group, and embryonic club, at the hub of global governance was also an important cause of the G20's strong performance in 2005 and of the major move toward elevating it to the leaders' level.

Internally, the appearance of Hu Jintao to address the opening of the Xianghe meeting confirmed the support of the G20 at the leaders' level, and showed a leader's personal buy-in to the group, from a significant member of the group. At the leaders' level, only George Bush prevented the group from becoming a summit-level global governance group.

Externally the global governance network around the G20 hub grew. At the finance level, APEC finance ministers met in Jeju, Korea, on September 8–9 and Commonwealth finance ministers met in Barbados on September 18–20. On November 15–16, immediately before the APEC summit in Busan, Korea, finance ministers focused mostly on trade, as they had at the G20 in China the previous month. However, they also dealt with food and agriculture, corruption, counterterrorism, health, natural disasters, and energy (APEC 2005b). Beyond finance, the ministerial Gleneagles Dialogue was established, with membership that largely overlapped with the G20. Health ministers from all the G20 members except Saudi Arabia, with the addition of several countries, met for the first time to deal with the shock of avian influenza. That meeting took place in Ottawa on October 25, just following the G20's Xianghe meeting on October 15–16 (International Meeting of Health Ministers 2005).

At the leaders' level, the G20-centred network expanded even more. At the 2005 Commonwealth Heads of Government meeting in Malta on November 25–27, 38 of the 52 participants discussed a wide range of issues, including their shared political values, terrorism, UN reform, arms control, and human rights (Commonwealth Heads of Government 2005). APEC leaders met on November 18–19 in Busan to discuss trade, human security, and the future of the organization (APEC 2005a). At the fourth Summit of the Americas, on November 4–5 in Mar del Plata, Argentina, the 34 members focused on job creation and democracy (SOA 2005).

Beyond finance and economics, at the summit of the North Atlantic Treaty Organization in Brussels on February 22, the leaders of six G7 countries and Turkey reaffirmed their commitment to collective defence and shared values and discussed regional security issues in Afghanistan, Iraq, the Balkans, Russia, Ukraine, and the

Broader Middle East. The Shanghai Cooperation Organisation, founded in 2001, held its fifth summit on July 5 in Astana, Kazakhstan. Led by Russia and China, members focused on strengthening cooperation in security, the economy, disaster relief, education, tourism, and media relations (Xinhua 2010). The third summit of the Organisation of Islamic Cooperation, with 57 emerging and developing members, took place on December 7–8, in Makkah Al Mukarramah, Saudi Arabia. Leaders discussed terrorism, trade, development, energy, and regional concerns in Iraq, Cyprus, Sudan, and elsewhere.

The year 2005 also saw the creation of two consequential regional organizations that combined the G20's advanced and emerging members and thus strengthened its network reach. The annual American-initiated North American leaders summit among the US, Canada, and Mexico first took place at Waco, Texas, on March 23, with George Bush as host. The Chinese-inspired East Asian Summit held its first meeting in Kuala Lumpur on December 14, gathering the leaders of Japan, China, Korea, and Indonesia, with Russia as an invited guest. The latter brought countries beyond the G20 further into the G20-centred governance net.

Conclusion

G20 diplomacy during 2005 and at the Xianghe gathering had three important effects: it helped move the annual G20 meetings and its agenda forward, especially in the architectural issue of IFI reform; it elevated China's engagement in the group; and it furthered discussions and debates on elevating the G20 to the leaders' level.

China championed issues that were important at home and abroad, including development, demographics, and IFI reform. Reform of the Bretton Woods institutions was key. The members ensured that this topic would remain on the agenda at future meetings. Eventually they were able to reach a compromise on the matter—something they were unable to do in other multilateral institutions, including the IMF and World Bank themselves and the G7/8 too.

The Xianghe meeting was also critical for more fully engaging China. It showed that the Chinese were more than mere participants, followers, or free riders in the G20. They could host, chair, and set the agenda as a full equal in the group. This was a clear departure from their role as an outsider in the meetings of G7 finance ministers and central bank governors and at the summits of G8 leaders.

In 2005, the idea of having a G20 summit gathered force and almost achieved its goal. There was still debate on whether the G20 was the right forum, what issues it should tackle, and when the first summit might be held. However, the first G20 summit, when it occurred in 2008, was rooted in the considerable consensus forged in 2005, during the campaign that came so close to success.

References

Asia-Pacific Economic Cooperation. 2005a. "Busan Declaration — Towards One Community: Meet the Challenge, Make the Change." Leaders' declaration, Busan, November 18–19. Available at: www.apec.org/Meeting-Papers/Leaders-Declarations/2005/2005_aelm.aspx. Accessed: July 2012.

Asia-Pacific Economic Cooperation. 2005b. "Joint Statement — Towards One Community: Meet the Challenge, Make the Change." Ministerial meeting, Busan, November 15–16. Available at: www.apec.org/Meeting-Papers/Ministerial-Statements/Annual/2005/2005_amm.aspx. Accessed: July 2012.

Åslund, Anders. 2006. "Russia's Challenges as Chair of the G8." Policy Brief No. 06-3, March, Institute for International Economics, Washington DC. Available at: www.iie.com/publications/pb/pb06-3.pdf. Accessed: July 2012.

Baum, Richard and Shevchenko, Alexei. 2001. "Bringing China In: A Cautionary Note." In *The New Great Power Coalition: Toward a Concert of Nations*, ed Rosecrance, Richard. New York: Rowman and Littlefield, 327–44.

Bergsten, C. Fred. 1998. "The New Agenda with China." *International Economic Policy Briefs* 98(2): 1–2.

Blair, Tony. 2010. *A Journey*. London: Random House.

Bradford, Colin I. and Linn, Johannes F. 2004. "Global Economic Governance at a Crossroads: Replacing the G7 with the G20." Brookings Institution Policy Brief 131. Available at: www.brookings.edu/papers/2004/04globaleconomics_bradford.aspx. Accessed: July 2012.

Brown, Gordon. 2005. "Statement at the Conclusion of G7 Finance Ministers Meeting." London, December 3. Available at: www.g8.utoronto.ca/finance/fm051203_brown.htm. Accessed: July 2012.

Brzezinski, Zbigniew. 1996. "Let's Add to the G7." *New York Times*, June 25, p. A11.

Canada. 2005a. "Joint Declaration by Canada and China." Beijing, January 20. Available at: epe.lac-bac.gc.ca/100/205/301/prime_minister-ef/paul_martin/06-02-03/www.pm.gc.ca/eng/news.asp@id=397. Accessed: July 2012.

Canada. 2005b. "Joint Declaration by Canada and India." Delhi, January 18. Available at: epe.lac-bac.gc.ca/100/205/301/prime_minister-ef/paul_martin/06-02-03/www.pm.gc.ca/eng/news.asp@id=391. Accessed: July 2012.

Commission on Global Governance. 1995. *Our Global Neighbourhood: The Report of the Commission on Global Governance*. Oxford: Oxford University Press.

Commonwealth Heads of Government. 2005. "Final Communiqué." Malta, November 25–27. Available at: www.thecommonwealth.org/Templates/Internal.asp?NodeID=147565. Accessed: July 2012.

Cooper, Andrew F. 2007. "The Logic of the B(R)ICSAM Model for G8 Reform." CIGI Policy Brief No. 1, Centre for International Governance Innovation, Waterloo ON. Available at: www.cigionline.org/publications/2007/5/logic-bricsam-model-g8-reform. Accessed: July 2012.

Cooper, Andrew F., Antkiewicz, Agata, and Shaw, Timothy M. 2006. "Economic Size Trumps All Else? Lessons from BRICSAM." Centre for International Governance Innovation, Waterloo ON. Available at: www.cigionline.org/publications/2006/12/economic-size-trumps-all-else-lessons-bricsam. Accessed: July 2012.

Cooper, Andrew F. and English, John. 2005. "Introduction." In *Reforming from the Top: A Leaders' 20 Summit*, eds English, John, Thakur, Ramesh, and Cooper, Andrew F. Tokyo: United Nations University Press.

Cooper, Andrew F. and Kirton, John J., eds. 2009. *Innovation in Global Health Governance: Critical Cases*. Farnham: Ashgate.

Cooper, Andrew F., Kirton, John J., and Schrecker, Ted, eds. 2007. *Governing Global Health: Challenge, Response, Innovation*. Aldershot: Ashgate.

Costello, Peter. 2008. *The Costello Memoirs: The Age of Prosperity*. Melbourne: Melbourne University Press.

de Brouwer, Gordon and Yeaman, Luke. 2007. "Australia's G20 Host Year: A Treasury Perspective." Treasury, Australian Government, Canberra. Available at: www.g20.utoronto.ca/biblio/debrouwer-yeaman_2007.pdf. Accessed: July 2012.

Desai, Seema. 2006. "Expanding the G8: Should China Join?," January. Foreign Policy Centre, London. Available at: fpc.org.uk/fsblob/749.pdf. Accessed: July 2012.

DeYoung, Karen. 2006. "Terrorist Attacks Rose Sharply in 2005, State Dept. Says." *Washington Post*, April 29. Available at: www.washingtonpost.com/wp-dyn/content/article/2006/04/28/AR2006042802181.html. Accessed: July 2012.

Dobson, Hugo. 2004. *Japan and the G7/8, 1975–2002*. London: RoutledgeCurzon.

Dolfman, Michael L., Fortier Wasser, Solidelle, and Bergman, Bruce. 2007. "The Effects of Hurricane Katrina on the New Orleans Economy." *Monthly Labor Review* 130(6): 3–18. Available at: www.bls.gov/opub/mlr/2007/06/art1exc.htm. Accessed: July 2012.

Economist. 1998. "Welcome to China, Mr Clinton." January 25. Available at: www.economist.com/node/137669. Accessed: July 2012.

Fues, Thomas. 2007. "Global Governance Beyond the G8: Reform Prospects for the Summit Architecture." *Internationale Politik und Gesellschaft* 2: 11–24. Available at: www.fes.de/ipg/inhalt_d/pdf/03_Fues_US.pdf. Accessed: July 2011.

G7 Finance Ministers and Central Bank Governors. 2005a. "Statement by G7 Finance Ministers and Central Bank Governors." September 23. Available at: www.g8.utoronto.ca/finance/fm050923.htm. Accessed: July 2012.

G7 Finance Ministers and Central Bank Governors. 2005b. "Statement of G7 Finance Ministers and Central Bank Governors." London, February 4–5. Available at: www.g8.utoronto.ca/finance/fm050205_statement.htm. Accessed: July 2012.

G8. 2006. "Global Energy Security." St. Petersburg, July 16. Available at: www.g8.utoronto.ca/summit/2006stpetersburg/energy.html. Accessed: July 2012.

G8 Research Group. 2004. "2003 Evian Final Compliance Report." Available at: www.g8.utoronto.ca/evaluations/2003evian_comp_final. Accessed: July 2012.

G8 Research Group LSE/Oxford. 2007. "The G8 and Climate Change since Heiligendamm: Final Compliance Report for the G8 and Outreach Five Countries." Available at: www.g8.utoronto.ca/oxford/g8rg-lseox-final-2007-080720.pdf. Accessed: July 2012.

G8 Research Group Oxford. 2007. "Governing Global Climate Change: St. Petersburg Compliance Report for the 'G8 Plus Five' Countries." Available at: www.g8.utoronto.ca/oxford/2006compliance-ox.pdf. Accessed: July 2012.

G20 Finance Ministers and Central Bank Governors. 2005a. "Communiqué." Xianghe, Hebei, China, October 16. Available at: www.g20.utoronto.ca/2005/2005communique.html. Accessed: July 2012.

G20 Finance Ministers and Central Bank Governors. 2005b. "G20 Reform Agenda 2005." Xianghe, Hebei, China, October 16. Available at: www.g20.utoronto.ca/2005/2005reform.html. Accessed: July 2012.

G20 Finance Ministers and Central Bank Governors. 2005c. "G20 Statement on Global Development." Xianghe, Hebei, China, October 16. Available at: www.g20.utoronto.ca/2005/2005development.html. Accessed: July 2012.

G20 Finance Ministers and Central Bank Governors. 2005d. "G20 Statement on Reforming the Bretton Woods Institutions." Xianghe, Hebei, China, October 16. Available at: www.g20.utoronto.ca/2005/2005bwi.html. Accessed: July 2012.

Guebert, Jenilee. 2008. "China's Compliance with G8 Commitments." G8 Research Group, Toronto.

Gurría, Angel. 2005. "A Leaders' 20 Summit?" In *Reforming from the Top: A Leaders' 20 Summit*, eds English, John, Thakur, Ramesh, and Cooper, Andrew F. Tokyo: United Nations University Press, 63–71.

Hodges, Michael R. 1999. "The G8 and the New Political Economy." In *The G8's Role in the New Millennium*, eds Hodges, Michael R., Kirton, John J., and Daniels, Joseph P. Aldershot: Ashgate.

Holbrooke, Richard. 2005. "China Makes Its Move." *Washington Post*, May 27. Available at: www.washingtonpost.com/wp-dyn/content/article/2005/05/26/AR2005052601540.html. Accessed: July 2012.

Ibbitson, John. 2005. "The Prime Minister's Passion for the L20." *Globe and Mail*, February 22.

International Meeting of Health Ministers. 2005. "Ottawa 2005: Global Pandemic Influenza Readiness." October 25, Ottawa. Available at: www.who.int/mediacentre/events/2005/05_Ottawa_Canada_Ian_Shugart.pdf. Accessed: July 2012.

Jayawardena, Lal. 1989. "World Economic Summits: The Role of Representative Groups in the Governance of the World Economy." *Journal of the Society for International Development* 4: 17–20.

Kirton, John J. 1999. "The G7 and China in the Management of the International Financial System." Paper prepared for "China in the 21st Century and the World," sponsored by the China Development Institute, the China International Center for Economic and Technical Exchange, and the National Institute for Research Advancement, Japan, November 11–12, Shenzen. Available at: www.g8.utoronto.ca/scholar/kirton199903. Accessed: July 2012.

Kirton, John J. 2001a. "The G7/8 and China: Toward a Closer Association." In *Guiding Global Order: G8 Governance in the Twenty-First Century*, eds Kirton, John J., Daniels, Joseph P., and Freytag, Andreas. Aldershot: Ashgate, 189–222.

Kirton, John J. 2001b. "The G20: Representativeness, Effectiveness, and Leadership in Global Governance." In *Guiding Global Order: G8 Governance in the Twenty-First Century*, eds Kirton, John J., Daniels, Joseph P., and Freytag, Andreas. Aldershot: Ashgate, 143–72.

Kirton, John J. 2004a. "Getting the L20 Going: Reaching Out from the G8." Paper prepared for a workshop on "G20 to Replace the G8: Why Not Now?" sponsored by the Brookings Institution, Institute for International Economics, and the Centre for Global Governance, September 22, Washington DC. Available at: www.g8.utoronto.ca/scholar/kirton2004/kirton_040922.html. Accessed: July 2012.

Kirton, John J. 2004b. "Toward Multilateral Reform: The G20's Role and Place." Paper prepared for a conference on "The Ideas-Institutional Nexus: The Case of the G20," sponsored by the Centre for International Governance Innovation, United Nations University, FLASCO, and the University of Waterloo, May 19–21, Buenos Aires. Available at: www.g8.utoronto.ca/scholar/kirton2004/kirton_g20_2004.pdf. Accessed: July 2012.

Kirton, John J. 2005a. "From G7 to G20: Capacity, Leadership and Normative Diffusion in Global Financial Governance." Paper prepared for the International Studies Association convention, March 1–5, Honolulu. Available at: www.g8.utoronto.ca/scholar/kirton2005/kirton_isa2005.pdf. Accessed: July 2012.

Kirton, John J. 2005b. "The Future of the G8." In *G8 Summit 2005: Mapping the Challenges*, ed Fraser, Maurice. London: Newsdesk Publications. Available at: www.g8.utoronto.ca/newsdesk/G8-2005.pdf. Accessed: July 2012.

Kirton, John J. 2007. "Facing Global Trade Imbalance: Cooperation and Development." Paper prepared for a conference sponsored by the Global Trade Development Forum and the Sixth Annual Academic Meeting on China and the World Trade Organization, November 9–12, Beijing.

Kirton, John J. 2008. "From G8 2003 to G13 2010? The Heiligendamm Process's Past, Present, and Future." In *Emerging Powers in Global Governance: Lessons from the Heiligendamm Process*, eds Cooper, Andrew F., and Antkiewicz, Agata. Waterloo ON: Wilfrid Laurier University Press, 45–79.

Kirton, John J. 2010. "The Group of Eight's Legacy, Limitations, and Lessons." In *The New Dynamics of Summitry: Innovations for G20 Summits*, eds Bradford,

Colin I., and Lim, Wonhyuk. Washington DC and Seoul: Brookings Institution Press and Korea Development Institute, 17–60.

Kirton, John J. and Kokotsis, Ella. 2004. "An Evaluation of the G8's Commitment to the Kananaskis Pledges." Discussion paper prepared for a meeting of the Council on Foreign Relations G8 Africa Round Table, February 4, Washington DC. Available at: www.g8.utoronto.ca/scholar/kirton2004/kirton_africa_040204.html. Accessed: July 2012.

Kirton, John J. and Panova, Victoria. 2007. "Coming Together: The Evian Legacy." In *Corporate, Public and Global Governance: The G8 Contribution*, eds Fratianni, Michele, Savona, Paolo, and Kirton, John J. Aldershot: Ashgate, 201–30.

Knabb, Richard D., Rhome, Jamie R., and Brown, Daniel P. 2006. "Tropical Cyclone Report: Hurricane Katrina, 22–30 August 2005." August 10, National Hurricane Center. Available at: www.nhc.noaa.gov/pdf/TCR-AL122005_Katrina.pdf. Accessed: July 2012.

Kokotsis, Ella. 2005. "Explaining Compliance with G20 Commitments: The Democratic Institutionalist and Concert Equality Models Compared." Paper prepared for the annual International Studies Association convention, March 1–5, Honolulu. Available at: www.g8.utoronto.ca/scholar/kokotsis_isa2005.pdf. Accessed: July 2012.

Lesage, Dries. 2007. "Globalisation, Multipolarity, and the L20 as an Alternative to the G8." *Global Society* 21(3): 343–61.

Martin, Paul. 2005a. "Address to the Canada-China Business Council." Beijing, January 21. Available at: epe.lac-bac.gc.ca/100/205/301/prime_minister-ef/paul_martin/06-02-03/www.pm.gc.ca/eng/news.asp@id=399. Accessed: July 2012.

Martin, Paul. 2005b. "A Global Answer to Global Problems." *Foreign Affairs* 84(3): 2–6. Available at: www.foreignaffairs.com/articles/60792/paul-martin/a-global-answer-to-global-problems. Accessed: July 2012.

Martin, Paul. 2010. "Address to the 2010 Couchiching Conference on 'Watershed Moment or Wasted Opportunity'." August 6, Geneva Park, Canada.

Martinez-Diaz, Leonardo. 2007. "The G20 after Eight Years: How Effective a Vehicle for Developing-Country Influence?" Global Economy and Development Working Paper No. 12, Brookings Institution, Washington DC. Available at: www.brookings.edu/papers/2007/1017development.aspx. Accessed: July 2012.

MI5. 2006. "Report of the Official Account of the Bombings in London on 7th July 2005." May 11. Available at: www.mi5.gov.uk/output/news/reports-on-7-7-bombings-published.html. Accessed: July 2012.

Pan, Letian. 2005. "Hu Calls for Strengthening Global Cooperation." Beijing, October 16. Available at: english.gov.cn/2005-10/16/content_78172.htm. Accessed: July 2012.

Smyser, W.R. 1993. "Goodbye, G7." *Washington Quarterly* (Winter): 15–28.

Summit of the Americas. 2005. "Declaration of Mar Del Plata: Creating Jobs to Fight Poverty and Strengthen Democratic Governance." November 5, Mar Del Plata, Argentina. Available at: www.summit-americas.org/iv_summit/iv_summit_dec_en.pdf. Accessed: July 2012.
Thakur, Ramesh. 2007. "India's Rising and Shining: Will It Prove a False Dawn?," Centre for International Governance Innovation, Waterloo ON. Available at: www.cigionline.org/publications/2007/7/indias-rising-and-shining-will-it-prove-false-dawn. Accessed: July 2012.
ul Haq, Mahbub. 1994. "The Bretton Woods Institutions and Global Governance." In *Managing the World Economy*, ed Kenen, Peter B. Washington DC: Institute for International Economics, 409–18.
Vickers, Brendan. 2006. "Heading Toward the G8 St. Petersburg Summit: What's In It for Africa?" *Global Insight* (63): 1–4.
Wheatley, Alan and Love, Brian. 2005. "Oil Dominates G20 Talks as Yuan Takes Back Seat." Reuters, October 16.
Whyman, William E. 1995. "We Can't Go On Meeting Like This: Revitalizing the G7 Process." *Washington Quarterly* 18(3): 139–65.
Wilson, Dominic and Purushothaman, Roopa. 2003. "Dreaming with BRICs: The Path to 2050." Goldman Sachs, New York. Available at: www.goldmansachs.com/our-thinking/topics/brics/brics-reports-pdfs/brics-dream.pdf. Accessed: July 2012.
World Health Organization. 2012. "Cumulative Number of Confirmed Human Cases for Avian Influenza A(H5N1) Reported to WHO, 2003–2012." July 6, Geneva. Available at: www.who.int/influenza/human_animal_interface/H5N1_cumulative_table_archives/en/index.html. Accessed: July 2012.
Xinhua. 2010. "Shanghai Cooperation Organization Summits." *China Daily*, June 9. Available at: www.chinadaily.com.cn/china/2010sco/2010-06/09/content_9955838.htm. Accessed: July 2012.

Chapter 9
Strengthening Sustainability, Melbourne 2006 and Kleinmond 2007

Introduction

In 2006 and 2007, the Group of 20 (G20) finance ministers and central bank governors met for the eighth and ninth times. The 2006 meeting was held on November 18–19 in Melbourne, Australia. The 2007 meeting was held on November 17–18 in Kleinmond, South Africa. Both meetings worked to further reforms of the international financial institutions (IFIs), coordinate macroeconomic policies, and address energy security and climate change.

Voice and vote reform at the International Monetary Fund (IMF) and World Bank remained high on the agenda, following from the 2005 meeting in China. Climate change and energy also gained momentum. In 2006, the Australians pushed for a much stronger institutionalization of the G20. They worked closely with the South Africans to carry their priorities onward in 2007.

By 2007, a new global financial crisis was brewing. It had yet to be addressed by the Group of Seven (G7), the Group of Eight (G8), or the International Monetary Fund (IMF). The G20's importance as a global economic and financial governor was thus growing as well. While it would not be until 2008 that the G20 was elevated to the leaders' level, the 2006 and 2007 meetings helped pave the way by highlighting the G20's role and success in the world.

The G20's Advance in 2006–2007

This chapter argues that the 2006 and 2007 G20 meetings were substantial successes, primarily in expanding the G20 agenda, furthering progress on key issues, and advancing solutions to challenges that could not be solved elsewhere. As non-G8 members, Australia and South Africa saw the particular importance and advantage of hosting successful meetings. They addressed issues that needed the assent of the broader membership that the G20 offered. IFI reform, climate change, energy, and development needed to be dealt with in this group of advanced and emerging equals.

Melbourne 2006

The Challenge

The theme of the eighth G20 meeting on November 18–19, 2006, held in Melbourne, was "Building and Sustaining Prosperity." As chair, Australia had two main objectives. The first was to pursue global development and growth. The second, a rational choice for an advanced country outside the G7 and G8 club, was to strengthen the G20 as an economic and financial forum. In Melbourne, for the first time, climate change came onto the G20 agenda in its own right, while energy and minerals took centre stage. This made Melbourne the G20's first energy-environment meeting. Melbourne competed for global political attention with the Asia-Pacific Economic Cooperation (APEC) leaders' forum, which met the same weekend in Hanoi. APEC was a summit-level international organization, attended in 2006 by 21 countries, 10 of which were also members of the G20. At the APEC meeting, leaders addressed free trade, acknowledged the importance of the Doha round of trade negotiations at the World Trade Organization (WTO), and put the idea of a Pacific free trade area on the table (APEC 2006). In an institutionally crowded world, the G20 thus still had to prove its unique worth as a ministerial-level body in relation to summit-level competitors, and to forge a working relationship with them, especially as many—including APEC—also contained an annual meeting of finance ministers.

Competing Assessments The Melbourne meeting inspired a debate among three major schools of thought. The first school saw it as a failure for not adequately addressing development. The second school saw the meeting as a selective success on issues such as energy and a failure on others, including climate change (Agence France Presse 2006). The third school argued that the meeting had been a success, essentially in domestic political management. The Australian Treasury hailed the gathering as "the most important economic forum ever held in Australia" (Hoy 2006).

The Argument The Melbourne meeting was successful in reaching the chair's two main goals: pursuing relevant and practical issues that supported global development and growth and establishing the G20 as a key forum on economic and finance issues. Discussions on energy and extractive industries and even climate change were innovative and productive. Democratic principles were affirmed as never before or since. A historic agreement to reform the IMF was confirmed. Institutional advances came in the form of a chair's manual and the introduction of study groups. However, the meeting did not make any real advance on other issues that the Australians had added, particularly climate change.

These advances were driven less by new shocks than by the failure of the multilateral organizations alone to advance key issues such as IFI reform, Doha, and climate change control. They were further inspired by new plurilateral competitors, notably the British-initiated Gleneagles Dialogue, the US-initiated Major Economies Meeting on Energy Security and Climate Change (MEM), and the Asia Pacific Partnership on clean energy and climate change. A key cause was the hosting by Peter Costello, a highly experienced and committed Australian finance minister and a G20 founder and eight-year veteran who had had two full years to prepare the event.

Planning and Preparations

Preparations for the 2006 meeting began in November 2004, just after Australia had been chosen as the host. At an early stage, Australia suggested establishing informal study groups to collect technical analyses on some of the issues that would be examined by the finance ministers and their deputies. Australia organized a study group on demographic change and labour mobility (G20 2008).

Australia set out three major objectives for the 2006 meeting. The first was to address global economic issues in a way that supported sustainable development. The second was to further institutionalize the G20 summit as a global economic forum, with a focus on encouraging rule-strengthening, market-orientated national policies, and on facilitating international cooperation. The third was to take advantage of hosting the G20 for domestic political management and to enhance Australia's international reputation (de Brouwer and Yeaman 2007, 31).

By the beginning of 2006, Australia had begun to outline the specifics of the agenda. It sought to integrate development more comprehensively into the agenda. Unlike China in 2005, where development had been the stand-alone theme, Australia wanted to embed and highlight development within a broader agenda.

Prior to the meeting, five issues appeared on the agenda. First, following up on the 2005 meeting, Australia confirmed that reform of the Bretton Woods institutions would remain a top priority for 2006 (Costello 2008). In 2005, Costello had noted the problem of Asian representation within the IMF. This cause was taken up among the G7 by Canada, the United Kingdom, and Japan, but opposed by the continental Europeans, who were overrepresented at the IMF.

The second issue was the world economy, a perennial staple of G20 meetings. Following up on the progress made at Berlin in 2004 and at the 2005 annual meeting of the IMF in Singapore, Australia was committed to continuing the discussion on economic policy reform. Third, Australia wanted to highlight the challenges of demographic change. Fourth, energy security was identified as an important issue well suited to a G20 discussion, given the mix in the group of energy- and mineral-exporting countries (Australia, Brazil, Canada, Indonesia, and Saudi Arabia) and key consumer countries (China, Europe, India, Japan, Korea, and the United States). Finally, development aid and aid effectiveness were slated for discussion, particularly since the "Paris Declaration on Aid Effectiveness" had been released in 2005 by the Organisation for Economic Co-operation and Development ([OECD] 2005).

At the Deputies' Meetings To prepare for the Melbourne meeting, the deputies met twice in Australia, in March and in October. The meetings were hosted by Martin Parkinson, Australia's G20 deputy finance minister. These meetings, in turn, were supported by three workshops. One was in February in Tokyo on reform of the Bretton Woods institutions. The second was in June in Banff, Canada, on energy and resources. The third was in July in Sydney on financial markets and demographic change. The workshops brought in experts on each of the issues. Background papers were made available by the Australian government. The meetings were valuable for testing out ideas before the meeting itself.

At the Meeting

At Melbourne, Australia as chair wanted to strike a balance between the legacy issues and the newer concerns it had chosen to champion (G20 2008, 106). Energy and minerals markets were the key new issues that Australia brought to the table (Martinez-Diaz 2007). The participants discussed each of the five agenda issues but focused particularly on IMF reform and energy security.

Global Economic Outlook On the state of the world economy, the G20 ministers were generally optimistic. They noted that it had expanded at above average rates for the fourth consecutive year, although they predicted that it would decline a little in the upcoming year. They reiterated that stable growth rates depended on open trade and ongoing adjustments to monetary and fiscal policy. On trade more directly, they were unequivocal in their support for the Doha Development Agenda, calling it "essential" for open trade market stability and sustained reductions in poverty. While the G20 called for the WTO to resume talks, it had nothing new or constructive to contribute to the stalled negotiations (G20 Finance 2006).

Domestic Economic Reform In true G20 spirit, the finance ministers and central bank governors had a broad ranging and pragmatic discussion on domestic economic reform. They shared their previous experiences and focused on practical ways to implement the reforms contained in the "G20 Accord for Sustained Growth" (see G20 Finance 2004).

Reform of the Bretton Woods Institutions On IFI reform, the G20 members affirmed their commitment to deliver. This was a legacy of China's chair in 2005. G20 members had come to consensus on the first stage of reform, which was confirmed in Singapore when the IMF had agreed to a G20-led review (G20 Finance 2006; de Brouwer and Yeaman 2007, 36). A G20 working group on reform of the IMF argued that, despite the criticism of quota increases as inadequate, these reforms were an essential first step. There was an agreement that quota share should increase for China, Korea, Mexico, and Turkey.

Global Energy and Minerals Markets Energy and minerals formed the first of the many new issues on the agenda at Melbourne. The issue of energy had been the centrepiece of the G8's St. Petersburg Summit in the summer. The G20 finance ministers and bank governors specified ways to strengthen energy and mineral markets, including reducing fiscal subsidies for resources and promoting more transparency from extractive firms and resource countries (de Brouwer and Yeaman 2007, 36). They presciently warned that "global demand for energy and minerals commodities [was] set to increase significantly over coming decades driven by a strong world economy, rising incomes, and ongoing industrialisation and urbanisation in many economies" (G20 Finance 2006). They agreed that "enhancing global trade by strengthening markets, and ensuring sustainability by promoting investment and encouraging efficiency, are the best ways to deliver lasting resource security."

The G20 finance ministers and bank governors concluded that treating energy supply as a security issue creates tension as countries move to secure stable energy sources for themselves. Collective action is thus overwhelmed. This was seen to "weaken stable access to supply or demand, raise the political heat and focus on securing national interests through any available means, destabilise international relations, and potentially increase the risk of conflict" (de Brouwer and Yeaman 2007, 36). Rapid industrialization and urbanization in China and other emerging powers, as well as persistently strong growth in other industrial economies, increased the demand for energy and mineral commodities, squeezed spare production capacity, raised commodity prices, and made the G20—comprising both key global producers and consumers of energy—the proper forum to respond (Parkinson 2006). The G20 agreed that "the most sustainable way to address resource security is to make sure that markets work as well as they can," with the implication that large investments would have to be made in the future on the supply side (de Brouwer and Yeaman 2007). "The recognition that the solution to securing a stable and predictable supply of energy and minerals need not be a zero-sum strategic game" showcased a growing consensus about the need for finding collective, rather than national, solutions to these multidimensional problems (Parkinson 2006).

The G20 also encouraged the work of the Extractive Industries Transparency Initiative (EITI), which aimed at ensuring that revenue from energy sectors contributed to sustainable development instead of getting lost to corruption or mismanagement. In that spirit, the G20 called for the Joint Oil Data Initiative (JODI) to be extended beyond the oil sector to apply to other energy sectors and develop a common definition of energy reserves.

In its treatment of energy and minerals, the Melbourne G20 broadly supported what the G8 St. Petersburg Summit had done (Kirton 2010). Yet it had these principles endorsed by a broader group of countries, including the key energy producer, Saudi Arabia.

Climate Change Melbourne was the first time the G20 seriously considered climate change, although the issue itself was primarily discussed in the context of energy security (McMillan 2006). The ministers endorsed international policy frameworks and actions, well-functioning markets, clear price signals, open trade and investment, market transparency, good governance, effective competition among firms, investment in new supply, efficiencies and new technologies, the use of alternative and renewable energy sources, and knowledge and resources flowing across borders (G20 Finance 2006). The G20 found it difficult to extend its climate governance into the decisional domain, thus inspiring the US-led creation in 2007 of a very similar forum—the 17-member MEM devoted to energy and climate change. Melbourne's difficulty on climate change was due to the insistence of the emerging members that climate change be acted upon only in the fully multilateral United Nations Framework Convention on Climate Change, which is dominated by developing countries, rather than the plurilateral G20 where emerging economies were evenly balanced by established ones.

Demographic Change, Migration, and Health Care Emerging demographic challenges had been addressed by the G20 in previous meetings. In 2006 the finance ministers and bank governors added the financial market aspects of demographic change. They considered improving the portability of social services such as healthcare benefits in order to reduce the transaction costs for migration, particularly for temporary workers. Migration and health came onto the G20 agenda together in this way.

Political Security While not noted in Melbourne's communiqué, G20 members universally condemned North Korea for its October nuclear tests (Australian Associated Press 2006a). The G20 thus in practice, if not publicly, became a global security governor in the high-politics domain of nuclear proliferation.

Achievements

Melbourne's most notable success was getting the IMF to agree to a package of reforms including quota increases for the most significantly underrepresented G20 members, namely China, Korea, Mexico, and Turkey. The G20 worked out a two-stage approach to reform to be implemented in subsequent years. It was a significant vote of confidence that the international economic community looked to the G20 to produce IMF reform.

The G20 thus helped break the longstanding stalemate in the IMF regarding quota reform. It did so because of the G20's broad, equal representation from key established and emerging economies alike. Having the key emerging countries at the table increased the legitimacy of the forum and its decision. The G20 also represented 90 percent of the world's gross domestic product (GDP), 80 percent of world trade, and two thirds of the world population, so a deal done here would be overwhelmingly accepted at the IMF. The involvement of middle powers such as Australia helped ease pressures and tensions among the big players. The G20 also reached consensus in other areas where other established international organizations were stuck, notably on tax havens where the OECD could not act.

The second substantial outcome came on energy and mineral markets. Costello concluded that "the biggest breakthrough in relation to this meeting was in relation to energy and minerals markets" (Chappell 2006). It was important that the finance ministers discussed energy markets in terms of sustainable development and a fair distribution of profits. Integrating equitable development ideas into the broader agenda was one of the key successes. Costello linked energy security with global security more broadly than just sustainable development, emphasizing that without "market production in a way which can guarantee emerging giants of economies access to the energy and minerals that they need, the differences between countries, the friction and dislocation could be quite severe—not just to the economy but beyond that" (Brinsden 2006). The G20 worked toward making the markets work as well as they could, for security and development reasons. The discussion of energy security, an interesting and innovative topic, made the G20 a global security governor even more.

On climate change specifically, China revealed one significant policy shift during the meeting. Zhou Xiaochuan, governor of the People's Bank of China, stated that his country would now support a carbon tax, despite acknowledging that environmentally pricing the energy market might be difficult for developing countries. Zhou confirmed that China would be encouraging cleaner, greener energy (Murdoch 2006). This was a considerable breakthrough in climate change discussions, since China, a large and fast-growing economy, had been particularly reticent on a global energy pricing regime.

There were advances in other areas. On demographic change, the G20 came up with a few specific initiatives to gain more information about this looming challenge, but did not offer any firm commitments. It was significant, however, that the topic was discussed in the context of international markets. The G20 ministers also expressed concern about the failure of the Doha trade negotiations. All agreed on the importance of aid effectiveness and the Millennium Development Goals for development financing. Neither of these affirmations was new or innovative. Nevertheless, it was important that all the countries reached agreement on questions of development. That the G20, where almost half of the members were developing countries, could issue statements on these meant a deepening of core principles and integration among the members.

The 2006 meeting thus broadened the G20 agenda, integrating emerging country concerns and economic development questions into the larger concept of financial stability. The G20 recognized that it was increasingly necessary to include emerging country concerns because of the increasing inter-connectivity of countries and markets. Global imbalances, at the root of many of the topics, were just that—global. The perceived ability of the G20, as one of many international forums, to answer global problems with global solutions made it more important on the international scene.

The Australian meeting also succeeded in further institutionalizing the forum. By introducing study groups and drafting a G20 policy manual to help guide future chairs, Australia helped ensure the enhanced usefulness and effectiveness of the group.

Dimensions of Performance

A systematic assessment of Melbourne's performance of the six dimensions of G20 governance confirms its substantial success.

Domestic Political Management In domestic political management, Australia, as 2006 host, used the G20 meeting to advance its interests and reinforce its government's reputation as an advocate for sustainable policy and as an open and flexible member of the G20. Australia was a wealthy, mid-sized economy that was relatively powerful compared to its small population. Yet it was located on an isolated continent, far away from the historic centres of wealth and security. It was not a member of the G7/8, despite earlier efforts by America's Ronald Reagan and Japan to have it added to this club. Because of this geopolitical and international institutional isolation, Australia constantly sought to join and strengthen international institutions that would allow it to have more global influence. These included the Asia-Pacific Partnership on Clean Development and Climate and MEM that began around this time (Fullilove 2010). In the "Treasury Perspective Report," Gordon de Brouwer and Luke Yeaman (2007, 31) reported that the second "strategic objective" of the Melbourne meeting was to "strengthen the position of the G-20 as a pre-eminent forum in the global economic and financial policy architecture," presumably because this was the one key forum to which Australia belonged.

Australia's particular concerns were given high priority on the agenda. Peter Costello stated early on that he intended to use the ministerial to advance one of his oldest areas of interest, the demographic challenge. For Australia, that challenge was an aging population. The G20 meeting gave Australia the chance to consider the effects of its domestic concerns at a global level. Costello challenged the finance ministers and central bank governors to examine the implications of this challenge: "What will it do to the movement of labour? What will it do to ... capital flows? What will it do to trade balances and exchange rates?" (Uren 2006). The G20 agenda was shaped by the domestic concerns of the host country.

At the same time Melbourne issued three communiqué compliments (see Appendix D). All went to non-G8 members.

Deliberation In its deliberations, Melbourne's performance was substantial (see Appendix E). The meeting produced two documents—the communiqué itself and the G20 reform agenda. The two statements were prolific: at 3,477 words, an increase from the year before and the third highest ever. The 36 paragraphs issued were greater than the year before, although less than the number produced in Montreal in 2000 and Berlin in 2004.

Continuing on from the meeting in China, the discussions were once again heavily rooted in macroeconomics, which took a majority 58 percent of the communiqué, IFI reform, and trade. However, climate change also surged on the agenda in a significant way for the first time.

Direction Setting In its direction setting, Melbourne was an outstanding success. Democratic host Australia further embedded the shared democratic values of the G20 in a major way. The references to shared democratic principles soared to a new high of 22, more than three times as many as ever before or since (see Appendix F-1). There were eight to good governance, seven to transparency, four to surveillance and monitoring, two to information and knowledge exchange, and one to the international mobility of ideas.

Decision Making In its decision making Melbourne performed strongly as well. The G20 made 10 commitments (see Appendix G). This was more than the eight in China the year before. It tied with the 2004 Berlin meeting for the second highest to date after Ottawa in 2001. The commitments fell rather evenly across a broad range of issues: macroeconomics, IFIs, trade, socioeconomics, energy, and terrorism. Once again, the most substantive commitment was on reform of the Bretton Woods institutions. Here the G20 promised to complete a comprehensive set of reforms, including implementing a new quota system and increasing votes.

Delivery Substantial advances were made in delivering these decisions. There was an effort to ensure that members would comply with their commitments. Members were asked to monitor their progress and review the actions that they had already undertaken to support promises, in particular on Bretton Woods reform. The G20 also issued two reports noting progress on past initiatives to combat terrorist financing and to observe standards and codes and the stability of their financial systems. Also, all the commitments made in 2006 were due for completion, at least in part, by the next meeting. Such a one-year timetable suggested that implementation was more likely to come.

Development of Global Governance In the development of global governance, Melbourne also did well (see Appendix C-1). Internally, there were five references to the G20, a drop from eight in each of the previous two years. The G20 study group format was used for the first time and proved to be a useful tool for encouraging frank and informal debate. Despite their value, however, ongoing study groups could be time consuming. The G20 recommended the number of groups be limited to one per year. There was also an effort by the Australian hosts to further institutionalize the G20 forum.

Externally, there were 32 references to other international institutions, the second highest number ever. They were led by the IMF. The International Energy

Agency, the EITI, and the Global Forum on Taxation were referred to for the first time. Australia sought to use the G20 to overcome deadlocks in other forums, notably the IMF. This was the antithesis of the choice that had been made to focus on the easy subjects at the G20's start in 1999.

Causes of Performance

Several forces highlighted by the systemic club model drove this particular pattern of substantial G20 performance at Melbourne.

Shock-Activated, Equalizing Vulnerability The first cause, shock-activated, equalizing vulnerability, helped broaden the G20's agenda and achievements beyond the finance and economic field and deepen its democratic consensus too. One area where a potential shock was gathering force was in energy and mineral markets. Another shock that arose was in nuclear proliferation, with North Korea's explosion on October 9, 2006. Members were drawn together by the shocks felt in their home countries: 16 out of 20 members suffered terrorist attacks in 2006, with fatalities in 11 countries (see Appendix J). Melbourne's commitments on energy and terrorism came as a result.

In finance, the material shocks of the Asian financial crisis were long gone, as the global economy had now rapidly expanded for several years. G20 members were optimistic about continuing growth. Although there was no immediate financial or economic shock influencing Melbourne, G20 markets were increasingly interconnected, an interdependence from which vulnerabilities could flow. The communiqué referred to the "deeper linkages … being forged between nations through trade, investment and the movement of people and capital" and to "shared challenges" that had arisen due to market globalization (G20 Finance 2006). This awareness of growing interdependence contributed to the macroeconomic, IFI reform, and sustainable development advances.

International Institutional Failure The second cause, international institutional failure, also played a role, especially in broadening the G20 agenda and securing IFI reform. IMF governance arrangements by themselves failed to keep pace with the changes in the world economy, eroding the IMF's effectiveness and authority. The quotas of fast-growing emerging markets, including Asia, no longer represented their increasing economic weight. The IMF was unable to reform itself or induce its members to provide the new resources the IMF needed. Because the G20 represented more than 60 percent of the voting power of the IMF, it was considered an appropriate and legitimate body to oversee the institutional reform. And once again, the IMF's predictions significantly underestimated the growth the global economy enjoyed in 2006 (see Appendix J-1).

The informal plurilateral G7/8 proved no more responsive to the emerging countries in 2006. Russia as host of the G8 summit only reluctantly repeated the Gleneagles invitation to the Group of Five (G5) without adding to its or others' participation in any important way, beyond iterating the G5 formula for a second year. Moreover, at the first two G8 finance ministers' meetings Russia held in 2006 it invited no outsiders (see Appendix J-3). In June 2006, it invited only Australia, China, India, Korea, Nigeria, and South Africa.

One widely shared failure, embracing the G20 too, was the inconclusive dialogue about bubbles that might be brewing in domestic financial markets. When the Germans raised concerns about the US real estate market, the Americans responded with concerns about German markets. Even if they had agreed on what bubbles were brewing where, it was not clear what to do about them.

Predominant, Equalizing Capabilities The third cause, predominant, equalizing capabilities, substantially contributed to the G20's success in 2006. To be sure, its global predominance again slightly declined, to a still predominant 78 percent (see Appendix K). But its Gini coefficient strongly rose. Its ratio of relative capability between its strongest and weakest members strongly declined, both for the second year in a row.

Democratic Convergence The fourth cause, democratic convergence, contributed a little as G20 members continued their domestic democratic character for another year (see Appendix L). The G20's common commitment to the democratic values of openness and transparency was central in 2006. As a veteran full democracy, G20 host Australia was also in a better position than G8 host Russia, as a new and partial democracy, to champion these core values.

Political Control, Capital, Continuity, Competence, and Commitment The fifth cause, political control, capital, continuity, competence, and commitment, had a mixed effect. There was a significant changeover in G20 officials in 2006 (see Appendix M-2). Argentina, Brazil, Canada, Germany, Italy, Japan, Korea, and the US had all appointed new finance ministers since their last meeting. Australia, Italy, Korea, Turkey, and the United States all had new central bank governors. Continuity was stronger among non-G8 members than G8 ones.

However, continuity, competence, and commitment as a finance minister was highest where it counted most, in the person of Peter Costello as the G20's host and chair (see Appendix M). Costello, a G20 founder, was chairing the eighth G20 ministerial he had attended. He also brought high political competence, in his tenth year as Australia's elected and appointed finance minister (see Appendix M-2). In this regard, he surpassed Canada's Paul Martin as chair in 1999, 2000, and 2001. Moreover, as the finance minister of a non-G8 country, Costello was strongly committed to making Australia's G20 a globally central club.

Controlled Club Participation as a Network Hub The sixth cause, controlled club participation as a network hub, contributed too. Internally, after the Melbourne meeting ended, several of its participants said it was one of the friendliest meetings, and one of the most significant (Australian Associated Press 2006b).

Germany's Peer Steinbrück reported that ministers did not agree on any specific strategy for improving energy security, nor was any possible solution discredited (Brown 2006). The discussion was open and interesting, even when it did not lead to conclusions or commitments.

Externally, the G20 served as a hub for a growing network of global governance in 2006. The meeting was held right after the APEC ministerial in Vietnam on November 15–16. It also took place one year before Australia would host APEC. As host, Australia was in a strong position to address both developed and emerging market concerns, as it was a longstanding member of the OECD's Development Assistance Committee as well as a non-G8 member. Melbourne followed the second G8-related ministerial meeting of the Gleneagles Dialogue on climate change, clean energy, and sustainable development and the G8 St. Petersburg Summit, both of which focused on issues such as energy.

Other groups with memberships that overlapped with the G20 expanded in the lead-up to and following the Melbourne meeting. In September 2006, the leaders of India, Brazil, and South Africa (IBSA) met for the first time. In September 2007, the first MEM—with 17 of the G20 members—would take place.

At the individual level of the four finance ministers who had continuously been members since the G20's founding, three—Australia's Peter Costello, Britain's Gordon Brown, and South Africa's Trevor Manuel—were members of the Commonwealth club. Together with Saudi Arabia's Al-Assaf, they represented all the G20's G8, G5, and other groups.

Kleinmond 2007

The Challenge

South Africa hosted the next and ninth G20 meeting, on November 17–18, 2007, in Kleinmond, just as the great global financial crisis of 2007–09 was gathering force. Its theme was "Sharing—Influence, Responsibility, and Knowledge." This expressed South Africa's objective to continue the G20's emphasis on sustainable economic development and multilateral cooperation on finance issues. There were three main issues at the meeting: the commodity cycle and its impact on financial stability, creating fiscal room for growth and development, and the continuing reform of the Bretton Woods bodies.

This was the first time that a G20 meeting had been held in Africa, adding another layer of pressure on the group to address systemic global imbalances in the international financial and development architecture. The meeting was the first for the new heads of both the World Bank and the IMF, and particularly significant since reform of those institutions had been a recurring theme of the recent G20 meetings. Robert Zoellick, who had become president of the World Bank on July 1, 2007, brought a particular interest in growth in Africa. Dominique Strauss-Kahn became the managing director of the IMF on November 1, 2007.

Competing Assessments The Kleinmond meeting inspired a familiar debate among three competing schools of thought. The first school suggested that the G20 had failed to address substantial issues. For example, the weak US dollar went unaddressed (Dickie et al. 2007). A second school saw the G20 just as non-prescient and non-proactive as other international economic forums. After the meeting, participants—including Russian finance minister Alexei Kudrin—said that the G20 had already successfully "passed the risk zone," signalling that members were unprepared for the severe downturn that was coming (Interfax 2007). The third school argued that the 2007 meeting was a success. The G20 was able to anticipate and address the coming global financial crisis before all its competitors, save for the Bank for International Settlements (Kirton 2010).

The Argument South Africa's Kleinmond meeting was substantially successful in several important respects, above all in the strong decisional performance it produced. It identified the turbulence in global financial markets. While it did not prevent the imminent financial crisis, it went beyond most other international organizations by publicly recognizing that there were problems percolating in the global economy. It advanced IFI reform. It included components of African outreach. The South Africans used their position as chair to host sideline meetings that included African and G20 officials. The discussions at these meetings influenced the final communiqué.

These successes were due to the small shocks coming from failing financial institutions in Britain and the US, to the IMF and G8's failure to foresee and prevent the coming storm, to the strongly equalizing capabilities of G20 members, to the continuity and competence of the highly respected chair Trevor Manuel at his ninth meeting, and to the growth of the G8-centred network as the MEM and the Heiligendamm Dialogue Process arrived.

Plans and Preparations

South Africa faced particular challenges in hosting the G20 meeting. Initially it had even doubted it would be able to host but was convinced to do so at the supportive urging of its closest friends in the group. As the only African member of the G20, South Africa unofficially represented the entire continent. Unsurprisingly, the economic and fiscal challenges faced by the continent were specific items on the agenda.

Early on in the planning, it seemed that G20 legacy issues would take centre stage, and that the meeting would thus focus on reform of the IMF and the World Bank. Manuel had begun to set his priorities soon after the 2006 meeting. He declared that there was "still a case to be made for the IMF and World Bank to exist," but that they needed to "become more relevant" (Dow Jones International News 2006). South Africa also signalled that it would follow up on the work carried out by Australia on commodity cycles, sovereign wealth funds, and hedging (G20 2008).

Three G20 workshops were held leading up to Kleinmond. The first, in Brazil in March 2007, addressed the completion of the second stage of the IMF reform. The second workshop, in May 2007 in Washington, dealt with commodity cycles and financial stability, expanding the discussion on energy security at the 2006 meeting. The third workshop, hosted by Turkey in Istanbul in July 2007, was on the role of public finance management in supporting economic growth. Each of the themes explored at these workshops contributed directly to the agenda at Kleinmond (G20 2008).

At the Meeting

Global Economic Outlook At Kleinmond in November 2007, G20 ministers and governors were considerably less optimistic about the prospects for the global economy than they had been in Melbourne the year before. They acknowledged the "recent financial market disturbances," a reference to the sub-prime mortgage crisis and collapse of the US housing market, which had begun only a few months earlier (G20 Finance 2007a). With that in mind, they stressed the importance of sound macroeconomic policy and agreed to work on improving their understanding of the transmission of financial shocks.

The G20 also recognized that rising food and energy prices could be a source of market pressure. The communiqué did not represent the full extent of their free and open discussions. After the meeting, participants hinted that the unprecedentedly weak American dollar had dominated the discussions. The new director of the IMF, Dominique Strauss-Kahn, revealed that currency imbalances had been a topic of discussion, but added that "the more discreet these discussions are, the more effective [they are]" (MacNamara and Russell 2007).

The G20 Reform Agenda On the reform agenda, finance ministers and central bank governors translated their ideas from the "G20 Accord for Sustained Growth" from Berlin in 2004 into concrete policy actions for each country. The reform agenda outlined some of the domestic policies that each country would take to contribute to the more global commitments made previously by the G20 (G20 Finance 2007b). The original accord had been a landmark achievement for the G20. Translating those agreements into policy through coordinated action was an equally significant step forward.

Fiscal Elements of Growth and Development Much of the discussion centred on the idea of fiscal space and the frameworks to be implemented in order to use that space effectively. Fiscal space could be used to finance social and economic development over the long term and provide a key organizing principle for expenditure programs. The G20 participants openly discussed these ideas, and the importance of sharing experiences and lessons learned. Without establishing any firm commitments, they agreed to continue these discussions next year. They assessed, in a foretaste of the future, the role of counter-cyclical fiscal policies as a tool for stabilizing and sustaining economic growth.

Commodity Cycles Participants also discussed commodity prices and financial stability. They affirmed their conviction that well-functioning markets would encourage economically efficient renewable energy sources. They were concerned with commodity price volatility. They emphasized the importance of sound macroeconomic policy to mitigate the effects of drastic price changes. They agreed that good governance, transparency, and appropriate institutional frameworks were all important for long-term macroeconomic stability. The participants reiterated their support for both the EITI and JODI.

Energy and Climate Change The participants also addressed possible actions to mitigate climate change in the context of financial stability and growth. They discussed the links between GDP growth and the potential of biofuels and clean technology, and noted the benefit of exploring these links further. The meeting also took note of two important reports, one on climate change prepared by a UK-led study group.

Bretton Woods Reform The G20 reported further progress on IMF reform. They noted that the "forum's efforts in 2007 have contributed to a convergence of views among the IMF's members" (G20 Finance 2007a). The participants reiterated their commitment to quota and voice reform, promising to try to reach an agreement on all elements by spring 2008.

The G20 Institution The meeting took note of a report on the history of the G20, which had been written by a study group led by Canada, as conceiver and continuing custodian of the group.

Achievements

The leitmotif of Kleinmond was global power imbalances. This theme was developed through the suggested reforms of the Bretton Woods institutions and in discussions about the relationship between fair global trade and long-term macroeconomic stability. The participants committed to reach an agreement on quota and voice reform by the spring of 2008.

The fact that the meeting was held in Africa was significant. South African finance minister Trevor Manuel declared that the G20 meeting was "probably the most significant gathering of economic policy makers we've ever had in South Africa" (Paterson 2007). By having the meeting in the G20's poorest country and on the world's poorest continent, a major step toward full institutional equality was made.

The full impact and scope of the meeting was not immediately apparent. The falling US dollar had been a significant topic of discussion, but did not make its way into the communiqué. It did, however, become clear to the finance ministers and bank governors that their efforts to control the credit markets through traditional fiscal policy was not working, and that something else needed to be done. Less than a month after the G20 meeting, the Bank of Canada, the US Federal Reserve, the European Central Bank, and the Swiss National Bank announced an unprecedented injection of billions of dollars into the financial markets. It was reported that the finance ministers and bank governors had begun working on this coordinated action, centred in the G7, at the Kleinmond meeting (Conway and Aldrick 2007). In this way, the G20 had become a rapid crisis-response global governor in the finance field, at least in the minimum sense as a hub where a smaller club could agree to act.

Dimensions of Performance

A systematic assessment of the six dimensions of G20 governance confirms Kleinmond's substantial success.

Domestic Political Management On domestic political management, as a member of the troika of the past, present, and future hosts, South Africa contributed significantly to the scope and shape of the meeting to good effect at home. Unsurprisingly, therefore, the agenda reflected some of South Africa's particular views and dissatisfactions with the G20 itself.

The meeting played directly into domestic politics in South Africa. Trevor Manuel (2007) laid out the plans for his G20 meeting in his February 2007 budget speech. He stressed its historic significance for South Africa. The domestic public opinion ratings for South African president Thabo Mbeki, which had dropped a significant 14 points before the meeting, started to rebound at the end of November (Angus Reid Global Monitor 2007). Kleinmond offered four communiqué compliments, the third highest thus far (see Appendix D-1). These were evenly balanced between G8 and non-G8 members.

Deliberation In its deliberation, the meeting was a strong success. Kleinmond produced a communiqué and a reform agenda, with a total of 3,858 words, continuing the upward trend that began in 2005 (see Appendix E). This was the second highest number of words ever issued, and nearly twice the overall average. Just as in 2006, macroeconomic policy, IFI reform, and climate change were the three dominant topics.

Direction Setting In its direction setting, however, there was a significant step back to only a solid performance. The group made only five references to the G20's democratic values (see Appendix F). This was the fewest since 2003. But in its democratic direction setting, Kleinmond still performed at about the G20's nine-year average. It affirmed the importance of transparency and now good governance again.

Decision Making In its decision making, Kleinmond performed strongly. It doubled to 20 the number of commitments the G20 had made the previous year. This was the second highest number ever made and came close to the 24 in 2001 in first place. Kleinmond commitments were led by those in macroeconomics with nine, followed by IFIs with five, energy with three, trade with two, and socioeconomics with one.

Delivery In its delivery, Kleinmond was less successful, beyond the coordinated G7-centred monetary intervention that came in its wake. Its communiqué made only three references to the G20 and 20 references to other international institutions (see Appendix C-1). Two reports were issued that noted progress on terrorist financing and observance with codes and standards and financial system stability. However, there was no commitment to monitor progress or review implementation on their pledges. This was a step back from past years.

Development of Global Governance The development of G20-centred global governance saw only a modest advance. Internally, there were only three references to the G20. To further the institutionalization of the G20, the South Africans worked closely with the troika, particularly the Australians who had hosted the year before. And they worked to draft a history of the group that was put forward to the ministers and bank governors for review at the meeting. Externally, with 20 references to international institutions, they expanded outreach, adding a home region approach. They hosted several meetings with additional African countries to feed into the G20 process.

Causes of Performance

Once again, the systemic club model accounts well for the G20's substantial success in 2007, above all in the decisional domain.

Shock-Activated, Equalizing Vulnerability The first cause, shock-activated, equalizing vulnerability, arose again in some force for the first time since 1999 in its classic form of financial crisis. At Kleinmond a new financial crisis was looming on the horizon, this time coming from the advanced Atlantic rather than the emerging Asian region. When the G20 finance ministers and bank governors met in November 2007, the US sub-prime mortgage crisis was just starting (Savona et al. 2011). After several years of consistent economic growth, the world economy was just starting to enter a period of considerable slow down.

The G20 recognized the fragile world economy: "the recent financial market disturbances have highlighted the importance of sound macroeconomic and financial policies and continued vigilance" (G20 Finance 2007a). The newest economic shock encouraged collective action among G20 members, increasingly aware of their interconnected markets.

Additional shocks came from energy and food (see Appendix I). The price of oil spiked sharply from its 2006 high of $77.05 a barrel to a 2007 high of $99.16. Food prices also rose sharply, leading to food riots that killed many in several poor countries. However, the fewest number of members suffered terrorist attacks since the creation of the group in 1999. There were no major natural disasters requiring collective action.

International Institutional Failure The second cause, international institutional failure, was relevant too. Despite the disturbances in the financial markets, both the IMF and the G8 failed to recognize the need for improved supervision. In its April 2007 *World Economic Outlook*, the IMF declared that, "the world economy still looks well set for continued robust growth in 2007 and 2008" (IMF 2007, 1). This was correct for 2007, but not 2008.

Although German chancellor Angela Merkel had wanted to address hedge funds at the G8 summit she hosted in Heiligendamm in June 2007, only the G20 anticipated and attempted to address the imminent financial crisis (Kirton 2010). More generally, at Heiligendamm, it became evident that sustained and expanded participation was necessary for effective and successful governance. The G8 tried to address this by launching the Heiligendamm Dialogue Process or Outreach Five (O5). This was the beginning of deliberate efforts to include and consult with the emerging countries of Brazil, China, India, Mexico, and South Africa—all G20 members—on energy, development, and cross-border investment, among other issues. The older G8 recognized it was not inclusive enough to deal with these issues on its own. Yet at the G8 summit and its new Heiligendamm Dialogue Process, it included only some of the G20 members, on a discretionary, partial basis, with equality among the 16 members only at the officials' level below.

Predominant, Equalizing Capabilities The third cause, predominant, equalizing capabilities, contributed a great deal. In 2007, the G8 represented 57 percent of global GDP, while the non-G8 members represented 20 percent in 2007, a significant shift from the year before (see Appendix K).

Advanced and emerging economies also continued to grow closer in terms of relative economic capability. The Gini coefficient again sharply rose and the relative capability ratio of the strongest to the weakest member again sharply declined (see Appendix K).

Democratic Convergence The fourth cause, G20 members' domestic democratic character, largely continued to accumulate for yet another year (see Appendix L). However, there was a major democratic reversal in Russia, whose score dropped from six to four. The G20's 2007 decline in democratic direction setting was consistent with this reversal in Russia.

Political Control, Capital, Continuity, and Competence The fifth cause, political control, capital, continuity, competence, and commitment, also had the hypothesized effect. Chair Trevor Manuel set a new high for continuity, political competence, and commitment, having been a part of the G20 since its beginning in 1999. He thus had a strong understanding of the process, diplomacy, and topics needed to host a successful meeting. Elsewhere, there were several significant shifts. Most notably in Alistair Darling there was a new British exchequer for the first time since the creation of the group, as founder Gordon Brown had finally followed Paul Martin in graduating from finance minister to leader at home. There were also new finance ministers in Argentina, China, France, Mexico, and Japan. However, now veteran US treasury secretary Henry Paulson came to Kleinmond, unlike the year before when deputy treasury secretary Robert Kimmitt represented the United States.

Controlled Club Participation as a Network Hub The sixth cause, controlled club participation as a network hub, counted. Internally, since the G20's creation in 1999, South Africa had been recognized as a leader within the group. Several advanced and emerging economies had repeatedly advocated that South Africa host a meeting. Even though Trevor Manuel called the G7 "passé," he had the respect of both G8 and non-G8 members.

Externally, the G20 meeting followed the G7 finance gatherings in February, April, and October; a meeting of the finance ministers of the Association of Southeast Asian Nations (ASEAN) in April; the G8 finance ministers' meeting in May; the APEC ministerial in Australia in September; and the meeting of Commonwealth finance ministers in October. It tied together the discussions that had been held in these various forums throughout the year and laid a foundation for debates that would be held in 2008.

Conclusion

The Melbourne and Kleinmond meetings took place just as the instabilities causing the great financial crisis of 2007–09 began. The G20 recognized these instabilities, and thus started to consider the counter-cyclical fiscal policies that would be needed in response. But more importantly, the meetings helped prove the G20's worth as a group that non-G8 members could successfully host and lead. They thus gave central attention to the critical emerging countries and their priorities. In addition, the meetings were key in achieving the important first stages of IMF voice and vote reform.

The Australian and South African meetings showed that the G20 had outperformed comparable international institutions, notably the IMF and the G8's Heiligendamm Dialogue Process. The G20 thus started to establish its effectiveness, legitimacy, and usefulness in the eyes of its G8 and non-G8 members, outside countries, and broader international organizations—making the G20 the choice for all its members as the group to respond to the great global financial and economic crisis that erupted in full force the next year.

References

Agence France Presse. 2006. "Economic Leaders to Act on Energy Security But Not Climate Change." November 19.

Angus Reid Global Monitor. 2007. "South Africans Divided on Mbeke's Tenure." December 13. Available at: www.angus-reid.com/polls/29613/south_africans_divided_on_mbekis_tenure. Accessed: July 2012.

Asia-Pacific Economic Cooperation. 2006. "Ha Noi Declaration: Towards a Dynamic Community for Sustainable Development and Prosperity." Leaders' declaration, Ha Noi, November 18–19. Available at: www.apec.org/Meeting-Papers/Leaders-Declarations/2006/2006_aelm.aspx?t=1. Accessed: July 2012.

Australian Associated Press. 2006a. "G20 'Universally' Condemns N. Korea Nuclear Tests." November 19.

Australian Associated Press. 2006b. "Melbourne G20 Hailed a Success." *Sydney Morning Herald*, November 20. Available at: www.smh.com.au/news/NATIONAL/Melbourne-G20-hailed-a-success/2006/11/20/1163871298527.html. Accessed: July 2012.

Brinsden, Colin. 2006. "G20 Baton Handed to South Africa." Australian Associated Press, November 19.

Brown, Owen. 2006. "G20 Didn't Exclude Any Energy Reform Strategy — Germany." Dow Jones, November 19.

Chappell, Trevor. 2006. "G20 Dialogue on Energy, Minerals Was a Breakthrough — Costello." Australian Associated Press, November 19.

Conway, Edmund and Aldrick, Philip. 2007. "Rescue Bid Cooked Up under the Cover of G20 Event." *Daily Telegraph*, December 13.

Costello, Peter. 2008. *The Costello Memoirs: The Age of Prosperity*. Melbourne: Melbourne University Press.

de Brouwer, Gordon and Yeaman, Luke. 2007. "Australia's G20 Host Year: A Treasury Perspective." Treasury, Australian Government, Canberra. Available at: www.g20.utoronto.ca/biblio/debrouwer-yeaman_2007.pdf. Accessed: July 2012.

Dickie, Mure, Guha, Krishna, and Garnham, Peter. 2007. "Chinese Join Chorus of Alarm on Weak Dollar." *Financial Times*, November 20. Available at: www.ft.com/intl/cms/s/0/067f2a4c-970c-11dc-b2da-0000779fd2ac.html#axzz20iSIum2u. Accessed: July 2012.

Dow Jones International News. 2006. "G20 to Focus on IMF, World Bank." November 22.

Fullilove, Michael. 2010. "With Friends in High Places: Australia's G20 Membership." *Australian*, March 13. Available at: www.brookings.edu/research/opinions/2010/03/13-australia-fullilove. Accessed: July 2012.

G20. 2008. "The Group of Twenty: A History." Available at: www.g20.utoronto.ca/docs/g20history.pdf. Accessed: July 2012.

G20 Finance Ministers and Central Bank Governors. 2004. "G20 Accord for Sustained Growth." Berlin, November 21. Available at: www.g20.utoronto.ca/2004/2004growth.html. Accessed: July 2012.

G20 Finance Ministers and Central Bank Governors. 2006. "Communiqué." Melbourne, November 19. Available at: www.g20.utoronto.ca/2006/2006communique.html. Accessed: July 2012.

G20 Finance Ministers and Central Bank Governors. 2007a. "Communiqué." Kleinmond, South Africa, November 18. Available at: www.g20.utoronto.ca/2007/2007communique.html. Accessed: July 2012.

G20 Finance Ministers and Central Bank Governors. 2007b. "G20 Reform Agenda 2007: Agreed Actions to Implement the G20 Accord for Sustained Growth." Kleinmond, South Africa, November 18. Available at: www.g20.utoronto.ca/2007/2007reform.html. Accessed: July 2012.

Hoy, Greg. 2006. "Costello Brothers Clash over G20." Transcript, November 20, Australian Broadcasting Corporation. Available at: www.abc.net.au/7.30/content/2006/s1793207.htm. Accessed: July 2012.

Interfax. 2007. "Russian Economy Over Risk Zone Overall — Kudrin." November 19.

International Monetary Fund. 2007. "World Economic Outlook: Spillovers and Cycles in the Global Economy." Executive Summary, April, Washington DC. Available at: www.imf.org/external/pubs/ft/weo/2007/01/pdf/exesum.pdf. Accessed: July 2012.

Kirton, John J. 2010. "The G20 Finance Ministers: Network Governance." In *Rising States, Rising Institutions: Can the World Be Governed?*, eds Alexandroff, Alan S., and Cooper, Andrew F. Washington DC: Brookings Institution Press, 196–217.

MacNamara, William and Russell, Alec. 2007. "G20 Silent on Dollar Impact on World Markets." *Financial Times*, November 19. Available at: www.ft.com/intl/cms/s/0/2c783062-962c-11dc-b7ec-0000779fd2ac.html#axzz20iSIum2u. Accessed: July 2012.

Manuel, Trevor. 2007. "Budget Speech 2007 by the Minister of Finance." February 21. Available at: www.info.gov.za/speeches/2007/07022115261001.htm. Accessed: July 2012.

Martinez-Diaz, Leonardo. 2007. "The G20 after Eight Years: How Effective a Vehicle for Developing-Country Influence?" Global Economy and Development Working Paper No. 12, Brookings Institution, Washington DC. Available at: www.brookings.edu/papers/2007/1017development.aspx. Accessed: July 2012.

McMillan, Stuart. 2006. "Free Trade and Energy on Regional Meeting Agendas." *National Business Review*, November 24.

Murdoch, Scott. 2006. "China Says Yes to Carbon Trading." *Advertiser*, November 19. Available at: www.adelaidenow.com.au/business/china-says-yes-to-carbon-trading/story-e6frede3-1111112550015. Accessed: July 2012.

Organisation for Economic Co-operation and Development. 2005. "The Paris Declaration on Aid Effectiveness: Ownership, Harmonisation, Alignment, Results, and Mutual Accountability." Paris. Available at: www.oecd.org/dataoecd/11/41/34428351.pdf. Accessed: July 2012.

Parkinson, Martin. 2006. "The G20: Addressing Global Challenges." Presentation to the Australian Business Economists Luncheon, November 9, Sydney. Available at: www.g20.utoronto.ca/biblio/parkinson_2006.pdf. Accessed: July 2012.

Paterson, Damian. 2007. "G20 Meeting Not Just More Idle Chatter." *Pretoria News*, November 16.

Savona, Paolo, Kirton, John J., and Oldani, Chiara, eds. 2011. *Global Financial Crisis: Global Impact and Solutions*. Farnham: Ashgate.

Uren, David. 2006. "Costello Plots Resources Pact." *Australian*, January 3.

PART IV
Creating the Summit Club, 2008–2010

Chapter 10
Soaring to the Summit, Washington 2008

Introduction

The Challenge

On November 14–15, 2008, the heads of the world's 19 systemically significant countries and the European Union assembled in Washington DC for the Summit on Financial Markets and the World Economy. It was the first ever summit of the Group of 20 (G20). It showed that the financial and economic crisis then gripping the globe was such a threat that it needed leaders rather than just finance ministers and central bank governors, who had met the week before, to respond. US president George W. Bush, in convening, hosting, and chairing the summit, acknowledged that the United States alone could not solve the unprecedented problem born in the USA. Moreover, to craft an effective response to this twenty-first century global financial crisis, the world needed more than the broadly multilateral old International Monetary Fund (IMF) or even the exclusive, elite, newer Group of Seven (G7) or Group of Eight (G8) club, even with its recent addition of the Group of Five (G5).

Emerging powers readily agreed to help the United States, its G7 partners, and the global community combat this crisis. The G20 gathering substituted for a G8 summit that had failed for several years to deal effectively with finance, macroeconomics, and trade. This first G20 summit also delved deeply and intrusively into the internal world of firms, where company managers had long wielded control, by addressing matters as detailed as executive pay. The summit's assembly, actions, and achievements marked the birth of a new leader-level G20 institution that less than a year later was to become the self-proclaimed permanent, premier centre for its members' international economic cooperation. It arose in an intensely interconnected world where finance was now globalized and driven by the private sector, and where economic power was passing from the established countries to the emerging ones (Altman 2009).

For citizens shocked by imploding financial firms and plummeting stock markets, economic growth, and employment, and for managers, governors, and scholars, several key questions immediately arose (Wolf 2008; Rotman School of Management 2008; Kirton 2008c; Alexandroff and Kirton 2010). Could any intergovernmental forum, no matter how powerful, prescient, and propelled by crisis, govern this new interconnected, complex, uncertain world of globalized private finance? If so, did this hastily called G20 summit get the diagnosis, prescription, and sequencing of its decisions, their delivery, and the development of a new global economic governance right? More specifically, did it do enough to start the process of responding adequately to the cascading crisis and risks for the years beyond? Finally, did adding the diverse and numerous emerging powers as equals at the leaders' level help or harm in accomplishing these tasks?

Competing Assessments

The sudden, surprising advent of the G20 summit and the urgent importance of its work gave rise to a great debate among five major competing schools of thought about the performance of the inaugural event and the causes that lay behind. The original schools of thought about the G20 of finance ministers and central bank governors re-emerged, often more vocally, to account for the new leaders' forum.

The first school, reminiscent of those who had originally considered the G20 redundant amid the many international financial regulatory bodies already at work, judged the Washington Summit to fall well short of success. Richard Duncan (2008) argued that the cause of the crisis lay in the fact that "the 37-year experiment with fiat money and floating exchange rates has failed catastrophically … The time has come to convene a forum of the world's leaders to hammer out and begin the transition to a new rule-based international monetary system predicated on sound money and balanced trade. Current Group of 20 efforts fall well short of what is required." A variant considered the summit to be an opportunity lost due to its incorrect diagnosis and denial of the real causes of the crisis. Kenneth Rogoff wrote that "anyone looking for the G-20 to issue a mea culpa on the global financial crisis will be sadly disappointed" (Lander 2008). The leaders "curiously downplay the huge culpability of the political leadership in the U.S. and Europe."

A second school, containing rejectionists, focused on the summit's failure to deliver the bold decisions made, while admiring its badly needed fiscal stimulus and trade liberalization thrusts. Jim O'Neill of Goldman Sachs concluded that the "world will be a better place" if the G20 achieved its large to-do list by March, but while the G20 statement focused on future plans and lacked specificity the near-term situation remained grim (Zeng 2008). *The Economist* argued that the United States and Germany did not produce the swift, substantial, sustained fiscal stimulus they had agreed to at the summit and that Russia, India, and even France immediately violated their commitment to renounce protectionist actions for the next 12 months (*Economist* 2008c, 2008d, 2008a, 2008b).

One variant, in the spirit of the American leadership model of G8 governance, pinned all hope on the new American president-elect, arguing that before Barack Obama arrived little could be done (Putnam and Bayne 1987). The *Sunday Times* editorialists said that despite the summit's good work in calling for fiscal stimulus and on the Doha round, such big decisions were easier said than done and would await Obama's inauguration on January 20, 2009 (*Sunday Times* 2008). Former IMF chief economist Simon Johnson concluded that the decisions were "plain-vanilla stuff they could have agreed on without holding a meeting," and asked

"What's new, except that this is the G-20 instead of the G-7?" (Lander 2008). However, he added that Obama might go to the next summit with "strong evidence of American action."

Another variant saw great potential in the summit, drawing parallels to the creation of the Bretton Woods institutions in 1944 and expressing optimism that the G20 might bring about a reimagining of the international financial system. They were disappointed, however, with the result, arguing that "the policy agenda did not in fact go much beyond pre-existing international initiatives" (Helleiner and Pagliari 2009, 276).

A third school, composed of reinforcers, emphasized the leaders' call for economic stimulus. David Smith and Jonathan Oliver (2008) concluded that "though some way short of a global action plan, it did give the green light for countries keen to shield their economies from the worst of the downturn" through fiscal stimulus and interest rate reductions. Some focused on domestic political management, noting how the summit gave leaders international justifications for changing domestic policies. Peter Woolstencroft noted that Canada's Prime Minister Stephen Harper now had "a G20 umbrella to protect himself" should he wish to retreat from previous promises not to run a deficit (Laghi 2008). Among practitioners, in 2010 Brazilian president Luiz Inácio Lula da Silva (2010) wrote about the G20 success in helping the global economy rebound after the worst economic recession since the Great Depression. Developing economies were increasingly part of global solutions, he argued, and the G20 could be the forum to achieve substantial reform of the multilateral system. The American hosts also judged their summit to be a big success (Hennessey 2008).

A fourth school focused on the development of global governance, calling the summit a step in the right direction toward the required new revolutionary global regime to govern finance. Walter Mattli and Ngaire Woods (2008) claimed that "nothing less than a new global architecture for the regulation of banking and finance is required," and that "a proposal made during the G20 Washington summit to establish international 'supervisory colleges for all major cross-border financial institutions'" was the correct move.

A fifth school, containing replacers, considered the summit to be the first step in the eventual substitution of the new G20 for the old G8. Paul Martin (2008) argued that the full inclusion of emerging market governments was now necessary to resolve the deepening financial crisis. Because the G8 countries were no longer the most powerful, there must be a new level of international cooperation to deal with the current global concerns.

Puzzles

These schools generally agreed that the Washington Summit did better on fiscal stimulus, trade anti-protection, and perhaps preliminary G20 institutionalization than on reform of the exchange rate regime and financial regulation. They saw the summit as more successful in domestic political management, deliberation, direction setting, and the development of G20 governance than in detailed decision making and delivery.

Yet the implications of the arrival of G20 summitry were not fully explored. None of the early accounts offered a comprehensive account of the first G20 summit's preparations, production, and performance across its entire agenda and all its governance dimensions. None presented a complete, coherent, multilevel conception of the causes of its performance. The two international systemic factors advanced as the causes of failure—the presence of fiat money and floating exchange rates—were unconvincing, since they had not produced a financial crisis and a G20 summit during the previous 36 years that they had dominated global finance. And at the other, individual end of the level of analysis spectrum, it seemed implausible that a particular US president was a necessary and sufficient cause of the failure or success of a new summit of 20 systemically significant equals, governing a world where the US no longer predominated and now served as the source of the crisis that threatened to take all down.

The Argument

This chapter argues that the first G20 summit was a strong success, in its combined performance across all six dimensions of international institutional performance. Such success was caused by the unprecedented scale, speed, spread, scope, and societal impact of the 2007–08 sequence of financial shocks and the ensuing vulnerability in the American-Atlantic core that this shock sequence showed in stark relief. It came also from the failure of the established multilateral and plurilateral institutions to predict, prevent, and respond adequately on their own to these shocks and from the sudden shift in relative capabilities from the badly battered established countries to the less affected large emerging ones. The unifying desire of the G8 members to preserve market democracy and social advance led the leaders of the US, France, and the rest of the G8 to transcend their domestic political weaknesses, and to catalyse a gathering at the leaders' level of a still constricted G20 group. This diverse group was commonly committed to social and political stability, had proven it could cope with financial crises during the past decade, and had become the centre of a multidimensional, leader-level, global governance network by 2008.

The Origins

The Campaign for an L20

The intellectual and policy leadership to produce a G20 summit had first arisen in the campaign of Canadian prime minister Paul Martin in 2004–05 to create a Leaders' 20, or L20. Martin's proposal was to take the G20 finance ministers forum that he, as Canada's finance minister, had co-invented in response to the

Asian-turned-global financial crisis of 1997–99 and turn it into a leaders-level institution that would meet as necessary to deal with any of the most critical issues the global community faced (Kirton and Koch 2008; Martin 2008; Summers 2008; English et al. 2005).

Such a summit did not take place before Martin stepped down as prime minister, following the electoral defeat of his Liberal Party of Canada on January 23, 2006. US president George Bush had rejected his call. But Martin's personal pitches to his G8 colleagues had attracted several converts, including Jacques Chirac of France. All G20 leaders were familiar with the concept and the underlying arguments for the value of a meeting, and all but Bush had agreed when the financial crisis reached a new and more dangerous phase in the autumn of 2008.

The Sarkozy Suggestion

Suggestions for holding a special leaders' meeting started to emerge in the international arena when the US investment bank Lehman Brothers filed for bankruptcy on September 15, 2008, and plummeting stock prices, collapsing banks, and frozen credit cascaded in its wake (Paulson 2010). French president Nicolas Sarkozy was the first to call publicly for a summit to cope with this new, acute phase of a financial crisis that had begun in less intense form the year before. At the United Nations General Assembly (UNGA) in New York City on September 23, Sarkozy suggested a gathering of the G7 or G8, probably along with a few select outsiders led by China, India, and Brazil. He said:

> Let today's major powers and the powers of tomorrow unite to shoulder together the responsibilities their influence gives them in world affairs … We cannot wait any longer to turn the G8 into the G13 or G14, and to bring in China, India, South Africa, Mexico, and Brazil. Italy is proposing a major step in this direction at the next summit which it will host. It is right to do so! ... I am convinced that it is the duty of the heads of state and government of the countries most directly concerned to meet before the end of the year to examine together the lessons of the most serious financial crisis the world has experienced since that of the 1930s. (Sarkozy 2008)

Sarkozy separately suggested the summit be held in New York, on the grounds that that was where the global crisis had begun.

During UNGA, Jean-David Levitte, Sarkozy's personal representative, or sherpa, called all his colleagues in the G8 to make the case that his president's proposal was serious and that he hoped they would react positively. Yet many of his fellow sherpas had not spoken to their leaders and were not involved in finance matters, where their finance departments led. Sarkozy's call initially met with skepticism, partly because of his reputation for grandstanding and calling for summits on any subject. It took a little time for some to realize the seriousness of the crisis, whether a summit-level response was required, and whether a larger group than the G8 was needed. Sarkozy had not specified who would be invited.

Britain's Gordon Brown was no such skeptic. He had known since early 2008 that Sarkozy believed that more than the G7 was needed to deal with the crisis (Brown 2010). However, who would be invited had not yet been agreed. Brown reports that during a visit to Sarkozy's country house, the two concluded that the G20 would be best and that they should work together to get G20 membership for Spain and the Netherlands. They also considered jointly proposing a leaders' meeting of the G20.

At the UN on September 25, Brown called a meeting with the leaders who were still in New York: Lula of Brazil, Kevin Rudd of Australia, who had listened to and congratulated Sarkozy on his UNGA speech, as well as several other, mostly European non-G20 members, and José Manuel Barroso, the head of the European Commission. They discussed the gathering storm and what the institutional response should be. They agreed that more than the G8 was needed, that the G20 chair should pass from Brazil to the United Kingdom before the scheduled date of January 1, 2009, and that Brown would pitch the idea to Bush and Sarkozy would follow up (Brown 2010). The next day Brown met with Bush at the White House. Brown noted Bush's "real appetite" for a G20 meeting to address banking, jobs, and living standards, but the US president wanted more than just talk. Brown highlighted the many financial sector issues that leaders needed to address, took responsibility for securing an agreed policy, noted that the G20 of finance ministers and central bank governors existed so they would not be creating a new forum, and suggested that the summit could make progress on trade. Bush stipulated that any meeting would have to be in Washington, as he would not travel during the presidential handover.

Miguel d'Escoto Brockmann, the newly elected president of the General Assembly and the former foreign minister of Nicaragua, also suggested a summit to deal with the crisis. But unlike Sarkozy, who spoke at UNGA's opening for only seven minutes, d'Escoto's long and rambling inaugural speech dealt with many matters other than the crisis. Although his and Sarkozy's calls seemed to fall on deaf ears, d'Escoto subsequently organized several special sessions on the crisis, including one in October 2008, set up a task force, and sought to mobilize for this purpose the major meeting on financing for development already scheduled for the end of November and early December in Qatar. d'Escoto tried almost single-handedly to move things quickly at the UN, but did not receive much support. When the G20 eventually chose to meet at the leaders' level, he insisted such a meeting should be held, early and urgently, with all UN member states.

By the beginning of October, Sarkozy and UN secretary general Ban Ki-moon had agreed that such a summit should be hosted at the UN headquarters in New York. The Americans were understandably reluctant to have the French and the UN control the process, and to hold it in New York to encourage the view that Wall Street and thus the US was to blame for the crisis. They preferred to show that the

White House, with support from the IMF in Washington, was controlling a crisis caused by the markets.

The American Reaction

By Monday, October 6, with American and global markets plummeting even after Congress had just passed the Troubled Assets Relief Program (TARP) and with more than $2 trillion in stock market value erased, the White House began to consider whether Bush should call a summit to confront the crisis (Paulson 2010, 334–5). The White House pondered inviting different sets of between seven and 24 countries. It decided to avoid the negotiations and lobbying involved in assembling an ad hoc group by going with the established G20, despite the fact that banking centres such as Switzerland and Singapore would be left out. At lunch on that Monday, US treasury secretary Henry Paulson told Dan Price, the president's assistant for international affairs, Steve Hadley, the president's assistant for national security affairs, and Keith Hennessey, the president's assistant for economic affairs, that such a summit should take place as soon as possible after the presidential election on November 4. Bush should also call his fellow leaders to ask them to send their finance ministers to a special G20 gathering during the semi-annual meetings of the World Bank and IMF that were starting that week. They decided to ask the Brazilian chair of the G20 to assemble the finance ministers' group on Saturday, October 11.

On Tuesday, October 7, as Europe continued to suffer and Iceland appeared on the verge of default, Gordon Brown, in a phone call with George Bush, suggested that Bush, consider gathering the leaders of the G20 to discuss the deepening crisis. Although he was receptive, Bush was focused on having the G7 finance ministers' meeting at the IMF–World Bank sessions come up with a coordinated plan (Paulson 2010, 159). The question by then was less whether to hold such a summit but rather when, where, with whom, on what agenda, and with what level of ambition and achievement in mind.

That day, the central banks of the US, the UK, Japan, and Switzerland, and the European Central Bank (ECB) acted together to provide US dollar liquidity to aid a US financial system that was seizing up. The central banks of China and Sweden also acted in support.

In preparation for the G7 finance ministers' meeting on Thursday, October 9, US Federal Reserve governor Ben Bernanke offered Paulson nine initiatives that were already being considered or contained in the draft G7 communiqué that the Americans had prepared. US finance deputy David McCormick then inserted these initiatives into an appendix entitled "The Action Plan." That afternoon, as Iceland closed its stock market and took control of its biggest bank, Paulson met with Bush to discuss his role in the G8 and G20 ministerial meetings in the following days (Paulson 2010; Brown 2010).

On Friday, October 10, Shoichi Nakagawa, Japan's fourth finance minister in two years, urged Paulson in a bilateral meeting to inject government capital into America's struggling banks (Paulson 2010, 347–51). At the G7 finance ministers' meeting starting at 2 pm that afternoon in the Cash Room at the Treasury Department, the Europeans angrily blamed the US for allowing Lehman to fail and thus causing their problems at home. However, they quickly backed off their position when it was pointed out that several of their institutions were highly indebted and very vulnerable as a result. There was some discussion of having leaders meet to deal with the crisis. Mervyn King, governor of the Bank of England, suggested replacing the draft communiqué with a punchy one-page document. McCormick and his fellow finance deputies then produced another draft, which the finance ministers adjusted in one round. Its central message was that the G7 would not let any more banks fail. When it was released that day, the seven-point statement lifted the mood of the ministers, but not the stock markets. The latter continued to plunge while the spread between the London inter-bank offered rate (LIBOR) and the overnight indexed swap (OIS) widened. The severity of the worldwide crisis became clear.

Early on Saturday, October 11, at 7 am in the Roosevelt Room, Bush met with G7 finance ministers for the first time. He acknowledged that the crisis had started in the United States, and said that he wanted to start fixing it before he left office in three months. Bush ruminated on the idea of having leaders meet to cope with the crisis. He was not thinking in terms of only the G7 leaders, but there was no sense of who else he felt should attend. He and the ministers then walked out into the Rose Garden at the White House, where the press were waiting. Bush noted how severe the crisis was and what he was doing in response and, with the G7 finance ministers standing behind him, endorsed their action plan (Paulson 2010, 352–3).

During that day, meetings of the finance ministers of both the IMF and the western hemisphere were held. At 6 pm the G20 finance ministers met at the IMF, with Brazil's Guido Mantega in the chair. Henry Paulson and the ECB's Jean-Claude Trichet led off, emphasizing the success of the G7 at its meeting and the US desire to solve its problems. Bush entered around 6:20 pm. He acknowledged America's role in causing the financial problems, declared America's responsibility and its resolve, and concluded that "now is the time to solve this crisis" (Paulson 2010, 354–5; Kirton 2008a). It was another unprecedented move, signalling the gravity of the crisis, US willingness to explore forums beyond the G7 for international cooperation, and Bush's implicit choice of the G20 as his preferred one.

Not all participants were pleased with their encounter with Bush. To be sure, it was the first time Bush had met with the finance ministers of both the G7 and the G20 and one other group. But the G20 encounter seemed to some to be only a photo opportunity. As a result, there was reportedly a great deal of disappointment, if not anger. Mantega, as chair of the G20, had held a meeting in Brazil in September. Another was scheduled for November. In Washington, G20 finance ministers had been forced to reschedule their meetings to accommodate Bush who, in the views of some, did not want to engage with them substantively. In contrast, Bush's meetings with the G7 finance ministers and another group had been more than just a photo op. At the G20 meeting Bush entered into a gathering already in progress, apparently expecting to take centre stage. Mantega insisted on continuing to discuss the item under consideration, and then adjourned the meeting to accommodate Bush, had the group photo taken, and resumed the meeting in the president's presence. Bush then found a reason to leave.

At both the G7 and G20 meetings, the discussions about having a summit included questions of how many and which leaders should attend. But nothing was determined. Canadian finance minister Jim Flaherty felt it was necessary to have a summit, given the seriousness and uncertainty of the situation. None of the G7 members had any answers, beyond the post-Lehman conviction that no more banks must be allowed to fail and that they needed to get leaders involved. Flaherty felt that a realistic assessment of the global economy meant that the leaders of Brazil, Russia, India, and China—the BRICs—as well as the G7 must be there.

Australian Prime Minister Kevin Rudd, who had been concerned about global conditions since the start of 2008 and was intensely worried, felt strongly that the international institutional response should come from a summit of the G20, rather than of a G14 or G8. Rudd felt the group needed a broad set of middle economies included, and that the established structure of the G20 already existed. The middle economies, including neighbouring Indonesia from Asia, would avoid polarization between the G8 and the BRICs. The G20 offered five members from Europe, five from the Americas, five from Asia, and five from elsewhere, giving global legitimacy compared to the smaller, more Eurocentric groups. Anything short of the G20 would in practice be the G8 plus the G5, an inadequate group even if Australia secured an invitation for itself.

Armed with these arguments, Rudd led the campaign for a G20 response rather than the smaller G14 that Sarkozy strongly sought and that the World Bank's Robert Zoellick had initially proposed, or a G8 one, which the Japanese preferred. The French argued that smaller numbers would make agreement easier, while their opponents felt it would enhance French influence in the group. Those favouring a G20 suspected that Japan sought a G8 in order to maximize Japan's voice and keep any Asian rivals out.

Waking up in the middle of the night to place phone calls to fellow leaders and others, Rudd conducted an intense, tough, diplomatic campaign against the French. He focused on the US, which was initially considering a G14. Rudd also focused on the UK and China, which strongly supported a wider group, and Germany, which was comfortable with the concept as well. Mexico was strongly supportive, as it recoiled at the thought of Brazil alone speaking for Latin America in a G14. When Lula seemed to support the G14 during a news conference with a visiting Sarkozy, Rudd phoned Lula right away, to learn that Lula had felt trapped in this public venue. Italy's Silvio Berlusconi seemed to support any leader who called. Harper's Canadians did not appear to be natural supporters of a G20.

In regard to the summit agenda, Rudd also focused on the US, arguing that the agenda should be comprehensive, dealing with all financial regulatory repair work, fiscal stimulus, and long-term generators of economic growth. In practice, most of the agenda setting for Washington was done by the White House, Britain's

Number 10 Downing Street, the German chancellery led by Jens Weidmann, China's He Yafei, and Rudd and his Australian team. They were highly active in the communiqué-drafting process for Washington, and for London and Pittsburgh beyond.

The week following the G7 and G20 meeting, the Americans revived their plans for hosting a summit. Paulson (2010, 373) emphasized the importance of reaching out to the developing world. He and deputy treasury secretary Robert Kimmitt felt that if a summit was going to be held, it should include the leaders of the G20 members.

In Quebec City at the Francophonie Summit on October 17, 2008, Canada's Prime Minister Stephen Harper met with Sarkozy and endorsed his call. The idea to expand G7 membership for such a summit was also taken up by Giulio Tremonti, Italy's economy minister, although the exact nature of the new group was still not fixed.

On October 18, Sarkozy, along with finance minister Christine Lagarde and European Commission president José Manuel Barroso, left to meet Bush, Paulson, and secretary of state Condoleezza Rice at Camp David (Paulson 2010; Brown 2010). Sarkozy advocated a summit smaller than the G20, arguing that the shared values among the G8 members would make consensus easier to reach. He sought to focus the summit on more technical details, distrusting the "experts [who] got us into trouble in the first place" (Paulson 2010, 375). Bush, however, insisted on a more inclusive group and a focus on the broad principles of regulatory and institutional reform. Following the Camp David meeting, Bush, Sarkozy, and Barroso released a joint statement saying that they would invite other world leaders to a special summit that would take place after the US elections (White House 2008). Ban Ki-moon offered to host the event at the UN in New York. But Bush had insisted to Sarkozy that it be held in Washington and that the Bretton Woods bodies would play a supporting role.

Two days later, on October 20, Brown telephoned Bush to push for an invitation to all G20 countries, for Spain and the Netherlands, and for more Africans than just South Africa. Brown (2010) reports he and Bush made progress on this.

On October 22, the US announced that it would host a summit in Washington on November 14–15. Participants would include the G20 leaders, the IMF managing director, the president of the World Bank, the UN secretary general, and the chair of the Financial Stability Forum (FSF). By the end of the month, it was confirmed that the main meeting would be held in Washington's National Building Museum.

The Washington meeting was officially called the "Summit on Financial Markets and the World Economy." The name accurately identified the agenda: the current financial crisis and its impact on the global economy. Participants would review progress made in addressing the financial crisis in recent weeks, examine the underlying causes of the crisis, and come to consensus on principles for reforming regulatory and institutional regimes in global finance. They would lay the framework for actions to come on financial regulation and institutional reform.

Participants might also discuss trade, investment, and the need for open market economies. Australia, Germany, and the World Bank indicated that they would like to discuss the Doha Development Agenda. The leaders would review a range of proposals put forward by several countries for how best to address the financial crisis. Indeed, some predicted that the meeting would be a "Bretton Woods II." But IMF managing director Dominique Strauss-Kahn and others cautioned that no drastic reforms would come.

Partners' Reactions

The reaction from the invited non-G7 countries was generally favourable. Many G20 leaders rapidly accepted Bush's invitation. Chinese president Hu Jintao was the first to do so (Paulson 2010, 375). When Bush had called China to discuss having a summit, China did not know when or where it would be or who to send. France had suggested October 2008. China could send one of three individuals: the vice premier in charge of economic affairs, the premier, or the president himself. China finally decided to send Hu. The Chinese had been caught unprepared by the call for a summit. Thus at Washington, Hu said simply: "If we run our own house in order, that is China's biggest contribution." Subsequently, others started to ask China what its proposals were.

Canada's Conservative prime minister Harper, as a close colleague of the Americans, eagerly accepted. Canada had concluded that the G20 could work. To be sure, Canada was attached to the G8 club, and would host its summit in 2010. It felt that the G7 finance ministers' forum had worked well in responding to the crisis in its October meeting. Yet even before October 2008, in memos from Department of Finance officials that convinced Flaherty, Canada had calculated that there was a danger of getting caught by a new architecture of a "G4," "G3," or "G10" that did not include Canada. Given the tough task of measuring who fit in the global top 10 based on economic weight, Canada concluded that the G20 was safe because it put Canada in the middle of the pack. In response to the crisis, Canada preferred to support a G20 summit, where it was a prominent member, rather than run the risk of America or others deciding upon an ad hoc architecture that would cast Canada aside. Moreover, Flaherty was comfortable with the G20 finance forum, having been involved in it since his appointment in early 2006. He would be the only G7 finance minister along with France's Lagarde to attend the annual ministerial in Brazil in early November 2008, just before the summit's start. He took to Brazil a Canadian proposal to strengthen the G20 institution, in part by making it more of a decision-making body.

Korea was even more supportive of Bush's call. In very early November, Daniel Price, Bush's sherpa for the summit, called his Korean counterpart Ahn Ho-young for a 30-minute conversation to solicit views on what Korea wished to see happen at the summit. The Koreans were well prepared. When they had first heard Sarkozy's speech, they had concluded that any such gathering must be a meeting of the G20, and not the G7, a "G13," or even "G16" without Korea. They argued that the world was facing a financial crisis, that the G20 had functioned well since 1999 to deal with the financial crisis then, and that any number between seven and 20 would produce great displeasure on the part of those left out. They advanced this argument through diplomatic channels with the G7 members and through finance channels with some of them prior to October 18. When the US announced on October 22 that it would be the leaders of the G20, the Koreans were very relieved. They had already prepared a five-point memo outlining their position. Making the G20 summit permanent was point number one. On November 4, an hour-long conversation between Dan Price and his Korean colleague concluded with Ahn sending that memo to Price.

The leaders of Australia, India, Italy, South Africa, Brazil, and Japan also quickly accepted Bush's call. Others were hesitant. Saudi Arabia was concerned that it would be blamed for high oil prices and pressured into making contributions to fund poorer countries. Paulson (2010, 376) called Saudi finance minister Ibrahim al-Assaf to reassure him this would not be the case. Brazil suggested that it would participate as a spokesperson for the developing and emerging worlds, as did China. This gave rise to a conception of the meeting as a way to protect the South from a crisis created in the North and to reform the international financial institutions (IFIs) to give emerging and developing countries the greater voice and vote they had long felt they deserved.

Other leaders not included in the initial invitation indicated they wanted to come. Spain's José Zapatero was the most insistent. Rudd and others were not supportive, judging that this would mean too many Europeans in the group. The Spanish pressed Sarkozy who, in an act of European solidarity, declared that France would give up the "second seat" it claimed as the current president of the European Council, so that Zapatero could come. Spain tried to mobilize its old colonies in the Americas to support its case (Beattie 2010).

Here Mexican president Felipe Calderón was key in securing for Spain the invitation it sought (Kirton 2012). Calderón, with a master's degree in economics, had entered office as a very domestically oriented president. He felt fortunate that Mexico had been included in the G20 and the summit invitation list. Calderón consulted with Zapatero, and then pressed Spain's case with Bush and subsequently Obama. Calderón's intervention had the intended effect and Zapatero was invited. Within North America, this was a far cry from 1994 when Mexico had been the country under attack and the consumer of financial security. More broadly, it was Mexico that now helped secure for its former imperial master a place in the top-tier group, and a place secondary in status to the full, top-tier membership that Mexico had enjoyed in the G20 at the finance and leader levels from the start. Indeed, in the lead-up to the summit, Calderón consulted with his North American partners, the US and Canada—both G7 members—rather than what some Mexicans saw as the Latin American "loose cannons" of Brazil and, above all, Argentina.

Jan Peter Balkenende, prime minister of the Netherlands, also solicited an invitation. It was difficult to turn down since as a traditional financial centre and G10 member, the Netherlands had a better case than Spain for being at the table discussing financial regulatory reform. Sarkozy thus surrendered the seat of his own finance minister, the impressive Christine Lagarde, so that Balkenende could attend. In the end, Balkenende flew to Washington but had to return to Amsterdam immediately on learning of the death of his father. The Netherlands was represented at the summit by finance minister Jan Cornelis de Jager.

Venezuela, Poland, and others also solicited summit invitations but were not successful.

Sarkozy suggested that Miroslav Kalousek, the Czech Republic's finance minister, participate in the process, on the grounds that the Czech Republic would take over the EU presidency from France in 2009. This suggestion was refused. Several African countries and civil society organizations noted that Africa and other poor countries would be underrepresented. Seven African heads strongly suggested that Congolese president Denis Sassou Nguesso attend. Nguesso said that it was "unacceptable" that Africa was not invited to a summit that would consider the future of the global financial system (Agence France Presse 2008c).

There was speculation over whether the US president-elect would participate in the meeting, which would take place a mere 10 days after the American presidential election on November 4. It was suggested that he be represented at the meeting even if he was not physically present. The White House confirmed that the president-elect was welcome to participate if he so chose. In the end, however, Barack Obama, who had won the election, chose not to attend, on the grounds that the US had only one president at a time.

UN secretary general Ban Ki-moon said he would attend if invited. He was and did. Ban stressed the importance of listening to the poor developing countries that were not represented. He signalled the need for a non-exclusive multilateralism, emphasizing that the G20 must take the needs and voices of the developing countries into account in reforming the international architecture (Agence France Presse 2008d).

Several participants scheduled bilateral meetings at the summit. Russian president Dmitry Medvedev planned to meet with the leaders from Germany, China, and the UK. Japanese prime minister Taro Aso, Korean president Lee Myung-bak, and Australian prime minister Kevin Rudd, among others, tried to arrange meetings with the US president-elect. Obama, however, said he would not meet with any of the participants, although his advisors might. Some leaders also tried to arrange bilateral meetings with Bush. He, too, announced he would not meet with any leaders on the sidelines of the event.

Each of the leaders would be accompanied by a personal representative or sherpa. Canada chose its G8 sherpa, Len Edwards, who then became involved along with Canada's team from the Department of Finance. Indian prime minister Manmohan Singh chose Montek Singh Ahluwalia, deputy chair of the planning commission, to be by his side. Turkish prime minister Recap Tayyip Erdoğan would be accompanied by state minister and deputy prime minister Nazım Ekren, state minister Mehmet Şimşek, and undersecretary of the treasury Ibrahim Çanakcı. Australian treasury secretary Wayne Swan confirmed that he would be involved in the preparatory process. Finance ministers from China, Japan, and Korea were also scheduled to be in Washington ahead of the summit.

Brazil chose as its sherpa its ambassador in Washington, Marco Aurélio Garcia, an outspoken former university professor who had been with Lula for many years and was a close personal friend. Foreign Minister Celso Amorim went to the Washington Summit with Lula, advised the president, and gave him papers but had no specific role. As most issues concerned finance, Mantega was in the ministerial lead. Marcos Galvão was Brazil's G20 finance deputy and deputy minister of finance.

G20 Finance Ministers' and Central Bank Governors' Meeting

Part of the preparations for the summit was the regularly scheduled annual meeting of the G20 finance ministers and central bank governors, taking place in São Paulo, Brazil, on November 8–9, one week before the summit's start. Spain put much pressure on Brazil to allow it to attend. The Spanish said they were going to travel to São Paulo. Mantega replied that they would not be allowed into the meeting.

The evening before the meeting, the BRIC countries met and issued their own statement. After the top officials of the BRIC countries and also South Africa and Mexico met, Brazilian finance minister Guido Mantega announced that the participants had concluded that there must be a reform of the international financial system, particularly within the Bretton Woods institutions (Clendenning 2008). The current G7 system was "not sufficient," he stated, and needed to reflect the increasing weight of emerging markets (Burleigh 2008). The BRIC countries promised "to take all necessary steps to lessen the impact of the recent turmoil on economic activity, aiming to preserve medium and long-term growth."

Some countries held bilateral discussions (Kirton and Guebert 2009). There had been suggestions that the first G20 summit might signal a "Bretton Woods II" agreement, the details of which would be worked out at São Paulo. However, expectations for São Paulo were soon scaled back. Paulson did not attend, and David McCormick, undersecretary of the treasury for international affairs, took his place. At the meeting Flaherty stressed the importance of sound domestic financial reform—a refrain that Canada continued to emphasize. Canada's constant message was "fix the banks" first.

The São Paulo meeting's long scheduled and carefully prepared agenda of fiscal policies to stimulate economic growth, public-sector spending efficiency, and social inclusion now assumed centre stage. The other core issues on its inherited agenda—commodity markets, conventional clean energy, and biofuels—remained relevant. But the crisis brought the G20's core mission of securing financial stability to the forefront again. The G20's rapidly rising emerging economies—led by China—now had the resources, experience, confidence, and sense of inclusion to help rescue the reeling established countries, led by America, where the current crisis had begun.

To the existing agenda was added the new crisis in the credit market and financial sector as a whole. This theme of "financial stability and the world economy" began with a consideration of the causes of the crisis and its contagion. It then proceeded through the effectiveness of the policy measures already taken, the impacts of financial market stress on developing countries, preventive measures to be taken at present and later, and prospects for the future. São Paulo participants sought to fine-tune the agenda for the Washington Summit and reduce the initial differences among the Europeans, North Americans, Asians, and the emerging countries beyond.

São Paulo sought to provide a down payment on one key component—further reform of the Bretton Woods bodies. Brazil felt it was time to push the views and voices of emerging markets in the IMF, the World Bank, and other international financial institutions. For the first time they offered specific details on IMF voice and vote reform, asked for benchmarks to measure progress, and demanded an expanded FSF, which they soon got. The Brazilian push to increase the place and power of emerging and developing countries matched the mood of the majority of participants and the needs of the world outside.

The meeting featured a minimally adequate if very light slate of finance ministers, and most central bank governors, from the members. The dense schedule of meetings in their network included the European Union in Belgium on November 4, Asia-Pacific Economic Cooperation (APEC) in Peru on November 5–6, and the G20 in Washington on the eve of the summit itself. A few of the members, such as Trevor Manuel of South Africa, had attended continuously since the G20 had started in 1999. While the chair of the current gathering had less global experience, recognition, and respect, Mantega had chaired the G20's first emergency meeting on October 11 and done so reasonably well.

The finance ministers of the two biggest economies, America and Japan, did not attend. Nor did anyone from President-Elect Obama's economic team. China chose at the last minute not to send its finance minister, Xie Xuren, following the lead of America, Japan, Germany, and Britain. However, at the meeting of the BRIC finance ministers on November 7, China indicated it would contribute more money to the IMF and World Bank, commensurate with the enhanced voice and vote it sought. Korea's demanding legislature forced its finance minister to stay home, even though the G20, now governed by a troika of past, present, and future chairs, would choose Korea as its chair for 2010. France's Lagarde and Canada's Flaherty did attend, to lead the G7 side.

On the day before the G20 gathering, the IBSA group of India, Brazil, and South Africa met, with Mexico included as a guest. Also, the first ever formal meeting of the finance ministers of the BRICs welcomed the historic G20 summit. Their statement called for many measures at the core of the G7 consensus—international coordination, countercyclical policies, regulatory and supervisory reform, transparency, credit access, demand stimulation, capital flows, trade and investment, anti-protectionism and the conclusion of the badly overdue Doha round (BRIC Finance Ministers 2008). It also emphasized issues long accepted by the G20—employment support, social inclusion, poverty reduction, infrastructure investment, assistance for low-income countries, and reform of the multilateral and financial institutions, inter alia, to give developing countries a greater voice and vote. It further asked the G7 to broaden the membership of the FSF.

Lula came to the G20 meeting. In his speech he called for expanded participation in the FSF, vote and voice reform of the IMF and World Bank, and stronger economic and social protection for the poor. Canada sought to strengthen the G20 finance institution itself, by having it become more action oriented and meet more frequently, with more influential timing and a direct role in the G20 summit itself.

The ministerial meeting made substantial advances on most fronts (Kirton 2008b). It largely endorsed the G7's approach to reforming the international financial system, adopting most of the principles and half of the actions the FSF had agreed on in its October 10 report. The G7 members in return accepted most of the emerging countries' key demands. The G20 communiqué declared that "the FSF must expand to a broader membership of emerging countries," "emerging and developing economies should have greater voice and representation" in the Bretton Woods institutions, and financial stability and global growth had "poverty reduction and social inclusion" as equal priority goals (G20 Finance 2008).

The G20 finance ministers and central bankers welcomed the November 14–15 summit as an "important step in enhancing international cooperation," called for global solutions and principles, pledged their readiness to help in preparation and implementation, and committed themselves to focusing on "concrete policy outcomes" and considering more frequent and well-timed ministerial meetings (G20 Finance 2008). They promised "comprehensive, coordinated and timely measures." But they cautiously endorsed additional fiscal stimulus only for countries where circumstances permitted and with due regard for "fiscal sustainability" over the long term.

The G20 in balanced fashion attributed the causes of the crisis to poor market practices, inconsistent government macroeconomic policy, and inadequate countries' regulation (as distinct from all blaming the G7 or America alone). It pledged to "work together to take all necessary actions" to solve the credit and financial crisis in all its members, and to support employment, resist trade and investment protectionism, and promptly and ambitiously conclude the Doha round. It further called for flows of official development assistance (ODA) to be maintained and for the Bretton Woods bodies to help the poor more. Its communiqué made six references to the G20 (one to the forthcoming summit and five to the finance ministers' forum). It made 15 to other international institutions, led by the IMF with eight, the World Bank and Bretton Woods institutions with three each, and the FSF with one.

Competing Positions

As the Washington Summit approached, key members still publicly had distinctly different approaches to its agenda and architecture.

United States

At one end of the spectrum stood the US. Its approach was to go slow, go long, go limited, and go light, following the work started in the spring by the FSF.

"Go slow" meant holding the summit well before Bush left office but after it was known who the next president would be. It further meant having the summit as the first of several summits to come. The purpose of that first summit would be primarily to agree on the principles, an agenda, and a mandate for several new working groups to be established to report back to subsequent gatherings, some of which need not be held at the leaders' level or as special, stand-alone G20 summits, separate from the already existing G8 ones. A few quick actions could also come.

Here the US was largely making a virtue of necessity—the logistical burden of organizing an unprecedented summit of 20 leaders, the need to associate in some way the next president's administration with its work, the immediate need to create confidence in still fragile financial, economic, and political markets, and the recognition that crisis management, prevention, and systemic reform would take much more than one meeting to get right.

"Go long" gave President-Elect Obama, his administration, and the new Congress time to get installed in office, organize themselves, devise an effective American strategy and positions, and conduct the diplomacy necessary to deliver a successful result. This would likely involve a process longer than a year, and perhaps much longer should the immediate crisis and its moment of opportunity diminish. Timing depended in part on the appointment of the new treasury secretary, with a choice of Lawrence Summers allowing for faster movement than many other appointees would. Moreover, Obama had no particular personal expertise, experience, or interest in financial and economic matters. It would thus take some time for him to get up to speed. Since the crisis had started in America, and was still hitting hard there, Obama had a particular incentive to get it done right rather than to get it done fast.

"Go limited" reinforced this "go long" approach. America wanted to focus narrowly on stopping the current financial crisis, preventing a return, identifying its causes and its contagion for these purposes, and combating the economic slowdown that it brought. The US initially showed little enthusiasm for burdening this already formidable agenda with a long list of things to regulate, or taking up outstanding issues on trade, development, and IFI reform.

"Go light" meant reforming the current system rather than revolutionizing or replacing it as a whole. This involved relying in the first instance on voluntary industry self-regulation and government supervision, rather than government regulation, control, or ownership. It also meant staying with essentially national regulation, with appropriate international communication, cooperation, and coordination, rather than leaping into any internationally harmonized common regulation, let alone one controlled by a supranational authority beyond the sovereign United States. America's central aim was to defend and reinforce market-oriented capitalism, rather than replace it with something else.

America had allies within the G7. Neither Japan nor Canada had experienced banking or financial crises over the past year. They thus felt no need to rush into a rapid, revolutionary response. Both had proven domestic policy models they sought to export. Indeed, Japan noted with some satisfaction that its secure banks were now buying up beleaguered American ones.

Europe

At the other end of the spectrum among the G7 stood Europe, led by France, followed in varying degrees by Britain, Germany, and Italy. While there were discernable differences within "team Europe," it largely sought to go fast, go short, go wide, and go deep.

"Go fast" meant holding the first and subsequent summits as quickly as possible, so solutions could be found and implemented very soon. Signals from Paris suggested that the Washington Summit's successors could come as soon as a week after the first, or at least immediately after the new US president was installed. The French pushed for quick decisions at Washington as well.

"Go short" meant concluding the summit process and its outcomes as soon as possible, within a matter of months, in German chancellor Angela Merkel's view. The European fear was that a long delay would lead to the dissipation of political will and focus, especially as the September 15 high point of financial panic passed into more familiar economic recessionary concerns.

"Go wide" meant including a comprehensive range of subjects in the agenda and action plan, in recognition of the tight interconnection among those subjects. Within the finance field this included not only hedge funds but also the overall architecture of global rules and a global regulator. Germany felt that, while financial regulation was understandably the main topic, the agenda should be broader. Merkel had proposed a "financial market charter" that contained many good components, to guide her approach. She also had a particular personal interest in issues of the environment, climate change, energy, trade, and the Doha round.

"Go deep" meant moving as much as possible toward a single set of global rules and a single global regulator. This was a concept comfortable for members of the somewhat supranational 27-member EU, especially those in it since the start who felt they could use the larger entity to exert their will on a wider stage. Sarkozy saw a Bretton Woods II for the twenty-first century, with a single global market regulator, while Silvio Berlusconi's Italy wanted to abolish hedge funds. Others wanted new international authorities, modified market principles, and major increases in IMF funding. The fall-back French position was much greater international regulatory coordination now, to evolve into supranational authority later.

As the São Paulo ministerial opened, there had been considerable trans-Atlantic accommodation, largely brought by European adjustments to the American position. Thus the Washington preparations moved toward agreement on the causes of the recent crisis, common principles to avoid a recurrence, and a few specific actions such as greater transparency and regulation in financial markets, coverage for credit defaults, and perhaps hedge funds. It seemed that American minimalism rather than French maximalism would prevail. Europe was divided, with none of the old EU members fully supporting the French. Most of the newer members from Central and Eastern Europe, cherishing their recent freedom from the Soviet Union, were on the minimalist side. Some older EU members, led by Spain, put more energy into getting invited to the summit than in engaging in the substance of what the summit might do.

China

The non-G7 emerging members of the G20 were also divided. Mexico, with memories of the peso crisis of 1994, had some sympathy for the French approach. China had none at all. With no immediate financial crisis at home, a single party-run state, and a thousand years of history including a well-remembered colonized phase, China had little desire to turn any of its sovereign authority over domestic finance to a European- or American-dominated global regulator outside.

China was important due to its sheer economic size, rapid and resilient growth, massive foreign exchange reserves of almost $2 trillion, and lack of any real banking crisis or financial stress at home. Yet it also had a strong incentive to act and adjust, with its growth projected to drop, its stock market plunging, its factories closing, and many of its workers newly unemployed, heightening the spectre of social unrest.

Through an announcement by Premier Wen Jiabao on November 4, China signalled at an early stage that it would actively participate in the Washington Summit and bear its global responsibility there. At the seventh Asia–Europe Meeting (ASEM) held on October 24, Hu Jintao had called for enhanced international policy coordination, strengthened cooperation, and a common response. He also noted that China's domestic growth contributed to economic growth and financial stability abroad. China had joined with G7 countries and Switzerland in simultaneous monetary policy action, although with a degree of coordination less intense than that among the G7 members themselves. Yet both Hu and Wen noted that keeping China's own economy growing was the greatest global contribution China could make, even as Britain's Gordon Brown identified China's foreign exchange reserves as an attractive source of new funding for the IMF. China's three guiding principles were, first, to keep its own house in order; second, to contribute to global action; and, third, to join international collective action.

At a November 6 briefing about Hu's trip to Washington for the summit, Vice Foreign Minister He Yafei said China expected a fair, inclusive, and efficient international financial system (Xinhua 2008). China saw the agenda as dealing with the causes of the crisis, evaluating the international response, and charting the way ahead for financial supervision and its reform. China's position centred on three points: all countries should act quickly on financial supervision, confidence, and economic growth; reform of the IFIs should reflect economic change, improve developing country representation, and select senior officials by fair comparison; and developed countries should consider and help developing countries in their crisis response.

China viewed the Washington meeting as timely. China would take a constructive stand and seek to reach consensus on a common response. Because the crisis had a more serious impact on developing countries, especially the most undeveloped ones, through declining investment and ODA, the developed world should assist them.

Rich countries, the IFIs, and the World Bank should help. Restoring consumer confidence and stabilizing global financial markets were the immediate priorities. The summit was just the start of a longer process of global financial system reform. The US should keep its free trade policies intact.

Brazil

Brazil's key initiative, backed by other emerging countries, was to put governance on the table. While there was a need to tackle the crisis and improve financial regulations, Brazil felt that it was not responsible for the crisis. While Brazil would come to help and accept the agenda, it asked to change the way global finance governance was structured.

One way to do so was to deepen the reform of the IMF and World Bank immediately, rather than wait for the second round until 2013 as had previously been agreed. Brazil's recommendation appeared in the Washington communiqué as the agreement on a comprehensive reform of IFIs.

Another very important way was to open previously closed financial forums to rising powers. Brazil was excluded from the G7, the FSF, the Basel Committee on Banking Supervision (BCBS), the technical committee of the International Organization of Securities Commissions (IOSCO), and the International Accounting Standards Board (IASB). Brazil asked to join not only the FSF but the BCBS too. At the FSF, Brazil and the BRICs demanded three chairs each: one for finance, one for the central bank, and one for the securities commission, just as the G7 members had.

Plans and Preparations

Lead-up Leaders' Discussions

Prior to the Washington Summit there were several other summits, with a dense, overlapping network of interaction as the cumulative result. In late October, Brown met Sarkozy to work out a common European position. Brown and Merkel planned a meeting on the global economy and reforms for financial markets. Medvedev spoke with Rudd and met with Berlusconi. Aso sent representatives, among them Yoshiji Nogami, to the G20 countries, including the G8 members and Indonesia.

Obama spoke by telephone with the leaders of Australia, Britain, Canada, France, Germany, Japan, Korea, and Mexico, as well as Israel, to discuss the economic crisis, among other topics. Harper spoke by phone with Singh, underscoring the need for real dialogue and unity among G20 members. In October, the ASEM summit in Beijing addressed several issues for the Washington Summit's agenda. At their November 7 EU summit, the Europeans agreed to produce a proposal to give emerging economies more voice, curb short-term behaviour in European markets, and ensure greater oversight of credit rating agencies and increased accountability and transparency in global financial markets. The day before the G20 summit Medvedev, Sarkozy, and Barroso were scheduled to meet at an EU-Russia summit.

From the start, the Americans had planned, and their partners had expected, that the November 14–15 summit would be the first of several. There was speculation that the second summit could happen as early as November 21 at the United Nations or sometime between February and April 2009 in Paris. The Europeans sought to meet again within 100 days to meet with the new US president as soon as possible. The next summit would likely take place outside the United States. In the meantime, working groups would develop the principles from the first summit to be decided on by leaders at subsequent ones, until the crisis was under control.

Sherpas' and Finance Deputies' Meetings

For the November summit, Dan Price chaired the sherpa meetings, all held in Washington. The main one took place along with the summit, with the sherpas arriving the day before the leaders' main day. The finance ministers and their deputies played a major part at this stage, with the sherpas and leaders following their lead. The work on the financial sector, above all the work on fixing the banks, was important.

Price had to put the summit together in a great hurry. To do this he had to knock heads together in a very forthright, indeed outspoken way. It was an experiment, because while the finance ministers and deputies of all the members of this group had sat around the table, neither the sherpas nor the leaders ever had. Among the sherpas, those of the G8 countries, especially Britain's Jonathan Cunliffe, were very literate on the key issues at hand. Their experience and expertise would show in the final result.

With so little time, preparations for the Washington Summit were very rushed. The G20 sherpas and finance deputies came to consensus on much of the draft communiqué one week before the summit. However, it took until Thursday, November 13, for a consensus on a college of supervisors for the biggest international banks to emerge. That day Mario Draghi, chair of the FSF, and Dominique Strauss-Kahn, managing director of the IMF, finally agreed on the respective roles and relationships of their institutions within the strengthened global financial architecture that the G20 summit would put in place (Engelen 2008). The FSF would create the standards, which the IMF would then monitor and enforce. The draft communiqué passages on trade liberalization remained rather routine.

Starting in the afternoon of November 14, the finance deputies met to draft sections of the leaders' communiqué and its action plan. The IMF played a key role as it was to carry out much of the ensuing work. The IMF thus had to stay heavily involved to ensure that it would be able to deliver what the G20 leaders would task it to do.

The finance deputies' text was subject to review at the sherpa level, where it was put under a microscope. As this was the first time the sherpas had prepared a G20 document, some sherpas paid close interest to the wording, including the text that came from finance deputies. Work was already well advanced once the leaders started dinner that evening.

One source of difficulty was the standoff between the US and China on the role played by imbalances in causing the crisis. China drew a "red line" and would not budge, refusing to accept the word "imbalances" in the communiqué because it felt that was an implicit reference to the renminbi. The US, for its part, did not want to take all the blame for causing the crisis. This opening exchange led to the long-term discussion of how to avoid similar problems going forward, with future G20s engaging ever more productively on the imbalances issue.

Another difference arose over trade. France, supported by Brazil, asked that all agree that they would meet, perhaps at the leaders' level, in the immediate future, to get Doha done. But the US had already said in the draft that the leaders were prepared to intervene to this end. After a debate on the trade language, the US words prevailed.

Brazil's demand to join the BCBS encountered some resistance. The argument was that the finance ministers at Washington could not ask for Brazil to be admitted to a central bankers' group. In the end, at the London Summit in April 2009, Brazil and the rest of the BRICs got into the FSF with three chairs each, and into the BCBS and the IASB through a central bank official operating in a personal capacity. This was the first time a Latin American country had become a member of the IASB.

At the Summit

The G20 summit began on the evening of November 14 with a working dinner at the White House. It was soon clear from the dynamics of the discussion that some leaders had not worked out how serious and systemic the unfolding crisis would be. Those of the US, UK, Germany, China, and Australia sought to convince their colleagues of the urgency of the task at hand.

The working part of the dinner began with statements from the heads of four international organizations: the UN, the IMF, the World Bank, and the FSF. Each was given five minutes for his remarks. Ban's speech slanted toward the South and advanced traditional points. He attempted to position the UN as a key player with a seat at the table. He offered the UN as the next G20 summit host.

Strauss-Kahn, speaking for a little longer than five minutes, made four points. First, the crisis was far from over. Advanced economies would face negative growth and emerging markets were being severely hit by drying-up financial flows and weakened demand. The situation was deteriorating. The risk was that it would get worse.

Second, policy actions to support growth must be taken now. G20 members should use all possible tools at their disposal. Inflation was no longer a risk in the biggest economies. In several countries there was room for additional monetary and substantial fiscal easing. Members should resist protectionism, a temptation all too easy in this environment. It was extremely important to resist it at the highest political level, since nothing would be worse for growth. There must be additional fiscal expansion wherever possible. Strauss-Kahn said that he would meet with each leader to outline the specific policy actions each could take regarding fiscal and monetary policies. IMF analysis showed that coordinated fiscal stimulus would make their policy response to the crisis more effective, but not all countries should do the same thing at the same time. However, in pursuing nationally appropriate measures in each economy, it would improve the effectiveness of the actions if trading partners pursued them simultaneously. This was primarily from a regional perspective among countries integrated in this way.

Third, Strauss-Kahn made a plea for money. The financing needs of emerging markets must be urgently addressed. Market financing was scarce or non-existent. There was a need to act decisively and rapidly to support them. The IMF had sufficient lending capacity, as it had lent out only $50 billion of its $230 billion so far. But the situation could change rapidly as demands escalated over the next few months. Leaders needed to ensure that the international institutions created to provide counter-cyclical lending had adequate resources at any time. It was now time to think about how the international community could expand the IMF's resources. Strauss-Kahn thanked Aso for Japan's intention to make a $100 billion loan available to the IMF. He asked who would be next. He said that he would clarify how much money each country could provide to the IMF for lending to emerging countries in his bilateral meetings with the leaders.

Fourth, work must begin on a new architecture for global collaboration for risk warning and for appropriate policy responses. Enhanced regulatory and supervisory rules and strengthened early warning systems were needed. The IMF was the place to build and operate more robust ones. But they needed to be followed by a commitment to act by policy makers when the warning system suggested action was required.

Strauss-Kahn's call for action was echoed by many around the table. There was strong support for fiscal stimulus by those countries that had room to stimulate. Many leaders indicated they would move forward with such programs in the coming days and weeks. Strauss-Kahn affirmed that the IMF stood ready to help them determine how much they could stimulate and how to maximize the effectiveness of the stimulus. The IMF already had action plans drawn up. There was a strong recognition of the severity of crisis facing the global economy.

At dinner, the main point made and accepted was, above all, the need to maintain orderly markets as it was still a dangerous time. It was necessary to back the banks and ensure there were no more international surprises. There was still a high degree of uncertainty apparent to all. Yet not all participants were on the same wavelength. From the start the emerging economies were less worried, as their financial systems were not imperilled. They were concerned about the collapse in the West because they were connected and affected, but their sense of urgency was less than that of the G7 members themselves.

That same evening, the G20 finance ministers, who had been having extensive phone conversations, were dining elsewhere at the same time as their leaders. In the morning the leaders of Canada and other countries would meet individually with their finance ministers to compare notes.

On Saturday, November 15, the leaders' working sessions took place in a very large room in the National Museum Building. Only country leaders spoke. Bush followed protocol order, with the King of Saudi Arabia leading off, as the only royalty in the room. Each leader was allowed to speak for the allotted five to seven minutes, without interruption or rejoinder. It took about two hours to reach Canada's Harper, who was seated directly opposite King Abdullah Bin Abdulaziz.

When calling on the leaders to speak, Bush skipped the Spanish prime minister and gave the floor to Sarkozy, although Zapatero was physically next in line. That was seen as a strong message. But after Sarkozy spoke, Sarkozy himself gave the floor to Zapatero and then to de Jager, the Dutch finance minister. The latter spoke for about 15 minutes, reading the text of his absent prime minister's speech. By this time, Lagarde had brought her seat up from the back to the front row.

Over lunch, there was a heated discussion. Leaders intervened forcefully to call for the restart and successful conclusion of the long-overdue Doha round and for a strong communiqué passage on trade overall. Sarkozy made a long intervention, saying that the leaders must get Doha done as their technicians had failed. Several leaders, including Rudd, replied that there was a vicious circle, with officials saying they needed a political mandate and leaders saying they lacked the technical expertise to conclude the deal themselves. Rudd and others felt that the

EU, and France within it, was the primary obstacle. The result was ambitious, detailed language on an anti-protectionist pledge for the following year and on concluding a modalities agreement by the end of 2008 to complete Doha. Despite this visible energetic unanimity, some at the table took this agreement with some skepticism, knowing that some of the leaders strongly advocating that Doha get done were the very ones preventing this outcome.

All agreed there should be a follow-up summit. At a break there was a discussion of where the summit should go next. Brown spoke of the need for one and offered to host it. He did so with considerable credibility, having been Britain's chancellor of the exchequer for 10 years.

In the plenary, several leaders made lengthy speeches. They went beyond their allotted time, covering a broad range of issues beyond the agenda and not making their positions clear. Berlusconi was relatively disengaged. He noted that Bush was about to retire, had been a great leader who had led the free world after September 11 in the war on terror, and congratulated him for that. But he did not comment on the economy. Sarkozy tried throughout the summit to impose his stamp on it. At the table he circulated his own set of key conclusions for the meeting, asking everyone to stick to the same song sheet.

Merkel, Rudd, and Harper stood out as being clear, focused, direct, and to the point. Even as discussions centred on the need for stimulus, Harper insisted on the need to address eventual exit strategies from the start. He also underscored the seriousness of the situation, the need for action now, and the need to restore confidence in the banking and financial system in those countries where such institutions had failed. He spoke forthrightly and effectively about the international economy. He was recognized as providing thoughtful interventions, especially on fiscal policy and on the banking and financial systems, as no Canadian institutions had failed. Canada would become known for its strong contributions on trade and for coming into summit meetings with positive statements on the need for G20 countries to resist the lure of protectionism.

Harper's vision of G20 governance was for more coordination and direction setting rather than decision making or the development of global governance. His government believed that sound financial regulation must begin "at home," and that international bodies could provide the necessary pressure to bring outlier countries in line (McCarthy 2008; Thorpe 2008a, 2008b; Agence France Presse 2008a, 2008b; Compte 2008; Menon 2008). While Harper participated actively in both the summit and the preparatory discussions with other leaders, he cautioned that there needed to be moderate expectations about the outcome.

During the summit, Canada took a middle-of-the-road or "balanced" approach. It included prudent market oversight with a light touch. Harper encouraged countries to adopt significant stimulus measures, but counselled against more "red-tape" regulation. He aligned himself more with Bush's defence of free market capitalism, rather than the European and Australian argument that the root of the crisis lay in deregulation and unchecked speculation. In regard to summit outcomes, Canada adopted its traditional role as an honest broker, urging leaders to find a middle ground between domestic and international regulation.

Many leaders had come to the summit eager to tell Bush directly that he was responsible for the financial crisis. Some BRIC leaders, unlike the Europeans, were at times critical of the US. In some respects it was a vindictive summit, with no one beyond Berlusconi expressing regrets that Bush would be leaving office soon. But all recognized the seriousness of the problem they collectively faced.

From Brazil, Lula pressed for global financial and economic governance reform. He was also engaged on the trade issue, with a surprising preference for and grasp of the details.

In Argentina the media reported that Cristina Fernández de Kirchner, along with others, was going to give Bush an earful in this regard. Kirchner arrived late for the photo, to the visible irritation of an always punctual Bush.

Some guest leaders added little to the discussions. Spain's Zapatero, with a crumbling economy and property sector and a problematic financial sector, added nothing, but did secure a short bilateral meeting with Bush. The Netherlands also added no value. Balkenende had returned home as soon as he had landed in Washington.

Sarkozy's spontaneity and sense of ownership continued to the end. On the final day his representative appeared at the meeting of the sherpas, who were reviewing the final communiqué. The French asked for a much shorter communiqué, which Sarkozy provided. When Price asked his fellow sherpas if they agreed, none did. Two hours later, the French reported that Sarkozy accepted the existing communiqué.

Achievements

The most striking achievements of the Washington Summit were that it won out among the competing international institutional concepts for responding to the crisis, and that it was held and worked. Moreover, it did so all at the hands of a long skeptical George Bush and a new president Barack Obama, who agreed to come to a second summit to be held very soon. Substantively, its standout success was mobilizing large-scale, simultaneous fiscal and monetary stimulus and establishing principles, a process, and tight deadlines to fix the banks and the financial system as a whole (Lukov 2010). To put the principles on financial regulatory reform into practice, it established four working groups that accomplished what participants thought was excellent work over the following four months.

Dimensions of Performance

The Washington Summit was a strong success, primarily in domestic political management, deliberation, direction setting, decision making, and the development of global economic governance. It created consensus in trade, fiscal stimulus, and international financial institution reform, where governments had considerable control. On private sector-driven finance, a subject that was not the leaders' area of experience and expertise, it put in place principles and a process to guide others in their work.

Domestic Political Management

In managing their domestic politics, the leaders used the summit for strong, short-term success (see Appendix D-2). Their attendance showed their voters that they were personally concerned with the crisis, were trying to solve it, and were a top-tier global player in the attempt. Simply being present was a matter of vital prestige and status for those leaders who felt they would be left out if a new or smaller ad hoc summit had been selected. It was even more significant for Spain and the Netherlands, where collapsing banks and a G10 position were at stake.

The Washington Summit also gave leaders a politically covered opportunity to alter established positions, especially on fiscal stimulus. Brown abandoned his venerable "golden rules" to introduce a major stimulus package, using the G20 summit and G7 consensus to justify the policy shift. Harper, who had just been re-elected on October 14, in part by pledging never to put Canada into a fiscal deficit, used the G20 as justification for the post-election move of his minority government to make such a move. His Speech from the Throne on November 19, 2008, explicitly referred to the G20 summit, but not to the earlier G8 one.

The summit also helped spark and sustain a boost in public opinion approval in several countries. Brown benefited the most. Merkel and Harper also enjoyed a public approval bounce. With regard to the leaders' satisfaction with the meeting, Singh was positive. On his return home, he noted his initial skepticism that the summit would be able to accomplish anything, but acknowledged that he had been won over by what it had done.

Only in its host was the summit's performance mixed. Bush used the summit to show his global leadership and to get his fellow Republicans to back large new fiscal stimulus. However, the legacy of the latter in the medium term was more negative, when Obama sought to control America's soaring deficits and debt.

Deliberation

In its deliberations, the summit was a substantial success. To be sure, it was a short face-to-face encounter, lasting less than 24 hours from the opening dinner on Friday evening to its concluding news conferences early Saturday afternoon. It was less than half as long as the 2008 G8 summit, which had lasted at least 48 hours over three days. Nonetheless, the mere fact that it was held for the first time among this very diverse group of leaders allowed personal conversations and relationships among them to start.

Publicly, the summit produced two documents, totalling 3,567 words (see Appendix C-2). This compared favourably with the first G8 summit (with six leaders) in 1975, which had generated one concluding document of 1,129 words. Washington's total, however, was less than the G8's 1975–2008 annual average of about 9,000 words.

The Washington documents covered a considerable range of issue areas. The emphasis was, in order, on financial regulation, the economy, trade, development, and IFI reform. The leaders also briefly ventured beyond those topics by declaring that "we remain committed to addressing other critical challenges such as energy security and climate change, food security, the rule of law, and the fight against terrorism, poverty and disease" (G20 2008). G20 governance at the leaders' level thus dealt with global-transnational and political-security issues from the very start. Although the documents did not directly state that the G20 leaders would address these issues through their summit, the call was reminiscent of the G20 finance ministers' statement in Montreal in 2000 that there was potentially no economically related issue that the forum would not take up (Kirton 2000).

Privately, the leaders' discussions consisted largely of set-piece speeches, with Argentina's Kirchner giving a very long, diffuse speech in Spanish. There was some disappointment at the White House and elsewhere that at the sessions, especially the opening dinner, participants generally only delivered speeches rather than engaged an open dialogue and exchange of views. But these discussions were marked by some personal commitment and passion. This was most evident on the trade discussion the next day. Here several leaders spoke about the threat of protectionism. As a result the communiqué passages on trade were specific and strong.

Direction Setting

In its principled and normative direction setting, Washington was a strong success. Its direction setting came most comprehensively and specifically in its principles to guide future decision making on financial stability, financial regulation, and economic growth. Those principles emphasized the benefits that open markets brought.

The principle of openness extended into the political domain. The communiqué made 12 affirmations of such values, covering six types (see Appendix F-2). In the lead was transparency, with five affirmations, followed by the rule of law and openness, with two affirmations each, and good governance, information/knowledge exchange, and accountability with one affirmation each. Moreover, it renewed the Montreal Consensus of 2000, by affirming the need to deal with a broad range of social and equity concerns.

These direction-setting achievements are highlighted alone among the six dimensions of performance in Bush's own recollection of what his summit achieved. He writes: "On November 15, every leader at the summit signed on to a joint statement that read: 'Our work will be guided by a shared belief that market principles, open trade and investment regimes, and effectively regulated financial markets foster the dynamism, innovation, and entrepreneurship that are essential for economic growth, employment, and poverty reduction'" (Bush 2010, 466).

Decision Making

In its collective decision making, Washington was also a strong success, as its principles were forwarded into many clear commitments. The summit produced 95 commitments, despite its emphasis on offering principles and work plans to guide the decisions that would take place only in several months' time. Those commitments dealt primarily with macroeconomics and financial regulation. Some were on trade. One was on development. There was also an ambitious agreement, in accordance with France's preferences, on tax havens, a problem the G7/8 had long tried but failed to solve.

The leaders' commitments at Washington were more than the G20 finance ministers had made in São Paulo the week before, although the number was much less than the 296 commitments made by the G8 leaders in Japan on a much broader agenda in July. The 95 Washington commitments were far more than the mere four commitments made by the G20 finance ministers at their first meeting in 1999 or the 14 the six G7 leaders had made at their first summit at Rambouillet in 1975. The G20 was thus transformed from primarily a discussion and direction-setting forum into a robust decision-making one. More generally, in contrast to the G8, there were few calls for the G20 summit to avoid acting as a *directoire*.

Delivery

In its delivery of these commitments, there was substantial success in the following four and a half months until the subsequent summit was held in London at the beginning of April 2009. At Washington, the leaders were well aware of the importance of their credibility and quick delivery on their promises. They demonstrated their personal commitment by agreeing to mount a second summit by April 30, 2009. This interval was shorter than the one between the first and second G7 summits in 1975, and similar to the recent regional European Council norm.

A further compliance-inducing move was the very short timeline the leaders set for getting many of their short-term decisions done: these commitments, they specified in their communiqué, were to be delivered by March 31, 2009. In the context of the G8, setting a short-term timetable of one year or less for delivery is often an important catalyst for getting members to comply (Kirton et al. 2010). Indeed, the G20's 95 commitments at Washington were laden with several G8-proven compliance catalysts: 39 commitments referred to a short-term timetable and 14 included a reference to the core international organization. Only 13 commitments referred to other international organizations, a catalyst that tends to bring G8 compliance down.

Some commitments were complied with within their short time frame, including the one to mount a second summit by April 30, 2009. Some, however, were quickly violated, such as the anti-protectionist pledge. Russia and India soon raised import duties on automobiles, France altered its Common Agriculture Policy plans, and the US introduced labelling requirements for Canadian meat. The ambitious commitment to produce a modalities agreement at the World Trade Organization by December 31, 2008, to get the overdue Doha Development Agenda done was not fulfilled. Indeed, trade ministers could not even hold a meeting by that date.

However, despite these imperfections, by the time the next summit started, G20 members had complied with their Washington anti-protectionist commitments at a level of +0.58, on a scale from −1.00 to +1.00, for a compliance rate of 79 percent (G20 Research Group and International Organizations Research Institute 2011). Subsequent analysis adding more data produced a score of +0.51 (75.5 percent) (see Appendix H-3). On the financial regulation commitment on market integrity, compliance was a robust +0.47 (73.5 percent). On fiscal stimulus, with most members mounting massive new discretionary stimulus within the following months, compliance came in at a high +0.75, or 87.5 percent.

Development of Global Governance

In the development of global governance, the Washington Summit was a very strong success, both within and beyond the G20. Internally, it was the first G20 summit. By the members deciding to hold a second one so soon, it suggested the start of an ongoing G20 summit institution. They also asked G20 trade ministers to play a role. Leaders created four official-level working groups, each co-chaired by an established country and an emerging one, to implement its decisions. The communiqué made five references to the G20: one to the summit, three to its finance ministers' component, and one to civil society.

At the civil society level, the G20 instructed its new task forces to engage in multistakeholder consultation with experts. Yet this was only on a functional, epistemic community basis, rather than a broadly multistakeholder one. Most of those people affected by the crisis were given no place in the G20's governance in response.

Externally, the summit instructed the FSF to broaden its membership and otherwise reform. It sent a similar reform message to the Bretton Woods institutions and other international regulatory and supervisory bodies, notably IOSCO and the nongovernmental IASB. It helped specify the relationship between these institutions in the strengthened global financial architecture. It created new bodies such as a college of supervisors for each global bank. In all, it made 40 references to outside international institutions, led by the IMF with 12; the FSF with eight; the World Bank with five; the IFIs with three; the Bretton Woods institutions, the World Trade Organization, the UN, and multilateral development banks with two each; and the Financial Action Task Force, the Organisation for Economic Co-operation and Development, the BCBS, and IOSCO with one apiece. In doing so, it helped strengthen a broader, multi-sectoral network to govern global economics and finance.

Causes of Performance

The Washington Summit's strong performance is well accounted for by the model of systemic hub governance.

Shock-Activated, Equalizing Vulnerabilities

The first cause—driving the initiation, institutionalization, and strong performance of the first G20 summit—was the sequence of severe financial shocks that exposed the shared economic vulnerability of all systemically significant countries, above all the most economically powerful United States, and in regard to the social and even political stability of some. This shock sequence was unprecedented in its surprise, severity, speed, spread, scope, and penetrative impact within sovereign polities and societies, and in its source from the American-Anglo-Atlantic core. Its source in the US, Britain, and Germany strongly equalized the vulnerability of the G20 members relative to the 1997–99 Asian-turned-global financial crisis, and offset in an equalizing way the distribution of relative capability among the 20 members.

On September 18, treasury secretary Henry Paulson and Federal Reserve governor Ben Bernanke had told Bush they were facing an unprecedented financial panic that it was the worst crisis since the Great Depression. Bush (2010, 440) decided to respond as "Roosevelt, not Hoover." In his words, "the strategy was a breathtaking intervention in the free market. It flew against all my instincts. But it was necessary to pull the country out of the panic … The financial crisis was global in scale, and one major decision was how to deal with it in the international arena" (458–9, 465).

The crisis also came with, and may have been importantly fuelled by, a less sudden but still severe energy shock. Above all that shock hit the US, Japan, Germany, Britain, and now net-oil-importing China. World oil prices had hit a historic nominal high, to make these leading powers more vulnerable. The rise also enhanced, in an equalizing way, the power of oil-rich Canada, Russia, Brazil, Indonesia, and Saudi Arabia lower down the G20's relative capability ranks.

New terrorist shocks also arrived, not just in America as in 2001 and Britain as in 2005, but now in rising Russia, India, and China with its Tibetan uprising. Terrorist vulnerability was spreading from the established G7 members to the emerging countries.

The possibility of an ad hoc "coalition of the willing" for crisis response had been offered by Sarkozy, in the form of a special inter-sessional G8 summit, with perhaps China and India and a few others added. But this choice would have left out Mexico and Turkey, which had been systematically significant victims of the

1994–2001 crises but were now stable providers of financial security for the one that began in 2007. The positions of Korea and Argentina had similarly reversed.

It was thus rational to choose the G20, a body that had been created to deal with a contagious global financial crisis in 1999, that had worked for an America under terrorist attack during Bush's first year in office, that had coped with the growing global economy and emerging energy and climate challenges at once, and that contained all the countries with the vulnerabilities and capabilities required to cope with the current shocks. Three facts explain why the 2008 financial shock caused the G20 to leap to the leaders' level while the 2001 terrorist shock for America had not done so: first, the 2008 shock fit neatly with the G20's 1999 core mission; second, the source of the 2008 shock lay in America rather than in Afghanistan; and, third, by 2008 the Bush administration had eight years of experience—rather than less than one in 2001—of seeing how the G20 could work for the United States and the world.

International Institutional Failure

The second cause of the G20 summit's creation and strong performance was the failure of UN and IMF hard law multilateralism and of the informal, plurilateral G7/8 and ministerial G20 to cope adequately with this new kind of shock sequence by themselves. American unilateralism would also not be an effective response to this globalized sequence of shocks, even though the sequence had erupted with full force in the US itself.

The old multilateral organizations were unable to deal with this financial crisis on their own due to legal inflexibility, mismatched mission, cautious bureaucratic culture, inadequate resources, and failure to reflect the true economic weight of the rising global powers. Among the many multilateral organizations governing global finance, only the Bank for International Settlements, through its chief economist William White, had seen the crisis coming and said so publicly, loud and clear.

The IMF's International Monetary and Financial Committee (IMFC) failed. As Gordon Brown judged his reforms to strengthen the IMFC, which he chaired from the start, in a way that acknowledged the IMFC's inadequacy. "The process was an improvement on what had gone before, when ministers simply read prepared statements, but the brutal assessment is that all the long-term studies of the G20 and the IMF yielded more diagnosis of the growing imbalances and the financial risk but little action" (Brown 2010, 80). The G20's Washington Summit, in contrast, gave the IMF's Strauss-Kahn the occasion and audience he needed to broadcast directly to national leaders his warning of the need for new resources and the need to put the IMF's technical analysis into policy effect.

The UN's soft warnings were also ignored, even though Kemal Derviş, the UN sherpa for Washington who played an important role in shaping Ban's interventions, had spent 30 years at the World Bank and was well acquainted with the IMF. The UN team behind him had been writing about different aspects of the impending crisis for some time. Warnings had arisen elsewhere within the UN system, including at the United Nations Conference on Trade and Development (UNCTAD), which had been regularly issuing similar warnings for a long time. The UN had conducted independent macroeconomic analysis, working directly with its members, notably with about 80 large economies. However, this work was largely ignored by the IMF. As the crisis loomed, the IMF's chief economist insisted that while it had spread from the sub-prime market segment to the jumbo mortgage market, it would stop there. UN economists could not understand why it would.

Among the informal plurilateral bodies, the G7 and G8 also importantly failed (Kirton 2010). In their approach to the crisis, G7 members had criticized an occasional private IMF warning that the collapse of the banking system could catalyse another Great Depression, a response that was a striking refusal to face reality in Strauss-Kahn's subsequent judgement (Talley 2010). The G7 finance ministers did take the lead at their October meeting. But the other G20 countries refused automatically to adopt frameworks that they had not been a part of creating. The new kind of extremely contagious financial crisis demanded a more inclusive group, including all the major economic world powers, in order to address it and approve a response by which all would abide.

At the summit level, the G8 had also failed to deal effectively with financial and economic issues, despite Angela Merkel's desire to address hedge funds in particular and economics more generally at the summit she hosted in 2007. The G8 had strikingly failed to foresee the coming crisis at its 2008 summit in Toyako-Hokkaido in July (Kirton 2010). When the crisis struck in full force that autumn, neither outgoing Japanese prime minister Yasuo Fukuda nor the incoming Taro Aso, as G7 and G8 chair, called for a special G8 summit to be held. What had worked at the Toyako Summit was Bush's creation of the Major Economies Meeting (MEM) to deal with climate change. This he had pioneered at the ministerial level and then raised to the leader level as part of the G8 Toyako Summit.

Behind lay another non-leader-level Bush creation for climate change—the Asia-Pacific Partnership-6, which became a seven-member group when Canada joined. Bush had also created the Security and Prosperity Partnership (SPP) with the leaders of Mexico and Canada in 2005, later known as the North American Leaders Summit. The ministerial Global Health Security Initiative in 2001, which added Mexico to the G7, had been created in response to the September 11 terrorist attacks on America. Those attacks had led the G20 to turn to address terrorist finance, proving its value to a new Bush administration and making it a bipartisan custodian of the group.

The path paved by Bush in pioneering increasingly expansive plurilateral summit institutions that worked with emerging economies, starting with neighbouring Mexico, and doing so on the basis of issue-specific variable geometry, helped lead Bush to choose the existing G20 for his 2008 Washington Summit in the end.

Predominant, Equalizing Capabilities

The third cause of the Washington Summit's creation and strong performance was the globally predominant capability of the G20 and the equalization of those capabilities among its members. The summit's effect was most evident in the swift, large-scale move to fiscal stimulus, IFI reform, and G20 institutionalization and in the slow start on financial regulation. Collectively, the G20 contained a strong majority of the world's money, economy, and population. Within it, the presence of rising, if financially closed, China—with its $2 trillion in foreign exchange reserves—was required by the financially open United States, rapidly acquiring $2 trillion in additional government debt. Strong stimulus was required from the US, China, Japan, and many others to stop the plunge in global economic growth and international trade. But on domestic financial regulation, the relevant specialized capabilities and expertise remained overwhelmingly within the old G7.

The G20's predominant, equalizing capability led Bush to select it over the G7 to be the summit-level group to respond to the unprecedented crisis at hand. He writes: "The question was which countries to invite. I heard that some European leaders preferred that we convene the G-7. But the G-7 included only two thirds of the global economy. I decided to make the summit a gathering of the G-20, a group that included China, Russia, Brazil, Mexico, India, Australia, South Korea, Saudi Arabia, and other dynamic economies … countries representing nearly 90 percent of the world economy" (Bush 2010, 465–67).

Democratizing Convergence

The fourth cause of the G20 summit's creation and strong performance was the democratic convergence among the diverse membership of the group. It best explains the quick success on trade and slowness on financial regulation. The first component of this convergence is clear in Bush's (2010, 459) conclusion that "the only way to preserve the free market in the long run was to intervene in the short run." The second component was clear in Bush's favourable response to the call for a summit from a pro-American Sarkozy representing an all democratic EU. Additional components embraced commitments shared by all G20 members. All were like-minded in regard to economic growth, open trade, and social stability—all domestic priorities increasingly under threat. The dominance of political democracy in all but two or three G20 members fostered the Washington Summit's principled consensus on the rule of law, transparency, and accountability (cf Ambrosio 2010, 387).

Yet it was difficult for non-democratic China and Saudi Arabia to accept domestically intrusive financial regulation and supervision from outside. This was the case even after the United States was finally prepared to relax its reflexive rejection of any infringement of state sovereignty and agree to submit to the review by the IMF's Financial Sector Assessment Program (FSAP), which it had resisted since the FSAP's invention 10 years earlier. The domestic reality and international consensus on shared sovereignty or enlightened sovereignty were now starting to arise in the largest democratic state.

Political Control, Capital, Continuity, Competence, and Commitment

The fifth cause of the summit's creation and strong performance was the robust, shock-reinforced domestic political control, capital, continuity, competence, and commitment of the leaders. To be sure, host George Bush was in his last lame-duck days and his party had just lost the presidency and both houses of Congress on November 4. In the UK, an unpopular Gordon Brown had no electoral mandate of his own (Mandelson 2010). Most of the other G7 leaders were governing with legislatures they did not control or with considerable mass public dissatisfaction (see Appendix M-1).

But political control, capital, and now compatibility with the US counted in creating the summit that Bush was to host. The combination was highest in France, with regional EU assistance. Sarkozy made the first call that was heard for a summit to be held. As Bush (2010, 456) recalls: "The turbulence came during France's turn as head of the European Union. Nicolas Sarkozy, the dynamic French president who had run on a pro-American platform, urged me to host an international summit. I grew to like the idea."

The G20 was also able to move quickly on fiscal stimulus, trade liberalization, and IFI reform due to the domestic support galvanized by the shock and severity of the crisis. In the United States, President-Elect Barack Obama and his Republican opponent for the presidency offered bipartisan support for the summit and its work (Paulson 2010).

Continuity and competence also counted. Bush had eight years of G8 summit experience. Singh and Hu had several years and a few in the MEM. Singh, Harper, and Brown combined considerable G7/8 involvement with their advanced economic expertise and experience. Harper had returned to office, despite the economic downturn, with a stronger minority government in the general election on October 14. Yet it was left to individuals other than those long personally committed to creating a G20 summit to produce the first one in the autumn of 2008.

Controlled Club Participation as a Network Hub

The sixth cause of the summit's creation and strong performance at Washington was the controlled participation within an established group, whose leaders, finance ministers, and central bank governors had become the hub of a multidimensional global governance network.

Internally, the 19 permanent country members, the EU, and the IMF and the World Bank already had a decade of proven performance at the finance level on trade, IFI reform of the Bretton Woods bodies, macroeconomics, and domestic financial reform. The G20 was the only group with the proven preparatory, consultative, and expert capacity and personal contacts among its ministers and bank governors to produce a successful summit within the available 24 days, especially given its built-in ministerial meeting in São Paulo in November and its first special gathering in Washington (Price 2009).

Bush likely trusted the G20 club due in part to its performance at the finance ministers' level when he had first taken office in 2001. The experience of the G8's Renewable Energy Task Force, abruptly ended by Bush when he took office, showed that a new Republican president not inclined toward multilateralism would not accept international institutions created by Democrats Bill Clinton and Larry Summers just before their party was voted out of office. But the first G20 meeting Bush encountered as president was the one that dealt quickly, flexibly, and decisively with terrorist finance, in the month after September 11.

The compact continuity of the G20 continued at the leaders' level. In the end Spain and the Netherlands were at Washington only as part of the European Union or French delegation. They did not contribute either positively or negatively to the success of the summit, beyond simply being there for the benefit of their voters back home. The G20's decade-long controlled, constructed, compact participation thus remained essentially intact as it rose to the leader level.

At this first meeting, the G20 was a leaders' club only in the institutional rather than the social-psychological sense. There were some slender signs of personal bonding in Berlusconi's retirement testimonial to Bush and in the broader shared passion on trade over lunch. However, several leaders, led by the BRICs, still blamed Bush and the West for the crisis. And the leaders had yet to all bond with one another and the whole and to change their interests and identities as a result of their personal devotion to their own valued group. As Bush (2010, 466) notes: "I knew it wouldn't be easy to forge an agreement among the twenty leaders. But with hard work and some gentle arm-twisting, we got it done. Responsibility for shaping the deal fell to Dan Price, a tenacious lawyer on the NSC [National Security Council] staff, and Dave McCormick, the capable undersecretary of the treasury for international affairs." Thus rational bargaining and gentle bullying, not personal bonding, drove the successful result.

Externally, at the leaders' level, most G20 heads had already travelled much of the road their finance ministers had paved in 1999. The G8 summit first began meeting regularly with the heads of multilateral organizations and outside countries in 2001, with the G8 Plus Five formula taking hold in 2005, after Bush's partial interruption in 2004. The Bush-created MEM was upgraded to the summit level in the summer of 2008. The Bush administration had performed well at the G8 in the summer of 2008 with the MEM embedded inside the experience. The MEM showed that a plurilateral summit gathering of 17 equal leaders from established and emerging economies could work well when focused on a single task. Only Saudi Arabia, Turkey, and Argentina had to be added to the MEM to get the G20 summit that Bush chose to govern economics and finance.

From the G20 host, more overlapping summit spokes had radiated inward and outward in recent years to show that established and emerging economies could work together. One was the regional SPP that Bush had invented in 2005. Another was the East Asian Summit (EAS) (Kirton 2006). At the trans-regional level was the older APEC leaders' meeting starting in 1993, the Summit of the Americas starting in 1994 and the biennial ASEM starting in 1996.

Conclusion

The Washington Summit was a strong success. The G20 rose to the summit level. The G20 prevailed among the many alternatives to emerge as the summit configuration of choice, to satisfy the participating leaders, and to induce them to hold a second one with the same members and agenda items in a few months' time. It performed best on fiscal stimulus, trade liberalization, money laundering, and G20 institutionalization, and on domestic political management, direction setting, decision making, and, above all, on the development of G20 governance. The G20 performed less well in managing the exchange rate regime and financial regulation and so delegated those issues to other international economic bodies. It did not even try to produce a new international monetary system or a Bretton Woods II on top of its more modest advances in developing global economic governance.

The causes of this particular performance are very well explained by the model of systemic hub governance. Like the G8 35 years before, the G20 emerged on the international scene from a financial crisis that neither the old multilateral organizations nor the now vulnerable established powers of the time could control on their own. A new globally predominant group of powers with internally equalizing capabilities was required to respond effectively. Its leaders were backed by sufficiently shared values and political support at home. But in the case of the new G20 summit, the need for a compact group of systemically significant countries at the hub of a global network was key.

The first G20 summit marked a turning point in global governance. Despite mixed reviews and skewed successes, the confidence with which the leaders met the critical challenge of the moment and agreed to meet again so soon shaped the way global financial crises and global economic policy would be addressed in the future. The promises made in Washington were to be completed by March 2009. The second G20 summit seemed from its inception to hold even greater potential than the first in producing concrete and clear results.

Beyond the policy substance of the summit, the first ever G20 leaders' meeting was significant for what it represented, both in the context of the increasingly serious economic crisis and in signalling a new era of inclusive economic governance. It was a significant achievement, bringing together diverse countries, from Saudi Arabia to Germany, to agree on the need for collective action to address the crisis and govern the global economy. Its communiqué embraced free-market principles and rejected protectionism, while recognizing the need for stronger domestic financial regulation and IFI reform. While some US officials continued to dispute the interpretation that the G20 represented an admission of weakness or loss of pre-eminence of the American economy, US treasury secretary Henry

Paulson (2010, 451) acknowledged the "vital fact of our interdependence." The first G20 summit was a turning point in global economic governance.

References

Agence France Presse. 2008a. "Canada Tempers Hopes for G20 Crisis Talks." November 7.

Agence France Presse. 2008b. "Canada Wants Home Remedies to Financial Crisis, Not Overhaul." November 5.

Agence France Presse. 2008c. "Congo President Plans to Attend G20 Economic Summit." October 30.

Agence France Presse. 2008d. "Les pays pauvres doivent être entendus au sommet du G20 (Ban Ki-moon)." October 24.

Alexandroff, Alan S. and Kirton, John J. 2010. "The 'Great Recession' and the Emergence of the G20 Leaders' Summit." In *Rising States, Rising Institutions: Challenges for Global Governance*, eds Alexandroff, Alan S., and Cooper, Andrew F. Washington DC: Brookings Institution Press, 178–95.

Altman, Roger C. 2009 (January/February). "The Great Crash, 2008: A Geopolitical Setback for the West." *Foreign Affairs* 88(1): 2–14.

Ambrosio, Thomas. 2010 (November). "Constructing a Framework of Authoritarian Diffusion: Concepts, Dynamics, and Future Research." *International Studies Perspectives* 11(4): 375–92.

Beattie, Alan. 2010. "International Economy: A Display of Disunity." *Financial Times*, October 22. Available at: www.ft.com/intl/cms/s/0/3ff4c528-de0f-11df-88cc-00144feabdc0.html#axzz215UCNXWY. Accessed: July 2012.

BRIC Finance Ministers. 2008. "Brazil, Russia, India, and China Finance Ministers Joint Communiqué." São Paulo, November 7. Available at: www.brics.utoronto.ca/docs/081107-finance.html. Accessed: July 2012.

Brown, Gordon. 2010. *Beyond the Crash: Overcoming the First Crisis of Globalization*. New York: Free Press.

Burleigh, Marc. 2008. "Key Emerging Economies Want Financial System Overhaul." Agence France Presse, November 7.

Bush, George W. 2010. *Decision Points*. New York: Crown Publishers.

Clendenning, Alan. 2008. "Big Emerging-Market Nations Unify to Demand Bigger Role in Fixing Global Finance System." Associated Press, November 7.

Compte, Michel. 2008. "Canada's PM Calls for Compromise at G20 Financial Crisis Talks." Agence France Presse, November 14.

Da Silva, Luiz Inácio Lula. 2010. "The G20 Moment." *New Perspectives Quarterly* 27(1): 33–34.

Duncan, Richard. 2008. "Bring Back the Link between Gold and the Dollar." *Financial Times*, November 23. Available at: www.ft.com/intl/cms/s/0/ba673d22-b977-11dd-99dc-0000779fd18c.html#axzz215UCNXWY. Accessed: July 2012.

Economist. 2008a. "The Coddle and Protect Policy." November 20. Available at: www.economist.com/node/12636308. Accessed: July 2012.

Economist. 2008b. "Miss World Goes Missing." November 20. Available at: www.economist.com/node/12641700. Accessed: July 2012.

Economist. 2008c. "No Time to Waste." November 20. Available at: www.economist.com/node/12637027. Accessed: July 2012.

Economist. 2008d. "Where's Angela?," November 20. Available at: www.economist.com/node/12637035. Accessed: July 2012.

Engelen, Klaus C. 2008 (September). "Rift Barely Acknowledged." *International Economy* 22(4): 10–11.

English, John, Thakur, Ramesh, and Cooper, Andrew F., eds. 2005. *Reforming from the Top: A Leaders' 20 Summit*. Tokyo: United Nations University Press.

G20. 2008. "Declaration of the Summit on Financial Markets and the World Economy." Washington DC, October 15. Available at: www.g20.utoronto.ca/2008/2008declaration1115.html. Accessed: July 2012.

G20 Finance Ministers and Central Bank Governors. 2008. "Communiqué of the Meeting of Finance Ministers and Central Bank Governors." São Paulo, November 9. Available at: www.g20.utoronto.ca/2008/2008communique1109.html. Accessed: July 2012.

G20 Research Group and International Organizations Research Institute. 2011. "2010 Seoul G20 Summit Final Compliance Report." November 6. Available at: www.g20.utoronto.ca/compliance/2010seoul-final. Accessed: July 2012.

Helleiner, Eric and Pagliari, Stefano. 2009 (June). "Towards a New Bretton Woods? The First G20 Leaders Summit and the Regulation of Global Finance." *New Political Economy* 14(2): 275–87.

Hennessey, Keith. 2008. "What Was Accomplished at the G20 Summit?" KeithHennessey.com (Blog). November. Available at: keithhennessey.com/2008/11/20/what-was-accomplished-at-the-g-20-summit. Accessed: July 2012.

Kirton, John J. 2000. "The Dynamics of G7 Leadership in Crisis Response and System Reconstruction." In *Shaping a New International Financial System: Challenges of Governance in a Globalizing World*, eds Kaiser, Karl, Kirton, John J., and Daniels, Joseph P. Aldershot: Ashgate, 65–94.

Kirton, John J. 2006. "East Asian Summitry and Regional Community Creation." In *The Road to East Asian Community*, ed Takita, Kenji. Tokyo: Chuo University Press, 61–88.

Kirton, John J. 2008a. "The G20 Takes Centre Stage." In *Growth, Innovation, Inclusion: The G20 at Ten*, eds Kirton, John J., and Koch, Madeline. London: Newsdesk, 16–17. Available at: www.g8.utoronto.ca/newsdesk/G20at10.pdf. Accessed: July 2012.

Kirton, John J. 2008b. "The Performance of the Meeting of the of G20 Finance Ministers and Central Bank Governors." São Paulo, November 9. Available at: www.g20.utoronto.ca/analysis/2008performance1109.html. Accessed: July 2012.

Kirton, John J. 2008c. "Prospects for the Meeting of G20 Finance Ministers and Central Bank Governors." São Paulo, November 8. Available at: www.g20.utoronto.ca/analysis/2008prospects1108.html. Accessed: July 2012.

Kirton, John J. 2010. "The Group of Eight's Legacy, Limitations, and Lessons." In *The New Dynamics of Summitry: Innovations for G20 Summits*, eds Bradford, Colin I., and Lim, Wonhyuk. Washington DC and Seoul: Brookings Institution Press and Korea Development Institute, 17–60.

Kirton, John J. 2012. "La gobernanza del G20 para el nuevo mundo." *Foreign Affairs Latinoamerica* 12(2): 8–21.

Kirton, John J. and Guebert, Jenilee. 2009. "A Summit of Substantial Success: The Performance of the G20 in Washington in 2008." March 7. Available at: www.g20.utoronto.ca/biblio/g20-2008-performance.pdf. Accessed: July 2012.

Kirton, John J. and Koch, Madeline, eds. 2008. *Growth, Innovation, Inclusion: The G20 at Ten*. London: Newsdesk. Available at: www.g8.utoronto.ca/newsdesk/G20at10.pdf. Accessed: July 2012.

Kirton, John J., Larionova, Marina, and Savona, Paolo, eds. 2010. *Making Global Economic Governance Effective: Hard and Soft Law Institutions in a Crowded World*. Farnham: Ashgate.

Laghi, Brian. 2008. "World Leaders Let Harper Off Deficit Hook." *Globe and Mail*, November 17. Available at: www.theglobeandmail.com/news/national/world-leaders-let-harper-off-deficit-hook/article663403. Accessed: July 2012.

Lander, Mark. 2008. "World Leaders Vow Joint Push to Aid Economy: Big Decisions Delayed." *New York Times*, November 16, p. 1. Available at: www.nytimes.com/2008/11/16/business/worldbusiness/16summit.html. Accessed: July 2012.

Lukov, Vadim. 2010. "G20 and G8 in Search of Solutions: Global Problems of Economy and Society." *International Affairs* 56(5): 58–76.

Mandelson, Peter. 2010. *The Third Man: Life at the Heart of New Labour*. London: HarperCollins.

Martin, Paul. 2008. "Time for the G20 to Take the Mantle from the G8." In *Growth, Innovation, Inclusion: The G20 at Ten*, eds Kirton, John J., and Koch, Madeline. London: Newsdesk, 22–27. Available at: www.g8.utoronto.ca/newsdesk/G20at10.pdf. Accessed: July 2012.

Mattli, Walter and Woods, Ngaire. 2008. "A New Architecture for Global Financial Regulation." Economists' Forum (Blog). *Financial Times*. November 19. Available at: blogs.ft.com/economistsforum/2008/11/a-new-architecture-for-global-financial-regulation/#axzz217HT8Uw1. Accessed: July 2012.

McCarthy, Shawn. 2008. "Harper Lines Up with Bush on Reform." *Globe and Mail*, November 14. Available at: v1.theglobeandmail.com/servlet/story/RTGAM.20081114.wibsummit14/front/Front/Front/. Accessed: July 2012.

Menon, Nirmala. 2008. "Canada Fin Min Sees Econ Stimulus by More Countries." Dow Jones International News, November 9.

Paulson, Henry M. 2010. *On the Brink: Inside the Race to Stop the Collapse of the Global Financial System*. New York: Grand Central Publishing.

Price, Daniel M. 2009. "Recovery and Reform." In *The G8 2009: From La Maddalena to L'Aquila*, eds Kirton, John J., and Koch, Madeline. London: Newsdesk, 24–26. Available at: www.g8.utoronto.ca/newsdesk/g8-2009.html. Accessed: July 2012.

Putnam, Robert and Bayne, Nicholas. 1987. *Hanging Together: Co-operation and Conflict in the Seven-Power Summit*. 2nd ed. London: Sage Publications.

Rotman School of Management, ed. 2008. *The Finance Crisis and Rescue: What Went Wrong? Why? What Lessons Can Be Learned*. Toronto: University of Toronto Press.

Sarkozy, Nicolas. 2008. "Speech delivered by H.E. Mr. Nicolas Sarkozy, President of the French Republic." 63rd session of the United Nations General Assembly, New York, September 23. Available at: www.un.org/en/ga/63/generaldebate/pdf/france-fr.pdf. Accessed: July 2012.

Smith, David and Oliver, Jonathan. 2008. "Fighting the Financial Inferno." *Sunday Times*, November 16.

Summers, Lawrence. 2008. "The Birth of the G20." In *Growth, Innovation, Inclusion: The G20 at Ten*, eds Kirton, John J., and Koch, Madeline. London: Newsdesk, 29–31. Available at: www.g8.utoronto.ca/newsdesk/G20at10.pdf. Accessed: July 2012.

Sunday Times. 2008. "Prudence Will Still Have a Role to Play." November 16.

Talley, Ian. 2010. "IMF Chief: Global Financial Crisis Has Washed Away Old Economic Order." Dow Jones, December 8.

Thorpe, Jacqueline. 2008a. "Canada, Bastion of Free Markets?" *National Post*, November 10. Available at: www.nationalpost.com/opinion/columnists/story.html?id=8ad4cc7b-3248-4bcd-b9c7-dc4fbbf1bde3. Accessed: July 2012.

Thorpe, Jacqueline. 2008b. "G20 Summit Looks to Market Overhaul." *National Post*, November 15, p. A1.

White House. 2008. "Statements by Bush, Sarkozy, EU Commissioner at Camp David: France, European Union Agree on a Summit to Address Financial Crisis." Washington DC, October 20. Available at: www.america.gov/st/texttrans-english/2008/October/20081020115655eaifas0.1981623.html. Accessed: July 2012.

Wolf, Martin. 2008. *Fixing Global Finance*. Baltimore: Johns Hopkins University Press.

Xinhua. 2008. "China Expects 'Fair, Inclusive' World Finance System." November 6. Available at: english.people.com.cn/90001/90776/90883/6528949.html. Accessed: July 2012.

Zeng, Min. 2008. "Support Seen for Dollar, Yen." *Wall Street Journal*, November 17. Available at: online.wsj.com/article/SB122687265714531785.html. Accessed: July 2012.

Chapter 11

Containing Contraction, London 2009

Introduction

The Challenge

On April 1–2, 2009, the leaders of the Group of 20 (G20) assembled in London's Docklands for their second summit, held a short four and a half months after their first in Washington DC (Kirton and Koch 2009b). The London Summit took place at the depth of the most severe global economic contraction since the Great Depression of the 1930s (Truman 2009b; Jha 2009). This summit was hosted by British prime minister Gordon Brown. Compared to George Bush when he hosted the first summit, Brown was a leader with a longer political future, extraordinary experience as a finance minister, and the status of a founding finance minister of the original G20 forum in 1999. London was the first G20 summit attended by newly elected US president Barack Obama and marked his arrival on the world stage (Bergsten 2009). With a fresh vision for fundamental change and a strong political mandate for the next four years, Obama was understandably the centre of attention. He arrived ready to broaden the summit agenda, mobilize massive new money, and support communiqué language on climate change.

Based on the mandate of the first G20 summit and on the comprehensive, detailed report that the G20 finance ministers had delivered, as directed, by March 31, 2009, London's leaders were due to make big decisions that would shape the state of the world's financial system and economy in the years ahead. Their comprehensive, interconnected agenda spanned fiscal, monetary and exchange rate policy, reform of international financial institutions (IFIs), the liberalization and financing of trade, investment, and infrastructure. It included regulation and supervision of banks, securities, accounting, credit ratings, derivatives, hedge funds, and private equity firms. The summit also sought to create a college of supervisors for global banks and an early warning system to help prevent financial crises from erupting again. Leaders would address new issues such as climate change. Above all, they would define the path for future G20 summits, thus helping bring to life a new continuing source of global financial and economic governance to stand alongside the old G8. G20 leaders would thus take a second step toward creating a new global finance and economic governance architecture for the world of the twenty-first century.

In the weeks leading up to London, several significant disagreements arose among G20 members, both within the established Group of Seven (G7) and Group of Eight (G8) and between the G7/8 and the major emerging country members. First, the earlier divide over priorities reappeared. Now it was between Obama, who wanted more fiscal stimulus quickly, and French president Nicolas Sarkozy and German chancellor Angela Merkel, who emphasized the need for stronger supranational financial regulation.

A second, broader division emerged between the established country members, who emphasized macroeconomic stimulus and financial regulation, and the emerging country members, who focused on trade liberalization, trade finance, economic development, and IFI reform to give rising powers greater voice and vote. The emerging countries, backed by development organizations led by the United Nations, wanted large-scale stimulus targeted to development. They argued that the great recession then rolling out in full force was harming the poorest countries most of all. In the lead-up to London a letter from Ban Ki-moon to Gordon Brown suggested a development-directed stimulus package of $1 trillion would do the job (*Financial Times* 2009).

A third divide arose between, on the one hand, the United Kingdom along with some other G7 members that wished to act on climate change at the summit and, on the other, some of the emerging countries that still stood opposed. British determination to put climate change on the agenda was driven in part by its Commonwealth associates from Africa. The leaders of several African countries had visited Brown to discuss their expectations for the summit (Millard 2009). They began not with development as expected, but with the urgent need for climate change control. They spoke eloquently about the melting ice on the top of Mount Kilimanjaro, citing it as a visible sign of the climate crisis that had already arrived and of the need for immediate action in response. Brown was persuaded by their entreaties and tried to use his G20 summit to advance the climate cause. He faced resistance, however, from several G20 members, including those leaders who felt that finance and economic issues should be the summit's sole focus. Resistance also came from those who felt that the G20 was the wrong forum to negotiate a climate change deal, and that the conferences and meetings of the parties to the United Nations Framework Convention on Climate Change were the only right place to do so.

In the end, the London Summit was a very strong success and was seen as such. The highly positive reaction may have come from a great sense of relief. Unlike in the 1930s, a second global summit had taken place and had generated a collective commitment to deal with the global financial and economic crisis head on. The London Summit dramatically mobilized an unprecedented $1.1 trillion in new money directed at fiscal stimulus and economic development. It faithfully delivered much of that money over the subsequent months and years.

Competing Assessments

The degree and causes of the London Summit's success aroused a debate among several schools of thought. Unusually for such debates, all schools saw its performance lie on the positive side of the spectrum.

The first school saw the summit as merely a mixed success, with its advances due to the unprecedented size of the global economic crisis it faced and Obama's mediatory skills. Some highlighted its "large increase in funding for troubled economies," its efforts to "clamp down on tax havens and to tighten financial regulations," but noted that "many declarations were of principles that have to be followed up—some at another G20 meeting that will be scheduled later this year" (Fidler et al. 2009).

A second school saw a general, development-for-democracy driven success. It argued that the new funding for the International Monetary Fund (IMF), the $250 billion increase in special drawing rights (SDRs), and the new trade finance were the result of fear that an "extended downturn will also increase the risk of the crisis expanding and deepening far beyond its current spread. In new democracies, whether in Africa or central and eastern Europe, this is a moment of genuine peril. In some poorer countries, it could even lead to war and famine … Hungary and Romania have already sought help from the IMF. More could follow" (*Financial Times* 2009).

A third school saw an interdependence-driven, developing country success. Laurence Norman and Clare Connaghan (2009) concluded that "developing economies came out as the main beneficiaries" because "massive new funding for the International Monetary Fund, accelerated reform of international financial institutions and a promise to ensure developing countries get equal treatment from global institutions amount to a significant reshaping of the balance of power in the world economy." This came because the established powers recognized that "in this interconnected, interdependent global economy, helping out emerging markets is, in fact, helping themselves."

A fourth school saw a short-term, policy-driven, confidence-creating success for the rich. Martin Sorrell (2009) concluded that recovery would soon come, due to the "dint of the scale of fiscal stimulus in the US, UK and elsewhere and even by the atmosphere surrounding Gordon Brown's seemingly triumphant Group of 20 nations summit … Yet we have never successfully articulated globalisation's advantages. Nor has everyone felt the benefits."

A fifth school went further, declaring London to be a historic success. Colin Bradford and Johannes Linn (2009, 16) judged it to be "the most successful summit ever" with its "unprecedented concerted fiscal expansion, which may be the turning point in addressing the worst recession since the Great Depression. It initiated significant national and international reforms in the oversight, supervision and regulation of financial systems and institutions. And it launched a process reform of the international financial institutions—such as the IMF and the World

Bank—which, among other things, should restore the IMF to its pivotal position in the global financial system along with the resources it needs to carry out this role."

A sixth school, even more ambitiously, saw the "replacement" of the G8 by the G20, as the G20 summit performed so well that the G8 one could and should now disappear. Choi Hee-nam (2009) welcomed the strengthening of the G20 framework, suggesting that the G20 might replace the G7 due to the increasing need for "close collaboration between advanced and emerging economies," and the G20's character as "an ideal forum with balanced representation" and with the management capability to address the major global financial issues. Brazilian foreign minister Celso Amorim boldly asserted that "the G8 has died. It doesn't represent anything anymore." He went on to say that "the G8 will always be important, but that it will not be able to replace the essential presence of China, Brazil or India" (Agence France Presse 2009).

The Argument

This chapter argues that the London Summit was a very strong success. It directly delivered $1.1 trillion in global financial support, much of which was aimed at developing countries. It expanded SDRs and IMF resources, helped deliver the previously promised fiscal stimulus and financial regulation, and put climate change on the G20 agenda. It admitted all G20 members as equals into the Financial Stability Board (FSB), a symbolically and politically important move as the first recognition by the G7 that this and other IFIs needed to be reformed to give emerging countries much greater voice. In this spirit London called for accelerated governance and voice reforms in the IMF and World Bank. It started to turn G20 summitry from an ad hoc crisis response to an ongoing global governance forum, with a new American president fully engaged.

This very strong performance was driven by the severe shocks of the Atlantic financial crisis now turning into a global economic one and by the social and ecological shocks it spurred in the developing world. Also relevant was the continuing failure of the IMF to reform on its own, and the rising relative capability of less crisis-scarred G20 members beyond the G8. An important cause was the new shock-generated fear that economic devastation would destroy not only development but also democracy in its wake, reversing the great democratic advances of 1994–2001 and even those of the Cold War victory from a decade before. Another key cause was the will and skill of its host Gordon Brown, with his deep personal commitment to poverty reduction globally, his Keynesian convictions, and his expertise and experience as a longstanding finance minister, G20 finance co-founder, and chair of the IMF's International Monetary and Financial Committee and of the G7 finance ministers. Such connections, along with those of the Commonwealth, Asia-Europe Meeting (ASEM), and the European Union, made the G20's London Summit even more of a global network hub.

Plans and Preparations

The preparations for the London Summit built on the proven success of the Washington Summit by following the path it had set (Alexandroff and Kirton 2010). The British had started preparing for their summit before they formally assumed the chair. Brown was assisted by his sherpa Jonathan Cunliffe, finance minister Alistair Darling, and by his political and official staff. Mark Malloch Brown, a minister of state in the Foreign and Commonwealth Office, was charged with consulting non-G20 members. Brown invited two African leaders beyond South Africa to attend the summit. He also invited the leaders of Spain and the Netherlands in their own right rather than as part of the EU. G20 preparations became the overall priority of the British government from January to April (Brown 2010).

International preparations for London began with Britain speaking to the United States, as Obama prepared to take over in Washington, and to other countries about the institutional character of the G20 in the future. According to Brown (2010, 116), they "agreed that it should emerge as the premier forum for economic cooperation." Brown met Obama shortly after his inauguration, but it was some time before the new administration, including the highly experienced Lawrence Summers as director of the National Economic Council, was installed and fully engaged (118). Brown also spoke repeatedly to Dominique Strauss-Kahn, the IMF's managing director, who led the call for immediate, far-reaching action, and to Robert Zoellick, president of the World Bank, who highlighted the effects of the crisis on low-income countries and agreed to establish a facility for trade finance at the World Bank in response.

The British hosts, at the finance officials' level, first focused on elaborating the details of financial regulations and similar subjects, following the principles, processes, and timelines that the Washington Summit had set down. To develop these details, four working groups had been established, each with one co-chair from an established member and one from an emerging member. The group on financial regulation was co-chaired by Tiff Macklem, associate deputy minister of Canada's Department of Finance, and Rakesh Mohan, deputy governor of the Bank of India. On the road to London, a fifth working group was added on employment. The first draft of the British plan for the summit based on this work program was technical, appearing to some as one drafted by junior IMF officials. It was composed of a long list of detailed steps each with seemingly limited advances. Even at a very late stage in the preparatory process, the plan was still based on detailed steps rather than larger ideas.

However, in order to address the scale of the global crisis and capture the attention of the British public concerned with their plummeting economy, the British government had long opted at the highest political level for a summit that would focus on broader, bolder ideas than financial and economic details. Based on a push from political staff, it decided that the London Summit needed to produce a major package of financial support.

A consensus emerged from outside the G20 as well as among key players inside on the need for large-scale financing, largely through the IFIs and for the consequent confidence that would come through such concerted global action (Brown 2010). After one proposed British solution proved legally impossible due to IMF rules, the British assembled a package of financing instruments that seemed sufficiently large to create the needed confidence, given that it added up to a bottom-line total of $1 trillion. Brown instructed an initially reluctant Cunliffe to secure the consent of his G20 colleagues on this package, with the $1 trillion total kept secret so it could have the maximum confidence-raising effect when revealed at the summit's end. To assist, Brown visited several of his G20 colleagues and had spoken to all by the time the summit began. The day before the summit, Brown and Australian prime minister Kevin Rudd, speaking at St. Paul's Cathedral, called for stronger ethics in the global economy and for meeting the needs of the poor, by reaching the Millennium Development Goals (MDGs) (Brown 2010).

By February UN staffers had also completed a list of proposed initiatives. In a letter dated March 20 to all the G20 leaders, Ban began by pointing to the prospect of a "severe crisis of global instability" with "profound consequences for the security and stability of us all." He called for leadership in four areas: "a truly global stimulus package that meets the needs of developing countries," trade, green growth and climate change, and a new international financial and economic architecture."[1] On the first he "estimated that the total financing needed to support developing countries through the crisis is at least US$ 1 trillion for 2009 and 2010." This included trade finance, an amount that could be raised by issuing additional SDRs.

On March 25, Brown met with Ban at the UN headquarters in New York. Brown asked the UN not to raise expectations for the summit. He specifically requested that the UN not publicize or even make public its letter. However, the press had already seen it. There was then a frantic effort to kill the release. By then Brown was crafting his big funding initiative for the summit. When the UN produced its $1 trillion figure, it reportedly inspired the ambitious British to raise the total amount in their initiative.

The UN's call for a global green new deal was first made in its draft letter in February 2009. It was strongly opposed by some at the UN. But the advocates got it into the letter. UN sherpa Kemal Derviş supported the advocates, who were opposed by the United Nations Development Programme (UNDP).

On the issue of a large, new allocation of SDRs, such a call had been made by the UN since 1969 as well as by the IMF for many years. But there was no political appetite among consequential members, led by the US and the UK. However, on the road to the London Summit—well before the public call on March 23 for a "super-sovereign reserve currency" by Zhou Xiaochuan, the governor of the People's Bank of China—the British, led by Brown, had been working to get this done.

1 A copy of this letter was published on the *Financial Times* website as a link from an article written by Harvey Morris (2009).

They had the full and close support of America's Summers and treasury secretary Timothy Geithner and the IMF staff. Brown pushed for an SDR allocation as a financing option, knowing he could not achieve it without the Americans, who had veto power in the IMF. Then the Americans started pushing it. When China's very knowledgeable, personally self-confident, relatively pro-western, reform-oriented Zhou (2009) published his essay, it provided important public support.

The British were not the only ones who felt that the UN letter complicated the situation. The $1.1 billion package had been largely assembled at the G20 finance ministers' meeting. For the IMF, which had been working with the US Treasury to mobilize real money, the UN initiative diverted attention from assembling the support package that was needed.

The formal agenda for London was still largely defined by the very detailed communiqué that the G20 had produced at Washington. Both the agenda and the communiqué contained a core agenda of five items: stimulus, financial regulation, IFI reform, trade and investment liberalization, and development. By the time the leaders arrived in London, chair and host Brown had succeeded in adding two new items: jobs, training, and social inclusion at the microeconomic level; and climate change.

A great drama played out publicly and to some extent privately leading up to the London Summit. Which of two agenda items would dominate? One was growth, with the United States under its new Democratic president Obama pushing for fast, simultaneous, large-scale international fiscal stimulus. The other was financial regulation, with the continental Europeans led by France and Germany demanding strong, even supranational, regulation of all financial industries, with particularly harsh measures against tax havens, hedge funds, and bankers' bonuses. Brown, in the transatlantic middle, had to balance both in order to produce a reasonable result.

The outcome of this drama, in this group of 20 equals, was driven in the first instance by the positions of the many other members beyond the Euro-American dualists. Within the G7 club, Japan—still the world's second most powerful country—had a strong need for new fiscal and monetary stimulus but none at all for new financial regulation. Italy, where the banks remained largely intact, was in much the same position. Its finance minister, Giulio Tremonti, aware of Italy's enormous debt burden, was reluctant to offer fiscal stimulus in his budget at home.

Canada was also reluctant to offer new fiscal stimulus. Its growth situation and prospects looked better than America's. Its financial system remained in sound shape beyond a small specific problem with non-bank asset-backed commercial paper and the fact that the country had 13 separate provincial and territorial securities regulators. Independent analysts regularly confirmed how good Canada's banks were on a global scale. Canada had already delivered a large fiscal stimulus in its January 2009 budget and so had no need for more discretionary stimulus so soon. Its priorities for the summit focused on the fundamentals. It brought a simple, straightforward message: "fix the banks first" and deliver the fiscal stimulus of 4 percent of members' gross domestic product (GDP) that the G20 had promised at Washington a few months before.

Canada, led by Prime Minister Stephen Harper and his finance minister, Jim Flaherty, were experienced, respectively, in macroeconomics and finance. They suspected that other issues highlighted by the British, notably the $1.1 trillion financial package and a global bank levy, were designed for dramatic domestic political impact in Britain rather than real economic global impact. Both British initiatives had been presented to the G20 members to consider before the finance ministers and central bank governors met at Horsham south of London on March 14–15. Canada had spoken against the global bank levy from the very start, considering it a bad idea, driven by a political desire to punish "bad banks," of which Canada and most G20 members had none. More broadly, Canada felt that issues such as money laundering and hedge funds, the latter occasionally advanced by some Europeans, were red herrings rather than core issues. Canada was comfortable with addressing the issue of money laundering through the adoption of standards and agreements for sharing tax information as produced by the Organisation for Economic Co-operation and Development (OECD). It regarded this as a successful approach. With regard to climate change, Canada judged the issue to be driven by Brown's domestic political concerns, but not a fundamental economic concern at that time—especially as publics around the world were worried about losing jobs and homes, and their interest in climate change was plummeting.

The Sherpa Meeting Sequence

There were two preparatory sherpa meetings, both held in London. The first, in mid-March at Lancaster House, was organized on short notice and was still rather ad hoc. There the sherpa process became more complicated, as the British brought in the World Bank, the IMF, the OECD, and the World Trade Organization (WTO) to sit at the sherpas' table. Everyone was crammed into a long, thin room, with British sherpa Jon Cunliffe chairing the meeting. Yet the sherpa process began to take on a standard practice. The British had thought it out and set it out well. In contrast, for the Washington Summit, US sherpa Daniel Price (2009) had to call his sherpa meetings on an urgent basis. Indeed, for Washington one meeting had been done over the phone, which was very awkward as participants found it hard to hear one another.

For London the sherpas tracked the four working groups set up to work on financial issues. Sherpas received reports from the IMF, the WTO, and the OECD. The main focus on follow up, among the many new issues, was financial sector regulation. Sherpas were accompanied by the finance deputies, so the meeting spent much time dealing with the various issues the deputies were working on.

From the start since the British had taken over, it was clear to many that the London Summit would be about Gordon Brown's domestic politics as much as the international challenge. The big outcomes played to his strengths: a desire to be the man who brought major international resources to deal with the financial crisis. There was an indication in the sherpa meeting that a package would be produced but not yet a discussion of a package that would total more than $1 trillion in all. Much of the package was produced by finance ministers, who were front and centre on this issue.

The sherpas realized that this was a step-by-step process. They worried whether the middle income countries at the table would have access to the international financial resources they needed to get through this difficult period. There was much discussion of the most vulnerable countries and people. Sherpas worried about everyone doing their part. They discussed SDRs and how to raise the necessary funds, although the issue was very technical and very much in the finance realm. A head of steam developed. With Brazil's Luiz Inácio Lula da Silva in Brazil and with China's leadership, Brown put much of his own personal credibility on the line to have his big financial package produced.

The sherpas were keen to receive the reports on the regulatory process and financing for development for the IMF and World Bank. There was a good report on stimulus measures, as it was important to ensure that they were adequate. While others were moving onto other issues, Canada continued to draw attention to fixing the banks and combating protectionism, which it considered the two most important.

As part of the $1.1 trillion package, $250 billion would come from a new allocation of SDRs. Although it was necessary to make some kind of a gesture to calm deteriorating markets, there was some back and forth on what that allocation would be. Cunliffe played to his strength, having been a G20 finance deputy and intimately familiar with the subject.

On climate change, seen by some as a minor issue, the British tried to introduce the issue at the first, mid-March sherpa meeting. The Europeans were catering to the newly installed administration in Washington and thought they had fertile ground to advance on climate change, in a way that they had not been able to at the Washington Summit chaired by George Bush. It was the first time the Americans had a position others wanted to pursue. This was to be Brown's moment to show leadership.

At the Summit

The Discussions

A few days before the summit started, the draft communiqué, without the headline $1 trillion figure, was leaked. Some felt this was done deliberately by the British, due to the poor domestic popularity facing their lame duck-looking government. The British began immediately to write a new communiqué, containing the content of the old one in a different form. Several sections would be drafted on the spot by the leaders themselves at London, in a way reminiscent of what Brown had done at the first IMFC meeting he chaired in Washington almost a decade before.

The summit started on April 1 with a reception for the leaders and their spouses hosted by Queen Elizabeth at Buckingham Palace, followed by a leaders-only dinner at 10 Downing Street. It continued the next morning with working sessions from breakfast to mid-afternoon.

Brown began the opening dinner by recalling the failed 1933 London Conference, the resulting depression, and the protectionism of the 1930s. He stated "that failure had foreshadowed all the other terrible events of that decade and the one to follow" (Brown 2010, 121). The first and defining frame for the entire summit was thus the direct link from economic depression to the replacement of democracy by dictatorship and the destructive world war and the Holocaust that came as a result. In response to Brown's invitation to others to comment on the world crisis, Obama spoke first, impressively accepting America's responsibility for initiating the crisis. Many other leaders followed, some speaking rather freely. The leaders listened to one another very respectfully and intensely as they considered what to do. There was unprecedented personal focus. Much of the consensus for the final communiqué was reached there. They left as scheduled at 9 pm in a "positive and determined[,] serious" mood (Brown 2010, 122).

Overnight Brown and his team worked to reduce disagreements flowing from some members' nervousness about the sheer scale of the $1 trillion package and Britain's desired inclusion of a numerical target for global growth. Portions of the new draft communiqué were distributed in sections. The sherpas went to bed at 2 am without knowing the context of the sections they had seen. After discussions with leaders the next morning, Brown moved toward securing agreement on the $1 trillion package, but not on the numerical target for global growth as a few G20 members would not accept a target or a number attached.

Around the table on April 2, instead of following the format of Washington, where each leader could speak in turn on whatever he or she wished, Brown (2010) focused the discussion tightly on each topic. Small groups would break out to negotiate and draft text on issues such as money laundering. In the view of some participants, the process was in disarray. Yet the leaders agreed on enough to allow a draft communiqué to be circulated in the morning, a document for which Brown had drafted the opening passages himself. Leaders then went through it, considering each paragraph in turn.

The meeting became stormy when Sarkozy threatened to walk out if the summit did not agree to the strong action against tax havens, which he had publicly identified in the lead-up to the summit as an important cause of the crisis (Brown 2010). Most G7 members and Australia's Rudd felt that tax havens were irrelevant to the serious, systemic issues facing the leaders. Non-G20 members had been insisting that there be no such action. A few emerging members of the G20 themselves opposed strong action. Brown, who considered tax havens a cause of tax leakage from treasuries and of a regulatory race to the bottom, sought a solution through reference to the OECD's list of non-compliant jurisdictions. But this aroused disagreement on several grounds. China's Hu Jintao was unhappy as China was not a member of the OECD. Obama and Rudd sought a compromise solution. The deadlock ended when, on the sidelines, Obama consulted with Hu, and then brought Sarkozy into the conversation. The compromise that finally came proposed using the OECD list as the instrument for identifying and publicly pressuring non-cooperative jurisdictions. China acquiesced, in part because the solution did not materially affect the interests of Hong Kong and Macau. The OECD list would be published simultaneously with the G20 communiqué.

On the overarching issue of enhancing economic growth through a reformed global governance architecture, India's Manmohan Singh suggested that Brown prepare a post-summit report on how international institutions could operate to enhance economic growth more effectively (Brown 2010). It was readily agreed that the next G20 summit would receive this report.

There were long delays while communiqué text that had been agreed was being photocopied for all the leaders to review. While they were waiting, Brown (2010) pressed on with discussions on the next item on the agenda. Throughout, Obama's calmness, understanding, and persuasiveness, culminating with an inspiring intervention at the summit's end, helped to unite all to provide the global leadership the world needed at that critical time.

At lunch at the convention centre, the leaders, finance ministers, and sherpas dined in three adjacent areas, with only curtains to divide them. Some sherpas were surprised to learn that Brown had decreed that the leaders themselves would write the final communiqué. Darling departed early to return to his regular office to work.

The negotiation of the texts went down to the wire. As Brown made his way to the concluding news conference, the last words were still being negotiated and written down. The fax machines that the sherpa teams were using created some technical difficulties, including shredding pages as they arrived. Officials were trying to draft text and listen to the leaders at the same time. Some sherpas felt it was a very unsatisfactory situation, as under such circumstances they could do neither task well. Brazilian officials had to stay up the entire night after the summit translating the communiqué into Portuguese, as Lula, along with many other leaders, did not speak English, the language in which the communiqué had been drafted and was being released.

Nonetheless, at the end of the summit, Brown strode to the podium in front of the media at the ExCel Centre to announce dramatically the $1.1 trillion package, to the audibly and visibly positive surprise of the journalists gathered there. The final news conference that evening commanded a TV audience of an estimated one billion people throughout the world (Brown 2010).

Members' Priorities, Roles, and Results

The newly elected US president Obama, the youngest leader at the summit, said he had come to listen and learn (Alexandroff and Kirton 2010). The US sought and secured its objectives on stimulus, financial regulation, and trade and investment. But it achieved only a small advance on climate change, in a passage that endorsed the UN but not the Major Economies Forum on Energy and Climate (MEF). The US led the campaign to get $500 billion in new loans for the IMF. Obama successfully mediated between Sarkozy and Hu on tax havens.

Japan also provided leadership. It secured the lighter financial regulation that it and the US preferred (Kirton 2009b). Its leadership in offering $100 billion for the IFIs in November 2008 saw the US and EU each pledge a $100 billion loan as part of London's $1.1 trillion package. This made Japan the equal of America and Europe in providing this key public good. Japan also advanced its climate change priority, following its G8 Toyako-Hokkaido Summit held the summer before.

France's major issue was tax havens, or non-cooperative jurisdictions. Although Sarkozy had publicly declared it to be his primary public concern in the immediate lead-up to the meeting, most other members, including Canada, felt it was not a primary cause of the financial and economic crisis, nor a solution to it. At the summit, however, the topic took up an inordinate amount of the leaders' time, due to Sarkozy's insistence as the meeting was drawing to a close that it be dealt with firmly. Brown was not pleased, as the issue was by no means his focus for the summit.

Canada, the least powerful G7 country, had some trouble keeping the summit's focus on fixing the banks, combating protectionism, strengthening regulatory systems, and ensuring the Washington Summit's fiscal stimulus would be delivered and would work. Canada had produced a strong stimulus budget at home. Others had done so, too. It wanted to keep the foot on the pedal of stimulus. Canada would support doing more only if it could fund its share of any new pledges within its recent budget. But in Canada's view, London was off track in its overall messaging, which focused on mobilizing massive money to finance the IMF and putting in place the resources to help countries' international financing needs. Harper felt that the G20 should not forget the need for financial regulation. Canada's mantra remained "fix the banks first" and "good regulation begins at home." It supported the approach of the Basel Committee on Banking Supervision (BCBS), with cooperation and common standards, rather than the supranational approach some Europeans sought. Canada was pleased that the London Summit endorsed the recommendations of the regulatory working group, co-chaired by finance deputy Tiff Macklem. It was also concerned about rising financial protectionism, given that some of the fixes for the banks put some international partners at a disadvantage and the US government now owned banks. The G20 was also starting to talk more about exit strategies, wisely in Harper's view. It was not too early to think about when they would be needed in regard to bank bailouts. In the end, Canada got much of what it sought.

China, the largest emerging country member, demonstrated that it was now willing to act as a global leader. Its economy was looking a little better, as its government had just produced a massive stimulus. Moreover, just over a week before the summit, bank governor Zhou had boldly proposed to move from a sole reliance on the US dollar to SDRs as the global reserve currency, with an altered basket of SDRs including the Chinese renminbi (Fratianni and Alessandrini 2009; Zhou 2009). This initiative was clearly in China's interest, as its large foreign exchange reserves were held largely in US dollar assets, and as it was concerned about a future US inflationary surge and corresponding American currency devaluation. Yet this was the important major policy proposal that China had publicly advanced for global governance reform. The London leaders' decision to allocate $250 billion in SDRs, while still based on the existing basket, was a clear Chinese success. The new allocation was only the third general SDR allocation ever, after the first one in 1970–72 and the second in 1979–81. It represented a massive increase in the current stock of 21.4 billion SDRs.

China avoided international intrusion into the supervision of its stable financial system, while obtaining full membership in the more inclusive FSB. China also successfully protected its sovereignty and desire to develop indigenous financial centres by having Hong Kong and Macau left outside the G20-strengthened tax haven regime. On the fight against protectionism, China and Canada were among the strongest participants and made important advances here. On climate change, China secured approval of its desired "common but differentiated" principle and the UN forum for the "beyond-Kyoto" negotiations.

Showing China's readiness to bear the burdens of global leadership as part of a collective top-tier club was its willingness to provide at least $40 billion of the IMF's $500 billion in new financial support. While this was much less than the US, Japanese, or collective European share, it showed that China would assume its global responsibilities and do so before it secured its commensurate international rights (Deudney and Ikenberry 2009). China would lend the IMF the money now, while its (and others') increased voice and vote in the IMF would only come later, by 2011 (Truman 2009a).

India, the second largest major emerging country, made a significant contribution to the summit. It welcomed the light approach to financial regulation, India's new membership in the FSB, and the affirmation of the UN's centrality on climate change. Only on fiscal stimulus, where India had advocated more money, did it as well as the US and Japan obtain less than it sought.

Brazil's priority remained IFI reform, especially on voice and vote in the IMF. It also favoured action on financial regulation. During the meeting among leaders on April 2, Lula and others refused to accept some of the proposals advanced by Brown.

Negotiating the Next Host

Toward the end of the London meeting there had been some debate about who would host the next summit. The question arose during the last-minute frenzy over the issue of tax havens and the content of the communiqué. There was some uncertainty about where the summit should go next. As the summit had already been held in the United States and then Europe, some thought it was now Asia's turn. Several countries put their names forward. Japan and in particular France wanted to host. There had already been some signals from the Americans that they would not mind hosting the next summit. But there was still a sense that somehow the next summit belonged to Asia. However, the Japanese were in the middle of another round of weak government and not capable of taking up the task. The Chinese were not interested. The Australians talked about possibly hosting the third summit. Several members, including the Canadians, had no preference about who should host and chair next.

Among all these considerations and claims, two stood out. The first was the perception that it was important to engage the new Obama administration and that, if the US was interested in hosting, it would be an effective way to ensure that the Americans were heavily involved. The second was that the US was at the centre of the crisis and thus could and should be at the centre of its cure. No one argued that the US would be a bad choice to host the next summit. Close observers would have noticed that at the London Summit Obama (2009) stated: "That this is just the beginning. Our problems are not going to be solved in one meeting; they're not going to be solved in two meetings. We're going to have to be proactive in shaping events and persistent in monitoring our progress to determine whether further action is needed."

Indeed, a key result of the London Summit, not directly announced by Brown or his colleagues at its conclusion, was defining the hosting sequence for several subsequent G20 summits. This insured the institutionalization of the fledgling forum, and doing so as a body in which both established and emerging economy members took the lead. In this process, Rudd, along with others, played an important part. Knowing that Obama did not instinctively like international summits, he sought to get the new US president institutionally and personally to consider G20 summitry as his own. Rudd also felt that the bold decisions made at London had to be delivered; otherwise G20 leaders would be held to account and their reputations would suffer. They needed to create a policy map for the future, to bring national budgets back to balance beyond short-term business cycles.

When the debate arose about where to hold the next summit, Rudd worried that there was an implicit deal between the British and the Japanese that Japan would host next. He was concerned that Japanese prime minister Taro Aso had a limited grasp of the substantive details of the G20's work and was more committed to the G8 than to the G20 as the world's central economic forum. There had also been a political deal between Obama and Korea's Lee Myung-bak that the latter would host the G20 at some stage. Moreover, hosting the G8 in 2010 and 2011 respectively were Canada and France, neither of which had seemed fully committed to the G20. Rudd, believing that G20 summitry needed a highly competent, fully committed chair, had offered Australia, an option that a majority of the sherpas had approved.

During the side meetings at London, Rudd approached Obama to say that despite the majority of the sherpas favouring Australia, the need was to indigenize the G20 summit within Asia as soon as possible, with Korea as the natural choice. Rudd recommended that the G20 should decide now on the next three hosts, with Obama holding the next summit, then Canada on the back of its G8 summit, and then Korea at the end of 2010. This would prevent the G20 from being derailed before the French G8 presidency in 2011, and would show that the G20 was not just a rich western club, as the Koreans were wedded to the G20 in a way that the Japanese were not. Obama indicated his approval, contingent on a significant G20 leader nominating him to host next.

Having been warned by Merkel that France would not support Australia, Rudd then approached Sarkozy. Rudd told Sarkozy that his strategic interest was to sustain the institution, that Obama was prepared to host it next as a strong chair, that France would host in 2011, that Obama would host only if a significant power recommended it at the leaders' table, and that Obama would appreciate it if Sarkozy nominated him.

At the leaders' table, to Aso's surprise, Sarkozy nominated Obama, who nominated the Canadians on the back of their G8 summit and then the Koreans. The leaders agreed to this leader-defined arrangement with no dispute.

Achievements

In the end, in Brown's (2005, 127) view, the London Summit succeeded in saving the world's economy at the most critical time, by giving the IFIs the new resources they required, by initiating the biggest and broadest banking reforms ever, and by catalysing swift, coordinated fiscal and monetary stimulus on a large scale. The leaders at London produced three documents. They dealt with several subjects, notably macroeconomic stimulus, financial support, financial regulation, IFI reform, and trade, as well as social inclusion and climate change. Among its many agreements, the summit mobilized $1.1 trillion in new money for economic stimulus and development and transformed the Financial Stability Forum (FSF) into the more inclusive, stronger Financial Stability Board.

Macroeconomic Policy

In their macroeconomic management, G20 leaders pledged fiscal and monetary stimulus that would be necessary to bring back growth. Beyond this "blank cheque" for stimulus, they decided to have the IMF consider what more money was needed, to renounce competitive currency devaluation, and to enhance IMF surveillance of the economies and financial sectors of G20 members. The "stimulus first" side thus had the edge in principle and, in the end, in messaging.

Financial Regulation

On financial regulation, the results were far less strong, statist, supranational, and speedy than some had wanted and more had feared.

First, the summit affirmed the fundamental principle of effective regulation, based on market principles, to restore lending and rebuild trust and confidence. The test was regulations that worked, with market participants as the ultimate referee. This was a remarkably light-touch approach. There were no explicit calls to punish those responsible for past problems, just moves to ensure that similar problems would not arise again. The singular concern was with putting out today's fire more than with addressing the systemic dangers that had caused it in the first place.

Second, the summit agreed that restoring domestic lending was essential for fiscal and monetary stimulus to restore growth. In addition to addressing the provision of liquidity, recapitalization, and impaired assets, G20 governments would take "all necessary actions to restore the normal flow of credit through the financial system and ensure the soundness of systemically important institutions" (G20 2009). This carte blanche for credit flows was an affirmation of the central message of Canadian finance minister Jim Flaherty. It was an encouragement to a slow-moving America, which had put stimulus first, to get on with core banking reforms.

Third, the G20 leaders called more loudly than they had at Washington for credible fiscal exit strategies. This was a sign that they recognized the dangers of financial protectionism and were already looking ahead to lending and trust being restored. It anticipated the subsequent call in the United States by Goldman Sachs and J.P. Morgan to be released from government control, as both had received bailouts.

Fourth, there was a demand for domestic regulatory systems that were not only strong but also consistent with internationally agreed high standards. The emphasis was more on the horizontal need for international consistency and cooperation than on the vertical degree of regulation or supervision itself. Regulation would be done in ways that, inter alia, supported "competition and dynamism" (G20 2009). Regulation and supervision would cover all systemically important institutions, instruments, and territories, with the details to be defined by the new FSB, the IMF, and the Financial Action Task Force (FATF) at the subsequent British-hosted meeting of G20 finance ministers and central bank governors in St. Andrews, Scotland, in November 2009.

IFI Reform

On IFI resources and reform, of the $1.1 trillion mobilized in new money, in addition to the new $250 million allocation of SDRs for the IMF, the World Bank received $100 billion. The leaders set firm deadlines for the vote and voice reform of the Bretton Woods institutions: spring 2010 for the World Bank and January 2011 for the IMF.

Trade

On trade and investment, the G20 leaders extended their anti-protectionist trade and investment pledge—the standstill provision—to the end of 2010 (Layton and Smith 2009). They added remedial action to correct any transgressions. They also added a promise to avoid fiscal and financial protectionism. They also innovatively mobilized at least $250 million for trade finance. To assist with accountability, they called for notification to and monitoring by the WTO and other institutions of national measures that might violate their anti-protectionist pledge.

Development, Food Security, and Social Security

To reinforce the development dimensions of the $1.1 trillion in new money, the G20 leaders endorsed the MDGs, as well as members' respective promises of official development assistance (ODA), including the pledge made at the 2005 G8 Gleneagles Summit to double ODA to sub-Saharan Africa by 2010. They further committed to mobilize money for food security through bilateral contributions and other international development infrastructures to assist the poorest countries. They also committed to foster employment and income support, for men and women alike.

Climate Change

On climate change, despite earlier disagreement, the leaders endorsed the principle of inter-generational equity and sustainability. They forged the link between the environment and the economy by pledging to "build an inclusive, green, and sustainable recovery" (G20 2009). Their specific commitment to climate change, however, was tacked on as the last article under the section "Ensuring a Fair and Sustainable Recovery for All." It confirmed only that the leaders would "address the threat of irreversible climate change, based on the principle of common but differentiated responsibilities." It called for a successful conclusion of the UN climate change conference planned for Copenhagen in December 2009.

Results

These results represented the outcome of a relatively balanced dynamic at the meeting, where the preferences and coalitions cut across the established and emerging power groups. The emerging powers and developing countries directly gained far more than they had from the first summit, specifically the $1.1 trillion in additional funding with a pro-development impact and the creation of the FSB.

Dimensions of Performance

A systematic assessment of the six dimensions of summit performance confirms that London was a very strong, striking success (see Appendix C-2).

Domestic Political Management

In its domestic political management the London Summit gave a nationally unpopular host Gordon Brown a badly needed boost in the polls (see Appendix D-2). It offered new hope for a while that he could win the general election that he would have to call within just over a year. However, while the summit was a short-term success for Brown, he was not ultimately able to leverage it adequately at home to win that election. The great glow of the London Summit proved very short lived.

Outside the G7-member host, the $1.1 trillion result was employed more successfully for domestic political rewards. India's Prime Minister Manmohan Singh used it in his competitive general election that came shortly after the summit. His London performance helped him secure an unexpectedly robust re-election result on May 13.

The London communiqué also issued one compliment. It went to another emerging country, Mexico, for its decision to seek a flexible credit line.

Deliberation

In its deliberation, London was a striking success. Its communiqué and two annexes contained 6,155 words, almost double the total of the Washington output (see Appendix E). Macroeconomic policy took up 27 percent, up from 18 percent at Washington. Development took 28 percent, up from 18 percent at Washington.

Moreover, London stood first by a wide margin as a summit where leaders were actively engaged doing deals at the summit itself and even personally drafting the communiqué language that reflected the results. The British decision on the eve of the summit to draft a new communiqué, to replace the leaked one, ensured that leaders were more involved. Brown was able to keep the conversation revolving around the leaders. He made good use of the breakfast meeting as well. It was an approach that advantaged the highly experienced British host.

Direction Setting

In its democratic direction setting, London was a strong success (see Appendix F-2). It did almost as well as Washington. London affirmed democratic principles 10 times, covering several types. These were led by surveillance monitoring with three affirmations, and transparency and accountability and international institutions with two apiece. On climate change, London also made the environment-economy link.

Decision Making

London's decision making was a strong success as well (see Appendix G). The leaders made 88 commitments, almost as many as Washington's 95. In the realm of financial regulation, three stood out, as follows.

On tax havens, a core concern of the continental Europeans, the G20 boldly proclaimed "the era of banking secrecy is over" (G20 2009). But all the G20 promised was to "stand ready to deploy sanctions" rather than actually unleash them against recalcitrant jurisdictions. The winners here were China and the other G20 members, such as Britain, with tax havens of their own in the Caribbean and elsewhere to protect.

On hedge funds, regulation and supervision would be applied only on institutions and activities that were "systemically significant" (G20 2009). They were thus subjected to the standard "all in" principle, rather than being singled out for special treatment as especially pernicious parts of the financial system. This was a far cry from the demand of the consequential Germans and Italians to abolish them outright. The United States and Britain, as home to most of the world's hedge funds, won here.

On accounting, the London commitment was for standards setters to work urgently with supervisors and regulators to devise an internationally consistent regime of high standards. G20 governors thus refrained from ordering these independent professionals how to practise their specialized and complex craft.

However, in overall terms, the relative decision making on financial regulation dropped, from the 58 commitments at Washington to only 22 at London. The big gains in decision making at London were on trade, development, macroeconomics, and IFI reform. Social causes, climate change, and energy also advanced, by securing commitments for the first time.

Delivery

In delivering its decisions in the six months after the summit, London did less well. On five assessed commitments, the compliance of its members was only +0.23 (61.5 percent) on a scale of −1.00 to +1.00, where −1.00 represents no implementation or action contrary to the commitment, 0 represents partial implementation or a work in progress, and +1.00 represents full implementation (International Organizations Research Institute 2009). While this performance was in the positive range, it was well below the Washington Summit's score and the G8's average of approximately +0.50 (75 percent). Subsequent analysis with additional countries and commitments assessed produced an overall score for London of +0.42 (71 percent) (see Appendix H-3).

The G8 members at London, with a score of +0.62 (81 percent) on the enhanced analysis, did better on the delivery of their assessed London commitments than the non-G8 ones, with only +0.25 (62.5 percent) (see Appendix H-3). Compliance was led by Britain at +1.00 (100 percent), followed close behind by Germany, France, Canada, and Australia. G7 compliance leadership was clear. On the key London commitment on voice and vote reform of the IMF, longer term compliance was complete. It was done eventually by its deadline of January 2011 due to the deal forged by the G20 for the Seoul Summit in November 2010.

Development of Global Governance

In the development of global governance, London was a very strong success. London did much to develop G20 governance. Internally, the leaders in their three documents made 12 references to the G20—two to their own summit and 10 to the finance ministers' forum. At its second summit, the G20 became an ongoing gathering rather than a one-time event. It helped deliver the results of the first summit, confirmed the value of this model, and set the precedent for the third summit that was soon to come. While some still saw the G20 summit as an ad hoc emergency measure, by publicly accepting the need for a third summit of the same sort and privately deciding the hosting order for the next four summits, the leaders took a decisive step on the path toward institutionalization. The sherpa process became standardized. On the road to London the G20 had created a new working group, on employment.

Externally, the London G20 vastly expanded its communiqué references to other international institutions to 116, about triple the 40 made at Washington (see Appendix C-2). Central to London's references was the IMF with 36 references, compared to the World Bank with 10 and the BCBS with seven. But the FSB with 23, compared to eight at Washington for its FSF predecessor, was the big winner. The G20 thus decided to govern more through its own plurilateral 1999 group and the plurilateral FSB, rather than rely only on the old 1944 IMF. In most cases, the G20 led with guidance to the other international institutions rather than expressions of support. One expression of support was for the British-hosted G8 Gleneagles Summit for its initiative to double ODA and otherwise help the poor.

By the much more material measure of which international institutions got the most new money, the IMF won by far, with $750 billion. The World Bank came second with $100 billion. Both the FSB and UN received nothing of consequence.

Causes of Performance

Shock-Activated, Equalizing Vulnerabilities

The first cause of London's very strong performance was high, shock-activated, equalizing vulnerability, as the American-centred financial crisis became a great economic recession on a global scale (see Appendix I). By the first quarter of 2009 severe financial system seizure had spread to Europe, leaving only the financial systems of Japan and Canada intact within the G7. The unprecedentedly high speed, spread, scope, scale, and severity of the financial crisis and its spillover to the real economies of all developed and many emerging and developing economies created the worst economic conditions since the Great Depression. Unlike the 1997–99 crisis, when a largely untouched G7 had ridden to the rescue of afflicted emerging countries, within the G8 there were few unaffected suppliers of financial and economic security on the systemic scale required to combat and contain a kind of crisis never seen before.

A second shock, seen strikingly in the melting mountaintops of Mount Kilimanjaro, was climate change. Its now visible, negative, chronic but cumulative consequences were arriving to afflict the poorer countries and peoples in the world. With the financial crisis assaulting the old rich and the climate crisis assaulting the long poor, it was up to the new rising rich, contained in the G20, to ride to the rescue of the global community as a whole.

International Institutional Failure

The second cause of London's very strong performance was the failure of the established multilateral organizations on their own to respond adequately to these unprecedented shocks, particularly in raising the massive new resources required to halt the great global recessionary plunge (see Appendix J-1).

The IMF did work effectively with the US and the British to put the SDR allocation in place for immediate liquidity injection, delivered through the New Arrangements to Borrow. Furthermore, the IMF's Dominique Strauss-Kahn had called—unusually for an IMF managing director—for a deficit-deepening fiscal stimulus of at least 2 percent of global GDP, a move that the G20 accepted and implemented.

Yet to combat the proliferating crisis, which had the domestic American housing and financial system at its core, the IMF had had only limited professional expertise and only $250 billion in resources to deploy. It also had a governance structure that had promised only a slightly greater share of voice and vote to the emerging powers with fewer problems and much more money (due to a deal done within the G20 finance ministers' forum). Its legally confined executive board and IMFC were unable to respond fast and fully to this new, fast-paced, shock sequence starting in America and Europe's financial system well beyond the commercial banks.

The UN's initiative, on the surface, seemed useful. Many elements of Ban Ki-moon's March 20 letter to G20 leaders, starting with the request for at least $1 trillion in new money, were directly reflected in the London communiqué and results. But behind the scenes, the IMF found it unhelpful. And the British and UN efforts were done at best in parallel and at worst in public competition. While Britain's Mark Malloch Brown provided a natural channel for communication and coordination, his relationship with Ban was not considered particularly close. Moreover, differences within the UN's G20 team limited the organization's impact. Nonetheless, the UN did reinforce the G20 process and made the mobilization of the package move more quickly, in part so that Brown could take credit for it himself.

More broadly the institutional characteristics of both the UN and IMF had long induced China to read the party line faithfully on behalf of the G77 developing-country members, rather than act as an individual with the flexibility and even free thinking useful for getting good deals done on time. Starting at London, the G20 summit allowed Chinese officials to act more in the latter fashion, as they could identify and associate with issue-specific allies and adversaries from individual colleagues around the table, whether they represented an established or emerging country back home or a fixed coalition in the world. This mattered more because the G20 was starting to direct the IMF.

Among the plurilateral institutions, the G20 finance forum was also constrained in its ability to act. It remained more of a consensus-oriented and conventional decision-making club rather than a rapid, revolutionary crisis-response one. This was especially so now that the leaders had assumed direct control. Nor had the FSF been up to the challenge, as the leading emerging powers of China, India, Brazil, Mexico, and South Africa were still left out.

The G8 itself had not responded to the crisis by springing into any inter-sessional action at the summit level in advance of its long-scheduled annual gathering in Italy in July (Kirton 2009a, 2009c; Kirton and Koch 2009a). It had left the field to the G20. The lack of response from the established multilateral organizations and newer plurilateral institutions in the face of the financial crisis left room for and indeed required the G20 summit to emerge as a new and effective forum.

Predominant, Equalizing Capabilities

The third cause of the summit's very strong success was the continuing collective predominance and major internal equalization of capability between the established and emerging countries, and among those countries within the G7/8 group (see Appendix K). The American economy, the world's largest, contracted at a seasonally adjusted annualized rate of 6.3 percent in the fourth quarter of 2008, and a further 6.1 percent in the first quarter of 2009. The contractions in the Japanese economy, the second largest, were estimated in late April 2009 at 3.1 percent for the year ending in March and, by the IMF, at 6.2 percent for 2009. For third-ranked Germany, the late April estimate was a lesser 5.4 percent contraction in 2009. For the 27 members of the EU, there was an even lower 4 percent contraction in 2009. However, the Bank of Canada predicted that Canada's economy, the smallest of the G7, would contract by more than 7 percent annualized in the first quarter of 2009, the biggest fall on record.

In sharp contrast to these significant declines within the G7, the largest emerging country, China, saw its growth fall only to almost zero in the fourth quarter of 2008. It predicted growth of at least 6.1 percent in the first quarter of 2009, with signs that growth would accelerate even more. India too seemed likely to maintain a growth rate of over 5 percent.

The only partial offset to these changes in the real economy came in short-term exchange rate moves. The US dollar received a temporary boost when those who needed to repatriate capital to cover their losses in the United States bought US dollars. But overall, the general shrinking of the developed countries' economies relative to the steady, albeit a little checked, growth of emerging markets, helped to equalize the relative capabilities among those countries, giving more scope for a G20 summit among equals.

Democratic Convergence

The fourth cause of London's very strong success was the domestic democratic convergence among G20 members, centred on their commitment to social and political stability and increasingly political openness. The G7/8 partners and particularly the EU were concerned with the economically devastated democracies among the new and prospective EU members in Eastern and Central Europe and elsewhere on the EU periphery. Among the emerging members, the newer democracies of Indonesia, Korea, and Mexico aroused concern. At their concluding news conferences at the London Summit, several of the G20 leaders noted that their common unifying fear was that economic distress would breed social unrest, political extremism, and authoritarianism, as it had in Europe and Japan during the Great Depression of the 1930s, with still vividly remembered results. China also had strong reasons to fear an intensification of its already worrisome domestic social instability, even if it did not share a common democratic ideal as its ultimate goal. Social and political stability as a unifying goal among G20 members contributed to the cohesion of the group. It concentrated their actions on stopping the recession in new democracies and developing states.

Political Control, Capital, Continuity, Competence, and Commitment

The fifth cause of London's very strong success was the substantial overall level of the political control, capital, continuity, competence, and commitment of the G20 leaders at home and abroad (see Appendix M). Within the G8, the leaders of the US and Britain, the former led by a newly elected and highly popular Barack Obama, had party control of their legislature and no immediately looming elections. The Japanese and German leaders, both with coalition governments, did not have party control and faced general elections in the fall. But Angela Merkel enjoyed considerable domestic support. She seemed likely to win her next election and would perhaps even be able to govern without her coalition partners from the Social Democratic Party. Beyond the G8, the consequential leaders were secure, save for India's Manmohan Singh, who faced a general election within weeks of the summit; going into the summit he was not thought likely to do better in this election than he had before, although he ended up with a strong showing. Generally speaking, in the face of the shocks, legislatures, central bankers, and voters were willing to give their leaders the benefit of the doubt. The major constraint from domestic politics came from a US Congress that appeared increasingly unwilling to authorize a second package of fiscal spending and bank bailouts.

Domestic political pressures in Britain also influenced the outcome of the London Summit. In the lead-up, the intervention of political staff in the British government helped shape a set of deliverables previously mired in the technical details of financial regulation into what became the $1.1 trillion package for global development.

Continuity was strong. All the G20 leaders except Obama were veterans of the Washington Summit held only 14 weeks before. Obama was not just another American president, but one whose mandate, style, and openness to international cooperation provided what many considered an attractive contrast to George Bush. Among the invited guests, Dutch prime minister Jan Peter Balkenende participated this time. The ratio of veterans to newcomers was very high. Most of those veteran leaders enjoyed a significant amount of political capital both domestically and internationally.

The leaders again had their G20-experienced finance ministers by their side. Leaders were able to benefit from the intense preparations and background knowledge within this still constricted group. Moreover, two key leaders—Brown and Singh—from established and emerging countries had extensive experience in the G20 finance ministers' club. Both also brought a deep personal commitment to poverty reduction. Brown, as Britain's chancellor of the exchequer, had significantly influenced the design and results of the British-hosted G8 Gleneagles Summit in 2005 in this way. He had an exceptional ability to orchestrate London's very strong success.

Brown brought his own deep convictions to London. He cared personally about poverty reduction and development, both in Britain and abroad, and he cared deeply about education and the details of financial regulation. Brown's commitment to these issues was significant in bringing about the $1.1 trillion for development and financial support, with its emphasis on protecting the poor.

At the sherpa level, Britain's Jon Cunliffe brought extraordinary expertise in economics and long experience in the G8 and G20 officials' forums. In early 2009, Kemal Derviş, who had been at the Washington Summit, had retired from the UN when his term as UNDP administrator was done. However, several senior colleagues insisted he continue to lead the UN's team into London. Derviş's advantage was not just that he was a sound economist, but also that he had solid diplomatic skills. Derviş attended all the sherpa meetings in London, at the insistence of those close to the secretary general. Nonetheless, not all his colleagues gave him their full support. Had those officials worked together as a team, the UN could have exerted more influence.

Controlled Club Participation as a Network Hub

The sixth cause of London's very strong performance was the controlled participation in the embryonic leaders' group that served as a global governance network hub (see Appendix N). Internally, full membership in the G20 summit stayed the same for the second time. Almost all leaders from Washington returned to deepen their personal relationships with one another, with Obama as the newcomer and with the group. Coalitions cutting across old divides reappeared, as seen in Mexican president Felipe Calderón's pre-summit consultations with Spain, the US, and Canada rather than with Brazil or Argentina. However, fixed caucuses were also evident. The finance ministers of the BRIC grouping of Brazil, Russia,

India, and China met before the summit to agree to ask for SDR bonds and the BRICs similarly consulted among themselves about how much money they would give to the IMF.

The British added to the Washington roster several discretionary, ad hoc invitees. They included Thailand as chair of Association of Southeast Asian Nations (ASEAN) and heads of several international organizations, for a total of 29 participants at London. While this made the group less compact, it was still controlled.

Externally, especially with these additions, the G20 leaders increasingly served as the hub of a global network that reached out to embrace all significant plurilateral summit institutions that included established and emerging countries and that had trans-regional reach. The individual and country connections came from both sides of the established and emerging country divide.

Among the established members, host Gordon Brown, having been an experienced finance minister, was deeply involved in several global financial networks. He was also an original member of the G20 forum and had participated in the G20 ministerials as well as the IMFC, as its sole founding chair, for many years, since 1999. He had participated in the quarterly G7 finance ministers' meetings since 1997 and, as a leader, in the annual G8 summit in 2008. India's Singh held a somewhat similar position in the emerging members' set.

At the official level, Korea and other emerging economies had joined the BCBS in March 2009.

Conclusion

The British government hoped to build on the highly successful results of London for the next G20 summit, including on the controversial issues of climate change, climate finance, and IMF voice and vote reform. The feedback Britain received from China on the results of the London Summit was highly critical of the European performance there. The Chinese attitude echoed the criticism that "it takes a lot of Europeans to speak with a single voice."

Nonetheless, the London Summit was a remarkable achievement in the change that it signalled in the prevailing view of the governance of international finance. At the final press conference of the summit, Brown (2009) summarized the achievements, not just of the April 2009 meeting, but of all the G20 meetings, as follows: "The old Washington consensus is over. Today we have reached a new consensus—that we take global action together to deal with the problems we face; that we will do what is necessary to restore growth and jobs; that we will take essential action to rebuild confidence and trust in our financial system, and to prevent a crisis such as this ever happening again." At London, the roles of the World Bank and the IMF were changed. No longer would their goals be to encourage the deregulation of the economy. Rather they would now serve as regulators and financial safety nets. The commonly understood Washington

Consensus, representing an unchecked faith in a self-regulating market, gave way to "managed globalization," where government regulation would contribute to and develop financial stability. Whereas the 1997–99 Asian-turned-global crisis had given way to the Montreal Consensus in 2000, now, a decade later, the American-turned-global crisis of 2007–09 had, at London, recreated the Montreal Consensus at the leaders' level to govern the world of the twenty-first century.

References

Agence France Presse. 2009. "Brazil Sees Chance to Alter World Decisions at BRIC Summit." June 14.

Alexandroff, Alan S. and Kirton, John J. 2010. "The 'Great Recession' and the Emergence of the G20 Leaders' Summit." In *Rising States, Rising Institutions: Challenges for Global Governance*, eds Alexandroff, Alan S., and Cooper, Andrew F. Washington DC: Brookings Institution Press, 178–95.

Bergsten, C. Fred. 2009. "Obama's 500-Day Report Card." *International Economy* 23(2): 10–19. Available at: www.international-economy.com/TIE_Sp09_Obama500Days.pdf. Accessed: July 2012.

Bradford, Colin I. and Linn, Johannes F. 2009. "Welcome to the New Era of G20 Global Leadership." In "G20 Summit: Recovering from the Crisis," G20 Summit Report No. 3, Brookings Institution, Washington DC. Available at: www.brookings.edu/research/reports/2009/09/17-g20-summit. Accessed: July 2012.

Brown, Gordon. 2005. "Statement at the Conclusion of G7 Finance Ministers Meeting." London, December 3. Available at: www.g8.utoronto.ca/finance/fm051203_brown.htm. Accessed: July 2012.

Brown, Gordon. 2009. "G20 Press Conference." London, April 3. Available at: tna.europarchive.org/20081209202104/http://www.number10.gov.uk/Page18934. Accessed: July 2012.

Brown, Gordon. 2010. *Beyond the Crash: Overcoming the First Crisis of Globalization*. New York: Free Press.

Choi, Hee-nam. 2009. "Enhancing Korea's Standing through the G20." *Korea Herald*, June 9.

Deudney, Daniel and Ikenberry, G. John. 2009. "The Myth of the Autocratic Revival: Why Liberal Democracy Will Prevail." *Foreign Affairs* 88(1): 77–93.

Fidler, Stephen, Davis, Bob, Mollenkamp, Carrick, and Weisman, Jonathan. 2009. "G20 in London: Measured Gains for G20." *Wall Street Journal Europe*, April 3.

Financial Times. 2009. "The First Bricks in a New World Order." April 3.

Fratianni, Michele and Alessandrini, Pietro. 2009. "The Common Purse." In *The G8 2009: From La Maddalena to L'Aquila*, eds Kirton, John J., and Koch, Madeline. London: Newsdesk, 52–53. Available at: www.g8.utoronto.ca/newsdesk/g8-2009.html. Accessed: July 2012.

G20. 2009. "Global Plan for Recovery and Reform." London, April 2. Available at: www.g20.utoronto.ca/2009/2009communique0402.html. Accessed: July 2012.

International Organizations Research Institute. 2009. "G20 London Summit Commitments Compliance Report 2009." September 18, Moscow. Available at: www.g20.utoronto.ca/analysis/hse/2009-london-compliance.pdf. Accessed: July 2012.

Jha, Pem Shankar. 2009. "Globe in a State." *World Today* 65(3): 4–7.

Kirton, John J. 2009a. "Coexistence, Co-operation, Competition: G Summits." *Aspenia* (43–44). Available at: www.g20.utoronto.ca/biblio/kirton-aspenia-2009.pdf. Accessed: July 2012.

Kirton, John J. 2009b. "A Committed Contributor: Japan in G8 and G20 Governance." Paper prepared for a workshop on "Japan (Still) Matters: What Role in the World," May 1, National Institute of Japanese Studies, Sheffield University, Sheffield. Available at: www.g8.utoronto.ca/scholar/kirton-japan-sheffield.pdf. Accessed: July 2012.

Kirton, John J. 2009c. "A Summit of Sound Success: Prospects for the G8 at L'Aquila 2009." July 6. Available at: www.g8.utoronto.ca/evaluations/2009laquila/2009prospects090706.html. Accessed: July 2012.

Kirton, John J. and Koch, Madeline, eds. 2009a. *The G8 2009: From La Maddalena to L'Aquila*. London: Newsdesk. Available at: www.g8.utoronto.ca/newsdesk/g8-2009.html. Accessed: July 2012.

Kirton, John J. and Koch, Madeline, eds. 2009b. *The G20 London Summit: Growth, Stability, Jobs*. London: Newsdesk. Available at: www.g8.utoronto.ca/newsdesk/g20london2009.pdf. Accessed: July 2012.

Layton, Duane and Smith, Tiffany. 2009. "Ditching Doha?" *International Economy* 23(2): 21–23. Available at: www.international-economy.com/TIE_Sp09_Layton.pdf. Accessed: July 2012.

Millard, Robin. 2009. "African Leaders Tell G20 Economic Crisis Threatens 'Chaos'." Agence France Presse, March 16.

Morris, Harvey. 2009. "Ban Ki-moon Urges $1,000bn for Developing World." *Financial Times*, March 26.

Norman, Laurence and Connaghan, Clare. 2009. "Developing Econs the Big Winners from G20 Ascent." Dow Jones Newswires, April 2.

Obama, Barack. 2009. "News Conference by President Obama." London Summit, April 2. Available at: www.whitehouse.gov/the-press-office/news-conference-president-obama-40209. Accessed: July 2012.

Price, Daniel M. 2009. "Recovery and Reform." In *The G8 2009: From La Maddalena to L'Aquila*, eds Kirton, John J., and Koch, Madeline. London: Newsdesk, 24–26. Available at: www.g8.utoronto.ca/newsdesk/g8-2009.html. Accessed: July 2012.

Sorrell, Martin. 2009. "The Pendulum Will Swing Back." *Financial Times*, April 8.

Truman, Edwin M. 2009a. "The G20 and International Financial Institution Reform: Unfinished IMF Reform." (Blog). *VoxEU*. January 28. Available at: www.voxeu.org/article/imf-reform-unfinished-agenda. Accessed: July 2012.

Truman, Edwin M. 2009b. "Globalization Goes into Reverse?" Realtime Economic Issues Watch (Blog). *Peterson Institute for International Economics*. January 30. Available at: www.petersoninstitute.org/realtime/?p=453. Accessed: July 2012.

Zhou, Xiaochuan. 2009. "Reform the International Monetary System." Beijing, March 23. Available at: www.pbc.gov.cn/publish/english/956/2009/20091229104425550619706/20091229104425550619706_.html. Accessed: July 2012.

Chapter 12
Institutionalizing Summitry, Pittsburgh 2009

Introduction

The Challenge

On September 24–25, 2009, the leaders of the Group of 20 (G20) assembled in Pittsburgh, Pennsylvania, for their third summit. This was the first chance for recently elected US president Barack Obama, enjoying strong popularity both at home and abroad, to host and chair a global summit. It was thus his first chance to make history at home on a central world stage (Kirton 2009; Kirton and Guebert 2009).

This Obama did in several ways. The Pittsburgh Summit proclaimed that the G20 would henceforth be the permanent premier forum for its members' international economic cooperation. It produced the new Framework for Strong, Sustainable, and Balanced Growth to help prevent economic crises from arising and to keep growth intensifying in the years ahead (Joicey and Pickford 2011). The leaders further pledged to phase out unsustainable fossil fuel subsidies as a major contribution to fiscal consolidation, energy security, and climate change control (Kirton and Boyce 2009). At Pittsburgh, the G20 summit thus graduated from being an ad hoc crisis response committee to being a permanent global governor of finance and economics.

Competing Assessments

The contribution and causes of the Pittsburgh Summit are a matter of considerable debate among three major competing schools of thought.

The first school, following the "rejectionist" tradition, saw failure. Paul Donovan (2009) pointed to the more than 100 protectionist measures that the G20 members had put in place since the London Summit, where the G20 had promised not to raise trade barriers. Lack of progress on climate change financing was a recurring theme, especially after the finance ministers and central bank governors met following Pittsburgh in St. Andrews, Scotland, in November 2009 (Giles 2009; Winning and Parkinson 2009). One variant of this school saw more self-congratulation than substance, as the finance ministers seemed pleased with the existence of the G20 forum, but had not yet achieved their central promises on shared policy objectives, such as mobilizing climate finance (Giles 2009).

A second school, in line with the "reinforcement" tradition, was composed of cautious optimists who had a realistic recognition of the substantial difficulties still faced by the group. Mark Weisbrot called the Pittsburgh shift in economic governance from the Group of Seven (G7) and Group of Eight (G8) to the G20 an important "symbolic change" (Johnson 2009). He acknowledged that there were rival blocs within the group, including the old G7 and the new BRIC grouping of Brazil, Russia, India, and China, which would continue to exercise more power. Steven Englander noted that G20 agreements carried more weight, now that emerging countries were at the table, even if this made diplomacy and decision making more difficult (Johnson 2009). Paolo Guerrieri concluded that on the key issue of managing global macroeconomic imbalances "the agreement reached at the G20 Summit in Pittsburgh in September 2009 [was] a first step in the right direction," but did not generate enough in terms of specific action and enforcement mechanisms (Guerrieri 2010, 690; see also Helleiner 2010, 634).

A third school saw modest success, constrained only by the marginal majority left out (Payne 2010). Jeffrey Sachs (2009) noted that in Pittsburgh, the leaders "spoke earnestly and with intelligence, moderation, and insight," due largely to Obama's gravitas and willingness to work with the rest of the world. The G20 was now "an experiment" on whose "makeshift scaffolding the success of the planet now rests." But Sachs also noted that more than two billion people were still not represented in the group and therefore it was still nowhere as legitimate as the United Nations. It also lacked expertise on issues such as climate change, financial regulation, and energy security. Donald Kaberuka, president of the African Development Bank, similarly said that the G20 was "important and irreversible," but its "unfinished business is to ensure the interests of low-income countries are taken into account" (Guha 2009).

The Argument

This chapter argues that the Pittsburgh Summit was a strong success. Its achievements came primarily in its proclamation of the G20 summit as an ongoing, premier economic forum for its members' international economic cooperation, its production of the framework, its promise to phase out fossil fuel subsidies, and its broadening of its social agenda. In particular, its self-proclaimed permanent pre-eminent place in the international institutional architecture represented a major victory for its non-G8 members, which now had an assured position in a permanent top-tier group. More broadly, the G20 appeared to be following the path of the G20 finance ministers and central bank governors, who at Montreal in 2000 had broadened the group's ambitions once the immediate economic crisis that had created the group had passed. Under Obama's leadership as host and chair, the G20 leaders successfully bonded to the fledgling group a new American president and administration from a party different from the one that had created the summit group less than a year before. And unlike the G20 finance forum in 2001, they did so without the shock of a new terrorist attack or similar assault on America itself.

Among the key causes of Pittsburgh's success were the sheer scale, deep domestic impact, and duration of the 2007–09 financial and economic shock sequence, especially in America where, most agreed, good growth and jobs would take a long time to return. Another cause was the mounting evidence that the International Monetary Fund (IMF), the G7/8, and other bodies would only act and reform effectively in response to the implicit competition, acceptance, and legitimization from the G20 summit and the G20's specific, highest level political direction to put the IMF's technical talents to best use. A further cause was the desire of the emerging members, rapidly rising relative to the crisis-ravaged American and European countries, for an assured, enhanced institutionalized place at the top and their growing willingness to accept the requisite responsibilities, including the democratic principles and practices cherished by the established countries in the group. Yet another cause was the competence of G20 founding father Lawrence Summers within the Obama administration, and the continuity of virtually all leaders, who were becoming personally attached to the closed group they had created. It was now tentatively acquiring more characteristics as a club and externally growing in its global sensitivity through its expanding network beyond.

Plans and Preparations

The G20's Pittsburgh Summit had a broader agenda than its predecessors. It built on the ambitious achievements of the London Summit in April 2009 and went well beyond in many ways.

Setting a Time and Place

The London communiqué had declared that the next summit would take place "by the end of this year" (G20 2009b). This passage had been inserted as a placeholder to get the issue out of the way, because there was no agreement on when the next summit would be held. There was a feeling it should take place within six months rather than leave it until the end of the year. After London, British prime minister Gordon Brown sent a follow-up letter to all the G20 leaders. Then the Americans picked up the process. The initial thought among the G20 partners was that the summit would again be held in Washington. It took some time for the Americans to decide that Pittsburgh was the place.

The G7 and G20 Finance Ministers' and Central Bank Governors' Meeting, April

After London, the debate among G20 members over hedge funds and accounting standards continued. To it were added the issues of bank stress tests and standards in the lead-up to and throughout the G7 and G20 finance ministers meetings held three weeks later, on April 24. In their communiqué, the G7 finance ministers directly endorsed what the G20 leaders had just done (G7 Finance 2009).

The meeting of the G20 ministers and bank governors, lasting less than two hours, was co-chaired by Britain's chancellor of the exchequer Alistair Darling and America's treasury secretary Timothy Geithner. It did not produce a communiqué. The focus was on setting priorities to implement the many leaders' commitments from London. It was also on global growth, in the immediate wake of the IMF's new, gloomy forecast that the global economy would contract by 1.3 percent in 2009.

At both meetings French finance minister Christine Lagarde sought to move to specifics, notably to define systemically significant hedge funds. The Europeans also disputed the methods behind the IMF's estimate that there were $4.1 trillion in bad assets on the books of the world's banks, with those in Europe being more burdened than most. Yet all seemed to agree that America was now moving with sufficient speed and skill to take care of its banks' impaired assets, thus meeting the essential prerequisite for a global recovery to begin. No demands for more intrusive banking regulation were voiced.

The good mood at the meetings was sustained by the fact that the implementation of the broad and deep London commitments seemed to be proceeding rather well. Japan had unveiled a major new program of fiscal spending, following its strong stimulus in 2008. Lagarde said she too would support a second stimulus package if need be. Her Canadian colleague Jim Flaherty signalled that he would also be prepared to stimulate further if necessary. And the G7 again promised to stimulate as much as was needed, to restore growth from the "green shoots" now visible.

Immediate action was taken on tax havens, with all three of the countries remaining on the blacklist issued by the Organisation for Economic Co-operation and Development (OECD) falling into line. This suggested there would be no need for sanctions against them. On trade, a report noted that in the three weeks since the London Summit, nine G20 members had violated their anti-protectionist pledge. But this list included measures being considered as well as actually taken. And four countries had taken liberalizing measures during this time. This record was better than that in the period following the G20's Washington Summit, perhaps reflecting the new London commitment to redress any protectionist moves.

On financial support, there was steady progress. As part of London's headline $1.1 trillion pledge, Japan, the US, and Europe (including Britain at $15 billion and France at $16 billion) had each promised $100 billion for the IMF. Canada pledged CA$10 billion, its traditional 10 percent of America's contribution. But China seemed to back off its early signal to give $40 billion. The Russians and Saudis remained reluctant to give anything at all. They looked to the alternative, approved in the London communiqué, of having the IMF float bonds instead. Only Canada clearly said it would consider giving more if the IMF asked.

G20 Finance Ministers' and Central Bank Governors' Meeting, September

The G20 finance ministers and bank governors met again in London on September 5 for a separate, stand-alone meeting. It was designed to follow up the leaders' Washington and London commitments and to prepare for the Pittsburgh Summit that would take place in a few weeks' time. Participants assessed their progress in delivering London's "Global Plan for Recovery and Reform" and the money that had been pledged for social protection and trade in low-income countries, trade financing, and the IMF's New Arrangements to Borrow. There was an agreement to support lending, which was to include addressing impaired assets and conducting more robust stress tests. The ministers agreed to promote employment and to address commodity price volatility. Coordinated but variable exit strategies were discussed. The ministers reiterated the G20's anti-protectionist pledge and their commitment to conclude the Doha Development Agenda. They also reaffirmed their commitment to reforming the international financial institutions (IFIs), including completing World Bank reforms by the spring of 2010 and the IMF quota review by January 2011 (G20 Finance 2009b). The ministers issued a separate statement on banking in which they agreed that more needed to be done in corporate governance and compensation, regulation and oversight for "systemically important firms," capital requirements, non-cooperative jurisdictions, coordination of international standards particularly on credit derivatives, credit rating agencies, hedge funds, and securities, and in developing a single, global set of accounting standards (G20 Finance 2009a).

G20 Sherpa Meetings

Washington, July

The first sherpa meeting for Pittsburgh was held in July, at Blair House in Washington DC. The American hosts identified the issues they wished the summit to address. One was correcting global imbalances, even though at the Washington Summit China had refused to allow the word "imbalances" to appear in the communiqué. A second was the concept of mutual assessment, to give life to the Framework for Strong, Sustainable, and Balanced Growth. A third was energy. The Americans were still scrambling with the physical preparations for their summit. They had not identified the location at the start.

Washington, September

The second sherpa meeting took place on September 10–11 at the State Department in Washington. It was a somewhat hectic affair, coming only two weeks before the Pittsburgh Summit. The Americans had distributed papers that they referred to as "building blocks." Helen Clark represented the United Nations secretary general, having replaced Kemal Derviş. (She remained the UN sherpa until May 2010.) To the surprise of some sherpas, representatives of other international organizations were also invited, including from the Asia-Pacific Economic Cooperation (APEC) forum. These guests sat behind the sherpas during the meeting but sat at the same table at dinner, in a small, cramped room at the State Department.

US sherpa Michael Froman, a smooth conductor, circulated his preparatory papers just enough in advance of the meeting to allow for informed discussions. The sherpas thus arrived in Washington prepared to comment. US finance deputy Lael Brainerd and her Treasury officials had met with the G20 finance deputies ahead of time. Froman left it to the finance officials to draft most of the text on all technical matters. These included financial regulations, IFI reform, and macroeconomic policy in its first version. The sherpas then focused on the economy, the overview text for the draft communiqué, and non-finance items including trade. The finance officials attended the sherpa meeting, having looked over the papers.

The idea of acting on fossil fuel subsidies arose in general terms. This was an idea to which Summers had been long attached. As director of the National Economic Council, he was in a position to have it put as a priority into the summit process, to ultimate success. It had also been pushed by a few, small, issue-focused American environmental nongovernmental organizations prior to the Pittsburgh Summit. The US Treasury Department took up the cause.

The American initiative on phasing out fossil fuel subsidies was presented by Mike Froman and David Lipton, the president's special assistant for international economic affairs, both from the White House. Right at the beginning the Americans complimented the Indonesians for what they had done to reduce their subsidies. India's sherpa Montek Singh Ahluwalia seemed pleased that the issue was on the table because his government had been trying to do this for a long time at home, where fossil fuel subsidies were especially regressive and went more to the rich than the poor. China did not disagree with the American overture. When the meeting ended with the summit agenda accepted, the Americans seemed pleased and surprised that they that had gotten so far with the fossil fuel subsidies initiative.

At the meeting, Froman called on the sherpas from Brazil, China, India, Mexico, and South Africa—whose officials had been working together under the G8's Heiligendamm Dialogue Process, which had become the Heiligendamm–L'Aquila Process at the 2009 G8 summit in July, and whose leaders had been meeting with the G8 as the G8 Plus Five—to ask if they preferred the G8 plus an undetermined group of invited countries (as distinct from the G8 Plus Five) or the G20 as the central future forum.

The five exchanged views on this subject. Brazil, China, and India had a clear preference for the G20. The Mexicans wanted to maintain the G8 Plus Five as they were custodians of the Heiligendamm–L'Aquila Process. Brazil felt that the G20 was working well. Brazil's experience with the G8 Plus Five had been less favourable because there was always an asymmetry between the G8 members and the other guests. It was not clear how a G8 Plus would work. Moreover, at the

Washington Summit, Brazilian president Luiz Inácio Lula da Silva had said it was important to consolidate the G20.

Within the G8 there proved to be some resistance to the G20 option. Italy and Russia initially preferred the G8 Plus. Canada was also somewhat uncomfortable with the G20 option, because it might dilute Canada's relative place and voice. It took a little time for Canada to let go of the G8-centric option. But having been at the centre of the creation of the finance G20, Canada well understood the advantages the G20 brought.

Out of these American consultations and consensus came the American initiative and the G20 agreement to make the G20 its members' permanent premier forum. Yet even when that announcement was made, some remained uncomfortable with the particular, if careful, American-crafted phrase that was used.

Another institutional initiative came from Brazil. During the Washington Summit Lula, as a former labour union leader, had taken time to meet with the head of the American Federation of Labor and Congress of Industrial Organizations (AFL-CIO). Lula then requested that labour issues be brought onto the G20 agenda. At London he had asked that the International Labour Organization (ILO) be invited to the next summit. In Obama, elected with significant trade union support, he found a receptive host.

Pittsburgh, September

The third sherpa meeting took place on September 23–24, immediately before the summit in Pittsburgh itself. The sherpas started discussions on the evening of September 23. Their meeting continued until 3 am the next day. The first evening sherpas saw for the first and last time the one long document produced by the Americans. It contained a summary, the communiqué with 31 points, and several annexes. The sherpas had expected it and were largely comfortable with its content.

The only major difficulty with both the draft communiqué and the sherpa meeting came on the issue of climate finance. This topic had been on the sherpas' agenda since the start, but the Americans had received little help in moving it ahead. They were pushing for an agreement on climate change control and its financing and to get the finance ministers to address the issue. It was still early enough in the Obama administration to instil hope in the Europeans that these issues could be advanced. The Canadians were also supportive, as long as the result did not eliminate the role of the private sector and did not focus unduly on public sources of finance. Most sherpas wanted to drive the financing discussion toward the role of the private sector. Yet Britain wanted the focus to remain on public sources. By the end of the lengthy discussion into the evening, almost everyone was able to find something to agree on.

The exception was China, which had been reluctant from the start. China argued that such negotiations should take place at the UN. It was not until lunch on September 24, when the leaders were meeting and their sherpas were reviewing the climate change text, that China vetoed the draft passage. Froman recognized that the discussion would not proceed any further and suggested dropping the proposed long paragraphs on climate finance. As a result, the communiqué contained only a short passage on climate change, with little substance.

Fossil Fuels The American initiative on fossil fuel subsidies had been contained in the preparatory papers distributed in advance. It was initially seen as a sensible proposal: consumer subsidies harmed price setting, in their effort to provide consumers with immediate shelter from high prices for electricity from fossil fuel plants. The initial wording referred to voluntary actions. Canada supported the initiative, as it applied to consumer subsidies only, of which Canada had none. However, the BRIC members objected to the American draft and produced an alternative text. At 3 am on September 24, a compromise was reached, with India and the US in the lead. The BRICs through India succeeded in including the world "rationalize" in the commitment, inserted before the "phase out" of the subsidies. The sherpas produced a work plan that pleased everyone, including the oil producers, notably Saudi Arabia.

Premier Economic Forum The decision to make the G20 the permanent premier forum for economic governance seemed, especially to those outside the BRICs, to have snuck into the draft text of the communiqué at this final sherpa meeting. Although all G20 members seemed to favour such a declaration, the Japanese in particular were nervous. The concept was connected to the discussion of which country would host the next summit and whether the agenda of the fledgling G20 summit should be broadened. The Americans suggested the term "economic," which became "our economic cooperation" in the communiqué. These were carefully chosen words that would not stake a claim that the forum was the world's permanent premier forum, but only the G20 members' one. The intention was not to presume to speak for others but to speak only about the group's own cooperation. Substantively, its work would be limited to the "economic" domain, thus leaving political security and other issues to other bodies, notably Japan's cherished G8.

The Framework for Strong, Sustainable, and Balanced Growth The Framework for Strong, Sustainable and Balanced Growth had been evolving throughout the sherpa process, based in part on the report that Gordon Brown had requested at the London Summit. The concept was discussed at the first two sherpa meetings, driven by the Americans with support from the British and the Germans, among others.

At London, the Germans had pushed for a charter of principles that would help guide members' cooperation, particularly a new international charter for economic behaviour to regulate markets and avoid "beggar thy neighbour" policies. German chancellor Angela Merkel's proposal had nine points, with general statements of intent that might be easy to negotiate but that would likely not, most partners thought, amount to much. She had tried to get her charter mentioned at London. The Germans had tried at Washington as well. It appeared again during the summer.

The Germans tried once more to create some momentum for their proposal on the way to Pittsburgh, but did not push very hard. In the end, it was overtaken by Pittsburgh's framework, which used harder-edged language. The framework was part of the evolution of the G20 from dealing with the financial nuts and bolts of the crisis to a broadened focus on macroeconomic issues. The idea was to turn the G20's attention to preventing a crisis from recurring.

Some, including Canada, had argued since the start that the G20 must first fix the financial system. In Canada's view, that was the primary goal, even when the summit became permanent. The question now was whether the G20 summit could survive the crisis. Once the crisis was over, one could call the G20 summit a permanent group, but what could it do? Would it continue to function in the crisis-induced, disciplined way that it had at the start? The work on the framework was a critical piece of the plan for the future of the permanent forum. Canada argued that the summit must discuss rebalancing international economic behaviour, addressing members' domestic savings and spending to get the balance right.

Financial Regulation On financial regulation, finance officials were working productively. But this issue had lost the pride of place it had enjoyed at Washington and London. Officials continued to follow up on the work on regulatory bodies and drive it forward, as well as attend to financing issues. But when the Pittsburgh Summit moved into the framework, financial regulation and development financing, while still important, were no longer a priority.

Canada did not want the Framework for Strong, Sustainable, and Balanced Growth to take the limelight away from finishing financial regulatory reform. Canada wanted, above all, to fix the banks, get the financial system working, and get the regulatory agenda sorted out. While Canada supported the framework, it was not at the top of its priority list.

IFI Reform IFI reform was another important issue for Pittsburgh. Finance ministers and officials had long tried to come up with a consensus on IMF quota reform. On the central issue of the IMF quota shift, the Americans had largely left the Europeans and emerging economies to come to an agreement among themselves. Britain was heavily involved, as it had a great deal at stake. The resulting communiqué text on a 5 percent shift was very carefully drafted.

The day before the summit began, a small group of finance ministers and deputies met to do a deal on reforming the IMF and World Bank. The group consisted of the US, which had consulted Japan and Canada, Britain, which had consulted the European members, and the BRICs. They arrived at a consensus for the leaders to consider and adopt.

Trade On protectionism, sherpas received another report concluding that G20 members had done well on resisting protectionist measures.

Leaders' Involvement

The leaders themselves were directly engaged in the lead-up to Pittsburgh. Gordon Brown (2010) used his report on international institutional reform to ask how to produce high growth and employment in the coming years and how the Pittsburgh Summit could best be used to this end. In August, he wrote Obama outlining ambitious ideas on a global growth strategy that involved coordinated action on imbalances, currency reserves, monetary and fiscal policy, and, perhaps, trade. Obama replied that they must work together to get such an agreement, and ordered his officials to produce a plan that could be melded with the British one. By the time the summit opened, G20 leaders were prepared to accept the concept. That became the Framework for Strong, Sustainable, and Balanced Growth.

At the Summit

At Pittsburgh, the summit was accompanied by two initiatives, one of a unilateral sort and the other a function of a smaller group.

On the eve of the summit, Canada unilaterally announced a contribution of $2.6 billion in callable capital to the African Development Bank. This idea had arisen in discussions between the Department of Finance and Bank of Canada as a mechanism to help the multilateral development banks (MDBs). Canada also had discussions with the Inter-American Development Bank about how to assist it in a similar way. Canada's move made the Pittsburgh Summit more of a success in the development domain.

During the summit, Obama, the host and chair, took time out to meet with Britain's Gordon Brown, France's Nicolas Sarkozy, and Germany's Angela Merkel to issue a public quadrilateral statement on Iran. In it the four leaders condemned Iran's nuclear program and violation of its international commitments. They indicated that they would impose another round of sanctions as a result. The US had previously said that this G20 meeting would serve as a deadline for Iranian compliant action, and as a convenient occasion for leaders to consider an appropriate response to what Iran had done by then. The US had considered raising the issue collectively among all the G20 members at Pittsburgh. However, in the end it chose this smaller coalition of the willing to act. Still, with the full G20 at the summit as a backdrop for this international political messaging, the G20 entered—if indirectly—into this traditional high political-security field.

The summit itself featured a full-strength agenda, embracing finance-economic issues, global-transnational subjects, and even political-security ones. Its agenda included macroeconomic policy, currencies, an economic charter for ethical finance, bankers' bonuses and other financial regulation, multilateral trade liberalization, IFI reform, climate change control, G20 institutionalization, development, food and health, and, on the sidelines, Iran's nuclear program. Its centrepiece was the Framework for Strong, Sustainable, and Balanced Growth.

Macroeconomic Policy and the Framework

The opening dinner saw a *tour d'horizon* of the economic situation. By September 2009, the global economy was starting to show signs of growth. Since it now appeared that the worst was over and that economic expansion would continue into 2010, the leaders looked two years ahead. Their attention quickly turned to the Framework for Strong, Sustainable, and Balanced Growth. With the new consensus and focus on the framework, discussion of Merkel's concept of a charter disappeared for good.

The issue of exit strategies returned. It was still too soon to judge the effects of the stimulus, although several national budgets with major fiscal stimulus had been announced. It was thus too early to conclude that the G20's stimulus strategy had worked.

The Germans and French, whose economies were now beginning to grow, sought a summit emphasis on withdrawing the major fiscal and monetary stimulus that seemed to be removing the threat of another great depression and reviving the global economy. Yet the United States, Britain, and Canada had economies that were still struggling, with unemployment rising or consumption and confidence sharply constrained. They argued that the still fragile recovery was the result of the unprecedented government stimulus that must be maintained until the private sector market, firms, and consumers started to function normally again. Backed by most other G20 members, this view won. Pittsburgh's main message became "stay the course" on stimulus rather than "rush to the exit" strategies. Nonetheless, firm plans were approved to create coordinated exit strategies that would be introduced over the next year if all went well. While work to construct the framework would start immediately, real action on exchange rate volatility and misalignments, international imbalances, and a global currency regime was left for later, when the economic recovery would reliably take hold.

Financial Regulation

The leaders paid only modest attention to financial regulation and supervision, making few innovative or ambitious moves. This regulatory work, driven by finance officials, did not have a high profile with the leaders. A step forward came from the call once again for strengthening and coordinating domestic financial regulations, beginning with banking capital and liquidity, and altering the structure of bankers' compensation to this end. Perhaps the most important summit promise was to start phasing in new rules for higher capital ratios for the world's systemically significant banks by the end of 2012. Most observers expected that the required level would rise from 4 percent of tier-one capital to 8 percent under the new rules.

The G20 leaders also set several other specific deadlines for follow-up work to be done by their finance ministers, central bankers, and others more expert and experienced in the specialized worlds of financial regulation than all but a few of the G20 leaders were. The principles that the leaders set for key issues such as derivatives, resolution regimes and accounting were very general. While the political pressures to highlight bankers' bonuses were understandable, few professionals felt bonuses were the key cause of the recent financial and economic crisis or a critical component of its cure. On financial regulation and supervision, Pittsburgh was thus largely a success not on policy substance or on innovative principles but on process, and domestic political management. Success in the latter potentially gave G20 governors the time and space to get the specialized solutions right.

On the controversial issue of imposing a bank levy, Brown, supported by Sarkozy and Merkel, inserted into the G20 statement the request for an IMF report by 2010 on a financial levy. Brown followed up at the G20 finance ministers' meeting in St. Andrews in Scotland in November 2009 (Brown 2010).

IFI Reform

On IFI reform the major issue was the contentious question of quota reform of the IMF. Leaders also dealt with replenishing the resources of the MDBs, which was not as divisive.

The G20 leaders discussed IFI reform at the opening dinner. Lula and others representing the developing world said that the proposal on the table did not go far enough. Brazil sought to get the greatest shift possible toward developing countries, while protecting some countries that had done well in the first round. China's Hu Jintao and India's Manmohan Singh were active in this debate. While these big emerging countries led, many others participated as well. The Americans had made up their mind to move ahead so were strongly pushing the Europeans, whose backs were against the wall as they had the most to lose. They were defending their interests without taking the moral high ground. Canada was relaxed as it would not lose any share. In the end, Obama asked the finance ministers to work out a better formula for reforming the IFIs.

This the finance ministers did, but not for long. They left it to their deputies to produce an agreement on the percentage of the quota to be shifted to the rising powers. After negotiations between the BRICs and the Europeans, with the US as intermediary, the finance deputies finally agreed on a shift of at least 5 percent. The sherpas then inserted that figure into the communiqué, which pleased Brazil. It was also a pleasure for the IMF, above all its managing director Dominique Strauss-Kahn, as the organization was particularly aware that now that the parameters had been set, the even more important and difficult details about who would give up what and who would get how much still needed to be negotiated and defined. However, even though the text was considered by some to be written in poor English, the 5 percent figure was a clear signal of where the process would go.

In the end, this result was a key part of Pittsburgh's success (Joicey and Pickford 2011). The Framework for Strong, Sustainable, and Balanced Growth took the headlines but reform of IMF governance was a major achievement, and perhaps an integrally interlinked one, too. It was certainly easier for the emerging members to engage more in a framework that was significantly supported by the policy and analytical advice of the IMF when they knew that they had just been promised a greater voice and vote in how the IMF was run.

G20 Institutionalism

At the opening dinner, Obama announced that now that the leaders had agreed to make their G20 summit their premier forum for international economic cooperation, they needed to examine more closely how the institution should work. This discussion did not take much time. The leaders, concurring, sought to have themselves included in a permanent summit, rather than a potential alternative that might exclude them, and in a summit that had now shown it would work.

Pittsburgh's greatest accomplishment in the institutional sphere was this decision to choose the G20 as the permanent primary centre of its members' international economic cooperation. It would finally give the central role to the emerging and established powers as equals, reflecting a predominance of capability and a broad array of the world's diversity on many dimensions. It would treat established and emerging powers as equals. It would add the new Financial Stability Board (FSB) to the IMF, the World Bank, and the World Trade Organization (WTO) as a fourth pillar of the global "civil service" to advise the G20 and implement what the leaders would collectively decide.

Climate Change

At Pittsburgh, Mexico's Felipe Calderón became the G20's leader on climate change. Sarkozy said he was worried that the forthcoming United Nations conference on climate change in Copenhagen in December would fail. He called for a special, issue-specific G20 summit on climate change to save the day. But Calderón proposed as an alternative a video conference among members on climate-friendly measures. He subsequently held one with a few key leaders, including Australia's Kevin Rudd, Denmark's Lars Løkke Rasmussen, and the UN's Ban Ki-moon. Subsequently, in Singapore at APEC Calderón called an early breakfast meeting with Rudd and Ban that, despite some tension with the Americans, Obama attended as well.

Achievements

The G20 gathering at Pittsburgh was a strong success. It was the third G20 summit within 12 months. All the leaders again attended, including China's Hu, who had had to leave Italy on the eve of the G8 L'Aquila Summit just a few months before in July. At Pittsburgh, the G20 leaders took up a broad agenda, covering key economic and development issues, as well as adding environmental issues such as climate finance, energy efficiency, food security, and, on the margins, the political-security issue of nuclear proliferation in Iran.

Pittsburgh's first policy accomplishment was to send a strong, unified message that all members of the G20 would stay the course on stimulus until a genuine, durable economic recovery driven by the private sector was assured. Second, it agreed that it was time to start to design the smart, sophisticated, well-tailored, market-sensitive exit strategies that could be implemented over the next year, as economic conditions allowed. Third, and more ambitiously, it created a framework to give the now growing global economy more balanced foundations, with consumers in key economic powers such as China, Germany, and Japan generating domestic demand and imports, while finally allowing Americans to accumulate savings at home. Fourth, the summit strengthened and improved the international coordination of domestic financial regulations by increasing bank capital and liquidity and adjusting the structure of bankers' compensation. Fifth, the summit made a major advance on IFI reform, pledging that there would be a shift from the established countries to the rapidly emerging ones of at least 5 percent of the quota share and resulting votes in the IMF, and that this would be done by the previously promised deadline of 2011. Sixth, it agreed to rationalize and phase out fossil fuel subsidies, an unprecedented agreement that promised major fiscal, carbon control, energy security, and human health rewards.

The summit also made some small progress on climate finance. It created principles to guide where the required money would come from, how it would be governed, and to whom it would go. This would help developing countries mitigate their carbon pollution and cope with the destructive consequences of the climate change already underway. These principles could be a useful step in breaking the stalemate in climate negotiations, which had focused primarily on funding, just in time for the UN climate change conference in Copenhagen, where environment ministers from 192 countries would discuss a more effective successor to the failing Kyoto Protocol regime.

The Pittsburgh Summit had its shortcomings. It advanced little on international trade. The G20 leaders promised to renounce new protectionist measures, rectify past action, deliver the overdue Doha Development Agenda, liberalize trade, reduce tariffs on environmentally enhancing and climate-friendly goods and services, and otherwise reduce barriers to trade and investment. None was a ground-breaking commitment. The "Leaders Statement" contained no concrete measures to put these promises into effect.

The summit directly addressed the critical issue of unemployment. However, it offered few actions to ensure that the current economic recovery generated the green jobs that would help reduce income and gender inequality in G20 countries and around the globe. On development, despite such welcome announcements as the Canadian contribution of an additional $2.6 billion to the African Development Bank, the summit as a whole did relatively little, apart from adding microfinance to its agenda, to mobilize new money to help the still struggling poor countries and peoples of the world. Nor did it deal with promoting health security, in the wake of the "swine" influenza and other pandemics afflicting the world.

Dimensions of Performance

A systematic assessment of the six dimensions of summit performance shows that Pittsburgh was a strong success. In some ways it was even more successful than the previous two summits had been. Only on domestic political management and delivery did Pittsburgh show no advance.

Domestic Political Management

In its domestic political management, Pittsburgh's performance was mixed. The summit did little to help its already popular host, Barack Obama, manage his politics at home. The summit took place in the shadow of the outcome and prospects of elections in the second and third most powerful countries: Japan on August 30, 2009, and Germany on September 27, 2009. Japan and other G20 countries found increasing domestic political advantage in staying the course on stimulus. In Germany, Merkel emerged much better off, with her party winning more seats than it had in 2005. The leaders of Korea and South Africa improved their post-Pittsburgh popularity. As at the Washington Summit, no countries were singled out for compliments in Pittsburgh's communiqué (see Appendix D).

Deliberation

In its deliberation, Pittsburgh's performance was very strong on paper but much less so in practice. In their recorded deliberations, the leaders issued 9,257 words—the most ever, more than double than Washington and a substantial increase from London (see Appendix E). Macroeconomic policy, domestic financial regulation, and development were once again the major topics.

However, the leaders' own discussions were a step back from London's personal engagement toward the standard speeches that had been delivered at Washington. There were too many people—54 altogether, including those from international organizations—at the table for effective interpersonal exchange. And while many individuals had been there before, the discussion was more stilted and obstructionist than at London, where the highly experienced chair had kept the conversation focused and flowing. The intimate discussions of London were lost. After Pittsburgh, the leaders themselves acknowledged that there were too many people at the table.

Direction Setting

In its direction setting, Pittsburgh's performance was very strong (see Appendix F-2). There was a large leap to a new high in the number of shared democratic principles affirmed by the members. The number almost tripled to 29 across six categories, most of which had appeared at the previous summits. The largest portion emphasized the importance of transparency, followed by surveillance and monitoring, openness, and information and knowledge exchange. The rule of law and accountability were endorsed as well.

With the US as host, this very strong democratic direction setting was not surprising. It was, however, especially significant as it came as part of the G20's decision to transform itself into its members' premier, permanent forum.

Decision Making

In its collective decision making, Pittsburgh's performance was also very strong (see Appendix G). It set a new high with 128 commitments made. Of these, 30 dealt with macroeconomics, 24 with financial regulation, 18 with energy (a huge jump from London's three), 15 with development, and 13 with international financial institutions. Others came on trade, socioeconomics, climate change, and corruption.

Several commitments stood out. The first was the leaders' promise to make the G20 the "premier forum for [their] international economic cooperation" (G20 2009a). The second was the launching of the Framework for Strong, Sustainable, and Balanced Growth. The third was the commitment to "phase out and rationalize over the medium term inefficient fossil fuel subsidies while providing targeted support for the poorest." But missing was any major collective mobilization of new money, in striking contrast to London's performance less than six months before.

Delivery

In delivering on its commitments, Pittsburgh was only a small success (see Appendix H-3). It performed less well than London had. Eight months after the Pittsburgh Summit, its compliance score of +0.28 (64 percent) was substantially lower than London's +0.42 (71 percent) in the six months after it was held (on a scale of −1.00 to +1.00, where −1.00 represents no implementation or action contrary to the commitment, 0 represents partial implementation or a work in progress, and +1.00 represents full implementation). After Pittsburgh the G8 members, with an average score of +0.56 (78 percent) of compliance with their G20 commitments, again did much better than the non-G8 members, whose +0.04 (52 percent) still kept them in the positive range. The Pittsburgh Summit as a whole performed poorly compared to the G8's L'Aquila Summit that year, as the L'Aquila Summit's compliance score was +0.53 (76.5 percent). The three North American members of the US, Canada, and Mexico, complied well with Pittsburgh's five commitments on clean energy and climate change.

Development of Global Governance

In its development of global governance, Pittsburgh's performance was very strong. Internally, the three leaders' documents made 47 references to the G20 institution, almost four times as many as at London. For the first time these were led by references to the summit itself, with 24, followed by those to the finance and other ministerial forums at 16, official-level bodies at six, and civil society bodies at one. The key decision was to institutionalize the G20 as the new permanent, premier forum for its members' international economic cooperation. Pittsburgh finally gave a central role to an institution that included emerging global powers as equals, recognizing the equalization of capability and multidimensional diversity in the group. The established and emerging powers were finally equals at the top.

The leaders looked forward to holding two summits the following year, even though the financial and economic crisis was starting to fade. These two would be hosted, for the first time, by first a non-imperial if still G7 member, Canada, and then a non-G7 and non-BRICs Asian one, Korea. The equality between established and emerging members had now reached the hosting and chairing of the group.

By agreeing to hold the next G20 summit at the same time and in the same country as the next G8 summit, long scheduled for Canada in June 2010, the division of labour and cooperation between the G8 and G20 were enhanced. Both the G8 and G20 finance ministers' platforms would now serve the new G20 summit. This cooperative spirit was evident in the Pittsburgh communiqué, which on several occasions noted, endorsed, built on, or promised to implement previous decisions of the G8.

At the ministerial level, the leaders asked their energy, environment, trade, and labour ministers to meet, review, or ensure progress on various commitments. At the officials' level they agreed to establish a G20 financial inclusion experts group to help "identify lessons learned on innovative approaches to providing financial services" for the poor (G20 2009a).

Externally, the Pittsburgh leaders' documents made a new high of 117 references to other international institutions, just one more than at London. Most were to the IMF with 34 and the World Bank with 14. These references, and those overall, were overwhelmingly positive. This trend showed that the G20 did much to identify and strengthen its relationship with the world's established multilateral organizations, and did so in a highly cooperative way. The G20's heavy reliance on the IMF to develop and implement the new framework was the leading case of this new close cooperation. Yet also an integral part of G20 governance was now the UN with eight references, the ILO with five, and the United Nations Conference on Trade and Development, the Food and Agriculture Organization, the International Fund for Agricultural Development, and World Food Programme with one each.

Strikingly, G20 leaders made four references—all positive and supportive—to the G8 system: one each to the 2005 Gleneagles Summit, the Major Economies Forum, the Global Partnership for Agriculture and Food Security, and the 2009 L'Aquila Summit. The leadership and learning of Obama and Brown were evident here.

Causes of Performance

The causes of Pittsburgh's strong performance are once again well captured by the model of systematic hub governance.

Shock-Activated, Equalizing Vulnerabilities

The first cause was the sheer scale, deep domestic impact, and duration of the recent economic and financial shocks, especially in host America where growth and jobs had taken a larger than expected plunge and were slow to return (see Appendix I). A report submitted by the ILO to the G20 leaders at Pittsburgh showed that by March 2009 the G20's unemployment rate had increased to 8.5 percent (ILO 2009). While unemployment had risen across the G20 members, the US was especially hard hit, with its rate rising from 5.8 percent in 2008 to 9.4 percent in 2009. America's high unemployment rate was lasting for an exceptionally long time. Turkey also took a big hit, with unemployment rising from 11.2 percent to 14.3 percent (OECD 2010). Government spending and thus growing deficits and debt levels also continued to increase in almost all the G20 members of the OECD, G8 and non-G8 alike. Most G8 and many non-G8 countries continued to suffer severely.

International Institutional Failure

A second cause of Pittsburgh's strong performance was the failure of the IMF, the G7/8, the G20 finance ministers and central bank governors, and other bodies to respond adequately to the crisis on their own. The IMF failed to predict global economic growth in 2009, forecasting a gain of more than 3 percent when a real drop of –0.6 percent came (see Appendix J-1). Little was achieved during the spring meetings of the World Bank and IMF at the end of April.

Obama and some other leaders had little faith that the G8 L'Aquila Summit and the process leading up to it would do much to help. While the G8 leaders did discuss economic issues at the summit, they mostly reiterated calls previously made by the G20. They were conscious of avoiding G8 moves that could offend the non-G8 members of the G20 and stifle progress at Pittsburgh. Most leaders were very disappointed in the G8 summit. The G7 finance ministers' forum had survived the advent of the G20 summit and the Obama administration, as its treasury secretary Tim Geithner saw value in continuing the old forum. His Canadian counterpart, Jim Flaherty, who was to host it in 2010, did too. Fewer commitments were being produced at the level of the G20 finance ministers, leaving the task for the leaders.

The international institutional failure of other bodies' was most clearly reflected in the leaders' decision to make the G20 the premier forum for their international economic cooperation and to continue to meet at the summit level two times in the following year. It was also reflected in the G20's commitment to reform the IFIs to make them more "legitimate and effective" (G20 2009a). These organizations were unable to do so on their own.

Predominant, Equalizing Capabilities

A third cause of Pittsburgh's strong performance was the globally predominant, equalizing capabilities of G20 members and the equalizing capabilities between the G8 and non-G8 members within (see Appendix K). All G8 economies continued to contract in 2009. Among the emerging members rising China retained the highest GDP growth rate at 9.1 percent, while Russia had fallen by –7.9 percent (IMF 2010). The emerging economies, particularly the BRICs, were climbing. A World Bank report released in July of GDP by rank showed that China had risen from fourth to third, changing places with Germany. Brazil had jumped from tenth to eighth place and Russia from eleventh to ninth.

The G20 with its equality across established and emerging powers was the well-matched forum for global economic governance. The IMF and G8, in their current forms, were out of date and unrepresentative of the new world economy.

Democratic Convergence

The fourth cause of Pittsburgh's strong performance was the G20 members' continuing convergence on a commitment to domestic political stability and openness and their corresponding conduct at home (see Appendix L-2). The motivating memory of the 1930s and '40s, so centrally vivid at London, remained, even if the Pittsburgh Summit's location made the memory less geographically and temporally prominent. Still, in their effort to seek out a stable economic system and employment-generating recovery, most G20 members continued to cherish their common democratic character at home. The choice of Korea to host a G20 summit in 2010, and to be the first non-G8 member to do so, revealed that the G20 was driven not only by equalizing capability among its established and emerging members but also by the democratic character shared by almost all.

Political Control, Capital, Continuity, Competence, and Commitment

The fifth cause of Pittsburgh's strong performance was the adequate political control, capital, continuity, competence, and commitment of the G20 leaders themselves. Host Obama with his recent election and party control of both legislative chambers, remained very popular. Germany's Merkel, who was facing an election right afterwards, was popular as well. It was the second G20 summit for Obama. Indeed, all the participants had been to a G20 summit except for the newly elected Jacob Zuma of South Africa and Yukio Hatoyama of Japan. By the leaders' side were their experienced G20 finance ministers and highly capable officials. In the host US this team included G20 founder Larry Summers, now leading Obama's National Economic Council. His initiative on the fossil fuel subsidy was one sign of his significant influence.

Controlled Club Participation as a Network Hub

The sixth cause of Pittsburgh's strong performance was the G20's controlled club participation as a network hub. The first component, arising internally, was the enhanced sense of belonging of the non-G8 members to the G20 summit group. They increasingly conceived of the G20 summit as a valued club that they too could soon lead. At Pittsburgh, Korea, now with support from China and Japan, became the favourite to host and chair a G20 summit in 2010. Mexico decided it wanted to host one after that. Even China signalled it might wish to host and chair in 2011, although it subsequently ceded that spot to France.

The second component was the growing number of countries and international organizations that were present at the G20 summit at the hub. They included as summit participants—many for the third straight time—the leaders of Spain, the Netherlands, ASEAN (represented by Thailand), the New Partnership for Africa's Development (represented by Ethiopia), the World Bank, the UN, the IMF, the FSB, the WTO, the ILO, and the OECD. Thus the G20 at the summit itself was increasingly reaching out to embrace a growing number of countries and institutions to serve as a central hub of global governance. However, this growing number came at the cost of compactness, and the lesser-than-London private deliberative performance that came as a result.

The third component, arising externally, was the way closely connected plurilateral summit institutions were used by G20 members to advance the G20's work. The fifth Summit of the Americas was held at the end of April 2009. Its participants noted that they were committed to addressing the current economic and financial crisis. When the Shanghai Cooperation Organisation met in Russia in June, participants discussed the need for improved international cooperation to deal with the economic crisis. The first BRIC summit was also held in Russia in June, solidifying the emerging economies of Brazil, Russia, India, and China as a distinct group and bringing together one G8 and three non-G8 members that were all part of the G20. The BRIC leaders discussed the economic situation and referred directly to the G20, thus solidifying its significance even before the G20 had declared itself to be the premier forum for its members' international economic cooperation (BRICs 2009).

At the G8 L'Aquila Summit in July, similar references were made to the G20, to the leaders' commitment to the new institution, and to the commitments that had been made at the G20 (G8 2009). The Major Economies Forum also met on the sidelines of the G8 summit to discuss climate change. L'Aquila, with up to 45 heads present for its culminating session, allowed G20 leaders to intensify their interpersonal relationships, do so on a broadening array of issues, and hold what was in effect the third G20 summit before the Pittsburgh Summit was held (Brown 2010). The somewhat negative reaction of some G20 members to L'Aquila's expanded gathering reinforced their conclusion that their own compact group of 20 was a more valuable forum.

Conclusion

Pittsburgh was a strongly successful summit with some standout achievements on several counts. It showed America's global leadership under Obama. It bonded the new Democratic president to the new body, making it as bipartisan as it had become at the ministerial level, in reverse partisan order, from 1999 to 2001. The attachment of America and all its partners was seen in the leaders' decision to make the G20 summit the permanent priority forum for their international economic cooperation. The leaders expanded the hosting and chairing of the forum from the two Anglo, imperial powers of old to Canada as a G8 country and to Korea as a non-G8 one and non-BRICs one beyond. They also broadened the agenda to include social and human security affairs and, on the margins, the hard security of nuclear nonproliferation as well.

These impressive institutional accomplishments were accompanied by equally significant substantive policy ones. Pittsburgh produced the Framework for Strong, Sustainable, and Balanced Growth that would guide members' future efforts at serious, coordinated macroeconomic and structural reform. Leaders agreed that 5 percent of the IMF quota would be shifted to rapidly rising states. And for the first time at a G20 summit leaders acted meaningfully on energy and the natural environment, with the promise to phase out fossil fuel subsidies.

These successes were driven by the sheer scale of the 2008 financial crisis and its follow-on economic shocks and by the fragility of the economic recovery just starting to appear. They were also fuelled by the willingness of more multilateral organizations and the G7/8 to allow and support the G20's economic lead, and the eagerness of the rapidly rising, emerging economies to address key economic issues through this group of equals. The leaders' common commitment to social stability through greater political openness and Obama's high political control and capital during his electoral honeymoon also helped. Of increasing importance was the growing attachment of virtually the same leaders, almost all meeting for the third time in less than a year, to one another and to their group as "their" central economic forum for good.

References

BRICs. 2009. "Joint Statement of the BRIC Countries' Leaders." Yekaterinburg, June 16. Available at: www.brics.utoronto.ca/docs/090616-leaders.html. Accessed: July 2012.

Brown, Gordon. 2010. *Beyond the Crash: Overcoming the First Crisis of Globalization*. New York: Free Press.

Donovan, Paul. 2009. "What Is the G20 Really Fighting For?" *Jakarta Post*, October 19.
G7 Finance Ministers and Central Bank Governors. 2009. "Statement of the G7 Finance Ministers and Central Bank Governors Meeting." Washington DC, April 24. Available at: www.g8.utoronto.ca/finance/fm090424.htm. Accessed: July 2012.
G8. 2009. "Responsible Leadership for a Sustainable Future." L'Aquila, Italy, July 8. Available at: www.g8.utoronto.ca/summit/2009laquila/2009-declaration.html. Accessed: July 2012.
G20. 2009a. "G20 Leaders Statement: The Pittsburgh Summit." Pittsburgh, September 25. Available at: www.g20.utoronto.ca/2009/2009communique0925.html. Accessed: July 2012.
G20. 2009b. "Global Plan for Recovery and Reform." London, April 2. Available at: www.g20.utoronto.ca/2009/2009communique0402.html. Accessed: July 2012.
G20 Finance Ministers and Central Bank Governors. 2009a. "Declaration on Further Steps to Strengthen the Financial System." London, September 5. Available at: www.g20.utoronto.ca/2009/2009banking0905.html. Accessed: July 2012.
G20 Finance Ministers and Central Bank Governors. 2009b. "Meeting of Finance Ministers and Central Bank Governors: Communiqué." London, September 5. Available at: www.g20.utoronto.ca/2009/2009communique0905.html. Accessed: July 2012.
Giles, Chris. 2009. "Finance Ministers Fall Short on Global Aims." *Financial Times*, November 9.
Guerrieri, Paolo. 2010. "Multipolar Governance and Global Imbalances." *International Affairs* 86(3): 681–92. doi: 10.1111/j.1468-2346.2010.00905.x.
Guha, Krishna. 2009. "Africa's Plea for Poor to Be Heard." *Financial Times*, September 26.
Helleiner, Eric. 2010. "A Bretton Woods Moment? The 2007–2008 Crisis and the Future of Global Finance." *International Affairs* 86(3): 619–36. doi: DOI: 10.1111/j.1468-2346.2010.00901.x.
International Labour Organization. 2009. "Promoting People, Promoting Jobs: A Survey of Country Employment and Social Protection Policy Reponses to the Global Economic Crisis." A report submitted to the G20 Leaders' Summit, Pittsburgh, 24–25 September, Geneva. Available at: www.ilo.org/public/libdoc/jobcrisis/download/protecting_people_promoting_jobs.pdf. Accessed: July 2012.
International Monetary Fund. 2010. "World Economic Outlook: Recovery, Risk, and Rebalancing." October, Washington DC. Available at: www.imf.org/external/pubs/ft/weo/2010/02/. Accessed: July 2012.
Johnson, Steven C. 2009. "G20 Means G7 No Longer Only Game in Town on Currencies." Reuters, September 29.

Joicey, Nicholas and Pickford, Stephen. 2011. "The International Monetary Fund and Global Economic Cooperation." In *New Economic Diplomacy: Decision-Making and Negotiation in International Economic Relations*, eds Bayne, Nicholas, and Woolcock, Stephen. Farnham: Ashgate, 283–302.

Kirton, John J. 2009. "Prospects for the Pittsburgh G20 Summit." *IBFed Newsletter*, Summer, pp. 3–4. Available at: www.g8.utoronto.ca/g20/biblio/kirton-ibfed.pdf. Accessed: July 2012.

Kirton, John J. and Boyce, Madeline. 2009. "Making History: G20 Governance from Pittsburgh to Muskoka." September 25. Available at: www.g20.utoronto.ca/analysis/2009performance0925.html. Accessed: July 2012.

Kirton, John J. and Guebert, Jenilee. 2009. "Prospects for the Pittsburgh Summit." In *The 2009 G20 Pittsburgh Summit: Sustaining Global Recovery*, eds Kirton, John J., and Koch, Madeline. London: Newsdesk, 28–29. Available at: www.g8.utoronto.ca/newsdesk/pittsburgh/kirton.html. Accessed: July 2012.

Organisation for Economic Co-operation and Development. 2010. "Government Final Consumption Expenditure in US Dollars." Economics: Key Tables from OECD, No. 2, December 13, Paris. doi: 10.1787/2074384x-2010-table2.

Payne, Anthony. 2010. "How Many Gs Are There in 'Global Governance' after the Crisis? The Perspectives of the 'Marginal Majority' of the World's States." *International Affairs* 86(3): 729–40. doi: 10.1111/j.1468-2346.2010.00908.x.

Sachs, Jeffrey. 2009. "America Has Passed On the Baton." *Financial Times*, September 29.

Winning, Nicholas and Parkinson, Joe. 2009. "G20 Fin Mins Come Up Short on Climate Change." Dow Jones, November 7.

Chapter 13
Containing the Eurocrisis, Toronto 2010

Introduction

The Challenge

The fourth summit of the Group of 20 (G20) was held in Toronto, Canada, on June 26–27, 2010. It was hosted and chaired by Canadian prime minister Stephen Harper. It was known that Korean president Lee Myung-Bak, whose country chaired and hosted the G20 finance ministers' and central bank governors' forum in 2010, would also host and chair the fifth G20 summit in Seoul on November 11–12, 2010.

The Toronto Summit was innovatively held the day after the Group of Eight (G8) summit in nearby Muskoka, leading many to focus on the relationship between the two groups and wonder if, and when, the newer, broader G20 might take over from the older, more exclusive G8. As the first summit after the leaders' Pittsburgh proclamation that the G20 was now the "premier forum for our international economic cooperation," there was intense pressure on them to live up to that ambitious label (G20 2009). Early in the spring of 2010, as the 2007–09 economic crisis receded, some felt that the G20 might also fade, as a crisis-response forum that had once succeeded but was now no longer needed. Yet when the first European sovereign debt shock from Greece emerged in January and then erupted in April, the Toronto Summit had a fresh financial crisis of its own to contain.

As it approached, the Toronto gathering seemed destined to be the most divisive summit to date. It pit the Americans against the Europeans on the questions of fiscal stimulus, exit, and consolidation, the Canadians against a coalition of Europeans and the United States over a global bank levy, and the advanced against the emerging members over controlling imbalances by making Pittsburgh's Framework for Strong, Sustainable, and Balanced Growth function well. While the G20 had successfully cooperated in unleashing large-scale, simultaneous stimulus when the 2008 crisis had hit, the effective exit strategies and fiscal sustainability now needed to contain the emerging Eurocrisis and support recovery were more difficult to obtain. Government spending comes easily, but cutbacks seldom do, especially before a robust recovery is underway.

Competing Assessments

These challenges gave rise to alternative forecasts in the commentaries leading up to Toronto. Some felt it was too soon to tell if Toronto would succeed. Sven Behrendt said that "the verdict is still out if the G20, facing singular national interests, can effectively translate principles into more concrete policies and develop a financial architecture that defends a dynamic global economy" (quoted in Dale 2010). Niu Xinchun similarly argued that it was easier for countries to reach agreement when they were all in crisis, but "selfish calculations" resumed once recovery came into view (quoted in Dale 2010).

Others felt that Toronto was a success before it started, due to its members' adjustment in advance, notably China's revaluation of its currency on the summit's eve (Subramanian 2010). Other "reinforcers" hoped that Toronto could advance climate change control after the failure of the United Nations at Copenhagen in December 2009 (McColl 2010). They also hoped that the G20 could erode some of the destructive bloc dynamics that existed within the UN system, give it and other international organizations some "healthy competition," and offer developing countries more involvement and acceptance of more responsibility (Patrick 2010). Some "replacers" saw Toronto as the moment when the G20 summit would take over from the G8 one (Currah 2010).

After the summit, the debate expanded into new schools of thought that now focused on Toronto's actual performance and the causes that lay behind.

Some saw failure in several forms. The first school saw the G8 gang up to impose its position on the larger G20, delay the developing countries' desired reform of the international financial institutions (IFIs), and fail to separate the agendas of the G8 and the G20 in a workable way (Garcia 2010; M.D. Nalapat quoted in Smith 2010). A second school saw failure in domestic political management and detailed decision making, due to disagreement among the members or simple ineptitude on their part (Masters 2010; Crook 2010; Schirm 2012). A third school saw the G20 making the wrong choice of austerity when the current growth and inflation figures and Keynesian logic called for stimulus instead (Makin 2010; Krugman 2010; Frank 2010).

A fourth school saw merely an agreement to disagree. This was due to the passing of the financial and economic crisis, lack of consensus on new dangers, the continuing dominance of markets over governments, the disunity of Europe, German chancellor Angela Merkel's dismal poll ratings, transatlantic rupture, the reluctance of the big states to cede sovereignty, the absence of effective and legitimate international institutions, and insufficient trust among the leaders (Stephens 2010; Roubini and Bremmer 2010).

A fifth school saw a mixed performance from muddled leaders. Martin Wolf (2010a, 2010b) identified steps forward and backward and a cautious shift to austerity, even though "in the first quarter of 2010, the GDP [gross domestic product] of every member of the Group of Seven leading countries was still below its pre-crisis peak." This shift to austerity was due to a global economy recovering more quickly than had been expected at London, the fiscal crisis in Greece, and the election of a Conservative-led coalition government in Britain. Moreover, policy makers only partially understood the interlinked nature of the problem, too often treated fiscal consolidation in isolation, and had a "widely held belief that this retrenchment will, via confidence effects, lead to a burgeoning of private spending," despite what the annual report of the Bank for International Settlements had said (Wolf 2010a). Sylvia Ostry (2010) saw useful progress on fiscal consolidation but doubted that it would be delivered, thought more was needed, and felt that Toronto failed on the big issues of creating a new institution for handling sovereign debt restructuring, imbalances, world income polarization, and climate change.

Several others saw success. A sixth school saw a G8-generated success, with "the old powers back in the saddle at Toronto" because they still accounted for at least 50 percent of the global economy, had much slower growth than the booming emerging economies and thus had the greatest need to adjust, and would not be bailed out by exchange rate changes from China (Pisani-Ferry 2010). Andrew Coyne (2010) expansively observed that in its economic consensus and commitments, the G20 at Toronto had become the new Organisation for Economic Co-operation and Development (OECD), as the G20's emerging economies adopted the principles and policies they had opposed when the Group of Seven (G7) had proposed them a mere 20 years before.

A seventh school saw a crisis-catalysed Canadian leadership success (Charlebois 2010; Clark 2010; Coyne 2010; Gotlieb 2010; Watson 2010). The needed tilt toward fiscal consolidation was accelerated by three factors: Stephen Harper as host, Canada's strong financial and economic position, and the erupting Eurocrisis. The Toronto Summit provided hard targets and timetables for fiscal sustainability, wisely rejected a bank levy, extended the anti-protectionist pledge, and created a comprehensive convergence on the Canadian model and international cover for Harper for any domestic austerity he might wish to impose.

An eighth school saw far-reaching success in crisis response (Kirton 2010b; Lee 2010; Stewart 2010; Lukov 2010a, 2010b). The Toronto G20 wisely put growth, jobs, and recovery first, calmed jittery markets with a pledge to cap deficits and debts in the medium term, advanced banking regulation, rejected the bank levy, forwarded the Framework for Strong, Sustainable, and Balanced Growth, reformed IFIs and especially the World Bank, came to sensible conclusions on financial safety nets and development, induced its largest members to adjust in an appropriate way, and solidified the role and status of the G20 as its members' premier economic forum. This was due to the spreading Eurocrisis, the uneven and uncertain global economic recovery, the looming deadlines for the Seoul Summit in November, and the successful division of labour between the G20 and G8.

The Argument

This chapter argues that the Toronto Summit was a strong success, especially in its core tasks of crisis response and macroeconomic policy management. It clearly affirmed the appropriate balance of stimulus now, exit soon, and fiscal consolidation a little later in order to convince markets to move back from the brink of a new global financial crisis erupting in the eurozone from Greece and to sustain the fragile recovery then underway. Toronto further provided momentum on the framework, sound bank regulations, anti-protectionism, and a new thrust on corruption, development, and financial safety nets. This performance was driven by the immediate second financial shock now from the eurozone, and now in the form of sovereign debt. It was reinforced by the slow progress of other bodies such as the Basel Committee on Banking Supervision (BCBS), and the solid political control of most leaders. It further flowed from the high continuity, competence, and personal commitment of host Stephen Harper, a professional economist devoted to balanced budgets, and veterans Nicolas Sarkozy from France, Angela Merkel from Germany, and Manmohan Singh from India. Moreover, the twin G8 and G20 summits induced the two bodies to work together in ways that strengthened the G20's position as a global network hub and as a group steadily moving toward becoming its leaders' valued club.

Plans and Preparations for Toronto

Negotiating the Chair

The decisions about when and where to hold the next G20 summit had been announced at Pittsburgh. There had been substantial negotiations about this long before. These had led to the unusual arrangement of holding the next G20 summit in tight tandem, in time and space, with the long scheduled G8 one. The first three G20 summits had been held in the US, in Britain, and in the US again. This exclusively Anglo-American hosting sequence seemed incongruent for a group of 20 equal members, especially when the centre of global economic power was shifting from the Atlantic to the Asia-Pacific region and from the established to the emerging powers in the world.

In the lead-up to the first summit in Washington, Japan had offered to host the next G20 summit and promised $100 billion in emergency loans for the International Monetary Fund (IMF). At London, where it was decided that the Americans would host the third G20 summit, it was obvious to most—and even in the end to a France that was eager to host—that the fourth summit should be held in Asia. Korea offered to host and received support from both Japan and China. All accepted the logic, especially as Korea was already scheduled to host the G20 finance ministers and bank governors in 2010. Korea proposed to hold the summit in April 2010, the same month as the London Summit the year before. Thus, as the

Pittsburgh Summit approached, it seemed likely that the next G20 summit would be in Korea in April 2010 (Lee 2009).

Barack Obama, however, had been planning to host a special, single-issue summit on nuclear security that would bring the leaders of up to 35 countries to Washington in the spring of 2010. The Americans first thought they might hold this summit in March but later settled on April. The same leaders were not likely to travel twice in the same month to both Washington and Korea. There was a broadly shared desire among G8 and G20 leaders to reduce the number of such meetings and the travel time involved. The US suggested that Korea host the G20 in February. Lee Myung-bak felt that was too soon.

The Canadians, as host of the G8 summit in Huntsville, Ontario, long scheduled for June 25–27, 2010, already knew that they would be working closely with Korea as the 2010 host of the G20 finance forum. They began discussions with Korea at an early stage. The relationship was good, aided by Leonard Edwards, Harper's sherpa for both the G20 and G8, who had formerly served as Canada's ambassador to Seoul. Harper and Lee met at the G8 L'Aquila Summit in July 2009, which Lee attended as a member of the Major Economies Forum (MEF). In their exploratory discussions they acknowledged the need for close cooperation between Canada as host of the G8 and Korea as chair of the G20 in 2010.

The Italians had held their G8 summit sandwiched between two G20 summits in April and September 2009. The L'Aquila G8 were thus caught in the middle of an economic discussion at a larger table. The Italians reacted by inviting many non-member leaders to their G8, up to 45 on the third day. The Canadians and others felt that this formula did not work. Canada gave much thought to finding an alternative that would still make the G8 worthwhile and valuable. The Canadians examined various ideas. The G8 summit dates had been announced and Canada could not move them. Canada knew there would be at least two summits—a G8 and a G20 one—in each of the following years. If one stuck with a six-month schedule for holding the G20 summit, which everyone thought would be necessary, that would leave Canada in the same position as the Italians, with its G8 summit in the summer of 2010 sandwiched between two G20 ones in the spring and fall. Canada concluded it needed a negotiated solution to the dilemma this posed.

On September 3–4, 2009, Edwards travelled to Korea for meetings with the Korean presidential administration. He returned to Korea in November. Several countries did not want to have too many summits. Some G8 countries, particularly the Americans, did not want three separate "G" summits in one year. If there were going to be three, they only wanted to travel twice. At the September meeting, with Harper's agreement, Edwards offered the formula whereby, given that Korea was chairing the G20 ministerial process for all of 2010, Korea would hold its G20 summit one year after Pittsburgh, and Canada would host a G20 summit back to back with the G8 one. The two would work together throughout 2010. Korea was attracted by the logic and Canada played on its good bilateral relationship. Harper was due to visit Korea in December.

At the sherpa meeting to prepare for Pittsburgh, held in Washington two weeks later, Il SaKong, Lee's chief financial advisor, came to meet Edwards and the Americans. After Il and Edwards met, the concept of their dual hosting seemed likely to secure Lee's approval. They then moved to the issue of timing. Edwards had successfully consulted with his colleagues by telephone to get support for the dual hosting concept.

Canada's hosting was then caught up in a larger discussion about who would host next. Sarkozy wanted to host the G20 in 2011 to launch his re-election campaign. With the French now in play, the Chinese became even more concerned. They saw G20 summits in Washington, London, Pittsburgh, then Canada, and next Korea. Until the G20 sorted out whether France would be the next host, China did not want to give a green light on Canada as host in 2010. At a UN meeting between Hu Jintao and Sarkozy, the Chinese agreed that France would host 2011. China backed off its bid to host because France had already secured the support of the United States, using the argument that Sarkozy needed to host in 2011 as part of his presidential re-election bid. China had argued that hosting should rotate either alphabetically by country name or by continent. But France had already assembled the support of 13 G20 members for its bid. China decided to support France as well.

The Mexicans then decided at Pittsburgh to seek the 2012 slot. Their competitors included Turkey as well as China, which hinted about its intentions at sherpa meetings. Russia had also mentioned at Pittsburgh that it wanted to host at some point. But it was not until the sherpas met in January 2010 in Mexico City that they tackled the issue in more detail. In the end, it was agreed that France would host the G20 summit as well as the ministerial process in 2011. With Canada hosting the G8 in 2010, and France also hosting the G8 in 2011, some felt this might have been a trade-off for these two upcoming G8 hosts having agreed at Pittsburgh to make the G20 the primary, permanent forum for its members' international economic cooperation. Those who shared that view felt that the G20 hosting rotation between developed and emerging countries would come soon enough, as it had for the finance ministers and central bank governors.

During Harper's visit to Korea in December, he and Lee held a more detailed discussion in the Blue House in Seoul. Harper told Lee that Canada would hold the G8 summit before its G20 one, as security and logistics dictated. Lee was comfortable with the decision although his officials were more concerned. Lee declined Harper's offer, made at Pittsburgh, that the two co-chair the Canadians' G20 summit as it would be too cumbersome. In response, Harper gave Lee preference in the speaking order for Toronto and allowed him to conclude the summit with a welcome to Korea. At the end of their meeting, on December 7, Harper publicly announced that the summit would be held in Toronto on June 26–27, with a subsequent summit to be held in Seoul in November (Office of the Prime Minister of Canada 2009).

Holding two summits in 2010 helped cement the institutionalization of the G20 summit, and establish the distinct roles of and complementary relationship between the G8 and the G20 summits. The arrangement would also encourage the integration of the G20 summit and the Asia-Pacific Economic Cooperation (APEC) summit by having the new Asian-led process, headed by two democratic powers in APEC, work together to mount the G20 summit in Seoul on November 11–12 and the APEC leaders' meeting immediately after on November 13–14 in Yokohama, Japan. For these twin summits in Asia, the G20 one would go first.

Negotiating the Physical Arrangements

The decision to hold the next G20 summit in tandem with the G8 in June 2010 raised immediate logistical and policy questions. The Canadians considered mounting both summits at their chosen G8 site at the small resort city of Huntsville in the scenic Muskoka region of Canada. But it became clear that for security and logistics reasons, they would have to hold the much larger G20 summit in downtown Toronto, Canada's largest city. Toronto would be able to house the more than 30 delegations and many thousands of people who would arrive. Furthermore, once the decision was made to hold the G20 summit after the G8 summit, it would take place on the weekend, thereby minimizing the disruption to Toronto's downtown business core.

The issue of sequencing was a contentious one. The Australians, Brazilians, and Chinese felt that the G20 should be held first. The Australians—particularly those close to Prime Minister Kevin Rudd—kept the issue alive. Seeing the G20 as their institution, they were more sensitive about the role of the G8 and the sequencing order than many of the developing members of the G20. The Australians, along with the Chinese, argued that holding the G8 summit first would make it appear that the old group was determining the G20 summit's agenda and outcomes. The Russians, on first learning of Canada's plan to hold back-to-back summits, also immediately responded negatively. They argued that there should be a decent interval, not only so that the G8 would not be seen to be dictating to the G20 but also so that the G8 decisions would not be overshadowed by the G20's. The Indians, however, were far less concerned about the sequence.

For the Canadians, logistics took priority. Canada felt the sequencing could work well either way. On one hand, Canada did not want it to seem that the G8 was defining the agenda and deliberations for the G20. On the other hand, since the leaders of Brazil, Russia, India, and China (BRIC), as well as the EU leaders, met before on the eve of the G8 summits as caucus groups to develop shared positions, having the G8 leaders meet prior to the G20 might help iron out some differences among the G8 members. That would make the short G20 meeting more productive.

At the sherpa meeting in Mexico in January 2010—the first meeting after Harper's announcement of the dates—China and a few others formally raised their previous concern about sequencing. But this was simply to send a message. The Canadians assured all that the two summits would be separate and distinct, and that the agendas, not the timing, would tell this tale.

Negotiating the Policy Agenda

On the policy substance of the summit, Harper (2009b) had first publicly, although indirectly, signalled his approach in late September 2009, just prior to the Pittsburgh Summit. He later elaborated with a speech to the World Economic Forum in Davos in January 2010 (Harper 2010b).

In September Harper had declared that his summit should focus on the economy and on following up on the G20 commitments already made. This meant addressing the financial system, stimulus and exit strategies, trade liberalization, IFI reform, and the Framework for Strong, Sustainable, and Balanced Growth (Harper 2009a, 2009b, 2010a; Edwards 2010). Canada was cautious about expanding the agenda, believing that the G20 first needed to deliver its existing commitments. More generally, Canada wanted to work with Korea to ensure that their two summits were complementary. One idea was that there should be a different thematic emphasis for each.

In determining its agenda, Canada began with two key concepts. First, it wanted to recognize that the G20 was a different forum from the G8 so the agenda should reflect that fact. Russia supported this approach. Second, Canada emphasized accountability, as it was doing for its G8 summit. It felt that delivering on past promises was particularly important for the new G20 summit as a permanent forum.

The G20 had asked the IMF to prepare reports that would help guide the Toronto Summit. The IMF was increasingly the main international organization that did the work for the G20 behind the scenes. It established the baseline for measurements and helped set the tone of the communiqués. For Toronto, the G20 had asked the IMF for a report on the global economy, an update on the Mutual Assessment Process (MAP) called for in the framework, and a frank report on IFI voice-and-vote reform.

The other issues included climate finance, particularly after the failures on this issue at Pittsburgh in September, at the G20 finance ministers' and bank governors' meeting in St. Andrews in November, and at the UN climate change conference in Copenhagen in December. Also considered for the Toronto agenda were energy subsidies, innovation, green growth, and employment.

St. Andrews Finance Ministers' and Central Bank Governors' Meeting, November

Preparations for the Toronto Summit began in practice at the regular annual meeting of G20 finance ministers and central bankers, hosted by the 2009 British chair in St. Andrews, Scotland, on November 6–7, 2009. The meeting was opened by British prime minister Gordon Brown. He put several bold proposals on the table, including a global bank levy (Brown 2010). This was opposed by those many G8 and G20 members whose banks had not failed. Russia supported any European and US move to impose such a tax on their own banks, calculating it would cause those banks to move to Russia to help build the global financial centre that Russia desired there.

Prior to the meeting Canada's minister of finance Jim Flaherty and US treasury secretary Tim Geithner had told Britain's chancellor of the exchequer Alistair Darling that Canada opposed a bank levy. To Darling's obvious discomfort, Brown's address at St. Andrews called strongly for such a tax. Brown then went before the media in Britain to repeat the call. Geithner was left to say politely that he did not think that Brown had done his political homework properly.

With the Americans now supporting a different form of bank levy and the Japanese remaining silent, Canada was the only G7 member left to oppose a uniform, global levy of the sort Brown had proposed. Canada argued, in a way that appealed to the emerging G20 members led by China and Indonesia, that a one-size-fits-all bank levy did not, in fact, fit all and that they should not have to pay, as none of their banks had failed at home. For the rest of 2009 and well into 2010, it appeared that the bank levy would be the most controversial issue that Toronto would have to address.

Much time at St. Andrews was taken by the ministers, and by their deputies immediately before, on the divisive issue of climate finance. They had little to show as a result. Exit strategies also took up much time.

Another focus was the framework. It was to be developed, the St. Andrews' ministers and bankers promised, in a way that was consistent with "efficient and resilient financial systems" as well as several other policy objectives (G20 Finance 2009). But no guidance was offered on how the links were to be forged.

There was discussion of strengthening financial systems, notably prudential supervision, identifying systemically important institutions, and dealing with tax transparency. Participants recognized that these and other elements all had to be part of a new framework. The St. Andrews communiqué dealt with financial regulation in only one of its seven paragraphs, which addressed bank capital, compensation, resolution regimes, and tax havens.

St. Andrews released a detailed 37-page progress report on the implementation of the work plan flowing from past G20 summits (UK Chair of the G20 2009). Of the 93 promises reviewed in this report, 54—well over half—dealt with financial regulation. The G20 system was thus moving steadily to improve accountability across the broad range of financial regulatory reform.

But such movement was compromised by the unilateral defections of some leaders, central banks, and legislatures from G20 commitments. These defections had arisen within days of the first G20 summit in the trade field. In the autumn of 2009 they had spread to monetary policy, with Australia unilaterally exiting from its monetary stimulus by raising its policy interest rates three times. In the lead-up to Pittsburgh there were unilateral defections over compensation from the Netherlands (an invited G20 participant). In the wake of St. Andrews, both Britain and France unilaterally imposed levies on bankers' bonuses, beyond the consensus and schedule that the G20 had agreed. Within the US, Japan, and the EU, moves toward strengthening and standardizing other financial sectors, including accounting, stalled.

The dynamic was evident in the traditional, well-understood area of banking capital. On December 17, 2009, the BCBS (2009b) released the consultative draft of its requested report on new rules for banking capital. While the US and Britain had sought a rapid move toward a higher level, Japan, France, and Germany had the committee declare it would "put in place appropriate phase-in measures and grandfathering arrangements for a sufficiently long period to ensure a smooth transition to the new standards" (BCBS 2009a). This suggested that the new rules might not come into effect for another 10 years, much longer than the G20 leaders had envisaged in their 2012 deadline. Together with other conditions, this slippage and uncertainty revealed that national preferences, notably the relatively poor quality of capital held by Japanese and continental European banks, were eroding the swift, strong collective action the leaders' sought. The leaders themselves would be required to return to this subject in 2010 to ensure that their Pittsburgh promise was kept.

As 2009 ended, growth and credit returned to most G20 economies. With them came a concern that the 2008–09 financial crisis and its impulse for unified action were rapidly wearing off. The eruption of new financial fears from Dubai and Greece and from Europe's banks only partially offset the return of confidence as 2010 began.

The Transition to the Canadian Host

The specific preparations for the Toronto G20 took place primarily at four sherpa meetings: Mexico City on January 12–14, Ottawa on March 18–19, the Spruce Meadows ranch just south of Calgary on May 24–25, and Toronto on June 23–24, just before the summit's start.

The Americans were slow to hand over the lead to the Canadians on institutional matters coming out of Pittsburgh. In following up on Pittsburgh, US sherpa Michael Froman wanted to ensure that the institutional decisions were taken forward. Edwards let Froman take the lead, as Canada and the US had a largely similar approach.

The Mexicans, as chair of the Group of Five (G5) of Brazil, China, India, Mexico, and South Africa had already called a meeting in Mexico City in mid January to discuss the G8 and G5's Heiligendamm–L'Aquila Process (HAP), which was the dialogue between the two groups launched at the 2007 German-hosted G8 Heiligendamm Summit and extended at the 2009 Italian-hosted L'Aquila Summit. Since 13 G20 members would attend that meeting, Edwards and Froman decided to call the first G20 sherpa meeting there to save on travel. Both the G5 and G20 meetings were chaired by Mexico's sherpa Lourdes Aranda Bezaury with Froman co-chairing the G20 one.

Sherpa Meeting 1: Mexico City, January As G20 hosts and chairs for 2010, the Canadians and Koreans agreed that the major item on the agenda for their meeting in Mexico City on January 12–14 was how to implement the leaders' agreement at Pittsburgh to make the G20 the permanent, premier forum for members' economic governance. The documents for the meeting were based on an American paper and a Canadian paper, both produced after the Pittsburgh Summit, which together provided a checklist of issues for the sherpas to discuss.

The most important agreement reached at Mexico City was the decision to stop talking about summit architecture and focus on substance, including delivering the promises already made. Edwards made it clear that Canada in 2010 would make a sharp separation between the G8 and G20 agendas and that Harper was determined that the G8 would not issue a statement on the economy (Harper 2010b).

Mexico proposed issuing an immediate statement on the earthquake that had struck Haiti on January 12. The sherpas engaged in a brief debate. While no one suggested that it be issued by the G8 and not the G20, the Canadians initially objected because it would signal that the G20's agenda was expanding beyond the finance and economic domain. Yet all soon agreed, given the emotion of the moment, that it was more important to show sympathy. While the earthquake was not strictly an economic issue, it was a compelling humanitarian shock that was difficult to ignore. With 20 members already sitting around the table when the earthquake erupted so close by, all of whose representatives could make the decision, there was no reason not to act. The Russian sherpa phoned his presidency to secure approval, which immediately came. Mexico then changed the wording of the draft statement to reflect this consensus. The statement was issued in the name of the G20 members, rather than their leaders or sherpas specifically.

On the delicate issue of G20 membership and participation, there was no consensus on expansion. Some saw a need to develop a procedure for selecting candidates for inclusion. Some proposed that invitations to guests be sent only to those approved by an overwhelming majority of members, rather than at the discretion of the chair. In the end the sherpas agreed to recommend to their leaders that the G20 would have 20 members—the existing ones, including the EU—in part because it would be too complicated to change. The chair each year would be allowed to invite a few guests at its choice, but only for that year. The EU was in a special category as far as regional organizations were concerned. The Spanish attended the Mexico City meeting in their capacity as head of the EU. The Dutch did not. The closed, compact, controlled character of the G20 group was thus confirmed.

There was a very strong feeling among almost all the sherpas that the international organizations, including the UN, should not have an equal seat with G20 leaders at the summit table but should be present only when they had a direct stake in the issue being discussed. Later, as the Toronto Summit drew near, some of the same sherpas who had expressed this view in Mexico City had their ambassadors in New York dress down Canada for not inviting the UN secretary general. The question of UN participation raised other concerns. Members of the Global Governance Group (3G)—an initiative launched by Singapore at the UN for small and medium-sized members to channel their views into the G20 process—argued that the secretary general spoke neither on behalf of non-G20 members nor the UN membership, but only on behalf of himself and the UN secretariat.

The sherpas agreed that G20 leaders should engage more directly among themselves at the summit. Some sessions would be held among the leaders only, without their finance ministers or central bank governors at their side. Communiqués would be short, clear, and concise so that the public could understand what was promised and could monitor the results. A two-member team, perhaps of the current and incoming chair, would be tasked to track compliance. A public G20 website would be created to report on compliance on an ongoing basis.

With the emergence of the G20, there was little need for the HAP. Mexico and some others sought support for continuing the process. At the HAP meeting, Aranda tried to move it forward so it could hand off its work to the G20. Mexico, and to some extent the Germans, as its originators in 2007, and the Italians, as its extenders, as well as the OECD, had been doing their best to keep it alive. They had been calling meetings without any authority, producing a confusing situation.

But the majority of HAP and G8 members were opposed. The overwhelming view was that with the advent of G20 summitry, the relationship between the emerging countries and the G8 ones had changed profoundly. China was adamant that there no longer was a G8-centred solar system, with the G8 as the sun deciding which countries would revolve around it as rotating or selective invitees. Rather, there was now and should only be a G20 with all members participating equally to discuss issues they chose and not just the ones selected by the G8 or even the G5. Russia, as a member of the G8, BRICs, and HAP, had initially welcomed the HAP as a way of accommodating more fully the interests of emerging countries. Russia had participated fully in all four HAP working groups. But by early 2010 Russia had concluded that the groups produced results that were more political, symbolic and declaratory than concrete. Russia thus joined all its BRIC partners in insisting that with the G20 summits now institutionalized, the HAP "solar system" must end. The US agreed. Mexico and South Africa, both HAP members but not BRIC members, were reluctant to let the HAP go. Canada, as a friend of Mexico, and many others were open to a sensible handover of some of the HAP work to the G20, but China's hard line put an end to this possibility.

It was suggested that G20 working groups be created. But this idea was refused, largely on the grounds that that the HAP's ones had not worked well, that working groups needed resources, and that the G20 should focus on its core agenda of financial reform. The Chinese and the Indonesians vehemently opposed a proposed G20 working group on intellectual property. The Koreans suggested a meeting of G20 officials to deal with migration, to prepare for their summit in November.

In the end, the sherpas determined that the HAP working groups' reports would be delivered to the G20 in Toronto, rather than to the G8 in Muskoka as initially intended. Then the Toronto G20 would decide whether to create G20 working groups to advance these issues.

On the question of a G20 secretariat, it was felt that there was no need for one now but that there might be in a few years. In the meantime, there would be an electronic secretariat, which would be a private, secure website for discussions among the G20 members. A few months earlier, in the late autumn, bogus messages had been sent in the name of the Canadian chair.

The order for hosting and chairing future G20 summits generated an extensive discussion. One option was for the leaders to go in reverse order from the current formula used at the finance ministers' and bank governors' level, which had grouped the 19 hosting countries into five "buckets" (G20 2008, 130). Under this scenario, some members would not have to wait 15 years for their turn to host, when their current leaders would be gone. Another proposal, supported by many, was to alternate hosting between advanced and emerging members. Russia proposed using the existing buckets and the advanced-emerging member rotation, with no special place for the BRICs, given the confrontations that would cause.

Immediate interests soon got in the way. Under the bucket system, Mexico would host in 2011, with Russia or Turkey slated for 2012. Russia and Turkey both said they wanted to host before 2014, with the Turks preferring 2012. But Russia and Turkey were both in the same bucket. China indicated it was interested in hosting in 2011, but later backed away. Australia wanted to host by 2014 or 2015.

When France, at Pittsburgh, secured a general agreement that it would host both the G20 leaders and the finance ministers and central bank governors in 2011, a reverse rotation emerged. The French had privately arranged with the Mexicans to support their bid for 2012. Mexican president Felipe Calderón was eager to host in 2012 for domestic political reasons, since he would be stepping down by the end of 2012. If Mexico were chosen for 2012, Russia and Turkey would compete for 2013. It was only at Toronto that Mexico was selected for 2012, when Turkey withdrew.

There was also a discussion about the timing of the G20 and G8 summits. One G7 member unofficially suggested that the G8 summit be held in July and the G20 one in November. It was left to France to decide the timing for 2011. Russia argued again that it was more important that the summits be separated in time than which one came first.

Sherpa Meeting 2: Ottawa, March The second sherpa meeting took place in Ottawa on March 18–19. It focused on Toronto's agenda, addressing policy substance for about 80 percent of the time. Yet it also dealt with the summit architecture and operation again. As at Mexico City, most of the architecture discussion dealt with participation. The consensus from Mexico City that membership would stay at 20 remained.

In considering the summit's agenda, the sherpas had available to them the results of an experts' meeting held in Ottawa the previous day, attended by Len Edwards, several senior members of the Korean team, and invited nongovernmental experts. The group's discussions were catalysed by research papers commissioned by both the Canadian and Korean sides (Canada-Korea G20 Seminar 2010).

The sherpas discussed institutional issues over dinner at the Museum of Civilization. Here the Mexico City package took harder shape and was more or less accepted. While participation and the upcoming chairs were issues that the sherpas could not conclusively resolve, a consensus to invite up to five participants emerged. It was agreed that there should be more representation from Asia and Africa. Spain, which was again at the meeting, was more or less accepted as a guest. That left two other seats, to be chosen by the chair. While not everyone agreed, the sense among the sherpas was that this formula would work. Those who did not like it would not be very upset about the chair acting on it for Toronto.

Canada used its prerogative as chair to make the decision for Toronto. It would invite a limited number of guests to meet a few objectives. The first objective was to increase the presence of Africa. Harper invited Ethiopia as the chair of the New Partnership for Africa's Development (NEPAD). NEPAD had been at previous summits. He also invited Malawi as the head of the African Union (AU), a first for both the country and the organization. For the second objective of increasing Asian representation, Harper invited Vietnam, the chair of the Association for Southeast Asian Nations (ASEAN). This was the third summit to which ASEAN's chair had been invited. Neither of these invitations were contentious.

The third objective was to deal with Europe. At Mexico City, there had been a discussion and clear desire among the sherpas that there should be fewer Europeans than the eight at Pittsburgh. The complexities of the EU and the recent Lisbon Treaty produced a chair, which was Spain, plus the president of the European Commission, which was José Manuel Barroso, and now a new president of the European Council, which was Herman Van Rompuy. The suggestion was made to scale back the European representation to seven or even six, given that there were already four permanent European members—Italy, Germany, France, and the UK—in the G20. From the beginning in 1999 there had been 19 countries and the EU. The Dutch and Spanish had been invited by George Bush to Washington, Gordon Brown to London, and Barack Obama to Pittsburgh. Now G20 members wanted Canada to tell these Europeans that they could not come. The Europeans suggested that the new European Council presidency and the commission presidency occupy one flag—two seats in one delegation. This would make five European "flags" plus the Spanish. Most non-Europeans still thought that was too many. However, the Spanish-speaking members and Brazil felt Spain should be present.

In the end, as chair of the European Union, Spain was invited as the fourth guest. For the fifth, Harper's officials offered several options. He chose the Netherlands, to the surprise of many. Some sherpas could not understand why he did, as it had been collectively determined that the Netherlands did not deserve a continuing place, although no European would say so directly. Some thought it was because the leader of the Netherlands was facing an election and considered continuing attendance at the G20 summit important for his electoral success at home. The leaders would also be joined by the heads of the UN, the IMF, the World Bank, and other international organizations.

As for the substantive discussion among the sherpas, Ottawa was a catch-up, coming six months after Pittsburgh. There was an update on the global economy that showed that the world was not yet in full recovery. The discussion touched on the question of continuing national stimulus measures. Canada had recently released its budget and was focusing the G20's agenda on continuing the stimulus as agreed.

The major item was a discussion on Pittsburgh's Framework for Strong, Sustainable, and Balanced Growth. This proved to be the trickiest substantive issue, especially given the politics over how much coordination there could be among its advocates. Canada's finance deputy Tiff Macklem and the Koreans took the lead. They brought in the IMF to strengthen the scenarios. Because the meeting preceded the IMF/World Bank spring meetings, the sherpas did not know where the scenarios from the IMF would lead. But they knew that they had to coordinate more than in the past—and to monitor the stimulus measures to see how well they worked. It was evident that many of the concerns expressed by China, which had initially considered the framework intrusive, were weakening. While Canada was getting good signals about the framework, much work still had to be done.

The session on the economic situation, the framework, and domestic financial regulation centred on Macklem's update. Canada wanted to convey the message that it was important not to forget regulatory reform, as Harper (2010b) had stressed in January at the World Economic Forum.

Although much had been happening behind the scenes on the issue of the bank levy, the issue did not take up much of the sherpas' time. They were waiting for the IMF's report due in April. Harper and Flaherty had been clear in public that Canada did not like the idea. It was regarded as an issue on which there were differences of opinion, to be worked on by finance officials.

The Eurocrisis was not directly discussed. The Greece situation was evident but not seen to be as fierce as it soon became. The March meeting thus set the scene, with the preparatory process for Toronto now well underway. The Canadian hosts were happy to come out of it with the sense all were working together to make the Toronto Summit succeed.

Following the meeting, the leaders of Canada, Korea, Britain, the US, and France, as the G20's pentarchy, sent a collective letter on March 29 to their colleagues to advance the "good progress" the G20 had made. The letter's theme was accountability and the need to implement the agreements already made. It covered growth and job creation, the framework, IFI reform, trade, clean energy and fossil fuels, and, above all, financial regulation. There was still no hint of the looming Eurocrisis or the need to confront it with a macroeconomic message with medium-term fiscal targets and timetables.

Sherpa Meeting 3: Spruce Meadows, May The third sherpa meeting took place on May 24–25 at the Spruce Meadows ranch, a 35-minute drive south of Calgary in Alberta. On the first day, the sherpas were scheduled to discuss the framework. But the erupting Eurocrisis captured their attention and clouded their conversation on all economic issues. On the second day, they discussed the other issues, including development, trade, fossil fuel subsidies, and food security. The Koreans distributed a draft paper on development, including the role of the private sector and the impact on the least developed countries. The sherpas agreed to recommend to leaders at Toronto the establishment of a development working group to prepare for Seoul. There was no sense that the Europeans were prepared to give up their IMF quota shares, as required to get the IFI voice and vote reforms done on time.

The sherpas were by now very much aware of the European difficulties on sovereign debt and European banks, and the lack of transparency. With the Europeans put on the spot, Canada's objective was to keep their feet to the fire but not to cause panic so that they could fix their own problems. The Europeans had taken some new steps to stabilize the situation and allocate more money with the help of the IMF. These were seen as useful.

After the IMF's April meeting, the scenarios for the framework were seen as too soft. Sherpas were waiting for new ones to come out in time for the meeting of the G20 finance ministers and governors scheduled for June 4–5 in Busan, Korea. The sherpas expected the choices to be stark. They intended to forge a consensus on policy measures for dealing with Europe's sovereign debt. There was much talk about fiscal consolidation and considerable differences of view. The Canadians and Europeans were united on its need, with the Europeans pushing hard and planning to take steps accordingly. The sherpas felt that the situation at the Toronto Summit could be very difficult as the crisis grew. Toronto was thus not just a stepping stone to Seoul but would have very important work of its own to do.

Spruce Meadows demonstrated that the crisis in Europe had refocused minds. None of the disagreements that could have erupted over the framework had done so. Even the Chinese and others were talking about the need to work together. The sherpas' sharpened focus would be even more evident later, after the British and German budgets came out. G20 members were moving quickly—in the case of Britain very quickly—to consolidate fiscally.

The discussion on the Framework for Strong, Sustainable, and Balanced Growth was now at a stage that required decisions. Resistance had previously come from China and, to some extent, Brazil. But now Brazil was facing a problem related to exchange rates. It was frustrated that China's opposition meant that the G20 could not mention exchange rates, not even at the summit. The Chinese had now come to terms with the fact that the framework and MAP were going to engage them as never before. The Indians, who had no banking problems at home, supported the Canadian approach that some countries needed to fix their banking system but also felt that too much blame was being put on the banks. They saw no need to over-regulate and opposed a bank levy.

The sherpas devoted time to several other issues. On fossil fuel subsidies, a group at the OECD had worked on a formula that did not go very far. As the sherpas delved deeper into the issue and finance officials were working with their energy colleagues, discussions extended into producer subsidies. Progress thus became more difficult. Producer subsidies were problematic for Canada, while consumer subsidies were not.

The Americans continued to try to get climate change onto the G20 agenda. The BRICs resisted. The World Bank proposed, as part of a paper on development, a passage on climate finance. The Indians objected, arguing that climate belonged to the UN and not the G20. The World Bank thus reframed the passage to cast it as part of development finance. The Indians accepted this, and it appeared in the Toronto communiqué as such.

Food security received a general reference. The sherpas touched on the Small and Medium-Sized Enterprises (SMEs) Challenge, but did not need to get involved as things were going forward on their own.

A discussion on development started. It aroused some of the "old speak" on development. The Koreans did not want the discussion to go in that direction but rather to be addressed with a priority on economic growth. The Indians and Vietnamese offered a little more of the traditional development rhetoric that still flourished at the UN and its Economic and Social Council.

The Korean paper on development proposed a partnership focused on the role of infrastructure as well as other issues. With Korea supported by Germany, the sherpas agreed to recommend that leaders establish a working group under the sherpas and a similar one on anti-corruption—the first time G20 working groups would operate outside of finance officials.

On financial safety nets the Koreans had convinced the British to join their cause. Out of deference to its 2010 hosting partner, the Canadians did not take a strong view, even though they felt that the issue needed careful consideration. Canadian experts said there was no real evidence that safety nets were needed or that governments ran current account surpluses to hedge against such risks. Countries did not deliberately self-insure. Yet the Koreans put it on the table and received support for moving forward.

The Americans raised the issue of anti-corruption. They felt that the UN Convention Against Corruption and the OECD Anti-Bribery Convention needed support. The discussion went beyond the topics of financial tax havens and terrorist finance, both already on the G20 agenda. Major efforts were needed outside the G8 on transparency. It was an issue to which no one would say no. It was important to the Americans. Canada came to support it.

On trade, Canada tried to eliminate nuisance tariffs and give duty-free access for the least developed countries. It ran into the usual resistance and could not come close to a consensus. Brazil's suggestion of a meeting of G20 trade ministers met with nervousness, including from the Canadian sherpa, because, some thought, he would have to organize it. In the end it was decided that the situation was not yet ripe for such a meeting.

Several international organizations were invited to Spruce Meadows to make interventions on specific issues, including the IMF's John Lipsky.

The Canadians had now made it known that they wished to drive toward fiscal consolidation. However, there was a clear tension among members (Schirm 2012). Among the finance deputies the division between the US and the rest of the G7, with Japan not being assertive, came out more strongly. Among the sherpas this division was more muted, and often overshadowed by the divide between the US and China.

Just before the Toronto Summit, Canada's team met with Harper to discuss the crisis in Europe, given his role as G20 chair. On June 17, a week before the summit, Harper sent his G20 colleagues a carefully worded letter highlighting the necessity of "getting [advanced countries'] fiscal houses in order" and calling for a promise to halve deficits by 2013 and stabilize the ratio of debt to GDP by 2016 (Reuters 2010). "It is imperative that we deliver credible and real measures that show we are committed to a sustained and durable recovery to the benefit of all," he wrote. "...Failure to deliver is not an option."

The hard targets and timetables on deficit and debt consolidation were always intended to apply only to the developed countries. Canada wanted Australia in that group and did not want to include those countries that from the outset needed to continue to stimulate while they could. The intention was never to put all the G20 in the same straitjacket.

Harper was taking a calculated risk. He did not shop this initiative around with other leaders in advance. He did use several calls to leaders inside and outside the G8 to gauge where different leaders were coming from. David Cameron, the new British prime minister, was talking about the need for austerity in Britain. Germany and the rest of the Europeans generally supported Canada's position. To be sure, Japan had concerns, not only at the prime ministerial level, where the very recently appointed Naoto Kan faced an upper house election in July in which the austerity message would be unpopular. Accommodating words were thus found for Japan. The general message received by Harper was to proceed.

Among all the discussions on this issue and despite a variety of opinions, Canada never encountered anyone who said this could not be done. To the contrary, everyone was willing to work together on it. Fiscal consolidation was seen as the right theme for the summit.

The selection of the targets themselves was viewed as appropriate ones that would work. People were working to make the initiative succeed. But the breakthrough would come only when the Americans signed on. The Canadians had been uncertain what their position would be. On June 16, Obama (2010) had also sent a letter to his fellow leaders arguing the case for "stimulus first," while leaving fiscal consolidation to the medium term. He was supported by Brazil.

Sherpa Meeting 4: Toronto, June The fourth sherpa meeting was held at the Metro Toronto Convention Centre in Toronto on June 23–24 immediately before the summit. Len Edwards chaired all the sessions. The finance deputies, who were also meeting, joined the sherpas in the afternoon.

The sherpa meeting was devoted to drafting the communiqué. As with the US, Canada as host had previously put out some preparatory papers, and one from the Department of Foreign Affairs and International Trade had been leaked to the media. But Canada kept its powder dry by not circulating a full draft until just before the sherpa meeting.

The dynamics at the sherpas' meeting at Toronto were not difficult. Some, however, felt that Edwards was not very accommodating in dealing with objections.

He often pushed things. Nonetheless, all understood that he was under pressure to meet deadlines.

On the first evening, the sherpas took a long time to work out what became paragraph four on the economy. Here balance was needed to identify the progress of the world economy, what the G20 as a group was trying to achieve, and why attention to fiscal consolidation for some was needed at the same time. The challenge was to identify the right balance between stimulating economic growth and controlling fiscal deficits and debt.

The Americans wanted a "stimulus first" message. This was easy to agree on as continuing with stimulus for 2010 was always part of the plan. But should the G20 continue to stimulate after 2010? The US sought strong references to the need for continued stimulus, so that they could take such action again. Canada argued that while stimulus should continue through the year, markets needed now to see signs that governments had plans to control their deficits once growth resumed. The Europeans wanted strong language that they must control their deficits now, as Germany and the UK had already moved to do.

The sherpa meeting was affected by developments at the finance deputies' meeting, which discussed the actual targets and the detailed annexes to the communiqué. The meetings were held in adjoining rooms, with some joint sessions. When the finance deputies came into the sherpas' room, the line was drawn. Mike Froman did not say much. But US finance deputy Lael Brainerd was adamant that the US opposed any emphasis on austerity, although she was less assertive than Obama had been in his letter.

Obama had redefined the issue as one of medium- to long-term fiscal sustainability, implying that the G20 should not be thinking about sustainability in the short term. That changed the outcome, so that fiscal consolidation became more medium term than it would have otherwise been. The US argued that recovery was not assured. It was not asking for a strong message, but arguing that the G20 had responsibilities for leadership.

As soon as it was known, from Obama's letter, that the US took a different position from the rest of the G7, there was the possibility of an alliance forming between the emerging countries, which usually did not coordinate their positions, and the US. However, there was never any such discussion among them. While Obama had always been consistent in his position, Sarkozy had been ambiguous in private. The US sherpa seemed to some to specialize in pushing the Chinese on everything.

The finance deputies' draft represented a compromise. The text veered toward "multitrackism"—everyone do their own thing with no coordination. Medium-term targets were suggested but were not binding. The sherpas were obliged to have the overall communiqué consistent with the appendices. In the end, the finance deputies worked out a fine balance that matched what sherpas had agreed to ahead of time.

On trade, the language was, as usual, carefully negotiated over a few hours. Canada secured consensus on the extension of the standstill for another three years and some good language on trade financing. The sherpas removed the reference to the end-of-year deadline for getting Doha done, as it was an unrealistic goal.

On development, in London in 2009 the G20 had asked the UN to examine vulnerability. The UN Global Pulse Initiative, launched in 2009, had not really delivered. In the meantime, other international organizations, particularly the World Bank, had been doing their own vulnerability work. British sherpa Jonathan Cunliffe, supported by UN sherpa Jomo Kwame Sundaram, secured for the UN one sentence in the final communiqué endorsing the Pulse Initiative. Argentina's proposal to double the allocation of special drawing rights at the IMF was quickly dismissed. The London allocations had not been fully used. The Argentineans, still violating their own IMF obligations, had little credibility.

As at the May sherpa meeting, the US tried to get the G20 to act on climate change. The BRICs objected. China, in particular, did not want to deal with the issue at the G20. The Chinese position had always been that countries should meet their obligations under the Kyoto Protocol and discussions should be carried out within the existing UN framework. Everything else was unacceptable. The Indians, from all the ministries other than finance, shared this vision. The sherpas of some of the smaller G20 members had received no instructions about how to deal with climate change at the G20. They felt that the G20 had a three-tier membership, with them in the third tier. Consequently, Ban Ki-moon's public priority for the G20 to advance climate change control at Toronto, proclaimed in Canada on the summit's eve, did not succeed.

Finance Ministers' Meetings: Washington, and Busan, June

To help prepare the summit, the G20 finance ministers and governors met in Washington on April 22–23 on the margins of the spring IMF/World Bank meetings and again in Busan, Korea, on June 4–5. They also issued a standalone statement in response to the European financial crisis on May 10, doing so one day after the G7 finance ministers had produced a more detailed one (G20 Finance 2010b; G7 Finance 2010).

In Washington, the G20 finance ministers cast aside their prepared agenda because of the Greek debt crisis that was beginning to erupt. The G7 finance ministers also meeting there had a frank and flurried discussion on the issue as well.

At Busan, some felt the meeting did not accomplish much (Wheatley 2010). Since the start of the year, both the G7 and G20 had agreed that a balanced exit strategy was necessary to keep the markets calm (*Financial Times* 2010). But the difficult questions regarding the timelines for withdrawing stimulus would be left to the sherpas and, ultimately, the leaders to decide. Canada prevailed in the bank levy debate: there would be no globally coordinated tax. Instead, individual countries could implement one as they saw fit (G20 Finance 2010a).

Another issue raised the question of whether the G20 should extend its agenda further into the political-security domain. At Busan and in the G20 finance process and sherpa meetings all the way to Toronto, Lael Brainerd suggested that since

Iran had been found in violation of its obligations set by the Financial Action Task Force and was financing terrorism, the G20 should identify it by name, as a prelude to imposing financial sanctions. All the others objected, some on the grounds that G20 communiqués had never singled out a specific state in this way. This view prevailed. All knew the real issue was whether the G20 would collectively support financial sanctions against Iran for its failure to meet its international obligations on its nuclear program. Brazil, Turkey, China, and India were opposed to such sanctions against Iran. Those that supported the substance of the US position on Iran also stood opposed, on the grounds that it would violate the G20's collective understanding not to address political-security subjects beyond terrorist finance and crime and corruption. Thus an informal, international institutional obligation of a procedural sort trumped the substantive policy preferences of the G20's most powerful member and its policy allies, on an issue where the high politics of peace and security were concerned.

Attendance

Immediately before the summit, there were a few alterations in the attendees. On June 2, Japanese prime minister Yukio Hatoyama resigned after only eight months in office. His finance minister and deputy prime minister Naoto Kan assumed office as prime minister on June 8. He attended both the G8 summit in Muskoka and the G20 summit in Toronto.

However, at Toronto the G20 leaders failed to match their G8 counterparts' perfect attendance record, maintained over the latter's 36-year life. Two leaders of members beyond the G8 chose not to come to the G20's fourth summit. On the Thursday before the Saturday evening summit's start, Australian prime minister Kevin Rudd was ousted by his governing Labour Party and Julia Gillard took his place. Gillard sent Wayne Swan, her new deputy prime minister and the former treasury secretary. Brazil's president, Luiz Inácio Lula da Silva, said he had to stay home due to heavy flooding in northeastern Brazil, and sent finance minister Guido Mantega. Lula was also thought to have waning enthusiasm for the G20, given its failure to advance Doha and its slow progress on reforming the IFIs and reducing imbalances. The influence of both countries suffered as a result.

The absence of two leaders, especially those who had been such leading figures in the G20 and who had at Pittsburgh just helped proclaim it as the permanent premier forum for their international economic cooperation, made it more difficult to reach this proclaimed goal.

G20 Compliance Momentum

As the summit approached, Harper's determination to make accountability its defining feature was reinforced by the rather modest progress its members were making in keeping the promises they had made at Pittsburgh. Compliance by the G20 with their Pittsburgh commitments was declining, compared to their delivery of their Washington and London ones, to a level substantially less than the G8 norm (International Organizations Research Institute and G20 Research Group 2010). Compliance with the G20 commitments by its G8 members was stronger than that by its non-G8 ones. Host Canada's compliance record was relatively strong (see Appendix H-3).

At the Summit

On June 26, the G8 leaders travelled from their rural resort in Muskoka to join their G20 colleagues in downtown Toronto. The G20 summit started with dinner discussions at the Royal York Hotel on the evening of June 26, and continued with working sessions at the Metro Toronto Convention Centre across the street the following day.

From Stimulus to Exit Strategies and Fiscal Sustainability

At the summit, Harper primarily sought agreement on reducing the ballooning fiscal deficits of developed countries. During the opening dinner, it appeared that his proposed targets and timetables on deficit and debt reduction might not be accepted. The dinner had been choreographed by Harper, who, as usual, had chosen which leader would speak on each subject in advance. Obama was unambiguous in arguing the case for continuing stimulus. His clearly stated priority was sustained recovery, because the recovery was not yet secure. Fiscal sustainability should thus come not in the short term, but only over the medium or long term.

Partly because of Obama's intervention, other leaders spontaneously revised their prepared remarks. All knew their positions and did not abandon them. But Sarkozy, looking for eye contact and approval from his colleagues, was very ambiguous in his remarks. Cameron, attending his first summit and also trying to make eye contact with everyone, was ambiguous as well.

Argentina's Cristina Fernández de Kirchner was particularly critical of the European's emphasis on austerity. The European response came from Sarkozy, who gave a particularly energetic defence. Although she was very disciplined at Toronto, her remarks about the need for stimulus did not command much attention. Brazil's Mantega supported Obama, but he was not a leader, not a compelling speaker, and not fluent in English. The Chinese and Indian leaders both tended to speak in "party congress" style, reading their talking points. Singh supported Obama. Other key emerging countries also expressed their concerns, arguing the pro-stimulus case.

Korea's Lee and Mexico's Calderón remained largely on Harper's side, but in a muted way. The IMF's Dominique Strauss-Kahn, who as usual had been invited to the summit, made balanced remarks that were almost indistinguishable from those of speakers arguing for fiscal consolidation.

After dinner, the negotiations continued among officials. Brazil and India, joined later by Argentina, indicated that they did not wish to be bound by any emphasis on fiscal consolidation. Edwards and Macklem told Harper that opposition to his signature initiative was mounting. Harper then activated his allies in Europe. He got Merkel to speak out publicly the first thing the next morning to say that the leaders had a deal on fiscal consolidation. He also spoke with Sarkozy, lining him up to make a forceful statement stressing the importance of fiscal consolidation at the morning session (Curry et al. 2010).

The next day, before the morning session, Merkel spoke to reporters, praising the draft communiqué and its specific proposals on fiscal consolidation. A little later Sarkozy addressed the leaders, urging them to instil confidence in investors that G20 countries were serious about tackling their deficits and debt (Curry et al. 2010). This combined backing from Germany and France, plus the support of Britain, whose prime minister had recently announced a serious deficit-reducing budget, brought several other countries onside. Russia's Dmitri Medvedev spoke, having been asked by Harper two months before to serve as one of the first interveners on this subject. Russia had a real stake in the issue, given the interdependence caused by the crucial concentration of Russia's exports on the European markets and thus its economic health. Japan, however, still did not wish to be persuaded to sign any austerity agreement for itself, due to its very high deficit and debt and its poor growth prospects.

In the end, an agreement was reached on the basis of what Harper had proposed: the numerical timetables and targets for debt and deficit reduction for the developed countries that he had formulated would go into the final communiqué, along with language that would exempt Japan. All developed countries except Japan thus committed to cut their deficits in half by 2013 and to stabilize or reduce their debt by 2016 as a share of GDP by. A few additional points addressed the differences about whether deficit spending or deficit cutting was the bigger risk to the fragile economy. The measures would be "tailored to individual country circumstances" and there would be no sanctions for countries that failed to meet the targets (G20 2010). Sarkozy noted that the measures were voluntary, and that each country would produce its own deficit-reduction plan. The agreement was about coordinated policies, not common ones.

With this clear, credible, medium-term message on fiscal consolidation to calm markets spooked by the Eurocrisis, the G20 was free to highlight the "growth first" message desired by Obama and key emerging country leaders. The opening of the communiqué highlighted this message, which permeated the entire text.

Amidst this drama, there was little discussion at the leaders' table of the Greek crisis itself. All agreed on the importance of dealing with it, as all were concerned. But the Europeans were eager to portray it as a small issue that they could handle, without assistance or advice from others.

Financial Regulation and Supervision

The second significant task at Toronto was to strengthen G20 members' domestic financial regulation and supervision in a more comprehensive, forward-looking, internationally coordinated way (Macklem 2011a, 2011b). The summit succeeded in injecting new momentum into this work and highlighting several key areas, led by the need for new capital standards for banks. The G20 noted the progress of the BCBS and assured investors that the new capital framework that should be agreed on before November would have "significantly higher" levels of capital, of "significantly improved" quality (G20 2010). In fact, agreement on the Basel III accord was reached a few months after the summit, in September, much earlier than anticipated, in part a result of the Toronto Summit's push.

On the broader array of issues, with both chambers of the US Congress having passed a comprehensive financial reform package, the US was likely to serve as a clear referent that would make it possible for other countries to develop their own policies and for the G20 to create a collective position. An annex to the communiqué offered some specifics. But many of the technical details and the big decisions were left for Seoul.

On the divisive issue of a global bank levy, its rejection at Busan was confirmed in an even more decisive way.

International Financial Institution Reform

The third task for Toronto was to reform the IFIs. The G20 had already pledged at Pittsburgh to shift at least 5 percent of the voting share at the IMF from the relatively shrinking established economies to the rapidly rising emerging ones. At Toronto, Medvedev spoke on this subject. It was a priority issue for Russia. The Toronto communiqué reiterated the Pittsburgh commitment and advanced the deadline for achieving it from the end of the year to the Seoul Summit in November. However, it did not indicate how the over-represented European countries would reduce their quota shares, and do so in ways that would help legislatures in all IMF member countries ratify the change. Nonetheless, in the end the increased pressure from the earlier deadline succeeded in getting the detailed deal done by Seoul, on the most difficult zero-sum issue the G20 faced.

Also important were the issues of expanding resources and improving governance at the IMF and the World Bank, and their role in any future large financial safety nets and support packages that countries within and beyond a fiscally embattled Europe might need. The summit made modest advances here. There was also a brief discussion of the IMF's mandate, which Korea had sought.

Toronto also celebrated the successful reforms for the World Bank announced in April. The Toronto Summit was effectively used as the pressure point to reach agreement on financing the regional development banks. More financing for the development funds of the World Bank and African Development Bank was agreed on. The G20 further agreed to write off all Haiti's official debt.

Trade and Investment

The fourth task was to liberalize trade and investment. This would fuel private sector-led growth and development, especially in the emerging and developing economies upon which future global prosperity would increasingly depend in a post-stimulus age.

The G20 leaders extended their commitment not to impose or raise barriers to trade and investment until the end of 2013, and to redress past protectionism moves. This extended date would bind, inter alia, the new US Congress due to be elected in November 2010.

In the trade discussion at lunch among the leaders alone, Cameron spoke first, at Harper's request. Cameron urged the G20 leaders to save the Doha deal. Obama responded that completing Doha would produce an increase of only one day's exports—which amounted to 0.03 percent of GDP. He added that Doha was not in the interest of the least developed countries. No one contradicted him. Merkel was particularly vigorous, showing her detailed knowledge of the subject. She asked Obama to clarify if the US position meant accepting everything that had already been agreed and just negotiating the few remaining points. WTO director general Pascal Lamy had proposed such an approach, with the additional outstanding items reduced to three, including subsidies and liberalization on environmental products and services. But the leaders agreed that the time to get Doha done had now come, by moving the negotiations into the end game.

They also endorsed regional and bilateral liberalization. The latter was a boost for Canada, which was negotiating a free trade agreement with the EU. It was also a boost for the Obama administration, which wanted to complete its own deal with Korea.

Development

Development was not addressed at length in the leaders' discussions. Yet it arose in almost every section of the communiqué. It was included prominently in the passage on the IFIs. There G20 leaders recognized their self-proclaimed compliance with the Pittsburgh promise to increase capital for the multilateral development banks by $350 billion. They noted the importance of ongoing reforms to increase transparency and accountability. The key task would now be ensuring that the multilateral and regional development banks had the funding needed to combat any economic slowdown and meet the Millennium Development Goals (MDGs) due in 2015. G20 leaders also created the Working Group on Development, tasked with outlining a development agenda and a multiyear action plan for adoption at Seoul (Bronnert 2011).

Climate Change and the Environment

Climate change was an issue that Mexico had insisted on placing on the G20 agenda. China agreed that Calderón could speak about the UN climate change conference that would take place in Cancún in December. Yet China remained adamant that climate change not be negotiated in the G20 forum, even as a supplement to the UN. The well-known Chinese position was that the G20 had been designed to deal with finance and should not discuss other issues, not even trade, as these were being dealt with elsewhere.

Climate change was scheduled to be discussed at lunch. However, at lunch the discussion on trade had lasted about an hour, leaving little time for other issues. When the topic of climate change finally arose, Calderón led off, at Harper's request. Calderón provided an update on plans and prospects for Cancún. Ban, who was present, admitted that Copenhagen had not been a success, but argued that the G20 must be more pragmatic at Cancún by not insisting on a comprehensive deal. Hu did not speak. All the other emerging country leaders who did, save for Calderón, supported China's position on climate change.

In summing up the session, Harper said it was clear that the UN process was a failure and that leaders had to look elsewhere for progress, to forums such as the MEF. He concluded by saying, with due respect to the UN secretary general, that there was no way the UN could make a deal. Harper thus had the G20 essentially endorse the American-invented and -led MEF. In their communiqué the G20 leaders merely thanked Mexico for hosting the Cancún climate change conference.

The leaders did reaffirm in the communiqué their Pittsburgh promise to phase out inefficient fossil fuel subsidies. But they did little to extend the definition or move the actual implementation ahead. They also noted their commitment to a green recovery.

The communiqué further referred, at Russia's initiative, to the accident at the Deepwater Horizon offshore drilling rig in the Gulf of Mexico in the United States. This was one of the worst ecological disasters in American history. Russia proposed the creation of a legally binding agreement on a marine life protection area, by working through a subgroup of the G20's Energy Working Group. Its proposal flowed from a broader Russian view that the G20 should begin with discussions, then move to consensus on principles, and then progress to decisions that could be converted into legally binding agreements and conventions in fully multilateral, legally authorized international organizations.

Financial Safety Net

The G20 agreed to establish a working group on financial safety nets. Korea had begun this initiative in July 2009. It argued that the Asian financial crisis of 1997–98 had led to a desire on the part of afflicted countries for self-insurance, with the result that, more than a decade later, Korea's foreign exchange reserves were 30 percent of its GDP and China's were 50 percent of its GDP. Britain had been one of the first supporters of Korea's initiative. Korea had sold the idea to others, one by one. There was still a long way to go. Yet already cooperation between a non-G8 member—Korea—and a G8 member—Britain—was leading the G20 into new fields. The working group was considered a significant step by Korea, which concluded that G20 members would not have agreed to it unless they were each ready to allocate bureaucratic resources to it.

To an important extent, this was a G20 reinforcement of what the IMF was already doing, including its work on precautionary credit lines and flexible credit lines. But the G20 had the potential to add more in ways that would further reduce the prospect of any Asian monetary fund emerging as an alternative to an international one, and reduce the instinct to self-insurance so that the Framework for Strong, Sustainable, and Balanced Growth and the MAP could more easily work.

Food and Agriculture

The issue of food and agriculture was shared by the G20 and G8. Toronto welcomed the launch of the Global Agriculture and Food Security Program, which was created to implement the G20's Pittsburgh pledges on food security. It also explicitly promised to implement the G8's L'Aquila Food Security Initiative and its principles. Both the Canadian G8 and G20 summits were thus used to help mobilize the promised money, and to apply the shared principles first specified by the G8, under Obama's leadership and the impact of the 2008 food crisis. The two groups thus worked well together in support of an American-led, shock-catalysed cause.

Corruption

Another advance came on corruption, an issue also shared by the G20 and G8. This US initiative, pioneered at Pittsburgh, saw the Toronto G20 leaders affirm the "rule of law." They also promised "to establish a Working Group to make comprehensive recommendations for consideration by Leaders in Korea" on issues that included "fighting corruption in the public and private sectors" and "protecting whistleblowers who stand-up against corruption" (G20 2010). These advances in good governance had a particular resonance in China as well as the US.

The Dynamic of G20 Diplomacy

The key outcomes achieved at Toronto were the result of issue-specific winning coalitions and adjustments that crossed basic G7/8 versus BRICs or emerging country divides (Schirm 2012). On the central issue of the macroeconomic message to contain the Eurocrisis, Canada initiated the position, the Europeans supported it, and the Americans, Japanese, Indians, and several emerging economies resisted. At the end, an exception was easily made for Japan. Obama's Americans accepted medium-term targets and timetables. Harper succeeded at the summit. Toronto's message succeeded in effectively containing the Eurocrisis for the following five months until the next G20 summit arrived, although it did not prevent other euro problems from erupting, in Greece and elsewhere. In the field of domestic financial regulation, on the divisive issue of a bank levy, the Europeans led, supported eventually by the Americans, but in the end were defeated by a Canadian-led coalition containing Japan, Australia, and almost all the emerging economies, with Korea trying to play a neutral, bridging role. This outcome showed that international institutions do make an autonomous difference in shaping outcomes. Had the bank levy issue been dealt with and decided at the G7 rather than the G20, the European-American coalition would more likely have won.

Dimensions of Performance

A systematic assessment of the summit's six dimensions of performance confirms the substantial success that Toronto achieved.

Domestic Political Management

In its domestic political management, Toronto's performance was strong. The declaration issued six compliments to member countries, far more than ever before (see Appendix D-2). Those compliments went to the US, the EU, Japan, Canada, Mexico, and Turkey. Four compliments thus went to the G8 and two to other G20 members.

The Toronto Summit, highly visible at home, immediately helped its host in the polls. Harper bounced from a pre-summit approval rating of 29 percent to a post-summit one of 31 percent. While this two-point gain was a very modest advance, Harper was the only G7 leader to enjoy any rise at all.

The media portrait of the summit's substance was generally favourable for its host. Most Canadian commentators felt that Harper's summit had got the macroeconomic approach and message right. The main message of halving medium-term fiscal deficits was welcomed by those leaders, such as Harper, Merkel, and Cameron, who wanted that goal, and by those such as Obama, who would be politically induced to join them soon. Indeed, Andrew Coyne's (2010) conclusion that the G20 converged on the Canadian model gave Harper the ideal assessment: the summit endorses what the host does and wants.

There were a few failures in domestic political management at Toronto. The first was the loss of the G20's perfect attendance record, as the leaders of Australia and Brazil chose not to come. However, their absence went largely unnoticed by the public and was not seen as a slight to Harper as summit host. The second was the response to the G20 on the streets of Toronto. The damage done to police cars and commercial property and the extensive arrests of protestors and bystanders commanded substantial attention in the local media, both at and after the summit itself. But as no one died at Toronto, unlike G20 and G8 summits before, the veteran global summit media corps sought their stories elsewhere. Subsequently, Harper felt sufficiently comfortable with Toronto's legacy and its media portrait that he chose to include his hosting of the G8 and G20 summits, along with the winter Olympics, in the list of Canada's annual accomplishments for 2010 that he featured in his 2011 New Year's Day address.

Less than a year after Toronto, in the campaign for the Canadian general election on May 2, 2011, the issue of Harper's hosting of the Toronto Summit arose recurrently, including in the televised leader debates. In the election, Harper's strongest critic of the Toronto Summit, Liberal Party leader Michael Ignatieff, saw his party fall from a strong second to a distant third place. Harper's Conservative government secured a majority for the first time.

Deliberation

In its deliberation, Toronto's performance was very strong on paper and, to a lesser degree in practice during the leaders' discussions. On paper, the 11,078 words in its documents were the most produced by a G20 summit thus far (see Appendix E). They had almost three times as many words as the first summit produced. The initial desire of the Canadian planners to produce only a two-page communiqué with some annexes had not survived the desire of the leaders, including Harper, to communicate to the world a message that was comprehensive, detailed, and thus credible and clear. Toronto also saw an important iteration and broadening of the G20's agenda. As about 80 percent of Toronto's agenda consisted of familiar issues, Toronto provided the desired bridge between the previous Pittsburgh and subsequent Seoul summits, while deepening the predictable and lengthening built-in agenda of the G20. The major additions came on the Korean-led new approach to development and Korea's other new issue of financial safety nets, both approved at Toronto as issues to be advanced at Seoul. The addition of development was important, given the need to supplement the G8's alleged focus on official development assistance (ODA) and to secure additional ODA donors from rising powers within the G20 beyond the G8 to contribute to the cause. In the views of some members such as Russia, given the tight link between trade and investment on the one hand and development on the other, the G20 was the proper place to deal with development in an effective way, as coherence between these two economic issues could be produced in a single place from the start.

In practice, as chair Harper ran a tight ship. An economist, he enjoyed the substance of the discussions very much. He chaired all the sessions. He intervened to make sure people stayed on time. Whereas at previous meetings, speakers had spoken too long, Harper imposed a five-minute rule on everyone. This system worked very well. Some interventions were spontaneous. Those who had speaking points, including Hu, Singh, and Lee, did not make long speeches. Unlike previous meetings when some might speak for as long as 15 minutes, this was a major advance.

There were fewer people sitting behind the leaders than anticipated, although there were still quite a few. The appropriate people sat at the leaders' table for the specific issue being discussed. Participants understood they were there to support country leaders, not as equals. Interventions were limited and pointed. Speakers exercised very strong judgement in how and when they intervened.

At the table in the meeting room and at the lunch and dinner there was more informality than in the past, if not any real spontaneous combustion. The trade discussion on the second day was the most relaxed and informal session, because leaders were siting close together in a small room having lunch. Generally, the summit itself was less staged than those before.

Still, with 33 leaders in the room it was difficult to get a real conversation going. When one person made a good point, someone else started talking about another subject. There was still an emphasis on political correctness rather than free, frank, and revealing exchange.

Direction Setting

In setting democratic directions, Toronto was a strong success (see Appendix F). It offered 12 affirmations of democratic principles and norms in its main declaration. This was a major decrease from the 29 at Pittsburgh, but higher than the nine at London and the same as at Washington. Here transparency came first with eight affirmations, followed by accountability with two, and the rule of law and openness with one each. Together with the annexes the leaders affirmed democratic principles 34 times.

Decision Making

In its decision making, Toronto was a substantial success. It produced 61 commitments (see Appendix G). This was fewer than all the previous summits, and the four-summit average of 93, but still a substantial number. A full 28 commitments at Toronto came on macroeconomics, reflecting the impact of the Eurocrisis from Greece. Trade, a Harper-Lee favourite, took 10 for second spot. Then came development in third with eight, domestic financial regulation with seven, IFI reform with five, and climate change with three. There were also commitments on accountability, socioeconomics, food and agriculture, energy, and good governance. There was thus considerable balance and substantial performance across the core economic domain.

Delivery

In the delivery of these commitments, Toronto's success was small. It seemed promising at the start. The commitments contained 18 of the catalysts that counted in raising G8 members' compliance with the commitments the similar G8 summit had made in the fields of finance and development, climate change, and health.

Setting specific medium-term targets and timetables for fiscal consolidation was considered by G20 members to be a major force in mobilizing compliance.

There were also several appeals to multilateral organizations to help monitor G20 compliance. But there was no other sign that accountability had, in fact, become a defining feature of the G20 summit as well as the Muskoka G8 one. Toronto did very little, relative to the G8's Muskoka Accountability Report and follow-on that the G8 summit twin had produced.

By late October, the Russian government's internal monitoring indicated that many G20 members were doing their best to fulfil their Toronto commitments. The UK was leading the way. Russia also saw itself as on track to exceed the medium-term fiscal consolidation target, by producing a balanced budget by 2014.

A systematic public assessment of the Toronto commitments by the G20 Research Group and Higher School of Economics, issued on the eve of the November Seoul Summit, showed a more modest performance (G20 Research Group and International Organizations Research Institute 2010). A broader assessment indicates that average compliance with Toronto's priority commitments was +0.28 (64 percent), the same as Pittsburgh's (see Appendix H-3). This suggested that the effect of the 2008 shocks were slowly and slightly wearing off in the delivery dimension, even with the new Eurocrisis from Greece. After Toronto, the G8 members of the G20 continued to comply more highly than non-G8 ones. Compliance with Toronto's priority commitments was led by Canada, the custodian of the summit's legacy, at +0.78 (89 percent). It was followed by the UK and Australia at +0.67 (83.5 percent), the EU at +0.57 (78.5 percent), and France, Italy, and Korea—the next host and chair—each at +0.56 (78 percent).

Development of Global Governance

In its development of global governance, Toronto was a strong success. Internally, the leaders' declarations made 71 references to the G20 as an institution, a substantial rise from the 47 at Pittsburgh. At Toronto there were 54 references to the G20 summit, 13 to its ministerial forums, and none to its civil society parts. Toronto announced that Mexico would be the chair and host two years hence, in 2012. It thus provided a two-year shadow of the future, and greater balance between the G8 and non-G20 members as hosts and chairs. In the new pentarchy, Mexico would immediately join Korea to work with France, Canada, the US, and the UK. The G20 also created its first working groups under the authority of the leaders with reporting through their sherpas, rather than through their finance ministers as before. At Toronto, the sherpas as well as the finance ministers had to approve any documents prepared from the finance side, as these were sent first to finance ministers and then to the sherpas for approval before being sent to the leaders themselves.

Externally, Toronto showed how the G20 had integrated itself as a steering committee into the landscape of international financial organizations. Its leaders' documents made 171 references to 28 other international institutions, a substantial rise from the 117 references at Pittsburgh. At Toronto these were led by the IMF at 35, the Financial Stability Board at 26, the World Bank at 19, the multilateral development banks at 16, and the BCBS at 12. Also featured were the IFIs at nine, the OECD at seven, the UN at six, and the International Labour Organization at five. There was one reference to the G8 and one to the Global Partnership for Agriculture and Food Security.

The G20 relied heavily on the IMF to provide reports on various matters and, in the case of the Framework for Strong, Sustainable, and Balanced Growth, to help support the general direction of the meeting. The IMF was also called upon to speak on every substantive item on the agenda except for trade. Dominique Strauss-Kahn spoke directly to the leaders on financial regulation, fiscal consolidation, the MAP, and progress on IMF reform. One senior official at the IMF noted that the sections of the 2010 communiqué on fiscal consolidation could have come directly from the IMF.

Toronto was the first G20 summit held in conjunction with the G8 one, tightening the relationship and network between the two. Despite Harper's clear desire to separate the agenda of the groups, there was considerable overlap. The G8 leaders spent the better part of their opening lunch discussing the economic situation, even if they made only slight reference to this subject in their communiqué. The communiqués of both bodies addressed trade, Haiti, corruption, climate change, development, and food and agriculture. Reinforcement of a somewhat reciprocal sort thus emerged.

Causes of Performance

Propelling this strong performance was the strength of many of the forces highlighted by the systemic hub model of G20 governance (Kirton 2010a).

Shock-Activated, Equalizing Vulnerabilities

First, the shock-activated vulnerability that produces a surge in demand for G20 governance and equalizes the vulnerability-capability configuration across all members arose in the lead-up to Toronto in several substantial ways (Masson and Pattison 2010) (see Appendix I).

In the finance-economic sphere, the aftermath of the unprecedented US-turned-global crisis of 2007–09 continued to be a concern. The weak job and housing markets in the US, the poor balance sheets of European banks that had not been stress tested, and, above all, the deepening fiscal deficits and debt burdens in Europe weighed heavily, even with a fragile and widespread recovery now underway. Both the UK and the US had acquired historically high peacetime fiscal deficits. Most G8 powers were still struggling from the consequences of the crisis, even if most other less-afflicted G20 members were booming once again.

As soon as G20 members had started to gain control of the financial credit crisis, in part through massive fiscal and monetary stimulus and direct financial support, a second financial shock struck in the form of sovereign debt and fears of rescheduling and default. Starting in the spring of 2010 in Greece, the contagion started moving to Portugal and Spain. It soon spread globally, moving from government debt to private financial markets and the real economy, with unprecedented speed and scope. It reached its peak in Europe on May 7–8 (Van Rompuy 2010). It immediately catalysed concerted EU action to assemble a financial support package that same weekend, a supportive G7 communiqué from finance ministers on May 9, and a shorter, more general one from G20 finance ministers on May 10. To be sure, this Eurocrisis was not as much of an immediate threat to the highly capable US, Japan, and China as it was to the European members of the G8. Yet as a contagious sovereign financial shock, it was readily recognizable to a G20 that had been created by a similar one in 1997–99.

The challenge in confronting this second shock, and the first one of its sort that had arisen in continental Europe, was compounded by the fact that the cure for the first—government spending—was the cause of the second. It was unclear how still struggling private firms and the market economy could now bail out crisis-affected G8 governments, in any reversal of the response to 2007–09. This second shock did bring G7 finance ministers quickly back into global financial governance in crisis-response mode, intensified ad hoc responses from the G20 finance ministers, and led the EU- and G7-controlled IMF to promise a major package—the second large springtime financial support package in as many years. Unlike London in 2009, however, this package was now offered only to one country in the developed world. The Greek-generated shock showed that Europe might now be as vulnerable as America in 2008 and Asia in 1997 had been.

This European-turning-global crisis added a new political dimension to the financial crisis, with the eruption of deadly protests in Greece and prospectively in Spain and Portugal along Europe's southern tier. The threat that such civil strife would attack the G20's core mission of maintaining financial and economic stability and thus social and political stability was muted by the fact that such protests arose primarily in the few OECD polities governed by left-of-centre governments. Elsewhere in Europe, notably in Britain, voters moved slightly to the right. Russia, whose democratic credentials some still doubted, stood with its new European and G20 partners, rather than siding with the troubled southern-tier countries and trying to lure them into a Russian sphere of influence, as the Soviet Union had during the Cold War when the Eurocommunism of the 1970s swept through Europe's south and helped bring the G7 summit to life.

In the energy-environment sphere arose the newest form of non-state shocks—natural disasters. Earthquakes in Haiti and Chile and the Icelandic volcano that grounded transatlantic air traffic reinforced recent memories of natural disasters from the G8 summit held in earthquake-devastated L'Aquila in 2009. Moreover, the great, deadly uncontrolled oil spill in the Gulf of Mexico that erupted on April 20, 2010, showed the vulnerability of many countries, and even the United States, to sudden, deadly, destructive disasters, both natural and human induced. The Gulf oil spill, and the resulting US ban on offshore oil drilling, compounded the energy-security vulnerability of the United States and other G20 members, and thus enhanced the relevance of Canada and Russia as energy superpowers. As a consequence, the 2010 Toronto Summit dealt with both Haiti and oils spills in its communiqué for the first time.

In the older security sphere, added to the ongoing war in Afghanistan was the unprovoked deadly North Korean attack on the Republic of Korea's *Cheonan* warship in March 2010. In the new security sphere, the narrowly thwarted terrorist attacks on an aircraft bound for Detroit on December 25, 2009, and in May on Times Square in New York City as well as the deadly assault on the Moscow subway that same month reminded all of how vulnerable both former superpowers continued to be. Terrorist finance thus reappeared in the communiqué.

Direct shocks were absent in the development, climate, food, and health areas. The outbreak of "swine" influenza that had erupted in April 2009 had faded by the summer and no new epidemic had arisen to take its place (Kirton and Guebert 2010). To be sure, the financial and economic crisis compounded the chronic challenges of food, nutrition, water, good governance, corruption, and vulnerable and insecure states. Escalating drug violence in Mexico was consistent with, if not a direct cause of, the initiative of its American neighbour on corruption.

International Institutional Performance

The Old Multilateral Organizations The second cause of Toronto's strong performance was the continuing, compounding failure of the established 1940s multilateral organizations to cope alone with these shocks and more chronic challenges.

In finance and economics, the IMF did not predict or prevent the Greek instalment of the Eurocrisis. It relied for many months on the hope that the regional EU could contain it all alone. The IMF finally offered to contribute $200 billion to the subsequently assembled support package. But this was an estimate, not a promise, of IMF support and the IMF did not convincingly possess the resources to make it certain should the need arise. The IMF was also unable to complete the second stage of its voice and vote reform, by getting the continental Europeans to give up the needed 5 percent of quota share.

With regard to energy, the environment, and natural disasters, the UN system did well on humanitarian relief in Haiti, even if it relied heavily for leadership from G8 members, especially the US, Canada, and France (Holmes 2010). The International Civil Aviation Organization did not visibly lead the response to the Icelandic volcano. The UN's small, selective energy and environment institutions were not key players on the Gulf oil spill. On climate change, the failure of the Copenhagen conference in December 2009 left it to the ad hoc Copenhagen Accord, and, ultimately, to the G8/G20 summits to come up with the $30 billion in "fast start" climate finance for 2010–12 that the accord had promised to produce.

Neither the G8 nor the G20, however, offered new money for climate finance at their 2010 summer summits to bail Copenhagen out.

Beyond lay the inability of the UN to advance adequately toward securing the eight MDGs. The leaders of all UN members had collectively proclaimed in September 2000 that these goals would be reached by 2015. In 2010, two thirds of the way through the timetable, it was left to the G20, as part of its new development agenda, to affirm the need for action now, to decide to add development as a new theme, and to create the Development Working Group for Seoul.

The Newer Plurilateral Institutions: G7/8 The newer plurilateral institutions were also inadequate on their own, even if the G8 provided important support through its summit held immediately before Toronto. The BCBS was making only slow progress on new rules for banking capital, liquidity, and leverage, and needed constant G20 pressure to produce whatever forward movement it had. The International Energy Agency (IEA) provided excellent information but no extra epistemic influence to bring to life the Pittsburgh promise to phase out fossil fuel subsidies. Although some G20 members suggested a greater role for the IEA on fossil fuel subsidies, and for the OECD on the G20's anti-corruption initiatives, those members of the G20 that were not also members of the IEA or OECD successfully resisted this.

In sharp contrast, the G7/8 performed well, in ways that fuelled the G20's success. G7 finance ministers had, under Flaherty's leadership, reverted to their original character of conducting an intimate "fireside chat," doing so quite literally in Iqaluit in the Canadian Arctic to start Canada's year as host. They subsequently grappled with the Greek-Eurocrisis and the need for a balanced fiscal exit strategy (*Financial Times* 2010). The G7 was quicker, when the Eurocrisis erupted, to issue a communiqué that was more detailed than the smaller, more general one issued by the G20 a day later on May 10.

Moreover, the G8's Muskoka Summit, held immediately before Toronto, helped the latter in an important way. For many years, the serious discussion of financial and economic matters within the G7/8 system had taken place at the G7 finance ministers' and central bank governors' forum, where Russia was not a regular member or participant, rather than at the G8 summit where it was. In normal years, Russia's finance minister Alexei Kudrin was invited only to G7 finance ministers' working lunches held as part of the twice-annual IMF/World Bank meetings, to discuss topics such as money laundering and terrorist finance. In the lead-up to Toronto in 2010, G20 members had generally agreed that the G20 summit—not the G8 one—would deal publicly with finance and economic affairs. However, they also realized that they could not prevent G8 leaders from spontaneously discussing finance and economic issues. The G20 leaders were prepared to accept this, as long as the G8 discussions or conclusions were not recorded in the G8 communiqué.

Such discussions on finance and economics arose at Muskoka in a semi-spontaneous way. The Canadians had warned their G8 colleagues that Harper as host and chair, who personally cared about economics, wished to bring these subjects up, as indeed he did at the summit's start. Muskoka's opening lunch focused on the Eurocrisis and the need for a credible macroeconomic response. This discussion helped firm up the G8's consensus, with America still ambivalent, that members would cut their fiscal deficits in half in the medium term, with due allowance for Japan. A potential sovereign debt crisis that was starting to appear within some G8/EU countries was thus in part contained by strong, swift action from those countries alone, before it could go global to harm the G20 and global community as a whole. But markets still needed the G20 summit message to calm them down.

More broadly, the Muskoka G8 acted on much of the G20's economic agenda in supportive ways. Trade, development, the MDGs, Haiti, and corruption were shared concerns, with mutual reinforcement rather than any rivalry or policy reversals taking place. Few non-G8 G20 members noticed or resented the G8's work on finance, economics, or the many other shared concerns. This was, in part, because Muskoka's signature achievement on maternal, newborn, and child health took the limelight, overwhelming outside attention to anything else.

Predominant, Equalizing Capability

The third cause—the G20's strong, shock-intensified moves toward collectively predominant and internally equal capability—also importantly influenced Toronto's strong success.

In 2009, the G20 members contained more than 77 percent of the world's GDP (see Appendix K). They accounted for 80 percent of the world's trade and two-thirds of the world's population. Capability among members was equalizing strongly. The G8 countries' share of global GDP had dropped from 67 percent a decade earlier to 55 percent. The GDP of four major emerging Asian, G20-only members—China, India, Indonesia, and Korea—had more than tripled since 1999. This surge was led by China, ranked seventh in GDP in 1999, fourth in 2006 (overtaking Italy, France, and the UK), third in 2007 (now ahead of Germany), and heading toward overtaking Japan for second place in 2010.

In the shorter term, the projected growth rates of countries within the G20 suggested that the most developed countries would lag behind the emerging ones in 2010. According to the IMF's *World Economic Outlook* published in April 2010, the US, Japan, and Europe were expected to have real GDP growth between 1 percent and 3 percent in 2010–11 (IMF 2010). Africa, Asia, and Latin America and summit host Canada were projected to have growth rates between 3 percent and 5 percent. China and India were expected to experience more than 5 percent growth.

Six weeks before the Toronto Summit, however, these underlying GDP trends were offset by strong, sudden currency changes. In response to the European-turning-global debt crisis, investors turned away from the euro, and the US dollar spiked. The euro, Canadian dollar, and other "commodity currencies" declined.

The leading position of the US was strengthened, if in a fragile, "flight-to-safety," export-inhibiting form.

This combination of equalizing capability in real GDP and a Eurocrisis-induced "safe haven" surge in the value of the US dollar strengthened the prospect of a US–emerging member pro-stimulus alliance at Toronto, and a resulting emphasis on stimulus now but not the headline message on fiscal consolidation in the medium term.

Democratic Convergence

The fourth cause—democratic convergence—also fostered Toronto's strong success. Many G20 members had made democratic advances from 2009 to 2010, with only Russia and South Africa going the other way (see Appendix L-2). Toronto's performance was reinforced by the domestic democratic convergence of the 2010 co-chairs, Canada and Korea. The G20 steering group pentarchy, which included the US, Britain, and France, also contributed to the strong democratic commonality within the group. So did all the invited guests except for Vietnam.

Within the G20 members there was a growing domestic consensus on the importance of financial stability and sustainable growth through economic openness, including transparency, accountability, good corporate and public governance, and the rule of law. The new emphasis on accountability to enhance effectiveness and legitimacy was one result of the domestic convergence on political openness that was slowly spreading throughout the members of the group. Acceptance of the US initiative against corruption was another result.

Political Control, Capital, Continuity, Competence, and Commitment

The fifth cause of the Toronto Summit's strong performance was the members' solid, if modest and mixed, domestic political control, capital, continuity, competence, and commitment (see Appendix M). These elements provided a push to strong performance, but also some of the constraints that kept performance from reaching a higher level.

Host Stephen Harper had a minority government and was still seeking the single national securities regulator that two leading Canadian provinces opposed. However, he did have collateral political capital acquired from the strong public support for his signature G8 Muskoka Initiative on Maternal, Newborn, and Child Health. A poll for World Vision by Ipsos-Reid, taken on November 11–16, 2009, showed that 88 percent of Canadians agreed that "Canada should use its influence in hosting the G8 and G20 to make sure that promises made to reduce childhood deaths are kept" and 87 percent believed that "despite the economic downturn, because Canada and other G8 countries made promises to reduce the number of child deaths by two thirds in poor countries by 2015, Canada should still keep this commitment" (Ipsos-Reid 2009). More directly, at 47 percent the first-ranked issue on which Canada should focus on the world stage was the "global economic recovery." Harper himself was a student of economics, a G8 and G20 summit veteran, and a G20 summit founder, attending his fourth G20 summit in less than two years. The summit's success on macroeconomics flowed from his political capital, continuity, and competence through experience and expertise, his personal commitment to balanced budgets and low debt, and his close connections with core European leaders.

Harper's fellow 2010 host, Korean president Lee Myung-bak, was in a more politically secure and a newly popular position at home. This was due in part to his firm response to the shock of the North Korean naval attack on the *Cheonan*. Lee was able to advance his priorities for development, a financial safety net, and trade at Toronto.

The other G20 leaders were less politically secure. In the US, Obama's Democratic party still controlled both congressional chambers, had just secured a victory on health care, and was likely to secure another victory on financial reform, but faced increasing partisan rancour. Unemployment in the US still hovered around 10 percent. The oil spill in the Gulf of Mexico was among the worst environmental catastrophes in US history. With the resulting sagging presidential popularity, public dissatisfaction with the soaring deficit, and mid-term congressional elections looming in November, Obama was unable to win his stimulus-centric case, even if he secured the summit's emphasis on growth first. Obama's political weakness also helped account for the summit's failure on climate change, as Congress increasingly resisted all his moves.

In the world's second and soon third most powerful country, Japan, the leader's political position was much less secure. Hatoyama's resignation, less than a month before the summit, was due in part to his plummeting popularity from his failure to agree with his American ally about its bases in Okinawa—an acute issue of Asian security considering the increasing tension on the nearby Korean peninsula (Kirton and Takase 2002). Kan, having just taken over as prime minister, arrived in Toronto with very little summit experience and none as a leader, with a difficult upper house election in a few weeks' time. As a former finance minister, however, he brought some economic experience. His deficit-reducing instinct helped Harper secure agreement on medium-term deficit and debt reduction targets. With the July election looming, Kan secured an exemption for Japan.

Among the other G8 members, political weakness also prevailed. Merkel's popularity was falling due to her handling of the Eurocrisis. The fall had led her to move unilaterally against naked short selling. Sarkozy was in a similar position, and had just lost key regional elections. Italy's Silvio Berlusconi, the ultimate G8 and G20 veteran who had hosted the G8 summit with some success in L'Aquila the previous year, was seeing his political control over his coalition government and his popularity fade fast. Britain's newly elected Cameron had a minority and coalition government—a very unusual experience for Britain.

The balance of domestic and personal power thus lay with the emerging member leaders. Hu Jintao was in firm control back home. He had gone to the G20 summit since the start and to the G8 ones since 2003 (save for 2004 and 2009).

Hu was due to retire in 2012, however, and there remained prospects of another domestic insurrection and ongoing civil strife in China.

Singh, recently re-elected with a surprisingly strong plurality, was equally a veteran of the G20 and, even more, the G8. He could keep coming to the summits as long as his health and currently supportive coalition partners allowed. He also led the G20 leaders in his expertise and experience as an economist and former finance minister, especially now that Britain's Gordon Brown, with his passion for poverty reduction and development, was gone. Singh had credibility when he spoke, particularly on the macroeconomic policy debate.

At the sherpa level, it was largely the same group preparing for their fourth summit in a row. The host sherpa had been involved in all the G20 summits and many G7/8 ones since 1988. The Indians were very practical pillars of strength, driven by Montek Singh Ahluwalia, a highly respected economist. In the preparatory process for Toronto the Chinese showed a sense of maturity. The Chinese sherpa was new since Pittsburgh and thus took a little time to grow into the role, but by Toronto he was a strong, subtle player. He was very blunt and clear on where he had room to be flexible and where he did not.

One or two sherpas, by nature, fussed over fine points. The more mature ones, who had much international experience and travelled with their leader, tended to do better. Those less experienced tended to dig in on small details and hold up the process.

Controlled Club Network Hub

The sixth cause of Toronto's strong success—the constricted, controlled participation that leaves leaders alone to be leaders with their only peers and desired partners in a club they cherish as their own—saw a notable advance on past summits.

The first component to advance was participation. In contrast to the large number of leaders present at Pittsburgh, in Toronto there were just over 30, with most staying in hotels within a block of their meeting place. Moreover, a full seat at the summit table was reserved for only the 20 members and a few invited guests. Virtually all the attending heads of multilateral organizations sat in the back row except when invited to come to the table for the discussion relating to their functional competence. At this smaller table in a smaller room, for the first time the finance ministers did not sit at the table with their leaders. Some chose to sit behind their leaders with the sherpas; others chose to stay out of the room. The only exceptions were the Canadian and Korean finance ministers, who were invited to the table for reporting the finance ministers' discussions and work, and who stayed there most of the day. Harper's choice of the Netherlands as the fifth guest for Toronto reinforced the continuity and compactness of the club.

The second component to advance was the skill of the chair. Harper's limiting interventions to five minutes prompted more spontaneity than at previous summits, even if there was still a long way to go.

A setback came on a third component—the attendance of the leaders at a meeting of the club they cared about more than anything else happening at home or abroad at the same time. Lula, a key personality in G20 summitry, and Gillard, from a country deeply involved in the G20, chose not to come, making Toronto the first summit to lose the G20's perfect summit attendance record at its fourth meeting. Lula was missed more because Brazil was such a major player and because Lula brought a point of view to the table that kept things interesting. Gillard was not missed as much. At Toronto Australia intervened on its usual topics of banks and trade, which played to its strong suits.

On the fourth component, a flexible cross-cutting alignment pattern rather than the rigidities from fixed blocs, Toronto again saw an advance. The meeting of the G8 summit immediately before the G20 one helped rather than hurt the G20 and caused no resentment from those absent from the G8. Moreover, there were several institutionalized subgroups within the G20, some of which cut across classic divisions and reached out to bring outside members into the club at the hub. The most cohesive and institutionalized were the EU with its 27 members, the decades-old G7 finance ministers' and central bankers' forum, and the G8 summit with Russia long a full member of the group. This made Russia the greater connector, for it was also a full member and the summit founder of the BRIC grouping, which had begun to meet regularly at the leaders' level too. The many deep divisions among BRIC members highly constrained their ability to act as a united bloc against the G7 within the G20 on the broad range of issues beyond IFI representation. In addition, Australia, Indonesia, Korea, Mexico, Turkey, Saudi Arabia, and South Africa, which belonged to neither the G8 nor the BRICs, acted at the G20 summits to mediate and add their weight to either side or any issue specific ad hoc coalition.

On the fifth component, the social-psychological sense of belonging to a valued club, there was another incremental advance. By 2010, the G20 summit had proven to be a club beyond the initial institutional sense of acting as a voluntary, exclusive, continuing collection with a known membership of leaders who valued being inside and who excluded those on the outside from some of the group's benefits. It was now starting to become a club in the social-psychological sense, even if its busy leaders now rationally calculated that they could reduce their club meetings to once a year from 2011 on. On a personal level, once heavily domestically oriented leaders such as Mexico's Calderón now felt at home in the G20. While those with long experience in the G7/8 felt it was too early to call the G20 a club in the same way as their older, smaller, more like-minded group, they saw the G20 as a club in the making. It had become a group of leaders who knew each other, who were ready to exercise discipline and to make concessions to produce a result that represented the group's outcome. They were moving away from statements of national interest or preference to reach across the table to find common ground. There was thus a real sense of a group, if not a G7/8-like club.

Pittsburgh and Toronto had confirmed this "groupism" at the leaders' level. It was based on a belief that there was a reason to meet, that the decisions taken were important enough not just for the leaders and their countries but for the world, and that members would exercise enough discipline to reach the required results. There was a healthy worry that if the G20 became too diffuse, lost focus, and thus became less interesting to the participants, it would fail. This sentiment was driven by leaders such as Manmohan Singh, who tended to think in the first instance of the global system and the good of the group, and Harper, with his new concept of "enlightened sovereignty." It was also driven by the key fact that an institutional club of the leaders of systemically significant states in a globalized world now knew at an interpersonal level that their self-interest was integrally connected with the health of the system and their group as a whole.

At the sherpa level, the personal sense of a common club was even stronger. At the January sherpa meeting in Mexico, a special statement had been proposed by Mexico, the chair and a country all too familiar with the devastation that earthquakes brought. So were several other members of the G20, notably Italy from L'Aquila, Indonesia and India from the December 2004 tsunami, Turkey, and China. The immediate outburst of emotional solidarity was the common bond that superseded any immediate rational calculation and prior institutional consensus that the G20 should not deal with such non-economic subjects (Linklater 2007). There was no desire to split hairs on this issue when so many lives had just been lost nearby. This spontaneous emotional solidarity strengthened the G20 club in several ways. It generated the first separate, inter-sessional statement ever issued by the G20 beyond finance. It showed that the G20 genuinely cared about one of the poorest countries and peoples in the world outside its own group. It underlined the common responsibilities of old and new donors of ODA, as almost all G20 members participated in humanitarian relief for Haiti. Russia, for example, immediately dispatched several large aircraft to shuttle UN relief supplies in. The Toronto Summit also acted on Haitian debt cancellation. In the end, however, the G20 did not turn itself into an institution to deal with "political" issues, as shown by the absence of any action on the far less emotional, still shock-free issue of Iran's nuclear program.

The previous two years had demonstrated how much participants who had not been used to this kind of gathering had been able to work together. In contrast to the G8, however, where sherpas tended to be more like-minded, the G20 still had some way to go in the way decisions were made, the extent to which fine points were important, and in the general impression to convey. While everyone had one or two sticking points, what prevailed was individuals who were willing to compromise or to give others a bit of room to get an agreement through. The maturity of the people sitting around the table for Toronto was evident.

Externally, in its position as a network hub, the G20 was strengthened by its novel twinning with the G8 in Muskoka and with APEC in Yokohama at the G20's Seoul Summit in November. Few G20 members or outsiders complained about the G8 summit immediately preceding the G20 summit, despite the substantial overlap between the agendas of the two.

To be sure, there were some gaps in the network. The absence of Lula meant that no BRIC summit was held. Nor was an MEF leaders' meeting held as part of the G8 summit at Muskoka. And at the ministerial level Russia remained out of the World Trade Organization, the OECD, and the IEA. At the official level, the HAP came to an end.

The Causal Combinations

Two central components of the Toronto Summit's strong performance show how this configuration of six causes combined to produce in large measure the observed result. The first is macroeconomic policy management and messaging to markets. Here the immediate, initial shock from the Eurocrisis was readily converted into the intended G20 governance result, with the help of the other causal factors lower on the systemic hub model's list. The recent sequence of severe shocks starting in America and rapidly spreading to engulf the world from 2007 to 2009 was joined by a fresh European one. The latter came in the form of sovereign debt and was thus readily recognizable to a G20 that had been created by and had controlled a similar shock sequence from Asia, Russia, the Americas, and the Middle East from 1997 through to 2002. A G20 tailor-made to control such shocks could, after its very strong London G20 performance, credibly convince markets that it could and would provide the major new money committed to rescue Europe and others, even though the IMF itself lacked such readily available funding on its own. That G20 guarantee was backed implicitly by China and other non-G8 members that had the money, especially in the form of deployable foreign exchange reserves at home. The rapidly growing non-G8 countries with low deficit and debt burdens and massive foreign exchange reserves made the G20 more a club of equals, in a way that was clear and credible to the outside world. With shared, status quo principles of financial stability, economic growth, and social and political stability, and with members' democratic convergence thus guaranteed in Greece, Europe, and beyond, Stephen Harper as G20 summit host and founder and an experienced leader could more easily secure the agreement on medium-term fiscal consolidation that he desired, and join with the non-G8 members to defeat a global bank levy. With the G8 and G20 summits held in tandem and working in the same direction on a shared economic and social agenda, the Toronto Summit became a hub that reached out through its members and participants to include, in its inspiration and influence, much of the world.

The second case is the phase-out of fossil fuel subsidies, as a contribution to fiscal consolidation, energy security, and climate change control. Here the strong sequence of shocks opened an opportunity for major achievements, but produced no new G20 performance in the end. The 2007–09 financial and ensuing economic crises had caused the G20 club to be elevated to the summit level in Washington, to add climate change to its agenda at London, and to promise at Pittsburgh to phase out fossil fuel subsidies. The European-going-global aftershock led Toronto to have advanced economy members except Japan commit to slashing their fiscal deficit in half by 2013. The energy shock from the Deepwater Horizon disaster in the Gulf of Mexico in the months leading up to Toronto offered an additional boost. Harper's promise that accountability would be the "defining feature" of the Toronto Summit should have internally reinforced the outside shock-driven call.

That Toronto did not seize the window of win-win-win opportunity opened by such shocks points first to the importance of international institutional failure as a cause. The full UN system had failed in full force at the Copenhagen conference in December 2009 and there was no sign it would succeed when it met again in Cancún in December 2010 (McColl 2010). Yet the latter meeting, which would come so soon after Seoul, offered an incentive for the G20 to leave climate change to the UN, just as China sought, and even though Ban Ki-moon himself promoted climate change as his priority for the Toronto G20 in the lead-up to the summit. To be sure, among the plurilateral institutions, on the eve of the summit, the IEA reliably reported that the world could simultaneously obtain more than half a trillion dollars in fiscal consolidation and achieve major reductions in carbon reduction simply by complying with the Pittsburgh commitments on fossil fuels (Tanaka 2010; Runnalls 2010). However, some key G20 members, including the major producers and consumers of Russia, Saudi Arabia, and China, were not part of this IEA club (Lesage et al. 2010). With a membership so small, the IEA was not invited to Toronto to pitch the case first hand, even though its OECD parent was there to promote its core economic concerns. Also absent was the secretariat of the United Nations Framework Convention on Climate Change, whose great failure at Copenhagen still paralyzed G20 members six months later. At this second step in the six-stage model of systemic hub governance, the push to success on phasing out fossil fuel subsidies thus stopped. Further down the causal ladder, no one made the connection between fossil fuels and democracy clear, even though the American-inspired agreements on corruption offered a convenient nest in which to raise the link between subsidies and corruption. And at the leaders' level, the host and most of his colleagues had low levels of commitment and competence on climate change.

Conclusion

At its 2010 Toronto Summit, the G20 faced high stakes (Bradford Jr. and Lim 2010). During the summit, the IMF reported that while the global economy was recovering at a rate faster than anticipated in Pittsburgh, the downside risks had intensified, the imbalances across a number of areas had increased, and the Eurocrisis threatened to bring a double-dip recession right away. The G20 could not afford to get its macroeconomic message and management wrong.

It did not. There was agreement on a timetable and targets for fiscal consolidation, and a recognition that members would need to implement member-specific strategies. This was effective in containing the Eurocrisis and keeping the fragile global recovery alive. It was a difficult macroeconomic balance to produce.

As the global economy moved shakily toward recovery, some members required immediate sovereign debt consolidation. Greece, Spain, Ireland, and Italy all needed to implement fiscal tightening policies right away. Others, including the United States and some European countries, needed to pursue a more medium-term strategy, given their slow rates of recovery and high unemployment levels. Considering the different fiscal positions and policy approaches, the G20 leaders succeeded in producing a clear, coordinated, credible plan that proved effective for the following five months, until the next G20 summit would be held.

Another important achievement was the sense that multilateral cooperation was alive and well. There had been a real fear that as countries entered into the recession, they would pursue severe protectionist policies, to the detriment of the global good, in order to try to mitigate their economic woes at home and reassure their domestic constituencies that they were prioritizing national needs. The great success of the G20's early years was providing enough collective international will for leaders to resist these tendencies. Together with large-scale, simultaneous stimulus and financial support, the result had been a rapid recovery. Toronto reinforced the thrust.

While the recession had exposed many of the imbalances that were already latent in the international financial system, the great hope for the future of the G20 was that the spirit of cooperation would extend into addressing these imbalances. A big winner at Toronto was Pittsburgh's Framework for Strong, Sustainable, and Balanced Growth. Canada had gone into its time as chair with making the framework work as its biggest concern. In the end the erupting Eurocrisis on sovereign debt took centre stage, but to the benefit of the framework itself. In large part, the Eurocrisis created the menu of policy options for the framework that were set out in the Toronto communiqué and the agreement to progress into a future phase of mutual assessment moving from a group-specific to country-specific assessment. In short, the crisis drove home the need for greater cooperation. At Toronto's end, the G20 had coped well not only with its founding American-turned-global financial crisis, but also with the European-turned-global one that had erupted in its wake. Toronto was thus a success both in responding to a current financial crisis as well as any G20 summit before, and, as the first summit after Pittsburgh, in providing a good model for the focus, participation, and meeting management for G20 summits to come.

References

Basel Committee on Banking Supervision. 2009a. "Consultative Proposals to Strengthen the Resilience of the Banking Sector Announced by the Basel Committee." Press release, December 17, Bank for International Settlements, Basel. Available at: www.bis.org/press/p091217.htm. Accessed: July 2012.

Basel Committee on Banking Supervision. 2009b. "International Framework for Liquidity Risk Measurement, Standards, and Monitoring: Consultative

Document." December 17, Bank for International Settlements, Basel. Available at: www.bis.org/publ/bcbs165.pdf. Accessed: July 2012.

Bradford, Colin I. and Lim, Wonhyuk, eds. 2010. *The New Dynamics of Summitry: Institutional, Policy, and Political Innovations for G20 Summits: Issues and Essays*. Seoul: Korea Development Institute.

Bronnert, Deborah. 2011. "Making Government Policy: The G8 and G20 in 2010." In *New Economic Diplomacy: Decision-Making and Negotiation in International Economic Relations*, eds Bayne, Nicholas, and Woolcock, Stephen. Farnham: Ashgate, 81–92.

Brown, Gordon. 2010. *Beyond the Crash: Overcoming the First Crisis of Globalization*. New York: Free Press.

Canada-Korea G20 Seminar. 2010. "Canada-Korea High-Level G20 Seminar: Report 2010." Norman Paterson School of International Affairs, Carleton University, March 17, Ottawa. Available at: www.g20.utoronto.ca/biblio/Canada-Korea-G20-2010-Report.pdf. Accessed: July 2012.

Charlebois, Sylvain. 2010. "Canada a Roadblock in Trade Talks." *National Post*, July 2. Available at: opinion.financialpost.com/2010/07/02/canada-a-roadblock-in-trade-talks. Accessed: July 2012.

Clark, Campbell. 2010. "Harper's Pro-Austerity Position Could Seal His Legacy — For Good or Bad." *Globe and Mail*, July 7. Available at: www.theglobeandmail.com/news/politics/harpers-pro-austerity-position-could-seal-his-legacy---for-good-or-bad/article1390298/. Accessed: July 2012.

Coyne, Andrew. 2010. "G20 Members: Embarking on a Great Experiment." *Maclean's*, July 5. Available at: www2.macleans.ca/2010/07/05/embarking-on-a-great-experiment/. Accessed: July 2012.

Crook, Clive. 2010. "A Graver Sin Than Fiscal Disarray." *Financial Times*, June 28.

Currah, Kel. 2010. "The G8: The Greatest Show on Earth." *G8/G20 Summit 2010*, June, pp. 32–33.

Curry, Bill, Waldie, Paul, Robertson, Grant, and Perkins, Tara. 2010. "Summit on the Brink: How Harper Saved His Deal." *Globe and Mail*, June 28.

Dale, Daniel. 2010. "What the Summit Pundits Said." *Toronto Star*, June 26.

Edwards, Leonard. 2010. "Looking Ahead to the G20 Seoul Summit: A Year of Canadian-Korean Partnership." Speech to the Annual General Meeting of the Korea-Canada Society, November 3, Ottawa.

Financial Times. 2010. "Financial Markets 'Do Not Understand the Euro'." December 5.

Frank, Robert H. 2010. "The Choices That Pay Us Back." *New York Times*, July 4. Available at: www.robert-h-frank.com/PDFs/EV.07.04.10.pdf. Accessed: July 2012.

G7 Finance Ministers and Central Bank Governors. 2010. "Statement of G7 Finance Ministers and Central Bank Governors." May 9. Available at: www.g8.utoronto.ca/finance/fm100509.html. Accessed: July 2012.

G20. 2008. "The Group of Twenty: A History." Available at: www.g20.utoronto.ca/docs/g20history.pdf. Accessed: July 2012.

G20. 2009. "G20 Leaders Statement: The Pittsburgh Summit." Pittsburgh, September 25. Available at: www.g20.utoronto.ca/2009/2009communique0925.html. Accessed: July 2012.

G20. 2010. "The G20 Toronto Summit Declaration." Toronto, June 27. Available at: www.g20.utoronto.ca/2010/to-communique.html. Accessed: July 2012.

G20 Finance Ministers and Central Bank Governors. 2009. "Communiqué." St. Andrews, Scotland, November 7. Available at: www.g20.utoronto.ca/2009/2009communique1107.html. Accessed: July 2012.

G20 Finance Ministers and Central Bank Governors. 2010a. "Communiqué: Meeting of G20 Finance Ministers and Central Bank Governors." Washington DC, April 23. Available at: www.g20.utoronto.ca/2010/g20finance100423.html. Accessed: July 2012.

G20 Finance Ministers and Central Bank Governors. 2010b. "Statement by the G20 Finance Ministers on the Euro Area Support Measures." May 10. Available at: www.g20.utoronto.ca/2010/g20finance100510.html. Accessed: July 2012.

G20 Research Group and International Organizations Research Institute. 2010. "2010 G20 Toronto Summit Final Compliance Report." November 14. Available at: www.g20.utoronto.ca/analysis/2010toronto-compliance.html. Accessed: July 2012.

Garcia, John. 2010. "The G20 Yields Only Unfulfilled Promises for Latin America." Council on Hemispheric Affairs, August 2. Available at: www.coha.org/the-g-20-yields-only-unfulfilled-promises-for-latin-america/. Accessed: July 2012.

Gotlieb, Allan. 2010. "Not Just Another Foreign-Policy Review." *Globe and Mail*, August 3. Available at: www.theglobeandmail.com/commentary/not-just-another-foreign-policy-review/article1387986/?page=all. Accessed: July 2012.

Harper, Stephen. 2009a. "The 2010 Muskoka Summit." In *The 2009 G8 Summit: From La Maddalena to L'Aquila*, eds Kirton, John J., and Koch, Madeline. London: Newsdesk, 18–19. Available at: www.g8.utoronto.ca/newsdesk/harper-2009.html. Accessed: July 2012.

Harper, Stephen. 2009b. "From Pittsburgh to Muskoka: Building a Sustainable Global Recovery." In *The 2009 G20 Pittsburgh Summit: Sustaining Global Recovery*, eds Kirton, John J., and Koch, Madeline. London: Newsdesk, 25–26. Available at: www.g8.utoronto.ca/newsdesk/pittsburgh/harper.html. Accessed: July 2012.

Harper, Stephen. 2010a. "Recovery and New Beginnings." In *G8 & G20: The 2010 Canadian Summits*, eds Kirton, John J., and Koch, Madeline. London: Newsdesk, 14–15. Available at: www.g8.utoronto.ca/newsdesk/g8g20/g8g20-harper-en.html. Accessed: July 2012.

Harper, Stephen. 2010b. "Statement by the Prime Minister of Canada at the 2010 World Economic Forum." Davos, January 28. Available at: www.g8.utoronto.ca/summit/2010muskoka/harper-davos.html. Accessed: July 2012.

Holmes, John. 2010. "Building Effective Humanitarian Responses for the 21st Century." In *G8 & G20: The 2010 Canadian Summits*, eds Kirton, John J., and Koch, Madeline. London: Newsdesk, 32–34. Available at: www.g8.utoronto.ca/newsdesk/g8g20/g8g20-holmes.html. Accessed: July 2012.

International Monetary Fund. 2010. "World Economic Outlook: Rebalancing Growth." April, Washington DC. Available at: www.imf.org/external/pubs/ft/weo/2010/01/. Accessed: July 2012.

International Organizations Research Institute and G20 Research Group. 2010. "2009 Pittsburgh G20 Summit Compliance Report." June 21. Available at: www.g20.utoronto.ca/analysis/Pittsburgh_G20_compliance_report.pdf. Accessed: July 2012.

Ipsos-Reid. 2009. "World Vision Child Health Factum." November, Toronto. Available at: www.worldvision.ca/About-Us/Newsroom/press-releases/Documents/World%20Vision%20Child%20Health%20Factum.pdf. Accessed: July 2012.

Kirton, John J. 2010a. "The G20 and Broader Multilateral Reform." Paper prepared for a conference on "What Role for the G20 in a Post-Crisis World?," July 15–16, Club of Madrid and Fundación para las Relaciones Internacionales y el Diálogo Exterior, Seoul. Available at: www.g20.utoronto.ca/biblio/kirton-fride-cdm.pdf. Accessed: July 2012.

Kirton, John J. 2010b. "In Substance, Summits Were a Success on Several Fronts." *Toronto Star*, June 28. Available at: www.g8.utoronto.ca/evaluations/2010muskoka/kirton-star.html. Accessed: July 2012.

Kirton, John J. and Guebert, Jenilee. 2010. "North American Health Governance: Shocks, Summitry, and Societal Support." *Revista Norteamericana* 5(1): 221–44. Available at: www.cisan.unam.mx/Norteamerica/PDFs%20COMPLETOS/Norteamerica%209.pdf. Accessed: July 2012.

Kirton, John J. and Takase, Junichi, eds. 2002. *New Directions in Global Political Governance: The G8 and International Order in the Twenty-First Century*. Aldershot: Ashgate.

Krugman, Paul. 2010. "Keynes in Asia." The Conscience of a Liberal (Blog). *New York Times*. July 24. Available at: krugman.blogs.nytimes.com/2010/07/24/keynes-in-asia. Accessed: July 2012.

Lee, Dong-hwi. 2009. "Third G20 Summit: International Political Economic Achievements and Prospects." IFANS Brief, October 12. Available at: www.g20.utoronto.ca/biblio/LEE-3rd-20091014-en.pdf. Accessed: July 2012.

Lee, Dong-hwi. 2010. "Assessment of the Toronto G20 Summit and Tasks Ahead in Preparing for the Upcoming Seoul Summit." IFANS Brief, July 13. Available at: www.g20.utoronto.ca/biblio/LEE-4-20100713-en.pdf. Accessed: July 2012.

Lesage, Dries, Van de Graaf, Thijs, and Westphal, Kirsten. 2010. *Global Energy Governance in a Multipolar World*. Farnham: Ashgate.

Linklater, Andrew. 2007. *Critical Theory and World Politics: Citizenship, Sovereignty, and Humanity*. Abdingdon: Routledge.

Lukov, Vadim. 2010a. "G20 and G8 in Search of Solutions: Global Problems of Economy and Society." *International Affairs* 56(5): 58–76.

Lukov, Vadim. 2010b. "Parnership for Progress: From the 2010 Muskoka-Toronto Summits to the Seoul Summit." Conference on "Partnership for Progress: From the 2010 Muskoka-Toronto Summits to Seoul Summit" at the State University Higher School of Economics, October 27, Moscow.

Macklem, Tiff. 2011a. "Global Financial Reform: Maintaining the Momentum." Remarks presented to the "G20 Workshop," Paris, July 7. Available at: www.bankofcanada.ca/2011/07/speeches/global-financial-reform. Accessed: July 2012.

Macklem, Tiff. 2011b. "The Role of the G20 in Sustaining the Recovery and Protecting Financial Stability." Remarks presented to the Federation of Indian Chambers of Commerce and Industry and the Indian Banks' Association, Mumbai, August 24. Available at: www.bankofcanada.ca/2011/08/speeches/role-g-20-sustaining-recovery. Accessed: July 2012.

Makin, John. 2010. "It Is Time to Face Down the Threat of Deflation." *Financial Times*, July 16.

Masson, Paul R. and Pattison, John C. 2010. "Financial Regulatory Reform: Using Models of Cooperation to Evaluate Current Prospects for International Agreement." Rotman School of Management, University of Toronto, Toronto. Available at: www.g20.utoronto.ca/biblio/G20reforms.pdf. Accessed: July 2012.

Masters, Brooke. 2010. "Move to Reassure Banks on Tough Rules." *Financial Times*, June 28.

McColl, Velma. 2010 (February). "Deconstructing Copenhagen." *Policy Options*: 22–28. Available at: www.irpp.org/po/archive/feb10/mccoll.pdf. Accessed: July 2012.

Obama, Barack. 2010. "Letter from the President to G20 Leaders." June 16, White House, Washington DC. Available at: www.whitehouse.gov/the-press-office/letter-president-g-20-leaders. Accessed: July 2012.

Office of the Prime Minister of Canada. 2009. "PM Announces G20 Leaders Will Meet in Toronto in 2010." Seoul, December 7. Available at: www.pm.gc.ca/eng/media.asp?category=1&featureId=6&pageId=26&id=3026. Accessed: July 2012.

Ostry, Sylvia. 2010. "Pessimism of the Intellect, Optimism of the Will." August 7, Available at: www.g20.utoronto.ca/biblio/ostry-cipa.html. Accessed: July 2012.

Patrick, Stewart. 2010. "G8, G20: A View of Canada's Summits." Council on Foreign Relations, June 21. Available at: www.cfr.org/canada/g8-g20-view-canadas-summits/p22463. Accessed: July 2012.

Pisani-Ferry, Jean. 2010. "Back to the G7?" By Invitation (Blog). *Economist*. June 29. Available at: www.bruegel.org/blog/detail/article/46-back-to-the-g7/. Accessed: July 2012.

Reuters. 2010. "Canada PM Harper's Letter to G20 on Deficits." June 18. Available at: www.reuters.com/article/2010/06/18/g20-canada-deficits-idUSN1817964220100618. Accessed: July 2012.

Roubini, Nouriel and Bremmer, Ian. 2010. "Sagging Global Growth Requires Us to Act." *Financial Times*, July 12.

Runnalls, David. 2010. "Fossil Fuel Subsidies and the G20." In *G8 & G20: The 2010 Canadian Summits*, eds Kirton, John J., and Koch, Madeline. London: Newsdesk, 164–65. Available at: www.g8.utoronto.ca/newsdesk/g8g20/g8g20-2010.pdf. Accessed: July 2012.

Schirm, Stefan A. 2012 (July). "Global Politics Are Domestic Politics: A Societal Approach to Divergence in the G20." *Review of International Studies*: 1–22. doi: dx.doi.org/10.1017/S0260210512000216.

Smith, Gordon. 2010. "The Last Thing We Need Is a G12 Competing with a G8." *Globe and Mail*, July 9. Available at: www.theglobeandmail.com/commentary/the-last-thing-we-need-is-a-g12-competing-with-a-g8/article4323467/. Accessed: July 2012.

Stephens, Philip. 2010. "Splintered Solidarity Has Put Global Governance in a Spin." *Financial Times*, July 1.

Stewart, James B. 2010. "One Good Review for the G20's Performance." *Wall Street Journal*, July 7. Available at: online.wsj.com/article/SB10001424052748704178004575351050968234196.html. Accessed: July 2012.

Subramanian, Arvind. 2010. "G20 Rules: Time for Germany Bashing." The Baseline Scenario (Blog). June 20. Available at: baselinescenario.com/2010/06/20/g-20-rules-time-for-germany-bashing. Accessed: July 2012.

Tanaka, Nobuo. 2010. "Fresh Momentum for Tackling Global Energy Challenges." In *G8 & G20: The 2010 Canadian Summits*, eds Kirton, John J., and Koch, Madeline. London: Newsdesk, 178–80. Available at: www.g8.utoronto.ca/newsdesk/g8g20/g8g20-2010.pdf. Accessed: July 2012.

United Kingdom Chair of the G20. 2009. "Progress Report on the Economic and Financial Actions of the London, Washington, and Pittsburgh G20 Summits." St. Andrews, Scotland, November 7. Available at: www.g20.utoronto.ca/2009/2009progressreport1107.pdf. Accessed: July 2012.

Van Rompuy, Herman. 2010. "Overcoming the Crisis in Europe and in the World." In *The G20 2010 Seoul Summit: Shared Growth Beyond Crisis*, eds Kirton, John J., and Koch, Madeline. London: Newsdesk, 30–31. Available at: www.g8.utoronto.ca/newsdesk/seoul/seoul-vanrompuy-en.htm. Accessed: July 2012.

Watson, William. 2010. "Canada's Moment." *National Post*, July 1. Available at: opinion.financialpost.com/2010/07/01/canadas-moment. Accessed: July 2012.

Wheatley, Alan. 2010. "G20 Strives to Cut Deficits Without Killing Growth." Reuters, June 3. Available at: in.reuters.com/article/2010/06/03/idINIndia-49012120100603. Accessed: July 2012.

Wolf, Martin. 2010a. "This Global Game of 'Pass the Parcel' Cannot End Well." *Financial Times*, June 29, p. 4.

Wolf, Martin. 2010b. "Why the Battle Is Joined over Tightening." *Financial Times*, July 18, p. 9.

PART V
Conclusion

Chapter 14
The Future of G20 Governance

In its first 12 years, from 1999 through to June 2010, the Group of 20 (G20) had become, in practice as well as proclamation, the centre of global economic governance for a globalized world. It was born in 1999 at the end of two years of international institutional experimentation, as one of three new bodies with which it had to compete and cooperate to thrive in an institutionally crowded world. It rapidly expanded its initial key mission, from promoting financial stability at its first meeting in Berlin in 1999 to making globalization work for all with its Montreal Consensus in 2000, and then at Ottawa in 2001 to combating the new, non-state threat of global terrorism that had just struck the United States. In its institutional leadership, initiative, and innovations, the G20 increasingly became a genuine group of advanced and emerging country equals, as its hosting moved to India in 2002, Mexico in 2003, Berlin in 2004, China in 2005, Australia in 2006, South Africa in 2007, and Brazil in 2008. Following a campaign that almost succeeded from 2004 to 2005, the G20 in 2008 finally leapt to the leaders' level, holding summits in swift succession in Washington DC in November 2008, London in April 2009, Pittsburgh in September 2009, and Toronto in June 2010, followed by Seoul in November 2010, Cannes in November 2011, and Los Cabos in June 2012. At Pittsburgh its leaders proclaimed that their G20 would become the permanent, priority forum for their international economic cooperation. In 2010 at Toronto, in its response to the erupting Eurocrisis, the G20 proved it had become, in practice, the centre of global economic governance for the world as a whole.

This rapid rise to centrality flowed first from the cascading cadence of crisis, in particular the sequence of shocks that showed all countries, including the United States as the most powerful, their equal vulnerability to new, non-state threats in a highly interconnected, complex, uncertain world. Yet the Asian-turned-global financial shocks of 1997–2002, the Afghanistan-turned-American terrorist shock of 2001, and the American-Atlantic-European-turned-global economic shocks of 2007–10 do not alone account for the G20's growth under the increasing leadership of emerging country members from 2002 to 2008, the particular path this process took, and the G20's primacy among other, often initially stronger international institutions in the end. These particular outcomes flowed from the failure of the old, formal multilateral organizations led by the International Monetary Fund (IMF) and the newer informal plurilateral institutions led by the Group of Seven (G7) and the Group of Eight (G8) to meet the new global governance demands on their own, and their success in providing the G20 with increasingly important support. These dynamics were further fuelled by the predominant, equalizing capabilities of the 19 systemically significant advanced and emerging countries and the European Union, which made the "G192" multilateral organizations too many and the G7/8 institutions too few to govern effectively the new, fast moving, fully globalized world.

Despite their multidimensional diversity, the G20 members benefited from their deepening domestic convergence on the values and practice of financial, economic, and social stability and openness, and on the democratic values of transparency, the rule of law, and accountability that came as a logical and recognized result. Essential to the success of the G20 were the political control, capital, continuity, competence, and commitment of particular individuals at the centre of its creation, operation, and ultimate centrality. They were led by Paul Martin and Lawrence Summers in 1999 and, in the end, by George W. Bush and Hu Jintao, who were willing to come along. Their personal inspiration and political investment led to the intense interaction, ultimately at the uniquely important leaders' level, that started to transform an efficient group governing from a rationally shared sense of exclusive global rights and responsibilities into an interpersonal club cemented by bonds among individuals who belonged to and cherished "their" G20 group.

The Cadence of G20 Governance from Creation to Centrality

This cadence of G20 governance, from its initial crisis-catalysed creation in 1999 to its global centrality by 2010, can be charted through the three distinct phases the international institutional journey took.

Phase 1: Generating the Group, 1999–2001

In its first phase, from 1999 to 2001, the G20 established itself as an effective group of operational equals, led largely by Canada, the United States, and other G7 members, governing to produce financial stability, globalization that worked for all, and the suppression of terrorist finance.

In this phase, the G20 emerged as a response to the Asian-turned-global financial crisis of 1997–99, after America alone had pioneered informal, ad hoc groupings and the Europeans more formal ones, in an effort to give emerging, if crisis-afflicted powers a greater place and voice. The G20 was largely conceived by Paul Martin, Canada's finance minister, who worked equally and essentially with American treasury secretary Larry Summers to design, define, and co-create the new group.

The group began operating as an annual meeting of finance ministers and central bank governors of the world's 19 most systemically significant countries, with institutional leadership residing in Canada as chair and Germany as host in 1999. That leadership then passed exclusively to Canada as chair and host in Montreal in 2000 and again, unexpectedly, in Ottawa in 2001 after the September terrorist attacks in the United States. In the latter instance, the G20 worked when other institutions could not. Thanks to the initiative of Canada—the least powerful member of the established G7—the G20 enabled a G7 meeting to take place as well, just after the G20 one was held.

With Canada continuously in the chair, the G20's mission and agenda broadened enormously during its first three years. It moved from providing the global public good of financial stability, whose absence had afflicted largely non-G7 countries, to the distributional desire to make globalization work for all, including the poorest in the world, to the security imperative of stopping terrorist finance in order to protect an America itself under direct and deadly attack from a new, non-state threat coming from one of the poorest places in the world. The G20's initial focus expanded from reforming international financial regulations within emerging states, through guiding the many dimensions and impacts of globalization, to focusing on the primary security threat to advanced and emerging countries alike in the twenty-first century world.

In doing so the G20 became not merely a forum for open dialogue in search of a new consensus beyond the old Washington Consensus but also a body that set innovative principled directions as well. In 2001 it became a major action-oriented decisional forum, whose commitments were quickly and reliably delivered by most of its members in the following months and years.

From the start there were signs that its emerging country members were increasingly influential within the group. Canada joined with the latter to delay and thus stop the majority G7's enthusiasm for capital account liberalization at the IMF and to add to the agenda the emerging members' priorities of development and globalization's dark side. Yet, on the whole, the initiatives and outcomes of G20 governance during its first three years were driven by its established G7 members, no more so than in November 2001 when the G20 in Ottawa took up terrorist finance in direct response to the September 11 attacks on the United States next door. Even so, the US and its G7 partners depended directly on a few of the emerging country members that understood how informal Islamic finance networks worked better than any G7 finance minister or central banker did.

The outcomes of the Ottawa meeting helped a G20 that had begun as a project of a Democratic administration in the US become a group valued by that of the new Republican president George W. Bush, who had arrived in office unsympathetic to the informal international institutions recently created by his now defeated political foe. It thus made the group a bipartisan asset and attachment within the United States. It showed that the G20 was needed not only by its emerging members, such as Indonesia and Korea, under attack from anonymous markets in the autumn of 1997, but also by its most powerful member, America, under direct deadly attack at home by the autumn of 2001. It also showed the skill and will of its Canadian visionary and co-founder, Paul Martin, still at the helm at that defining time.

Phase 2: Equalizing the Influence, 2002–2007

During its second phase from 2002 to 2007 the G20 became a more genuine group of equals in several ways.

The first was the equalization in hosting and chairing, and in the rights, responsibilities, learning, and socialization that such institutional leadership brought. Hosting moved almost entirely to the non-G8 members—India in 2002, Mexico in 2003, Germany in 2004, China in 2005, Australia in 2006, South Africa in 2007, and Brazil in 2008. This made the G20 a global group guided largely by mainstream middle powers, in the Westphalian conceptualization. In its first decade the finance G20 was never hosted by the two most powerful members of the G8 and indeed the world—the US and Japan—or by the most vigorous promoters and practitioners of free market capitalism and capital market-centred financial systems, the "imperial" United States and the United Kingdom. The leading non-G8 countries of India and China became early hosts and chairs. The non-G8 outliers in relative capability and political and economic systems—Saudi Arabia, Argentina, Indonesia, and Turkey—never did. Yet this preference for the mainstream middle powers made the hosting more global. The Atlantic powers of the first phase expanded during the second to embrace Asia with India, China, and Australia, the Americas with Mexico and Brazil, and Africa with South Africa, while continuing with Europe through Germany and leaving out only the Middle East through Turkey and Saudi Arabia.

The second equalization came with the G20's institutionalization through the addition of the troika system of the present, past, and future hosts and the bucket system for rotating the hosts. With the particular choice of more global, largely non-G8 hosts, this helped ensure that the emerging countries would have their influence as hosts built in for a longer time and in a more guaranteed and predictable way.

The third equalization came in the expanding agenda. Each host country in particular and the emerging countries in general added its preferred issues to the agenda in its year as chair and host. India and Mexico brought a greater concern with development. China emphasized trade and reform of the international financial institutions (IFIs).

The fourth equalization came in the ability of emerging countries to take initiatives that met with success within the G20 and in the institutions of global financial governance beyond. Whereas in phase one, the emerging markets and Canada had defensively helped stop the American initiative to change the IMF's charter to approve capital account liberalization, in phase two the emerging members went on the offensive to take initiatives that were also constitutional in character and that prevailed. The outstanding case was the first stage of voice and vote reform at the IMF, pioneered by the G20 and agreed to by all in 2008, even if its subsequent implementation was rather slow. This was an initiative that the Bretton Wood institutions born in 1944 and the G7 countries that dominated them had been unable alone to carry through to success, despite a serious attempt at IFI reform at the G7 summit in Halifax in 1995.

With these four equalizations, the G20 was well positioned to have George Bush pick it among the established and ad hoc alternatives, and to have the emerging members accept his choice, to leap to the leaders' level to combat the unprecedented global financial crisis that erupted in full force in the autumn of 2008.

Phase 3: Creating the Summit Group, 2008–2010

During its third phase, in another three, crisis-filled years from 2008 to 2010, the G20 became a summit-level, central, global governance group. Its relatively unscathed, rapidly rising emerging country members rushed to the assistance of the now afflicted, advanced American-Atlantic-European ones, and helped craft an agenda and achievements that increasingly reflected the views of the ascending powers. Together they succeeded in reducing and reversing the great American-turned-global economic crisis of 2007–09, in containing the European-going-global aftershock that erupted in the spring of 2010, in agreeing to balance global growth through mutual assessment and adjustment, in strengthening and converging their domestic financial regulation, in opening trade, in financing development, in phasing out fossil fuel subsidies, in advancing the second stage of IFI voice and vote reform, and in cutting the fiscal deficits and debts of most advanced members in the medium term.

To be sure, the crisis-catalysed leap to the leader level was led by the G7, first with the campaign of Paul Martin—by now prime minister of Canada—in 2004–05, then in September 2008 with French president Nicolas Sarkozy's suggestion of a summit at the UN in New York, then with the campaign of Britain's Gordon Brown, Australia's Kevin Rudd, and several others for a G20 summit, and finally with the decision of a long resistant George Bush to design, host, and chair a G20 summit in Washington on November 14–15, 2008. Gordon Brown's hosting of the second summit in London in April 1–2, 2009, broadened G20 leadership across the Atlantic, while Democratic president Barack Obama's hosting of the third in Pittsburgh on September 24–25, 2009, with Larry Summers at his side, again bonded US presidents on a bipartisan basis to the group, now in its summit form. Yet chairing and then hosting responsibilities soon shifted from the old "imperial" powers within the G7 to Canada, which chaired the fourth G20 summit in Toronto on June 26–27, 2010, and later that year to Korea—an emerging, Asian democracy that was neither a member of the G8's Group of Five countries of Brazil, China, India, Mexico, and South Africa, nor of the BRIC group of Brazil, Russia, India, and China—which hosted and chaired the fifth G20 summit in Seoul on November 11–12.

The institutionalization of the G20 summit that deepened its equality proceeded in other ways during these two years. The G20 leaders at Pittsburgh in 2009 proclaimed the G20 as the permanent premier forum for their international economic cooperation. The first meeting of the leaders' representatives, or sherpas, to prepare the following summit was held in Mexico. It concluded that the group needed to be a compact, leaders' gathering that reached out to major multilateral organizations and the poorest regions in the world. In 2010 the G20 confirmed that it wished to be a global governor as well as a crisis-response group. With its success so far, it could relax the intensity of its meetings from twice to once a year by 2011.

The increasing initial influence of the emerging members and the resulting equalization of initiative within the group were seen in the expansion of the agenda to embrace the concerns of the non-G7 members more fully. Thus the initial focus on domestic financial regulation and macroeconomic management at Washington quickly gave way to financial support at London, to IMF reform at Pittsburgh, and to Korea's two new initiatives, approved at Toronto, on an approach to development that did not focus on official development assistance and on stronger financial safety nets.

This increasing influence of emerging countries in setting the agenda carried through into the defining achievements of the group. This was clearest in the case of the replacement of the Financial Stability Forum (FSF) by the Financial Stability Board (FSB) and then in the case of IMF reform, where the Pittsburgh G20 promised to transfer at least 5 percent of the quota share from the old established powers largely in Europe to the new, emerging, largely Asian ones.

With this increase in emerging country influence and the overall equalization of leadership in the group, in its third phase the G20 slowly became more of a personal club of the leaders who created and came to it, not just a convenient forum for advancing domestic preferences but as a group that they valued for taking care of themselves, their citizens, and the global community as a whole.

The Causes of G20 Governance

The first cause of the G20's creation, continuation, and eventual centrality as a group—and one that was emerging as an interpersonal club—was crisis. Specifically, the key cause was the sequence of shocks that showed all members and outsiders the vulnerability of even the most powerful countries to the new, non-state threats arising in a densely interconnected, complex, uncertain, globalized world, defined by the demise and death of distance and delay. The sequence of market-originated, Asian-turned-global financial shocks from 1997 to 1998, which infected the United States itself with the collapse of the hedge fund Long-Term Capital Management in the autumn of 1988, caused the G20 finance ministers and central bank governors to come together as a new group in 1999. The deadly terrorist attacks targeted at America on September 11, 2001, and their anthrax aftermath caused the G20, alone among similar international institutions, to meet in Ottawa the following November, thus allowing other bodies to meet as well. A decade later, the Anglo/American-turned-global financial shocks of 2007–08, with the US at the epicentre by September 2008, caused the G20 to be elevated to the leaders' level for an intense schedule of summitry starting two months later. The absence of such finance or terrorist shocks on the United States in 2004–05 enabled George Bush to ignore the call of Paul Martin, despite his eventual support from all the other G20 leaders, for such summitry at that time. The financial shock of the Eurocrisis in its Greece phase in the spring of 2010 caused the Toronto Summit to produce its central achievement of containing the crisis, if not necessarily its specific formula of doing so through a macroeconomic message of stimulus now, exit soon, and fiscal consolidation according to specific targets and timetables in the medium term.

Such shocks, especially in their financial form, were necessary causes of the G20's creation in 1999 and especially of its leap to the leaders' level in 2008. But alone they were by no means enough to cause the many consequences that defined the particular path that the G20 took to reach its central place in global economic governance by 2010. Indeed, the shock sequence alone decreasingly determined the G20's emergence, with its particular membership. This is seen in the formidable international institutional competition in 1999, the shock-free Montreal mission and agenda expansions of 2000, the increasing influence of emerging members from 2002 to 2008, and the shock-free Pittsburgh proclamation of the G20 as its permanent, priority, post-crisis, international economic governance group.

The second cause important in explaining such outcomes is the failure of the old formal multilateral organizations from the 1940s and the more informal, plurilateral institutions from before and after 1997 to respond adequately to such shocks and to the new globalized world that lay behind. Indeed, as early as September 11, 2001, the terrorist shock on America dramatically showed that only the fledgling G20 forum could function, and that the G7 and IMF could work only because of it, in light of the terrorist trauma striking a newly vulnerable America and world. Yet even given the financial shock in America in September 2008, Nicolas Sarkozy and even George Bush in the beginning thought of the G7 or G8, or a G8 Plus Five, as the first international institutional line of defence, before soon realizing that they needed the established, effective G20, now in a new summit form. And it was only with the advent of G20 summitry that the IMF effectively abandoned its strategy, there since the start in 1999, of eliminating the G20 in favour of itself and its International Monetary and Financial Committee (IMFC). The IMF shifted to a new strategy of making itself indispensable to the G20's work and thus to a G20 that worked. It thus gave the G20 a critical, formal "G192" supporter, to go along with the critical, informal G7 ally the G20 also had. At a lower level, international institutional failure also explained why the G20's competitors and colleagues among the other 1999 creations—the G7-centric FSF and the IMFC—eventually faded. The first changed into a G20-like number and membership by 2010 in the form of the FSB. The IMFC, the IMF's 24-member executive board, or missing ministerial council were not needed for leadership in a world where the G20 leaders, finance ministers, and central bank governors worked so well.

Yet international institutional competition and cooperation, as essential supplements to sequential shocks, do not alone explain why these particular 20 members came to create a group that continued from 1999 to 2010 with an unchanged membership, unlike the recurrently expanding G7/8, IMF, and FSF. The third cause—globally predominant and internally equalizing capabilities—offers one important answer to this question. These 20 members gave the G20 the critical collective predominance and increasingly internal equality in the relative capabilities of its members that its international institutional alternatives lacked. Indeed, as realists have long claimed, relative capability continues to count for much, even in the much changed world of the twenty-first century. However,

Summers and Martin's creational consideration of which countries should be in or out of their new group, the continuing inclusion of South Africa and Argentina, and the closing of the list at 19 shows that there was more at work than merely rational actors reliably counting relative capability. Most fundamentally, the selection criterion was not only relative capability but also global connectivity, combined in the new criterion of systemic significance—a rational recognition by the two co-creators that the now globalized world had importantly changed from its Westphalian ontological origins in 1648.

Not all systemically significant candidates made it in as full members, as shown by the cases of Indonesia at the very start, Nigeria from 1999 on, and Spain from 2008 to 2010. Thus convergence on the domestic principles and practices of political openness and their components and consequences is a fourth cause of the G20's composition, operation, and, particularly, direction-setting performance. Nigeria, as with Indonesia at the beginning, needed to pass that additional test of behaving as a recognizable democratic polity. But by the time Nigeria did, the G20 was frozen in its familiar membership. Moreover, few agreed that a non-democratic Egypt should be added as a substitute, despite the old Westphalian logic where geographic location defined by territorial land counted most as the "representativeness" required for a group to work. With regard to quickly admitted Indonesia, and even Mexico, Korea, and Turkey, the democratic criterion was clear, if in varying degrees. The two non-democratic anomalies of Saudi Arabia and China had sufficient systemic significance to compensate for their democratic defects. The latter slowly moved from 1999 to 2010 toward more political openness and an acceptance of its component principles of transparency, free information exchange, accountability, and the rule of law. Both also shared with G20 members the core conviction about the centrality of political stability, based on underlying social stability and economic and financial stability. These were the shared values of the systemically significant winners in the world of 1999 to 2010. This was shown most clearly by Mexico, Korea, Indonesia, Turkey, and Argentina, as these economic losers from 1994 to 2002 became the winners from 2008 to 2010.

The slow move toward political openness among G20 members offers an inadequate explanation of the particular cadence of G20 governance, with its great leaps forward in 2001 and 2008–10 and its slowness, if not setbacks, at others times such as 2002. Here arises the fifth cause—the political capital, control, continuity, financial-economic competence, and personal commitment of the individual G20 ministers, bankers, and leaders. Important for the G20's punctuated pathway to high performance is the presence of Paul Martin, who was a CEO before entering politics and then Canada's finance minister from 1993 to 2002 and leader in 2003–06. Martin was accompanied by Larry Summers as the US treasury secretary in 1999–2001 and economic advisor to Barack Obama in 2009–10. They were aided by Gordon Brown, who was Britain's chancellor of the exchequer from 1997 to 2007 and leader from 2007 to 2010, George Bush as US president from 2001 to 2008, and Manmohan Singh, who had served as India's finance minister three times and had been the prime minister since 2004. The key individual was Martin, who co-created the G20 and put it on the path to sustained success from 1999 to 2001 and mounted the campaign to create a G20 summit that succeeded when, three years after he had left, the September 2008 shock struck and Bush finally agreed.

Yet G20 governance requires not just leadership by one, two, or a few committed individuals but collegiality of a certain sort among most, if it is to perform effectively as the group of equals it was designed to be. At both the level of ministers and governors and the level of leaders, the G20 increasingly became the efficient, effective, legitimate club at the hub of an expanding network of global governance. Here dense, diverse, overlapping combinations of advanced and emerging country representatives met intensively to execute their responsibilities and rights instrumentally and rationally to govern the globe for their individual, collective, and broader global good. In doing so they slowly started to bond together as individuals, moving the G20 toward an interpersonal club they cared about as a core element of their personal sense of interest and even identity in some respects.

The Contributions to International Relations Theory

This study of G20 governance offers five specific contributions to the larger study of global governance and international relations.

The first, in an international system that is rapidly transforming from its defining Westphalian foundations of sovereign, mutually exclusive, territoriality, is to highlight the need for much greater attention to the demand side of global governance and to how the transforming system of the twenty-first century generates new catalysts and requirements for responses from states and the many other types of actors now involved (Ruggie 1993; Kirton et al. 2005). In particular, in a globalized world, the oligopolistic array of state-centric actors led by the major powers and the mechanical, linear logic bred by their interactions to produce threats based on the balance of state power is being replaced as the source of demand for global governance by new, non-state sources of deadly, even existential threats. Those threats can arise anywhere and flow fast and freely to exert their unintended and uncontrolled destruction on even the most powerful states. In this world of equalizing vulnerability bred by an intense, interconnected, complex, uncertain non-state-inclusive system, the concepts of complex adaptive systems—with their emphasis on simultaneity, non-linearity, path dependence, and punctuated change—are important starting points on the demand side.

The second contribution is to suggest that international institutions deserve to stand alongside sovereign states as key actors in global governance and international politics. The 1648 Westphalian world without intergovernmental organizations or even institutions (beyond sovereign separation, monarchical intermarriage, and diplomacy) has now been replaced in the twenty-first century by a dense array of international institutions of a highly formal or highly informal character and of broadly multilateral, globally plurilateral, trans-regional, or restricted regional relevance and reach (Ikenberry 2001; Bayne 2011b; Kirton et al. 2010). To be sure, despite the demands bred by a global complex adaptive system, some issue areas such as energy or terrorism remain governed by few formal, multilateral organizations dedicated to the subject (Lesage et al. 2010). Yet many other areas, notably finance and economics, have a highly dense array that is growing rapidly. In such areas, the dynamics of creation, competition, cooperation, and extinction, long the staple of scholars assuming that states are the dominant actors in world politics, still deserve a central place, but now with international institutions standing alongside sovereign states as the actors consequentially involved (Kirton et al. 2005). Yet because these institutions are often composed of states that belong to many such institutions, for reasons well beyond regime nesting or forum shopping, it is important to identify the sociogram formed by their overlapping institutional network, to see which countries acquire and exert global influence and leadership by standing at the global hub (Raustiala and Victor 2004).

The third contribution is the need to move from rational incentive and choice conceptions to social-psychological ones to describe and explain collective club governance. This shift points in particular to how the intense interactions within valued club institutions can produce the personal bonds and thus the ensuing accommodation, adjustment, and solidarity among the individuals involved (Stephens 2010). It requires recognizing and tracing how rational incentives and choices and social-psychological processes combine in complex combinations to produce the observed outcomes not well explained by either one alone.

The fourth contribution is to highlight the effective, autonomous agency of individuals, at the official, ministerial, and, above all, leader level, in making international institutions and—through them—global governance work, especially in new systemic structural contexts such as that brought by a globalizing world. In the end it is individuals with a vision, personal commitment, and political skill who create the clubs that count, and work within them to make the club their own.

The fifth contribution is to highlight how global governance of an ontologically complex adaptive system requires moving epistemologically beyond considering causation in terms of relative salience, or even a sequential process of adding successive residuals to explain the causal gaps. The alternative is to start with a conception of a more complex causal configuration and cadence in which causes interrelate with all others simultaneously in ways that are difficult to predict compactly, as distinct from anticipate (Welch 2005).

The Future of G20 Governance

The future of G20 governance remains open-ended, if only because its fate lies in the hands of individuals who must react to and guide a complex, uncertain, rapidly changing world. The alternatives range across the broad options of redundancy, reform, reinforcement, and replacement in relation to the established

G7/8 system that was central to the G20 at its start and that remains relevant to global governance today. This broad quadrumvirate is also relevant in regard to a similar set of possible outcomes arising from a succeeding generation of informal institutions, ranging from a rapidly emerging BRICs to a "G2" of the US and China, through a "G4" of different states, to other configurations also un-created and as yet unconceived. The durability and dominant path of the G20 could also be bounded and shaped by the wide variety of recommendations about how it can and should be institutionally improved to govern the twenty-first century world more effectively and legitimately (Bradford and Lim 2010). However, the G20 has now acquired a powerful institutional and personal momentum sufficiently strong to guide it through even far-reaching forthcoming systemic changes and challenges, rather than leaving it just to react to and be easily replaced by outside transformations and centres to come. Given the firm foundation and formidable path laid from 1999 to 2010, the G20's future was further shaped by its following summits in Seoul, Korea, on November 11–12, 2010, in Cannes, France, on November 3–4, 2011, on June 18–19, 2012, in Los Cabos, Mexico, and on the road to St. Petersburg, Russia, in September 2013.

Seoul, Korea, November 2010

Indeed, the 2010 Korean-hosted Seoul Summit was a substantial success (Kirton 2010; Lee 2010; Bayne 2011a). It proved that an emerging economy member from Asia—and one beyond the BRICs—could design, chair, and host a summit that met the deadlines then due for the initiatives central to the G20's foundational mission of promoting financial stability by strengthening, at both the domestic and international level, the respective central pillars of the world's private banks and the IMF (Bayne and Woolcock 2011). It further delivered on the second mission, soon added through the Montreal Consensus, by adding the Seoul Development Consensus to help make globalization through G20 governance work better for all. Moreover, Seoul's second initiative from the host, on financial safety nets, constituted a pre-emptive response to the classic financial crises coming, not from Asia and Korea as in the distant decade before but now from Europe, out of Greece in the spring of 2010 and then out of Ireland on the eve of the summit itself.

The Seoul Summit did not respond well to the clear and present danger from Ireland so far away from Asia. This failure became clear in the weeks following the summit as this second instalment of the Eurocrisis in 2010 mutated into a substantial systemic threat. Had the G20 leaders at Seoul had more time together, by having a two-day summit, rather than the less than one-day summit that was the norm for G20 summitry, they could well have taken up the new crisis of the moment. They could thus have reacted in a way superior to that of the Europeans, left to do so on their own with a merely regional response to a contagious crisis in a now globalized world. When the G20 leaders were left alone together at Seoul, they moved the G20 from a rational, calculating club toward a personally cherished one. There were several spontaneous outbursts of applause for their beloved colleague Brazil's Luiz Inácio Lula da Silva, who would soon be leaving (Kirton 2011a). There were also personal condolences for their politically less loved colleague from Argentina, Cristina Fernández de Kirchner, on the recent death of her husband.

Cannes, France, November 2011

For France as host in 2011, from the start the G20 summit was central to the domestic political management of its entrepreneurial co-creator, Nicolas Sarkozy. He publicly set forth his objectives for his summit at an unusually early stage, in August 2010, well before the preceding Seoul Summit had even been held (Sarkozy 2010). No fewer than 12 new issues under three themes were added to the G20's broadening built-in agenda that now included Korea's two additions from Toronto and Seoul.

These new issues, with initiatives proposed on each, were very ambitious. The most modest was the institutionalization of the G20 itself, in the standard century-old way of adding a fixed secretariat to improve accountability and the relationship of the G20 with other international organizations. The proposals extended to a grand transformation of the enduring 1944 order, and of the hegemonic financial capability of the US that lay behind, through a reform of the international monetary system in which the unique status of the US dollar as the international reserve currency would be replaced by a new arrangement where other currencies had a consequential place. Most notably, Sarkozy's initiatives took G20 governance into the classic, core, political-security realm, on a proactive, institutionally architectural level, rather than a reactive, immediate, issue-specific one, by proposing to use the 2011 G20 summit to reform the United Nations Security Council at the UN's 1945 "constitutional" core.

Apart from the suggestion for a G20 secretariat, the French moved quickly to strengthen governance of the G20 as an institution in several ways. They faced the challenge of delivering their own and the world's highly ambitious agenda, and doing so despite an escalating Eurocrisis, through holding only one G20 summit in 2011 rather than two a year for the first time. They moved to deepen and broaden G20 governance at the ministerial level, by mounting the first meeting of G20 ministers of agriculture. They took up the Canadian challenge of chairing and hosting both the G20 and G8 summit in a single year, and thus further defining the relationship between the two bodies, now meeting at far more distant times and places than they had in 2010. And France would extend the G20's trend of having the host, as well as the group, at the hub of a global governance network, through its central role in the regular summit of la Francophonie and the Asia–European Union Meeting in 2011.

The Cannes Summit proved to be a substantial success (Kirton 2011b). It contained the financial crisis that reached critical levels in Greece and Italy on the eve of the summit, riding to the rescue of a European Union that had tried but failed repeatedly to cope on its own. The leaders endorsed a recipe for stronger, more sustained, and balanced growth by recommitting to medium-term fiscal consolidation first, short-term stimulus where possible, and substantially more exchange rate flexibility, respecting market fundamentals more than ever. The summit moved to augment the resources of the IMF, so it could credibly assist large countries in Europe or elsewhere that were afflicted by short-term market panic but were seriously committed to painfully needed reforms at home. It similarly strengthened the resources, role, and status of the FSB, and appointed as its new chair Mark Carney, who could be counted on to lead it in smarter, fairer, more inclusive financial regulation and supervision.

Less prominently but still importantly, the G20 finally effectively declared the decade-long Doha negotiations of the World Trade Organization to be dead, choosing instead to focus on smaller trade-liberalizing measures to provide relief to the poorest countries in the world. The G20 also rejected both a global financial transaction tax at a time when more inexpensive money was needed to flow from abroad to Europe, as well as a G20 secretariat that would transfer ownership of the club from the most powerful leaders in the world to international bureaucrats claiming to act in their name.

Los Cabos, Mexico, June 2012

For Mexico in 2012, its Los Cabos Summit was a significant success in moving the G20 from being not only a crisis-response committee to also being a steering committee (Kirton and Kulik 2012; Cooper 2012). It delivered a globally demanded and urgently desired double dividend, by both controlling an escalating Eurocrisis and advancing a priority and built-in agenda that it broadened in important ways.

To control the Eurocrisis, Los Cabos promised to support Greece's path to reform and sustainability and, through its euro area members, to take swift, specific short-term moves toward supranational European-wide banking regulation and deposit insurance, and "all necessary policy measures to safeguard the integrity and stability of the area" (G20 2012). To generate global growth and jobs, the summit set a credible strategy that emphasized stimulus now and fiscal consolidation soon, and to this end mandated more discretionary and automatic fiscal stimulus, monetary policy, and a broad array of structural reforms. In support, it strengthened employment and social protection, trade and investment, the international financial architecture, financial regulation and inclusion, food security and commodity price volatility, development, green growth, corruption, and G20 governance and accountability, while for the first time addressing gender issues and the proliferation of weapons of mass destruction.

This double dividend, embedded in at least 95 clear commitments in the core 14-page communiqué, was driven above all by the sequence of severe and spreading shocks erupting in Europe, led by Spanish bond yields escalating well before G20 leaders met to turn the tide. Support came from the key international institutions, notably the IMF in helping raise $456 billion in new resources, the

G8's Camp David Summit a month earlier in pioneering a fiscally responsible global strategy for growth and jobs, the G7 finance ministers' accommodating statement on the eve of the Los Cabos Summit in response to the pro-European, pro-austerity results of the elections in Greece, and the BRICS summit—now with South Africa as a member—on June 18 that supported Europe, new IMF resources, and the G20 itself. G20 leaders recognized that they had the predominant share of the world's economy and responsibility, even if accelerating growth in North America and slowing growth in Europe and the BRICS exacerbated inequalities within the G20. G20 members' growing convergence on political openness, promised by transitions in political leadership in Russia and China, strengthened the solidarity of the group. Among the many new leaders, looming elections, and political transitions, there was a strong core of committed G20 summit founders and veterans, led by Mexican president and host Felipe Calderón, who were able and willing to lead. This personal bond was reinforced by an intense summit interaction within and overlapping the G20. This made the G20, as an institution and its leaders as individuals, the embryonic club at the hub of a dense, expansive network of global governance as a whole.

Institutionally, the first contribution of Los Cabos to global governance came from repeating and thus further reinforcing the new tradition in G20 summitry of rotating the chair and host between an advanced G8 member and an emerging non-G8 one (Calderón 2010). This confirmed the core institutional expression of the equality among all categories and countries within the summit-level club. By doing so in the fifth year of G20 summitry, Mexico repeated its contribution at the level of finance ministers and central bank governors, through hosting that forum in its fifth year in 2003. Mexico was thus the first emerging member to host the G20 at both the ministerial and leader levels in different years, thus benefiting from the experience that such a repetition brought. It also pointed the way to a rotation among very broadly defined geographic regions, with the summit moving from the Americas and then Asia in 2010, to Europe in 2011, and back to the Americas for 2012.

Mexico institutionalized the precedent, set by Korea, of having the G20's non-G8 hosts come from democratic polities, and from those outside the more powerful emerging countries in the recently established BRICs. This tradition will be reinforced by the G20 being hosted by Russia in September 2013 and then moving back to the Asia-Pacific region in November 2014 in Australia.

Finally, Mexico took up the challenge of hosting the G20 summit in tandem with a G8 one, this time on a regional rather than national basis, as the US hosted the G8 exactly a month earlier, on May 18–19 in Camp David, Maryland, in the lead-up to Barack Obama's presidential re-election bid. Mexico, a key member of the Summit of the Americas since its 1994 start and the North American Leaders' Summit since it began in 2005, further enriched the position of the host of the group as a hub of a network of global governance beyond.

The Longer Term

What lies ahead for G20 governance over the longer term in both the ideational and institutional realms? The challenge will be for the G20 to retain its relevance in an increasingly crisis-ridden, institutionally crowded world. Will performance as assessed against the key criteria of effectiveness, accountability, and legitimacy ultimately favour the new G20, the old G8, the newer BRICS, or some other group? How will its performance shape the relationship between the new G20 and old G8 in a redundant, rejection, reinforcement, or replacement way?

In the ideational realm, the answer to these questions lies in the G20's growing devotion to the democratic values at the core of the G8. This devotion can be seen most broadly by recalling that the cadence of G20 governance is defined and driven by global financial crises—the 1997–99 one from Asia that created the G20 at the ministers' and bank governors' level and the 2008–10 one from America and the Atlantic that catalysed the G20 at the leaders' level and continued it as a permanent primary forum. One of the great surprises of both crises was their failure, despite the great economic and social devastation in all the hardest hit countries, to generate sharp surges of civil strife or shifts to the political right reminiscent of the Great Depression of the 1930s and the Weimar-to-Hitler radicalization that such crises brought. In the 1997–99 crisis, the striking result was the move from dictatorship to democracy in Indonesia and the durability of democracy in the rising emerging countries to which it had recently come. In the 2008–10 crisis, the United States at the epicentre moved from Bush's Republicans to Obama's "New Deal" Democrats in the presidency, Senate, and Congress. In all other G20 members incumbent governments were returned with stronger pluralities (Canada, India), moved slightly to the right but well within the range of normal politics (Britain, Germany), or shifted slightly to the left (Japan, Russia). Even in China, the crisis produced more moves to political openness and "democracy" from the streets rather than repression from the top, compared to the dark days at Tiananmen Square in 1989. Nowhere did the dictatorship dog bark. Everywhere the democracy one did. Against the deep dark backdrop of the fascism and Stalinism of the 1930s, why was it so different this time?

Among the many possible answers, two explanations stand out. The first is that the democratic revolution brought by the G7/8 since 1975 was so successful that it proved durable, even when financial crises struck Greece, Portugal, Spain, and Italy in post-communist Europe, with no signs of a return to Euro-communism in sight. The second is that the G8's democratic revolution did not end in 1997–99, or even 2006, when Russia was finally accepted as a full member of the G8 summit club. Rather, it was extended through the G20 into the twenty-first century, into the emerging powers of the new era, and thus throughout the world. Almost from the start, G20 governance was not only about financial stability and economic growth, but also about open democracy, individual liberty, and social advance—about globalization that worked for all in these pre-eminently political and very human ways.

In the institutional realm, the key also lies in the G20's growing devotion to democracy, as this will define the G20's long-term relationship with the more durable and continuing G8. The new vulnerabilities and shocks brought by globalization, notably a succession of financial crises since 1994 and the terrorist shocks since September 11, 2001, catalysed the creation in 1999 and subsequent continuation of a broader, more collectively capable G20 to help provide global governance in finance, economics, and related fields. The G20's expanded number and range of systemically important countries as members increased the capacity, effectiveness, and resulting legitimacy of this new global centre of collective leadership. In 2008, the American-turned-global financial crisis finally inspired the G20 to leap to the leaders' level, a move that brought new challenges and new potential for impact.

With non-democratic China and Saudi Arabia as core members from the start, however, and stability, growth, equity, and openness as key principles, to what extent will the G20 be able to help diffuse the democratic principles its G8 members share? How much and why has the G20 been able to extend the G7/8's commitment to open democracy, individual liberty, and social advance? Since the elevation of the G20 to the leader level, these questions take on added importance.

An analysis of the G20's performance since its 1999 start suggests that the G20 has indeed assisted in diffusing democratic values. The vulnerability and shocks bred by globalization, in an experience shared increasingly by all members, substantially help to explain this trend. So does the deepening institutionalization of the G20 as a balanced, autonomous, valued forum led by experienced, democratic hosts. The substantial G20 performance in democracy diffusion as well as in its domestic political management, deliberative, decisional, delivery, and development of global governance dimensions has only intensified since the G20 began its summits. Should current trends continue, the G20 and all its members could in the longer run become devoted to democracy along with the G8 and all its members, if in distinctly different ways. With such shared social purpose to trump the dynamics of relative power and the transaction costs of large numbers of more diverse members, over the longer run, in a fusion of equals each equally committed to the same core values, the G20 and G8 could well become one (Ruggie 1983).

References

Bayne, Nicholas. 2011a. "The Decline of the G8 Summit and Lessons for the G20." In *New Economic Diplomacy: Decision-Making and Negotiation in International Economic Relations*, eds Bayne, Nicholas, and Woolcock, Stephen. Farnham: Ashgate, 249–62.

Bayne, Nicholas. 2011b. "Plurilateralism and Multilateralism: Comparing Institutions." In *The New Economic Diplomacy: Decision-Making and*

Negotiation in International Relations, eds Bayne, Nicholas, and Woolcock, Stephen. Aldershot: Ashgate, 205–29.

Bayne, Nicholas and Woolcock, Stephen. 2011. "The Future of Economic Diplomacy." In *New Economic Diplomacy: Decision-Making and Negotiation in International Economic Relations*, eds Bayne, Nicholas, and Woolcock, Stephen. Farnham: Ashgate, 359–78.

Bradford, Colin I. and Lim, Wonhyuk, eds. 2010. *Toward the Consolidation of the G20: From Crisis Committee to Global Steering Committee*. Seoul and Washington DC: Korea Development Institute and Brookings Institution.

Calderón, Felipe. 2010. "The G20 as a Lever for Global Development." In *The G20 2010 Seoul Summit: Shared Growth Beyond Crisis*, eds Kirton, John J., and Koch, Madeline. London: Newsdesk, 18–19. Available at: www.g8.utoronto.ca/newsdesk/seoul/seoul-calderon-en.html. Accessed: July 2012.

Cooper, Andrew F. 2012. "The G20 as the Global Focus Group: Beyond the Crisis Committee/Steering Committee Framework." June 19. Available at: www.g20.utoronto.ca/analysis/120619-cooper-focusgroup.html. Accessed: July 2012.

G20. 2012. "G20 Leaders Declaration." Los Cabos, June 19. Available at: www.g20.utoronto.ca/2012/2012-0619-loscabos.html. Accessed: July 2012.

Ikenberry, G. John. 2001. *After Victory: Institutions, Strategic Restraint, and the Rebuilding of Order after Major Wars*. Princeton: Princeton University Press.

Kirton, John J. 2010. "A Summit of Substantial Success: The Performance of the G20 at Seoul." Seoul, November 13. Available at: www.g20.utoronto.ca/analysis/101113-kirton-seoul-perf.html. Accessed: July 2012.

Kirton, John J. 2011a. "Brazil's Contribution to G20 and Global Governance." Paper prepared for keynote address to the 16th ENERI Conference, Brasilia, May 18–19. Available at: www.g20.utoronto.ca/biblio/kirton-eneri-110518.html. Accessed: July 2012.

Kirton, John J. 2011b. "Cannes 2011: A Summit of Substantial Success." Cannes, November 4. Available at: www.g20.utoronto.ca/analysis/111104-kirton-cannes-perf.html. Accessed: July 2012.

Kirton, John J., Fratianni, Michele, Rugman, Alan M., and Savona, Paolo. 2005. "New Perspectives on the G8." In *New Perspectives on Global Governance: Why America Needs the G8*, eds Fratianni, Michele, Savona, Paolo, and Kirton, John J. Aldershot: Ashgate, 231–56.

Kirton, John J. and Kulik, Julia. 2012. "A Summit of Significant Success: G20 Los Cabos Leaders Deliver the Desired Double Dividend." June 19. Available at: www.g20.utoronto.ca/analysis/120619-kirton-success.html. Accessed: July 2012.

Kirton, John J., Larionova, Marina, and Savona, Paolo, eds. 2010. *Making Global Economic Governance Effective: Hard and Soft Law Institutions in a Crowded World*. Farnham: Ashgate.

Lee, Myung-bak. 2010. "The Road to Seoul: Shared Growth Beyond Crisis." In *The G20 2010 Seoul Summit: Shared Growth Beyond Crisis*, eds Kirton,

John J., and Koch, Madeline. London: Newsdesk, 10–11. Available at: www.g8.utoronto.ca/newsdesk/seoul/seoul-lee-mb-en.html. Accessed: July 2012.
Lesage, Dries, Van de Graaf, Thijs, and Westphal, Kirsten. 2010. *Global Energy Governance in a Multipolar World*. Farnham: Ashgate.
Raustiala, Kal and Victor, David G. 2004 (April). "The Regime Complex for Plant Genetic Resources." *International Organization* 58(2): 277–309.
Ruggie, John G. 1983. "International Regimes, Transactions, and Change: Embedded Liberalism in the Postwar Economic Order." In *International Regimes*, ed Krasner, Stephen D. Ithaca: Cornell University Press, 195–232.
Ruggie, John G. 1993. "Territoriality and Beyond: Problematizing Modernity in International Relations." *International Organization* 47(1): 139–74.
Sarkozy, Nicolas. 2010. "Plans for France's G20 Summit in 2011." In *The G20 2010 Seoul Summit: Shared Growth Beyond Crisis*, eds Kirton, John J., and Koch, Madeline. London: Newsdesk, 16–17. Available at: www.g8.utoronto.ca/newsdesk/seoul/seoul-sarkozy-en.html. Accessed: July 2012.
Stephens, Gina. 2010. "Information and Communication: G8 Institutionalization and Compliance in the DOT Force." In *Making Global Governance Effective: Hard and Soft Law Institutions in a Crowded World*, eds Kirton, John J., Larionova, Marina, and Savona, Paolo. Farnham: Ashgate, 201–15.
Welch, David. 2005. *Painful Choices: A Theory of Foreign Policy Change*. Princeton: Princeton University Press.

Bibliography

Abbott, Kenneth W., Keohane, Robert, Moravcsik, Andrew, Slaughter, Anne-Marie, and Snidal, Duncan. 2000. "The Concept of Legalization." *International Organization* 54(3): 401–20.

Adler, Emanuel. 1997. "Seizing the Middle Ground: Constructivism in World Politics." *European Journal of International Relations* 3(3): 319–63.

Adler, Emanuel. 2002. "Constructivism and International Relations." In *Handbook of International Relations*, eds Carlsnaes, Walter, Risse, Thomas, and Simmons, Beth A. London: Sage Publications, 95–118.

Adler, Emanuel and Barnett, Michael, eds. 1998. *Security Communities*. Cambridge: Cambridge University Press.

Adler, Emanuel and Haas, Peter M. 1992. "Conclusion: Epistemic Communities, World Order, and the Creation of a Reflective Research Program." *International Organization* 46(1): 367–90.

Agence France Presse. 2004. "After Five Years, G20 Forum Still Teething." November 16.

Agence France Presse. 2004. "Eichel Criticizes Argentina's Pullout from G20 Meeting." November 19.

Agence France Presse. 2004. "Exchange Rate Developments Could Come Up at Central Bankers' Meeting." November 10.

Agence France Presse. 2004. "Italy Supports Canadian Plans for a G20 Summit, Cooperation on Africa." October 15.

Agence France Presse. 2004. "Russia Blocking Paris Club Debt Relief for Iraq." November 21.

Agence France Presse. 2004. "Snow Pleased by G20 'Broad Endorsement' of Pro-growth Agenda." November 21.

Agence France Presse. 2004. "US Sees Growing Importance of G20; Wants to Avoid Dollar Spat." November 16.

Agence France Presse. 2004. "Wolfensohn Says Economic Powers Should Formalize G20 to Consult." September 24.

Agence France Presse. 2006. "Economic Leaders to Act on Energy Security But Not Climate Change." November 19.

Agence France Presse. 2008. "Canada Tempers Hopes for G20 Crisis Talks." November 7.

Agence France Presse. 2008. "Canada Wants Home Remedies to Financial Crisis, Not Overhaul." November 5.

Agence France Presse. 2008. "Congo President Plans to Attend G20 Economic Summit." October 30.

Agence France Presse. 2008. "Les pays pauvres doivent être entendus au sommet du G20 (Ban Ki-moon)." October 24.

Agence France Presse. 2009. "African Ministers Demand G20 Seat." October 4. Available at: www.pambazuka.org/aumonitor/comments/2564. Accessed: July 2012.

Agence France Presse. 2009. "Brazil Sees Chance to Alter World Decisions at BRIC Summit." June 14.

Alexandroff, Alan S. and Kirton, John J. 2010. "The 'Great Recession' and the Emergence of the G20 Leaders' Summit." In *Rising States, Rising Institutions: Challenges for Global Governance*, eds Alexandroff, Alan S., and Cooper, Andrew F. Washington DC: Brookings Institution Press, 178–95.

Altman, Roger C. 2009 (January/February). "The Great Crash, 2008: A Geopolitical Setback for the West." *Foreign Affairs* 88(1): 2–14.

Amato, Giuliano. 2008. "From Bretton Woods to the G20." In *Growth, Innovation, Inclusion: The G20 at Ten*, eds Kirton, John J., and Koch, Madeline. London: Newsdesk, 29–31. Available at: www.g8.utoronto.ca/newsdesk/G20at10.pdf. Accessed: July 2012.

Ambrosio, Thomas. 2010 (November). "Constructing a Framework of Authoritarian Diffusion: Concepts, Dynamics, and Future Research." *International Studies Perspectives* 11(4): 375–92.

Angus Reid Global Monitor. 2007. "South Africans Divided on Mbeke's Tenure." December 13. Available at: www.angus-reid.com/polls/29613/south_africans_divided_on_mbekis_tenure. Accessed: July 2012.

Arrighi, Giovanni and Silver, Beverly. 1999. *Chaos and Governance in the Modern World System*. Minneapolis: University of Minnesota Press.

Asia-Pacific Economic Cooperation. 2005. "Busan Declaration — Towards One Community: Meet the Challenge, Make the Change." Leaders' declaration, Busan, November 18–19. Available at: www.apec.org/Meeting-Papers/Leaders-Declarations/2005/2005_aelm.aspx. Accessed: July 2012.

Asia-Pacific Economic Cooperation. 2005. "Joint Statement — Towards One Community: Meet the Challenge, Make the Change." Ministerial meeting, Busan, November 15–16. Available at: www.apec.org/Meeting-Papers/Ministerial-Statements/Annual/2005/2005_amm.aspx. Accessed: July 2012.

Asia-Pacific Economic Cooperation. 2006. "Ha Noi Declaration: Towards a Dynamic Community for Sustainable Development and Prosperity." Leaders' declaration, Ha Noi, November 18–19. Available at: www.apec.org/Meeting-Papers/Leaders-Declarations/2006/2006_aelm.aspx?t=1. Accessed: July 2012.

Åslund, Anders. 2006. "Russia's Challenges as Chair of the G8." Policy Brief No. 06-3, March. Institute for International Economics, Washington DC. Available at: www.iie.com/publications/pb/pb06-3.pdf. Accessed: July 2012.

Åslund, Anders. 2009. "The Group of 20 Must Be Stopped." *Financial Times*, November 26. Available at: www.iie.com/publications/opeds/oped.cfm?ResearchID=1549. Accessed: July 2012.

Australian Associated Press. 2006. "G20 'Universally' Condemns N. Korea Nuclear Tests." November 19.

Australian Associated Press. 2006. "Melbourne G20 Hailed a Success." *Sydney Morning Herald*, November 20. Available at: www.smh.com.au/news/NATIONAL/Melbourne-G20-hailed-a-success/2006/11/20/1163871298527.html. Accessed: July 2012.

Authers, John. 2003. "G20 Meeting Upbeat over Outlook for World Economy." *Financial Times*, October 28.

Bailin, Alison. 2005. *From Traditional to Group Hegemony: The G7, the Liberal Economic Order, and the Core-Periphery Gap*. Aldershot: Ashgate.

Baker, Andrew. 2006. *The Group of Seven: Finance Ministries, Central Banks, and Global Financial Governance*. London: Routledge.

Baker, Andrew. 2010. "Restraining Regulatory Capture? Anglo-America, Crisis Politics, and Trajectories of Change in Global Financial Crisis." *International Affairs* 83(3): 647–63.

Barnett, Michael and Finnemore, Martha. 1999. "The Politics, Power, and Pathologies of International Organizations." *International Organization* 53(4): 699–732.

Barnett, Michael and Finnemore, Martha. 2004. *Rules for the World: International Organizations in Global Politics*. Ithaca: Cornell University Press.

Basel Committee on Banking Supervision. 2009. "Consultative Proposals to Strengthen the Resilience of the Banking Sector Announced by the Basel Committee." Press release, December 17, Bank for International Settlements, Basel. Available at: www.bis.org/press/p091217.htm. Accessed: July 2012.

Basel Committee on Banking Supervision. 2009. "International Framework for Liquidity Risk Measurement, Standards, and Monitoring: Consultative Document." December 17, Bank for International Settlements, Basel. Available at: www.bis.org/publ/bcbs165.pdf. Accessed: July 2012.

Baum, Richard and Shevchenko, Alexei. 2001. "Bringing China In: A Cautionary Note." In *The New Great Power Coalition: Toward a Concert of Nations*, ed Rosecrance, Richard. New York: Rowman and Littlefield, 327–44.

Bayne, Nicholas. 2001. "Managing Globalisation and the New Economy: The Contribution of the G8 Summit." In *New Directions in Global Economic Governance: Managing Globalisation in the Twenty-First Century*, eds Kirton, John J., and von Furstenberg, George M. Aldershot: Ashgate, 171–88.

Bayne, Nicholas. 2003. "Impressions of the Evian Summit, 1–3 June 2003." June 3. Available at: www.g8.utoronto.ca/evaluations/2003evian/assess_bayne030603.html. Accessed: July 2012.

Bayne, Nicholas. 2010. *Economic Diplomat*. Durham UK: Memoir Club.

Bayne, Nicholas. 2011. "The Decline of the G8 Summit and Lessons for the G20." In *New Economic Diplomacy: Decision-Making and Negotiation in International Economic Relations*, eds Bayne, Nicholas, and Woolcock, Stephen. Farnham: Ashgate, 249–62.

Bayne, Nicholas. 2011. "Plurilateralism and Multilateralism: Comparing Institutions." In *The New Economic Diplomacy: Decision-Making and Negotiation in International Relations*, eds Bayne, Nicholas, and Woolcock, Stephen. Aldershot: Ashgate, 205–29.

Bayne, Nicholas and Woolcock, Stephen. 2011. "The Future of Economic Diplomacy." In *New Economic Diplomacy: Decision-Making and Negotiation in International Economic Relations*, eds Bayne, Nicholas, and Woolcock, Stephen. Farnham: Ashgate, 359–78.

Beattie, Alan. 1999. "New Forum to Supplement G7 Work." *Financial Times*, September 27.

Beattie, Alan. 2010. "International Economy: A Display of Disunity." *Financial Times*, October 22. Available at: www.ft.com/intl/cms/s/0/3ff4c528-de0f-11df-88cc-00144feabdc0.html#axzz215UCNXWY. Accessed: July 2012.

Beauchesne, Eric. 1999. "Martin Warns against Complacency." *Montreal Gazette*, September 26, p. A9.

Beeson, Mark and Bell, Stephen. 2009. "The G20 and International Economic Governance: Hegemony, Collectivism, or Both?" *Global Governance* 15(1): 67–86.

Ben-Ishai, Elizabeth, Aburto, Daniella, Fiorello, Carrie, Harrison, Judah, and Dolkar, Karma. 2002. "G20 in New Delhi: Fight Trade Barriers and Money Laundering." *G8 Bulletin*, November 18–24. Available at: www.g8.utoronto.ca/g8bulletin/vol6/issue12.htm. Accessed: July 2012.

Bergsten, C. Fred. 1998. "The New Agenda with China." *International Economic Policy Briefs* 98(2): 1–2.

Bergsten, C. Fred. 2009. "Obama's 500-Day Report Card." *International Economy* 23(2): 10–19. Available at: www.international-economy.com/TIE_Sp09_Obama500Days.pdf. Accessed: July 2012.

Bergsten, C. Fred and Henning, C. Randall. 1996. *Global Economic Leadership and the Group of Seven*. Washington DC: Institute for International Economics.

Best, Jacqueline. 2003. "From the Top–Down: The New Financial Architecture and the Re-embedding of Global Finance." *New Political Economy* 8(3): 383–84.

Birdsall, Nancy and de la Torre, Augusta. 2001. "Washington Contentious." *Politica Internazionale* 29 (January-April): 97–104.

Blair, Tony. 2010. *A Journey*. London: Random House.

Blustein, Paul. 2001. *The Chastening: Inside the Crisis That Rocked the Global Financial System and Humbled the IMF*. New York: PublicAffairs.

Bradford, Colin I. and Lim, Wonhyuk, eds. 2010. *Toward the Consolidation of the G20: From Crisis Committee to Global Steering Committee*. Seoul and Washington DC: Korea Development Institute and Brookings Institution.

Bradford, Colin I. and Lim, Wonhyuk, eds. 2010. *The New Dynamics of Summitry: Institutional, Policy, and Political Innovations for G20 Summits: Issues and Essays*. Seoul: Korea Development Institute.

Bradford, Colin I. and Linn, Johannes F. 2004. "Global Economic Governance at a Crossroads: Replacing the G7 with the G20." Brookings Institution Policy Brief 131. Available at: www.brookings.edu/papers/2004/04globaleconomics_bradford.aspx. Accessed: July 2012.

Bradford, Colin I. and Linn, Johannes F. 2009. "Welcome to the New Era of G20 Global Leadership." In "G20 Summit: Recovering from the Crisis," G20 Summit Report No. 3, Brookings Institution, Washington DC. Available at: www.brookings.edu/research/reports/2009/09/17-g20-summit. Accessed: July 2012.

BRIC Finance Ministers. 2008. "Brazil, Russia, India, and China Finance Ministers Joint Communiqué." São Paulo, November 7. Available at: www.brics.utoronto.ca/docs/081107-finance.html. Accessed: July 2012.

BRICs. 2009. "Joint Statement of the BRIC Countries' Leaders." Yekaterinburg, June 16. Available at: www.brics.utoronto.ca/docs/090616-leaders.html. Accessed: July 2012.

Brinsden, Colin. 2006. "G20 Baton Handed to South Africa." Australian Associated Press, November 19.

Bronnert, Deborah. 2011. "Making Government Policy: The G8 and G20 in 2010." In *New Economic Diplomacy: Decision-Making and Negotiation in International Economic Relations*, eds Bayne, Nicholas, and Woolcock, Stephen. Farnham: Ashgate, 81–92.

Brown, Gordon. 2005. "Statement at the Conclusion of G7 Finance Ministers Meeting." London, December 3. Available at: www.g8.utoronto.ca/finance/fm051203_brown.htm. Accessed: July 2012.

Brown, Gordon. 2009. "G20 Press Conference." London, April 3. Available at: tna.europarchive.org/20081209202104/http://www.number10.gov.uk/Page18934. Accessed: July 2012.

Brown, Gordon. 2010. *Beyond the Crash: Overcoming the First Crisis of Globalization*. New York: Free Press.

Brown, Owen. 2004. "China Watch: Yuan Grumbles at G20, But No Moves Likely." Dow Jones International News. November 19.

Brown, Owen. 2006. "G20 Didn't Exclude Any Energy Reform Strategy — Germany." Dow Jones, November 19.

Bryant, Ralph C. 2003. *Turbulent Waters: Cross-Border Finance and International Governance*. Washington DC: Brookings Institution Press.

Brzezinski, Zbigniew. 1996. "Let's Add to the G7." *New York Times*, June 25, p. A11.

Buchanan, Allen and Keohane, Robert O. 2006. "The Legitimacy of Global Governance Institutions." *Ethics and International Affairs* 20(4): 405–37.

Buchanan, James M. 1965. "An Economic Theory of Clubs." *Economica* 32(125): 1–14.

Burleigh, Marc. 2008. "Key Emerging Economies Want Financial System Overhaul." Agence France Presse, November 7.

Bush, George W. 2010. *Decision Points*. New York: Crown Publishers.

Business Times Singapore. 2004. "US Dollar Danger Ahead." October 8.

Calderón, Felipe. 2010. "The G20 as a Lever for Global Development." In *The G20 2010 Seoul Summit: Shared Growth Beyond Crisis*, eds Kirton, John J., and Koch, Madeline. London: Newsdesk, 18–19. Available at: www.g8.utoronto.ca/newsdesk/seoul/seoul-calderon-en.html. Accessed: July 2012.

Canada. 2005. "Joint Declaration by Canada and China." Beijing, January 20. Available at: epe.lac-bac.gc.ca/100/205/301/prime_minister-ef/paul_martin/06-02-03/www.pm.gc.ca/eng/news.asp@id=397. Accessed: July 2012.

Canada. 2005. "Joint Declaration by Canada and India." Delhi, January 18. Available at: epe.lac-bac.gc.ca/100/205/301/prime_minister-ef/paul_martin/06-02-03/www.pm.gc.ca/eng/news.asp@id=391. Accessed: July 2012.

Canada-Korea G20 Seminar. 2010. "Canada-Korea High-Level G20 Seminar: Report 2010." Norman Paterson School of International Affairs, Carleton University, March 17, Ottawa. Available at: www.g20.utoronto.ca/biblio/Canada-Korea-G20-2010-Report.pdf. Accessed: July 2012.

Canada. Department of Finance. 1999. "Finance Minister Paul Martin Chosen as Inaugural Chairperson of New Group of Twenty." Press Release 99–080, Washington DC, September 25. Available at: www.g8.utoronto.ca/finance/fm992509.htm. Accessed: July 2012.

Canada. Department of Finance. 2000. "New G20 Forum: Backgrounder." Available at: www.g20.utoronto.ca/g20backgrounder.htm. Accessed: July 2012.

Canada. Governor General. 2004. "Speech from the Throne to Open the First Session of the 38th Parliament of Canada." October 5. Available at: www.pco-bcp.gc.ca/index.asp?lang=eng&page=information&sub=publications&doc=a archives/sft-ddt/2004_2-eng.htm. Accessed: July 2012.

Canada. Standing Committee on Foreign Affairs and International Trade. 2000. "Evidence." Ottawa, May 18. Available at: www.parl.gc.ca/HousePublications/Publication.aspx?DocId=1040280&Language=E&Mode=1&Parl=36&Ses=2. Accessed: July 2012.

Carin, Barry and Mehlenbacher, Alan. 2010. "Constituting Global Leadership: Which Countries Need to Be Around the Summit Table for Climate Change and Energy Security?" *Global Governance* 16(1): 21–38.

Cerny, Philip G. 1995. "Globalization and the Changing Logic of Collective Action." *International Organisation* 49(4): 595–625.

Chappell, Trevor. 2006. "G20 Dialogue on Energy, Minerals Was a Breakthrough — Costello." Australian Associated Press, November 19.

Charlebois, Sylvain. 2010. "Canada a Roadblock in Trade Talks." *National Post*, July 2. Available at: opinion.financialpost.com/2010/07/02/canada-a-roadblock-in-trade-talks. Accessed: July 2012.

Choe, Wongi. 2010. "The Role of Korea in G20 Process and the Seoul Summit." Paper prepared for an international conference on "G20 Seoul Summit: From Crisis to Cooperation," Korean Association of Negotiation Studies, May 20, Seoul. Available at: www.g20.utoronto.ca/biblio/choe-kans.pdf. Accessed: July 2012.

Choi, Hee-nam. 2009. "Enhancing Korea's Standing through the G20." *Korea Herald*, June 9.

Clark, Campbell. 2010. "Harper's Pro-Austerity Position Could Seal His Legacy — For Good or Bad." *Globe and Mail*, July 7. Available at: www.theglobeandmail.com/news/politics/harpers-pro-austerity-position-could-seal-his-legacy---for-good-or-bad/article1390298/. Accessed: July 2012.

Clendenning, Alan. 2008. "Big Emerging-Market Nations Unify to Demand Bigger Role in Fixing Global Finance System." Associated Press, November 7. Accessed: July 2012.

Cohn, Theodore. 2000. *Global Political Economy: Theory and Practice*. New York: Longman.

Commission on Global Governance. 1995. *Our Global Neighbourhood: The Report of the Commission on Global Governance*. Oxford: Oxford University Press.

Commonwealth Heads of Government. 2005. "Final Communiqué." Malta, November 25–27. Available at: www.thecommonwealth.org/Templates/Internal.asp?NodeID=147565. Accessed: July 2012.

Compte, Michel. 2008. "Canada's PM Calls for Compromise at G20 Financial Crisis Talks." *Agence France Presse*, November 14.

Conway, Edmund and Aldrick, Philip. 2007. "Rescue Bid Cooked Up under the Cover of G20 Event." *Daily Telegraph*, December 13.

Cook, Peter. 1999. "Time Will Tell Whether There's a Need for a G20, Peter Cook Says." *Globe and Mail*, December 15.

Cooper, Andrew F. 2007. "The Logic of the B(R)ICSAM Model for G8 Reform." CIGI Policy Brief No. 1, Centre for International Governance Innovation, Waterloo ON. Available at: www.cigionline.org/publications/2007/5/logic-bricsam-model-g8-reform. Accessed: July 2012.

Cooper, Andrew F. 2010. "The G8-G20 Partnership." In *G8 & G20: The 2010 Canadian Summits*, eds Kirton, John J., and Koch, Madeline. London: Newsdesk, 306–07. Available at: www.g8.utoronto.ca/newsdesk/g8g20. Accessed: July 2012.

Cooper, Andrew F. 2010. "The G20 as an Improvised Crisis Committee and/or a Contested 'Steering Committee" for the World.' *International Affairs* 86(3): 741–57.

Cooper, Andrew F. 2012. "The G20 as the Global Focus Group: Beyond the Crisis Committee/Steering Committee Framework." June 19. Available at: www.g20.utoronto.ca/analysis/120619-cooper-focusgroup.html. Accessed: July 2012.

Cooper, Andrew F. and English, John. 2005. "Introduction." In *Reforming from the Top: A Leaders' 20 Summit*, eds English, John, Thakur, Ramesh, and Cooper, Andrew F. Tokyo: United Nations University Press.

Cooper, Andrew F. and Kirton, John J., eds. 2009. *Innovation in Global Health Governance: Critical Cases*. Farnham: Ashgate.

Cooper, Andrew F. and Subacchi, Paola. 2010. "Overview." *International Affairs* 86(3): 607–17.

Cooper, Andrew F., Antkiewicz, Agata, and Shaw, Timothy M. 2006. "Economic Size Trumps All Else? Lessons from BRICSAM." Centre for International Governance Innovation, Waterloo ON. Available at: www.cigionline.org/publications/2006/12/economic-size-trumps-all-else-lessons-bricsam. Accessed: July 2012.

Cooper, Andrew F., Kirton, John J., and Schrecker, Ted, eds. 2007. *Governing Global Health: Challenge, Response, Innovation*. Aldershot: Ashgate.

Costello, Peter. 2008. *The Costello Memoirs: The Age of Prosperity*. Melbourne: Melbourne University Press.

Coyne, Andrew. 2010. "G20 Members: Embarking on a Great Experiment." *Maclean's*, July 5. Available at: www2.macleans.ca/2010/07/05/embarking-on-a-great-experiment/. Accessed: July 2012.

Crockett, Andrew. 2004. "Progress towards Greater International Financial Stability." In *The IMF and Its Critics: Reform of Global Financial Architecture*, eds Vines, David, and Gilbert, Christopher L. Cambridge: Cambridge University Press, 36–58.

Crook, Clive. 2010. "A Graver Sin Than Fiscal Disarray." *Financial Times*, June 28.

Culpeper, Roy. 2000. "Systemic Reform at a Standstill: A Flock of 'Gs' in Search of Global Financial Stability." Paper presented at Critical Issues in Financial Reform: Latin-American/Caribbean and Canadian Perspectives, Munk Centre for International Studies, University of Toronto, June 1–2, Toronto. Available at: www.g8.utoronto.ca/scholar/culpeper2000. Accessed: July 2012.

Currah, Kel. 2010. "The G8: The Greatest Show on Earth." *G8/G20 Summit 2010*, June, pp. 32–33.

Curry, Bill, Waldie, Paul, Robertson, Grant, and Perkins, Tara. 2010. "Summit on the Brink: How Harper Saved His Deal." *Globe and Mail*, June 28.

Cutler, A. Claire, Haufler, Virginia, and Porter, Tony, eds. 1999. *Private Authority and International Affairs*. Albany: State University of New York Press.

Da Silva, Luiz Inácio Lula. 2010. "The G20 Moment." *New Perspectives Quarterly* 27(1): 33–34.

Daily Telegraph. 2004. "G20 Host Adds to Status." November 22.

Dale, Daniel. 2010. "What the Summit Pundits Said." *Toronto Star*, June 26.

de Brouwer, Gordon and Yeaman, Luke. 2007. "Australia's G20 Host Year: A Treasury Perspective." Treasury, Australian Government, Canberra. Available at: www.g20.utoronto.ca/biblio/debrouwer-yeaman_2007.pdf. Accessed: July 2012.

de Larosière, Jacques. 2005. "From Mexico to Argentina: What Have We Learned from Two Decades of Debt Crises?" Monograph Series, Number 3, Princeton Institute for International and Regional Studies. Available at: www.asmp.fr/fiches_academiciens/textacad/larosiere/mexico_argentina.pdf. Accessed: July 2012.

Dean, January. 2004. "Trade Minister Says PM's Right on Expanding G7." *Mississauga News*, April 21.

Desai, Seema. 2006. "Expanding the G8: Should China Join?," January. Foreign Policy Centre, London. Available at: fpc.org.uk/fsblob/749.pdf. Accessed: July 2012.

Deudney, Daniel and Ikenberry, G. John. 2009. "The Myth of the Autocratic Revival: Why Liberal Democracy Will Prevail." *Foreign Affairs* 88(1): 77–93.

Dewitt, David and Kirton, John J. 1983. *Canada as a Principal Power: A Study in Foreign Policy and International Relations*. Toronto: John Wiley and Sons.

DeYoung, Karen. 2006. "Terrorist Attacks Rose Sharply in 2005, State Dept. Says." *Washington Post*, April 29. Available at: www.washingtonpost.com/wp-dyn/content/article/2006/04/28/AR2006042802181.html. Accessed: July 2012.

Dickie, Mure, Guha, Krishna, and Garnham, Peter. 2007. "Chinese Join Chorus of Alarm on Weak Dollar." *Financial Times*, November 20. Available at: www.ft.com/intl/cms/s/0/067f2a4c-970c-11dc-b2da-0000779fd2ac.html#axzz20iSIum2u. Accessed: July 2012.

Dobson, Hugo. 2004. *Japan and the G7/8, 1975–2002*. London: RoutledgeCurzon.

Dodge, David. 2001. "Interview with Candida Tamar Paltiel." November 18. Available at: www.g8.utoronto.ca/oralhistory. Accessed: July 2012.

Dolfman, Michael L., Fortier Wasser, Solidelle, and Bergman, Bruce. 2007. "The Effects of Hurricane Katrina on the New Orleans Economy." *Monthly Labor Review* 130(6): 3–18. Available at: www.bls.gov/opub/mlr/2007/06/art1exc.htm. Accessed: July 2012.

Donovan, Paul. 2009. "What Is the G20 Really Fighting For?" *Jakarta Post*, October 19.

Doran, Charles. 1971. *The Politics of Assimilation: Hegemony and Its Aftermath*. Baltimore: Johns Hopkins University Press.

Dow Jones Chinese Financial Wire. 2004. "China Central Banker: Prepared to Talk on FX Rates at G20." November 19.

Dow Jones International News. 2006. "G20 to Focus on IMF, World Bank." November 22.

Duncan, Richard. 2008. "Bring Back the Link between Gold and the Dollar." *Financial Times*, November 23. Available at: www.ft.com/intl/cms/s/0/ba673d22-b977-11dd-99dc-0000779fd18c.html#axzz215UCNXWY. Accessed: July 2012.

Economist. 1998. "Welcome to China, Mr Clinton." January 25. Available at: www.economist.com/node/137669. Accessed: July 2012.

Economist. 2008. "The Coddle and Protect Policy." November 20. Available at: www.economist.com/node/12636308. Accessed: July 2012.

Economist. 2008. "Miss World Goes Missing." November 20. Available at: www.economist.com/node/12641700. Accessed: July 2012.

Economist. 2008. "No Time to Waste." November 20. Available at: www.economist.com/node/12637027. Accessed: July 2012.

Economist. 2008. "Where's Angela?," November 20. Available at: www.economist.com/node/12637035. Accessed: July 2012.

Edwards, Leonard. 2010. "Looking Ahead to the G20 Seoul Summit: A Year of Canadian-Korean Partnership." Speech to the Annual General Meeting of the Korea-Canada Society, November 3, Ottawa.

El Economista. 2002. "Mexico to Preside over G20 During 2003." November 25.

Engelen, Klaus C. 2008 (September). "Rift Barely Acknowledged." *International Economy* 22(4): 10–11.

English, John, Thakur, Ramesh, and Cooper, Andrew F., eds. 2005. *Reforming from the Top: A Leaders' 20 Summit*. Tokyo: United Nations University Press.

Fagan, Drew. 2004. "PM's Plan Pushes UN to Sidelines." *Globe and Mail*, April 30, p. A1.

Fidler, Stephen, Davis, Bob, Mollenkamp, Carrick, and Weisman, Jonathan. 2009. "G20 in London: Measured Gains for G20." *Wall Street Journal Europe*, April 3.

Financial Stability Forum. 1999. "Announcement of the First Meeting of the FSF, Washington." April 6. Available at: www.financialstabilityboard.org/press/t_990414.htm. Accessed: July 2012.

Financial Times. 2009. "The First Bricks in a New World Order." April 3.

Financial Times. 2010. "Financial Markets 'Do Not Understand the Euro'." December 5.

Foster, Peter. 2003. "Far More New Faces than New Ideas." *National Post*, December 13.

Frank, Robert H. 2010. "The Choices That Pay Us Back." *New York Times*, July 4. Available at: www.robert-h-frank.com/PDFs/EV.07.04.10.pdf. Accessed: July 2012.

Fratianni, Michele and Alessandrini, Pietro. 2009. "The Common Purse." In *The G8 2009: From La Maddalena to L'Aquila*, eds Kirton, John J., and Koch, Madeline. London: Newsdesk, 52–53. Available at: www.g8.utoronto.ca/newsdesk/g8-2009.html. Accessed: July 2012.

Fratianni, Michele and Pattison, John C. 2001. "International Organisations in a World of Regional Trade Agreements: Lessons from Club Theory." *World Economy* 24(3): 333–58.

Fratianni, Michele, Salvatore, Dominick, and Savona, Paolo, eds. 1999. *Ideas for the Future of the International Monetary System*. Boston: Kluwer Academic Publishers.

Fratianni, Michele, Savona, Paolo, and Kirton, John J., eds. 2005. *New Perspectives on Global Governance: Why America Needs the G8*. Aldershot: Ashgate.

Fréchette, Louise. 1995. "The Halifax Summit: A Canadian Perspective." *North American Outlook* 5(3): 7–13.

Freytag, Andreas, Kirton, John J., Sally, Razeen, and Savona, Paolo, eds. 2011. *Securing the Global Economy: G8 Global Governance for a Post-Crisis World*. Farnham: Ashgate.

Friedman, Benjamin. 2006. "The Moral Consequences of Economic Growth." *Society* 43(2): 15–22.

Fues, Thomas. 2007. "Global Governance Beyond the G8: Reform Prospects for the Summit Architecture." *Internationale Politik und Gesellschaft* 2: 11–24. Available at: www.fes.de/ipg/inhalt_d/pdf/03_Fues_US.pdf. Accessed: July 2012.

Fullilove, Michael. 2010. "With Friends in High Places: Australia's G20 Membership." *Australian*, March 13. Available at: www.brookings.edu/research/opinions/2010/03/13-australia-fullilove. Accessed: July 2012.

G7. 1988. "Toronto Economic Summit Economic Declaration." Toronto, June 21. Available at: www.g8.utoronto.ca/summit/1988toronto. Accessed: July 2012.

G7. 1999. "G7 Statement." Cologne, June 18. Available at: www.g8.utoronto.ca/summit/1999koln/g7statement_june18.htm. Accessed: July 2012.

G7. 2001. "G7 Statement." Genoa, July 20. Available at: www.g8.utoronto.ca/g7/summit/2001genoa/g7statement.html. Accessed: July 2012.

G7 Finance Ministers and Central Bank Governors. 2005. "Statement by G7 Finance Ministers and Central Bank Governors." September 23. Available at: www.g8.utoronto.ca/finance/fm050923.htm. Accessed: July 2012.

G7 Finance Ministers and Central Bank Governors. 2005. "Statement of G7 Finance Ministers and Central Bank Governors." London, February 4–5. Available at: www.g8.utoronto.ca/finance/fm050205_statement.htm. Accessed: July 2012.

G7 Finance Ministers and Central Bank Governors. 2009. "Statement of the G7 Finance Ministers and Central Bank Governors Meeting." Washington DC, April 24. Available at: www.g8.utoronto.ca/finance/fm090424.htm. Accessed: July 2012.

G7 Finance Ministers and Central Bank Governors. 2010. "Statement of G7 Finance Ministers and Central Bank Governors." May 9. Available at: www.g8.utoronto.ca/finance/fm100509.html. Accessed: July 2012.

G8. 2000. "G8 Communiqué Okinawa 2000." Okinawa, July 23. Available at: www.g8.utoronto.ca/summit/2000okinawa/finalcom.htm. Accessed: July 2012.

G8. 2006. "Global Energy Security." St. Petersburg, July 16. Available at: www.g8.utoronto.ca/summit/2006stpetersburg/energy.html. Accessed: July 2012.

G8. 2009. "Responsible Leadership for a Sustainable Future." L'Aquila, Italy, July 8. Available at: www.g8.utoronto.ca/summit/2009laquila/2009-declaration.html. Accessed: July 2012.

G8 Research Group. 2004. "2003 Evian Final Compliance Report." Available at: www.g8.utoronto.ca/evaluations/2003evian_comp_final. Accessed: July 2012.

G8 Research Group LSE/Oxford. 2007. "The G8 and Climate Change since Heiligendamm: Final Compliance Report for the G8 and Outreach Five Countries." Available at: www.g8.utoronto.ca/oxford/g8rg-lseox-final-2007-080720.pdf. Accessed: July 2012.

G8 Research Group Oxford. 2007. "Governing Global Climate Change: St. Petersburg Compliance Report for the 'G8 Plus Five' Countries." Available at: www.g8.utoronto.ca/oxford/2006compliance-ox.pdf. Accessed: July 2012.

G20. 2008. "Declaration of the Summit on Financial Markets and the World Economy." Washington DC, October 15. Available at: www.g20.utoronto.ca/2008/2008declaration1115.html. Accessed: July 2012.

G20. 2008. "The Group of Twenty: A History." Available at: www.g20.utoronto.ca/docs/g20history.pdf. Accessed: July 2012.

G20. 2009. "G20 Leaders Statement: The Pittsburgh Summit." Pittsburgh, September 25. Available at: www.g20.utoronto.ca/2009/2009communique0925.html. Accessed: July 2012.

G20. 2009. "Global Plan for Recovery and Reform." London, April 2. Available at: www.g20.utoronto.ca/2009/2009communique0402.html. Accessed: July 2012.

G20. 2010. "The G20 Toronto Summit Declaration." Toronto, June 27. Available at: www.g20.utoronto.ca/2010/to-communique.html. Accessed: July 2012.

G20. 2012. "G20 Leaders Declaration." Los Cabos, June 19. Available at: www.g20.utoronto.ca/2012/2012-0619-loscabos.html. Accessed: July 2012.

G20 Finance Ministers and Central Bank Governors. 2000. "Communiqué." Montreal, October 25. Available at: www.g20.utoronto.ca/2000/2000communique.html. Accessed: July 2012.

G20 Finance Ministers and Central Bank Governors. 2001. "Communiqué." Ottawa, November 17. Available at: www.g20.utoronto.ca/2001/2001communique.html. Accessed: July 2012.

G20 Finance Ministers and Central Bank Governors. 2001. "G20 Action Plan on Terrorist Financing." Ottawa, November 17. Available at: www.g20.utoronto.ca/2001/2001communique.html#action. Accessed: July 2012.

G20 Finance Ministers and Central Bank Governors. 2002. "Delhi Communiqué." Delhi, November 23. Available at: www.g20.utoronto.ca/2002/2002communique.html. Accessed: July 2012.

G20 Finance Ministers and Central Bank Governors. 2003. "Economic Reform in this Era of Globalization: 16 Country Cases." October 26. Available at: www.g20.utoronto.ca/docs/economicreform.pdf. Accessed: July 2012.

G20 Finance Ministers and Central Bank Governors. 2003. "G20 Communiqué." Morelia, Mexico, October 27. Available at: www.g20.utoronto.ca/2003/2003communique.html. Accessed: July 2012.

G20 Finance Ministers and Central Bank Governors. 2003. "Mexico 2003: G20 Work Program." Available at: www.g20.utoronto.ca/2003/2003program.pdf. Accessed: July 2012.

G20 Finance Ministers and Central Bank Governors. 2004. "Communiqué." Berlin, November 21. Available at: www.g20.utoronto.ca/2004/2004communique.html. Accessed: July 2012.

G20 Finance Ministers and Central Bank Governors. 2004. "G20 Accord for Sustained Growth." Berlin, November 21. Available at: www.g20.utoronto.ca/2004/2004growth.html. Accessed: July 2012.

G20 Finance Ministers and Central Bank Governors. 2004. "G20 Reform Agenda." Berlin, November 21. Available at: www.g20.utoronto.ca/2004/2004reform.html. Accessed: July 2012.

G20 Finance Ministers and Central Bank Governors. 2004. "G20 Statement on Transparency and Exchange of Information for Tax Purposes." Berlin, November 21. Available at: www.g20.utoronto.ca/2004/2004transparency.html. Accessed: July 2012.

G20 Finance Ministers and Central Bank Governors. 2004. "G20 Workshop on Developing Strong Domestic Financial Markets." April 26–27. Available at: www.g20.utoronto.ca/docs/financialmarketsworkshop.pdf. Accessed: July 2012.

G20 Finance Ministers and Central Bank Governors. 2005. "Communiqué." Xianghe, Hebei, China, October 16. Available at: www.g20.utoronto.ca/2005/2005communique.html. Accessed: July 2012.

G20 Finance Ministers and Central Bank Governors. 2005. "G20 Reform Agenda 2005." Xianghe, Hebei, China, October 16. Available at: www.g20.utoronto.ca/2005/2005reform.html. Accessed: July 2012.

G20 Finance Ministers and Central Bank Governors. 2005. "G20 Statement on Global Development." Xianghe, Hebei, China, October 16. Available at: www.g20.utoronto.ca/2005/2005development.html. Accessed: July 2012.

G20 Finance Ministers and Central Bank Governors. 2005. "G20 Statement on Reforming the Bretton Woods Institutions." Xianghe, Hebei, China, October 16. Available at: www.g20.utoronto.ca/2005/2005bwi.html. Accessed: July 2012.

G20 Finance Ministers and Central Bank Governors. 2006. "Communiqué." Melbourne, November 19. Available at: www.g20.utoronto.ca/2006/2006communique.html. Accessed: July 2012.

G20 Finance Ministers and Central Bank Governors. 2007. "Communiqué." Kleinmond, South Africa, November 18. Available at: www.g20.utoronto.ca/2007/2007communique.html. Accessed: July 2012.

G20 Finance Ministers and Central Bank Governors. 2007. "G20 Reform Agenda 2007: Agreed Actions to Implement the G20 Accord for Sustained Growth." Kleinmond, South Africa, November 18. Available at: www.g20.utoronto.ca/2007/2007reform.html. Accessed: July 2012.

G20 Finance Ministers and Central Bank Governors. 2008. "Communiqué of the Meeting of Finance Ministers and Central Bank Governors." São Paulo, November 9. Available at: www.g20.utoronto.ca/2008/2008communique1109.html. Accessed: July 2012.

G20 Finance Ministers and Central Bank Governors. 2009. "Communiqué." St. Andrews, Scotland, November 7. Available at: www.g20.utoronto.ca/2009/2009communique1107.html. Accessed: July 2012.

G20 Finance Ministers and Central Bank Governors. 2009. "Declaration on Further Steps to Strengthen the Financial System." London, September 5. Available at: www.g20.utoronto.ca/2009/2009banking0905.html. Accessed: July 2012.

G20 Finance Ministers and Central Bank Governors. 2009. "Meeting of Finance Ministers and Central Bank Governors: Communiqué." London, September 5. Available at: www.g20.utoronto.ca/2009/2009communique0905.html. Accessed: July 2012.

G20 Finance Ministers and Central Bank Governors. 2010. "Communiqué: Meeting of G20 Finance Ministers and Central Bank Governors." Washington DC, April 23. Available at: www.g20.utoronto.ca/2010/g20finance100423.html. Accessed: July 2012.

G20 Finance Ministers and Central Bank Governors. 2010. "Statement by the G20 Finance Ministers on the Euro Area Support Measures." May 10. Available at: www.g20.utoronto.ca/2010/g20finance100510.html. Accessed: July 2012.

G20 Research Group and International Organizations Research Institute. 2010. "2010 G20 Toronto Summit Final Compliance Report." November 14. Available at: www.g20.utoronto.ca/analysis/2010toronto-compliance.html. Accessed: July 2012.

G20 Research Group and International Organizations Research Institute. 2011. "2010 Seoul G20 Summit Final Compliance Report." November 6. Available at: www.g20.utoronto.ca/compliance/2010seoul-final. Accessed: July 2012

Galtung, Johan. 1964. "Balance of Power and the Problem of Perception: A Logical Analysis." *Inquiry* 7(1–4): 277–94.

Gamble, Andrew. 2009. *The Spectre at the Feast: Capitalist Crisis and the Politics of Recession*. Basingstoke: Palgrave Macmillan.

Garcia, John. 2010. "The G20 Yields Only Unfulfilled Promises for Latin America." Council on Hemispheric Affairs, August 2. Available at: www.coha.org/the-g-20-yields-only-unfulfilled-promises-for-latin-america/. Accessed: July 2012.

Germain, Randall D. 2001. "Global Financial Governance and the Problem of Inclusion." *Global Governance* 7(4): 411–26.

Giles, Chris. 2009. "Finance Ministers Fall Short on Global Aims." *Financial Times*, November 9.

Giles, Chris. 2009. "G20 Yet to Deliver on Early Promise." *Financial Times*, November 8. Available at: www.ft.com/cms/s/0/8e834f02-cc63-11de-8e30-00144feabdc0.html#axzz1B4rYIUhT. Accessed: July 2012.

Gill, Stephen, ed. 1993. *Gramsci, Historical Materialism, and International Relations*. Cambridge: Cambridge University Press.

Globe and Mail. 1999. "The Surprising Legacy of the Minister of Finance Paul Martin's Triumph on the Deficit is Shadowed by Wrong-headed Policies Elsewhere." December 19.

Gotlieb, Allan. 2010. "Not Just Another Foreign-Policy Review." *Globe and Mail*, August 3. Available at: www.theglobeandmail.com/commentary/not-just-another-foreign-policy-review/article1387986/?page=all. Accessed: July 2012.

Grant, Kelly. 2010. "Paul Martin." *Globe and Mail*, May 31.

Griesgraber, Jo Marie. 2009. "Reforms for Major New Roles of the International Monetary Fund? The IMF Post-G20 Summit." *Global Governance* 15: 179–86.

Gruen, David, O'Brien, Terry, and Lawson, Jeremy, eds. 2002. *Globalisation, Living Standards, and Inequality: Recent Progress and Continuing Challenges*. Sydney, Australia: Reserve Bank of Australia. Available at: www.g20.utoronto.ca/biblio/rba-at-2002.pdf. Accessed: July 2012.

Guebert, Jenilee. 2008. "China's Compliance with G8 Commitments." G8 Research Group, Toronto.

Guerrieri, Paolo. 2010. "Multipolar Governance and Global Imbalances." *International Affairs* 86(3): 681–92. doi: 10.1111/j.1468-2346.2010.00905.x.

Guha, Krishna. 2009. "Africa's Plea for Poor to Be Heard." *Financial Times*, September 26.

Gupta, Surojit and Friel, Terry. 2002. "G20 Nations Unsure How to Cut Money for Terrorism." Reuters, November 24.

Gurría, Angel. 2005. "A Leaders' 20 Summit?" In *Reforming from the Top: A Leaders' 20 Summit*, eds English, John, Thakur, Ramesh, and Cooper, Andrew F. Tokyo: United Nations University Press, 63–71.

Hajnal, Peter I. 2007. *The G8 System and the G20: Evolution, Role, and Documentation*. Aldershot: Ashgate.

Hajnal, Peter I. 2007. "Summitry from G5 to L20: A Review of Reform Initiatives." CIGI Working Paper No. 20, March, Centre for International Governance Innovation, Waterloo ON. Available at: www.cigionline.org/publications/2007/3/summitry-g5-l20-review-reform-initiatives. Accessed: July 2012.

Hale, David. 2001. "Have Hedge Funds Become an Agent of Monetary Policy?," Zurich Financial Services, 13 June.

Harper, Stephen. 2009. "The 2010 Muskoka Summit." In *The 2009 G8 Summit: From La Maddalena to L'Aquila*, eds Kirton, John J., and Koch, Madeline. London: Newsdesk, 18–19. Available at: www.g8.utoronto.ca/newsdesk/harper-2009.html. Accessed: July 2012.

Harper, Stephen. 2009. "From Pittsburgh to Muskoka: Building a Sustainable Global Recovery." In *The 2009 G20 Pittsburgh Summit: Sustaining Global Recovery*, eds Kirton, John J., and Koch, Madeline. London: Newsdesk, 25–26. Available at: www.g8.utoronto.ca/newsdesk/pittsburgh/harper.html. Accessed: July 2012.

Harper, Stephen. 2010. "Recovery and New Beginnings." In *G8 & G20: The 2010 Canadian Summits*, eds Kirton, John J., and Koch, Madeline. London: Newsdesk, 14–15. Available at: www.g8.utoronto.ca/newsdesk/g8g20/g8g20-harper-en.html. Accessed: July 2012.

Harper, Stephen. 2010. "Statement by the Prime Minister of Canada at the 2010 World Economic Forum." Davos, January 28. Available at: www.g8.utoronto.ca/summit/2010muskoka/harper-davos.html. Accessed: July 2012.

Heine, Jorge. 2010. "Will They Have Table Manners? The G20, Emerging Powers, and Global Responsibility." *South African Journal of International Affairs* 17(1): 1–11.

Helleiner, Eric. 2010. "A Bretton Woods Moment? The 2007–2008 Crisis and the Future of Global Finance." *International Affairs* 86(3): 619–36. doi: DOI: 10.1111/j.1468-2346.2010.00901.x.

Helleiner, Eric and Pagliari, Stefano. 2009 (June). "Towards a New Bretton Woods? The First G20 Leaders Summit and the Regulation of Global Finance." *New Political Economy* 14(2): 275–87.

Helleiner, Eric, Woods, Ngaire, and Griffith-Jones, Stephany. 2010. "The Financial Stability Board: An Effective Fourth Pillar of Global Economic Governance?," Centre for International Governance Innovation, Waterloo ON. Available at: www.cigionline.org/sites/default/files/FSB%20special%20report_2.pdf. Accessed: July 2012.

Helleiner, Gerald. 2001. "Developing Countries, Global Financial Architecture, and the Group of Twenty: A Note." Prepared for the Governance Working Group of the Global Financial Governance Initiative. Available at: www.globaleconomicgovernance.org/wp-content/uploads/Helleiner%20on%20G20.PDF. Accessed: July 2012.

Helleiner, Gerald. 2001. "Markets, Politics, and Globalization: Can the Global Economy Be Civilized?" *Global Governance* 7(3): 243–63.

Hennessey, Keith. 2008. "What Was Accomplished at the G20 Summit?" KeithHennessey.com (Blog). November. Available at: keithhennessey.com/2008/11/20/what-was-accomplished-at-the-g-20-summit. Accessed: July 2012.

Hermawan, Yulius P., Sriyuliani, Wulani, Hardjowijono, Getruida H., and Tanaga, Sylvie. 2011. *The Role of Indonesia in the G20: Background, Role, and Objectives of Indonesia's Membership*. Jakarta: Friedrich-Ebert-Stiftung Indonesia Office. Available at: library.fes.de/pdf-files/bueros/indonesien/08365.pdf. Accessed: July 2012.

Hillman, Jennifer. 2010. "Saving Multilateralism: Renovating the House of Global Economic Governance for the 21st Century." Brussels Forum Paper Series, March. German Marshall Fund of the United States. Available at: www.gmfus.org/wp-content/files_mf//galleries/ct_publication_attachments/EconJenniferHillmanBFPaperSavingMultilateralism.pdf. Accessed: July 2012.

Hodges, Michael R. 1999. "The G8 and the New Political Economy." In *The G8's Role in the New Millennium*, eds Hodges, Michael R., Kirton, John J., and Daniels, Joseph P. Aldershot: Ashgate.

Holbrooke, Richard. 2005. "China Makes Its Move." *Washington Post*, May 27. Available at: www.washingtonpost.com/wp-dyn/content/article/2005/05/26/AR2005052601540.html. Accessed: July 2012.

Holling, Crawford. 1973. "Resilience and Stability of Ecological Systems." *Annual Review of Ecology and Systematics* 4: 1–23.

Holmes, John. 2010. "Building Effective Humanitarian Responses for the 21st Century." In *G8 & G20: The 2010 Canadian Summits*, eds Kirton, John J., and Koch, Madeline. London: Newsdesk, 32–34. Available at: www.g8.utoronto.ca/newsdesk/g8g20/g8g20-holmes.html. Accessed: July 2012.

Homer-Dixon, Thomas. 2001. *The Ingenuity Gap: Can We Solve the Problems of the Future?* Toronto: Vintage.

Hoy, Greg. 2006. "Costello Brothers Clash over G20." Transcript, November 20, Australian Broadcasting Corporation. Available at: www.abc.net.au/7.30/content/2006/s1793207.htm. Accessed: July 2012

Ibbitson, John. 2005. "The Prime Minister's Passion for the L20." *Globe and Mail*, February 22.

Ibbitson, John and Perkins, Tara. 2010. "How Canada Made the G20." *Globe and Mail*, June 18. Available at: www.theglobeandmail.com/news/world/g8-g20/news/how-canada-made-the-g20-happen/article1609690. Accessed: July 2012.

Ikenberry, G. John. 2001. *After Victory: Institutions, Strategic Restraint, and the Rebuilding of Order after Major Wars*. Princeton: Princeton University Press.

Interfax. 2007. "Russian Economy Over Risk Zone Overall — Kudrin." November 19.

International Labour Organization. 2009. "Promoting People, Promoting Jobs: A Survey of Country Employment and Social Protection Policy Reponses to the Global Economic Crisis." A report submitted to the G20 Leaders' Summit, Pittsburgh, 24–25 September, Geneva. Available at: www.ilo.org/public/libdoc/jobcrisis/download/protecting_people_promoting_jobs.pdf. Accessed: July 2012.

International Meeting of Health Ministers. 2005. "Ottawa 2005: Global Pandemic Influenza Readiness." October 25, Ottawa. Available at: www.who.int/mediacentre/events/2005/05_Ottawa_Canada_Ian_Shugart.pdf. Accessed: July 2012.

International Monetary Fund. 2001. "World Economic Outlook: The Global Economy After September 11." December, Washington DC. Available at: www.imf.org/external/pubs/ft/weo/2001/03. Accessed: July 2012.

International Monetary Fund. 2004. "World Economic Outlook: Advancing Structural Reforms." April, Washington DC. Available at: www.imf.org/external/pubs/ft/weo/2004/01. Accessed: July 2012.

International Monetary Fund. 2007. "World Economic Outlook: Spillovers and Cycles in the Global Economy." Executive Summary, April, Washington DC. Available at: www.imf.org/external/pubs/ft/weo/2007/01/pdf/exesum.pdf. Accessed: July 2012.

International Monetary Fund. 2010. "World Economic Outlook: Rebalancing Growth." April, Washington DC. Available at: www.imf.org/external/pubs/ft/weo/2010/01/. Accessed: July 2012.

International Monetary Fund. 2010. "World Economic Outlook: Recovery, Risk, and Rebalancing." October, Washington DC. Available at: www.imf.org/external/pubs/ft/weo/2010/02/. Accessed: July 2012.

International Organizations Research Institute. 2009. "G20 London Summit Commitments Compliance Report 2009." September 18, Moscow. Available at: www.g20.utoronto.ca/analysis/hse/2009-london-compliance.pdf. Accessed: July 2012.

International Organizations Research Institute and G20 Research Group. 2010. "2009 Pittsburgh G20 Summit Compliance Report." June 21. Available at: www.g20.utoronto.ca/analysis/Pittsburgh_G20_compliance_report.pdf. Accessed: July 2012.

Ipsos-Reid. 2009. "World Vision Child Health Factum." November, Toronto. Available at: www.worldvision.ca/About-Us/Newsroom/press-releases/Documents/World%20Vision%20Child%20Health%20Factum.pdf. Accessed: July 2012.

ITAR-TASS. 2003. "It Is Premature to Discuss Donations to Iraq—Kudrin." October 27.

Jayawardena, Lal. 1989. "World Economic Summits: The Role of Representative Groups in the Governance of the World Economy." *Journal of the Society for International Development* 4: 17–20.

Jha, Pem Shankar. 2009. "Globe in a State." *World Today* 65(3): 4–7.

Johnson, Pierre Marc. 2000. "Beyond Trade: The Case for a Broadened International Governance Agenda." *Policy Matters* 1(3): 4–36.

Johnson, Pierre Marc. 2001. "Creating Sustainable Global Governance." In *Guiding Global Order: G8 Governance in the Twenty-First Century*, eds Kirton, John J., Daniels, Joseph P., and Freytag, Andreas. Aldershot: Ashgate, 245–82.

Johnson, Steven C. 2009. "G20 Means G7 No Longer Only Game in Town on Currencies." Reuters, September 29.

Joicey, Nicholas and Pickford, Stephen. 2011. "The International Monetary Fund and Global Economic Cooperation." In *New Economic Diplomacy: Decision-Making and Negotiation in International Economic Relations*, eds Bayne, Nicholas, and Woolcock, Stephen. Farnham: Ashgate, 283–302.

Jokela, Juha. 2011. "The G20: A Pathway to Effective Multilateralism?" Chaillot Paper No. 125, April 21, European Union Institute for Security Studies. Available at: www.iss.europa.eu/publications/detail/article/the-g-20-a-pathway-to-effective-multilateralism. Accessed: July 2012.

Jones, Bruce, Pascual, Carlos, and Stedman, Stephen John. 2009. *Power and Responsibility: Building International Order in an Era of Transnational Threats*. Washington DC: Brookings Institution.

Kaiser, Karl, Kirton, John J., and Daniels, Joseph P., eds. 2000. *Shaping a New International Financial System: Challenges of Governance in a Globalizing World*. Aldershot: Ashgate.

Kant, Immanuel. 1991. "Perpetual Peace: A Philosophical Sketch." In *Kant: Political Writings*, ed Reiss, Hans Siegbert. Cambridge: Cambridge University Press, 93–130.

Katada, Saori N. 2001. *Banking on Stability: Japan and the Cross-Pacific Dynamics of International Financial Crisis Management*. Ann Arbor: University of Michigan Press.

Kelly, Paul. 2009. "Shift to G20 Was Matter of Time." *Australian*, September 27.

Keohane, Robert O. 1984. *After Hegemony: Cooperation and Discord in the World Political Economy*. Princeton: Princeton University Press.

Keohane, Robert O. 2002. *Power and Governance in a Partially Globalized World*. London: Routledge.

Keohane, Robert O. and Nye, Joseph S. 1977. *Power and Interdependence: World Politics in Transition*. Boston: Little, Brown.

Keohane, Robert O. and Nye, Joseph S. 1989. *Power and Interdependence*. 2nd ed. Glenview, IL: Scott, Foresman.

Kharas, Homi and Lombardi, Domenico. 2012. "The Group of Twenty: Origins, Prospects, and Challenges for Global Governance." Brookings Institution, Washington DC. Available at: www.brookings.edu/research/papers/2012/08/g20-global-governance-kharas-lombardi. Accessed: July 2012.

Kirton, John J. 1989. "Contemporary Concert Diplomacy: The Seven-Power Summit and the Management of International Order." Paper presented at the annual convention of the International Studies Association, 29 March–1 April, London. Available at: www.g8.utoronto.ca/scholar/kirton198901. Accessed: July 2012.

Kirton, John J. 1993. "The Seven Power Summits as a New Security Institution." In *Building a New Global Order: Emerging Trends in International Security*, eds Dewitt, David, Haglund, David, and Kirton, John J. Toronto: Oxford University Press, 335–57.

Kirton, John J. 1995. "The G7, the Halifax Summit, and International Financial System Reform." *North American Outlook* 5 (June): 43–66.

Kirton, John J. 1999. "Economic Cooperation: Summitry, Institutions, and Structural Change." In *Structural Change and Cooperation in the Global Economy*, eds Boyd, Gavin, and Dunning, John H. Cheltenham: Edward Elgar.

Kirton, John J. 1999. "The G7 and China in the Management of the International Financial System." Paper prepared for "China in the 21st Century and the World," sponsored by the China Development Institute, the China International Center for Economic and Technical Exchange, and the National Institute for Research Advancement, Japan, November 11–12, Shenzen. Available at: www.g8.utoronto.ca/scholar/kirton199903. Accessed: July 2012.

Kirton, John J. 2000. "The Dynamics of G7 Leadership in Crisis Response and System Reconstruction." In *Shaping a New International Financial System: Challenges of Governance in a Globalizing World*, eds Kaiser, Karl, Kirton, John J., and Daniels, Joseph P. Aldershot: Ashgate, 65–94.

Kirton, John J. 2001. "The G7/8 and China: Toward a Closer Association." In *Guiding Global Order: G8 Governance in the Twenty-First Century*, eds Kirton, John J., Daniels, Joseph P., and Freytag, Andreas. Aldershot: Ashgate, 189–222.

Kirton, John J. 2001. "The G20: Representativeness, Effectiveness, and Leadership in Global Governance." In *Guiding Global Order: G8 Governance in the Twenty-First Century*, eds Kirton, John J., Daniels, Joseph P., and Freytag, Andreas. Aldershot: Ashgate, 143–72.

Kirton, John J. 2001. "Guiding Global Economic Governance: The G20, the G7, and the International Monetary Fund at Century's Dawn." In *New Directions in Global Economic Governance: Managing Globalisation in the Twenty-First Century*, eds Kirton, John J., and von Furstenberg, George M. Aldershot: Ashgate, 143–67.

Kirton, John J. 2002. "Embedded Ecologism and Institutional Inequality: Linking Trade, Environment, and Social Cohesion in the G8." In *Linking Trade, Environment, and Social Cohesion: NAFTA Experiences, Global Challenges*, eds Kirton, John J., and Maclaren, Virginia W. Aldershot: Ashgate, 45–72.

Kirton, John J. 2002. "Global Community Outreach: The G20 and Africa." G8 Online, Lecture No. 9. Available at: www.g8.utoronto.ca/g8online/2002/english/2002/09.html. Accessed: July 2012.

Kirton, John J. 2004. "Getting the L20 Going: Reaching Out from the G8." Paper prepared for a workshop on "G20 to Replace the G8: Why Not Now?" sponsored by the Brookings Institution, Institute for International Economics, and the Centre for Global Governance, September 22, Washington DC. Available at: www.g8.utoronto.ca/scholar/kirton2004/kirton_040922.html. Accessed: July 2012.

Kirton, John J. 2004. "Toward Multilateral Reform: The G20's Role and Place." Paper prepared for a conference on "The Ideas-Institutional Nexus: The Case of the G20," sponsored by the Centre for International Governance Innovation, United Nations University, FLASCO, and the University of Waterloo, May 19–21, Buenos Aires. Available at: www.g8.utoronto.ca/scholar/kirton2004/kirton_g20_2004.pdf. Accessed: July 2012.

Kirton, John J. 2005. "From G7 to G20: Capacity, Leadership and Normative Diffusion in Global Financial Governance." Paper prepared for the International Studies Association convention, March 1–5, Honolulu. Available at: www.g8.utoronto.ca/scholar/kirton2005/kirton_isa2005.pdf. Accessed: July 2012.

Kirton, John J. 2005. "The Future of the G8." In *G8 Summit 2005: Mapping the Challenges*, ed Fraser, Maurice. London: Newsdesk Publications. Available at: www.g8.utoronto.ca/newsdesk/G8-2005.pdf. Accessed: July 2012.

Kirton, John J. 2005. "Toward Multilateral Reform: The G20's Contribution." In *Reforming from the Top: A Leaders' 20 Summit*, eds English, John, Thakur, Ramesh, and Cooper, Andrew F. Tokyo: United Nations University Press, 141–68.

Kirton, John J. 2006. "East Asian Summitry and Regional Community Creation." In *The Road to East Asian Community*, ed Takita, Kenji. Tokyo: Chuo University Press, 61–88.

Kirton, John J. 2007. "Facing Global Trade Imbalance: Cooperation and Development." Paper prepared for a conference sponsored by the Global Trade Development Forum and the Sixth Annual Academic Meeting on China and the World Trade Organization, November 9–12, Beijing.

Kirton, John J. 2008. "From G8 2003 to G13 2010? The Heiligendamm Process's Past, Present, and Future." In *Emerging Powers in Global Governance: Lessons from the Heiligendamm Process*, eds Cooper, Andrew F., and Antkiewicz, Agata. Waterloo ON: Wilfrid Laurier University Press, 45–79.

Kirton, John J. 2008. "The G8's Democratic Governance." ["In Portuguese."] *Cadernos Adenauer* 9: 39–60.

Kirton, John J. 2008. "The G20 Takes Centre Stage." In *Growth, Innovation, Inclusion: The G20 at Ten*, eds Kirton, John J., and Koch, Madeline. London: Newsdesk, 16–17. Available at: www.g8.utoronto.ca/newsdesk/G20at10.pdf. Accessed: July 2012.

Kirton, John J. 2008. "The Performance of the Meeting of the of G20 Finance Ministers and Central Bank Governors." São Paulo, November 9. Available at: www.g20.utoronto.ca/analysis/2008performance1109.html. Accessed: July 2012.

Kirton, John J. 2008. "Prospects for the Meeting of G20 Finance Ministers and Central Bank Governors." São Paulo, November 8. Available at: www.g20.utoronto.ca/analysis/2008prospects1108.html. Accessed: July 2012.

Kirton, John J. 2009. "Coexistence, Co-operation, Competition: G Summits." *Aspenia* (43–44). Available at: www.g20.utoronto.ca/biblio/kirton-aspenia-2009.pdf. Accessed: July 2012.

Kirton, John J. 2009. "A Committed Contributor: Japan in G8 and G20 Governance." Paper prepared for a workshop on "Japan (Still) Matters: What Role in the World," May 1, National Institute of Japanese Studies, Sheffield University, Sheffield. Available at: www.g8.utoronto.ca/scholar/kirton-japan-sheffield.pdf. Accessed: July 2012.

Kirton, John J. 2009. "London Summit: Acting for Change." In *The G20 London Summit: Growth, Stability, Jobs*, eds Kirton, John J., and Koch, Madeline. London: Newsdesk Publications, 26–27. Available at: www.g20.utoronto.ca/newsdesk/london. Accessed: July 2012.

Kirton, John J. 2009. "Prospects for the Pittsburgh G20 Summit." *IBFed Newsletter*, Summer, pp. 3–4. Available at: www.g8.utoronto.ca/g20/biblio/kirton-ibfed.pdf. Accessed: July 2012.

Kirton, John J. 2009. "A Summit of Sound Success: Prospects for the G8 at L'Aquila 2009." July 6. Available at: www.g8.utoronto.ca/evaluations/2009laquila/2009prospects090706.html. Accessed: July 2012.

Kirton, John J. 2010. "The G20 and Broader Multilateral Reform." Paper prepared for a conference on "What Role for the G20 in a Post-Crisis World?," July

15–16, Club of Madrid and Fundación para las Relaciones Internacionales y el Diálogo Exterior, Seoul. Available at: www.g20.utoronto.ca/biblio/kirton-fride-cdm.pdf. Accessed: July 2012.

Kirton, John J. 2010. "The G20 Finance Ministers: Network Governance." In *Rising States, Rising Institutions: Can the World Be Governed?*, eds Alexandroff, Alan S., and Cooper, Andrew F. Washington DC: Brookings Institution Press, 196–217.

Kirton, John J. 2010. "The G20 Summit as an International Negotiation Process: Shaping the Systemic Summit Club for Toronto and Seoul." Paper prepared for a conference on "G20 Seoul Summit: From Crisis to Co-operation" hosted by the Korean Association of Negotiation Studies and sponsored by the Institute of Foreign Affairs and National Security, May 19, Seoul. Available at: www.g20.utoronto.ca/biblio/kirton-kans.pdf. Accessed: July 2012.

Kirton, John J. 2010. "The G20, the G8, the G5, and the Role of Ascending Powers." Paper prepared for a presentation at a seminar on "Ascending Powers and the International System," December 14, Mexico City. Available at: www.g20.utoronto.ca/biblio/kirton-g20-g8-g5.pdf. Accessed: July 2012.

Kirton, John J. 2010. "The Group of Eight's Legacy, Limitations, and Lessons." In *The New Dynamics of Summitry: Innovations for G20 Summits*, eds Bradford, Colin I., and Lim, Wonhyuk. Washington DC and Seoul: Brookings Institution Press and Korea Development Institute, 17–60.

Kirton, John J. 2010. "In Substance, Summits Were a Success on Several Fronts." *Toronto Star*, June 28. Available at: www.g8.utoronto.ca/evaluations/2010muskoka/kirton-star.html. Accessed: July 2012.

Kirton, John J. 2010. "Potential Partnership in Global Economic Governance: Canada's G20 Summit from Toronto to Turkey." Paper prepared for a presentation at TEPAV, Ankara, and DEIK, Istanbul, Turkey, June 7–8, Available at: www.g20.utoronto.ca/biblio/kirton-turkey-2010.pdf. Accessed: July 2012.

Kirton, John J. 2010. "A Summit of Substantial Success: The Performance of the G20 at Seoul." Seoul, November 13. Available at: www.g20.utoronto.ca/analysis/101113-kirton-seoul-perf.html. Accessed: July 2012.

Kirton, John J. 2011. "Brazil's Contribution to G20 and Global Governance." Paper prepared for keynote address to the 16th ENERI Conference, Brasilia, May 18–19. Available at: www.g20.utoronto.ca/biblio/kirton-eneri-110518.html. Accessed: July 2012.

Kirton, John J. 2011. "Cannes 2011: A Summit of Substantial Success." Cannes, November 4. Available at: www.g20.utoronto.ca/analysis/111104-kirton-cannes-perf.html. Accessed: July 2012.

Kirton, John J. 2011. "G8 Sanctioning Success." In *Securing the Global Economy: G8 Global Governance for a Post-Crisis World*, eds Freytag, Andreas, Kirton, John J., Sally, Razeen, and Savona, Paolo. Farnham: Ashgate, 157–80.

Kirton, John J. 2012. "La gobernanza del G20 para el nuevo mundo." *Foreign Affairs Latinoamerica* 12(2): 8–21.

Kirton, John J. and Boyce, Madeline. 2009. "Making History: G20 Governance from Pittsburgh to Muskoka." September 25. Available at: www.g20.utoronto.ca/analysis/2009performance0925.html. Accessed: July 2012.

Kirton, John J. and Guebert, Jenilee. 2009. "Prospects for the Pittsburgh Summit." In *The 2009 G20 Pittsburgh Summit: Sustaining Global Recovery*, eds Kirton, John J., and Koch, Madeline. London: Newsdesk, 28–29. Available at: www.g8.utoronto.ca/newsdesk/pittsburgh/kirton.html. Accessed: July 2012.

Kirton, John J. and Guebert, Jenilee. 2009. "A Summit of Substantial Success: The Performance of the G20 in Washington in 2008." March 7. Available at: www.g20.utoronto.ca/biblio/g20-2008-performance.pdf. Accessed: July 2012.

Kirton, John J. and Guebert, Jenilee. 2010. "North American Health Governance: Shocks, Summitry, and Societal Support." *Revista Norteamericana* 5(1): 221–44. Available at: www.cisan.unam.mx/Norteamerica/PDFs%20COMPLETOS/Norteamerica%209.pdf. Accessed: July 2012.

Kirton, John J. and Koch, Madeline, eds. 2008. *Growth, Innovation, Inclusion: The G20 at Ten*. London: Newsdesk. Available at: www.g8.utoronto.ca/newsdesk/G20at10.pdf. Accessed: July 2012.

Kirton, John J. and Koch, Madeline, eds. 2009. *The G8 2009: From La Maddalena to L'Aquila*. London: Newsdesk. Available at: www.g8.utoronto.ca/newsdesk/g8-2009.html. Accessed: July 2011.

Kirton, John J. and Koch, Madeline, eds. 2009. *The G20 London Summit: Growth, Stability, Jobs*. London: Newsdesk. Available at: www.g8.utoronto.ca/newsdesk/g20london2009.pdf. Accessed: July 2011.

Kirton, John J. and Kokotsis, Ella. 2004. "An Evaluation of the G8's Commitment to the Kananaskis Pledges." Discussion paper prepared for a meeting of the Council on Foreign Relations G8 Africa Round Table, February 4, Washington DC. Available at: www.g8.utoronto.ca/scholar/kirton2004/kirton_africa_040204.html. Accessed: July 2012.

Kirton, John J. and Kulik, Julia. 2012. "A Summit of Significant Success: G20 Los Cabos Leaders Deliver the Desired Double Dividend." June 19. Available at: www.g20.utoronto.ca/analysis/120619-kirton-success.html. Accessed: July 2012.

Kirton, John J. and Panova, Victoria. 2007. "Coming Together: The Evian Legacy." In *Corporate, Public and Global Governance: The G8 Contribution*, eds Fratianni, Michele, Savona, Paolo, and Kirton, John J. Aldershot: Ashgate, 201–30.

Kirton, John J. and Takase, Junichi, eds. 2002. *New Directions in Global Political Governance: The G8 and International Order in the Twenty-First Century*. Aldershot: Ashgate.

Kirton, John J., Daniels, Joseph P., and Freytag, Andreas. 2001. "The G8's Contributions to Twenty-First Century Governance." In *Guiding Global Order: G8 Governance in the Twenty-First Century*, eds Kirton, John J., Daniels, Joseph P., and Freytag, Andreas. Aldershot: Ashgate, 283–304.

Kirton, John J., Daniels, Joseph P., and Freytag, Andreas, eds. 2001. *Guiding Global Order: G8 Governance in the Twenty-First Century*. Aldershot: Ashgate.

Kirton, John J., Fratianni, Michele, Rugman, Alan M., and Savona, Paolo. 2005. "New Perspectives on the G8." In *New Perspectives on Global Governance: Why America Needs the G8*, eds Fratianni, Michele, Savona, Paolo, and Kirton, John J. Aldershot: Ashgate, 231–56.

Kirton, John J., Larionova, Marina, and Savona, Paolo, eds. 2010. *Making Global Economic Governance Effective: Hard and Soft Law Institutions in a Crowded World*. Farnham: Ashgate.

Knabb, Richard D., Rhome, Jamie R., and Brown, Daniel P. 2006. "Tropical Cyclone Report: Hurricane Katrina, 22–30 August 2005." August 10, National Hurricane Center. Available at: www.nhc.noaa.gov/pdf/TCR-AL122005_Katrina.pdf. Accessed: July 2011.

Knight, Malcolm, Schembri, Lawrence, and Powell, James. 2004. "Reforming the Global Financial Architecture: Just Tinkering Around the Edges?" In *The IMF and Its Critics: Reform of Global Financial Architecture*, eds Vines, David, and Gilbert, Christopher L. Cambridge: Cambridge University Press, 124–56.

Kokotsis, Eleanore. 1999. *Keeping International Commitments: Compliance, Credibility, and the G7, 1988–1995*. New York: Garland.

Kokotsis, Eleanore and Kirton, John J. 1997. "National Compliance with Environmental Regimes: The Case of the G7, 1988–1995." Paper prepared for the annual convention of the International Studies Association, March 18–22, Toronto.

Kokotsis, Ella. 2005. "Explaining Compliance with G20 Commitments: The Democratic Institutionalist and Concert Equality Models Compared." Paper prepared for the annual International Studies Association convention, March 1–5, Honolulu. Available at: www.g8.utoronto.ca/scholar/kokotsis_isa2005.pdf. Accessed: July 2012.

Krasner, Stephen D. 1978. *Defending the National Interest: Raw Materials Investments and US Foreign Policy*. Princeton: Princeton University Press.

Krasner, Stephen D. 1983. *International Regimes*. Ithaca, NY: Cornell University Press.

Krugman, Paul. 2010. "Keynes in Asia." The Conscience of a Liberal (Blog). *New York Times*. July 24. Available at: krugman.blogs.nytimes.com/2010/07/24/keynes-in-asia. Accessed: July 2012.

Laghi, Brian. 2008. "World Leaders Let Harper Off Deficit Hook." *Globe and Mail*, November 17. Available at: www.theglobeandmail.com/news/national/world-leaders-let-harper-off-deficit-hook/article663403. Accessed: July 2012.

Lander, Mark. 2008. "World Leaders Vow Joint Push to Aid Economy: Big Decisions Delayed." *New York Times*, November 16, p. 1. Available at: www.nytimes.com/2008/11/16/business/worldbusiness/16summit.html. Accessed: July 2012.

Larionova, Marina, ed. 2012. *The European Union in the G8: Promoting Consensus and Concerted Actions for Global Public Goods*. Farnham: Ashgate.

Layton, Duane and Smith, Tiffany. 2009. "Ditching Doha?" *International Economy* 23(2): 21–23. Available at: www.international-economy.com/TIE_Sp09_Layton.pdf. Accessed: July 2012.

Le Boucher, Eric. 2003. "Pourquoi les antimondialistes gagnent du terrain." *Le Monde*, November 9.

Lee, Dong-hwi. 2009. "Third G20 Summit: International Political Economic Achievements and Prospects." IFANS Brief, October 12. Available at: www.g20.utoronto.ca/biblio/LEE-3rd-20091014-en.pdf. Accessed: July 2012.

Lee, Dong-hwi. 2010. "Assessment of the Toronto G20 Summit and Tasks Ahead in Preparing for the Upcoming Seoul Summit." IFANS Brief, July 13. Available at: www.g20.utoronto.ca/biblio/LEE-4-20100713-en.pdf. Accessed: July 2012.

Lee, Myung-bak. 2010. "The Road to Seoul: Shared Growth Beyond Crisis." In *The G20 2010 Seoul Summit: Shared Growth Beyond Crisis*, eds Kirton, John J., and Koch, Madeline. London: Newsdesk, 10–11. Available at: www.g8.utoronto.ca/newsdesk/seoul/seoul-lee-mb-en.html. Accessed: July 2012.

Lesage, Dries. 2007. "Globalisation, Multipolarity, and the L20 as an Alternative to the G8." *Global Society* 21(3): 343–61.

Lesage, Dries ed. 2010. "The Future of the G8 and G20" [Special issue]. *Studia Diplomatica* 63(2).

Lesage, Dries, Van de Graaf, Thijs, and Westphal, Kirsten. 2010. *Global Energy Governance in a Multipolar World*. Farnham: Ashgate.

Linklater, Andrew. 2007. *Critical Theory and World Politics: Citizenship, Sovereignty, and Humanity*. Abdingdon: Routledge.

Luce, Edward. 2002. "G20 Countries Disagree on Debt Defaults." *Financial Times*, November 25.

Lukov, Vadim. 2010. "G20 and G8 in Search of Solutions: Global Problems of Economy and Society." *International Affairs* 56(5): 58–76.

Lukov, Vadim. 2010. "Parnership for Progress: From the 2010 Muskoka-Toronto Summits to the Seoul Summit." Conference on "Partnership for Progress: From the 2010 Muskoka-Toronto Summits to Seoul Summit" at the State University Higher School of Economics, October 27, Moscow.

Macklem, Tiff. 2011. "Global Financial Reform: Maintaining the Momentum." Remarks presented to the "G20 Workshop," Paris, July 7. Available at: www.bankofcanada.ca/2011/07/speeches/global-financial-reform. Accessed: July 2012.

Macklem, Tiff. 2011. "The Role of the G20 in Sustaining the Recovery and Protecting Financial Stability." Remarks presented to the Federation of Indian Chambers of Commerce and Industry and the Indian Banks' Association, Mumbai, August 24. Available at: www.bankofcanada.ca/2011/08/speeches/role-g-20-sustaining-recovery. Accessed: July 2012.

MacNamara, William and Russell, Alec. 2007. "G20 Silent on Dollar Impact on World Markets." *Financial Times*, November 19. Available at: www.ft.com/intl/cms/s/0/2c783062-962c-11dc-b7ec-0000779fd2ac.html#axzz20iSIum2u. Accessed: July 2012.

Mahapatra, Rajesh. 2002. "G20 Ministers Agree on Early Removal of Trade Barriers and Phasing Out Subsidies." Associated Press, November 23.

Makin, John. 2010. "It Is Time to Face Down the Threat of Deflation." *Financial Times*, July 16.

Mandelson, Peter. 2010. *The Third Man: Life at the Heart of New Labour*. London: HarperCollins.

Manuel, Trevor. 2007. "Budget Speech 2007 by the Minister of Finance." February 21. Available at: www.info.gov.za/speeches/2007/07022115261001.htm. Accessed: July 2012.

Martin, Paul. 2000. "Statement by the Honourable Paul Martin, Minister of Finance for Canada, to the Institute for International Economics." Washington DC, April 14. Available at: www.collectionscanada.gc.ca/webarchives/20071122055106/www.fin.gc.ca/news00/00-031e.html. Accessed: July 2012.

Martin, Paul. 2001. "Globalization, Terrorism, and the World Economy." Speech delivered at a luncheon organized by the Reinventing Bretton Woods Committee and The Conference Board of Canada, Ottawa, November 16. Available at: www.collectionscanada.gc.ca/webarchives/20071122093833/http://www.fin.gc.ca/news01/01-105e.html. Accessed: July 2012.

Martin, Paul. 2004. "Speech by the Prime Minister." Address at a lunch at the Woodrow Wilson Center for International Scholars sponsored by the Center for Global Development, Washington DC, April 29. Available at: epe.lac-bac.gc.ca/100/205/301/prime_minister-ef/paul_martin/05-10-06/www.pm.gc.ca/eng/news.asp@id=192. Accessed: July 2012.

Martin, Paul. 2005. "Address to the Canada-China Business Council." Beijing, January 21. Available at: epe.lac-bac.gc.ca/100/205/301/prime_minister-ef/paul_martin/06-02-03/www.pm.gc.ca/eng/news.asp@id=399. Accessed: July 2012.

Martin, Paul. 2005. "A Global Answer to Global Problems." *Foreign Affairs* 84(3): 2–6. Available at: www.foreignaffairs.com/articles/60792/paul-martin/a-global-answer-to-global-problems. Accessed: July 2012.

Martin, Paul. 2008. *Hell or High Water: My Life In and Out of Politics*. Toronto: McClelland and Stewart.

Martin, Paul. 2008. "Speaking Notes for the Right Honourable Paul Martin." Canada 2020 and Financial Times: View from the Top, Toronto, September 29. Available at: canada2020.ca/files/Canada_2020_Martin_Speech_FINAL.pdf. Accessed: July 2012.

Martin, Paul. 2008. "Time for the G20 to Take the Mantle from the G8." In *Growth, Innovation, Inclusion: The G20 at Ten*, eds Kirton, John J., and Koch, Madeline. London: Newsdesk, 22–27. Available at: www.g8.utoronto.ca/newsdesk/G20at10.pdf. Accessed: July 2011.

Martin, Paul. 2010. "Address to the 2010 Couchiching Conference on 'Watershed Moment or Wasted Opportunity'." August 6, Geneva Park, Canada.

Martinez-Diaz, Leonardo. 2007. "The G20 after Eight Years: How Effective a Vehicle for Developing-Country Influence?" Global Economy and Development Working Paper No. 12, Brookings Institution, Washington DC. Available at: www.brookings.edu/papers/2007/1017development.aspx. Accessed: July 2012.

Masson, Paul R. and Pattison, John C. 2010. "Financial Regulatory Reform: Using Models of Cooperation to Evaluate Current Prospects for International Agreement." Rotman School of Management, University of Toronto, Toronto. Available at: www.g20.utoronto.ca/biblio/G20reforms.pdf. Accessed: July 2012.

Masters, Brooke. 2010. "Move to Reassure Banks on Tough Rules." *Financial Times*, June 28.

Mattli, Walter and Woods, Ngaire. 2008. "A New Architecture for Global Financial Regulation." Economists' Forum (Blog). *Financial Times*. November 19. Available at: blogs.ft.com/economistsforum/2008/11/a-new-architecture-for-global-financial-regulation/#axzz217HT8Uw1. Accessed: July 2012.

McCarthy, Shawn. 2004. "Ottawa Still Supports UN, Graham Says." *Globe and Mail*, May 1.

McCarthy, Shawn. 2008. "Harper Lines Up with Bush on Reform." *Globe and Mail*, November 14. Available at: v1.theglobeandmail.com/servlet/story/RTGAM.20081114.wibsummit14/front/Front/Front/. Accessed: July 2012.

McColl, Velma. 2010 (February). "Deconstructing Copenhagen." *Policy Options*: 22–28. Available at: www.irpp.org/po/archive/feb10/mccoll.pdf. Accessed: July 2012.

McMillan, Stuart. 2006. "Free Trade and Energy on Regional Meeting Agendas." *National Business Review*, November 24.

Meltzer, Allan H. 2000. "Report of the International Financial Institutions Advisory Commission." United States Congress, Washington DC.

Menon, Nirmala. 2008. "Canada Fin Min Sees Econ Stimulus by More Countries." Dow Jones International News, November 9.

Meyer, Laurence, Doyle, Brian, Gagnon, Joseph, and Henderson, Dale. 2004. "International Coordination of Macroeconomic Policies: Still Alive in the New Millennium?" In *The IMF and Its Critics: Reform of Global Financial Architecture*, eds Vines, David, and Gilbert, Christopher L. Cambridge: Cambridge University Press, 59–105.

MI5. 2006. "Report of the Official Account of the Bombings in London on 7th July 2005." May 11. Available at: www.mi5.gov.uk/output/news/reports-on-7-7-bombings-published.html. Accessed: July 2012.

Millard, Robin. 2009. "African Leaders Tell G20 Economic Crisis Threatens 'Chaos'." Agence France Presse, March 16.

Morgenthau, Hans Joachim. 1948. *Politics among Nations: The Struggle for Power and Peace*. New York: Knopf.

Morris, Harvey. 2009. "Ban Ki-moon Urges $1,000bn for Developing World." *Financial Times*, March 26.
Mukherji, Biman. 2002. "Worldwide Trade to Benefit from G20 Pledge." Agence France Presse, November 24.
Murdoch, Scott. 2006. "China Says Yes to Carbon Trading." *Advertiser*, November 19. Available at: www.adelaidenow.com.au/business/china-says-yes-to-carbon-trading/story-e6frede3-1111112550015. Accessed: July 2012.
Norman, Laurence and Connaghan, Clare. 2009. "Developing Econs the Big Winners from G20 Ascent." Dow Jones Newswires, April 2.
O'Neill, Jim and Hormats, Robert. 2004. "The G8: Time for a Change." Global Economics Paper No. 112, Goldman Sachs, New York.
Obama, Barack. 2009. "News Conference by President Obama." London Summit, April 2. Available at: www.whitehouse.gov/the-press-office/news-conference-president-obama-40209. Accessed: July 2012.
Obama, Barack. 2010. "Letter from the President to G20 Leaders." June 16, White House, Washington DC. Available at: www.whitehouse.gov/the-press-office/letter-president-g-20-leaders. Accessed: July 2012.
Office of the Prime Minister of Canada. 2009. "PM Announces G20 Leaders Will Meet in Toronto in 2010." Seoul, December 7. Available at: www.pm.gc.ca/eng/media.asp?category=1&featureId=6&pageId=26&id=3026. Accessed: July 2012.
Oneal, John R. and Russett, Bruce. 1999. "The Kantian Peace: The Pacific Benefits of Democracy, Interdependence, and International Organizations." *World Politics* 52(1): 1–37.
Organisation for Economic Co-operation and Development. 2005. "The Paris Declaration on Aid Effectiveness: Ownership, Harmonisation, Alignment, Results, and Mutual Accountability." Paris. Available at: www.oecd.org/dataoecd/11/41/34428351.pdf. Accessed: July 2012.
Organisation for Economic Co-operation and Development. 2010. "Government Final Consumption Expenditure in US Dollars." Economics: Key Tables from OECD, No. 2, December 13, Paris. doi: 10.1787/2074384x-2010-table2.
Organski, A.F.K. and Kugler, Jacek. 1980. *The War Ledger*. Chicago: University of Chicago Press.
Ostrom, Elinor. 2009. "Beyond Markets and States: Polycentric Governance of Complex Economic Systems." Nobel Prize lecture, December 8. Available at: www.nobelprize.org/nobel_prizes/economics/laureates/2009/ostrom_lecture.pdf. Accessed: July 2012.
Ostry, Sylvia. 2010. "Pessimism of the Intellect, Optimism of the Will." August 7, Available at: www.g20.utoronto.ca/biblio/ostry-cipa.html. Accessed: July 2012.
Pan, Letian. 2005. "Hu Calls for Strengthening Global Cooperation." Beijing, October 16. Available at: english.gov.cn/2005-10/16/content_78172.htm. Accessed: July 2012.

Parkinson, Martin. 2006. "The G20: Addressing Global Challenges." Presentation to the Australian Business Economists Luncheon, November 9, Sydney. Available at: www.g20.utoronto.ca/biblio/parkinson_2006.pdf. Accessed: July 2012.

Paterson, Damian. 2007. "G20 Meeting Not Just More Idle Chatter." *Pretoria News*, November 16.

Patrick, Stewart. 2010. "G8, G20: A View of Canada's Summits." Council on Foreign Relations, June 21. Available at: www.cfr.org/canada/g8-g20-view-canadas-summits/p22463. Accessed: July 2012.

Paulson, Henry M. 2010. *On the Brink: Inside the Race to Stop the Collapse of the Global Financial System*. New York: Grand Central Publishing.

Payne, Anthony. 2010. "How Many Gs Are There in 'Global Governance' after the Crisis? The Perspectives of the 'Marginal Majority' of the World's States." *International Affairs* 86(3): 729–40. doi: 10.1111/j.1468-2346.2010.00908.x.

Penttilä, Risto E.J. 2009. "Multilateralism Light: The Rise of Informal International Governance." Centre for European Reform, London. Available at: www.cer.org.uk/pdf/penttila_essay_july09.pdf. Accessed: July 2011.

Perez, Santiago. 2003. "G20 Summit Ends, Sees Global Economic Recovery Underway." Dow Jones, October 27.

Persaud, Avinash. 2010. "The Locus of Financial Regulation: Home versus Host." *International Affairs* 86: 637–646).

Pisani-Ferry, Jean. 2010. "Back to the G7?" By Invitation (Blog). *Economist*. June 29. Available at: www.bruegel.org/blog/detail/article/46-back-to-the-g7/. Accessed: July 2012.

Polanyi, Karl. 1944. *The Great Transformation: The Political and Economic Origins of Our Time*. New York: Farrar and Rinehart.

Porter, Tony. 2000. "The G7, the Financial Stability Forum, the G20, and the Politics of International Financial Regulation." Paper presented at the annual convention of the International Studies Association, March 15, Los Angeles. Available at: www.g8.utoronto.ca/g20/biblio/porter-isa-2000.pdf. Accessed: July 2012.

Porter, Tony. 2003. "Technical Collaboration and Political Conflict in the Emerging Regime for International Financial Regulation." *Review of International Political Economy* 10(3): 520–51.

Postel-Vinay, Karoline. 2011. *Le G20, laboratoire d'un monde émergent*. Paris: Les Presses de Sciences Po.

Price, Daniel M. 2009. "Recovery and Reform." In *The G8 2009: From La Maddalena to L'Aquila*, eds Kirton, John J., and Koch, Madeline. London: Newsdesk, 24–26. Available at: www.g8.utoronto.ca/newsdesk/g8-2009.html. Accessed: July 2012.

Putnam, Robert and Bayne, Nicholas. 1984. *Hanging Together: Co-operation and Conflict in the Seven-Power Summit*. 1st ed. Cambridge MA: Harvard University Press.

Putnam, Robert and Bayne, Nicholas. 1987. *Hanging Together: Co-operation and Conflict in the Seven-Power Summit*. 2nd ed. London: Sage Publications.

Raustiala, Kal and Victor, David G. 2004 (April). "The Regime Complex for Plant Genetic Resources." *International Organization* 58(2): 277–309.

Reuters. 2004. "Highlights: G20 Delegates' Comments on FX." November 21.

Reuters. 2010. "Canada PM Harper's Letter to G20 on Deficits." June 18. Available at: www.reuters.com/article/2010/06/18/g20-canada-deficits-idUSN1817964220100618. Accessed: July 2012.

Rogoff, Kenneth. 2010. "Technology, Complexity, Economy, Catastrophe." *Globe and Mail*, June 2. Available at: www.theglobeandmail.com/news/opinions/technology-complexity-economy-catastrophe/article1588565. Accessed: July 2012.

Rotman School of Management, ed. 2008. *The Finance Crisis and Rescue: What Went Wrong? Why? What Lessons Can Be Learned.* Toronto: University of Toronto Press.

Roubini, Nouriel and Bremmer, Ian. 2010. "Sagging Global Growth Requires Us to Act." *Financial Times*, July 12.

Rubin, Robert E. and Weisberg, Jacob. 2003. *In an Uncertain World: Tough Choices from Wall Street to Washington*. New York: Random House.

Ruggie, John G. 1983. "International Regimes, Transactions, and Change: Embedded Liberalism in the Postwar Economic Order." In *International Regimes*, ed Krasner, Stephen D. Ithaca: Cornell University Press, 195–232.

Ruggie, John G. 1993. "Territoriality and Beyond: Problematizing Modernity in International Relations." *International Organization* 47(1): 139–74.

Runnalls, David. 2010. "Fossil Fuel Subsidies and the G20." In *G8 & G20: The 2010 Canadian Summits*, eds Kirton, John J., and Koch, Madeline. London: Newsdesk, 164–65. Available at: www.g8.utoronto.ca/newsdesk/g8g20/g8g20-2010.pdf. Accessed: July 2012.

Sachs, Jeffrey. 1998. "Global Capitalism: Making It Work." *Economist*, September 12, pp. 23–25.

Sachs, Jeffrey. 2009. "America Has Passed On the Baton." *Financial Times*, September 29.

Salai-i-Martin, Xavier and Mohapatra, Sanket. 2003. "Poverty, Inequality, and the Distribution of Income in the Group of 20." *Economic Roundup* Autumn. Available at: archive.treasury.gov.au/documents/580/HTML/docshell.asp?URL=Poverty_Inequality.asp. Accessed: July 2012.

Salvatore, Dominick. 2000. "The Present International Monetary System: Problems, Complications, and Reforms." *Open Economies Review* 11(1): 133–48.

Sandler, Todd and Tschirhart, John T. 1997. "Club Theory: Thirty Years Later." *Public Choice* 93(3): 335–55.

Sarkozy, Nicolas. 2008. "Speech delivered by H.E. Mr. Nicolas Sarkozy, President of the French Republic." 63rd session of the United Nations General Assembly,

New York, September 23. Available at: www.un.org/en/ga/63/generaldebate/pdf/france-fr.pdf. Accessed: July 2012.

Sarkozy, Nicolas. 2010. "Plans for France's G20 Summit in 2011." In *The G20 2010 Seoul Summit: Shared Growth Beyond Crisis*, eds Kirton, John J., and Koch, Madeline. London: Newsdesk, 16–17. Available at: www.g8.utoronto.ca/newsdesk/seoul/seoul-sarkozy-en.html. Accessed: July 2012.

Sautter, Christian. 2008. "Fundamental Principles for Global Financial Governance." In *Growth, Innovation, Inclusion: The G20 at Ten*, eds Kirton, John J., and Koch, Madeline. London: Newsdesk, 32–34. Available at: www.g8.utoronto.ca/newsdesk/G20at10.pdf. Accessed: July 2012.

Savona, Paolo, Kirton, John J., and Oldani, Chiara, eds. 2011. *Global Financial Crisis: Global Impact and Solutions*. Farnham: Ashgate.

Schirm, Stefan A. 2012 (July). "Global Politics Are Domestic Politics: A Societal Approach to Divergence in the G20." *Review of International Studies*: 1–22. doi: dx.doi.org/10.1017/S0260210512000216.

Scholte, Jan Aart. 2003. "Governing Global Finance." In *Governing Globalization: Power, Authority and Global Governance*, eds Held, David, and McGrew, Anthony. Cambridge: Polity Press, 189–208.

Schwab, Klaus. 2003. "Address to the Plenary Session of the World Economic Forum: Africa Economic Summit 2003." June 12, Durban.

Scoffield, Heather. 2000. "Globalization Must Deal with Poverty: Martin." *Globe and Mail*, October 25.

Shanghai Institutes of International Studies Working Group. 2009. "The Reform of International Financial System and China's Policy Options." *Global Review* (3): 40–54.

Shorr, David and Wright, Thomas. 2010. "The G20 and Global Governance: An Exchange." *Survival: Global Politics and Strategy* 52(2): 171–98.

Simmons, Beth. 2000. "The Legalization of International Monetary Affairs." *International Organization* 54(3): 573–602.

Slaughter, Anne-Marie. 1997. "The Real New World Order." *Foreign Affairs* 76(5): 183–97.

Slaughter, Anne-Marie. 2004. *A New World Order*. Princeton: Princeton University Press.

Slaughter, Anne-Marie. 2005. "Government Networks, World Order, and the L20." In *Reforming from the Top: A Leaders' 20 Summit*, eds English, John, Thakur, Ramesh, and Cooper, Andrew F. Tokyo: United Nations University Press, 281–95.

Slaughter, Anne-Marie. 2009. "America's Edge: Power in the Networked Century." *Foreign Affairs* 88(1): 94–113.

Smith, David and Oliver, Jonathan. 2008. "Fighting the Financial Inferno." *Sunday Times*, November 16.

Smith, Gordon. 2004. "An Idea Whose Time Has Come." *Globe and Mail*, October 22, p. A19.

Smith, Gordon. 2010. "The Last Thing We Need Is a G12 Competing with a G8." *Globe and Mail*, July 9. Available at: www.theglobeandmail.com/commentary/the-last-thing-we-need-is-a-g12-competing-with-a-g8/article4323467/. Accessed: July 2012.

Smyser, W.R. 1993. "Goodbye, G7." *Washington Quarterly* (Winter): 15–28.

Snidal, Duncan. 1985. "The Limits of Hegemonic Stability Theory." *International Organisation* 39(4): 579–614.

Soederberg, Susanne. 2002. "On the Contradictions of the New International Financial Architecture: Another Procrustean Bed for Emerging Markets?" *Third World Quarterly* 23(4): 607–20.

Sorrell, Martin. 2009. "The Pendulum Will Swing Back." *Financial Times*, April 8.

Steinbruner, John D. 2002. *The Cybernetic Theory of Decision: New Dimensions of Political Analysis*. Princeton: Princeton University Press.

Stephens, Gina. 2010. "Information and Communication: G8 Institutionalization and Compliance in the DOT Force." In *Making Global Governance Effective: Hard and Soft Law Institutions in a Crowded World*, eds Kirton, John J., Larionova, Marina, and Savona, Paolo. Farnham: Ashgate, 201–15.

Stephens, Philip. 2010. "Splintered Solidarity Has Put Global Governance in a Spin." *Financial Times*, July 1.

Stewart, James B. 2010. "One Good Review for the G20's Performance." *Wall Street Journal*, July 7. Available at: online.wsj.com/article/SB10001424052748704178004575351050968234196.html. Accessed: July 2012.

Subramanian, Arvind. 2010. "G20 Rules: Time for Germany Bashing." The Baseline Scenario (Blog). June 20. Available at: baselinescenario.com/2010/06/20/g-20-rules-time-for-germany-bashing. Accessed: July 2012.

Summers, Lawrence. 2008. "The Birth of the G20." In *Growth, Innovation, Inclusion: The G20 at Ten*, eds Kirton, John J., and Koch, Madeline. London: Newsdesk, 29–31. Available at: www.g8.utoronto.ca/newsdesk/G20at10.pdf. Accessed: July 2012.

Summit of the Americas. 2005. "Declaration of Mar Del Plata: Creating Jobs to Fight Poverty and Strengthen Democratic Governance." November 5, Mar Del Plata, Argentina. Available at: www.summit-americas.org/iv_summit/iv_summit_dec_en.pdf. Accessed: July 2012.

Sunday Times. 2008. "Prudence Will Still Have a Role to Play." *Sunday Times*, November 16.

Suskind, Ron. 2004. *The Price of Loyalty: George W. Bush, the White House, and the Education of Paul O'Neill*. New York: Simon and Schuster.

Talley, Ian. 2010. "IMF Chief: Global Financial Crisis Has Washed Away Old Economic Order." Dow Jones, December 8.

Tanaka, Nobuo. 2010. "Fresh Momentum for Tackling Global Energy Challenges." In *G8 & G20: The 2010 Canadian Summits*, eds Kirton, John J., and Koch, Madeline. London: Newsdesk, 178–80. Available at: www.g8.utoronto.ca/newsdesk/g8g20/g8g20-2010.pdf. Accessed: July 2012.

Thakur, Ramesh. 2007. "India's Rising and Shining: Will It Prove a False Dawn?," Centre for International Governance Innovation, Waterloo ON. Available at: www.cigionline.org/publications/2007/7/indias-rising-and-shining-will-it-prove-false-dawn. Accessed: July 2012.

Thomas, Andrea. 2004. "Dollar Decline Bedevils G20 Officials, Little Relief Seen." *Globe and Mail*, November 18.

Thomas, Andrea. 2004. "Germany's Eichel Sees G20 Progress on Debt Restructuring." *Globe and Mail*, November 20.

Thorpe, Jacqueline. 2008. "Canada, Bastion of Free Markets?" *National Post*, November 10. Available at: www.nationalpost.com/opinion/columnists/story.html?id=8ad4cc7b-3248-4bcd-b9c7-dc4fbbf1bde3. Accessed: July 2012.

Thorpe, Jacqueline. 2008. "G20 Summit Looks to Market Overhaul." *National Post*, November 15, p. A1.

Truman, Edwin M. 2009. "The G20 and International Financial Institution Reform: Unfinished IMF Reform." (Blog). *VoxEU*. January 28. Available at: www.voxeu.org/article/imf-reform-unfinished-agenda. Accessed: July 2012.

Truman, Edwin M. 2009. "Globalization Goes into Reverse?" Realtime Economic Issues Watch (Blog). *Peterson Institute for International Economics*. January 30. Available at: www.petersoninstitute.org/realtime/?p=453. Accessed: July 2012.

ul Haq, Mahbub. 1994. "The Bretton Woods Institutions and Global Governance." In *Managing the World Economy*, ed Kenen, Peter B. Washington DC: Institute for International Economics, 409–18.

United Kingdom Chair of the G20. 2009. "Progress Report on the Economic and Financial Actions of the London, Washington, and Pittsburgh G20 Summits." St. Andrews, Scotland, November 7. Available at: www.g20.utoronto.ca/2009/2009progressreport1107.pdf. Accessed: July 2012.

United Nations Development Programme. 2010. "The Real Wealth of Nations: Pathways to Human Development." Human Development Report 2010. Available at: hdr.undp.org/en/reports/global/hdr2010/chapters/. Accessed: July 2012.

Uren, David. 2004. "Costello Backs Bid to Power Up G20." *Australian*, May 3.

Uren, David. 2006. "Costello Plots Resources Pact." *Australian*, January 3.

Van Rompuy, Herman. 2010. "Overcoming the Crisis in Europe and in the World." In *The G20 2010 Seoul Summit: Shared Growth Beyond Crisis*, eds Kirton, John J., and Koch, Madeline. London: Newsdesk, 30–31. Available at: www.g8.utoronto.ca/newsdesk/seoul/seoul-vanrompuy-en.htm. Accessed: July 2012.

Vickers, Brendan. 2006. "Heading Toward the G8 St. Petersburg Summit: What's In It for Africa?" *Global Insight* (63): 1–4.

von Furstenberg, George M. 2001. "Assembling a New Financial Architecture: The G7's 2001 Role and Response." Paper presented at the conference on Assembling a New International Financial Architecture: The Deeper Challenges, LUISS University, July 17, Rome.

von Furstenberg, George M. 2001. "US Dollarization: A Second-Best Form of Regional Currency Consolidation." In *Guiding Global Order: G8 Governance in the Twenty-First Century*, eds Kirton, John J., Daniels, Joseph P., and Freytag, Andreas. Aldershot: Ashgate, 45–54.

von Furstenberg, George M. and Daniels, Joseph P. 1992. *Economic Summit Declarations, 1975–1989: Examining the Written Record of International Cooperation*. Princeton: Princeton University Press.

Wade, Robert. 2009. "From Global Imbalances to Global Reorganisations." *Cambridge Journal of Economics* 33(4): 539–62. doi: 10.1093/cje/bep032. Accessed: July 2012.

Wade, Robert and Vestergaard, Jakob. 2010. "Judging G20 by Output Ignores Input Problems." *Financial Times*, October 22. Available at: www.ft.com/intl/cms/s/0/2581209c-5f0b-11e0-a2d7-00144feab49a.html#axzz1mClv38ck.

Wade, Robert and Vestergaard, Jakob. 2010. "Overhaul the G20 for the Sake of the G172." *Financial Times*, October 22. Available at: www.ft.com/intl/cms/s/0/a2ab4716-dd45-11df-9236-00144feabdc0.html#axzz1mClv38ck. Accessed: July 2012.

Waki, Natsuko. 2004. "Japan Says G20 Too Large But Possible to Expand G7." Reuters, November 21.

Wallerstein, Immanuel. 1979. *The Capitalist World-Economy*. Cambridge: Cambridge University Press.

Wang, Guoxing. 2009. "Financial Crisis: Its Impacts on International Economic System and Geopolitics." *Global Review* 3: 24–38.

Wang, Jing and Goodman, Matthew P. 2012. "Prudence and the G20." *Global Economics Update* 1(6): 1–2. Available at: csis.org/files/publication/120802_Simonchair_newsletter_August2012.pdf. Accessed: August 2012.

Watson, Sheri. 2003. "G20 Bulletin." October 28. Available at: www.g8.utoronto.ca/g20bulletin/g20v2n1.htm. Accessed: July 2012.

Watson, William. 2010. "Canada's Moment." *National Post*, July 1. Available at: opinion.financialpost.com/2010/07/01/canadas-moment. Accessed: July 2012.

Weiss, Martin A. 2005. "Iraq: Debt Relief." March 11, Federation of American Scientists, Washington DC. Available at: www.fas.org/sgp/crs/mideast/RS21765.pdf. Accessed: July 2012.

Welch, David. 2005. *Painful Choices: A Theory of Foreign Policy Change*. Princeton: Princeton University Press.

Wheatley, Alan. 2010. "G20 Strives to Cut Deficits Without Killing Growth." Reuters, June 3. Available at: in.reuters.com/article/2010/06/03/idINIndia-49012120100603. Accessed: July 2012.

Wheatley, Alan and Love, Brian. 2005. "Oil Dominates G20 Talks as Yuan Takes Back Seat." Reuters, October 16.

White House. 2008. "Statements by Bush, Sarkozy, EU Commissioner at Camp David: France, European Union Agree on a Summit to Address Financial Crisis." Washington DC, October 20. Available at: www.america.gov/st/

texttrans-english/2008/October/20081020115655eaifas0.1981623.html. Accessed: July 2012.

Whyman, William E. 1995. "We Can't Go On Meeting Like This: Revitalizing the G7 Process." *Washington Quarterly* 18(3): 139–65.

Wicks, Nigel L. 2003. "Governments, the International Financial Institutions, and Cooperation." In *The New Economic Diplomacy: Decision-Making and Negotiation in International Economic Relations*, eds Bayne, Nicholas, and Woolcock, Stephen. Aldershot: Ashgate, 261–74.

Williamson, John. 1997. "The Washington Consensus Revisited." In *Economic and Social Development into the XXI Century*, ed Emmerji, Louis. Washington DC: Inter-American Development Bank, 48–61.

Wilson, Dominic and Purushothaman, Roopa. 2003. "Dreaming with BRICs: The Path to 2050." Goldman Sachs, New York. Available at: www.goldmansachs.com/our-thinking/topics/brics/brics-reports-pdfs/brics-dream.pdf. Accessed: July 2012.

Winning, Nicholas and Parkinson, Joe. 2009. "G20 Fin Mins Come Up Short on Climate Change." Dow Jones, November 7.

Wolf, Martin. 2008. *Fixing Global Finance*. Baltimore: Johns Hopkins University Press.

Wolf, Martin. 2010. "This Global Game of 'Pass the Parcel' Cannot End Well." *Financial Times*, June 29, p. 4.

Wolf, Martin. 2010. "Why the Battle Is Joined over Tightening." *Financial Times*, July 18, p. 9.

Wolfers, Arnold. 1962. "National Security as an Ambiguous Symbol." In *Discord and Collaboration: Essays on International Politics*, ed Wolfers, Arnold. Baltimore: Johns Hopkins University Press, 147–65.

World Health Organization. 2004. "Summary of Probable SARS Cases with Onset of Illness from 1 November 2002 to 31 July 2003." Geneva. Available at: www.who.int/csr/sars/country/table2004_04_21/en. Accessed: July 2012.

World Health Organization. 2012. "Cumulative Number of Confirmed Human Cases for Avian Influenza A(H5N1) Reported to WHO, 2003–2012." July 6, Geneva. Available at: www.who.int/influenza/human_animal_interface/H5N1_cumulative_table_archives/en/index.html. Accessed: July 2012.

Xinhua. 2008. "China Expects 'Fair, Inclusive' World Finance System." November 6. Available at: english.people.com.cn/90001/90776/90883/6528949.html. Accessed: July 2012.

Xinhua. 2010. "Shanghai Cooperation Organization Summits." *China Daily*, June 9. Available at: www.chinadaily.com.cn/china/2010sco/2010-06/09/content_9955838.htm. Accessed: July 2012.

Zacher, Mark and Sutton, Brent. 1996. *Governing Global Networks: International Regimes for Transportation and Communication*. Cambridge: Cambridge University Press.

Zeng, Min. 2008. "Support Seen for Dollar, Yen." *Wall Street Journal*, November 17. Available at: online.wsj.com/article/SB122687265714531785.html. Accessed: July 2012.

Zhou, Xiaochuan. 2009. "Reform the International Monetary System." Beijing, March 23. Available at: www.pbc.gov.cn/publish/english/956/2009/20091229104425550619706/20091229104425550619706_.html. Accessed: July 2012.

G20 Appendices

Appendix A: Schools of Thought on G20/G8 Governance

		Dominance	
		G8 Dominant	*G20 Dominant*
Relationship	*Conflictual (zero sum)*	Redundant	Replacement
	Cooperative (positive sum)	Rejectionist	Reinforcement

Appendix B: G20 Finance Ministerial and Summit Meetings

B-1: G20 Meetings of Finance Ministers and Central Bank Governors, 1999–2012

Germany, 1999
    December 15–16, Berlin, Germany
Canada, 2000
    October 24–25, Montreal, Canada
Canada, 2001
    November 16–17, Ottawa, Canada
India, 2002
    November 23, New Delhi, India
Mexico, 2003
    October 26–27, Morelia, Mexico
Germany, 2004
    November 20–21, Berlin, Germany
China, 2005
    October 15–16, Beijing, China
Australia, 2006
    November 18–19, Melbourne, Australia
South Africa, 2007
    November 17–18, Kleinmond, South Africa
Brazil, 2008
    October 11, Washington DC, United States
    November 8–9, São Paulo, Brazil
United Kingdom, 2009
    March 14–15, Horsham, England
    April 24, Washington DC, United States
    September 4–5, London, England
    November 6–7, St. Andrews, Scotland
Canada and Korea, co-chairs, 2010
    April 22–23, Washington DC, United States
Korea, 2010
    June 4–5, Busan, Korea
    October 9–10, Washington DC, United States
    October 22–23, Gyeongju, Korea
France, 2011
    February 18–19, Paris, France
    April 14–15, Washington DC, United States
    August 8, conference call
    September 22, Paris, France
    September 23, with development ministers, Paris, France
    October 14–15, Paris, France

Mexico, 2012
  February 25–26, Mexico City, Mexico
  April 19–20, Washington DC, United States
  November 4–5, Mexico City, Mexico

B-2: G20 Summits, 2008–2012

United States, 2008
  November 14–15, Washington DC, United States
United Kingdom, 2009
  April 1–2, London, England
United States, 2009
  September 24–25, Pittsburgh, United States
Canada, 2010
  June 26–27, Toronto, Canada
Korea, 2010
  November 11–12, Seoul, Korea
France, 2011
  November 3–4, Cannes, France
Mexico, 2012
  June 18–19, Los Cabos, Mexico

Appendix C: G20 Performance, 1999–2010

C-1: G20 Finance Ministers and Central Bank Governors

	Domestic Political Management		Deliberation			Direction Setting	Decision Making	Delivery	Development of Global Governance	
	members %	Average # references	# days	# documents	# words	Democracy	# commitments	Compliance catalysts	Internal	External
1999 Berlin	0	0.00	2	1	472	3	4	5	4	6
2000 Montreal	50	0.50	2	2	2,504	2	7	0	7	18
2001 Ottawa	0	0.00	2	2	1,646	4	24	3	6	31
2002 New Delhi	5	0.05	2	1	989	5	2	–1	2	6
2003 Morelia	10	0.10	2	1	1,188	3	6	4	4	14
2004 Berlin	25	0.25	2	4	3,971	6	10	7	8	21
2005 Xianghe	5	0.05	2	4	3,462	6	8	3	8	39
2006 Melbourne	15	0.15	2	2	3,477	22	10	2	5	32
2007 Kleinmond	20	0.20	2	2	3,858	5	20	6	3	20
2008 Washington	0	0.00	2	1	257	1	4	2	1	2
2008 São Paulo	15	0.15	2	1	1,737	5	27	3	6	15
2009 Horsham	0	0.00	1	2	1,661	4	18	4	3	15
2009 London	0	0.00	2	2	1,382	7	27	7	5	20
2009 St. Andrews	10	0.10	2	1	1,276	5	22	14	5	37
2010 Washington	0	0.00	2	2	2,085	5	10	5	11	37
2010 Busan	5	0.05	2	1	1,524	14	18	9	8	28
Total	–	0.10	31	29	31,489	97	217	73	86	341
Average	10	0.10	1.94	1.81	1,968	6.06	13.56	4.56	5.38	21.31

C-2: G20 Leaders

	Attendance %	Domestic Political Managment		Deliberation			Direction Setting	Decision Making	Delivery	Development of Global Governance	
		members %	Average # references	# days	# documents	# words	Democracy	# commitments	Compliance score	Internal	External
2008 Washington	100	0	0	2	2	3,567	12	95	0.53	0	40
2009 London	100	5	0.05	2	3	6,155	9	88	0.42	12	116
2009 Pittsburgh	100	0	0	2	2	9,257	29	128	0.28	47	117
2010 Toronto	90	30	0.3	2	4	11,078	12	61	0.28	71	171
Total	n/a	n/a	n/a	8	11	30,057	62	372	–	130	444
Average	97.50	8.75	8.75%	2.00	2.75	7,514	15.50	93.00	0.35	32.50	111.00

Note: n/a = not applicable

Appendix D: Domestic Political Management

D-1: G20 Finance Ministers and Central Bank Governors

	Communiqué Compliments		
	Number	Spread	
		G8	Non-G8
1999 Berlin	0	0	0
2000 Montreal	10	4	6
2001 Ottawa	0	0	0
2002 New Delhi	1	0	1
2003 Morelia	2	1	1
2004 Berlin	5	3	2
2005 Xianghe	1	0	1
2006 Melbourne	3	0	3
2007 Kleinmond	4	2	2
2008 Washington	0	0	0
2008 São Paulo	3	1	2
2009 Horsham	0	0	0
2009 London	0	0	0
2009 St. Andrews	2	1	1
2010 Washington	0	0	0
2010 Busan	1	1	1
Total	32	13	20
Average	2	0.81	1.25

D-2: G20 Leaders

	Communiqué Compliments			Editorial Approval		Public Approval Change (Host)	National Policy Address (Host)
	Number	Spread		Host	New York Times		
		G8	Non-G8				
2008 Washington	0	0	0	0	NA	+2.0%	0
2009 London	1	0	1	−1	0	+5.0%	1
2009 Pittsburgh	0	0	0	0	0	−1.0%	0
2010 Toronto	6	3	3	0	NA	+2.0%	3
Total	7	3	4	−1	0	–	4
Average	1.75	0.75	1	−0.50	0	+2.0%	1

Notes: Scoring: +1 = positive editorial; 0 = neutral editorial; −1 = negative editorial; NA = not available; related editorial not found. National policy address = total number of G20 mentions in host national policy addresses in the immediate lead-up to and follow-up of the summit.

Appendix E: Deliberation: G20 Communiqué Conclusions

Year	# Words	# Paragraphs	# Documents	% Macroeconomics
Ministerials				
1999 Berlin	472	6	1	69.60
2000 Montreal	2,504	38	2	19.90
2001 Ottawa	1,646	31	2	30.60
2002 New Delhi	989	10	1	53.90
2003 Morelia	1,188	9	1	69.10
2004 Berlin	3,971	40	4	48.10
2005 Xianghe	3,462	35	4	62.70
2006 Melbourne	3,477	36	2	58.30
2007 Kleinmond	3,858	26	2	79.90
2008 Washington	257	5	1	44.70
2008 São Paulo	1,737	17	1	74.60
2009 Horsham	1,661	34	2	18.80
2009 London	1,382	20	2	45.30
2009 St. Andrews	1,276	16	1	37.20
2010 Washington	2,085	41	2	56.10
2010 Busan	1,524	18	1	47.50
Subtotal	31,489	382	29	816.30
Average	1,968	23.88	1.81	51.02
Summits				
2008 Washington	3,567	82	2	17.80
2009 London	6,155	164	3	27.40
2009 Pittsburgh	9,257	129	2	30.00
2010 Toronto	11,078	192	4	33.40
Subtotal	30,057	567	11	109
Average	7,514	141.75	2.75	27.15
Total	61,546	949	40	925
Average	3,077	47.45	2.00	46.25

Note: Percentages are calculated using the number of words per issue divided by the total number of words in the documents for each meeting. Totals exceed 100% because of overlap among issues.

% Financial Regulations	% Reform of International Financial Institutions	% Trade	% Development	% Climate	% Terrorism
0.00	37.20	8.10	0.00	10.70	0.00
12.50	24.10	12.30	12.60	0.00	0.00
1.80	15.20	18.70	41.60	0.00	56.30
8.40	33.20	6.20	45.00	0.00	12.50
15.60	53.30	23.80	35.10	0.00	12.70
2.40	13.50	9.30	7.60	11.30	4.10
0.00	21.00	14.80	58.20	4.70	0.00
0.80	13.20	18.50	10.70	4.50	3.90
3.40	19.30	4.00	9.20	10.30	0.00
65.60	28.00	0.00	24.10	0.00	0.00
14.20	36.90	11.60	60.00	3.60	0.00
46.20	41.30	2.40	13.10	0.00	0.00
5.80	62.20	18.20	43.20	3.60	10.30
73.90	76.80	0.00	48.40	13.90	9.60
28.10	67.30	1.60	73.90	4.70	6.80
33.40	80.30	14.70	46.40	0.00	2.80
312.10	622.80	164.20	529.10	67.30	119.00
19.51	38.93	10.26	33.07	4.21	7.44
100.00	29.40	12.00	17.80	1.70	2.80
66.60	45.40	16.10	27.60	1.00	0.00
100.00	38.30	9.70	24.50	9.70	4.10
50.00	41.00	4.60	34.50	7.40	2.50
317	154	42	104	20	9
79.15	38.53	10.60	26.10	4.95	2.35
629	777	207	634	87	128
31.44	38.85	10.33	31.68	4.36	6.42

Appendix F: G20 Direction Setting

F-1: G20 Ministerial Democratic Direction Setting

Value	1999 Berlin	2000 Montreal	2001 Ottawa	2002 New Delhi	2003 Morelia	2004 Berlin[a]	2005 Xianghe	2006 Melbourne	2007 Kleinmond	2008 Washington	2008 São Paulo	2009 Horsham	2009 London	2009 St. Andrews	2010 Washington	2010 Busan
Transparency	1	2	1	1		3	3	7	2		1	1	3	3	2	6
International mobility of ideas	1							1								
Access to ideas in all countries	1															
Good governance			1	1	1		1	8	3		1	1	1	1	1	2
Accountable international institutions			1													
Surveillance/Monitoring				1		1		4			2	1	1			1
Rule of law[b]				1												
Support of NEPAD				1												
Information/Knowledge exchange			1		2		2	2						1	2	3
Accountability						1					1		1			
Creditor rights						1										
Openness[c]										1		1	1			1
Multistakeholder consultation																1
Total	3	2	4	5	3	6	6	22	5	1	5	4	7	5	5	14
Type spread	3	1	4	5	2	4	3	5	2	1	4	4	5	3	3	6

Note: Main communiqué only. NEPAD = New Partnership for Africa's Development.

[a] Excludes institution building and legal mechanisms.

[b] Includes legal framework.

[c] Includes political, societal, cultural, informational, and educational openness but excludes economic openness.

F-2: G20 Summit Direction Setting: Democracy

Value	2008 Washington	2009 London	2009 Pittsburgh	2010 Toronto
Transparency	5	2	14	8
International mobility of ideas				
Access to ideas in all countries				
Good governance	1	1		
Accountable international institutions		2		
Surveillance/Monitoring		3	8	
Rule of law[a]	2		1	1
Support of NEPAD				
Information/Knowledge exchange	1		2	
Accountability	1		1	2
Creditor rights				
Openness[b]	2	1	3	1
Multistakeholder consultation				
Total	12	9	29	12
Type spread	6	5	6	4

Notes: Main communiqué only. Excludes corruption and inclusion.

[a] Includes legal framework.

[b] Includes political, societal, cultural, informational, and educational openness but excludes economic openness.

Appendix G: G20 Decision Making: Commitments

	Total Commitments	Macroeconomics	Financial Regulations	Reform of International Financial Institutions	Trade	Development	Socioeconomic	Climate Change	Energy	Accountability	Terrorism	Corruption	Other
Ministerials													
1999 Berlin	4	2	0	2	0	0	0	0	0	0	0	0	0
2000 Montreal	7	3	0	1	0	2	1	0	0	0	0	0	0
2001 Ottawa	24	2	0	1	1	0	0	0	0	0	20	0	0
2002 New Delhi	2	0	0	0	0	1	0	0	0	0	1	0	0
2003 Morelia	6	2	0	0	1	0	0	0	0	0	1	2	0
2004 Berlin	10	4	0	0	1	1	0	0	0	0	0	1	0
2005 Xianghe	8	0	0	2	4	2	0	0	0	0	0	0	0
2006 Melbourne	10	2	0	2	2	1	1	0	1	0	1	0	0
2007 Kleinmond	20	9	0	5	2	0	1	0	3	0	0	0	0
2008 Washington	4	4	0	0	0	0	0	0	0	0	0	0	0
2008 São Paulo	27	12	2	7	1	4	0	0	0	1	0	0	0
2009 Horsham	18	5	5	6	1	1	0	0	0	0	0	0	0
2009 London	27	7	15	2	1	1	0	0	0	0	0	0	0
2009 St. Andrews	22	7	6	5	0	1	0	2	1	0	0	0	0
2010 Washington	10	2	4	0	0	3	0	0	1	0	0	0	0
2010 Busan	18	7	3	4	0	2	0	0	0	1	0	0	1
Subtotal	217	68	35	37	14	19	3	2	6	2	23	3	1
Average	13.56	4.30	2.20	2.30	0.88	1.20	0.19	0.13	0.38	0.13	1.40	0.19	0.06
Summits													
2008 Washington	95	8	58	12	5	5	0	0	0	1	0	4	2
2009 London	88	14	22	15	16	12	3	1	3	2	0	0	0
2009 Pittsburgh	128	30	24	13	9	15	7	3	18	0	0	2	2
2010 Toronto	61	15	11	4	9	8	2	3	1	2	0	3	3
Subtotal	372	67	115	44	39	40	12	7	22	5	0	9	7
Average	93.00	16.75	28.75	11.00	9.75	10.00	3.00	1.75	5.50	1.25	0.00	2.25	1.75

Appendix H: G20 Delivery: Compliance

H-1: 2003 Morelia G20 Compliance

Country	Trade	Crisis	Codes	Abuse	Offshore Financial Centres	Terrorism	Total
Australia	+1.00	0.00	0.00	+1.00	–1.00	0.00	+0.17
Canada	+1.00	n/a	0.00	+1.00	0.00	+1.00	+0.60
China	0.00	n/a	n/a	n/a	+1.00	+1.00	+0.67
India	+1.00	0.00	0.00	+1.00	n/a	0.00	+0.40
Indonesia	0.00	n/a	0.00	+1.00	+1.00	0.00	+0.40
Japan	+1.00	0.00	n/a	+1.00	n/a	0.00	+0.50
Korea	0.00	n/a	n/a	n/a	n/a	0.00	0.00
Russia	+1.00	n/a	0.00	+1.00	n/a	+1.00	+0.75
South Africa	+1.00	0.00	0.00	+1.00	0.00	+1.00	+0.50
United States	0.00	n/a	0.00	+1.00	0.00	0.00	+0.20
Total Average	+0.60	0.00	0.00	+1.00	+0.17	+0.40	+0.42
G8 Average (4)	+0.75	0.00	0.00	+1.00	0.00	+0.50	+0.51
Non-G8 Average (6)	+0.50	0.00	0.00	+1.00	+0.25	+0.33	+0.36

Note: n/a = not available.

H-2: 2003 Evian G8 Compliance for Selected G20 Countries

	China	India	Korea	Australia	South Africa	Average
Crime/Terrorist finance	+1.00	0.00	0.00	+1.00	+1.00	+0.60
Debt	0.00	–1.00	n/a	0.00	0.00	–0.25
Development	n/a	0.00	0.00	0.00	0.00	0.00
Energy	+1.00	+1.00	+1.00	+1.00	+1.00	+1.00
HIV/Infectious diseases	+1.00	–1.00	+1.00	0.00	+1.00	0.40
Information and communications technology	0.00	0.00	0.00	0.00	+1.00	+0.20
Marine environment	+1.00	+1.00	+1.00	+1.00	+1.00	+1.00
Terrorism	+1.00	0.00	+1.00	+1.00	0.00	+0.60
Trade	+1.00	0.00	+1.00	0.00	+1.00	+0.60
Transport security	+1.00	+1.00	+1.00	+1.00	0.00	+0.80
Weapons of mass destruction	+1.00	+1.00	0.00	0.00	+1.00	+0.60
World economy	0.00	0.00	0.00	0.00	+1.00	+0.20
Average	+0.73	+0.17	+0.55	+0.42	+0.67	+0.48

Note: The average score by issue area is the average of all countries' compliance scores for that issue. The average score by country is the average of all issue area compliance scores for a given country. The overall compliance average is an average of the overall issue average and overall country average. n/a = not available.

H-3: G20 Summit Compliance

	Average (Total)	**2008 Washington[a]**	**2009 London[b]**	**2009 Pittsburgh[c]**	**2010 Toronto[d]**
Argentina	–0.16 (33)	–0.25 (4)	–0.18 (11)	–0.20 (10)	0.00 (8)
Australia	+0.69 (34)	+0.75 (4)	+0.90 (11)	+0.50 (10)	+0.67 (9)
Brazil	+0.21 (31)	+1.00 (3)	+0.73 (11)	–0.50 (10)	+0.29 (7)
Canada	+0.73 (39)	+0.75 (4)	+0.90 (11)	+0.60 (15)	+0.78 (9)
China	+0.03 (32)	+0.00 (4)	–0.18 (11)	0.00 (9)	+0.38 (8)
France	+0.74 (36)	+0.25 (4)	+0.90 (11)	+0.77 (13)	+0.56 (9)
Germany	+0.74 (33)	+1.00 (4)	+0.90 (11)	+0.70 (10)	+0.50 (8)
India	–0.20 (32)	+0.00 (4)	–0.10 (11)	–0.30 (10)	–0.29 (7)
Indonesia	–0.42 (33)	+0.25 (4)	–0.73 (11)	–0.50 (10)	–0.13 (8)
Italy	+0.50 (34)	+1.00 (4)	+0.64 (11)	+0.20 (10)	+0.56 (9)
Japan	+0.37 (32)	+0.75 (4)	+0.09 (11)	+0.56 (9)	+0.50 (8)

	Average (Total)	2008 Washington[a]	2009 London[b]	2009 Pittsburgh[c]	2010 Toronto[d]
Korea	+0.65 (31)	0.00 (1)	+0.73 (11)	+0.70 (10)	+0.56 (9)
Mexico	+0.15 (36)	+0.50 (4)	0.00 (11)	+0.36 (14)	–0.14 (7)
Russia	+0.20 (37)	+0.25 (4)	+0.18 (11)	+0.20 (15)	+0.14 (7)
Saudi Arabia	–0.03 (30)	0.00 (1)	+0.09 (11)	–0.10 (10)	–0.13 (8)
South Africa	+0.57 (32)	+1.00 (4)	+0.81 (11)	+0.70 (10)	–0.14 (7)
Turkey	+0.24 (29)	+1.00 (1)	+0.73 (11)	–0.20 (10)	0.00 (7)
United Kingdom	+0.90 (39)	+1.00 (4)	+1.00 (11)	+0.90 (15)	+0.67 (9)
United States	+0.49 (39)	+0.25 (4)	+0.18 (11)	+0.73 (15)	+0.33 (9)
European Union	+0.60 (32)	+1.00 (4)	+0.80 (11)	+0.40 (10)	+0.57 (7)
All	+0.35 (674)	+0.53 (70)	+0.42 (220)	+0.28 (225)	+0.28 (160)
G8	+0.59 (321)	+0.69 (36)	+0.62 (99)	+0.56 (112)	+0.51 (75)
Non-G8	+0.16 (353)	+0.39 (34)	+0.25 (121)	+0.04 (113)	+0.10 (85)

Notes: The number in parentheses is the number of assessed commitments conducted for the individual country. Scores are based on compliance reports conducted by the G20 Research Group at the University of Toronto, the International Organizations Research Institute at the National Research University Higher School of Economic, Moscow, and the Center for Dialogue and Analysis on North America at the Tecnologico de Monterrey in Mexico City.

[a] Commitments covered trade, specifically resisting protectionism (3), and domestic financial regulation, specifically strengthening regulatory oversight (1).

[b] Commitments covered macroeconomics, specifically restoring growth and jobs (1); trade, specifically resisting protectionism (7); domestic financial regulation (1); and development, specifically ensuring a fair and sustainable recovery for all (3).

[c] Commitments covered macroeconomics, specifically stress tests (1); trade, specifically resisting protectionism (2); financial and regulatory reform (1); reform of the international financial institutions, specifically the International Monetary Fund (1) and multilateral development banks (1); development, specifically official development assistance (2); climate change, specifically clean technologies (1) and the United Nations Framework Convention on Climate Change (1); energy, specifically fossil fuels (1); market transparency (1); investment stimulus (1); access (1); and corruption (1).

[d] Commitments covered macroeconomics, specifically advanced economies (1), deficit countries (1), and surplus economies (1); trade, specifically resisting protectionism (1); domestic financial regulation, specifically market infrastructure (1), reform of the international financial institutions, specifically the International Monetary Fund (1); development, specifically financing (1); food and agriculture, specifically the L'Aquila Food Security Initiative (1); energy, specifically fossil fuels (1); corruption, specifically the United Nations Convention Against Corruption (1); climate change, specifically the green recovery (1) and the United Nations Framework Convention on Climate Change (2).

Appendix I: Shocks, Vulnerability, and Interdependence

I-1: Shocks

Year	Finance/Economics				Energy/Ecology				
	New York Stock Exchange			Events	Oil Price (US$)			Events	Food Price Index
	Eve	High	Low		Eve	High	Low		
1997		5,438.18	4,118.15	Thailand, Indonesia, Korea		26.55	17.60	Sea of Japan oil spill; North Korean famine (1996–98); Indonesia fires	113.5
1998		6,352.17	5,045.78	Russia, United States, Brazil		25.55	10.82	Turkey earthquake	103.7
1999	6683.34	7,011.65	6,092.27		25.87	28.03	11.38	France oil spill	91.1
2000	6791.40	7,164.55	6,094.91		34.90	37.22	23.91	India earthquake; South Africa oil spill; Brazil oil spill	89.5
2001	6130.50	7,048.13	5,331.38	Turkey, Argentina	17.50	32.21	17.50		92.3
2002	5214.12	6,445.01	4,452.49		27.00	32.68	18.02		90.2
2003	5851.14	6,469.50	4,418.62		29.99	37.96	25.25	Europe heat wave; Southern India heat wave	98.3
2004	7002.91	7,273.18	6,211.33		46.30	56.37	32.49	Indian Ocean tsunami (December)	111.5
2005	7362.59	7,867.59	6,902.51		62.61	69.91	42.16	Hurricane Katrina, US	114.7
2006	8897.17	9,188.17	7,708.11		55.90	77.05	55.90		122.4
2007	9701.38	10,387.17	8,811.55		94.81	99.16	50.51		154.1

2008 Washington[a]	5,704.13	9,781.57	4,607.47		77.44	145.31	30.28	China earthquake	190.9
2008 São Paulo[a]	5,871.98				61.06				
2008 Washington[b]	5,715.79				58.31				
2009 Horsham	4,721.00	7,288.23	4,181.75		46.22	81.03	34.03	Fires, Australia	151.5
2009 London[b]	4,978.98				48.49				
2009 Washington[a]	5,372.10				48.46				
2009 London[a]	6,546.60				67.90				
2009 Pittsburgh	6,964.69				68.74				
2009 St. Andrews	6,950.14				79.64				
2010 Washington[a]	7,644.67	7,743.74[c]	6,355.83[c]	Greece	82.78	86.54[d]	64.78[d]	Deepwater Horizon oil spill, Gulf of Mexico, US; Russian heat wave	179.1
2010 Busan	6,860.39				74.62				
2010 Toronto	6,763.93				78.45				

Notes: Finance refers to country's need for international financial support and/or firms' need for financial support from national or international government. Eve refers to the last reported day before the meeting.

[a] Ministerial.

[b] Summit.

[c] For the period January 1, 2010–August 16, 2010.

[d] For the period from January 1, 2010–August 10, 2010.

I-2: Shock Characteristics

	Subject	Status	Source	Spread	Speed	Scale: Deaths	Scale: Destruction	Democracy in Doubt
Political Security								
Afghanistan	War	Old-New	BMENA (Afghanistan)	Bilateral border (Pakistan); regional (BMENA)				Yes
Korea: *Cheonan*	War	Old	Asia (North Korea)	Bilateral border		49		
New York City	Terrorism	New	Yemen–United States	Africa–America		0	0	
Detroit: December 25, 2009	Terrorism	New	United States			0	0	
New York City (May)	Terrorism	New	United States			0	0	
Moscow Subway	Terrorism	New	Russia	Not applicable		38		Yes
Energy-Environment								
Haiti	Environment	New natural disaster	Americas	Dominican Republic		30,000–50,000		
Chilean earthquake	Environment	New natural disaster	Americas			300		
Icelandic volcano	Environment	New natural disaster	Europe (Iceland)	Europe–North America	2 weeks	0		
Gulf of Mexico	Environment-Energy	New human accident	United States	America–Mexico	3 months	11		
Finance-Economy								
2007–09 American–Atlantic	Banking-Finance	New	United States–Britain–Germany	Global	18 months	0		No
Greece debt	Sovereign debt	Old	Greece	Europe	Weeks	3		Yes
European debt	Sovereign debt (bank)	Old (New)	Europe	Global	1 day	0		Yes

Note: BMENA = Broader Middle East and North Africa.

I-3: G20 Terrorism Shocks

Year	# of G20 Countries Attacked	% of G20 Countries Attacked	# of G20 Countries That Suffered Fatalities	% of G20 Countries That Suffered Fatalities	Total Attacks on G20	Total Fatalities in G20
1997	17	89.5%	10	52.6%	607	1,327
1998	16	84.2%	8	42.1%	197	585
1999	16	84.2%	11	57.9%	520	1,210
2000	16	84.2%	8	42.1%	449	985
2001	15	78.9%	7	36.8%	498	3,883
2002	14	73.7%	7	36.8%	304	1,068
2003	15	78.9%	7	36.8%	367	1,071
2004	13	68.4%	7	36.4%	236	1,063
2005	13	68.4%	9	47.4%	302	816
2006	16	84.2%	11	57.9%	315	860
2007	11	57.9%	7	36.4%	271	760
2008	14	73.7%	7	36.4%	868	968
Average	14.7	77.2%	8.3	43.4%	441.2	1,216.3

Source: Global Terrorism Database <http://www.start.umd.edu/gtd/>.

Notes: Excludes the European Union.

Appendix J: International Institutional Performance

J-1: Predictive Accuracy of the International Monetary Fund

Year	Spring	Fall	Actual
1999	2.3	3.0	3.4
2000	3.4	3.5	4.7
2001	3.9	4.2	2.2
2002	3.9	3.5	3.0
2003	4.0	3.7	3.9
2004	4.1	4.1	5.1
2005	4.4	4.3	4.9
2006	4.4	4.3	5.4
2007	4.7	4.9	5.0
2008	4.9	4.8	3.0
2009	3.8	3.0	−0.6
2010	1.9	3.1	5.1

Source: International Monetary Fund (1999–2011), *World Economic Outlook*, world output tables.

Notes: Percentage range in real gross domestic product. Actual = from the fall report of the following year.

J-2: Multilateral Organizations' Head/Chair/Location by Country

Year	G20	International Monetary Fund	International Monetary and Financial Committee	World Bank	Bank for International Settlements	Basel Committee for Banking Supervision
1999	**Germany/Canada**	**France**	**United Kingdom**	**United States**	**United Kingdom**	**United States**
2000	**Canada**	**Germany**	**United Kingdom**	**United States**	**United Kingdom**	**United States**
2001	**Canada**	**Germany**	**United Kingdom**	**United States**	**United Kingdom**	**United States**
2002	India	**Germany**	**United Kingdom**	**United States**	**United Kingdom**	**United States**
2003	Mexico	**Germany**	**United Kingdom**	**United States**	**Canada**	Spain
2004	**Germany**	Spain	**United Kingdom**	**United States**	**Canada**	Spain
2005	China	Spain	**United Kingdom**	**United States**	**Canada**	Spain
2006	Australia	Spain	**United Kingdom**	**United States**	**Canada**	Netherlands
2007	South Africa	**France**	**Italy**	**United States**	**Canada**	Netherlands
2008	**United States**	**France**	Egypt	**United States**	Spain	Netherlands
2009	**United Kingdom/ United States**	**France**	Egypt	**United States**	Spain	Netherlands
2010	**Canada**/Korea	**France**	Egypt	**United States**	Spain	Netherlands

Continued ...

	Organisation for Economic Co-operation and Development	G10	G33	G7	Financial Stability Forum/ Board
1999	**Canada**	Sweden	Not applicable	**Germany**	**United Kingdom**
2000	**Canada**	Switzerland	Not applicable	**Japan**	**United Kingdom**
2001	**Canada**	**Germany**	Not applicable	**Italy**	**United Kingdom**
2002	**Canada**	**France**	Not applicable	**Canada**	**United Kingdom**
2003	**Canada**	**Canada**	Indonesia	**France**	**United States**
2004	**Canada**	**United States**	Indonesia	**United States**	**United States**
2005	**Canada**	**France**	Indonesia	**United Kingdom**	**United States**
2006	Mexico	**Italy**	Indonesia	**Russia**	**Italy**
2007	Mexico	**Japan**	Indonesia	**Germany**	**Italy**
2008	Mexico	Netherlands	Indonesia	**Japan**	**Italy**
2009	Mexico	Not applicable	Indonesia	**Italy**	**Italy**
2010	Mexico	Not applicable	Indonesia	**Canada**	**Italy**

Note: G7 members are in bold.

J-3: Outside Participation at G7 Finance Ministers' Meetings

	Australia	Brazil	China	India	Israel	Korea	Kuwait	Nigeria	Norway	Palestine	Russia	Saudi Arabia	Singapore	South Africa	United Arab Emirates	European Community	International Monetary Fund	Middle East Quartet	World Bank	World Trade Organization
1992 April											1									
1992 September											1									
1995 April											1					1				
1995 October											1					1				
1997 September																	1			
1998 February																	1			
1998 April																	1			
1998 May											1					1	1		1	1
1998 October																1	1		1	
1999 February																1	1			
1999 April																1	1			
1999 September																1	1			
2000 January																1	1			
2000 April																1	1			
2000 September																1	1			
2001 February											1					1	1			
2001 April											1					1				
2004 October			1																	
2005 February			1																	
2005 September		1	1	1							1			1						
2005 December		1	1	1	1					1								1		
2006 January[b]											1									
2006 February[b]											1									
2006 June[b]	1		1	1		1		1			1			1						
2007 February			1								1									
2007 May[b]	1	1	1	1		1		1			1									
2007 October			1			1	1		1		1	1	1		1					
Total	2	3	8	4	1	3	1	2	1	1	14	1	1	2	1	12	27[b]	1	2	1

Notes:

[a] Signifies G8 finance ministers meeting.

[b] Includes attendance at 15 meetings prior to April 1992.

Appendix K: G20 Capability: Gross Domestic Product

Country	1999	2000	2001	2002	2003	2004	2005	2006	2007	2008	2009	2010
Argentina	283.69	284.47	269.05	102.74	129.54	153.02	183.00	214.03	262.09	328.13	310.35	369.99
Australia	412.142	399.54	377.361	423.56	539.114	654.981	732.095	777.974	945.596	1,054.59	991.852	1,245.31
Brazil	586.92	644.28	554.41	505.71	552.24	663.55	881.75	1,089.16	1,366.22	1,650.39	1,622.31	2,142.93
China	1,083.28	1,198.48	1,324.81	1,453.83	1,640.96	1,931.65	2,256.92	2,712.92	3,494.24	4,519.95	4,990.53	5,930.39
India	453.66	476.35	487.80	510.29	590.97	688.74	808.67	908.47	1,152.81	1,251.37	1,253.98	1,597.95
Indonesia	140.00	165.02	160.45	195.66	234.86	256.84	285.74	364.28	432.19	510.96	538.70	708.35
Korea	461.81	533.39	504.58	575.93	643.76	721.98	844.87	951.77	1,049.24	931.41	834.06	1,014.89
Mexico	566.17	671.93	709.94	705.51	700.24	759.56	848.55	951.79	1,035.32	1,094.03	881.84	1,035.40
Saudi Arabia	161.17	188.69	183.26	188.80	214.86	250.67	315.76	356.63	385.20	476.94	377.20	451.39
South Africa	133.105	132.964	118.563	111.357	168.22	219.426	246.956	261.175	285.805	274.186	284.236	363.475
Turkey	249.82	266.44	195.55	232.28	303.26	392.21	482.69	529.19	649.13	730.32	614.42	734.59
Canada	661.25	724.91	715.44	734.65	865.90	992.23	1,133.76	1,278.61	1,424.07	1,502.68	1,337.58	1,577.04
France	1,457.07	1,331.59	1,340.27	1,458.20	1,796.68	2,055.36	2,137.95	2,259.58	2,586.77	2,842.55	2,631.92	2,562.76
Germany	2,133.84	1,891.93	1,882.51	2,013.69	2,428.45	2,729.92	2,771.06	2,905.45	3,328.59	3,640.73	3,307.20	3,286.45
Italy	1,209.70	1,107.25	1,124.67	1,229.51	1,517.40	1,737.80	1,789.38	1,874.72	2,130.24	2,318.16	2,116.63	2,060.89
Japan	4,432.60	4,731.20	4,159.86	3,980.82	4,302.94	4,655.82	4,571.87	4,356.75	4,356.35	4,849.19	5,035.14	5,488.42
Russia	195.91	259.70	306.58	345.13	430.29	591.18	763.70	989.93	1,299.70	1,660.85	1,222.69	1,487.29
United Kingdom	1,503.12	1,480.15	1,471.10	1,614.41	1,862.27	2,202.50	2,283.31	2,448.11	2,813.95	2,657.31	2,180.65	2,263.10
United States	9,353.50	9,951.48	10,286.18	10,642.30	11,142.23	11,853.25	12,622.95	13,377.20	14,028.68	14,291.55	13,938.93	14,526.55
Total G20 GDP	25,478.76	26,439.75	26,172.38	27,024.38	30,064.19	33,510.68	35,960.95	38,607.73	43,026.18	46,585.29	44,470.20	48,847.16
Total non-G8 GDP	4,531.77	4,961.54	4,885.77	5,005.67	5,718.02	6,692.62	7,886.98	9,117.38	11,057.83	12,822.28	12,699.47	15,594.66
Total G8 GDP	20,946.99	21,478.21	21,286.61	22,018.71	24,346.17	26,818.06	28,073.97	29,490.35	31,968.35	33,763.01	31,770.73	33,252.50

Total Global GDP	31,326.85	32,299.02	32,090.91	33,357.75	37,484.38	42,136.20	45,571.19	49,342.42	55,677.54	61,166.63	57,760.76	63,074.93
% Global GDP – G20	81%	82%	82%	81%	80%	80%	79%	78%	77%	76%	77%	77%
% Global GDP – non-G8	14%	15%	15%	15%	15%	16%	17%	18%	20%	21%	22%	25%
% Global GDP – G8	67%	66%	66%	66%	65%	64%	62%	60%	57%	55%	55%	53%
Highest G20	9,353.50	9,951.48	10,286.18	10,642.30	11,142.23	11,853.25	12,622.95	13,377.20	14,028.68	14,291.55	13,938.93	14,526.55
Lowest G20	133.11	132.96	118.56	102.74	129.54	153.02	183.00	214.03	262.09	274.19	284.24	363.48
Ratio G20	70.27	74.84	86.76	103.59	86.02	77.46	68.98	62.50	53.53	52.12	49.04	39.97
Highest non-G8	1,083.28	1,198.48	1,324.81	1,453.83	1,640.96	1,931.65	2,256.92	2,712.92	3,494.24	4,519.95	4,990.53	5,930.39
Lowest non-G8	133.11	132.96	118.56	102.74	129.54	153.02	183.00	214.03	262.09	274.19	284.24	363.48
Ratio non-G8	8.14	9.01	11.17	14.15	12.67	12.62	12.33	12.68	13.33	16.48	17.56	16.32
Highest G8	9,353.50	9,951.48	10,286.18	10,642.30	11,142.23	11,853.25	12,622.95	13,377.20	14,028.68	14,291.55	13,938.93	14,526.55
Lowest G8	195.91	259.70	306.58	345.13	430.29	591.18	763.70	989.93	1,299.70	1,502.68	1,222.69	1,487.29
Ratio G8	47.74	38.32	33.55	30.84	25.89	20.05	16.53	13.51	10.79	9.51	11.40	9.77
Gini coefficient – all	0.54	0.54	0.55	0.56	0.54	0.53	0.56	0.61	0.76	0.75	0.67	0.77
Gini coefficient – non-G8	0.33	0.33	0.34	0.36	0.32	0.30	0.30	0.39	0.66	0.65	0.51	0.62
Gini coefficient – G8	0.80	0.81	0.81	0.81	0.81	0.81	0.83	0.83	0.83	0.83	0.83	0.43

Sources: GDP: International Monetary Fund. 2012. "World Economic Outlook Database." Washington DC, April. Available at: www.imf.org/external/pubs/ft/weo/2012/01/weodata/index.aspx. Accessed: July 2012. Gini coefficient: Wessa.net. Available at: www.wessa.net. Accessed: July 2012.

Note: GDP = gross domestic product.

Appendix L: Common Principles of Democracy

L-1: Polity IV: Authority Trends

	1999	**2000**	**2001**	**2002**	**2003**	**2004**	**2005**	**2006**	**2007**	**2008**
Argentina	7	8	8	8	8	8	8	8	8	8
Australia	10	10	10	10	10	10	10	10	10	10
Brazil	8	8	8	8	8	8	8	8	8	8
Canada	10	10	10	10	10	10	10	10	10	10
China	−7	−7	−7	−7	−7	−7	−7	−7	−7	−7
France	9	9	9	9	9	9	9	9	9	9
Germany	10	10	10	10	10	10	10	10	10	10
India	9	9	9	9	9	9	9	9	9	9
Indonesia	−7	6	6	6	6	6	8	8	8	8
Italy	10	10	10	10	10	10	10	10	10	10
Japan	10	10	10	10	10	10	10	10	10	10
Korea	6	8	8	8	8	8	8	8	8	8
Mexico	6	6	8	8	8	8	8	8	8	8
Russia	3	3	6	6	6	6		6	4	4
Saudi Arabia	−10	−10	−10	−10	−10	−10	−10	−10	−10	−10
South Africa	9	9	9	9	9	9	9	9	9	9
Turkey	7	7	7	7	7	7	7	7	7	7
United Kingdom	10	10	10	10	10	10	10	10	10	10
United States	10	10	10	10	10	10	10	10	10	10

Notes: The "Polity Score" captures this regime authority spectrum, which spans fully institutionalized autocracies through mixed or incoherent authority regimes to fully institutionalized democracies on a 21-point scale from −10 (hereditary monarchy) to +10 (consolidated democracy). Excludes the European Union.

Sources: Polity IV Project: Political Regime Characteristics and Transitions, 1800–2010. Monty Marshall and Keith Jaggers, principal investigators. www.systemicpeace.org/polity/polity4.htm. Accessed: July 2012.

L-2: Freedom House Scores

	1999			2000			2001			2002			2003			2004		
	R	L	S	R	L	S	R	L	S	R	L	S	R	L	S	R	L	S
Argentina	2	3	F	1	2	F	3	3	P	3	3	P	2	2	F	2	2	F
Australia	1	1	F	1	1	F	1	1	F	1	1	F	1	1	F	1	1	F
Brazil	3	4	P	3	3	P	3	3	P	2	3	F	2	3	F	2	3	F
Canada	1	1	F	1	1	F	1	1	F	1	1	F	1	1	F	1	1	F
China	7	6	N	7	6	N	7	6	N	7	6	N	7	6	N	7	6	N
France	1	2	F	1	2	F	1	2	F	1	1	F	1	1	F	1	1	F
Germany	1	2	F	1	2	F	1	2	F	1	1	F	1	1	F	1	1	F
India	2	3	F	2	3	F	2	3	F	2	3	F	2	3	F	2	3	F
Indonesia	4	4	P	3	4	P	3	4	P	3	4	P	3	4	P	3	4	P
Italy	1	2	F	1	2	F	1	2	F	1	1	F	1	1	F	1	1	F
Japan	1	2	F	1	2	F	1	2	F	1	2	F	1	2	F	1	2	F
Korea	2	2	F	2	2	F	2	2	F	2	2	F	2	2	F	1	2	F
Mexico	3	4	P	2	3	F	2	3	F	2	2	F	2	2	F	2	2	F
Russia	4	5	P	5	5	P	5	5	P	5	5	P	5	5	P	6	5	N
S. Africa	1	2	F	1	2	F	1	2	F	1	2	F	1	2	F	1	2	F
S. Arabia	7	7	N	7	7	N	7	7	N	7	7	N	7	7	N	7	7	N
Turkey	4	5	P	4	5	P	4	5	P	3	4	P	3	4	P	3	3	P
UK	1	2	F	1	2	F	1	2	F	1	1	F	1	1	F	1	1	F
US	1	1	F	1	1	F	1	1	F	1	1	F	1	1	F	1	1	F

	2005			2006			2007			2008			2009			2010		
	R	L	S	R	L	S	R	L	S	R	L	S	R	L	S	R	L	S
Argentina	2	2	F	2	2	F	2	2	F	2	2	F	2	3	F	2	2	F
Australia	1	1	F	1	1	F	1	1	F	1	1	F	1	1	F	1	1	F
Brazil	2	2	F	2	2	F	2	2	F	2	2	F	3	4	P	2	2	F
Canada	1	1	F	1	1	F	1	1	F	1	1	F	1	1	F	1	1	F
China	7	6	N	7	6	N	7	6	N	7	6	N	7	6	N	7	6	N
France	1	1	F	1	1	F	1	1	F	1	1	F	1	2	F	1	1	F
Germany	1	1	F	1	1	F	1	1	F	1	1	F	1	2	F	1	1	F
India	2	3	F	2	3	F	2	3	F	2	3	F	2	3	F	2	3	F
Indonesia	2	3	F	2	3	F	2	3	F	2	3	F	4	4	P	2	3	F
Italy	1	1	F	1	1	F	1	1	F	1	2	F	1	2	F	1	2	F
Japan	1	2	F	1	2	F	1	2	F	1	2	F	1	2	F	1	2	F
Korea	2	3	F	2	3	F	1	2	F	1	2	F	2	2	F	1	2	F
Mexico	2	2	F	2	3	F	2	3	F	2	3	F	3	4	P	2	3	F
Russia	6	5	N	6	5	N	6	5	N	6	5	N	4	5	P	6	5	N
S. Africa	1	2	F	2	2	F	2	2	F	2	2	F	1	2	F	2	2	F
S. Arabia	7	6	N	7	6	N	7	6	N	7	6	N	7	7	N	7	6	N
Turkey	3	3	P	3	3	P	3	3	P	3	3	P	4	5	P	3	3	P
UK	1	1	F	1	1	F	1	1	F	1	1	F	1	2	F	1	1	F
US	1	1	F	1	1	F	1	1	F	1	1	F	1	1	F	1	1	F

Notes: Each country is assigned a numerical rating from 1 to 7 for political rights (R) and an analogous rating for (L); a rating of 1 indicates the highest degree of freedom and 7 the lowest level of freedom. These ratings determine the status (S) of a country as free (F), partly free (P), or not free (N).

Sources: Freedom House, www.freedomhouse.org.

Appendix M: G20 Members' Political Capacities

M-1: Leaders' Political Support in G20 Countries

Country	Leader	Date	Polling Company	Approval (%)	Disapproval (%)	Net
		May 2010	Poliarquía Consultores	29		
Argentina	Cristina Fernández de Kirchner	Dec. 2009	Poliarquia Consultores	19	54	−35
		Aug. 2009	Poliarquia Consultores	23	53	
		May 2, 2010	Newspoll/The Australian	39	50	−11
Australia	Kevin Rudd	Apr. 18, 2010	Angus Reid	50	41	
		Mar. 28, 2010	Angus Reid	51	39	
		Mar. 14, 2010	Angus Reid	48	41	
		Apr. 2010	Angus Reid	76	5	+71
Brazil	Luiz Inácio Lula da Silva	Mar. 2010	Angus Reid	75	5	
		Feb. 2010	Angus Reid	76	5	
		May 2010	Angus Reid	29	48	−19
Canada	Stephen Harper	Apr. 2010	Ekos	33	49	
		Mar. 2010	Angus Reid	29	49	
China	Hu Jintao	n/a	n/a	n/a	n/a	n/a

		Jun. 25–28, 2010	TNS Sofres	26		
		Jun. 3–4, 2010	ViaVoice	34	64	−30
France	Nicolas Sarkozy	May 5, 2010	CSA/Le Parisien	37	58	
		Apr. 2010	CSA/Le Parisien	34	59	
		Mar. 2010	CSA/Le Parisien	36	58	
		May 2010	Infratest dimap	58	42	+16
Germany	Angela Merkel	Apr. 2010	Infratest dimap	55	44	
		Jan. 2010	Infratest dimap	59	39	
India	Manmohan Singh	n/a	n/a	n/a	n/a	n/a
		Sep. 2009	Angus Reid	84	16	+68
Indonesia	Susilo Bambang Yudhoyono	Mar. 2009	Angus Reid	80	20	
		Nov. 2008	Angus Reid	62	38	
		Jul. 2010	IPR Marketing/La Repubblica	39	55	
Italy	Silvio Berlusconi	Jun. 2010	IPR Marketing/La Repubblica	41	54	−13
		Apr. 2010	IPR Marketing/La Repubblica	44	54	
		Mar. 2010	IPR Marketing/La Repubblica	44	54	
		Jul. 2010	Kyodo News	43		
Japan	Naoto Kan	Jun. 26, 2010	Nikkei	50	33	+17
		Jun. 21, 2010	Kyodo	59	30	
		Jan. 2010	Korea Research Center	52		
Korea	Lee Myung-bak	Oct. 2009	Korea Society Opinion Institute	33	53	−20
		Oct. 2008	Korea Society Opinion Institute	24	64	

Continued ...

Country	Leader	Date	Polling Company	Approval (%)	Disapproval (%)	Net
Mexico	Felipe Calderón	Mar. 1 2010	Angus Reid	45	53	−8
		Nov. 2009	Angus Reid	52	46	
		Aug. 2009	Angus Reid	54	37	
Russia	Dmitry Medvedev	May 2010	Yury Levada Analytical Center	70		
		Apr. 2010	Yury Levada Analytical Center	73	25	+48
		Mar. 2010	Yury Levada Analytical Center	75	22	
		Feb. 2010	Yury Levada Analytical Center	77	21	
		Jan. 2010	Yury Levada Analytical Center	75	23	
Saudi Arabia	Adbullah Bin Abdulaziz	n/a	n/a	n/a	n/a	n/a
South Africa	Jacob Zuma	Feb. 2010	TNS Research Surveys	43	41	+2
		Nov. 2009	TNS Research Surveys	58	23	
		Sep.2009	TNS Research Surveys	53	19	
		Jun. 2009	TNS Research Surveys	57	13	
Turkey	Tayyip Erdoğan	Aug. 03, 2009	MetroPOLL Strategic and Social Research Center	58	38	+20
United Kingdom	David Cameron	Jun. 23–25, 2010	Angus Reid	54	32	+22
		May 21–24, 2010	Angus Reid	54	25	

United States	Barack Obama	Jun. 25–27, 2010	Angus Reid	44	50	−6
		Jun. 18–20, 2010	Gallup	49	44	
		May 25–26, 2010	Angus Reid Public Opinion	48	45	
		May 21–23, 2010	CNN/ORC	51	46	
		Apr. 22–25, 2010	ABC/Washington Post	54	44	
		Mar. 23–26, 2010	USA Today/Gallup	53	43	
European Union	José Manuel Barroso	Apr. 2010	Harris Interactive	34		n/a
		Nov. 2009	Harris Interactive	37		
Net Average						+7.8

Notes: Wording includes: “Do you have a positive or negative opinion of xxx?”; “Do you have confidence in xxx to face the country’s problems”; “Do you approve or disapprove of xxx performance?; “Are you satisfied with the political work of xxx?”; “Indicate whether you have a very good, somewhat good, somewhat poor or a very poor opinion of xxx”; “Do you have confidence in xxx?”. n/a = not available.

M-2: Political Continuity by Minister

	1999	2000	2001	2002	2003	2004
Argentina	Roque Fernandez	José Luis Machinea	Domingo Cavallo	Roberto Lavagna	Roberto Lavagna	Roberto Lavagna
Australia	Peter Costello	Peter Costello	Peter Costello	Peter Costello	Peter Costello	Peter Costello
Brazil	Pedro Malan	Pedro Malan	Pedro Malan	Pedro Malan	Antonio Palocci	Antonio Palocci
Canada	Paul Martin	Paul Martin	Paul Martin	John Manley	John Manley	Ralph Goodale
China	Xiang Huaicheng	Xiang Huaicheng	Xiang Huaicheng	Xiang Huaicheng	Jin Renqing	Jin Renqing
France	Christian Sautter	Laurent Fabius	Laurent Fabius	Francis Mer	Francis Mer	Nicolas Sarkozy
Germany	Hans Eichel	Hans Eichel	Hans Eichel	Hans Eichel	Hans Eichel	Hans Eichel
India	Yashwant Sinha	Yashwant Sinha	Yashwant Sinha	Manmohan Singh	Manmohan Singh	P. Chidambaram
Indonesia	Bambang Sudibyo	Prijadi Praptosuhardjo	Boedino	Boedino	Boedino	Yusuf Anwar
Italy	Giuliano Amato	Vincenzo Visco	Giulio Tremonti	Giulio Tremonti	Giulio Tremonti	Domenico Siniscalco
Japan	Kiichi Miyazawa	Kiichi Miyazawa	Masajuro Shiokawa	Masajuro Shiokawa	Sadakazu Tanigaki	Sadakazu Tanigaki
Korea	Bong-Kyun Kang	Nyum Jin	Nyum Jin	Yun-chur Jeon	Jin-Pyo Kim	Hun Jai Lee
Mexico	Angel Gurría	Angel Gurría	Francisco Gil Díaz	Francisco Gil Díaz	Francisco Gil Díaz	Francisco Gil Díaz
Russia	Mikhail Kasyanov	Alexei Kudrin	Alexei Kudrin	Alexei Kudrin	Alexei Kudrin	Alexei Kudrin
Saudi Arabia	Ibrahim Al-Assaf	Ibrahim Al-Assaf	Ibrahim Al-Assaf	Ibrahim Al-Assaf	Ibrahim Al-Assaf	Ibrahim Al-Assaf
South Africa	Trevor Manuel	Trevor Manuel	Trevor Manuel	Trevor Manuel	Trevor Manuel	Trevor Manuel
Turkey	Sümer Oral	Sümer Oral	Sümer Oral	Kemal Unakıtan	Kemal Unakıtan	Kemal Unakıtan
UK	Gordon Brown	Gordon Brown	Gordon Brown	Gordon Brown	Gordon Brown	Gordon Brown
USA	Lawrence Summers	Lawrence Summers	Paul O'Neill	Paul O'Neill	John Snow	John Snow
European Union	Pedro Solbes Mira	Pedro Solbes Mira	Pedro Solbes Mira	Pedro Solbes Mira	Pedro Solbes Mira	Pedro Solbes Mira
# Changes		6	5	6	5	6

Note: Represents who was finance minister at the time of the annual G20 ministerial meeting and not who attended the meeting.

2005	2006	2007	2008	2009	2010	# Changes
Roberto Lavagna	Felice Miceli	Miguel Peirano	Carlos Fernández	Amadou Boudou	Amadou Boudou	7
Peter Costello	Peter Costello	Peter Costello	Glenn Swan	Glenn Swan	Glenn Swan	1
Antonio Palocci	Guido Mantega	Guido Mantega	Guido Mantega	Guido Mantega	Guido Mantega	2
Ralph Goodale	Jim Flaherty	Jim Flaherty	Jim Flaherty	Jim Flaherty	Jim Flaherty	3
Jin Renqing	Jin Renqing	Xie Xuren	Xie Xuren	Xie Xuren	Xie Xuren	2
Thierry Breton	Thierry Breton	Christine Lagarde	Christine Lagarde	Christine Lagarde	Christine Lagarde	5
Hans Eichel	Peer Steinbrück	Peer Steinbrück	Peer Steinbrück	Peer Steinbrück	Wolfgang Schäuble	2
P. Chidambaram	P. Chidambaram	P. Chidambaram	P. Chidambaram	Pranab Mukherjee	Pranab Mukherjee	3
Yusuf Anwar	Sri Mulyani Indrawati	Sri Mulyani Indrawati	Sri Mulyani Indrawati	Sri Mulyani Indrawati	Agus Martowardojo	4
Giulio Tremonti	Tommaso Padoa-Schioppa	Tommaso Padoa-Schioppa	Giulio Tremonti	Giulio Tremonti	Giulio Tremonti	6
Sadakazu Tanigaki	Koji Omi	Fukushiro Nukaga	Fukushiro Nukaga	Hirohiso Fujii	Yoshihiko Noda	6
Duck-soo Han	O-kyu Kwon	O-kyu Kwon	Man-Soo Kang	Jeung-hyun Yoon	Jeung-hyun Yoon	8
Francisco Gil Díaz	Francisco Gil Díaz	Agustín Carstens	Agustín Carstens	Agustín Carstens	Ernesto Cordero	3
Alexei Kudrin	Alexei Kudrin	Alexei Kudrin	Alexei Kudrin	Alexei Kudrin	Alexei Kudrin	1
Ibrahim Al-Assaf	Ibrahim Al-Assaf	Ibrahim Al-Assaf	Ibrahim Al-Assaf	Ibrahim Al-Assaf	Ibrahim Al-Assaf	0
Trevor Manuel	Trevor Manuel	Trevor Manuel	Trevor Manuel	Pravin Gordhan	Pravin Gordhan	1
Kemal Unakıtan	Kemal Unakıtan	Kemal Unakıtan	Kemal Unakıtan	Mehmet Şimşek	Mehmet Şimşek	2
Gordon Brown	Gordon Brown	Alistair Darling	Alistair Darling	Alistair Darling	George Osborne	2
John Snow	Henry Paulson	Henry Paulson	Henry Paulson	Timothy Geithner	Timothy Geithner	4
Joaquín Almunia	Joaquín Almunia	Joaquín Almunia	Joaquín Almunia	Joaquín Almunia	Olli Rehn	3
4	7	8	5	7	6	

M-3: Leader Continuity in G8/G20 Countries

G7	# changes	1975 Rambouillet	1976 San Juan	1977 London	1978 Bonn
Canada	0	–	Pierre Trudeau	Pierre Trudeau	Pierre Trudeau
France	0	Valéry Giscard d'Estaing	Valéry Giscard d'Estaing	Valéry Giscard d'Estaing	Valéry Giscard d'Estaing
Germany	0	Helmut Schmidt	Helmut Schmidt	Helmut Schmidt	Helmut Schmidt
Italy	1	Aldo Moro	Aldo Moro	Giulio Andreotti	Giulio Andreotti
Japan	1	Takeo Miki	Takeo Miki	Takeo Fukuda	Takeo Fukuda
United Kingdom	1	Harold Wilson	James Callaghan	James Callaghan	James Callaghan
United States	1	Gerald Ford	Gerald Ford	Jimmy Carter	Jimmy Carter
European Union	0	–	–	Roy Jenkins	Roy Jenkins
Total	4	0	1	3	0
Average	0.5	0	0.14	0.38	0

G20	# changes	2008 Washington	2009 London	2009 Pittsburgh	2010 Toronto
Argentina	0	Cristina Fernández de Kirchner	Cristina Fernández de Kirchner	Cristina Fernández de Kirchner	Cristina Fernández de Kirchner
Australia	1	Kevin Rudd	Kevin Rudd	Kevin Rudd	Julia Gillard
Brazil	0	Luiz Inácio Lula da Silva	Luiz Inácio Lula da Silva	Luiz Inácio Lula da Silva	Luiz Inácio Lula da Silva
Canada	0	Stephen Harper	Stephen Harper	Stephen Harper	Stephen Harper
China	0	Hu Jintao	Hu Jintao	Hu Jintao	Hu Jintao
France	0	Nicolas Sarkozy	Nicolas Sarkozy	Nicolas Sarkozy	Nicolas Sarkozy
Germany	0	Angela Merkel	Angela Merkel	Angela Merkel	Angela Merkel
India	0	Manmohan Singh	Manmohan Singh	Manmohan Singh	Manmohan Singh
Indonesia	0	Susilo Bambang Yudhoyono	Susilo Bambang Yudhoyono	Susilo Bambang Yudhoyono	Susilo Bambang Yudhoyono
Italy	0	Silvio Berlusconi	Silvio Berlusconi	Silvio Berlusconi	Silvio Berlusconi

Japan	2	Taro Aso	Taro Aso	Yukio Hatoyama	Naoto Kan
Korea	0	Lee Myung-bak	Lee Myung-bak	Lee Myung-bak	Lee Myung-bak
Mexico	0	Felipe Calderón	Felipe Calderón	Felipe Calderón	Felipe Calderón
Russia	0	Dmitry Medvedev	Dmitry Medvedev	Dmitry Medvedev	Dmitry Medvedev
Saudi Arabia	0	Abdullah Bin Abdulziz	Abdullah Bin Abdulziz	Abdullah bin Abdul Aziz	Abdullah Bin Abdulziz
South Africa	1	Kgalema Motlanthe	Kgalema Motlanthe	Jacob Zuma	Jacob Zuma
Turkey	0	Recep Tayyip Erdoğan	Recep Tayyip Erdoğan	Recep Tayyip Erdoğan	Recep Tayyip Erdoğan
United Kingdom	1	Gordon Brown	Gordon Brown	Gordon Brown	David Cameron
United States	1	George W. Bush	Barack Obama	Barack Obama	Barack Obama
European Union	0	José Manuel Barroso	José Manuel Barroso	José Manuel Barroso	José Manuel Barroso
Total	6	0	1	2	3
Average	0.3	0	0.05	0.10	0.15

M-5: Competence of G20 Leaders in 2008–2010

Country	Head	Ministerial Experience	Professional Experience	Education
Argentina	Cristina Fernández de Kirchner	None	None	Law studies
Australia	Julia Gillard	Education, employment, social inclusion, 2007–10	Lawyer	Law
Australia	Kevin Rudd	None	Government official (foreign affairs)	Chinese history and language
Brazil	Luiz Inácio Lula da Silva	None	Business	None
Canada	Stephen Harper	None	Accountant	MA, economics
China	Hu Jintau	None	None	Engineering
France	Nicolas Sarkozy	Budget, 1993–95; Interior, 2002–04, 2005–07; Economy, finance, and industry, 2004	Lawyer	Law
Germany	Angela Merkel	Environment, nature conservation, and nuclear safety, 1994–98; Women and youth, 1991–94	None	PhD, physics
India	Manmohan Singh	Finance, 1991–96	Economist, International Monetary Fund Governor, Reserve Bank of India, 1982–85	PhD, economics
Indonesia	Susilo Bambang Yudhoyono	Politics, social, and security, 2000–04; Mines and energy, 1999–2000	None	PhD, agricultural economics
Italy	Silvio Berlusconi	None	Business	Law studies
Japan	Naoto Kan	Finance, 2010; Deputy prime minister, 2009–10; Minister of state, economic and fiscal policy, national strategy, science and technology policy 2009–10; Health and welfare, 1996	None	University

Country	Head	Ministerial Experience	Professional Experience	Education
Japan	Yukio Hatoyama	None	None	PhD, engineering
Japan	Taro Aso	Foreign affairs, 2005–07; Internal affairs and communications, 2003–05; Economic and financial policies, 2001	Business	Graduate studies, economics
Korea	Lee Myung-bak	None	Mayor, Seoul Business	Business Administration
Mexico	Felipé Calderón	Secretary, energy, 2003–04	Director, National Bank of Public Works and Services (BANOBRAS)	MA, economics MPA
Russia	Dmitry Medvedev	First deputy prime minister, 2005–08	Lawyer	Law
Saudi Arabia	Abdullah Bin Abdulazziz	Chair of the Supreme Economic Council	None	No formal university studies
South Africa	Jacob Zuma	Deputy president, 1999–2005	None	No formal education
South Africa	Kgalema Motlanthe	None	None	No university studies
Turkey	Recep Tayyip Erdoğan	None	Mayor, Istanbul	Business administration
United Kingdom	David Cameron	None	Business, government official (finance)	Philosophy, politics, and economics
United Kingdom	Gordon Brown	Finance, 1997–2008	None	PhD, history
United States	Barack Obama	None	Lawyer Professor Senator	Law
United States	George W. Bush	None	Business Governor	MBA

Appendix N: Controlled Club Participation

N-1: Country Leaders Participating at G20 Summits

Summit	Spain	Netherlands	Singapore	African Union	ASEAN	NEPAD	Total
2008 Washington	1	1					2
2009 London	1	1			1 (Thailand)	1 (Ethiopia)	4
2009 Pittsburgh	1	1			1 (Thailand)	1 (Ethiopia)	4
2010 Toronto	1	1		1 (Malawi)	1 (Vietnam)	1 (Ethiopia)	5
2010 Seoul	1		1	1 (Malawi)	1 (Vietnam)	1 (Ethiopia)	5
Total		4	1	1	3	3	16

Note: ASEAN = Association of Southeast Asian Nations; NEPAD = New Partnership for Africa's Development.

N-2: Multilateral Organizations Participating at G20 Summits

	IMF	World Bank	United Nations	Financial Stability Forum/Board	WTO	ILO	OECD	Total
2008 Washington	1	1	1	1				4
2009 London	1	1	1	1	1			5
2009 Pittsburgh	1	1	1	1	1	1	1	7
2010 Toronto	1	1	1	1	1	1	1	7
2010 Seoul	1	1	1		1	1	1	
Total	4	4	4	4	3	2	2	

Notes: Executive heads only: IMF = International Monetary Fund; WTO = World Trade Organization; ILO = International Labour Organization; OECD = Organisation for Economic Co-operation and Development.

N-3: Ministerial Financial Forum Membership

	Paris Club (1956)[a]	**OECD (1960)**	**G10 (1962)**	**BCBS (1974)**	**G7 (1975)**	**G8 (1997)**	**G22 (1997)**	**G33 (1999)**	**IMFC (1999)**	**G20 (1999)**[b]	**FSF (1999)**[c]	**FSB (2009)**[d]
Algeria									x			
Argentina				x			x	x	x	x		x
Australia	x	x		x			x	x	x	x	x	x
Austria	x	x										
Belgium	x	x	x	x				x	x			
Brazil				x			x	x	x	x		x
Canada	x	x	x	x	x	x	x	x	x	x	x	x
Chile		x						x				
China				x			x	x	x	x		x
Côte d'Ivoire								x				
Czech Republic		x										
Denmark	x	x							x			
Egypt								x				
Estonia		x										
Finland	x	x										
France	x	x	x	x	x	x	x	x	x	x	x	x
Gabon									x			
Germany	x	x	x	x	x	x	x	x	x	x	x	x
Greece		x										
Hong Kong				x			x	x			x	x
Hungary		x										
Iceland		x										
India				x			x	x	x	x		x
Indonesia				x			x	x	x	x		x
Ireland	x	x										
Israel		x										
Italy	x	x	x	x	x	x	x	x	x	x	x	x
Japan	x	x	x	x	x	x	x	x	x	x	x	x
Korea		x		x			x	x		x		x
Luxembourg		x		x								
Malaysia							x	x				
Mexico		x		x			x	x		x		x
Morocco								x				
Netherlands	x	x	x	x				x	x		x	x
New Zealand		x										

Norway	x	x										
Poland		x					x	x				
Portugal		x										
Russia	x			x		x	x	x	x	x		x
Saudi Arabia				x				x	x	x		x
Singapore				x			x	x	x		x	x
Slovak Republic		x										
Slovenia		x										
South Africa				x			x	x	x	x		x
Spain	x	x		x				x	x			x
Sweden	x	x	x	x				x				
Switzerland	x	x	x	x				x	x		x	x
Thailand							x	x				
Turkey		x		x				x		x		x
United Arab Emirates									x			
United Kingdom	x	x	x	x	x	x	x	x	x	x	x	x
United States	x	x	x	x	x	x	x	x	x	x	x	x
Total	19	34	11	27	7	8	22	33	25	19	12	24

Notes: Date in brackets refers to date of founding. Refers to membership as of 2012 or the last year of functioning. OECD = Organisation for Economic Co-operation and Development; BCBS = Basel Committee on Banking Supervision; IMFC = International Monetary and Financial Committee; FSF = Financial Stability Forum; FSB = Financial Stability Board.

[a] There are 13 associated members of the Paris Club, which participate in negotiation sessions, subject to the permanent members and the debtor country: Abu Dhabi, Argentina, Brazil, Korea, Israel, Kuwait, Mexico, Morocco, New Zealand, Portugal, South Africa, Trinidad and Tobago, and Turkey.

[b] The European Union is the 20th member of the G20.

[c] The following international organizations and standard-setting bodies were members of the Financial Stability Forum, which was superseded by the Financial Stability Board in 2008: Bank for International Settlements, Basel Committee on Banking Supervision, Committee on Payment and Settlement System, Committee on the Global Financial System, European Central Bank, International Accounting Standards Board, International Association of Insurance Supervisors, International Monetary Fund, International Organization of Securities Commissions, Organisation for Economic Co-operation and Development, and World Bank.

[d] The following international organizations and standard-setting bodies are members of the Financial Stability Board: Bank for International Settlements, Basel Committee on Banking Supervision, Committee on the Global Financial System, Committee on Payment and Settlement Systems, European Central Bank, European Commission, International Accounting Standards Board, International Association of Insurance Supervisors, International Monetary Fund, International Organization of Securities Commissions, Organisation for Economic Co-operation Development, and the World Bank.

N-4: G20 Network through Plurilateral Institutions

	UNSC	IMF Board	IMFC	OECD	FSB	G24	G77	ASEAN +3	Total
Argentina					x	x			2
Australia				x	x				2
Brazil			x		x	x	x		4
Canada		x	x	x	x				4
China	x	x	x		x	x	x	x	7
France	x	x	x	x	x				5
Germany		x	x	x	x				4
India			x		x	x	x		4
Indonesia			x		x			x	3
Italy		x	x	x	x				4
Japan		x	x	x	x			x	5
Korea			x	x	x		x[a]	x	4
Mexico			x	x	x	x	x[a]		4
Russia	x	x	x		x				4
Saudi Arabia		x	x		x				3
South Africa			x		x	x	x		4
Turkey				x	x				2
United Kingdom	x	x	x	x	x				5
United States	x	x	x	x	x				5
Total	5	10	16	11	19	6	6	4	

Notes: UNSC = Permanent Five members of the United Nations Security Council; IMF = International Monetary Fund; IMFC = International Monetary and Financial Committee; OECD = Organisation for Economic Co-operation and Development; FSB = Financial Stability Board; ASEAN = Association of Southeast Asian Nations.

[a] Mexico and Korea were founding members of the G77, but left after joining the Organisation for Economic Co-operation and Development in 1994.

N-5: G20 Network through Plurilateral Summit Institutions

	G8[a]	MEM	Commonwealth	Francophonie	ASEM	OSCE	APEC	SOA	SCO	NATO	OIC	Total
Argentina								x				1
Australia		x	x				x					3
Brazil	x	x						x				3
Canada	x	x	x	x		x	x	x		x		8
China	x	x			x		x		x			5
France	x	x		x	x	x				x		6
Germany	x	x			x	x				x		5
India	x	x	x		x				x[b]			5
Indonesia		x			x		x				x	4
Italy	x	x			x	x				x		5
Japan	x	x			x		x					4
Korea		x			x		x					3
Mexico	x	x					x	x				4
Netherlands					x	x				x		3
Russia	x	x				x	x		x		x[b]	6
Saudi Arabia		x										1
South Africa	x	x	x									3
Spain					x	x				x		3
Turkey						x				x	x	3
United Kingdom	x	x	x		x	x				x		6
United States	x	x				x	x	x		x		6
European Union	x	x			x							3
Total	14	18	5	2	12	10	9	5	3	9	3	

Notes: Includes plurilateral summit institutions of trans-regional reach containing members from the developed and emerging/developing world.

MEM = Major Economies Meeting; ASEM = Asia–European Union Meeting; OSCE = Organization for Security Cooperation in Europe; APEC = Asia Pacific Economic Cooperation; SOA = Summit of the Americas; NATO = North Atlantic Treaty Organization; SCO = Shanghai Cooperation Organisation; SOA = Summit of the Americas; OIC = Organisation of Islamic Cooperation.

[a] Includes Plus Five members.

[b] Observer.

N-6: G20 Leaders' Network

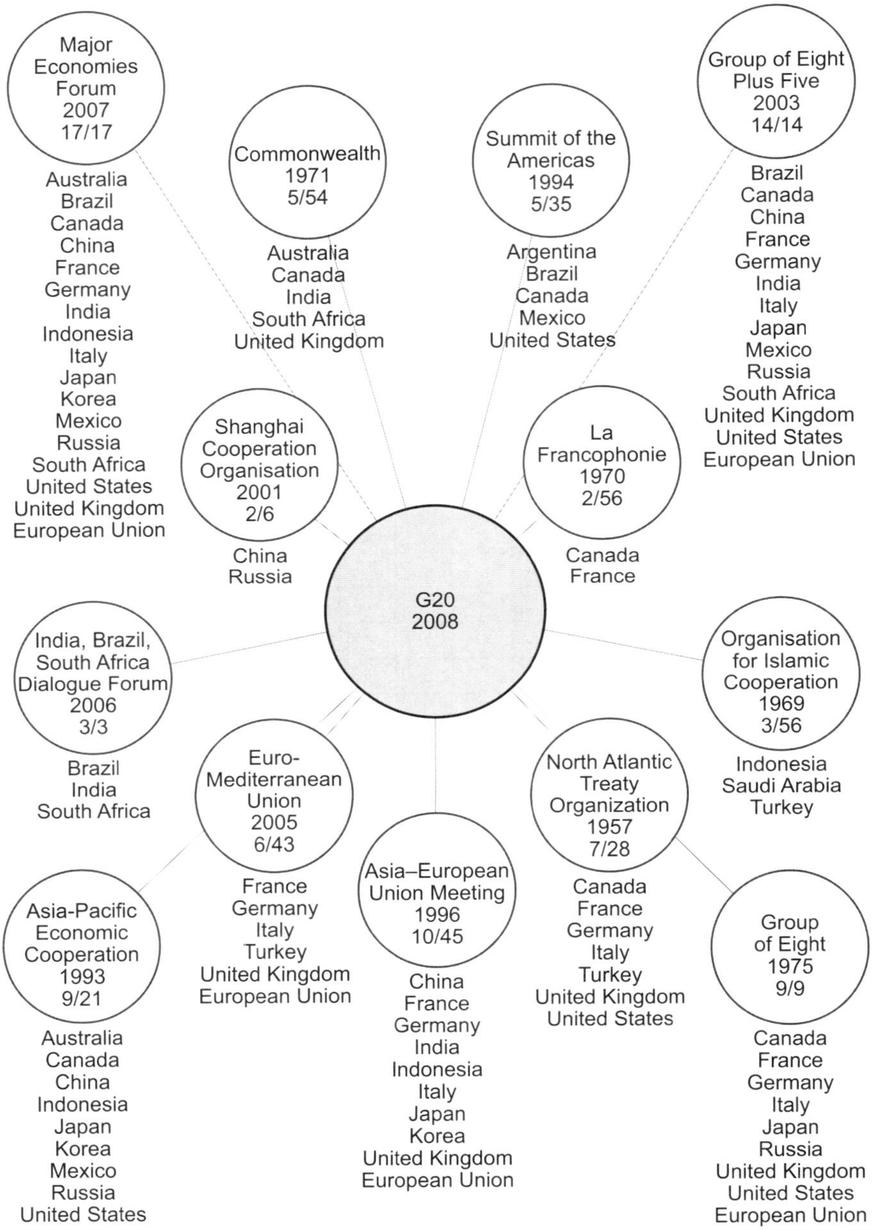

Index

Global Finance Series

Full series list

The European Union in the G8
Promoting Consensus and Concerted Actions for Global Public Goods
Edited by Marina Larionova
ISBN 978-1-4094-3323-1

European Union Economic Diplomacy
The Role of the EU in External Economic Relations
Stephen Woolcock
ISBN: 978-0-7546-7930-1

The New Economic Diplomacy
Decision-Making and Negotiation in International Economic Relations
Edited by Nicholas Bayne and Stephen Woolcock
ISBN: 978-1-4094-2541-0

Financial Crisis Management and the Pursuit of Power
American Pre-eminence and the Credit Crunch
Mine Aysen Doyran
ISBN: 978-1-4094-0095-0

Global Financial Crisis
Paolo Savona, John J. Kirton and Chiara Oldani
ISBN 978-1-4094-0271-8

Sovereign Wealth Funds and International Political Economy
Manda Shemirani
ISBN 978-1-4094-2207-5

Securing the Global Economy
G8 Global Governance for a Post-Crisis World
Edited by Andreas Freytag, John J. Kirton, Razeen Sally and Paolo Savona
ISBN 978-0-7546-7673-7

Debt Relief Initiatives
Policy Design and Outcomes
Marco Arnone and Andrea F. Presbitero
ISBN 978-0-7546-7742-0

Making Global Economic Governance Effective: Hard and Soft Law Institutions in a Crowded World
Edited by John Kirton, Marina Larionova and Paolo Savona
ISBN 978-0-7546-7671-3

G8 against Transnational Organized Crime
Amandine Scherrer
ISBN 978-0-7546-7544-0

Governing Global Derivatives
Challenges and Risks
Chiara Oldani
ISBN 978-0-7546-7464-1

Financing Development
The G8 and UN Contribution
Edited by Michele Fratianni, John J. Kirton and Paolo Savona
ISBN 978-0-7546-4676-1

The G8 System and the G20
Evolution, Role and Documentation
Peter I. Hajnal
ISBN 978-0-7546-4550-4

Corporate, Public and Global Governance
The G8 Contribution
Edited by Michele Fratianni, Paolo Savona and John J. Kirton
ISBN 978-0-7546-4046-2

Elements of the Euro Area
Integrating Financial Markets
Edited by Jesper Berg, Mauro Grande and Francesco Paolo Mongelli
ISBN 978-0-7546-4320-3

New Perspectives on Global Governance
Why America Needs the G8
Edited by Michele Fratianni, John J. Kirton, Alan M. Rugman and Paolo Savona
ISBN 978-0-7546-4477-4

Global Financial Crime
Terrorism, Money Laundering and Offshore Centres
Edited by Donato Masciandaro
ISBN 978-0-7546-3707-3

Sustaining Global Growth and Development: G7 and IMF Governance
Edited by Michele Fratianni, Paolo Savona and John J. Kirton
ISBN 978-0-7546-3529-1

Governing Global Finance
New Challenges, G7 and IMF Contributions
Edited by Michele Fratianni, Paolo Savona and John J. Kirton
ISBN 978-0-7546-0880-6